D0331204

Looking Back at Law's Century

LOOKING BACK AT LAW'S CENTURY

Edited by

Austin Sarat
Bryant Garth
Robert A. Kagan

CORNELL
UNIVERSITY PRESS

ITHACA AND
LONDON

First published 2002 by Cornell University Press

Printed in the United States od America

Library of Congress Cataloging-in-Publication Data

Looking back at law's century / edited by Austin Sarat, Bryant Garth, Robert A. Kagan.
p. cm.
Includes bibliographical references and index.
ISBN 0-8014-3957-4 (cloth : acid-free paper)
1. Law—United States—History—20th century—Congresses. I. Sarat, Austin. II. Garth, Bryant G. III. Kagan, Robert A.
KF371.A2 L66 2002
349.73—dc21
2002005493

Cornell University Press strives to use environmentally responsible suppliers and materials to the fullest extent possible in the publishing of its books. Such materials include vegetable-based, low-VOC inks, and acid-free papers that are recycled, totally chlorine-free, or partly composed of nonwood fibers. For further information, visit our website at www.cornellpress.cornell.edu.

Cloth printing 10 9 8 7 6 5 4 3 2 1

Contents

Acknowledgments

This volume grew out of a conference—Law2000—held in October 1999. We are grateful to all the participants for their interest and enthusiasm. Special thanks go to Karen Underwood for her help in organizing that event. We are grateful for the generous financial support provided by the American Academy of Arts and Sciences, the Charles Hamilton Houston Forum on Law and Social Justice of Amherst College, the Offices of the Dean of the Faculty and the President of Amherst College, the Center for Law and Society at the University of California, Berkeley, and the American Bar Foundation.

Contributors

GUYORA BINDER, Law, SUNY-Buffalo
MARIANNE CONSTABLE, Rhetoric, University of California at Berkeley
OWEN FISS, Law, Yale University
BRYANT GARTH, American Bar Foundation
ROBERT W. GORDON, Law, Yale University
CAROL GREENHOUSE, Anthropology, Princeton University
ROBERT A. KAGAN, Political Science and Law, University of California at Berkeley
LAURA KALMAN, History, University of California at Santa Barbara
MORTON KELLER, History, Brandeis University
DAVID KENNEDY, Law, Harvard University
MARTHA MINOW, Law, Harvard University
WILLIAM J. NOVAK, History, University of Chicago
AUSTIN SARAT, Political Science and Law, Jurisprudence, and Social Thought, Amherst College
JONATHAN SIMON, Law, University of Miami
KENDALL THOMAS, Law, Columbia University

Looking Back at Law's Century

INTRODUCTORY ESSAY

Facilitating and Domesticating Change

DEMOCRACY, CAPITALISM, AND LAW'S DOUBLE ROLE IN THE TWENTIETH CENTURY

Robert A. Kagan, Bryant Garth, and Austin Sarat

PUTTING LAW IN TIME

THE TASK OF THIS BOOK is to put law in time, to look back at a century of tremendous legal change, of inspiring legal developments and profound failures. The last hundred years—what we might in retrospect characterize as "law's century"—took us from the Progressive Era's optimism about law and social engineering to current concerns about our hyperlegalist society, from Wilsonian idealism to the worldwide spread of democracy, the rule of law, and the idea of human rights. At the dawn of a new century the story we hear about law is mainly a triumphal one (Carothers 1998). Law has maintained (or regained) its status as the key language of governance in our country (Friedman 1990), making lawyers and legal scholars central players in political and economic life. The United States, the most "legal" of countries, has succeeded in making its version of the state the point of reference for much of the world. Thus it should not be surprising that rule-of-law projects are now central to the agenda of the U.S. Department of State, the World Bank, the International Monetary Fund (IMF), and many others (Trubek 1996), or that the spread of this U.S. model highlights the potential role for law in social movements, in protecting human rights, and in promoting economic growth.

Any observer of the economy and the state in the United States during the twentieth century would recognize that law has played a crucial role in both responding to and initiating social change (Friedman 1985b). Law's prominence has been largely a product of underlying social, economic, and cultural changes, but it is also a measure of the success of particular actors in promoting their position and the position of law in political and economic life. The success of this project is seen in the fact that law, as if fulfilling a kind of Tocquevillian prophecy, has become the hegemonic language in social struggles both here and abroad (see, for example, McCann 1994; also Sarat and Scheingold 2001).

Increasingly, therefore, politics has operated on the terrain of law. But the terrain is not entirely neutral, for it affects the nature of politics. Law plays what we see as a double role—both facilitating and containing social and political change, both advancing and domesticating challenge (McCann and Silverstein 1998). Litigation provides one way for marginalized social actors to insist on the legitimacy of their demands for inclusion, equal treatment, and respect. Yet as Scheingold (1999; 2001, 22) explains, the legalization of politics "privileges a liberal democratic agenda built around accommodation with states, basic human rights, and incremental legalism." Thus it is seldom an apt vehicle for accomplishing redistributive or substantively egalitarian projects.

Moreover, even as it channels political life through the more orderly embankments of due process, reasoned adjudication, and legal accountability, law also legitimates the use of official coercion and penal action, outlaws disruptive modes of protest, reinforces economic and class differences, and helps to entrench existing power arrangements. And of course, law's glittering promises often are merely the manifestation of "symbolic politics," promises betrayed by failures of the governmental will and financing that are needed to make them realities. In sum, while the legal contests implicated in many of the important political, social, and cultural events of the twentieth century were part of a story of major transformations of social and legal justice, as is commonly understood, the double role of law—as well as the recurrence of war, economic troubles, and political reaction—ensured that the story was not one of linear progress.

Seeking to understand the changing position of law and the ways in which critical issues in law today engage with the past, this volume reflects on law's multifaceted story as it has played itself out in different domains of legal policy—and legal scholarship. It starts in the present with two ambitions: to find tools to help us understand where we are at the start of the twenty-first century, and to look at what has become our legal stock to see what it does and does not offer in the way of resources for the new century. Each of the contributors thus takes the present moment seriously in part by looking back in time, as if reading the past to assess future possibilities. Our interest here is therefore less in the creation of definitive historical accounts than in thinking about law in relation to time and in helping to create and preserve a useable memory of the twentieth century and its law both for scholars seeking to understand the position of law and for scholars seeking to put law to work for themselves.[1]

Millennial speculation, we suspect, will be as fleeting in its impact as it is now rampant. Yet as we thought about how we might talk about the law of the twentieth century, we were drawn back to an examination of what people were saying about law at the end of the nineteenth. And, like any reader of that period, we were especially drawn to the writing of Oliver Wendell Holmes. Holmes (1897, 61) started his classic "Path of the Law" by announcing that "when we study law we are not studying a mystery" and then moved on to suggest that the focus of legal study should be "prediction, the prediction of the incidence of the public force through the instrumentality of the courts." He fought hard to distinguish law from morality and invited us to think about law from "the bad man's point of view" (Holmes 1897, 78). Holmes (1897, 63) wrote in praise of "theory" and proclaimed that "The remoter and more general aspects of the law are those which give it universal interest." He argued that the validity of law should be based not on particular moralities but on principles of sufficient generality to build its claim to universality. The success of law in the twentieth century in the United States has made it unnecessary for contemporary commentators to continue to argue that it is distinct from morality and special interests. Law is taken for granted.

Frederick Schauer (1998, 73), a prominent constitutional scholar, points out that Holmes's belief that we should make prediction the center of legal thought was premised on a confidence that legal outcomes could be placed into discrete categories, "the discovery of which would enable us to predict future decisions with some degree of reliability." Schauer quite persuasively argues that, even if that were the case in 1897, more than one hundred years later the law is infinitely more complex not just in terms of the number of general legal categories, but also "in the number of legal topics and doctrines that are specific to pre-legal social, economic, cultural, and technological categories" (Schauer 1998, 82). With the universalism of the law now taken for granted, scholars such as Schauer can insist on a law that recognizes its links to contingent social practices. The scholars who have contributed to this volume have much more in common with Schauer than with Holmes on this point.

LAW'S CENTURY

Law's century witnessed both the spread of legal ideals to societies where law once played little role and the growing penetration of law into new domains of social life in societies already committed to the rule of law. Thus nation-states all over the world today employ law to maintain order and to enhance the legitimacy of their authority, policies, and actions. While in these countries there is enormous variation in what this formal deference to law means in practice, over the last hundred years the geographical domain of commitment to the rule of law—the view that law should be even-handed, reliable, and democratically responsive, binding on the powerful as well as the weak, and available for ordinary people to vindicate deeply felt injustices (Hendley 1996)—has expanded dramatically. In 1900, only 6 of the 43 countries then recognized as nation-states were what would now be termed constitutional democracies, in which political legitimacy is explicitly based on the rule of popularly validated law. In 1998, 117 of the 193 recognized nation-states claimed to be constitutional democracies (Emmott 1999).

Furthermore, reflecting on the post–World War II establishment and increasing assertiveness of constitutional courts in Europe, Canada, Israel, India, Korea, South Africa, Hungary, and beyond (Cappelletti 1989; Stone 1992), scholars have written of *The Global Expansion of Judicial Power* (Tate and Vallinder 1995) and *The Rights Revolution* (Epp 1998). These books recount scores of government policies and actions struck down by judges as violative of constitutional rights and principles. The World Bank and the International Monetary Fund have increasingly demanded (and often funded) strengthened legal institutions in less developed countries as a condition for financial aid (Rowat, Malik, and Dakiolis 1995). A reasonable approximation of the rule of law, in short, defined more or less according to the separation of powers found in the United States, has become an essential ticket to recognition as a "modern" nation.

Another illustration of what we call the double role of law, however, is the fact that the triumph of law in the international arena, and especially a U.S. conception of law, has raised concerns about the imposition of models that are foreign and alien to the settings for which a transformation is sought. One example of this is played out in the domain of human rights. Some commentators here and elsewhere, while acknowledging the significance of human rights in political struggles around the world, worry that reliance on human rights by political movements exemplifies a kind of legal imperialism in which Western ideas and institutions take on an unhealthy prominence (Pollis and Schwab 1979). As the "rights industry" flourishes and the export of American ideas of rights grows dramatically, we hear claims that the spread of the rule of law is the latest manifestation of neocolonialism, that it reflects a particularly insidious form of cultural imperialism.[2] At the very moment when possibilities for realizing the rule of law seem particularly promising, therefore, one encounters questions about the fit between human rights and respect for cultural difference and the integrity of cultural traditions (Shute and Hurley 1993), worries about whether the virtues of the rule of law are, in truth, culture specific, and doubts about the effectiveness of the rule of law in protecting subject populations from abuse (Bell 1992).

While these concerns have some validity, they generally do not do justice to the complexity of the national and international dynamic that contributes to the promotion of legal universalism and the triumph of the U.S. model. In varying degrees in different countries, U.S.–dominated discourse about the rule of law has become the basis for *indigenous* criticisms and reforms. The extension of U.S. ideals of law is much more complicated than the imperialism critique usually recognizes.

In societies already committed to the rule of law, throughout the twentieth century law's domain grew deeper as well as wider, penetrating more and more spheres of social and economic life. In 1900, the United States was a democracy only for white males, and millions of African Americans were excluded from the protections of the rule of law, especially but not exclusively in southern states. In 1900, there were no public defenders' offices providing representation for criminal defendants. The federal Bill of Rights did not impose restrictions on police interrogations or prison conditions. There were no public interest law firms, no class actions for violations of antidiscrimination law. There was no income tax law, no bank deposit insurance law, no social security law. There were no laws regulating the filling in of wetlands, or industrial air pollution, or the safety of new medicines, or the accuracy of financial statements for new corporate stock offerings.

By the end of the century, thousands of American citizens each day were making telephone calls to police departments, workplace safety inspectorates, and environmental agencies whose officials fanned out into the community to enforce legal rights and duties. In 1960, there was one lawyer for every 627 people in the United States. By 1995, the ratio had grown more than 100 percent, to 1:307. Litigation among business corporations grew rapidly (Nelson 1990; Galanter and Rogers 1991), as did government regulation, and law firms serving corporate clients swelled to enormous proportions (Galanter and Palay 1992). Welfare recipients, confronting a complex array of jurisdictional and procedural rules, rights, and restrictions, told interviewers that "the law is all over" (Sarat 1990). By the end of the century, the threat of legal liability permeated the operations of universities, public school systems, hospitals, and municipal governments, as well as tobacco companies, land developers, and product manufacturers. Moreover, the penetration of images of law into our cultural lives was also greater (Sarat 2000). Television viewers by the millions watched nightly dramas portraying the moral dilemmas of police officers and defense lawyers, plus news programs laced with accounts of legal transgressions and legal victories. In the United States and a number of other democracies, tens of millions of ordinary individuals had come to think of themselves as rights-bearing citizens for whom "the law" signifies not only official constraints and demands but also a universally available set of entitlements (Ewick and Silbey 1998).

These kind of quick "then and now" comparisons, while undeniably significant, nonetheless obscure the much more complicated, nonlinear story to which we alluded earlier. Throughout the twentieth century, even in the United States, costly and cumbersome legal procedures were often inaccessible to the poor and to members of politically marginal minority groups. American law has legitimated the internment of loyal Japanese Americans during World

War II and the executions of hundreds of homicide defendants, many of whom received inadequate representation. Legal systems even in the places where legal legitimacy counts the most often do not come close to the ideals that are supposed to be embraced.

In the United States and elsewhere, there continue to be many instances in which the role of political parties, religious or ethnic authority, some form of clientelism or familial capital is far more important than law in governing the state or the economy. Post-communist governments, for example, have shown not only how difficult it is to build a legal order that will prove itself effective according to internationally acceptable standards, but also how enduring longstanding practices can be. Thus corporation managers in Russia, for example, continue to rely on oligarchs and their mafias rather than on the courts (Hendley 1999) to handle their disputes. Despite the tremendous attention to the effort to make General Pinochet accountable to international human rights standards, the politicians in power today in Chile, including many who were persecuted by Pinochet, have similarly preferred to keep negotiations involving key issues of political power in the hands of the political elite.

The leaders of these countries all embrace the rule of law, but what it means in practice depends on structures of power that have been in place for many years. The ascendancy of the U.S. model of law also faces more direct challenges. European legal scholars accustomed to a strong state have complained of the "juridification" of everyday life (Teubner 1987). Alexander Solzhenitsyn, after defecting to the United States, reasserted the importance of religious authority (Berman 1980, 8): "I have spent all my life under a Communist regime and I will tell you that a society without any objective legal scale is a terrible one indeed. But a society with no other scale but the legal one is also less than worthy of man. Whenever the tissue of life is woven of legalistic relationships, this creates an atmosphere of spiritual mediocrity that paralyzes man's noblest impulses."

Thus at the end of law's century, while seemingly ascendant in the political life of nations everywhere, law was at the same time under serious challenge, sometimes of the overt kind exemplified by Solzhenitsyn, sometimes by the dogged resistance of social and political forms in the face of pressures to change. This simultaneous ascendancy and challenge is another element of the double role of law, one that is likely to remain constant as the new century unfolds.

DYNAMICS OF LEGAL CHANGE: "INSIDE" AND "OUTSIDE" FACTORS

Accounts of change in the law during the twentieth century are often linked to developments in national legal traditions. In this perspective, legal systems, at least in democratic regimes, are regarded as relatively autonomous from the world of politics—realms in which lawyers, judges, and legal academics, bolstered by the aura of professionalism, dominate the formulation of legal ideas, norms, and reforms.[3] Hence legal changes, it is assumed, reflect changing currents in a nation's "elite legal culture," as yesterday's novel dissenting opinion, law review article, or law reform committee's report, gradually gathering intellectual support, becomes today's majority opinion or revised statutory code.

Other analysts, however, trace legal change to seismic shifts in the "external" spheres of politics and economics (Friedman 1985a). The extreme version of this approach is that of Marxists (and some of their intellectual descendants), for whom legal autonomy and professionalism are only myths, a smokescreen of words and rituals that mask the coercive aspects of law and its subservience to the power and interests of capital (Collins 1982). But many non-Marxist social scientists too believe that judges and lawmakers, especially in democratic societies, are responsive to popular political attitudes and demands (whose development legal officials do not control), to the policy preferences of political elites, or even to the interests of major actors in the economy. In this view, a nation's distinctive legal norms, institutions, and practices may be polished and rewrapped at the retail level by legal professionals, but the basic production process is dominated by political and economic forces.

More recently, some sociolegal scholars and historians have promoted a more complex view of legal change, emphasizing the interaction of "inside" and "outside" forces, and also suggesting that the relationship between "law" and "society" is so intertwined that it hardly makes sense to think of them as separate spheres (Gordon 1984; Engel 1993). Legal elites are important in this perspective, as they subtly adapt the law to deflect criticisms and threats from powerful economic actors and from political movements, thereby preserving the prerogatives and independence of lawyers and judges. Moreover, factions within the legal elite, each sympathetic to different political and economic interests, compete for influence over legal development, as do other professionals (such as economists, psychologists, scientists, or criminologists) who seek to penetrate institutions that forge legal and regulatory norms (Dezalay and Garth 1996).

In addition to the influence of legal elites on political movements and public opinion, legal constraints and legal ideas have a "constitutive" role in society, shaping the way markets work, political ideas are formulated, and the struggle for power is channeled (see Sarat and Kearns 1993; Gordon 1984). Thus, in the twentieth century, law came to permeate social life. Law-thought and legal relations (or emanations from such thought and relations) dominate—or at least seek to dominate—self-understanding and one's understanding of one's relations to others.

The triumph of law is marked by the fact that we are not merely pushed and pulled by laws that impinge on us from the "outside." Rather, when law is successful in constituting our categories of thought, it means that we have internalized law's "meanings" and its representations of us, so much so that our own purposes and understandings can no longer be extricated from them. As a consequence, law's "demands" tend to seem natural and necessary, and hardly like demands at all. In its strongest form, the constitutive perspective suggests that law "colonizes our souls," thereby making its demands ours at the same time that it reinforces the illusion of independence from law (Sarat and Kearns 1993). "(T)he power exerted by a legal regime consists less in the force that it can bring to bear against violators of its rules than in its capacity to persuade people that the world described in its images and categories is the only attainable world in which a sane person would want to live" (Gordon 1984, 108).

Looking back at the broad sweep of the twentieth century, it seems obvious but nonetheless worthwhile to observe that law has been shaped most profoundly, and in turn has helped structure, two powerful "extralegal" developments—the halting rise of more extensive, competitive, and inclusive democratic political processes, and the construction of more productive and competitive capitalist economies. It is to these developments and their place in the story of law's century that we now turn.

DEMOCRACY AND TWENTIETH-CENTURY LAW

In his essay in this volume, Owen Fiss asserts, "The political conception of liberty has grown in importance in the course of the twentieth century because our commitment to democracy has grown." Fiss is surely correct in emphasizing the notion that law has increasingly been shaped by democratic politics. But the relationship between democratic politics and law has also been contentious and complex. Democracy fuels the growth of law and is, in turn, protected by it. Yet law also acts as a brake on democratic forces. Here again we confront the dual role of law in the twentieth century.

Against the ideal of democratically shaped law, American legal scholars often have arrayed a contravening ideal—the notion of law as a realm at least partially insulated from democratic politics, shaped by legal elites, particularly judges and legal scholars, whose claim to formulate the law is based on their expertise in legal tradition, deliberative rationality, or policy analysis. After all, the constitutionalism that Fiss celebrates depends on the authority of courts to strike down democratically enacted legislation that impinges on legal rights, as defined by judges—a form of judicial supremacy borne of the American Founding Fathers' mistrust of democratic politics. In the American political tradition, law was to be not only an instrument of democratic governance but also a constraint on the irrational passions and financial influences that could corrupt democratic politics.

Other democracies have not always seen things the same way. Late-eighteenth-century French revolutionaries understandably viewed the judiciary as a conservative, antidemocratic institution inclined to oppose governmental measures designed to advance the public welfare (Rosenthal 1992). In the nineteenth century and much of the twentieth, most democratic regimes—in Europe, the British Commonwealth, South America—adopted a similar theory: it was the elected legislature's job to make policy and write it into legislation, the judge's job to apply it faithfully and accurately to resolve individual disputes. In the early years of the twentieth century, many American progressives, not unlike French Revolutionaries, viewed American judiciaries as antidemocratic bastions of reaction, all too willing to invalidate laws regulating the labor market as unconstitutional "class legislation" or as restrictions on a judicially invented "freedom of contract" (see Commager 1943). In the 1960s, political conservatives denounced the "Warren Court" for judicial imperialism, this time on behalf of liberal causes, and later decried the construction of a political culture addicted to "rights talk" (Glendon 1991). Thus in the United States politicians and legal scholars have continued to struggle with the "counter-majoritarian difficulty" (Bickel 1962; Ely 1980; Peretti 1999), debating the appropriate boundaries of judicial power in a democratic polity.

Nevertheless, for all the disagreement about the details, by the year 2000 judicial review and the constraint of democratic politics was more widely accepted in the United States than it had been a century earlier, and as significantly, that practice had spread to many other democracies. In the wake of Nazism, Communism, and imperialism, active constitutional courts were established in a growing number of democracies, from Germany, Hungary, and Poland to India, Canada, Korea, Israel, South Africa, and Chile. The European Court for Human Rights imposed legal changes on democratic governments in England, Norway, and Germany. By 2000, in a world of increasingly pluralistic democracies, court-enforced legal protections for ethnic and political minorities, as well as for individual rights, had become part of the dominant conception of democracy.

At the same time, as Fiss suggests, over the course of law's century, despite many ebbs and flows, law was shaped by the social movements and partisanship unleashed by increasingly competitive democratic politics, and a more responsive legal system, in turn, increasingly diverted political action toward the pursuit of democratic change, particularly in the United States. Perhaps the most important consequence of this democratic influence was a shift in the dominant concept of law (Friedman 1985b). At the beginning of the century, legal scholars, judges, and politicians generally thought of law in formal terms—the product of a semi-autonomous realm in which legal technicians applied rules or precedents to particular disputes. Law emphasized what Max Weber called formal rationality, as opposed to substantive (policy-oriented) rationality (Rheinstein 1967). Judges were not to be concerned with broader questions of social justice. The disjunction was captured by the famous

Anatole France aphorism, "The law, in its majestic equality, forbids the rich as well as the poor to sleep under bridges, to beg in the streets, and to steal bread."

That remains true in 2000 no less than in 1900. Indeed, in the densely developed modern metropolis, it may now be even harder for a homeless person to find a public place in which to spend the night (Waldron 1991). Yet in the decades that followed France's jibe, legal elites began to address that cruel irony. Prodded by socialist and labor movements in Europe and the United States, they called on lawmakers and judges to attend to the often unequal *consequences* of formal law. Legal scholars, educators, lawyers, and judges gradually came to advocate what Philippe Nonet and Philip Selznick (1978) later labeled a transition from "autonomous law" to "responsive law"—a mode of legal thought that demands attention to the social consequences of law and legal procedures, including their disparate, disadvantageous impact on the poor or on political, racial, and ethnic minorities.

In democratic societies, therefore, legal discourse was explicitly linked to issues of social justice. After the New Deal in the United States, protection for the rights of "discrete and insular minorities" and political dissidents came to be a central focus of constitutional jurisprudence. When a lawyer before the Supreme Court cited a ruling precedent, Chief Justice Earl Warren was said to have responded, "Yes, but is it fair?" Looking beyond the formal equality of the late-nineteenth-century "separate but equal" doctrine, the Court emphasized the actual social inequalities reinforced by legally segregated public schools and held them unconstitutional (see Sarat 1997). A democratically driven focus on unequal consequences was employed to reform the institutions of democracy itself. The Supreme Court commanded the redrawing of electoral district lines to ensure equal representation for all geographical areas. Congress, looking at the racially biased consequences of ostensibly neutral voting registration rules, enacted the Voting Rights Act, ending the disenfranchisement of African Americans in southern states.

In the wake of World War II, the new national constitutions formulated in Europe, and in many other new nations that followed their model, gave prominence to social and economic rights as well as to formal political and legal equality. In the United States, the breadth and generosity of welfare state benefits lagged considerably behind those provided by post–World War II democracies in western Europe and Canada (McFate 1995). But Franklin Delano Roosevelt's New Deal, Lyndon Johnson's War on Poverty, and many decisions of the Warren Court (Melnick 1993) created numerous new legal entitlements—from Social Security to Medicare, Medicaid, disability benefits, and aid for dependent children—all of which injected new values into the traditionally individualistic spirit of American law. Government-funded legal services for criminal defendants and the poor, along with the establishment of law enforcement and regulatory agencies that would respond to citizen complaints for the price of a telephone call, made access to law more universal than it had been early in the century.

But the story of democratization in the twentieth century and of law's role in it is by no means a singular one. Even as law stimulated and responded to democratic pressures, it helped to contain and neutralize them (Scheingold 1974). Throughout the twentieth century, political pressures for greater equality competed with broad political support for capitalist economic systems—particularly in the United States (McClosky and Zaller 1984). If capitalism's appeal lay in its capacity to increase incomes, opportunities, and wealth for the society at large, it also tended to widen the gap between the rich and the poor. The dominant welfare state compromise, embodied in a complex and always politically contested body of law, was to guarantee a "social minimum" rather than anything approximating equality of condition. Thus the legal rights and services of the modern welfare state did not come close to eliminating the economic and social inequality that Anatole France lamented or the regulation and restrictions that continue to accompany it. "The myth of rights" proclaimed the elasticity of legal doctrine and the ability of legal decisions to reshape society. Yet legal ideology helped to mystify and reify social relations, to make inequality seem inevitable, necessary, natural, and just.

Law's relationship to democratization has not gone unchallenged. The rise of identity politics has been associated with criticism of universalizing notions of citizenship and rights. As the twentieth century drew to a close we witnessed the growing assertiveness of racial, ethnic, and other social groups both in the United States and abroad, demanding recognition of their distinctive histories and traditions as well as opportunities to develop and maintain the institutional infrastructure necessary to preserve them. As Charles Taylor notes, "the development of the modern notion of identity has given rise to a politics of difference" (1992, 38). Where once it seemed that the ideal of American citizenship and law was found in the promise of integration and in the hope that none of us would be singled out for, let alone judged by, our race or ethnicity, today integration is often rejected and new terms of inclusion are sought (Natapoff 1996, 751). Critics allege that integration is a mask for cultural domination (if not a form of cultural genocide) and that it signals the triumph of dominant identities over the rich mosaic of social and cultural difference. Integration is now often taken to mean assimilation, which threatens to submerge the identity and history of subordinated racial, gender, sexual, or ethnic groups.

Advocates of cultural pluralism promote cultural autonomy for themselves; for the larger society they advocate pluralism. The cultural pluralism they seek refers to a "loosely connected set of attitudes and practices sharing . . . the notion that American society should be understood as a collection of diverse cultural groups rather than as a single, unified national body or as simply an aggregate of atomized individuals. . . . [It] implies that government must recognize and respect if not nurture the diversity and integrity of racial and ethnic communities" (Peller 1997, 372). Policies providing such recognition and respect include bilingual education, university programs in areas such as African-American, Asian-American, Hispanic, and Jewish Studies, legal acceptance of so-called cultural defenses, and exemptions for particular groups from the reach of otherwise valid positive law. Instead of seeking to transcend our differences and locate the basis of citizenship in the most abstract and universalized common traits, law should, so the argument goes, seek a form of citizenship that recognizes difference but nonetheless claims equality (Mouffe 1995, 39). At the end of the twentieth century, law seems uncertain about how to respond to these challenges and about how to define the terms of inclusion in a democratizing community.

And there is surely another underside to the democratization story. With the greater responsiveness of law to the voting public's fears and concerns came an increase in law's capacity to order and regulate behavior and to impose a more effective network of surveillance. In the last three decades of the twentieth century, the United States witnessed a dramatic escalation of punitiveness, an escalation focused especially on racial minorities. According to the Bureau of Justice Statistics, at the end of 1996, 5.5 million people were in prison, in jail, or on probation. That number constituted about 2.8 percent of all adult residents of the country. Moreover, for every 100,000 African-American males, 3,209 were in prison or jail; for every 100,000 Hispanic males, 1,273 were incarcerated. The comparable figure for whites was 386 per 100,000. Extending the rights of citizenship and encouraging political participation—which included more responsiveness to the demands of minorities in the inner cities for greater security—thus went hand in hand with severe impositions in the lives of other citizens. From Richard Nixon's "law and order" rhetoric to Bill Clinton's pledge to represent people who "work hard and play by the rules," crime has been such an important issue that some now argue that we are being "governed through crime" (Simon 1997). Crime has been crucial in the processes of demonizing young black males and using them in the pantheon of public enemies to replace the "evil empire (Tonry 1995)" (Simon 1997, 15).

Interestingly, the populist politics of law and order expanded during an era in which government action in other areas of our social and economic life came under political attack. When, as President Bill Clinton announced, "The era of big government [was] over," emphasis was increasingly placed on freedom and responsibility as a prevailing cultural ethos. Yet this era also is associated with the dramatic escalation of state investment in the apparatus of punishment. At a time when citizens were skeptical that government activism could be appropriate or effective, punishment provided one arena in which the state could redeem itself by taking action with clear and popular results. In this area, democracy and populist sentiment triumphed over the technocratic rationality of legal elites; here law, instead of restraining that sentiment, became its tool.

CAPITALISM AND TWENTIETH-CENTURY LAW

If the last hundred years was law's century, it surely was capitalism's century too. Between the year 1500 and 1825, according to a study published by the International Monetary Fund ("Road to Riches" 1999, 10), gross domestic product in western Europe rose from about $750 per capita income to about $1,250, calculated in 1900 prices. Then economic take-off occurred. In 1900, GDP per capita had leapt to about $3,750. But in the next hundred years, aside from the loss of altitude in the 1930s, the take-off extended into the economic stratosphere. By 2000, GDP in Europe had soared to $17,500. The technological changes mobilized, financed, and disseminated by competitive capitalist systems led to unheard-of increases in economic and geographical mobility, longevity, standards of living, and comfort. In the last thirty years of the century, technological revolutions in transportation and electronic communication, along with shrinking trade barriers, generated a more intensely competitive global capitalism. The socialist alternative, seemingly on the ascendancy at the twentieth century's dawn, ultimately faded. More and more nations adopted explicitly pro-capitalist political economies.

Dynamic capitalism affected legal change in many important ways. First, law served as capitalism's handmaiden, adapting to the imperatives of an ever-changing business world. Sometimes this meant that the law helped business firms (especially certain politically connected firms) circumvent the market by obtaining particular immunities, tax breaks, or special rents. But overall and over time, law tended to construct and legitimate markets, spurring aggregate economic growth and innovation. Throughout the twentieth century, as in the nineteenth, lawyers were deployed to protect property rights, punish dishonesty, reinforce managerial prerogatives vis-à-vis labor, and enhance the reliability of contractual commitments. Judges and legislatures constantly reworked the law to provide business firms and investors remedies against new forms of fraud and betrayal, and to accommodate the needs of new kinds of enterprises, from franchisers and multinational corporations to venture capitalists and computer software inventors. Corporations called on platoons of corporate lawyers to serve as "transaction cost engineers," drafting agreements and security arrangements that reduced risks and thereby encouraged investments (Gilson 1984). Toward the end of the century, courts and legislatures dismantled regimes that protected firms from competition in transportation, financial services, and telecommunications, substituting more efficiency-oriented legal regimes (Vogel 1996). Indeed, in a world in which capitalism constantly battered down traditional social arrangements, law seemed more and more necessary. As an American secretary of the treasury wrote:

> In a world without courts, one lends money to one's brother-in-law and relies on one's wife's parents to enforce the agreement. In a world without borders, arms-length formal contracts become ever more critical to innovation and growth. So too the means of reliably enforcing them. In such circumstances the American preference for rules over understandings and for law over custom, emerges as a major strength. (Summers 1999, 28)

Secondly, especially in democratic capitalist systems, law was constantly called on to ameliorate the sudden economic losses, social disruptions, physical hazards, and inequities that flow from what Joseph Schumpeter called the "creative destruction" of capitalism. Particularly in the last third of the century, capitalist enterprises were compelled by law to "internalize" the previously "externalized" costs of production—to pay tort damages for harms caused by dangerous machines and substances; to provide compensation insurance for workplace injuries and install workplace safety measures; to mitigate some of the environmental and social disruptions that accompany building projects; to install and maintain expensive pollution control equipment; to pay taxes for unemployment and retirement insurance; and, in varying degrees (usually less in the United States), to guarantee employees' rights against arbitrary dismissal, severance pay, paid vacations, and maternal leave.

These market-tempering and redistributive measures were enacted because political movements and organizations, such as labor unions and environmental advocacy groups, loudly demanded them. They were not enacted without a struggle, and even at the end of the century, the protections provided struck many as inadequate. Yet some business enterprises and associations, as well as many basically pro-capitalist political leaders, legal scholars, and judges, recognized that at least in democratic polities, legal measures that promised to soften the harsh blows of capitalism were essential to capitalism's legitimacy and preservation. Here again we see law's dual role.

Scarcely more than a third of the way through the twentieth century, the U.S. Supreme Court abandoned the rear-guard efforts of legal conservatives to erect constitutional barriers against government regulation of business and labor relations, thereby legitimating the expansion of regulation at both the state and federal levels of government. And once within a more tightly regulated business world, particular corporations and their lawyers quickly learned to lobby and litigate for protective regulations that gave them an advantage over their cut-rate competitors. Political coalitions between regulatory advocacy organizations and firms that were comfortable with regulation became a recurrent feature of the political landscape (Vogel 1995), steadily adding to the scope and stringency of the waves of environmental, safety, and health regulations enacted by late-twentieth-century governments.

Third, the remarkable increase in aggregate wealth that accompanied market-driven technological and managerial innovations generated both the justification for serious legal controls on capitalism and the government's capacity to enforce them. In the depths of the Great Depression of the 1930s, when coal mines and manufacturing firms were losing money and laying off workers, judges were reluctant to order them to take the costly measures necessary to abate environmental nuisances (*Versailles v. McKeesport Coal*, 1935). By the 1970s, after two and a half decades of growing corporate profits and overall prosperity, legislatures leapt to enact strict, costly-to-comply-with pollution control rules, and courts were willing, by and large, to enforce them. To the legal historian Lawrence Friedman (1985b), the visibly enlarged capacity of business firms to pull off extraordinary feats of organization, production, and technological wizardry gave rise to rising popular expectations of "total justice"—the notion that because rich organizations (and societies) at last had the financial and technical means to build in safeguards and compensate the victims of accidents and of capitalism's creative destruction, they should be compelled by law to do so. Similarly, wealth-generating capitalist economies were able to finance unprecedented levels of government activity, making possible the ever larger government bureaucracies, police departments, regulatory inspectorates, tax collection agencies, and law departments that could project law's rights, imposing duties and threats more pervasively into the corporate board rooms and factory floors—as well as the schools and households—of late-twentieth-century society.

In the United States, a distinctive political culture, suspicious of concentrated economic power and concentrated government authority alike, has produced a particularly heavy reliance on law and litigation to police the business world. Compared to European market-oriented systems, populist-inspired antitrust laws and bank regulations have bolstered a style of capitalism that generally has been more decentralized and competitive than most European market-oriented economies (Roe 1991). Through most of the twentieth century, American markets have been less often dominated by cartels, huge banks, government agencies, nationalized companies, or corporatist deals between powerful industry associations and labor federations than other markets throughout the world. Regulation of opportunism in commercial relations in the United States, accordingly, has been left more fully to the realms of contract law and private litigation. Martin Shapiro observes:

> America may use so many lawyers in business and governmental dealings less because we have a special affection for lawyers, than because economic and political power has been widely dispersed among scattered, disparate elites who cannot get together at their club or country

> house, because they do not have one, and who would find that they had little in common upon which to build mutual trust even if they did have a meeting place. Where there are no gentlemen, there have to be contracts, rather than gentlemen's agreements. (1993, 42)

Similarly, government regulation of business in the United States has been uniquely formal and legalistic (Kagan 1997; Kagan and Axelrad 2000).

Democratic pressures for tougher business regulation in the last third of the century, when combined with popular distrust of government and corporate power, led to administrative doctrines and regulatory statutes that constrained American regulators with much more detailed substantive and procedural rules and more searching judicial review than one finds in the regulatory systems of other economically advanced democracies. For similar reasons, the United States was distinctive in developing legal doctrines that foster business accountability through lawsuits by "private attorneys general" and massive class actions by entrepreneurial private lawyers. The American combination of political demands for more government regulation and mistrust of government thus accelerated the penetration of economic life by more detailed laws, legal demands, and lawyers. As Guyora Binder's essay in this volume puts it:

> Americans have many more lawyers per capita than any similar society, and it is tempting to see these lawyers as freelance bureaucrats regulating matters that would be left to officials elsewhere. We set our lawyers watching our government bureaucrats, and we have other lawyers designing, advising, and watching the private bureaucracies—business and nonprofit corporations—that handle most of our affairs. The American version of modernity has been shaped by a "due process" revolution that formalizes decision making not only in government but in private institutions as well.

At the end of the twentieth century, however, American exceptionalism seemed to be fading. Intensified global competition, along with the political and economic dominance of American government and business, was pressuring other economically advanced nations to reshape their political economies, making them a bit more like that of the United States and hence more susceptible to American-style legal accountability. From western Europe to Australia, New Zealand, and Chile, governments busily privatized nationalized enterprises, opened up financial markets, and questioned closed-door governance by corporatist government-business-labor bodies. Freer markets, as Stephen Vogel (1996) shows, generally led to enactment of more legal rules and more formal modes of regulation. Litigation rates in Europe rose (Sellers 1995; Markesenis 1990). American lawyers were quick to push European and Asian businesses toward more legalistic contracts and more adversarial methods of litigation (Garth and Dezalay 1995; Kagan 1997). Capitalism's growth, especially (but not exclusively) in democratic nations, seemed to accelerate the continuing exfoliation of law as well.

While capitalism depends on law and expands its density, it should be noted that it also constrains law's role in certain ways. By the end of the twentieth century, the imperatives of economic efficiency had become the reigning test for labor law and for governmental health, safety, and environmental regulations—and hence an upper limit on their stringency. Law's success in protecting markets also entrenched private corporate dominance over how profits and savings should be invested (and disinvested) and how wide a variety of social services were provided, virtually squelching serious consideration of alternative social and legal arrangements. Law thus protected and promoted capitalist development at a substantial cost to its own transformative possibilities.

OVERVIEW OF CHAPTERS

The chapters that follow each engage with the dual role of law and the tensions of democratization and capitalism that mark law's century. Some do so by explicitly focusing on these issues, while others take up questions whose salience is heightened by the interplay of law, democracy, and capitalism in the twentieth century. The categories our authors use in thinking about law's century are, for the most part, social, economic, cultural, or technological rather than doctrinal. They could/should have been many things. In choosing the former genre over the latter we do not mean to say that doctrinal categories could not or would not produce an interesting conversation. But as participants in various communities of interdisciplinary legal scholarship, we come to this enterprise with a distinct desire to connect stories of law in the twentieth century with stories of its politics, its economy, its culture. While we do not imagine for a moment that the categories into which this book is organized are comprehensive, or even representative, we hope that they point the way toward, or facilitate, the connection of those two kinds of narratives.

Each of the three essays in the first section of this volume—Citizenship, Rights, and Politics—calls attention to the role of law in responding to, and advancing, the claims of citizenship and of political democracy; each suggests that law in the twentieth century extended rights as a way of building a more inclusive and vibrant political community. Owen Fiss's "The Idea of Political Freedom" traces these developments in the domain of the First Amendment's protection of speech. His essay tells the story of changes in our understanding of free speech as a way of connecting developments in the law of the First Amendment with a larger story of the intensification of the ideal of democracy in the last century.

On Fiss's account, two changes were central in this area of law. First was the displacement of what he calls the "authority" question from its preeminent place in constitutional law. While this question still plays a role, it has been superseded by a constitutional jurisprudence that assumes the basic legitimacy of governmental regulatory power—except when it violates specific constitutional prohibitions, such as the First Amendment's restrictions on government control of speech and the Fourteenth Amendment's guarantee of due process and equal protection of the laws. In the twentieth century, however, the Court has interpreted those restrictive clauses more broadly. These shifts, Fiss argues, reflect an ever deepening commitment to political freedom and democracy as guiding principles of constitutional adjudication.

The second development Fiss contends marks twentieth-century free-speech jurisprudence is the displacement of a natural, or prepolitical, conception by a political conception of freedom. Law has been pushed by democratic forces and has advanced democracy by insisting on the priority of the political as a justification for protecting speech. As the twenty-first century opens, he argues, Americans have a much deeper and more profound commitment to democracy than they did a century ago. This commitment is manifested not only by the enfranchisement of women and blacks but by a deeper and more profound commitment to advancing robust political debate. Anxiety about preserving order or state authority, Fiss argues, has given way to a political conception of freedom.

A less triumphant picture of twentieth-century law emerges, however, when we shift from the First Amendment to the fate of human rights in the global arena. Here law's double role is amply on display, helping to fuel the development of human rights discourse during the twentieth century while at the same time restricting political action and political mobilization. Martha Minow draws attention to this double role of law when she notes that the twentieth century spawned the concept of human rights even as it was all too often characterized by their violation without remedy. One important reason for this, David Kennedy's essay in this volume reminds us, is that international law also enshrined the principle of unfettered state sovereignty, rendering illegitimate external intervention into the internal affairs of nation-states, even as oppressive twentieth-century governments used the new technologies of totalitarianism to crush human freedom and dignity. Yet in Minow's view, what was truly remarkable in the area of international human rights was the political energy that fueled various efforts to provide more effective remedial devices.

Minow claims that the legacy of institutional innovation will be the key contribution of international law in the twenty-first century. Her essay charts the proliferation of devices used to provide more effective remedies and protection of human rights. The increasing prominence of these devices reflects the larger trends of the twentieth century noted earlier. One factor has been the determined effort of lawyers and legal scholars—mostly those from rich democracies, but also some third-world lawyers educated in Europe and the United States—to carve out a larger role for their ideology in the harsh world of global *realpolitik*. Another factor has been what Fiss called "a deepening of our commitment to democracy," as democratic electorates, responding to televised images of human rights violations around the world, increasingly pushed their governments to "do something" about the horrors they saw on the tube.

Yet while Fiss confidently points to the growth of democracy and political freedom in the United States, Minow reminds us that the struggle to attain the rule of law is still ongoing in many parts of the world. What she sees as characteristic of the turn-of-the-century situation is a mixed picture of international legal institutions policing selected violations of rights and increased democratization of the struggle for meaningful rights in the work of nongovernmental organizations. NGOs, Minow contends, bring the beliefs of ordinary people to the struggle for rights, dignity, and citizenship.

The third essay in this section, by Kendall Thomas, provides a stark reminder that that struggle is by no means resolved in the United States. When the focus is on the history of law's engagement with issues of racial justice, the picture Thomas paints is, in its texture, more like Minow's than like Fiss's. In the context of race, Thomas contends, the connection between law, rights, and citizenship is still a highly contested terrain. Increasing access to robust political engagement of the kind that Fiss values should be, in Thomas's view, the touchstone in assessing the role of law in promoting racial justice in the twenty-first century.

As Thomas sees it, the record on this score is not good. But more importantly, he contends, attention has rarely been directed to the question of the racial dimensions of politics and citizenship. Instead all sides of the debate about race and law's role in remedying racial injustice have been preoccupied with what Thomas calls a "moral conception" of race, particularly whether it is moral or immoral to use race as a factor in remedying past discrimination. That, we might point out, is yet another illustration of what we have called the double role of law. The legal enshrinement of the nondiscrimination principle, which had wide moral resonance, was the key to the assault on overt racial discrimination in education, employment, law enforcement, and politics. Yet that legal principle has been of only limited efficacy in overcoming the economic and social "inequalities of condition" that have burdened African Americans, and indeed has been successfully invoked in court by white persons complaining that racial preferences in affirmative action programs designed to ameliorate social inequalities are unconstitutional violations of the nondiscrimination principle.

Thomas argues that at the start of the twenty-first century we need what he calls a "political conception of racial justice." This conception calls attention to questions of access to the means of political power and to social relations of domination. Calling attention to law's double role in imposing draconian penalties on black communities through the criminal justice system even as it combats overt discrimination, Thomas asks us to think in new ways about law's complex relation to race. His analysis, like that of Fiss and Minow, takes citizenship seriously and directs attention to the impact of law and policy on the political integrity of black civic publics.

While Thomas's essay ends with an extended reflection on the racial dimensions of crime, justice, and punishment in the United States, Jonathan Simon begins the next section of this book—"Law and the Constitution of Selves and Society"—by providing a broad historical overview of those subjects. His and the other essays in this section describe ways in which citizens and political actors are formed, at least in part, through their interactions with law. Simon argues that issues of crime, justice, and punishment in the twentieth century were played out "largely around the problem of 'self-control,' meaning both the control of individual selves and the capacity of the individual self to exercise control in accordance with the demands of social coordination." Throughout the criminal justice system, Simon points to the emergence of what he calls "new rationalities" of governance that infused the law and practices of crime, justice, and punishment. Those rationalities depended on social science expertise and were directed at reconceiving individual deviance and ultimately at the project of reconstituting individual behavior. He traces the development of new rationalities in three arenas of law—the early-twentieth-century juvenile court movement, the mid-century reform of the law of homicide, and the late-century debate about the maximum-security prison.

The juvenile court movement emerged as part of a developing societal interest in the moral and social lives of individuals, reflecting Progressive reformers' optimism about social reform through systematic study and expertise and some legal reformers' vision of less formal, sociologically sensitive modes of adjudication. Yet juvenile courts, Simon notes, also were part of an apparatus of surveillance aimed, in particular, at the urban poor.

The law of homicide, as it evolved in the last century, increasingly focused on the centrality of dangerousness as the key to judgments about culpability and punishment. Various reform efforts, most prominently the drafting of the *Model Penal Code* and the expansion of the legal category of manslaughter, were geared toward what Simon calls a "new subject for criminal law," not so much a moral being as one who could be given legal incentives to be a prudent manager of risk.

The third area Simon reviews involves the maximum-security prison. In this area law confronts its failure as a mechanism of socialization, surveillance, and risk management. Moreover, Simon shows how the increased responsiveness to democracy and to democratic forces and pressures that Fiss notes in the area of free-speech law manifested itself in the area of crime and criminal justice in escalating severity. Here again law's double role becomes visible, responding to popular demands for greater freedom and security but only at the price of harsher control for others.

Guyora Binder's essay takes Simon's interest in the legal constitution of selves and generalizes it beyond the domain of criminal justice, exploring the ways in which the metaphors embedded in legal thought contain implicit models of society and individual capacity. Changes in legal metaphors thus mark changes in both law and the broader culture. Binder begins with Maine's famous pronouncement that the " 'movement of the progressive societies has hitherto been a movement from Status to Contract' " and contrasts the prominence of contract as a metaphor for social interaction in the late nineteenth century with its declining significance in the twentieth. In the course of the more urban, industrialized twentieth century, contract was subordinated to government regulation and the metaphors of individual and economic rights were replaced by analysis of social conflicts in terms of competing "interests," which governments and courts somehow had to "balance."

More generally, examining the development of twentieth-century legal thought, from legal realism to law and economics, Binder argues that we are left with a "redescription of society as a kind of discursive or semiotic process without any necessary origin or referent in subjective meaning." In such a situation the focus of both law and politics is less on weighing the particular concerns of individuals and more on designing "appropriate conditions for self-representation." At the start of the twenty-first century, Binder claims, "we have come to see society more as a discursive forum than as a marketplace envisioned by Maine." This transformation marks the difference between modernism and postmodernism, between law as a medium for representing selves constituted outside it and law as deeply engaged in defining and enabling the subjects it purports to represent. Yet, even as we come to understand law in this way Binder, echoing Robert Cover, calls on us to remember the violence with which law traffics every day, a violence that does more than provide another stage for the play of representation and the performance of identity.

This same interest in the way the legal constitution of selves and society at the start of the twenty-first century plays out in the shadow of violence marks Carol Greenhouse's exploration of "Law, Identity, and the Dream of Time." Her essay connects the concern for identity that is at the center of this section of our book back to the theme of citizenship in the first section. Indeed, Greenhouse claims that citizenship materializes in issues of identity/difference. The linkage between citizenship and identity is made most vivid in the idea of the nation, with its claims of inclusion and exclusion, belonging and denial. Greenhouse uses the tragic killing of Won-Joon Yoon as a touchstone for these reflections. Yoon was murdered in Bloomington, Indiana, as one of a series of murders across the Midwest carried out by a racist hate-monger.

For Greenhouse this killing marks one way in which difference is given meaning. But it also becomes the occasion for her to ask whether it is possible to imagine a temporality that does not subscribe to nationalism's desire for the end of difference. Against the image of identity and difference that fuels hate crimes, Greenhouse presents another found in the gathering of Bloomington residents at Yoon's memorial service. There she says one could see the embeddedness of state, nation, citizenship, and culture as well as the stark fact that, at the end of the twentieth century, they can no longer be contained within a single national imagining. At this gathering a message from the president of the United States was read. In it he called for the enactment of Anti–Hate Crimes legislation. In this moment, Greenhouse notes, the possibility of a legal response to hatred's desire for the obliteration of difference allowed a community gathered in mourning to imagine itself as a plebiscite. Here law helped provide a way of constituting selves and society in a different relation to difference.

Greenhouse draws on Hannah Arendt and Alexis de Tocqueville to suggest that law and politics can open up new possibilities for the kind of performativity that Binder notes has become so important in figuring identity. Law, she notes, provides the place where citizenship and identity meet. Greenhouse asks her readers to consider whether and how people incorporate the state into their own self-understandings and agency. Citizenship, she claims, brings state and self together. As she puts it, "Within the empirical domain of U.S. citizenship, the federal and the personal borrow each other's signs." In the end, it is to law's imagined presence in our lives that Greenhouse suggests we must attend if we are to understand the complex ways we become particular kinds of selves and if we are to chart new possibilities for the social.

In the next section of this book—"Regulatory Processes in the Economy and Society"—William Novak's essay, "The Legal Origins of the Modern American State," emphasizes the constitutive role of law in enhancing the legitimacy of the modern administrative state. Novak takes issue with the conventional wisdom, forged by historians associated with the early-twentieth-century Progressive movement, which characterized American law and courts as obstacles to the establishment of a modern social-welfare state, at least until the end of the New Deal. The Supreme Court's 1905 *Lochner* decision, the symbolic center of the conventional account, Novak points out, was far from representative. During the late nineteenth and early twentieth centuries, state and federal legislatures, under political pressure to soften the harsh externalities of a growing capitalistic economy, enacted scores of regulations, from antitrust and public utilities laws to legal regimes promoting safety in food processing, banking, railroads, tenement housing, and workplaces. The U.S. and state supreme courts *upheld* the constitutionality of the vast majority of those laws, explicating and constitutionalizing government "police powers."

In the course of these court battles over regulation, Novak argues, American law was fundamentally transformed: law was redefined in a more positivist mold, as the command of the sovereign rather than as a prepolitical "brooding omnipresence in the sky," to use Holmes's derisive term, and "constitutional law replaced the common law . . . as the final authority on the legitimacy of exertions of state power and expressions of individual right." Moreover, Novak observes, the constitutional dialogue surrounding new forms of regulation was the key to the construction and acceptance of a "newly juridified constitutional state," characterized by more centralization of governmental power, a new conception of individual rights against the state, and the expansion of governmental bureaucratic administration. The new public law thus laid the foundation for the growth of the federal welfare-regulatory state in the New Deal and in the 1960s.

The late-nineteenth-century and Progressive-era demand for new regulatory laws and agencies was stimulated in large part by the rise of the large business corporation—the subject of Morton Keller's chapter, "Law and the Corporation." Keller tells us that American law has been concerned simultaneously with fostering corporate organization and with regulating it. By the first decade of the twentieth century, Keller notes, corporate lawyers and courts had built a new framework of corporation law that established the legitimacy of the corporate form, and in a way that maximized entrepreneurial and managerial freedom and authority. State governments competed to make their corporation law attractive to industrialists. Neither the antitrust laws, nor the Federal Trade Commission, nor the extensive environmental, safety, and antidiscrimination regulations enacted in the latter part of the twentieth century made much of a dent in those early legal arrangements and conceptions of corporate governance—or in the almost unquestioned acceptance of corporations as an appropriate vehicle for entrepreneurial activity. Unlike their counterparts in western Europe and Japan, American corporate managers generally have not been subjected to superordinate structures such as strong industry associations, government-fostered cartels, or dominant banks.[4] Forms of corporate governance that empower additional stakeholders, such as the labor-management "co-determination" mandated by post–World War II Germany, never made significant inroads in the United States. This too is evidence of the powerful constitutive effects of American law, entrenched in this instance not only by lawyers and legal scholars but also, as Keller points out, by the neoclassical economic analysis that become preeminent in the latter part of the century.

On the other hand, Keller describes a competing populist tradition, mis trustful of concentrated corporate power, that focused legal development on specific types of corporate misbehavior or social consequences. During the New Deal, new laws regulated deceptive stock market and unfair labor practices. During the 1960s and 1970s, many realms of corporate decision making were subjected to detailed regulations—discrimination in hiring and promotions, pollution control, worker and product safety, the management of health care and pension plans, and more. In recent decades, the rise of massive class action lawsuits generated additional regulatory pressures. At the same time, Keller observes, corporations, their lawyers, and their political allies have won legal controls on regulation—such as mandatory cost-benefit analysis and "rationality review" of new regulations in the courts—that ensure that the new regulatory and liability regimes, with rare exceptions, do not stray far beyond criteria of economic efficiency and technological feasibility, while populist attempts to silence the political voice of business corporations have been rejected by the courts.

Marianne Constable's chapter, "The Rhetoric of Community: Civil Society and the Legal Order," reflects on ways in which the late-twentieth-century administrative state regulates and reconstitutes the nature of community and individual behavior. During the 1960s and 1970s, she notes, the growing administrative-regulatory state was transformed by "the politics of rights," expanding individuals' and public interest groups' capacity to challenge governmental decisions in administrative hearings and in court. But in the last decades of the century, Constable observes, the rhetoric of rights was supplemented by the rhetoric of community involvement. As the tasks of government grew, rule by "command and control" no longer seemed sufficient. To regulate social activity, governments relied more and more on "intermediate institutions"—health maintenance organizations; certified public accountants; professional and industry associations; local nonprofit housing, drug treatment, and welfare-to-work organizations; and so on. The "business community," the "scientific community," the "educational community," and various ethnic and racial "communities" were called upon to act responsibly and cooperatively with government in advancing public purposes.

The new ideal of the "responsible community member," Constable suggests, was double-sided. On one hand, it provided a rhetoric through which government called upon citizens to take responsibility for their own and their communities' governance, whether as participants in the census, as choosers and monitors of their own diets and health care plans, as parents prodded from welfare dependency into the job market, or as local agencies and businesses that could facilitate that process. On the other hand, to enlist particularized communities into the governance process also intensified the pervasiveness of government control, while fragmenting older civic ideals of a unified polity. The new administrative-regulatory state thus monitors social and economic life ever more closely, making it simultaneously more democratic (in the sense of attentiveness to citizens' habits and preferences) and, in Constable's view, more insidious and omnipresent.

The concluding section of the book concentrates on lawyers, law professors, and the marketing of law. It begins with a chapter by Robert Gordon, who traces the internal story of the U.S. legal profession and the "troubles"—even crises—it now faces in what looks like a moment of triumph. In a rich essay that touches on numerous aspects of the legal profession, he also situates the developments of the twentieth century in the long history of lawyers who seek both to serve clients and to gain positions of power in the state and the economy. He shows the ways that lawyers in the United States have come to embody the double role of law. They develop rules and institutions that protect and legitimate the position of powerful clients through regulations that also offer space to challenge those clients. As Gordon points out, these activities make both corporate lawyers—now converted into lawyer-statespersons—and their clients respectable.

Gordon suggests that the role of the corporate lawyer-statesperson, which has survived many challenges in the twentieth century, may be disappearing today. The profession is divided, with a small public interest bar on one side and a massive corporate bar increasingly preoccupied only with the work that is done directly for their clients on the other. What little corporate investment there is in institution-building and statesperson behavior, he suggests, is focused outside the United States on exporting the rule of law and models of U.S. legal practice to other countries. If Gordon is correct, and the awesome power of the corporate law firms is channeled domestically only to clients' instrumental needs, it will be harder for the legal profession to make the case that the law should be respected for its availability to all sides in the struggle for political and economic power. Law's legitimacy and therefore its position might be threatened.

Laura Kalman's chapter highlights a similar precariousness in the legal academy and its relationship to practicing lawyers, judges, and other academic disciplines. She explores the tensions and conflicts that have occurred as the various parts of the profession converge and diverge around what their roles should be. Practicing lawyers and legal academics are divided by differences about how and whether social scientific expertise should be used. Practitioners tend to reject social science, while academic lawyers tend to mobilize social scientific approaches to challenge legal formalism and the rationales for prevailing legal practices. At the same time, the academic disciplines the legal scholars appropriate tend to resent the law professors' encroachments and their lack of schooling in the proper disciplinary methods. The conflicts have not been resolved, and they could potentially threaten the legitimacy of law within the academy and the profession, each seemingly pulling in different directions. Nevertheless, Kalman asserts, the conflicts involved in these particular crises are not insurmountable. Interdisciplinary scholarship is increasing, and along with that increase comes growing mutual respect within the law and other disciplines. Whether or not Gordon is right about the potential decline of the lawyer-statesperson, Kalman's chapter shows that the still relatively prestigious statesperson role, itself a product and producer of the legitimacy of law, can be strengthened and affirmed if the academy can succeed in drawing the insights and expertise of social science into law and legal practice.

David Kennedy's chapter focuses on the history of international law, especially in the post–World War II period. He takes up the challenge of the international lawyer acting as legal statesperson from the United States. The role has been given considerable prominence recently through the strength of the United States and its approach to law and governance. Ambitious lawyers see opportunities to invest in international activities. Kennedy emphasizes, however, that the doctrine of international law is limited by its absorption of conventional wisdom grounded in social science as well as ideas about markets and democracies. He also points out that the presumed challengers of conventional wisdom are themselves trapped in the traditional categories and arguments of international law, such as formalism versus informalism, or state sovereignty versus internationalism.

Kennedy suggests that a creative examination of international law doctrines informed by the histories that have generated them can open up new legal spaces. He envisions a strengthening and transformation of the progressive statesperson role. He seeks, therefore, to reinvent the field of international law and to strengthen the position of the international lawyer—to respond to growing concerns about inequality in the emerging global economy. Kennedy wants to build the international rule of law, but he also wants to ensure that it reflects a set of political values that are not given sufficient prominence today.

Kennedy's point reflects a truism about law that was often neglected in the twentieth century. While we have witnessed the triumph of the rule of law, and while the rule of law both fosters and challenges democracy and capitalism, it is capable of countless substantive meanings. On the one hand, it is fairly easy to say that the rule of law is missing in contexts where the authority of law is ignored or easily dismissed. Reflecting on the failure of the rule of law in the Soviet empire, for example, Martin Krygier cautioned, "The rule of law is not a panacea. There are countless problems it does not and cannot solve. There are values with which it conflicts, and there are problems it generates itself. Moreover, its elements are nowhere fully or uniformly realized . . . and [sometimes] gives potent and often misleading ideological cover for exploitative and oppressive realities" (1990, 645). Yet comparing the Communist experience with the West's experience of democratically responsive yet partially autonomous and reliable legal systems, Krygier notes, one is reminded that "law . . . is capable of being a shield against government, not merely its sword," as well as "an important source of signals and nodes of cooperation, a rich and valuable contributor to the texture of everyday life, and an important source of security and stability to many people who never give it a thought." Both aspects of law's domain, its limits and its contributions, are reflected in this volume's essays.

The essays also convey the protean nature of law in a rapidly changing social order. While we speak of the rule of law or law's century, changes have been dramatic over the past hundred years. In the course of the twentieth century, various schools of legal thought and constitutional interpretation rose, fell, and evolved, as did the policies and conceptions of legal subjects that suffused the ever-growing body of positive law. We came to use the terms "statute," "contract," "regulation," "property," "crime," "rights," and "lawyer" to encompass types of commands, agreements, government activities, individual claims, and legal roles that could hardly have been imagined in 1900. In the unpredictable century to come, we can foresee only that the law will continue to be characterized by a relative stability in terminology combined with plasticity, ubiquity, and a wide variety of consequences that can follow legal change. In any case, the double-sidedness of law will remain evident. Forces for change may be dramatic or radical, but legal professionals will domesticate those forces by pouring new ideas and theories into relatively traditional legal categories and concepts. The essays in this volume document law's recent successes not only in managing change, but also in shaping our thinking about change. Whether it will make sense a century from now to maintain law in such a privileged place in the United States—or to promote it in other societies with very different histories—remains to be seen.

NOTES

1 As an ideal type, the turn from history to memory is to move from the disciplined effort to marshal evidence about the "truth" of the past to the slippery terrain on which individuals and groups invent traditions and record partisan versions of the past on the basis of which they seek to construct particular conditions in the present. "Memory," Pierre Nora claims, "is life, borne by living societies founded in its name. It remains in permanent evolution, open to the dialectic of remembering and forgetting, unconscious of its successive deformations, vulnerable to manipulation and appropriation. . . . history, on the other hand, is the reconstruction . . . of what is no longer" (1989, 10). It is true, however, that each generation rewrites history in light of its own concerns and approaches—inventing traditions in a different way.

2 "The 'cultural' side," as Gary Peller (1997, 193) explains, "reflects the notion that colonialism is not always imposed by visible material force nor according to the boundaries of formally constituted nation-states." "The 'imperialism' side," Peller continues, "embodies the understanding that disparate power is at issue."

3 For a description and critique of this position see Unger 1976.

4 Mark Roe (1991, 10) points out that American law, fueled by Populist mistrust of concentrated power, has long insisted on preserving the autonomy of corporate managers by sharply limiting ownership shares in individual corporations by large aggregations of capital such as banks, insurance companies, pension funds, and mutual funds.

REFERENCES

Bell, Diane. 1992. "Considering Gender: Are Human Rights for Women, Too? An Australian Case." In *Human Rights in Cross-Cultural Perspectives: A Quest for Consensus*, ed. Abdullahi Ahmed An-Na'im. Philadelphia: University of Pennsylvania Press.

Berman, Ronald, ed. 1980. *Solzhenitsyn at Harvard: The Address, Twelve Early Responses and Six Later Reflections*. Washington, D.C.: Ethics and Public Policy Center.

Bickel, Alexander. 1962. *The Least Dangerous Branch: The Supreme Court at the Bar of Politics*. Indianapolis: Bobbs-Merrill.

Cappelletti, Mauro. 1989. *The Judicial Process in Comparative Perspective*. Oxford: Clarendon Press.

Carothers, Thomas. 1998. "The Rule of Law Revival," 77 *Foreign Affairs* (1998).

Collins, Hugh. 1982. *Marxism and the Law*. Oxford: Clarendon Press.

Commager, Henry Steele. 1943. *Majority Rule and Minority Rights*. New York: Peter Smith.

Correa, Jorge. 1993. "The Judiciary and the Political System in Chile." In *Transition to Democracy in Latin America: The Role of the Judiciary*, ed. Irwin Stotsky. Boulder, Colo.: Westview Press, 1993.

Dezalay, Yves, and Bryant Garth. 1996. *Dealing in Virtue: International Commercial Arbitration and the Construction of a Transnational Legal Order*. Chicago: University of Chicago Press.

Ely, John Hart. 1980. *Democracy and Distrust: A Theory of Judicial Review*. Cambridge: Harvard University Press.

Emmott, Bill. 1999. "Freedom's Journey: A Survey of the 20th Century," *The Economist*, September 11.

Engel, David. 1993. "Law in the Domains of Everyday Life: The Construction of Community and Difference." In *Law in Everyday Life*, ed. Austin Sarat and Thomas Kearns. Ann Arbor: University of Michigan Press.

Epp, Charles. 1998. *The Rights Revolution: Lawyers, Activists and Supreme Courts in Comparative Perspective*. Chicago: University of Chicago Press.

Ewick, Patricia, and Susan S. Silbey. 1998. *The Common Place of Law: Stories from Everyday Life*. Chicago: University of Chicago Press.

Friedman, Lawrence. 1985a. *A History of American Law*, 2d ed. New York: Simon and Schuster.

———. 1985b. *Total Justice*. New York: Russell Sage Foundation.

———. 1990. *The Republic of Choice: Law, Authority, and Culture*. Cambridge: Harvard University Press.

Galanter, Marc, and Thomas Palay. 1992. *Tournament of Lawyers: The Transformations of The Big Law Firms*. Chicago: University of Chicago Press.

Galanter, Marc, and Joel Rogers. 1991. "A Transformation of American Business Disputing? Some Preliminary Observations." Working Paper DPRP 10–3, Institute for Legal Studies, University of Wisconsin, Madison.

Garth, Bryant, and Yves Dezalay. 1995. "Merchants of Law as Moral Entrepreneurs: Constructing International Justice from the Competition for Transnational Business Disputes," 29 *Law & Society Rev* 27.

Gilson, Ronald. 1984. "Value Creation by Business Lawyers: Legal Skills and Asset Pricing," 94 *Yale Law Journal* 239.

Glendon, Mary Ann. 1991. *Rights Talk: The Impoverishment of Political Discourse*. New York: Free Press.

Gordon, Robert. 1984. "Critical Legal Histories," 36 *Stanford Law Review* 57.

Hendley, Kathryn. 1996. *Trying to Make Law Matter: Legal Reform and Labor Law in the Soviet Union*. Ann Arbor: University of Michigan Press.

———. 1999. "Rewriting the Rules of the Game in Russia: The Neglected Issue of the Demand for Law," 8 *East European Constitutional Review* 89.

Holmes, Oliver Wendell. 1897. "The Path of the Law," 10 *Harvard Law Review* 61.

Kagan, Robert A. 1997. "Should Europe Worry about Adversarial Legalism?" 17 *Oxford Journal of Legal Studies* 165.

Kagan, Robert A., and Lee Axelrad, eds. 2000. *Regulatory Encounters: Multinational Corporations and American Adversarial Legalism.* Berkeley: University of California Press.

Krygier, Martin. 1990. "Marxism and the Rule of Law: Reflections after the Collapse of Communism," 15 *Law & Social Inquiry* 633.

Markesenis, Basil. 1990. "Litigation Mania in England, Germany and the USA: Are We So Very Different?" 49 *Cambridge Law Journal* 233.

McCann, Michael. 1994. *Rights at Work: Pay Equity Reform and the Politics of Mobilization.* Chicago: University of Chicago Press.

McCann, Michael, and Helena Silverstein. 1998. "Rethinking Law's "Allurements": A Relational Analysis of Social Movement Lawyers in the United States." In *Cause Lawyering: Political Commitments and Professional Responsibilities*, ed. Austin Sarat and Stuart Scheingold, 261–292. New York: Oxford University Press.

McClosky, Herbert, and John Zaller. 1984. *The American Ethos: Public Attitudes toward Capitalism and Democracy.* Cambridge: Harvard University Press.

McFate, Katherine. 1995. "Trampolines, Safety Nets, or Free Fall? Labor Market Policies and Social Assistance in the 1980s." In *Poverty, Inequality, and the Future of Social Policy: Western States in the New World Order*, ed. Katherine McFate, Roger Lawson, and William Julius Wilson. New York: Russell Sage Foundation.

Melnick, R. Shep. 1993. *Between the Lines: Interpreting Welfare Rights.* Washington, D.C.: Brookings Institute.

Mouffe, Chantal. 1995. "Democratic Politics and the Question of Identity." In *The Identity in Question*, ed. John Rajchman. New York: Routledge.

Natapoff, Alexandra. 1996. "Madisonian Multiculturalism," 45 *American University Law Review* 751.

Nelson, William. 1990. "Contract Litigation and the Elite Bar in New York City, 1960–1980," 39 *Emory L. Rev.* 413.

Nonet, Phillippe, and Philip Selznick. 1978. *Law and Society in Transition: Toward Responsive Law.* New York: Harper & Row.

Nora, Pierre. 1989. "Between Memory and History: *Les Lieux de Memoire*," 26 *Representations* 8.

Peller, Gary. 1997. "Cultural Imperialism, White Anxiety, and the Ideological Realignment of *Brown*." In *Race, Law, & Culture: Reflections on* Brown v. Board of Education, ed. Austin Sarat. New York: Oxford University Press.

Peretti, Terry Jennings. 1999. *In Defense of a Political Court.* Princeton, N.J.: Princeton University Press.

Pollis, Adamantia, and Peter Schwab. 1979. "Human Rights: A Western Construct with Limited Applicability." In *Human Rights: Cultural and Ideological Perspectives*, ed. Adamantia Pollis and Peter Schwab. New York: Praeger.

Rheinstein, Max. 1967. *Max Weber on Law in Economy and Society.* New York: Simon & Schuster.

"Road to Riches, The." 1999. *The Economist*, December 31, 9.

Roe, Mark. 1991. "A Political Theory of American Corporate Finance," 91 *Columbia L. Rev.* 10.

Rosenthal, Jean-Laurent. 1992. *The Fruits of Revolution.* Los Angeles: UCLA Press.

Rowat, Malcolm, Waleed Malik, and Maria Dakiolis, eds. 1995. *Judicial Reform in Latin America and the Caribbean*, World Bank Technical Paper no. 20. Washington, D.C.: The World Bank.

Sarat, Austin. 1990. "'The Law Is All Over': Power, Resistance and the Legal Consciousness of the Welfare Poor," 2 *Yale J. Law & Humanities* 343.

———. 1997. *Law, Race, and Culture: Reflections on* Brown v. Board of Education. New York: Oxford University Press.

———. 2000. "Imaging the Law of the Father: Loss, Dread, and Mourning in *The Sweet Hereafter*," 34 *Law and Society Review* 3.

Sarat, Austin, and Thomas Kearns. 1993. "Beyond the Great Divide: Forms of Legal Scholarship and Everyday Life." In *Law in Everyday Life*, ed. Austin Sarat and Thomas Kearns. Ann Arbor: University of Michigan Press.

———. 2000. "The Unsettled Status of Human Rights: An Introduction." In *Human Rights: Concepts, Contests, Contingencies*, ed. Austin Sarat and Thomas Kearns. Ann Arbor: University of Michigan Press.

Sarat, Austin, and Stuart Scheingold. 2001. *Cause Lawyers and the State in a Global Era*. New York: Oxford University Press.

Schauer, Frederick. 1998. "The Path of Law Today: Prediction and Particularity," 78 *Boston University Law Review* 773.

Scheingold, Stuart A. 1974. *The Politics of Rights*. New Haven, Conn.: Yale University Press.

———. 1999. "Taking Weber Seriously: Lawyers, Politics, and the Liberal State," 24 *Law and Social Inquiry* 1061–1081.

———. 2001. "Cause Lawyering and Democracy in Transnational Perspective: A Postscript." In *Cause Lawyers and the State in a Global Era*, ed. Austin Sarat and Stuart Scheingold. New York: Oxford University Press.

Sellers, Jeffery. 1995. "Litigation as a Local Political Resource: Courts in Controversies over Land Use in France, Germany and the United States," 29 *Law & Society Review* 475.

Shapiro, Martin. 1993. "The Globalization of Law," 1 *Indiana J. of Global Legal Studies* 37.

Shute, Stephen, and Susan Hurley. 1993. "Introduction." In *On Human Rights: The Oxford Amnesty Lectures 1993*, ed. Stephen Shute and Susan Hurley. New York: Basic Books.

Simon, Jonathan. 1997. "Governing through Crime." In *The Crime Conundrum: Essays on Criminal Justice*, ed. Lawrence Friedman and George Fisher. Boulder, Colo.: Westview Press.

———. 1997. "Governing through Crime in a Democratic Society," unpublished paper, 15.

Stone, Alex. 1992. *The Birth of Judicial Politics in France*. New York: Oxford University Press.

Summers, Lawrence H. 1999. "The New Wealth of Nations: Lessons from the 1990s," 53 *Bulletin of the American Academy of Arts and Sciences* 26.

Tate, C. Neal, and Torbjorn Vallinder. 1995. *The Global Expansion of Judicial Power.* New York: New York University Press.

Taylor, Charles. 1992. *Multiculturalism and "The Politics of Recognition."* Princeton, N.J.: Princeton University Press.

Teubner, Gunther. 1987. *Juridification of Social Spheres*. Berlin: Walter de Gruyter.
Trubek, David. 1996. "Law and Development: Then and Now," unpublished manuscript.
Tonry, Michael. 1995. *Malign Neglect: Race, Crime, and Punishment in America*. New York: Oxford University Press.
Ulc, Otto. 1972. *The Judge in a Communist State*. Athens: Ohio University Press.
Unger, Roberto. 1976. *Law in Modern Society: Toward a Criticism of Social Theory*. New York: Free Press.
Versailles v. McKeesport Coal. 83 *Pittsburgh Legal Journal* 379 (1935).
Vogel, David. 1995. *Trading Up: Consumer and Environmental Regulation in a Global Economy*. Cambridge: Harvard University Press.
Vogel, Steven. 1996. *Freer Markets, More Rules: Regulatory Reform in Advanced Industrial Countries*. Ithaca, N.Y.: Cornell University Press.
Waldron, Jeremy. 1991. "Homelessness and the Issue of Freedom," 39 *UCLA Law Review* 295.

PART I
Citizenship, Rights, and Politics

The Idea of Political Freedom

Owen Fiss

OVER THE LAST TWO centuries, our conception of state power has shifted. In the nineteenth century, we conceived of the state as an artificial entity constructed by the members of society to serve distinct and limited purposes. The Constitution, according to this view, was an instrument of creation. It brought the state into being, and the constraints it imposed on the state derived from this constructive endeavor. The first and foremost question of constitutional law was one of authority: is the state empowered to act?

In the twentieth century, particularly after the New Deal, the state was conceived in more organic terms: as a structure of existence immanent within the community whose welfare it sought to further. Authority was presumed, and the principal constitutional inquiry was whether the state had violated some specific prohibition. In that respect, the First Amendment, the subject of this chapter, is exemplary. It declares that "Congress shall make no law abridging the freedom of speech, or of the press." In the twentieth century, this provision of the Bill of Rights became one of the focal points of constitutional litigation and was forged into a powerful tool for invalidating state and federal regulations even when authority was otherwise manifest.

Today, any transgression of the First Amendment prohibition is construed to mean that the state exceeded its authority. In the nineteenth century, however, the question of authority arose not from the application of a specific prohibition, but from an understanding of the inherent limits on the state's authority to pursue certain ends. Those limits were intrinsic or internal to the authority itself; they were derived from the very purposes for which states were created. The limits imposed on state authority by the First Amendment, by contrast, are extrinsic. They place limits on state power even when it was assumed that the law in question served public purposes.

The doctrine of "enumerated powers," so prominent in nineteenth-century

The author wishes to acknowledge the many important contributions of William Fick and Matthew Lindsay to this essay.

constitutional litigation, was an attempt to preserve the intrinsic limits of state authority. It required the Supreme Court to locate a grant of authority in the Constitution that would allow Congress to enact the measure in question. The doctrine of "substantive due process" was of like effect, though it had its greatest force in the context of state and local legislation. Admittedly, the states possessed a power—the police power—that the federal government lacked, but in the nineteenth and the early twentieth century, the Supreme Court understood that power in much the manner of the enumerated powers of the federal government—that is, as a species of constructed, as opposed to organic, authority. Although the states could enact measures to further the "health, welfare, or morals" of the public, each of the seemingly expansive terms in this formula became a narrow pigeonhole restricting the scope and permissible purpose of any law.

In the most famous substantive due process case of all—*Lochner v. New York* (1905)—the Supreme Court struck down a New York statute imposing a ceiling on the hours worked in bakeries, on the ground that the state had exceeded the limits on its authority. Justice Rufus Peckham's majority opinion acknowledged that protecting the health of workers—the only justification for the law that he could countenance—was a permissible end for the state, yet he thought the relationship between that end and the means adopted by the legislature to achieve it was unacceptably incongruent. If restricting the number of hours worked in bakeries, were an acceptable means of protecting the health of workers, there would be, he feared, no effective limit to the power of the state. As the basis of this decision, Peckham relied on the Due Process Clause, which prohibits the state from depriving any person of "life, liberty, or property without due process of law." The Due Process Clause was not treated, however, like the First Amendment, as a prohibition, but more in the nature of the Ninth Amendment, as a codification of the general idea that the rightful reach of the state over the individual is limited (Fiss 1993, 158–60).

The distinction between the authority and prohibition inquiries that distinguish the nineteenth and twentieth centuries represented not only a difference in constitutional method, but also, and perhaps more fundamentally, a difference in the understanding of liberty. From the authority perspective, liberty was what remained to the individual once the state had reached the outer bounds of its authority. Liberty was a residue. This kind of liberty might be characterized as a prepolitical or natural liberty because it belonged to the individual standing outside of, or apart from, the organized political community. It was the liberty an individual might enjoy in the state of nature imagined by the social contract theorists of the eighteenth century and before.

From the perspective of the First Amendment, another type of liberty emerges: a right that the individual enjoys as a member of the community and that is essential to the effective functioning of that community. The extent of the state's capacity to regulate speech is drawn not along the lines of the intrinsic limits of its authority, or at the outer boundaries of the individual's domain of natural freedom, but rather in a fashion calculated to further the functioning of the political system. Speech is protected on the theory that free and open debate on public issues is an essential precondition of democratic self-government. Accordingly, the freedom the First Amendment has given rise to might well be conceived as a political freedom: first, because it belongs to individuals as participants in the political system, and second, because it serves the needs and interests of that system.

Driven by the imperatives implicit in the idea of political freedom, the Supreme Court has over the course of the twentieth century invalidated many laws that manifestly serve public purposes and that were otherwise within the scope of state authority. The Court saw itself as a bulwark of our political freedom. Even more remarkably, given the nineteenth-century understanding of constitutionalism and its emphasis upon limiting the state, the idea of political freedom led the Court to call upon the state to act affirmatively to protect and even enrich public debate.

FREE SPEECH AS A NATURAL LIBERTY

The intellectual traditions out of which *Lochner* arose have great resiliency, and, as illustrated by the 1969 decision *Stanley v. Georgia*, continued to surface in the application of the First Amendment. In these cases, state regulation was deemed to have intruded into a domain that naturally belonged to the individual, and the Amendment was used as a formal basis to invalidate state action in a manner reminiscent of *Lochner*. The specific content of First Amendment law and the idea of political freedom played no role in the Court's analysis.

The petitioner in *Stanley v. Georgia* was convicted for possessing obscene films in the privacy of his home. In defending the constitutionality of the state law underlying the prosecution, Georgia drew on precedent that allowed it to criminalize the production and public distribution of obscene material. The state acknowledged a difference between these public activities and the mere possession of obscenity in the privacy of one's home but defended its authority in terms of "the right to protect the individual's mind from the effects of obscenity" (*Stanley*, 565).

Justice Marshall's opinion for the Court flatly denied that this was a permissible end of government. The state, he said, "cannot constitutionally premise legislation on the desirability of controlling a person's private thoughts" (*Stanley*, 566). Put differently, the state had exceeded the limits on its authority and intruded into a domain of liberty—in this instance not freedom of contract, but rather, in Marshall's terms, the individual's "right to read or observe what he pleases" (*Stanley*, 568). Marshall also rejected the state's attempt to justify the statute on grounds that might be regarded as more legitimate, such as preventing destructive sexual behavior or crimes of sexual violence. In much the spirit of Peckham's analysis in *Lochner*, Marshall feared that to allow these admittedly public purposes to justify the application of coercive state power would destroy all sense of limits upon government authority.

In reaching this conclusion Marshall and the modern Court may have been giving expression to the two ideologies—liberalism and capitalism—that have shaped so much of our constitutional history and that have nourished the ideal of the limited state. These ideologies have helped keep alive the notion of the state as a structure of power with internal limits. Even more plausibly, the persistence of the authority question may also be seen as a response to a uniquely dangerous twentieth-century phenomenon—totalitarianism (Primus 1996 and 1999). Although Thurgood Marshall and many of the other justices who served during the last half century were not likely to be drawn to the conception of state power underlying *Lochner*, Hitler's Germany, Stalin's Soviet Union, and Mao's China surely represented powerful negative examples. For them, the challenge was to acknowledge the state as an organic entity, an expression of the political community, without tolerating excesses made vivid by the specter of totalitarianism.

Jed Rubenfeld has proposed an antitotalitarian principle to explain Supreme Court decisions invalidating laws that criminalize abortions and prohibit the distribution of contraceptives. The state, he argues, should not be able to write the script of a woman's life by denying her the capacity to have sex without having children (Rubenfeld 1989). More recently, Rubenfeld applied this principle to the Takings Clause. He argued that the state would be "taking," as opposed to merely "regulating," property when it actually tried to *use* the property of a citizen (Rubenfeld 1993). The totalitarian state is one that refuses to recognize any intrinsic limits on its authority and intrudes into domains that properly belong to the individual. This same fear of totalitarianism can explain the Court's judgment in some free-speech cases such as *Stanley v. Georgia,* and could also account for the continued vitality of the authority question in the twentieth century.

Although *Stanley v. Georgia* involved conduct occurring in the home, and for that reason might be seen simply as a case about privacy rights, much like decisions regarding contraceptives or abortion, the concern for limits on state authority that is evident in that decision extends far more broadly, and has in fact informed a number of cases involving regulation of speech in public places. One such case arose from the effort of a state to establish a code of etiquette in the public square. The Supreme Court responded to that effort in *Chaplinsky v. New Hampshire* (1942) with the famous "fighting words" doctrine. The Court did not deny the communicative character of certain offensive or derisive utterances, but rather, by linking the speech to the disruption of the public order, framed the question of constitutionality as an inquiry into the grounds for state authority.

The statute at issue in *Chaplinsky* provided that "no person shall address any offensive, derisive or annoying word to any other person who is lawfully in any street or other public place, nor call him by any offensive or derisive name" (*Chaplinsky*, 569). The authority of the state to enact such a code of etiquette, even for public places, was open to question. What business does the state have in setting the terms of public interactions? In order to answer that question, the Supreme Court began its analysis by adopting the interpretation of the New Hampshire court that confined the statute to words "which by their very utterance inflict injury or tend to incite an immediate breach of the peace" (*Chaplinsky*, 572). It was the risk of a breach of the peace, the Supreme Court concluded, that permitted the state to prohibit Chaplinsky from calling a law enforcement official with whom he was engaged in an argument "a God damned racketeer" and "a damned Fascist" (*Chaplinsky*, 569). New Hampshire was not trying to establish a code of etiquette, but rather to avoid breaches of the peace, which was clearly within its authority.

The Court's recent response to the regulation of commercial advertising provides another instance in which a concern about state authority has shaped the development of free-speech law in a public context. Surely, a statute prohibiting misleading or false advertising would serve a manifest public purpose—to preserve the integrity of the market and the capacity of consumers to make meaningful choices. It would thus fall within the authority of the state. Likewise, few would dispute the authority of the state to ban advertising in order to depress the demand for an illegal substance, such as cocaine. On the other side of the line, a state law that prohibited advertising about a product or activity of unquestionable legality seems excessive. Imagine, for example, a law that prohibited any form of advertising about the price of computers. In such a case, all of the justices would probably agree that the state had exceeded its authority. What have divided the Court in recent years, in cases such as *44 Liquormart v. Rhode Island* (1996) or *Central Hudson Gas and Electric Corp. v. Public Service Commission of New York* (1980), are advertising regulations aimed at suppressing demand for products—for example, alcohol or electricity—that remain legal and unrationed, but the consumption of which many believe should be discouraged.

A controlling majority of the justices believe that such regulations on commercial speech are invalid, or at least presumptively invalid. They deny that the state has any authority to suppress the demand for a product that has not itself been declared illegal. Another bloc is hesitant to require the state to ban a product as a precondition for banning its advertisement. The purposes served by an outright prohibition—for example, public health—may be more effectively served by a strategy that reduces the public desire to use or want such a product. Yet even for this particular group of justices, the forcefulness of their inquiry into the instrumental connection between means and ends reflects doubt as to the warrant for state authority. Is the ban on advertisement at issue a reasonably effective mechanism for suppressing demand, or does it serve other, improper ends, such as protecting one group of competitors over another?

Still another branch of First Amendment jurisprudence informed by the concern for the limits on state authority can be found in the Court's effort—largely taking shape in the late 1950s and 1960s—to protect artistic activity. This area of the law returns us to *Stanley v. Georgia*, but outside the context of a private home. Imagine a state law that prohibited the sale or distribution of abstract expressionism. Of course, any such enactment would smack of totalitarianism and would be deemed far beyond the scope of state authority.

A more plausible regulation might seek to restrict public dissemination of sexually explicit material. Policy makers have offered a wide variety of rationales to justify such laws. They prevent sexual violence, avoid affronts to public sensibilities, prevent the objectification of women, and shield children from material that might disrupt the normal development process. These rationales, especially when taken collectively, help to build the warrant for state authority so lacking in *Stanley v. Georgia* and my abstract expressionism example. Yet doubts generated by a fear of totalitarianism persisted and put the state to the task of producing justifications for the regulation of artistic expression. These doubts also account for the boundaries the Supreme Court has placed on the regulation of obscenity; namely, that the materials subject to prohibition appeal to a prurient interest in sex, be patently offensive, and lack serious aesthetic, social, or political value (*Miller v. California* [1973]).

In an important article published in 1971, Robert Bork struggled with the regulation of art and analyzed it in terms of the First Amendment theory of Alexander Meiklejohn. According to Meiklejohn, the value of speech derives from the contribution it makes to democracy (Meiklejohn 1960 and 1961). Robust debate advises citizens of the available political alternatives and the arguments for and against each. Meiklejohn conceived of free speech as an adjunct to the right to vote. On various occasions, critics challenged Meiklejohn with the example of art: if the goal of the First Amendment is strictly political, then why protect art? Professor Bork dismissed Meiklejohn's famous answer—that we need to read *Ulysses* in order to vote—as a principle with no limits. Such an instrumental argument would lead, Bork feared, to an "analogical stampede," since nearly any human activity could be swept within its reach (Bork 1971, 25).

Unprepared to abandon the Meiklejohn theory, Bork felt—at least in 1971, before he was nominated to the Supreme Court and buckled under questioning from the Senate Judiciary Committee—that he had no alternative but to leave art outside the protection of the First Amendment. As a result, he proposed a principle that would limit First Amendment protection to speech explicitly about government—speech related to a political campaign, or praising or criticizing a government policy or agency.

Many, including myself, believe that there is much more truth to Meiklejohn's instrumental rationale for protecting art than Bork had allowed. Putting that objection aside, however, Bork could be faulted also for overlooking the possibility of protecting art through an inquiry into authority. Short of embracing the totalitarian state, or identifying some very specific threat to the public welfare, it is hard to understand what reason the state would have for regulating the production or distribution of art. Bork's lapse can readily be explained by the fact that his First Amendment analysis formed part of a broader argument that repudiated *Lochner* and, more pointedly, the 1965 decision of *Griswold v. Connecticut*, which invalidated a state ban on dissemination of information on contraceptives. *Griswold* was the indispensable precursor of the soon-to-be-decided *Roe v. Wade* (1973), which struck down laws that criminalized abortions.

The use of the First Amendment to protect a right not to speak provides a final example of the authority question at work. This branch of First Amendment doctrine has its roots in *West Virginia State Board of Education v. Barnette* (1943), which denied the state the power to compel schoolchildren who were Jehovah's Witnesses to salute the flag. In this case, decided at the height of the Second World War, the interest of the state in compelling the activity—the promotion of patriotism—was understandable, and the absence of authority in the classic nineteenth-century sense was far from manifest. To justify its decision, which banned the state from compelling flag salutes, the Court invoked principles, almost religious in nature, holding the conscience of the individual to be inviolate.

The lack of state authority to coerce speech became clearer in *Wooley v. Maynard* (1977), a striking contemporary use of this doctrine. In that case, New Hampshire imprinted the state motto, "Live Free or Die," on each and every license plate. The state prohibited those who might be offended by carrying such a message on their cars—for example, Jehovah's Witnesses—from obscuring the words. The Supreme Court held New Hampshire's policy to be unconstitutional. In the Court's eyes, the state was simply using individuals and their property to propagate its own views. The state would be condemned on much the same terms Rubenfeld had proposed in his analysis of the takings clause and abortion decisions: by using individuals as instruments of its policy, the state was acting much like a totalitarian government. All sense of limits was gone.

THE POLITICAL CONCEPTION OF FREE SPEECH

In the various branches of First Amendment law that I have identified—the rule of *Stanley v. Georgia*, "fighting words," commercial speech, art, and the right not to speak—the authority question played an important role. Whether out of fear of the excesses of totalitarianism or out of respect for traditional liberal or capitalist principles, the Court operated on the assumption that the state, even a democratic state responsive to majority wishes, has intrinsic limits to its authority. The task remained of identifying those limits.

For the most part, however, the authority question has played a relatively minor role in the evolution of First Amendment doctrine in the twentieth century. Most free speech decisions were handed down in the period following the New Deal and the Second World War, at a time when state power was conceived as immanent within the community it served. As a result, the Court's analyses typically began with the assumption that the law served proper public purposes; the principal question then became whether the law violated the prohibition of the First Amendment.

Central to this enterprise has been a functional interpretation of the First Amendment—largely adumbrated by Alexander Meiklejohn in 1948, and before him by Justice Brandeis in *Whitney v. California* (1927)—that conceives of freedom of speech an instrument of democracy. It is posited that free and open discussion of issues of public concern is an essential precondition for exercising the power of self-government in an intelligent and reflective way, and that freedom of speech, like freedom of the press, is protected for this reason. Under this theory, the First Amendment protects the right of individuals or organizations to participate in public debate—to express their views freely—in order to maintain and strengthen the power of self-determination of the collectivity. Speech serves democracy, and because of this instrumental relationship, speech takes on a distinctly political cast.

Although prepolitical or natural liberty derived from authority limitations has played a role in the evolution of First Amendment doctrine in the twentieth century, from a historical perspective it has a vestigial quality. Distinctly twentieth-century developments—above all, the emergence of the totalitarian state—may have revived a concern with the authority question, but the persistence of that concern should be seen as the continuation of a nineteenth-century tradition in First Amendment garb. The political conception of free speech, by contrast, had an entirely different trajectory. The twentieth century largely belonged to the political. The idea of political freedom grew in importance and centrality throughout the twentieth century, and it did so because our commitment to democracy also grew.

The enfranchisement of women and blacks and the elimination of literacy and property qualifications for voting were a reflection and affirmation of our growing democratic commitment, as were the Second World War and, arguably, the cold war. At the end of the twentieth century, democracy had a claim to our allegiance that far transcended any such claim it might have had at its beginning. In 2000, in contrast to 1900, we assumed that the only legitimate form of government is a democratic one—any deviation requires explanation. It was thus only natural that the conception of free speech that views speech as an instrument of democracy achieved an increasingly prominent place in First Amendment jurisprudence, and that it achieved an affirmative or compelling quality in much the same way that democracy itself did.

If, as I suggested, *Stanley v. Georgia* might be taken as the symbol of natural liberty, *New York Times v. Sullivan* should be seen as representing the idea of political freedom. The decision was handed down in 1964, during one of the fiercest and most inspiring democratic struggles of the century. The case arose from a libel proceeding brought by a police commissioner of Montgomery, Alabama, against the *New York Times* for publishing an advertisement on behalf of Martin Luther King Jr. and his followers. The advertisement, which appeared in the *Times* in 1960, at an early phase of the civil rights era, charged the Montgomery police with launching a wave of terror against Dr. King and student protestors. Titled "Heed Their Rising Voices," it sought financial contributions from the readers of the *Times*.

An Alabama jury had rendered a $500,000 verdict against the *Times*. The Supreme Court set aside this verdict and announced what has become known as the "actual malice" standard for libel cases: false statement of facts about public officials—in this instance, that Dr. King had been arrested seven times, when in truth he was arrested only four times—are actionable only if it can be shown that the speaker knew the statement was false or spoke with reckless disregard for the truth. Commissioner Sullivan could make no such showing.

In thus protecting a carelessly uttered falsehood, the Supreme Court was not making a point about the limits of state authority; clearly there was sufficient public purpose to warrant a state to protect its officials from the injury to reputation that might come from false statements, even those uttered carelessly. Rather, the Court was affirming the right of Dr. King's supporters, and derivatively, the newspaper that carried their words, to participate in public debate in a swift and forceful manner. The protection of careless falsehoods stemmed from the desire of the Court to make the promise of political freedom real and from a recognition that political activists and the media need a margin of error, or, as Justice Brennan put it in his majority opinion, "breathing space." The Court feared that if political activists and the media could be held liable for carelessly uttered falsehoods, they might be disinclined to exercise their right to participate in public debate altogether, and that if they thus declined to speak we would all suffer. In thus affirming the ideal of political freedom, the Court was unanimous, although Justices Black, Douglas, and Goldberg, anxious to ward off the slightest discouragement to the exercise of political liberty, would have gone further and shielded the speaker from liability even for a deliberate lie.

In justifying the ruling in *New York Times v. Sullivan*, Justice Brennan evoked "a profound national commitment to the principle that debate on public issues should be uninhibited, robust, and wide-open" (*Sullivan*, 270). This phrase has been quoted repeatedly by the Supreme Court and celebrated on numerous occasions by many scholars, most notably by Harry Kalven Jr., the principal proponent of the Meiklejohn theory of the First Amendment during the 1960s and early 1970s (Kalven 1964 and 1987). (Meiklejohn died in 1964 at age ninety-two; Kalven died in 1974 at age sixty.) Constant repetition may have resulted in Brennan's language seeming limp today, but at the time it powerfully conveyed the affirmative, alluring dimension of political freedom (Brennan 1965). Because the strength of democracy depends on the quality of public debate, a mandate devolves on the Court to enhance the robustness of public debate and thus the vitality of democracy.

In addition to the actual malice standard of *Sullivan* itself, the Court's so-called "strict scrutiny" doctrine likewise reflects the affirmative and compelling character of political freedom. Under this doctrine, it is not sufficient for the state to show that a law threatening the robustness of public debate serves a merely legitimate interest. It must also show that the interest is especially urgent and that the method chosen by the legislature is narrowly tailored to serve that end, so that no more speech is sacrificed than is necessary. In this way, an enormous burden of justification is placed on the state, and it would be fair to comment, as stated in another context, that strict scrutiny is usually "fatal in fact" to a challenged statute (*Adarand Constructors v. Peña* [1995], 237). Under a regime that protects natural liberty only, however, the imposition of such a stringent burden would be inexplicable, for the police power requires only that the law serve a legitimate, as opposed to a compelling, end.

The Court's concern with political freedom likewise finds expression in its singling out the content of speech for special First Amendment protection. In early cases, the Supreme Court made no distinction between state laws that curtailed a speaker's access to the public and those that regulated the content of speech. Whenever a law impaired the vitality of public debate, a very heavy burden of justification fell upon the state. In the 1939 decision *Schneider v. State*, for example, the Court struck down ordinances that prohibited leafleting or handbilling on public streets, even though such regulations kept the streets of the city free of litter, thus serving both aesthetic and health purposes. Although the Court acknowledged that these interests were legitimate, it concluded that they were insufficiently weighty to justify interference with a liberty that Justice Roberts, the author of the Court's opinion, described as lying "at the foundation of free government by free men" (*Schneider v. State*, 151).

Starting in the 1970s, the Supreme Court erected a sharp distinction between access regulations (variously called "time, place, and manner regulations") and content regulations. Aside from the time-honored categories of state censorship of obscenity and libel, the regulation of speech on the basis of its content has become a sufficient condition for strict scrutiny. In most instances, it has also become a necessary condition for such exacting review. The only exception to this rule appears to consist of laws banning all speech in a particular place—for example, in front of the Supreme Court. In my view, the rule that makes content regulation a necessary condition for strict scrutiny seems misguided, for the very reasons articulated in *Schneider*. Yet the heavy emphasis upon content regulation as a trigger of strict scrutiny represents another manifestation of the allure of political freedom, for such a concern stems from a fear that the state is somehow suppressing an idea or otherwise skewing public debate. In guarding against content regulation the Court is seeking to preserve the integrity of public debate and thus the conditions for true collective self-determination.

In addition to the doctrine of strict scrutiny and the actual malice requirement of *New York Times v. Sullivan*, the rules crafted by the Court in the last half century under a doctrine called "First Amendment Due Process" also reflect the affirmative dimensions of the idea of political freedom. First Amendment Due Process consists of a number of special procedural rules that seek to protect against interferences with public debate. Three are of special interest. These rules are buried in the technical interstices of the Court's work, but they play a crucial role in the protection of speech and thus reflect an understanding of the integral connection between robust public debate and democracy.

One strand of First Amendment Due Process emerges in cases where the Supreme Court, contrary to normal appellate procedure, undertakes an independent assessment of the facts underlying a free speech claim. The practice has its roots in the case of *Fiske v. Kansas* (1927). The state statute in question proscribed criminal syndicalism—advocacy of violence to effectuate political or economic change—and it was applied to the speech of an organizer for the Industrial Workers of the World, one of the most radical labor unions of the period. In the course of a state criminal trial, the prosecution cited the preamble of the organization's manifesto, which spoke of class struggle and the necessity for workers to organize and "take possession of the earth and the machinery of production, and abolish the wage system" (*Fiske*, 383). The Supreme Court looked at the preamble and concluded that, contrary to the view of the state courts, it provided an insufficient factual basis for concluding that the defendant had violated the criminal syndicalism statute. In proceeding in this way, the Court undoubtedly drew some of its guidance from Justice Brandeis, who in a companion case, *Whitney v. California*, linked free speech to democracy and laid the foundation for the injection of the idea of political freedom into the First Amendment jurisprudence.

Traces of First Amendment Due Process are also evident in the "prior restraint" doctrine, which creates a doubly strong presumption against the validity of injunctions aimed at speech. All restraints against political speech are disfavored, but those imposed by injunctions, as opposed to other legal instruments such as criminal statutes or damage awards, are especially suspect. In the modern period, the rule against prior restraint received its most dramatic statement in the Pentagon Papers case (*New York Times vs. United*

States, 1971), in which the Court denied the Nixon administration an injunction against publication of a Department of Defense study of United States involvement in Vietnam up to 1968. The study was classified "Top Secret" but had already been leaked to the press. In denying the injunction, a majority of the Court made clear that its action in no way precluded a criminal prosecution (*New York Times v. United States* [1971]).

The "overbreadth doctrine" represents yet another example of First Amendment Due Process. Although it first emerged in 1940 in *Thornhill v. Alabama*, which involved state interference with labor picketing, it received its most emphatic statement during the political struggles of the civil rights era. In the 1965 case of *Dombrowski v. Pfister*, civil rights activists in Louisiana had been charged with violation of a state law that had made it a criminal act to organize or participate in subversive activities. Rather than defend themselves in state criminal proceedings, the accused brought suit in federal court for an injunction against the enforcement of the statute, which would, of course, bring the state court prosecution to an end.

In sustaining the federal court injunction, the Supreme Court did not decide that the plaintiffs were acting within the permissible parameters of the First Amendment. They in fact may have been engaged in the kind of subversive advocacy that can be constitutionally proscribed. Rather, the Court found the statute invalid because it swept within its scope speech that was clearly constitutionally protected—it was overbroad. In voiding the statute on this ground, the Court was, in effect, granting the plaintiffs the power to vindicate the rights of others. In other words, the Court departed from its usual practice of only judging a particular application of a statute, and instead issued an injunction against all possible applications. The Court justified this procedural innovation in the name of "the transcendent value to all society" of constitutionally protected free speech (*Dombrowski*, 486).

THE DUTY OF THE STATE TO PROTECT FREE SPEECH

The affirmative character of political freedom operated as a premise underlying First Amendment Due Process, the doctrine of strict scrutiny, and the actual malice rule. Sometimes the premise was articulated, as in *Dombrowski* and *Sullivan*, both written by Justice Brennan. Sometimes, as in the Pentagon Papers case, it remained implicit. In either instance, the idea of political freedom formed the justification for rules that enhance protection for speech. There is, however, another branch of First Amendment jurisprudence that took shape in the course of the twentieth century in which the imperative or positive quality of political freedom was more formally recognized. I am here referring to the affirmative obligation imposed upon the state to protect speech. This obligation is unintelligible in the context of natural liberty, which, after all, consists of nothing more than what is reserved to the individual after the state has reached the limits of its authority. It fits comfortably, however, with the notion of political freedom and represents perhaps its most distinctive achievement.

Historically, this branch of First Amendment law can be traced to the period following the Second World War and, more particularly, to the dissent of Justice Black in *Feiner v. New York* (1951), which gave rise to the protection against the "heckler's veto." The importance of this idea was first underscored by Harry Kalven (Kalven 1965, 140–41) and is now firmly a part of the First Amendment lexicon and treated as majority doctrine. Feiner was the prototypical soap-box orator. Standing on a street corner in Syracuse, New York, he addressed a group of seventy-five to eighty persons, urging them to attend a meeting of the Young Progressives of America. He denounced various public officials, including President Truman and the mayor of Syracuse, and spoke forcefully for the cause of civil rights. As he put it, "The Negroes don't have equal rights; they should rise up in arms and fight for their rights" (*Feiner*, 330). The listeners that gathered filled the sidewalk and eventually spilled into the street. They soon became restless, pushing and shoving one another. One onlooker said to a policeman, "If you don't get that son of a bitch off, I will go over and get him off there myself" (*Feiner*, 330). The police asked Feiner to stop speaking, and when he refused, they arrested him. Feiner was later charged with disorderly conduct, which, under state law, followed from a refusal to heed a police order to disperse.

In an opinion by Chief Justice Vinson, the Court upheld Feiner's conviction and treated the police directive to Feiner as a reasonable attempt to maintain order. As Vinson put it, "This Court respects, as it must, the interest of the community in maintaining peace and order on its streets" (*Feiner*, 320). What Vinson overlooked was the impact this state action, however authorized it might have been, would have upon public debate. It would, in essence, provide hecklers with a veto. This point was not lost on Justice Black, who read the First Amendment as a command to protect public debate. As he saw it, the police should not have capitulated to the threat posed by the heckler, but rather made "all reasonable efforts" to protect the speaker. "Their duty," Justice Black said, referring to the police, "was to protect petitioner's right to talk, even to the extent of arresting the man who threatened to interfere" (*Feiner*, 327).

During the civil rights era, the rule denying hecklers a veto became deeply woven into our political and legal culture. It was well understood that the police had an affirmative responsibility to protect civil rights demonstrators from being silenced by angry, hostile mobs. As the hecklers grew in both number and hostility, so did the responsibility of the state. In *Williams v. Wallace* (1965), for example, Judge Frank M. Johnson Jr. ordered the state police to provide sufficient protection to Dr. King and his legion so that they could march on the state highway from Selma to Montgomery. In a number of decisions during this same time—*Edwards v. South Carolina* (1963), *Cox v. Louisiana* (1965), and *Gregory v. City of Chicago* (1969)—the Supreme Court set aside convictions of civil rights activists that were largely predicated on the hostile reaction such speech would elicit from whites.

Today street corners are not a significant site of communicative activity. Public debate is largely shaped by the mass media—newspapers, magazines, and above all, television. Protest activity that occurs on the street is largely staged for the evening news. Yet the principles derived from Feiner's poignant encounter on the streets of Syracuse have continuing vitality insofar as they point to the affirmative obligation of the state to protect and promote free and open discussion. In Feiner's case, that affirmative obligation required the police to protect his right to speak by arresting the heckler. In the context of the mass media, it meant that the state had to require the media to cover events or present views that they might otherwise slight due to market or other considerations. It required the state to curb what I describe elsewhere as managerial censorship—namely, decisions media managers might make in pursuit of legitimate goals, such as maximizing profits, but which impair the flow of politically meaningful information to the public (Fiss 1999).

In 1969, when the idea of political freedom implicit in *Sullivan* held full sway, the Court in *Red Lion Broadcasting v. FCC* (1969) unanimously sustained the FCC's attempt to curb managerial censorship by instituting the fairness doctrine. That doctrine required broadcasters to cover issues of public importance in a balanced and fair way. It also gave electoral candidates an opportunity to respond to editorials and provided a right of reply to individuals who might be personally attacked in a program. In upholding the FCC's fairness doctrine, the Supreme Court shifted the focus from the speakers—the mass media—to the listeners, and in so doing they were guided by the need of citizens to hear all sides.

In the years immediately following this decision, a period of American history characterized by attacks on "big government" and the resurgence of laissez-faire economics, the validity of the fairness doctrine fell into doubt and the *Red Lion* decision lost its generative force (*CBS v. Democratic National Committee* [1973]; *Miami Herald Publishing Co. v. Tornillo* [1974]). In 1981, the Supreme Court upheld a regulation requiring broadcasters to provide access to candidates for federal elective office (*CBS v. FCC* [1981]). Yet that case stuck out as a lonely exception. In 1987, the FCC itself repudiated the principal branch of the fairness doctrine (*Syracuse Peace Council v. WTVH* [1987]; *Syracuse Peace Council v. FCC* [1989]), and soon thereafter President Reagan vetoed a Congressional attempt to reinstate it. The fairness doctrine has never been reinstated, but a 1992 measure by Congress brought the principles of *Red Lion* once again into play, this time in the context of cable television.

By the 1990s, television had become the most significant means by which the public learns of political issues and becomes acquainted with political candidates. Moreover, cable operators had obtained an increasingly large share of the television market—60 percent in 1992. Congress feared that a further decline in the over-the-air broadcasting component of the television industry might result in its eventual collapse, and thus leave a good number of American homes—some 40 percent in 1992—with no television at all. Although some of the persons who depended on over-the-air broadcasts were simply not willing to pay the fees for cable service, many lived in communities not served by cable or could not afford cable fees. In response to these developments, in 1992 Congress enacted a law that required cable operators to carry a certain number of over-the-air broadcast channels as part of their offerings to subscribers. Congress hoped this would ensure the continuing viability of the broadcast industry and thus provide all Americans with access to television and the information it provides.

In the 1997 *Turner Broadcasting v. FCC* decision, a narrow majority of the Supreme Court upheld these so-called "must carry" requirements. Writing for himself and three other members of the Court, Justice Kennedy relied on antitrust principles in upholding the 1992 law. He thought the statute would counter predatory practices by cable operators that disfavored over-the-air broadcasters. The danger of such predatory practices arose, he felt, from the fact that many cable programmers, an alternative source of television programs, were owned by cable operators.

In a concurring opinion providing the crucial fifth vote needed for a majority, Justice Breyer eschewed the antitrust rationale. Drawing on *Red Lion* and Brandeis's concurrence in *Whitney v. California*, Breyer defended the law in terms of political freedom. His concern was wholly with the consequences to democracy of a collapse of the over-the-air broadcasting industry. He worried that such a development would leave as many as 40 percent of American homes without television. Breyer argued that in enacting the 1992 law, Congress, much like the policeman following Justice Black's mandate to protect the speaker, might have imposed upon the speech interest of the cable operators, but only to enrich public debate and further democratic self-government.

In *Feiner*, the heckler did not have much to say. Presumably he did not like Feiner's message, but rather than wait his turn to speak, he threatened to stop Feiner from speaking if the police did not. Such a threat hardly contributes to public debate. In this regard, Breyer's *Turner Broadcasting* concurrence moved beyond Black's *Feiner* dissent, for the speech interests put in jeopardy by the 1992 Cable Act are significantly greater. Requiring cable programmers to carry the programs of over-the-air broadcasters necessarily entailed a displacement of a number of programs developed by cable programmers. As a result, the First Amendment interests of the displaced cable operators and the consumers who might have viewed those programs would be adversely affected. Breyer understood, however, that some sacrifice of those interests was necessary to further the larger democratic purposes of the First Amendment. If the state did not intervene and the broadcast industry collapsed, the First Amendment interests of all the homes without cable would suffer immensely. As he put it, speech was on both sides of the equation.

In its willingness to sacrifice what might be deemed genuine First Amendment interests, Breyer's concurrence in *Turner Broadcasting* represented a more powerful expression of the generative character of political freedom than Black's dissent in *Feiner*: the state may act to promote political freedom even if some speech interests are sacrificed. In January 2000 Justice Breyer applied this same approach to sustain a Missouri law that imposed limits on financial contributions to candidates for state office (*Nixon v. Shrink Missouri Government PAC* [2000]). In *Turner Broadcasting* and this more recent campaign finance case Justice Breyer expressed these views in a separate concurrence. In *Turner Broadcasting* he spoke only for himself, though in *Shrink Missouri Government* he gained the support of Justice Ginsburg.

It is important to note, however, that in another respect the question before the Court in *Turner Broadcasting* and *Shrink Missouri Government* was narrower than the one in *Feiner*. The immediate question before the Court in *Turner Broadcasting* and *Shrink Missouri Government* was one of permissibility—was the action taken by the state to enhance public debate consistent with the First Amendment? In *Feiner*, Black did not pause on that issue, perhaps because the speech interests represented by the heckler were so slight; instead he focused entirely on the duty of the state to further public debate. His claim was not simply that the police should have refrained from arresting the speaker, but more significantly, that they must protect the speaker by arresting the heckler. Recall his words: "Their duty was to protect petitioner's right to talk, even to the extent of arresting the man who threatened to interfere" (*Feiner*, 327).

Black's assertion of a duty to protect public debate represents the fullest recognition of the imperatives latent in the idea of political freedom and rests on two propositions. First, private actors—for example, the heckler in a crowd—can threaten public debate just as much as state actors. Second, the state may sometimes be the only power in society capable of keeping these forces at bay. Neither proposition denies that state power might be used for purposes of suppressing public debate. Rather, they reflect the belief that the effect on public debate of censorship by so-called private actors—not just the heckler, but also the managers of the media or the economically powerful—is not qualitatively different from state censorship, and that the threat posed to democracy by such actions might sometimes warrant expanding the regulatory authority of the state.

These ideas became a standard part of First Amendment doctrine during the heyday of *New York Times v. Sullivan* in a series of cases that involved not the mass media, but shopping centers. At first blush, it may seem odd for a law as grand as the First Amendment to have been tested in such a mundane setting, but not once it is understood that in the decades following *Feiner*, the suburban shopping center—and later, its cousin, the downtown mall—rendered Feiner's street corner obsolete as a political forum. As a result of suburbanization and the reconfiguration of urban spaces, no one remained on the street corner. Because political activists seek to persuade the public—speech is not a cathartic activity—they took their cause to shopping centers and malls.

At first the Court was prepared to let the law follow the speaker (*Amalgamated Food Employees Union v. Logan Valley Plaza* [1968]). In a rather dramatic turnabout in the 1970s, however, the Court refused to guarantee the access of speakers to shopping centers or malls (*Lloyd Co. v. Tanner* [1972]). The Court allowed local governments to guarantee speaker access, but there was no obligation for them to do so. To justify this result, Justice Stewart pointed to the fact that the shopping centers and malls were privately owned and managed. He condescendingly reminded us that "the First and Fourteenth Amendments safeguard the rights of free speech and assembly by limitations on state action, not on action by the owner of private property" (*Hudgens v. NLRB* [1976], 519).

Contrary to Stewart's suggestion, the turnabout in Supreme Court doctrine represents not a belated discovery of the so-called state action requirement of the First Amendment, but a weakening of the commitment to the idea of political freedom. The affirmative duty of the state does not require that any of the entities threatening public debate—the hostile crowd, the owners of the shopping centers, or the managers of the media organizations—be treated as the state itself or as agents of the state (though any clever lawyer could find many ways in which these entities are involved with or dependent upon the state). Rather, the simple point, and the one that I believe underlies Black's imposition on the state of a duty to act in *Feiner*, is that sometimes inaction by the state is tantamount to action. A police officer's decision to turn a blind eye to the heckler, and thus to enable him to beat up and silence Feiner, represents an act of the state.

Admittedly, under state law the police have a duty to maintain order, and there may be no corresponding duty for the state to act in the shopping center or media cases. It was not, however, the police's duty to maintain order that transformed the inaction into action. That particular duty is a state law duty, and in any event it does not explain why the heckler, as opposed to the speaker, should be arrested. Although as a purely conceptual matter a duty to act is needed in order to transform inaction into action, that duty does not derive from some specific statute. Rather, it derives from an assessment of the interests that would be harmed by inaction, the opportunity for the state to take action that would prevent those harms, and the interests that might be jeopardized if the state were to decline to act. In assessing the interests that would be harmed by the inaction, it must be emphasized that the metric is decidedly a federal constitutional one, and that the final tally will reflect, above all, the Court's assessment of the importance or value of political freedom. No wonder the Court's turnabout in the shopping center cases occurred at roughly the same time that the Court retreated from *Red Lion.*

LIBERALISM IN THE SERVICE OF DEMOCRACY

In the shopping center, media, and related cases efforts have sometimes been made to block the affirmative exercise of state power or to deny the state's duty to act by invoking the idea of natural liberty. For example, in the mid-1980s a public utility company successfully attacked a state law that required it to provide a consumers' group access to its billing envelope four times a year, on the theory that the law abridged the company's right not to speak and the principle of *West Virginia State Board of Education v. Barnette* (*Pacific Gas & Electric Co. v. Public Utility Commission* [1986]). Soon thereafter, the FCC used this decision to declare the fairness doctrine unconstitutional (*Syracuse Peace Council v. WTVH; Syracuse Peace Council v. FCC*).

Decisions such as these represent a misappropriation of the idea of natural liberty, which should not be seen as a free-floating anxiety about the welfare of the individual that the justices may invoke whenever they take issue with a regulation. Rather, it is the residue that belongs to the individual after state authority has reached its outer limit. Accordingly, the crucial question should have been whether the challenged regulations served a public purpose. Clearly, they did. They sought to enhance public debate—not only a legitimate purpose, but (from a constitutional perspective) a highly commendable one. The regulations in question sought to strengthen the democratic system and thus stood on grounds very different from those requiring schoolchildren to salute the flag or forcing Jehovah's Witnesses to carry the motto "Live Free or Die" on their automobiles. Specific objections might be raised to such regulations when applied to the media: for example, that they actually impoverished, rather than enriched, public debate by discouraging speakers from taking controversial stands (for fear of provoking a response). But such objections are heavily fact-dependent and do not deny the authority of the state to act at all. They simply claim that the regulations are counterproductive.

For this reason, I contend—in some instances contrary to the Court—that natural liberty is not antithetical to political freedom. The most distinctive achievement of the idea of political freedom lies in its capacity to permit, or even to compel, affirmative action by the state. Properly understood, natural liberty is no bar to such action since the public purpose of the action is manifest. Going further, one can discern in the Court's decision over the latter part of the twentieth century a category of cases in which political and natural liberty supplement one another. This occurred whenever political liberty was used, in the tradition of the *Sullivan* decision, to impose limits on state authority in order to insure robust public debate. The 1994 decision in *City of Ladue v. Gilleo* represents a striking illustration of this tie between political and natural liberty.

Like *Stanley v. Georgia, Ladue* involved the home, and thus provoked strong suspicion of any state intervention. *Ladue* differed from *Stanley v. Georgia*, however, because the home was used not as a sanctuary for indulging sexual fantasies, but as a site of political protest. A citizen had hung a sign in the window of her house protesting the war against Iraq. The 8½-by-11-inch sign simply read: "For Peace in the Gulf." In protecting this protest activity, Justice Stevens, writing for a unanimous Court, recognized the political character of the speech. Residential signs, he observed, play an important part in political campaigns. Their importance in public debate stems not just from the content of the message, which can of course be conveyed by countless other means (letters, handbills, bumper stickers, etc.). It also arises from the fact, he noted, that residential signs "are an unusually cheap and convenient form of communication. Especially for persons of modest means or limited mobility, a yard or window sign may have no practical substitute" (*City of Ladue*, 56).

Although this line of analysis, expressive as it was of the value of political freedom, might have been sufficient to justify protecting the speaker, Justice Stevens did not stop there. He went on to root the decision in the principle of natural liberty as well. Although Stevens acknowledged the role of the state in controlling the use of the public streets, he insisted that "its need to regulate temperate speech from the home is surely much less pressing" (*City of Ladue*, 58). He also recognized that "a special respect for individual liberty in the home has long been part of our culture and law" and observed that "most Americans would be understandably dismayed, given that tradition, to learn that it was illegal to display from their window an 8-by-11-inch sign expressing their political views" (*City of Ladue*, 58). In making these observations, Justice Stevens made no distinction between natural and political liberty.

Concern for the impact of the state's intervention on both types of liberty has not been confined to intrusions into the home. Occasionally it has also been present in cases involving attempts to regulate conduct in the public square. *Chaplinsky* could have been one such instance, for the "fighting words" uttered in that case were politically charged. Remember, he called the local marshal a "God damned racketeer" and "a damned Fascist." In sustaining the conviction, however, the Court paid no special heed to the political character of the offensive language. In contrast, the Court grasped the point when an analogous issue surfaced in the early 1970s, after the *Sullivan* decision and the tumultuous and ennobling protest activities of the civil rights era.

In 1968, shortly after the assassination of Dr. King, the concern of many activists shifted from civil rights to the Vietnam War; both the means and rhetoric of protest activity shifted along with it. When an antiwar activist named David Cohen appeared in the Los Angeles Courthouse wearing a jacket bearing the words "Fuck the Draft," he was convicted under a statute that made it a crime to "maliciously and willfully disturb the peace or quiet of any person [by] offensive conduct." In sustaining the conviction, the state court put a *Chaplinsky*-like gloss on the statute, defining "offensive conduct" as "behavior which has a tendency to provoke others to acts of violence" (*Cohen v. California* [1971], 16).

Justice Harlan wrote the majority opinion in *Cohen v. California* overturning the conviction. He fully understood the exigencies of public debate and the political significance of Cohen's particular choice of words. "Words," Harlan said, "are often chosen as much for their emotive as their cognitive force" (*Cohen*, 26). Harlan saw the expletive as a means of conveying strong emotions—it was like an exclamation point—and recognized that this emotive quality might have been the more important element in the message conveyed. He also feared that penalizing particular words created the risk of suppressing ideas.

In addition to the concerns about political freedom, Harlan fully understood the impact of Cohen's arrest on the scheme of natural liberty, and he was equally repelled by it: "Surely the State has no right to cleanse public debate to the point where it is grammatically palatable to the most squeamish among us" (*Cohen*, 25). Harlan recognized that the expletive Cohen used might be thought especially offensive, but he bemoaned the possibility of drawing such distinctions. As he put it, "Indeed, we think it is largely because governmental officials cannot make principled distinctions in this area that the Constitution leaves matters of taste and style so largely to the individual" (*Cohen*, 23).

The dissenters invoked *Chaplinsky* and sought to locate the basis for state authority in the risk of violence raised by the slogan on Cohen's jacket. Harlan strongly disputed this point, insisting that "we have been shown no evidence that substantial numbers of citizens are standing ready to strike out physically at whoever may assault their sensibilities with execrations like that uttered by Cohen" (*Cohen*, 23). Of course, there was no such showing in *Chaplinsky* either—as far as I can tell, the marshal just brushed off the insults leveled at him. Harlan also distinguished *Chaplinsky* on the ground that Cohen's words were not directed to anyone in particular and thus could not be regarded "as a direct personal insult" (*Cohen*, 20). This observation seems valid, but it is not at all clear why a direct personal insult is required to establish the predicate for state authority, which, of course, was the whole point of *Chaplinsky* and the "fighting words" doctrine.

The state court sustained the conviction of Cohen on the ground that wearing a jacket with "Fuck the Draft" on it had a tendency to provoke others to act violently. Harlan did not dispute the existence of this tendency—it could be present even if the utterance were not a direct personal insult—so much as deny its constitutional sufficiency. In contrast to Justice Frank Murphy, the author of *Chaplinsky*, Justice Harlan was unwilling to accept the mere tendency of words to provoke a violent response as a justification for state authority. Such a reluctance on the part of Harlan and the others who formed the majority in *Cohen* might have been due to a growing disenchantment with state power—not just as a matter of philosophical predilections, but as one of the legacies of the Vietnam War and the decision-making process that resulted in America's involvement in that war. Or it might have stemmed from an understanding of the implications of Cohen's action for political freedom and the view that public debate in a democracy worthy of our admiration must be "uninhibited, robust, and wide-open." The civil rights era was a lesson in the need for political freedom, and the Vietnam War taught us to be skeptical of state authority.

Skepticism is always in season. It may be all the more appropriate when applied to efforts by the state to justify itself, especially in light of Vietnam, Watergate, or the countless other abuses of governmental power here and abroad that have marred the twentieth century. *Cohen* and *Ladue* are a tribute to this skeptical tradition, but only because they worked to further democracy. Denying the power of the state to prohibit the display of a 8½ × 11 sign reading "For Peace in the Gulf" or to prohibit an antiwar protester from wearing "Fuck the Draft" on the back of his jacket acknowledged the limits on state power, yet these rulings also enriched public debate.

This was no small feat. The First Amendment was invoked in each of these cases to save forceful expressions of dissent at moments when the nation demanded loyalty. In the time of war, liberalism, understood as the doctrine that proclaims intrinsic limits on the state, served democracy. But this happy coincidence should not obscure a more profound truth affirmed by the history of the First Amendment in the twentieth century: democracy is not self-sustaining. As Black's dissent in *Feiner* boldly revealed, democracy sometimes needs the help of state action, and when it does, liberalism should not stand in its way. Every state intervention demands public justification, of course, but the pursuit of democracy amply supplies it.

REFERENCES

Bork, Robert. 1971. "Neutral Principles and Some First Amendment Problems," 47 *Indiana Law J.* 1.

Brennan, William J. Jr. 1965. "The Supreme Court and the Meiklejohn Interpretation of the First Amendment," 79 *Harvard Law Review* 1.

Fiss, Owen M. 1993. *Troubled Beginnings of the Modern State, 1888–1910.* New York: Macmillan.

———. 1999. "The Censorship of Television," 93 *Northwestern University Law R.* 1215.

Kalven, Harry Jr. 1964. "The *New York Times* Case: A Note on 'The Central Meaning of the First Amendment,'" 1964 *Supreme Court Review* 267.
———. 1965. *The Negro and the First Amendment.* Chicago: University of Chicago Press.
———. 1987. *A Worthy Tradition: Freedom of Speech in America.* New York: Harper & Row.
Meiklejohn, Alexander. 1960. *Political Freedom: The Constitutional Powers of the People.* New York: Harper. [Reprinted with minor changes from Alexander Meiklejohn, *Free Speech and Its Relation to Government* (1948).]
———. 1961. "The First Amendment Is an Absolute," 1961 *Supreme Court Review* 245.
Primus, Richard. 1996. "A Brooding Omnipresence: Totalitarianism in Postwar Constitutional Thought," 106 *Yale Law J.* 423.
———. 1999. *The American Language of Rights.* Cambridge: Cambridge University Press.
Rubenfeld, Jed. 1989. "The Right of Privacy," 102 *Harvard Law J.* 373.
———. 1993. "Usings," 102 *Yale Law J.* 1077.

CASES CITED

44 Liquormart v. Rhode Island, 517 U.S. 484 (1996).
Adarand Constructors v. Peña, 515 U.S. 200 (1995).
Amalgamated Food Employees v. Logan Valley, 391 U.S. 308 (1968).
CBS v. Democratic National Committee, 412 U.S. 94 (1973).
CBS v. FCC, 453 U.S. 367 (1981).
Central Hudson Gas & Electric Co. v. Public Service Commission of New York, 447 U.S. 557 (1980).
Chaplinsky v. New Hampshire, 315 U.S. 568 (1942).
City of Ladue v. Gilleo, 512 U.S. 43 (1994).
Cohen v. California, 403 U.S. 15 (1971).
Cox v. Louisiana, 379 U.S. 536 (1965).
Dombrowski v. Pfister, 380 U.S. 479 (1965).
Edwards v. South Carolina, 372 U.S. 229 (1963).
Feiner v. New York, 340 U.S. 315 (1951).
Fiske v. Kansas, 274 U.S. 380 (1927).
Gregory v. City of Chicago, 394 U.S. 111 (1969).
Griswold v. Connecticut, 381 U.S. 479 (1965).
Hudgens v. NLRB, 424 U.S. 507 (1976).
Lloyd Co. v. Tanner, 407 U.S. 551 (1972).
Lochner v. New York, 198 U.S. 45 (1905).
Miami Herald Publishing Co. v. Tornillo, 418 U.S. 241 (1974).
Miller v. California, 413 U.S. 15 (1973).
New York Times v. Sullivan, 376 U.S. 254 (1964).
New York Times v. United States (Pentagon Papers case), 403 U.S. 713 (1971).
Nixon v. Shrink Missouri Government PAC, 528 U.S. 377 (2000).

Pacific Gas & Electric Co. v. Public Utility Commission, 475 U.S. 1 (1986).
Red Lion Broadcasting v. FCC, 395 U.S. 367 (1969).
Roe v. Wade, 410 U.S. 113 (1973).
Schneider v. State, 308 U.S. 147 (1939).
Stanley v. Georgia, 394 U.S. 557 (1969).
Syracuse Peace Council v. WTVH, 2 F.C.C.R. 5043 (1987).
Syracuse Peace Council v. FCC, 867 F. 2d 654 (D.C. Cir. 1989).
Thornhill v. Alabama, 310 U.S. 88 (1940).
Turner Broadcasting v. FCC, 520 U.S. 180 (1997).
West Virginia State Board of Education v. Barnette, 319 U.S. 624 (1943).
Whitney v. California, 274 U.S. 357 (1927).
Williams v. Wallace, 240 F. Supp. 100 (M.D. Ala. 1965).
Wooley v. Maynard, 430 U.S. 705 (1977).

Instituting Universal Human Rights Law

THE INVENTION OF TRADITION IN THE TWENTIETH CENTURY

Martha Minow

"THE AGE OF HUMAN rights is upon us," begins a 1999 *New York Times* article (Rieff 1999, 36–37).[1] The article claims that elite leaders and policy makers have embraced the concept of international human rights. In this concept, each individual is entitled to freedom from torture, murder, arbitrary detention, slavery, and discrimination on the basis of race, sex, ethnicity, or religion. Moreover, states violate international law if they engage in genocide, slavery or slave trade, murder, torture or other cruel or degrading treatment, prolonged arbitrary detention, systematic racial discrimination, or a consistent pattern of gross violations of international human rights (Reiff 1999, 37; see also Steiner and Alston 1996).[2] The actual meaning of human rights, though, cannot be assessed apart from the institutions and practices necessary for enforcement, and these are both less clear and less well established than the substantive vision.[3] If the twentieth century spawned the concept of human rights, it was also much characterized by their violation without commensurate remedy or sanction. Thus, it may be more apt to suggest that the age of human rights rhetoric is upon us, challenging people to realize or else ignore the rhetoric.

Enforcement alternatives are neither obvious nor appealing to many ordinary citizens. Deploying combat troops to keep peace or to stop crimes of aggression and violence in certain far-off lands seldom generates support in domestic politics in the United States and elsewhere, absent immediate jeopardy to domestic security; tangible jeopardy to local lives outweighs in most people's imaginations the value of protecting the rights of unknown and foreign peoples. Also, post-Vietnam skepticism makes especially Americans doubt that the government is disclosing all the facts in making the case for military intervention.[4] Trade sanctions against a regime that violates human rights are often opposed by voters if the result pinches consumers and others mobilized by interest groups who fear retaliation (Rieff 1999, 41).

Perhaps this mixed or negative reception may stem from deeper skepticism about human rights. It is understandable to be skeptical about whether human rights can bear weight beyond the political calculus of powerful nations. In addition, human rights in international contexts can seem amorphous, naïve, and quixotic given the lack of sovereign power, a police force, or an established enforcement mechanism. The advocates of human rights have generated innovative institutions and practices, yet the successive and multiple nature of these innovations can contribute to the sense that human rights are merely ideal aspirations and, in practice, insecure.

Yet this tradition of institutional innovation may be the most significant legacy of the human rights movement. Even more than the underlying horrors of mass killings and regimes of torture—which, sadly, are not unique to this past century—the century bequeaths a tradition of innovation, building temporary and also perhaps more lasting institutions devoted to the articulation and enforcement of human rights. Ad hoc international tribunals, domestic court jurisdiction over international law violations, networks of nongovernmental organizations producing reports with the power to shame governments, truth commissions, a permanent international criminal court, and unique variants on these structures for individual circumstances—each reflects the creative application of political will and legal vision.

Taken together, these innovations transform the role of law in the world, the meaning of state sovereignty, and the status of individuals. Yet rather than clarifying and entrenching human rights through lasting institutions, this wave of innovations launches a movement of novelty, with all the excitement, improvisation, and uncertainty that novelty implies.[5] As a result, the meaning and capacity of human rights to inspire faith and commitment may be unclear and limited—even though the dream of human rights may yet inspire new forms of formal and informal innovation by nations and by individuals.

Precisely how the history of implementation for human rights is told reflects and affects a range of possible ideas about them. Has there been a stirring, unidirectional movement toward the endorsement and enforcement of human rights? Or has the topic instead generated struggles in domestic and international politics and law with no reality beyond the self-interest of particular groups and nation-states? Without attempting to provide a worldwide and century-wide social and intellectual history, I examine here how people turned to and built the idea of human rights with innovative responses to mass atrocities and violence. People invented human rights institutions in the cauldron of hopes for individuals caught in terrifying circumstances and concern for those far away from them. These innovations had to take their place amid clashes between idealism and national self-interest, amid international tensions. The innovations stand ready to be celebrated, castigated, ignored. They offer concrete demonstrations of the power of the idea of human rights to mobilize political will and legal instruments, and in that respect they create a legacy for the future (Dawes 1999, 250).[6]

Assessing the journey of human rights ideas and practices depends in part, however, on the map upon which they are placed. Human rights could be located on the terrain of war and international affairs. Then, their shape and effectiveness would have to be compared with other tools developed to contain wars and guide international relations, tools such as arms control treaties, trade treaties, and geopolitical power negotiations. Human rights protection groups use state-to-state agreements to ensure protection for individuals; how does this approach stack up when compared with state-to-state contacts dealing with commerce and war?

Human rights can be situated in the narrative of rights as philosophical and legal concepts and as repository and inspiration for human self-understanding. Then, international human rights would have to be tested in light of conventions developed for assessing the coherence or foundations of rights, or critical approaches to rights notions, or for assessing empirically the pervasiveness of rights in human imaginations. Human rights can alternatively find a home in the repertoire of responses to human suffering; they thus appear as part of twentieth-century responses, including therapeutic, artistic, pedagogic, media sensationalist, and theological. The arrival of rights rhetoric—and institutional innovations—as responses particularly to violence notably links the seemingly distant spheres of international affairs and intrafamily abuse. This essay sits uncomfortably at the margins of each of these maps, a point to which I return at the end.

FROM THE LAW OF NATIONS TO THE NUREMBERG AND TOKYO TRIALS

In his famous and controversial 1917 speech calling for "peace without victory," President Woodrow Wilson invoked a vision of a just and secure peace, rather than a new balance of power (Wilson 1917, 66). This vision replaces the familiar method of forcing peace terms upon a vanquished foe with efforts to insure an equality of rights among nations, organized to secure lasting peace (Wilson 1917, 67–68). In Wilson's view, lasting peace would also depend upon government by the consent of the governed who themselves must enjoy inviolable security of life, of worship, and of industrial and social development (Wilson [1917, 68], discussing Poland as an example).

In direct response, Elihu Root warned that Wilson's vision neglected the fact that half the military power of the world supported a different view, a view that rights stem from the state and thus that the exigencies of the state are superior to all individual rights (Root 1918, 70). Moreover, warned Root, Wilson's vision would call for preventing wars by preparing for war (Root 1918, 73). Only with a buildup of force and a willingness to use it could each nation contribute to an organized effort to enforce peace (Root 1918). Root thus keenly anticipated not only the United States' entrance into the Great War, now known as World War I, but also the danger that violent aggression itself would surpass the vision of peace founded in respect for the rights of each individual and the equality of nations governed with their citizens' consent. Instead of this vision, civil liberties were wildly suppressed at home in the United States and the victors imposed on the losers vindictive peace terms with compromises observers warned would lay the ground for future violent conflict (Editorial 1919, 184–85). The Senate refused to ratify the Versailles treaty and thus quashed Wilson's dream of a peace-securing organization of nations, which had proceeded as far as a plan for the League of Nations. Many people pressed for prosecution of individuals in the wake of wartime atrocities, including the murder of many civilians in France and elsewhere, the launching of zeppelins that killed civilians in London, and the sinking of the *Lusitania* with the loss of 1,200 civilians on it. Even though the Versailles treaty called for prosecutions and prescribed an international court to try the German Kaiser and national or national military courts to prosecute others, almost no trials ensued and those that did produced little or no punishment (Nino 1996, 3–5).[7]

This series of debates and events prefigured many of the themes surrounding the development of human rights over the course of the century. Idealistic visions of global peace, founded upon respect for individual rights and for states' legitimacy derived from the consent of the governed, collided with unstable national and international relations, brutal totalitarian states of great military power, and wars of aggression. Efforts to use a legal model of criminal responsibility for individual perpetrators ran into political and practical obstacles. Struggles to create new institutions to promote and secure respect for human rights, however impressive compared with their predecessors, produced more an idea than a practiced reality.

As horrific as the Great War was, World War II introduced violence and degradation of human beings on a scale and in a form that defied comprehension. Winston Churchill and Joseph Stalin both urged summary execution of the Axis leaders. Nonetheless, the Allies decided to hold trials, and in so doing, to establish a body of transnational rules to guarantee peace and human rights with institutions sufficiently strong to enforce those rules. What emerged was an International Military Tribunal, empowered to prosecute major war criminals of the Axis countries for crimes against peace, war crimes, and crimes against humanity (Steiner and Alston 1996, 100–101).[8]

Both the substance and the procedure of this plan were novel. Customary law had developed the notion of crimes against the law of nations, but only restricted examples, such as piracy on the high seas, had strong consensus ("Comment on the Nuremberg trials," in Steiner and Alston 1996, 99). The failed League of Nations had not even tried to ban war. The Kellogg-Briand pact of 1927, combined with the charter authorizing the post–World War II tribunal, offered the ingredients of an international norm against wars of aggression. Customary law and treaties did exist to govern excessive conduct during war but without clearly leading to individual criminal responsibility (Steiner and Alston 1996, 99–100). Crimes against humanity, however, appeared first for the World War II tribunals as an almost entirely invented category. It presented many ambiguities, including whether it applied to conduct committed outside the context of the war. The invention of a tribunal composed of judges from each of the four major Allied powers departed from any national military court previously involved in enforcing the laws of war (Steiner and Alston 1996, 101).

This lack of precedent led to charges that the resulting trials—in Nuremberg and in Tokyo—imposed norms retroactively, selectively, and in a politicized fashion (see Minow 1998, 29–47 reviewing these charges). The tribunal itself tried to narrow its prosecutions of crimes against humanity to those committed in conjunction with wars of aggression, and to norms announced in prior treaties against wars of aggression; still the norms and procedures for the Nuremberg and Tokyo trials departed from the past, particularly in imposing criminal liability for wars of aggression. Indeed, the Nuremberg trials are widely credited with establishing that there is no injustice in punishing defendants who knew they were committing a wrong condemned by the international community, even in the absence of a highly specified international law (Marquadt 1995, 82). The Nuremberg trials fundamentally stand for the principle that in matters of individual criminal liability international law takes precedence over claims of obligation to obey state law (Marquadt 1995).

At the same time, the Nuremberg trials involved highly limited, even selective prosecutions, with an initial group of only twenty-four defendants to stand in for the thousands involved in causing the deaths of more than twenty million people and the unspeakable suffering of many more.[9] The Tokyo trials also engaged in a limited number of highly symbolic prosecutions. These trials then generated charges of ethnic bias when the resulting sentences seemed more severe than those issued at the Nuremberg trials.

While plans for the trials developed, so did Allied agreement to establish "a general international organization, based on the sovereign equality of all peace-loving states" (*Annals of America* 1976, 321, quoting Moscow Conference of 1943). Radically departing from the League of Nations, the United Nations combined a commitment to maintain international peace and security with hopes to promote and encourage respect for human rights, fundamental freedoms, and self-determination of all peoples.[10] Critics at the time charged that the new organization jeopardized the sovereignty of individual nations (Vandenberg 1945, 7956–57, quoting and critiquing an editorial opposing the United Nations Charter). Although its supporters endeavored to rebut the charge, the challenge to national sovereignty emerged as a crucial feature of the human rights movement associated with the United Nations and other human rights institutions.

COLD WAR, NGOS, AND RULE OF LAW IDEOLOGY

Eleanor Roosevelt, who headed the UN Commission on Human Rights that drafted the Universal Declaration of Human Rights of 1948, explained that the United Nations was meant to operate once war ended; but peace never came, so the UN had to proceed amid many unexpected political problems (Roosevelt 1949, 613). She referred in large part to what came to be known as the cold war, the protracted tension between the United States and its allies on the one hand and the Soviet Union and its sphere of influence on the other (Glendon 1998, 1160).[11] For Roosevelt and other human rights advocates, precisely because of this global conflict, the issue of human rights took on great importance. Yet however fervent the commitment to human rights, the content of these rights was to be defined neither by the past nor by any particular nation or tradition. Instead, the content of human rights—exemplified by the UN Universal Declaration of Human Rights—reflected an intense negotiation process among drafters from eight nations and then debates among representatives of all the United Nations member states (Glendon 1998, 1160–62; Ignatieff 1999, 59).[12]

The document echoes many early declarations of rights and speaks of recognizing the rights and dignity inherent in human beings. Nonetheless, as Mary Ann Glendon observes,

> By expressly including women, by alluding to freedom from want, and by evoking the U.N. Charter's commitment to better standards of life, the Preamble signals from the outset that this document is not just a "universalization" of the traditional eighteenth century "rights of man," but part of a new "moment" in the history of human rights. (Glendon 1998, 1164)

The announced rights included some aiming at protection of individuals from physical interference, others concerning people's relations with others and within civil society, still others restricting the power of states to interfere with individual liberties, and finally a set of economic and social commitments addressing rights to work—and to work under reasonable conditions with a decent standard of living—and educational rights. Once this last kind of "new rights" became part of the package, courts could not be the sole institutions charged with implementing human rights (Glendon 1998, 1168); indeed, courts are largely irrelevant to any human rights protections in large parts of the world. Working out what could ensure such protections became even more difficult because the nation state could not be the sole vehicle for realizing the kinds of rights embodied in the document. Apparently, the Declaration's drafters understood that the hearts and will of people—shaped by culture and history—are the most effective means for advancing human rights (Glendon 1998, 1170). Responsibility for protecting human rights, therefore, must attend not only to nation states but to families, civil society, labor organizations, professions, international organizations, and a global international order (Glendon 1998).

The ambition of the document stands in sharp contrast to its influence, at least for the firsttwo decades after its adoption. Although the United Nations grew in size and personnel, it had little influence in a world dominated by the cold war. National sovereignty also persisted as a nearly absolute barrier to international review; each state operated according to the notion of reciprocal respect between nations, founded upon treating matters within borders as beyond any other nation's concern. Yet, perhaps ironically, the UN's very impotence left room for other actors to help realize human rights (Glendon 2001, 218).

The leading alternative that emerged in the 1960s and 1970s was advocacy by nongovernmental organizations (NGOs) that cultivated consciousness about human rights, sometimes by means that the drafters of the Declaration would have applauded and sometimes by means (e.g., advancing special interests) that they would have deplored. In forming nongovernmental organizations, advocates of human rights in several parts of the world invented new ways to combine the grass-roots organizing strategies of social movements, the best versions of muckraking reportage in investigative journalism, and the shaming techniques of deeply religious small towns. They halted potential controversy about the scope and definition of human rights by targeting extrajudicial killings, torture, group oppression, and political imprisonment, violations even skeptics would have difficulty disputing. And they focused on the situations of specific, named individuals, giving the sometimes abstract notion of human rights individual human faces (see generally Steiner and Alston 1996, 456–99; Korey 1999). In a way revealing the "power of the weak," nongovernmental organizations also contributed to the view of human rights as challenges to conventional pillars of power (Janeway 1980).[13]

British lawyer Peter Benenson launched Amnesty International in 1961 with a newspaper appeal about forgotten prisoners.[14] Within a year, it had chapters in seven countries and sent delegations to four nations to advocate for some 210 prisoners. By 1999, it had sections in fifty-five countries and more than 1,000,000 members. It developed the practices of issuing reports about the conditions and treatment of prisoners of conscience, about extrajudicial execution, and about the "disappearance" of individuals in suspected human rights violations. Amnesty International mobilized supporters to use increasingly sophisticated communications technologies (such as electronic mail and fax) to send appeals about people facing immediate danger, and organized networks of physicians, lawyers, and others to bring expertise, pressure, and visibility to the problems. As a leading inventor of the techniques of nongovernmental organizations to advocate for and, through public pressure, enforce human rights, Amnesty International grew from a budget of approximately $20,000 in the 1960s to more than a thousand times that size in 1998.[15]

Human Rights Watch, founded in 1978 as Helsinki Watch, followed the same path but with a broader scope of human rights concerns. Spreading its documentation of abuses through partnerships with local organizations and lobbying national governments and centers of influence including the United Nations, the European Union, and the World Bank, Human Rights Watch by 1999 had a budget of $15 million.[16] The influence of such organizations on the United States has been considerable at least with regard to its stance toward other nations, if not toward criticisms of human rights issues within the country. Foreign aid programs now include human rights conditions, and the State Department has an Assistant Secretary for Democracy, Human Rights, and Labor as well as an Ambassador at Large for War Crimes Issues (Rieff 1999, 37).[17]

Yet the brilliance and successes of the NGOs depended upon their status outside governments and their apparent ties to ordinary people wishing to express outrage at human rights violations (although many of the groups actually engage chiefly elites and some assist multinational corporations with their public relations).[18] Bypassing state-to-state international relations, the NGOs introduced a kind of human rights enforcement dependent on the beliefs of ordinary people and their power to pressure and shame governments. In a real sense, the broad vision of human rights imagined in the Universal Declaration previewed and required the development of some strategy of this ilk in order to tie human rights enforcement to ordinary people and to generate a sense of international community quite different from that produced by an assembly of sovereign state representatives.

The technique of documenting abuses and shaming the offenders worked especially well during the cold war as waged by the Reagan administration, for the West's ideology of democracy and civil liberties created a baseline for shame. Aryeh Neier, who ran Human Rights Watch in its crucial early years, explained how Reagan-era officials like Jeanne Kirkpatrick and Elliott Abrams had to "pretend that everyone on our side in the cold war was *not* violating human rights. That allowed Human Rights Watch to point out the gap between pretense and practice. It created enormous embarrassment" (Rieff 1999, 38). The techniques of exposure and embarrassment work far less well when the targets are dictatorships or other nondemocracies that have not even a hypocritical or superficial commitment to civil liberties and other human rights.

During the 1960s and 1970s, another human rights strategy pursued by the nongovernmental organizations and others turned to the novel idea of seeking enforcement of international human rights in national courts. Most national courts, when asked to consider suits arising from the conduct of other nations during war or other violence, concluded that foreign states and their agencies acting in their governmental capacity had immunity from suit (Cassese 1988, 150). But a few domestic courts took different tacks.[19]

Israel prosecuted and convicted Adolph Eichmann for his conduct during World War II with review by its then barely decade-old Supreme Court. That court concluded that even though partly framed in terms of specific crimes against the Jewish people, the indictment involved crimes against humanity always recognized by the international community and thus was not in violation of the ban against ex post facto punishment (Lahav 1997, 154; Nino 1996, 14–16). The trial performed certain nation-building tasks for the fledgling state of Israel but also demonstrated the authority and symbolic commitment of a nation to enforce international human rights, however much it might breach them in practice in the years to come.

Before becoming the first president of the appeals chamber of the International Criminal Tribunal for the Former Yugoslavia and the International Criminal Tribunal for Rwanda, Antonio Cassese celebrated the 1963 decision of a Tokyo court that addressed the international law dimensions of claims brought by individuals for compensation for suffering caused by the bombings of Hiroshima and Nagasaki (Cassese 1988, 153–56, discussing the decision in the *Japanese Annual of International Law* 8 [1964]). The plaintiffs knew that American courts would never touch the question of whether dropping the bombs violated international law[20]; therefore the plaintiffs sued Japan in a Japanese court for waiving all claims of its citizens and the nation in its 1951 peace treaty with the United States (Cassese 1988, 154). The Tokyo court reached the question of international law's application to the bombings; found them violations of international law, which banned indiscriminate bombing of undefended cities; and called for legislative action even in acknowledging the exemption of foreign states from jurisdiction (Cassese 1988, 155–56).

Perhaps the most celebrated civil lawsuit generating a judgment by a national court on a human rights violation committed elsewhere is *Filartiga v. Pena-Irala*, a decision reached by the United States Court of Appeals for the Second Circuit.[21] A Paraguayan police inspector, Pena-Irala, ordered the seizure and torture of the son of a doctor who provided a hospital and medical care for very poor residents in an area of Paraguay. The dictatorial government apparently had concluded that no one but a revolutionary would provide such service to poor people and assumed that Dr. Filartiga was involved with guerrilla activity (Cassese 1988, 157). The son died following electric shock torture. Efforts to seek justice within Paraguay failed. When one of the doctors obtained political asylum in the United States, she was informed that Pena-

Irala had also come to the United States after being ousted by the government. The daughter and her father, Dr. Filartiga, filed suit in a United States court for compensation for the torture of her brother.

Conventionally, a United States court would find no basis for jurisdiction over torture in Paraguay of a Paraguayan by a Paraguayan official. But the plaintiffs' lawyers used a 1789 statute authorizing suits in United States district courts over torts committed by an alien in violation of the law of nations or a treaty of the United States.[22] Assisted by a friend-of-the-court brief filed by the Department of Justice—itself influenced by President Jimmy Carter's commitment to human rights—the court of appeals rejected the district court's refusal of jurisdiction. In addition, the court found torture violative of a rule of customary international law and thus supplied the substantive law otherwise lacking, given that the United States had not signed any treaty or convention against torture. The district court ruled in favor of the Filartigas. Even though Pena-Irala by that time had left the United States, and thus avoided paying the $375,000 damages award, the decision created a bold statement against torture and a dramatic, inventive use of domestic civil court jurisdiction to condemn and attempt to remedy human rights violations.[23]

Other United States courts have not always followed, and indeed have at times disagreed with, the *Filartiga* decision.[24] Nonetheless, it represents an innovative mechanism for enforcing and broadcasting human rights in several respects: use of a domestic court to articulate and enforce norms of international human rights; use of civil court jurisdiction; and collaboration between the executive branch—which supported judicial review in this case—and the independent judicial branch. The case also indicates a judicial willingness to limit the power of individual defendants to claim act of state or sovereign immunity because they acted as state officials. Innovative and symbolic, civil domestic court jurisdiction still falls considerably short of international criminal prosecutions, the model set forth by the Nuremberg and Tokyo trials.

INVENTING HUMAN RIGHTS INSTITUTIONS

Many would say that any response other than criminal trials fails to implement the vision of international human rights enforcement, though of course only certain kinds of rights are amenable to individual adjudication. In the absence of an international process to bring trials, and without domestic political will to prosecute human rights violations especially in nations where they are chronic, articulation and enforcement of human rights have required creative alternatives. One notable alternative is the development of truth commissions: commissions of inquiry exposing and documenting torture, murders, and other human rights violations that otherwise would be denied and covered up by repressive regimes. The Brazilian report *Brasil: Nuca Mas* documented 144 political murders, 125 disappearances, and more than 1,800 incidents of torture following a risky secret investigation led by religious groups (see Weschler 1990). The enormous public reaction in Brazil, making the report a best seller, contributed largely to the decision of President Sarney to sign the United Nations Convention against Torture in 1985 (Nino 1996, 34). The UN sponsored the creation of a truth commission for El Salvador, demonstrating the availability of this mechanism in international as well as domestic initiative and form.

Other inquiries have taken more public forms, collecting testimony from survivors and issuing public reports tracing the causes of the violence. The most dramatic example is South Africa's Truth and Reconciliation Commission (TRC), created by the first democratically elected parliament after the negotiated transition from apartheid. Because that negotiation included a promise for a process to grant amnesty to participants in past conflicts, the TRC established a committee to receive applications from individuals seeking amnesty for politically motivated human rights violations and gave amnesty to only a few hundred of the 7,000 applicants, only under conditions specified by statute.[25] The TRC also collected statements from survivors of violence on all sides of the preceding conflicts. Some 22,000 offered statements, and many appeared in public hearings that were broadcast throughout the nation. A lightning rod for controversy especially among opponents of amnesty, the TRC nonetheless provided dramatic and unforgettable proof of human rights violations that had been denied by members of the apartheid government while giving voice to many who survived violence at the hands of secret police, other government officials, and opposition groups. The TRC also offered concrete and symbolic occasions for reconciliation between individuals on different sides of the past conflicts. Yielding a five-volume report as well as memorable national broadcasts of live testimony, the TRC most remarkably indicated a path for creating truthful accounts of the past from which the nation could proceed (Minow 1998, 52–90, 127–32). Yet the demand for individual responsibility and punishment through criminal prosecutions for human rights violations persisted among many in South Africa and elsewhere. And the language of reconciliation offended many who sought retribution for or at least acknowledgment of what could never be brought back or healed.

The fiftieth anniversary of the Nuremberg trial process—and the end of the cold war and fall of the Soviet Union in 1989—inspired dignitaries around the globe to celebrate it as the launch of an international movement for human rights founded in the rule of law. Yet the Nuremberg tribunal failed to launch its most obvious sequel—the holding of further international trials following genocide and torture—until more than forty years had passed. No international legal response followed mass murders in Cambodia, South Africa, Kurdistan, Argentina, Chile, China, the Soviet Union, or elsewhere until the UN Security Council authorized creation of first the International Criminal Tribunal for the former Yugoslavia, and then the International Criminal Tribunal for Rwanda.[26] The council also faced head-on the issue of governing law and acknowledged that international law contained gaps in treating criminal wrongs. Accordingly, the council authorized the new tribunals to resort to the domestic law of the affected nation to fill in any gaps, although this rendered ambiguous the precedent to be established internationally (Minow 1998, 38).

Although ad hoc and temporary, these two international tribunals departed from the Nuremberg and Tokyo models in several respects. They emerged from the authority of the standing institution, the Security Council of the United Nations, rather than from the military command of victors following a war. Perhaps they represented intentionally weak gestures after international failures to stop the mass violence they sought to address. The tribunal addressing the former Yugoslavia operated amid ongoing peace negotiations with some of the potential targets of prosecution. In the case of the tribunal addressing the genocidal destruction of some 800,000 people within Rwanda,[27] the United Nations stretched authority derived from Nuremberg precedents, the Hague and Geneva Conventions, and two Protocols of 1977 to apply to a conflict *within* one nation (Minow 1998, 34–35).[28] The UN also required complex innovations in the establishment of procedural rules to be administered by judges trained in very different legal systems. Given governmental controls over media in the former Yugoslavia and technological devastation in Rwanda, the most likely audiences for these tribunals existed outside the most affected nations.

Despite slow progress, cumbersome procedures, and widespread uncertainty about their effectiveness, these two tribunals no doubt helped to generate support in many nations for establishing a permanent International Criminal Court (ICC), originally envisioned soon after the Nuremberg trials. In 1998, 120 of the world's nations—but not the United States—voted for the creation of such a court with jurisdiction over genocide, crimes against humanity, war crimes, and the crime of aggression (Slaughter 1999, 7–8).[29] Despite early active support for the court, the United States declined to endorse it, chiefly because of the fears that (1) U.S. military personnel could face charges for political reasons; (2) the UN Security Council retained too much control over prosecutions; (3) jurisdiction remained too ambiguous especially under the crime of aggression; and (4) the relationship between the court and national courts was unclear (Slaughter 1999, 8). In the waning days of the Clinton administration, the United States did sign the authorizing statute, but President George W. Bush strongly opposed Senate ratification. Nonetheless, plans for the ICC proceeded.

These recent innovations—truth commissions and international criminal tribunals—seem incompatible with each other to some, but compatible to others. Some argue that criminal trials proceed through retribution and punishment, with a hope of deterrence, while truth commissions seek truthful accounts and a mechanism to permit the society to deal with the past without the recriminations and enmity generated by trials (Bolton 1999, 37–38, 48). Others believe that a nation or region could benefit from both, perhaps at different times; a truth commission could help identify people to prosecute or could follow initial prosecutions to enable a broader understanding of the conflicts, the victims' experiences, and the roles of all sectors in society (Minow 1998, 87–90). Separately and together, they represent innovations in the expression and implementation of human rights norms.

As the century closed, the United Nations developed still another institutional form, this time as an effort to bring leaders of the Khmer Rouge to justice before the by then aged individuals died and eluded accountability. The Cambodian government rejected use of an independent criminal tribunal as a violation of its sovereignty. In response, the UN proposed that it would select an independent prosecutor and international judges to be joined by Cambodian judges selected by the Cambodian government (Shenon 1999).[30] Stalled politically within Cambodia, whose government opposed trials of high Khmer Rouge leaders, by 2002 this hybrid of international and domestic responses lost UN endorsement, while illustrating the flexibility, pragmatism, and unpredictability of the tradition of innovation characterizing human rights institutions throughout the century.

Meanwhile, persistent critiques challenge the UN and its related formal international institutions and practices as bureaucratic, unduly segmented and technical, unresponsive, and ineffective (see, e.g., Scott 1999). And global media coverage of atrocities introduced the idea—and perhaps the experience—of "compassion fatigue" while demonstrating continuing, unspeakable forms of human cruelty and aggression.

A LEGACY OF NOVELTY

The meaning of a right cannot be determined unless we know how and when it is enforced. What practical effects, besides stirring hopes, come with rights that lack institutional implementation? This practical perspective, itself a contribution of twentieth-century thinkers, challenges claims that the twentieth century has produced a revolution in international, universal human rights. The century has witnessed remarkable deployment of the rhetoric of human rights and a series of institutional innovations but no stable process for enforcing or realizing individual freedom from torture, murder, discrimination, or collective aggression. Indeed, the technologies of mass destruction produced in the twentieth century include not only the atomic bomb but also the radio and television, capable of extraordinary manipulation by unscrupulous leaders who have stimulated mass hatreds and face-to-face machete murders in the name of ethnic pride.

The institutional innovations in human rights have contributed some notable accomplishments. The Nuremberg and Tokyo trials, flawed as they were, dramatically demonstrated a commitment to attribute responsibility even for mass crimes to the actions of particular human beings, actions warranting accountability and punishment. The United Nations—and perhaps most impressively, its Universal Declaration of Human Rights—reached new levels of international collaboration in the commitment to recognize the worth and dignity of each human being with no state's sovereignty a rationale for anything less. Nongovernmental organizations mobilized large numbers of supporters to care about the human rights of often distant people and to show how not just troops but also broadcast facts alongside public and private pressure can constrain abuses by oppressive governments. Domestic judiciaries proved occasionally responsive especially to civil claims of human rights violations and thus opened avenues for integrating human rights enforcement within domestic legal systems. Regional authorities established transnational courts and commissions with some enforcement powers (see, e.g., Tomuschat 1992). Weakening doctrines of immunity, these courts even imposed external constraints to curb state sovereignty in the name of human rights.

Commissions of inquiry and reconciliation initiated national processes of acknowledgment of human rights violations without the strengths and weaknesses of criminal trials. Public truth telling and materials for fashioning truthful national narratives afforded opportunities for national healing and perhaps preventive educational work. When operating within a domestic sphere, such commissions do not challenge state sovereignty. Yet they may generate domestic support for international human rights.

Two International Criminal Tribunals created for individual countries revived the ideas of the Nuremberg Trials and paved the way for 120 nations to endorse the creation of a permanent international criminal court. Yet with the United States declining to support that court, and with the resistance of nations like Cambodia to pursue responses to mass violence, further alternatives will be needed. It is here that the tradition of innovation launched during the twentieth century appears a potential strength. That tradition straddles domestic and international, courts and commissions, governmental and nongovernmental, punitive and preventive. These ambiguities hamper human rights if they are understood simply as counterparts to positive rights, enforced by domestic police and courts. Yet these ambiguities offer real hope for effectuating the bolder ambitions of human rights as ideas available to every person and dependent upon the beliefs and hopes of ordinary people. Given the failures of nation states to protect individuals from terror, murder, discrimination, and national aggression, human rights will need more than state power for their realization.

CODA

If human beings, rather than law and its development, become the center of inquiry, it is far from clear that the twentieth century will be described as the age of human rights; nor would human rights seem adequate as a response to the suffering and trauma of those years. Neil Belton's 1998 book, *The Good Listener,* covers much of the same chronological period as this chapter and some of its same concerns, but through the lens of the life of Helen Bamber, a British Jew who spent her life working with survivors first of World War II and then of successive mass atrocities (Belton 1998). Recalling her relief work right after the war with survivors of the concentration camps, she said,

> "My feeling about death, there, was almost of relief; there were times when I wanted people to die. We cling onto people nowadays; now I try so hard to stop people committing suicide. I'm not sure we had that feeling there. There was so much death; so much talk of death. I think that when memories came back, and the whole horror was open in a way that it was not when they were freezing and starving—I think that people didn't fight sometimes to live, when it all became clear." (Belton 1998, 88)

Some survivors, she found, needed to tell, over and over, what had happened to them; "it wasn't so much grief as a pouring out of some ghastly vomit like a kind of horror" (1998, 89). Many found unbearable not what happened to them, but "what they had not been able to prevent" from happening to others (1998, 91). Returning home to England, Bamber worked with refugees and learned that normal sympathy and consolation were impotent because nothing could replace the parents and loved ones who had been lost. Bamber observed of one survivor, "You could never touch him: he held on as fiercely to the pain as to his independence" (1998, 142).

The Universal Declaration of Human Rights emerged in 1948 and forty-eight countries signed on. But shortly thereafter, torture in postwar Algeria made Bamber realize the horrors could happen again: "Perhaps there is something more realistic in the assumption of human evil than in the hope that declarations can change impulses and hatreds" (1998, 171). Bamber turned to campaigning against the separation of any children from their families when treated by English hospitals because she remembered this separation and loss as the worst cruelty for children in the concentration camps (1998, 194, 197).[31]

Bamber became an activist with Amnesty International. She had been moved to act after the 1973 military coup in Chile, but she was also frustrated by Amnesty's reluctance to look beyond the individual prisoner to those who built the cell and armed the guards, and to campaign more broadly for human rights (1998, 211–19).

Agitating and campaigning for human rights did not seem enough to Bamber, especially after she encountered Luis Minoz, a Chilean survivor of torture. He himself explained that after gaining asylum in Britain, "You come out a different person. I was afraid of myself. You're meeting somebody inside yourself that you don't know; you are totally disconnected" (1998, 226). Minoz was suicidal. Bamber listened to him and was struck when he said that the torturers took his clothes and wore them when they were torturing him. Bamber reflected, "It's as though they want you to feel you are torturing yourself; something that you've honoured and bought and worn, your leather jacket, your jeans, your shirt; they are suggesting to you that they have completely removed your personality, and it reversed everything, takes a personality and destroys everything a person loves, like playing music while torturing" (1998, 226).

For someone like Helen Bamber, the idea of human rights becomes a touchstone for mobilizing against this kind of horror. Still, "human rights" could not capture her commitment to trying to understand the profound devastation to unique and vibrant individuals inflicted by torture and murder—and to persist in advocacy even with the knowledge that the devastation and the motives for it could never really be fully understood. Lobbying for human rights could signal and in turn solicit commitments to provide sustained physical and emotional aid to survivors, but it does not necessarily point toward something else that seems equally crucial: assisting survivors in relocating and expressing their own strengths and creative potential (1998, 291–93).[32] Broadcasting human rights abuses and lobbying against them remains crucial but insufficient both to prevent the abuses and to assist survivors in the slow and difficult work of reclaiming their lives (1998, 286).

Bamber and others started an organization for the treatment of refugees from atrocity. Fusing human rights and therapy, political analysis and interpersonal empathy, the Medical Foundation for the Care of Victims of Torture gathers and preserves the personal narratives from survivors and works to examine torture and mass atrocities as systematic and political, not merely the acts of individual sadists. The Foundation works as a human rights organization to apply political pressure against torture while also offering help to survivors. As the author of Bamber's biography writes, "serious enforcement of international law would go a long way to eliminating torture. But relying on legal instruments alone is insufficient. Attention to the results of torture—the effects on other human beings—is a powerful reminder of the cost of regressing to a situation where excuses for torture seem plausible" (1998, 324).

I end this discussion with the example of an individual witness to vile human atrocities, a witness who has struggled to respond. The language of human rights, the fledgling international institutions and start-up nongovernmental agencies, offered Bamber an important, but insufficient, mode of response. She struggled to amplify a further, therapeutic response. What witnesses do in response, and in prevention, will tell the tale for the future.

NOTES

1 See also Ignatieff 1999, 58: "Human rights has become the major article of faith of a secular culture that fears it believes in nothing else."

2 See also American Law Institute 1987, summarizing customary international law of human rights. Much broader notions of human rights have been offered over time, and crucially include economic and social rights, which may be inextricable from real prevention of mass violence. Nonetheless, it is the human liberty elements that I address here. See generally Gordon 1998.

3 "Covenants without the Word are but Words, and of no strength to secure a man at all" (Hobbes 1968, 223).

4 Thanks to Mary Ann Glendon for this point.

5 It could be said that the underlying problem is lack of political will to effectuate international human rights, yet this only shifts the perspective on the institutional innovations to one of surprise at the success of small groups in the absence of sufficient political will to realize the promise of such innovations.

6 "Lacking the signatures of belief and affirmation, words do indeed require Hobbes' sword for actualization. But treated as real in the overlapping consensus of a non-exclusionary intersubjective discourse, they become real: real without coercion, and with the key feature of susceptibility to argument." (Dawes 1999, 250.)

7 Nino notes that Holland refused to turn the Kaiser over to the Allies for prosecution, Germany refused to turn over other offenders, and German Supreme Court trials produced acquittals, modest sentences, and the conclusion by the French and Belgians that the trials were invalid.

8 For a thoughtful overview of the historical developments, see Meron 1998.

9 Subsequent trials took place but involved only a tiny fraction of the perpetrators. See Sprecher 1999.

10 UN Charter, chapter 1, article 1.

11 When the General Assembly of the United Nations began its deliberations on the Declaration of Human Rights, Soviet relations with the West were deteriorating. The Berlin blockade heated tensions, and armed conflicts broke out in Greece and in Korea.

12 Ignatieff argues that the origin of the Declaration depended upon the accident of circumstances, postponing ideological arguments that arose during the cold war.

13 I am suggesting here that nongovernmental organizations contribute to the use of human rights to bypass and ultimately subvert the usual instrumentalities of state-to-state dealings in international law. Dawes (1999, 234) argues that modern human rights notions generate two very different views of international law: the first sees human rights as subverting the foundations of the world community and traditional political institutions; the second sees human rights as dependent upon the instruments of state power.

14 This information is from the Web page of Amnesty International, http://www.web.amnesty.org (visited August 23, 1999).

15 See Rieff 1999, 37. Amnesty International's Web site indicates that in 1961, its first year, the organization spent £6,040; in 1999, its expenditures totaled £16,859,000 (see www.amnesty.org, visited 28 August 2001). The London *Guardian* recently reported that Amnesty's annual budget totals £19.5 million (Barton 2001, 66).

16 See Reiff 1999, 37; http://www.hrw.org (visited August 23, 1999).

17 See also Korey 1999, discussing the role of grass-roots groups in demanding rights of emigration for Soviet Jewry and in pressing for UN reports on human rights violations in South Africa

and elsewhere. See also http://www.state.gov/www.about state/biography/scheffer.html (visited August 23, 1999; no longer available) describing David John Scheffer, the first person to hold the post of Ambassador at Large for War Crimes Issues, appointed May 22, 1997 by President Clinton, and sworn in August 5, 1997.

18 The vast number of people in the world may be understandably too distracted by their own life circumstances to become engaged with problems in other parts of the world, so the "ordinary people" recruited by the NGOs typically fall in the small percentage of the world's population that already enjoys relative material comfort and political freedoms.

19 Following World War II, and again following the fall of communist regimes after 1989, Germany and several eastern European countries undertook a limited number of domestic criminal prosecutions for violations of their own domestic laws and emerging international norms (see Nino 1996, 10–14, 16–26; Rosenberg 1995, 261–305, 340–51).

20 Legal doctrines of political question (rendering an issue nonjusticiable because it is reserved to the elected branches) and sovereign immunity would shield the decision from judicial review.

21 See 630 F.2d 86 (2d Cir. 1980).

22 Alien Tort Claim Statute, 28 U.S.C. sec. 1350 (1994). See also Torture Victim Protection Act, 28 U.S.C. sec. 1350 note (1994). See also Burley 1989.

23 The court of appeals also had to address claims of immunity for an act of state. The court rejected the claims in a less than coherent fashion; Cassese suggests that a better explanation for its decision to reject the immunity claim is the view that crimes against humanity, even when committed by an agent of a state, do not excuse the individual perpetrator from individual responsibility (Cassese 1988, 161).

24 See, e.g., Tel-Oren v. Libyan Arab Republic, 726 F.2d 774 (D.C. Cir. 1984), cert. denied, 470 U.S. 1003 (1985). For a comprehensive treatment of these cases and of the power of U.S. courts to reach conduct outside its territory, see Note 1985.

25 The applicant had to disclose fully the facts of violations as well as demonstrate that their motive was political and that the means used were commensurate with that goal.

26 The creation of these ad hoc tribunals helped to trigger debates about responses to Cambodia's period of terror and to newly unfolding events in Kosovo and East Timor.

27 Simultaneous with the international tribunal activity, Rwanda undertook domestic trials that drew sharp international criticisms for failing to ensure due process.

28 On the origin and scope of the Hague and Geneva Conventions and the Two Protocols, see Steiner and Alston 1996, 69–70.

29 The court will take effect only after sixty nations sign and ratify the statute authorizing it; at this writing, eighty-two have signed and three have ratified.

30 Prior truth commissions have varied enormously in the composition of their members, the source of their originating authority, their relationship to criminal prosecution, and their scope and powers.

31 " 'We had normal—not Nazi—French boys doing unspeakable things to Algerians. What made them capable of it? I can't pretend that this sort of consideration drove my work for children in hospital, but I know that many of us did not want to be part of a society intent on fostering the destructive side of children's characters' " (Belton 1998, 197).

32 Bamber worked with psychotherapist John Schlapobersky to develop the notion of positive intervention rather than simply medicalizing the problem. Together they worked to evoke the individual's creativity and strengths.

REFERENCES

Annals of America. 1976. Vol. 16. Chicago: Encyclopaedia Britannica.

American Law Institute. 1987. *Restatement (Third) the Foreign Relations Law of the United States section 702*.

Barton, Laura. 2001. "Amnesty's Work Is Never Done," *Guardian* (London), 29 May 2001.

Belton, Neil. 1998. *The Good Listener: Helen Bamber, A Life Against Cruelty*. New York: Pantheon.

Bolton, John. 1999. "Speech Two: Reject and Oppose the International Criminal Court," in *Toward an International Criminal Court: Three Options Presented as Presidential Speeches*, ed. A. Frye. New York: Council on Foreign Relations.

Burley, Anne-Marie. 1989. "The Alien Tort Statute and the Judiciary Act of 1789: A Badge of Honor," 83 *AJIL* 461.

Cassese, Antonio. 1988. *Violence and the Law in the Modern Age*. Princeton, N.J.: Princeton University Press.

Dawes, James R. 1999. "Language, Violence, and Human Rights Law," 11 *Yale J. of Law & the Humanities* 215.

Editorial. 1919. "Peace at Any Price," reprinted in *Annals of America*, vol. 14. Chicago: Encyclopaedia Britannica.

Glendon, Mary Ann. 1998. "Knowing the Universal Declaration of Human Rights," 73 *Notre Dame L. Rev.* 1153.

———. 2001. *A World Made New: Eleanor Roosevelt and the Universal Declaration of Human Rights*. New York: Random House.

Gordon, Joy. 1998. "The Concept of Human Rights: The History and Meaning of its Politicization," 23 *Brook. J. Int'l L.* 689.

Hobbes, Thomas. 1968. *Leviathan*. New York: Penguin Books.

Ignatieff, Michael. 1999. "The Midlife Crisis," *New York Review of Books*, 29 May 1999.

Janeway, Elizabeth. 1980. *Powers of the Weak*. New York: Alfred A. Knopf.

Korey, William. 1999. *NGOs and the Universal Declaration of Human Rights: A Curious Grapevine*. New York: St. Martin's Press.

Lahav, Pnina. 1997. *Judgment in Jerusalem: Chief Justice Simon Agranat and the Zionist Century*. Berkeley: University of California Press.

Marquadt, Paul D. 1995. "Law without Borders: The Constitutionality of an International Criminal Court," 33 *Colum. J. of Transnational Law* 33.

Meron, Theodor. 1998. *War Crimes Law Comes of Age*. New York: Oxford University Press.

Minow, Martha. 1998. *Between Vengeance and Forgiveness: Facing History after Genocide and Mass Violence*. Boston: Beacon Press.

Nino, Carlos Santiago. 1996. *Radical Evil on Trial*. New Haven, Conn.: Yale University Press.

Note. 1985. "Predictability and Comity: Toward Common Principles of Extraterritorial Jurisdiction," 98 *Harv. L. Rev.* 1310.

Rieff, David. 1999. "The Precarious Triumph of Human Rights," *New York Times Magazine*, 8 August 1999.

Roosevelt, Eleanor. 1949. "The United Nations," reprinted in *Annals of America*, vol. 16. Chicago: Encyclopaedia Britannica.

Root, Elihu. 1918. "The European War and the Preservation of American Ideals," reprinted in *Annals of America*, vol. 15. Chicago: Encyclopaedia Britannica.

Rosenberg, Tina. 1995. *The Haunted Land: Facing Europe's Ghosts after Communism*. New York: Vintage.

Scott, Craig. 1999. "Reaching Beyond (Without Abandoning) the Category of 'Economic Social and Cultural Rights,'" 21 *Human Rights Quarterly* 633.

Shenon, Philip. 1999. "U.N. Plans Joint War Crimes Tribunal for Khmer Rouge," *New York Times*, 12 August 1999.

Slaughter, Anne-Marie. 1999. "Memorandum to the President," in *Toward an International Criminal Court: Three Options Presented as Presidential Speeches*, ed. A. Frye. New York: Council on Foreign Relations.

Sprecher, Drexel A. 1999. *Inside the Nuremberg Trial: A Prosecutor's Comprehensive Account*. Lanham, Md.: University Press of America.

Steiner, Henry J., and Philip Alston, eds. 1996. *International Human Rights in Context: Law, Politics, Morals*. Oxford: Clarendon Press.

Tomuschat, Christian. 1992. "Quo Vadis, Argentoratum? The Success Story of the European Convention on Human Rights—and a Few Dark Stains," 13 *Human Rights Law Journal* 401.

United Nations Charter. 1945. Chapter 1, article 1.

Vandenberg, Arthur H. 1945. *Congressional Record, 79 Cong., 1 Sess.*

Weschler, Lawrence. 1990. *A Miracle, A Universe: Settling Accounts with Torturers*. New York: Pantheon.

Wilson, Woodrow. 1917. "Peace Without Victory," reprinted in *Annals of America*, vol. 14. Chicago: Encyclopaedia Britannica

Racial Justice

MORAL OR POLITICAL?

Kendall Thomas

> In the present century, black people are believed to be totally different from whites in race and origin, yet totally equal to them with regard to human rights. In the sixteenth century, when blacks were thought to come from the same roots and to be of the same family as whites, it was held . . . that with regards to rights blacks were by nature and Divine Will greatly inferior to us. In both centuries, blacks have been bought and sold and made to work in chai6ns under the whip. Such is ethics; and such is the extent to which moral beliefs have anything to do with actions.
>
> —Giacomo Leopardi

INTRODUCTION

NEARLY ONE HUNDRED years ago, W.E.B. DuBois predicted that the problem of the twentieth century would be the problem of the color line (DuBois 1986, 372). Were he writing today, DuBois might well conclude that in the United States, the problem of the coming century will be the problem of the *color-bind* (Chávez 1998). Although Americans arguably remain "the most 'race-conscious' people on earth" (Marable 1995, 185), our national conversation about "race" now stands at an impasse. Our ways of talking, or refusing to talk, about race increasingly speak past the racialized dilemmas of educational equity, affirmative action, poverty, welfare reform, housing, lending, labor and employment discrimination, health and medical care access, environmental justice, immigration and asylum, or crime, policing, and punishment. The current deadlock in U.S. public discourse on racial justice reveals itself not only the arena of power politics; our predicament can also be seen in the creeping "paralysis of perspective" (Mamdani 1996, 3) that threatens to devitalize serious critical reflection on race and racism at the threshold of the twenty-first century.

Nonetheless, the broad sweep of our history and our present plight both suggest that "racialization" (Small 1999) continues to be a central fact of American life. Obviously, the claim that race remains a structuring principle in U.S. institutions and social relations need in no way assume an unbroken, unmodified continuity in the content or meanings of "racial formation in the United States" (Omi and Winant 1986). DuBois's time is not our own. We can admit the complex, changing, and contested character of contemporary racial formations and still recognize that race will likely figure in U.S. law and policy for many decades to come. Acknowledging the continuing relevance of race, in this chapter I ask whether the governing grammar of contemporary American debates about the content of racial justice will be adequate to the pressing tasks of the new century. Taking my point of reference from the ongoing controversy over the place of "color-blindness" and "race-consciousness" in U.S. constitutional discourse, I argue that it is not. The reasons behind this state of affairs, however, have less to do with the concept of race than with its specific discursive deployments.

I begin with a short and selective survey of the terminological terrain on which struggles over racial justice have been waged in American constitutional law. I then describe and discuss the limits of the normative vision that underwrites the dominant discourse on racial justice in our constitutional jurisprudence. Even in writings whose claimed concerns are much broader, the normative horizons of racial justice are more often than not drawn in and confined to moral terms. I criticize the dominant debate's almost obsessive focus on the *morality* of race, race-consciousness, and racial identification, and I sketch an alternative to the language of racial moralism. This competing account finds its conceptual center of gravity in the distinctively *political* dimensions of racial claims-making. Taking an example from the contentious dispute over race, criminal law, and black civic publics, I end by indicating more precisely how a political conception of racial justice can provide a conceptual vocabulary for thinking American constitutionalism out of its current color-bind.[1]

RACE AND RECOGNITION: THE "COLOR-BLINDNESS"/ "RACE-CONSCIOUSNESS" DEBATE

In the last quarter century, mainstream discussion of the forms of racial justice has increasingly come to revolve around a single normative question: is the use of race in public policy making defensible in our constitutional order? Broadly speaking, opinion on this issue has divided into two main camps. On one side are those who contend that race should never be used as a ground for imposing burdens or allocating benefits: ours is, or should be, a "color-blind" society whose public policy should impute no special significance to race. On the other side are those who argue that American constitutional norms do not categorically foreclose race-conscious decision making. While proponents of race-consciousness may disagree about the conditions under which reliance on race is legitimate, they reject the principle that race-based distinctions can never be condoned in our constitutional order.

The textual lodestar of the color-blindess principle in U.S. Supreme Court case law is the famous language from the first Justice Harlan's dissenting opinion in *Plessy v. Ferguson* (1896): "Our Constitution is color blind, and neither knows nor tolerates classes among citizens" (*Plessy*, 559).[2] On the current Court, this commitment to color-blindness has found its most passionate proponents in Justices Antonin Scalia and Clarence Thomas. In a series of increasingly strident pronouncements on the meaning of the Equal Protection Clause, Justice Scalia has denounced the use of race as a criterion in public decision making, even for putatively benign purposes. Scalia would forbid even those policies that are designed "to 'make up' for past discrimination"; concurring in *Adarand Constructors, Inc. v. Pena* (1995), Justice Scalia maintained that even putatively "benign" uses of race "reinforce and preserve for future mischief the way of thinking that produced race slavery, race privilege and race hatred" (239). In the same case, Justice Thomas acidly dismissed the notion that one could distinguish between "benign" and "malicious" uses of race; for Thomas, there is no constitutional difference between the two. "In each instance," he writes, race-conscious decision making "is race discrimination, plain and simple" (241).

Similar defenses of the color-blindness principle abound in the scholarly literature. The case for color-blindness has perhaps found its sharpest statement in critical discussions regarding the constitutionality of affirmative action. Writing more than twenty-five years ago (before the Supreme Court first squarely addressed the issue), the late Alexander Bickel argued that the unconstitutionality of race-consciousness was axiomatic:

> If the Constitution prohibits exclusion of blacks and other minorities on racial grounds, it cannot permit the exclusion of whites on similar grounds; for it must be the exclusion on racial grounds which offends the Constitution, and not the particular skin color of the person excluded. (Bickel 1975, 132–33)

For Bickel, the "lesson of the great decisions of the Supreme Court" and of "contemporary history" is that "discrimination on the basis of race is illegal, immoral, unconstitutional, inherently wrong, and destructive of democratic society" (133). In a roughly contemporaneous intervention, Richard Posner advanced a similar thesis. Posner maintained that the "proper constitutional principle" for assessing policies that accord "preferential treatment" to racial minorities was not "no 'invidious' racial or ethnic discrimination, but *no* use of racial or ethnic criteria to determine the distribution of government benefits and burdens" (Posner 1974, 25–26, emphasis added).

More recently, Abigail and Stephan Thernstrom contend in their *America in Black and White* that "[r]ace conscious policies make for more race-consciousness; they carry society backward. We have a simple rule of thumb: that which brings the races together is good; that which divides us is bad" (Thernstrom and Thernstrom 1997, 539). Although the Thernstroms concede that deep disagreement exists about "which policies have what effect," they leave little doubt regarding their own views. On the Thernstroms' account, race-consciousness is always and everywhere "bad": "[We] hold to Justice Harlan's belief that 'our Constitution is color-blind, and neither knows nor tolerates classes among citizens' " (ibid., quoting *Plessy*, 559).

Rejecting the demand for the immediate and categorical deracialization of public discourse, proponents of race-conscious decision making argue that the only way to transcend the American racial dilemma is precisely to take race into account. In one of the earliest constitutional defenses of race-conscious remedies, Justice Brennan counseled caution toward "[c]laims that law must be 'color-blind' or that the datum of race is no longer relevant to public policy" (Regents of the University of California v. *Bakke* (1978), 327). On Brennan's account, the color-blindness principle must instead "be seen as aspiration rather than as description of reality" (327). A rule of racial non-recognition would only "[mask] the reality that many 'created equal' have been treated within our lifetimes as inferior both by the law and by their fellow citizens" (327). More recently, Justice Stevens rejected the claim of Justices Scalia and Thomas in *Adarand* that "benign" and "invidious" race-based policies must be viewed in the same constitutional light: "There is no moral or constitutional equivalence between a policy that is designed to perpetuate a caste system and one that seeks to eradicate racial subordination" (*Adarand*, 243). For Stevens, the constitutional consistency toward race-conscious policies demanded by the *Adarand* majority would effectively "disregard the difference between a 'No Trespassing' sign and a welcome mat" (245).

In the contemporary scholarly literature, the constitutional defense of race-conscious policy making has received extended and sophisticated elaboration by a number of writers. I shall concentrate here on the work of Ronald Dworkin and Amy Gutmann, who have authored two of the most sustained recent reflections (from either side of the debate) on the moral case for and against color-blind constitutionalism.

Dworkin announces his project in the subtitle of *Freedom's Law*—he aims to defend "the moral reading of the American Constitution." As Dworkin describes it, the moral reading approaches the abstract clauses of the U.S. Constitution "on the understanding that they invoke moral principles about political decency and justice" (Dworkin 1996, 2). The equality principle of the Fourteenth Amendment figures centrally in Dworkin's defense of the moral reading. For Dworkin, the U.S. Supreme Court's decision in the famous *Brown v. Board of Education* (1954) case offers an exemplary instance of the moral reading on the ground. Dworkin argues that the outcome in *Brown* was "plainly required by the moral reading, because it is obvious now that official school segregation is not consistent with equal status and equal concern for all races" (Dworkin 1996, 13). Dworkin recognizes that his proffered moral reading of the words "equal protection of the laws" goes far beyond the interpretive tenets of originalism. As a practical matter, the men who wrote and ratified the Equal Protection Clause aimed for much less on the ground than "equal status and equal concern for all races": no one can doubt their commitment (or acquiescence) to continuing racial inequality. However, the moral reading asks "what the framers intended to say" in writing the Fourteenth Amendment, not "what they expected their language to *do*" (1996, 13). In Dworkin's account, the moral method of constitution reading not only permits but requires reparation of the framers' earlier interpretive error. Dworkin maintains that the *Brown* court properly corrected the mistake in understanding that led the framers of the Fourteenth Amendment to uphold race-based school segregation: "The moral reading insists that they misunderstood the moral principle that they themselves enacted into law" (1996, 13).[3] For Dworkin, *Brown* and its progeny restored racial equality jurisprudence to its proper moral basis: the principle of equal status and equal concern for every racial group.

Another thoughtful effort to establish the moral foundations of racial justice is undertaken in Amy Gutmann's "Responding to Racial Injustice" (Appiah and Gutmann 1996, 109). As it's the essay's title suggests, the question Gutmann poses and seeks to answer is how we should respond to the continuing problem of racial injustice in America. Although she takes the persistence of racial injustice in the contemporary United States as a factual premise, Gutmann does not dispute the notion that, as a normative matter, "color blindness is the ideal morality (for an ideal society)" (1996, 109). What Gutmann does deny is the claim that color-blindness represents *the* fundamental principle of justice against which any response to racial justice must be measured, even when it can be shown that color-blind policies maintain institutional patterns of racialized discrimination. For Gutmann, the principle that should inform our response to racial injustice is the norm of justice as fairness. Taking this principle of justice as her regulative ideal, Gutmann contends that one can offer a "color-blind" argument in favor of "color consciousness" in public policy making. Gutmann undertakes to advance a "moral case against racial injustice" (1996, 114) that recognizes the dangers of "race consciousness" without discounting the claims of what she calls "color consciousness." Gutmann endorses the social constructionist understanding that race is a "fiction" (1996, 113). As such, it ought to have no "morally relevant implications for public policy" (1996, 112). The same cannot be said for the notion of "color consciousness": "If we need not be color blind, we can be color conscious" (1996, 132). Gutmann maintains that the idea of "color consciousness" avoids the potential injustice of essentialist racial categories while recognizing "the ways in which skin color and other superficial features of individuals adversely and unfairly affect their life chances" (1996, 112). Taking employment, university admissions, and electoral redistricting as her examples, Gutmann seeks to show that color-conscious principles and policy are consistent with her preferred model of justice as fairness, as well as with the ideal (which she embraces) of a color-blind American future. Building on the moral principle of justice as fairness, Gutmann endorses "those (and only those) color conscious policies" that are "instrumentally valuable in overcoming racial injustice and consistent with counting all persons, whatever their skin color or ancestry, as civic equals" (1996, 177).

RACE, JUSTICE, AND THE LIMITS OF MORALISM

What interests me about the dispute between the advocates of color-blindness and the proponents of color-consciousness is not so much the language of the debate as the normative vision that undergirds it. One of the most fascinating aspects of the debate I've been discussing is the reliance by both sides on a fundamentally moral conception of race and its relevance for public policy. To be sure, these defenses of racial moralism are not always fully theorized; more often than not, they are couched in the language of moral intuition or an asserted moral consensus.[4] Nonetheless, the felt necessity to defend or attack color-blindness and color-consciousness in terms of the morality of race has become one of the more striking features of the dominant discourse.

In our legal doctrine, this moral idea of racial justice informs Justice O'Connor's concern in *City of Richmond v. J.A. Croson* (1989) with the "'personal rights' [of the *Croson* plaintiffs] to be treated with equal dignity and respect" by public decision makers (493). Similarly, a stated fidelity to "the moral basis of the equal protection principle" (*Adarand*, 240) animates Justice Thomas's insistence that racial classifications always "have a destructive impact on the individual and our society" (240): "I believe that there is a 'moral [and] constitutional equivalence' . . . between laws designed to subjugate a race and those that distribute benefits on the basis of race in order to foster some current notion of equality" (240, citations omitted).

Versions of the "moralizing style" are mobilized, as well, in the theoretical literature on the constitution of racial justice. We have seen that for Gutmann the morality in question has to do with the rights of individual moral personhood. Gutmann's moral conception of racial justice starts from the premise that "all human beings regardless of their color should be treated as free and equal beings, worthy of the same set of basic liberties" (Appiah and Gutmann 1996, 112–13).[5] Similarly, in Dworkin's "moral reading" of the Constitution, the "abstract moral principle" of racial justice to which the Equal Protection Clause gives expression is a larger, group-sensitive recognition of "equal status and equal concern for all races" (Dworkin 1996, 13).[6] Despite their differing views about the claims of color-blindness and color-consciousness, writers I have discussed share a reading of the Fourteenth Amendment as a constitutional statement about the morality or immorality of discrimination. They share the belief that questions of racial justice under our Constitution are properly approached from the moral point of view,[7] and they draw on the resources of racial moralism to defend their respective positions.

In my view, this "moral constriction"[8] of the public debate over racial justice fails to capture the distinctive and constitutive role of the political in racial claims-making. At its core, the moral vision that underwrites the dominant constitutional discourse on race provides a contemporary case study in the "displacement of politics" as we know it (Honig 1993). The moral concept of racial justice tries to capture and control the explosive, agonistic conflicts that characterize American racial politics. If it cannot altogether remove questions of racial power politics from its agenda, the racial moralism model can aspire to confine them within the dispassionate discursive boundaries of juridical settlement, bureaucratic administration, and deliberative legislation. If contemporary history teaches us anything about our racial dilemma, it is that conflicts over the forms and substance of racial injustice have been primarily contests about access to the means of political power, about social relations of domination, subordination, and resistance. These distinctively political dimensions of race in America resist the normative logic of the moral view that continues to predominate in public debates about racial justice.

This is not to say that the moral conception of racial justice has succeeded entirely in excluding politics from its discursive domain. We need only consider in this connection the terms of the Supreme Court's opinion in *Brown*, which Dworkin holds up as a shining example of the moral reading at its best. As I have noted, Dworkin interprets the Court's judgment as a ringing repudiation of the erroneous moral principle that had sanctioned state-imposed racial segregation in public education throughout most of the previous century. For Dworkin, the *Brown* Court took the Fourteenth Amendment as a textual marker for the moral precept that all racial groups have a claim to equal status and concern within our constitutional order. Dworkin's moral reading of *Brown* comports with the standard account of the case, which holds that the Court's chief constitutional concern was how enforced racial segregation made black schoolchildren *feel*.[9] Racially segregated public schools generated a "feeling of inferiority" among black students about "status in the community that may affect their hearts and minds in a way unlikely ever to be undone" (*Brown*, 494). On this account, the heart of the harm addressed in *Brown* was, at base, a moral harm. In responding to that harm, the Court drew on the "abstract moral principles" of the Fourteenth Amendment. I am not claiming the moral reading of *Brown* finds no basis in the text of the opinion. My point, rather, is that proponents of racial moralism have not paid sufficient attention to the fact that the *Brown* Court's defense of the equality principle sought support in another, very different justification:

> Today, education is perhaps the most important function of state and local governments. Compulsory school attendance laws and the great expenditures for education both demonstrate our recognition of the importance of education to our democratic society. It is required in the performance of our most basic public responsibilities, even service in the armed forces. It is the very foundation of good citizenship. (*Brown*, 493).

As this language suggests, the moral account of racial justice offers at best a partial explanation of the *Brown* opinion. The *Brown* Court explicitly stresses the political meaning and significance of public education for American life in the middle of the twentieth century. From this perspective, the exclusionary practices struck down in *Brown* threatened the "very foundation of good citizenship" in our constitutional democracy. Put another way, the racial segregation of public schools denied African Americans equal access to the means of civic or political *formation* necessary for "performance of our most basic public responsibilities." As a constitutional matter, then, *Brown* can be read not only or even primarily as a statement about moral personhood and rights in a moral community;[10] on this interpretation, the decision is equally a vindication of political citizenship and right to political society.[11]

To my mind, *Brown* is a specific (though incompletely theorized) instance of a broader principle of racial citizenship. The defense of that principle derives from an openly political understanding and a political reading of our racial Constitution. The moral conception of racial justice highlights the immorality of discrimination, whose incidence and effects it tries to control through ethical norms such as those that command "equal concern and respect" or obedience to the notion of "justice as fairness." The political conception of racial justice focuses squarely on the illegitimacy of a regime of civic subjugation that the Court, in the decade after *Brown*, labeled "White Supremacy" (*Loving v. Virginia* [1967], 11). The moral defense of racial justice seeks to "annihilate the political" (Schmitt 1976, 71) dangers of race by submitting disputes about racialized privilege and subordination to a "rational process of negotiation" (Mouffe 1993b, 49) and the ethical constraints of "agreed-upon, neutral rules" (48). The moral model thus seeks to build a normative firewall between racial justice-seeking and racial politics, toward which its basic attitude is one of anxious distrust. By contrast, the political account of racial justice starts from a candid recognition that the power and persistence of racial hierarchy warrant a sober (and sobering) "racial realism" (Bell 1995) about the limits of "moral politics" (Lakoff 1996). While it acknowledges the influence and achievements of the racial egalitarian ideal, the political account also insists that democracy in America remains a *racial* democracy. Because American political society is still in salient and significant ways a "racial polity" (Mills 1999, 17), a democratic conception of racial justice faces a double challenge: to review the problem of justice in light of the problem of politics, and at the same time to "rethink the political around the axis of race" (17).

The moral model concerns itself with the intersection of justice and virtue.[12] The political conception directs its concerns to the intersection of race and power. Unlike the moral conception of racial justice, the political perspective on racial justice-seeking refuses to deny the constitutive value and affirmative role that power, antagonism, and interest play in the life of racialized politics. It understands that racial justice-seeking in the late modern state takes place in a field of ongoing political conflict and contest, a domain in which we "cannot hope to achieve moral consensus" (MacIntyre 1981, 234) on questions of race. The political model thus attends to the agonistic dimensions of racial justice-seeking. Its normative account of justice and racial politics places full accent and emphasis on the power relations that subtend disputes and decision making about the distribution of burdens and benefits across racial publics. For the political conception of racial justice, the effort to translate the deep agreements of racial politics into the depoliticized language of rational morality cannot possibly achieve what we hope from it. The attempted moral mastery of racial politics does not make its "conflicts, antagonisms, relations of power, forms of subordination and repression simply disappear" (Mouffe 1993b, 49). The political conception of racial justice recognizes that because "[m]oral discourse is personal dialogue" (Pitkin 1972, 216), its decision rules embody a model of judgment that simply fails to wrestle with the large public questions of group privilege, inequality, and power that an adequate account of race, racism, and racial justice-seeking must engage.

I hope by now to have said enough to convey a sense of the normative boundaries that inform a properly political conception of racial justice. I turn now to a brief description of what I take to be the rudiments of its basic structure. In broad terms, the political conception of racial justice is a species of "democratic justice" (Shapiro 1999). A state committed to democratic justice in the "racial polity" must undertake at least three key tasks, the performance of which determines its political legitimacy. The first task is to secure and maintain for vulnerable racial publics equal and meaningful access to the processes of self-governance through which democratic political identities are formed and given expression. I have in mind here such formal rights as the right to vote and to run for elective office. The second task of constitutional democracy is to insure that the voices and interests of vulnerable racial publics are not excluded from the state institutions in which binding collective choices are discussed and made. For the political conception of democratic justice requires that the representation rights of vulnerable racial publics must not simply be given formal voice; they must be accorded real weight and value. From this perspective, legal and policy outcomes matter. This is not to say that vulnerable racial publics would necessarily win each and every dispute over the content of race-relevant law and policy. What the right of racial representation would require is an understanding that the process and product of state policy making cannot claim political legitimacy if the governing decision rules entrench racially segmented hierarchy and racialized democratic domination.

The third element of a political conception of racial justice is perhaps more controversial. A democratic understanding of racial justice-seeking would demand an ongoing effort to facilitate what Jane Mansbridge calls "enclaves of resistance" (Mansbridge 1996, 58) within vulnerable racial publics, a protected space for developing oppositional ideas about racial justice and its opposite. Mansbridge rightly argues that since "no democracy ever reaches the point at which justice is simply done, democracies need to recognize and foster enclaves of resistance" (58). Nancy Fraser aptly terms these venues for oppositional discussion and deliberation "subaltern counterpublics" (Fraser 1997, 81).

> The goals of these counterpublics include understanding themselves better, forging bonds of solidarity, preserving the memories of past injustices, interpreting and reinterpreting the meanings of those injustices, working out alternative conceptions of self, of community, of justice, and of universality, trying to make sense of both the privileges they wield and the oppressions they face, understanding the strategic configurations for and against their desired ends, deciding what alliances to make both emotionally and strategically, deliberating on ends and means, and deciding how to act, individually and collectively. (Mansbridge 1996, 58)

Like the relations of power they challenge, these subaltern counterpublics emerge and flourish beyond the formal boundaries of statist politics. Nonetheless, they play a decisive role in both validating and contesting the claim of the state to democratic legitimacy.

Ian Shapiro has identified at least four levels on which institutionalized oppositional counterpublics are a "defining criterion of democracy" (Shapiro 1996, 234). First, because periodic transfers of power are a necessary if not sufficient condition of democratic governance, oppositional political enclaves provide a site for potential alternative leaderships to organize and equip themselves to assume the reigns of democratic state power. Second, oppositional counterpublics help legitimate democratic politics by "attracting social dissent toward antigovernment forces within the regime rather than directing it at the regime's foundations." In this way, anger and alienation among civic counterpublics can be directed at particular power holders without resort to oppositional strategies that permanently or fundamentally threaten the broader culture of democratic politics. Third, institutionalized opposition advances the wider public interest by ensuring that there will always be members of the political society who stand ready to "ask awkward questions, shine light in dark corners, and expose abuses of power." Fourth and finally, the presence of effective oppositional counterpublics creates a space within democratic political culture that gives subordinated groups some reason to believe they are not doomed to suffocate under the weight of inherited injustices and "can challenge prevailing norms and rules with the realistic hope of altering them" (1996, 234–35).

Taken together, these elements of a political conception of racial justice create the conditions for polity in which democratic citizenship and racial citizenship are mutually constitutive and mutually transformative, in ways that might be positive for both.[13] I recognize that the conception of racial justice I have sketched here will be a source of deep political discomfort, particularly in its suggestion that vulnerable racial publics should be accorded a species of democratic "destabilization rights" (Unger 1997, 387–91). In theory (if not in actual practice), the modern American constitutional order is premised on the notion that democratic politics and racial politics are hostile at all points. The conception of racial justice-seeking elaborated here collides fundamentally with a vision of American political identity and American political ideas whose sheer taken-for-grantedness has made it almost impossible to question, much less dislodge. Nonetheless, I am persuaded that the political conception of racial justice I am defending is both a valid and a viable alternative to the magical thinking that characterizes the regnant status quo. Abandoning the idea that we can or must achieve a moral consensus for adjudicating disputes about race and power, the political conception proceeds from the belief that "there is no criterion for justice that is anterior to what democracy generates" (Shapiro 1996, 237–38). The political conception of racial justice thus enjoins us to look for democratic solutions to the problems of racialized hierarchy, privilege, and disadvantage in the domain of democracy itself. One possible point of entry here is by way of the concept of *democratic racial citizenship* and its normative commitment to the right of vulnerable racial publics "to survive and participate" (Shapiro 1999, 236) fully in the institutions of American constitutional democracy.

TAKING RACIAL CITIZENSHIP SERIOUSLY

I have said that the political conception of justice asks us to take the idea of democratic, race-conscious citizenship seriously. However, any effort to place the idea of citizenship at the center of political and legal discourse on race must acknowledge a threshold difficulty. For most of its history, American political culture has treated the concept of citizenship with indifference, if not outright contempt. This has been particularly true with respect to questions of racial justice. A 1973 article by the late Alexander Bickel illustrates my point. In "Citizenship in the American Constitution," Bickel deployed his formidable analytic and rhetorical skills to show that "the concept of citizenship plays only the most minimal role in the American constitutional scheme" (Bickel 1973, 369). For Bickel, this is part of the genius of our constitutional democracy. Bickel begins by noting that "the original constitution presented the edifying picture of a government that bestowed rights on people and persons, and held itself out as bound by certain standards of conduct in its relation with people and persons, not with some legal construct called citizen" (1973, 370). Bickel then turns his attention to the language of citizenship in the Civil Rights Act of 1866 and the Reconstruction Amendments. Bickel concedes that these two texts represented the first attempt in our constitutional history at "an authoritative definition of citizenship in American law" (372). On his account, however, these codifications of citizenship rights sought only to dispel Chief Justice Taney's mischievous linkage of rights and citizenship status in the *Dred Scott v. Sandford* (1837) case, whose constitutional vision had been repudiated with the Union victory in the Civil War.

In addition to his argument from the constitutional text, Bickel drew more broadly on normative political philosophy:

> Emphasis on citizenship as the tie that binds the individual to government and as the source of his rights leads to metaphysical thinking about politics and law, and more particularly to symmetrical thinking, to a search for reciprocity and symmetry and clarity of uncompromised rights and obligations, rationally ranged one next and against the other. Such thinking bodes ill for the endurance of free, flexible, responsive and stable institutions, and of a balance between order and liberty. . . . It is gratifying, therefore, that we live under a Constitution to which the concept of citizenship matters very little indeed. (Bickel 1973, 387)

Having surveyed the claims of citizenship theory in American constitutional practice, Bickel concludes that "[c]itizenship is at best a simple idea for a simple government" (387).

In the decade after Bickel celebrated its irrelevance for American constitutional law, the citizenship idea would become an object of renewed interest in normative political and legal theory. In the law schools, scholars such as Cass Sunstein and Frank Michelman explored the implications of the revival of civic republican thought for American constitutionalism. However, the call for the rehabilitation of the republican tradition met with some resistance among scholars of race and constitutional law. In a critical reply to Sunstein and Michelman, Preeta Bansal and Derrick Bell urge "skepticism" as "the necessary response" for people of color toward the urged revival of republican ideas of citizenship (Bansal and Bell 1988, 1609). Bansal and Bell argued that the civic republican faith "in the existence of shared values and the possibility of the common good" assumes "that a social consensus will emerge from 'reasoned' deliberation by individuals who think 'rationally' and who are capable of abstracting from their private experiences" (1610). In their view, "blacks have served as the group whose experiences and private needs have been suppressed in order to promote the 'common good' of whites" (1611). Accordingly, Bansal and Bell found little in the republican vision of citizenship that spoke to the dynamics of American racial politics. "What parts of the republican vision," they queried, "are capable of combating and subduing the by-now familiar priorities for whites in racial policymaking, priorities that have preserved for whites their perpetual power?" (1613).

The question Bansal and Bell raise here about the political use and abuse of the citizenship idea warrants an answer. Briefly stated, I believe that the beginnings of a response to their concerns can be found in the work of scholars who have rethought and reconstructed the narrative of republican citizenship in order to put it to new uses within a vision of multicultural justice and a democratic politics of difference. Theorists such as Iris Marion Young (Young 1990) have argued persuasively that there is no necessary conceptual connection between the idea of citizenship and the ideology of classical republicanism. The concept of citizenship, Young contends, can serve as a crucial tool in building a democratic political conception of racial justice for our contemporary multicultural polity. Properly understood, the citizenship idea places the very questions of racialized power relations that concern Bansal and Bell at the center of its normative concerns. In this respect, the language of citizenship can provide a grammar for racial claims-making that speaks directly to our own moment, when it is not so much the moral personhood or status but the political identity and station of racial minority publics whose future is in doubt.[14]

It should be noted in this connection that the citizenship idea figures prominently in those provisions of our Constitution around which so much of the U.S. debate over racial justice has revolved. As T. Alexander Aleinikoff demonstrates, the concept of citizenship was a crucial element in the architecture of the Reconstruction Amendments, whose terms continue to inform the project of racial claims-making in contemporary American political culture. In a careful contrarian reading of the dissent in *Plessy*, Aleinikoff argues that the ideal of color-blindness was not the primary source of the first Justice Harlan's constitutional objections to the segregation statute upheld by the *Plessy* majority. Harlan's target was not "racial classifications" but the "ideology of white supremacy" (Alienikoff 1992, 961). Moreover, the *Plessy* dissent must be read as "a discourse on the fundamental rights of citizenship, not the equal protection of the laws" (964). Harlan "painted a far grander picture than equal treatment; [he], in effect, portrayed the recent amendments as declaiming that the blessings of citizenship are to be respected in every jurisdiction of the United States" (964). For Aleinikoff, the *Plessy* dissent offers a "unifying account of the Civil War Amendments" as a whole. "[T]he 'freedom' guaranteed by the Thirteenth Amendment is linked to the fundamental-rights-protecting 'liberty' of the Fourteenth Amendment; the opposite of the slavery prohibited by the Thirteenth Amendment is the citizenship guaranteed by the Fourteenth Amendment" (974). Although he does not explicitly frame his argument in these terms, Aleinikoff makes a compelling case for a normative reorientation from a moral to a political reading of the Reconstruction Amendments and of the vision of justice as political freedom to which they give expression.[15] In this respect, Aleinikoff's reinterpretation of the *Plessy* dissent as a judicial defense of the "freedom of citizens" (*Plessy*, 557) and the "blessings of citizenship" (Aleinikoff 1992, 964) offers an insightful constitutional genealogy of the political conception of racial justice urged here.

The problem, as Aleinikoff himself admits, is that Harlan's idea of the "personal liberty of citizens" is too elusive to do the work that a political conception of racial justice would demand of it: "simply invoking 'liberty' is not enough" (1992, 976).[16] The challenge, then, is to specify precisely what an adequate *grundnorm* for a political conception of racial justice would look like. Taking my example from the vexed debate over racial disparities in the criminal law, I suggest that the "political freedom of vulnerable racial publics" might generate a useful normative framework for thinking about claims of racial injustice.

RACE, CRIME, AND POLITICAL JUSTICE: AN ANALYTIC EXPLORATION

In recent years, black conservative and neoliberal scholars have challenged the claim that racially disparate effects in the system of American criminal justice should be viewed as a problem of unlawful racial discrimination. To take one example, in *Race, Crime, and the Law*, Randall Kennedy contends that we ought not conclude that racial disparities in criminal law are racist without first determining whether the law harms black communities. Thus Kennedy asks, is "the black population hurt when traffickers in crack cocaine suffer longer prison sentences than those who deal in powdered cocaine or helped by incarcerating for longer periods those who use and sell a drug that has had an especially devastating effect on African-American communities?" (Kennedy 1998, 10).[17] Kennedy applies a utilitarian moral theory to determine when and how racial disparities in criminal law might raise a problem from the perspective of the antidiscrimination principle—in effect endorsing an essentially moral conception of racial justice.

The moral calculus that underwrites Kennedy's analysis of racially disparate treatment within the criminal justice system revolves around his twin notions of "racial reputation" and the "politics of respectability." For Kennedy, the "historically besmirched reputation" (1998, 13) of African Americans is one of the central reasons behind the nation's "indifference to their plight" (21). Kennedy writes:

> In American political culture, the reputation of groups, be they religious denominations, labor unions, or racial groups, matters greatly. For that reason alone, those dedicated to advancing the interests of African-Americans ought to urge them to conduct themselves in a fashion that, without sacrificing rights or dignity, elicits respect and sympathy rather than fear and anger from colleagues of other races. (21)

Kennedy argues that black Americans must make a renewed commitment to the "politics of respectability"[18]:

> The principle tenet of the politics of respectability is that, freed of crippling, invidious discriminations, blacks are capable of meeting the established moral standards of white middle-class Americans. Proponents of the politics of respectability exhort blacks to accept and meet these standards, even while they are being discriminated against wrongly (in hypocritical violation of these standards). They maintain that while some blacks succeed even in the teeth of discouraging racial oppression, many more would succeed in the absence of racial restrictions. Insistence that blacks are worthy of respect is the central belief animating the politics of respectability. One of its strategies is to distance as many blacks as far as possible from negative stereotypes used to justify racial discrimination against all Negroes. (17)[19]

Building on these two moral tenets, Kennedy goes on to examine such policies as the racially disparate effect of federal sentencing guidelines for crack cocaine and powder cocaine possession.[20] The governing statute imposes much harsher prison terms on crack cocaine offenders than it does on those convicted of powder cocaine offenses (the sentencing disparity is 100:1 for crack and powder cocaine violations respectively). For Kennedy, this "dramatic difference" (364) in sentencing does not necessarily run afoul of the antidiscrimination principle embodied in the Equal Protection Clause.

In defending this assertion, *Race, Crime, and the Law* offers a number of arguments against the "racial critique" of the crack–powder disparity. Most pertinent to our purpose, however, are those Kennedy develops in response to the claim (made by federal district court Judge Clyde Cahill) that the more severe punishment of crack offenders imposes "an increased burden on blacks as a class" (375). Kennedy questions the grounds on which this assumption rests. It might be that the longer incarceration of black crack offenders confers benefits on the largely African-American communities from which they are sent to prison. Imprisonment, in short, is both a burden and a benefit, writes Kennedy: "a benefit for those imprisoned and a good for those whose lives are bettered by the confinement of criminals who might otherwise prey on them" (375). Kennedy also challenges the notion that the crack–powder sentencing differential imposes a *racially discriminatory* burden. He notes that the challenged statute applies to anyone who violates its crack cocaine provisions without regard to race. Kennedy argues that Judge Cahill apparently believes that "black crack convicts represent blacks as a whole. They do not" (375–76). On Kennedy's analysis, the crack cocaine differential would only be racially discriminatory if it fell on the entire black population, as opposed to those "bad Negroes" (18) who actually break the law (376). Since it does not, it cannot properly be called racist, not least because it "could be" (376) that the enhanced sentencing of black crack addicts and dealers "helps" the vast majority of "good" African Americans, who not only gain "security [as] law-abiding blacks vis-à-vis criminals," but share the enhanced "reputation of blacks as a collectivity in the eyes of whites" (17).

Kennedy is careful to note that he is not endorsing the sentencing distinction between crack and powder cocaine. The differential, he concedes, may well be a policy mistake. His is a rather different claim, which answers the charge that the sentencing differential is racist. Kennedy concludes that "even if these policies are misguided, being mistaken is different from being racist, and the difference is one that greatly matters" (386). Curiously, Kennedy's concluding remarks fail to highlight a second, crucial legal difference between "mistaken" and "racist" drug policies: under current Supreme Court doctrine, the latter are clearly unconstitutional, while the former are not. Despite its racially disparate effects, a successful claim that the crack–powder sentencing distinction was "racist" in constitutional terms would have to prove that it had been adopted *intentionally* in order to imprison black convicts for a longer term than whites.[21]

The case Kennedy chooses to illustrate that point is the Supreme Court's decision in *Hunter v. Underwood* (1985). In *Underwood*, a unanimous Court voided a provision of the Alabama state constitution that disfranchised any person who was convicted of a crime of moral turpitude. The Court found that when it was enacted in 1901, the provision was aimed at removing black Alabamians from the state's voting rolls. Kennedy writes approvingly of the decision and argues that the Supreme Court was right to strike down Alabama's law, because "unjustified racial considerations" (Kennedy 1998, 376) had driven its initial adoption. Kennedy contends that little evidence exists to support a similar conclusion with respect to the crack–powder sentencing differential; it may be fairly inferred that he accordingly believes the distinction is constitutional, notwithstanding its differential racial impact.

However, it is not Kennedy's account and endorsement of the purpose requirement that makes his discussion of *Underwood* so intriguing in the instant context. I am rather more interested in the way Kennedy's preoccupation with the moral economy of racial reputation and respectability blinds him to a problem that lies right on the surface of the *Underwood* case. That problem has to do the political economy of racially disparate sentencing. Let me explain what I mean.

In the decade and a half since the Supreme Court rendered its judgment in *Underwood*, American society has witnessed an explosion in prison incarceration. From 1980 to 1994, the population of the United States grew by 9.8 percent (Golenpaul 1997, 829). During the same period, the number of men and women in jail or prison increased an astronomical 195.6 percent (Cole 1999, 148). Much of the growth in America's imprisoned population during these years was a result of the so-called "war on drugs." The number of drug offenders incarcerated for drug offenses in federal prisons increased nearly tenfold from 1980 to 1993, accounting for almost three-quarters of the overall increase in federal prisoners (1999, 145). The number of state prisoners incarcerated for drug offenses during the period under consideration grew at a similar rate (145).

The most striking aspect of this burgeoning incarceration rate is its racial cast. In 1992, the U.S. Public Health Service reported that 76 percent of the nation's self-reported illicit drug users were white, 14 percent were black, and 8 percent were Hispanic (Miller 1996, 81). Although the percentage of illegal drug users from each group roughly corresponded to their proportions in the general population, the incarceration rates tell an altogether different story. Between 1986 and 1991, the number of white drug offenders in state prisons increased by 110 percent, but the number of black drug offenders rose by 465 percent (Mauer 1997, 10). African Americans constitute 74 percent of those who are serving time for drug-related crimes (Huling and Mauer 1995, 12). If our current rates of incarceration remain stable, 28.5 percent of African-American men will do jail or prison time at least once during their lifetimes (Fellner and Mauer 1998, 13). A disproportionate number of these men will be casualties of the "war on drugs." As that war has been prosecuted, the crack–powder cocaine sentencing differential has effectively drawn a color line between the white crack-cocaine-using majority and the black offenders who make up the majority of Americans imprisoned for crack-related crimes.

In passing judgment on the racial demographics of drug-related incarceration, Kennedy would pose the following moral question: do the longer prison sentences meted out to African Americans who sell and use crack cocaine *help* or *hurt* the nation's black population? In Kennedy's moral conception of racial justice, this assessment would depend in significant measure on whether racially disparate prison terms for black crack offenders enhance the racial reputation of law-abiding African Americans in the eyes of whites. If the crack–powder cocaine sentencing differential in fact has led white middle-class Americans to believe that blacks have the capacity to "meet the established moral standards" to which they themselves subscribe, Kennedy would presumably conclude that the differential does not present a case of racial injustice, at least in the absence of evidence that it was intended to punish black crack offenders more harshly than their white powder-using counterparts.

My main concern here is not to stake out a substantive position in the debate over the crack cocaine–powder cocaine sentencing differential; I want, instead, to contest Kennedy's view of the normative terms on which that debate should proceed. As a normative matter, the political conception of racial justice advanced in this essay would approach the problem from another direction. The political model is not indifferent to the relative costs and benefits of racially disparate drug sentencing laws; it shares that much with the analysis offered in *Race, Crime, and the Law.* Aside from this, however, Kennedy's racial moralism and the political account of racial justice could not be more divergent. The political conception of racial justice would undertake a very different normative accounting of the costs and benefits racially disparate sentencing entails. The central task of the political conception of racial justice is not to determine how the disparate sentencing regime affects the racial reputation and standing of black "communities"; rather, it seeks to assess the impact of these laws on the political power of black civic publics.

The political conception of racial justice would thus pose a number of questions Kennedy's argument from racial moralism fails to ask, much less answer: Do these sentencing differentials increase or diminish African-American access to the means and modes of collective political action? Does the longer incarceration of blacks who are convicted of these crimes strengthen or weaken the political integrity and effectiveness of African-American civic publics? Do such laws enhance or undermine the institutions and practices through which black political identity and opinion are shaped and mobilized? What are the burdens and benefits of these policies in sustaining the social and cultural conditions of African-American citizenship?

In exploring these questions, one of the first issues on which the political conception of racial justice would focus is the impact on black civic publics of America's felony disfranchisement laws. A recent study of the subject commissioned by The Sentencing Commission and Human Rights Watch is instructive in this regard. The authors report that nearly four million Americans cannot vote because of felony convictions (Fellner and Mauer 1998, 7). Of that number, 1.4 million are black men (8). Viewed on a state-by-state basis, the picture is even more grim. 31 percent of the black men who live in Alabama and Florida are permanently disenfranchised. In Iowa, Mississippi, New Mexico, Virginia, and Wyoming, one in four black men are permanently excluded from the vote. In Washington State, one in four black men are currently or permanently disenfranchised. In Delaware and Texas a full 20 percent of black male citizens are either permanently or currently barred from the franchise. In four other states, 16–18 percent of voting-age black men are currently disenfranchised. In nine states, the figure stands between 10 and 15 percent (Fellner and Mauer 1998, 8–11). The authors estimate that if current incarceration rates remain stable, 28.5 percent of black men will do prison time at least once in their lifetime—a figure six times greater than that for white men (1998, 13). Since felony disenfranchisement policies apply as well to defendants who are convicted but not sentenced to prison, the report predicts that among the next generation of black American men, some 40 percent will probably lose the right to vote for life (13).[22]

These facts should give us pause.[23] The story they tell is only in part about the current and future evisceration of the black vote. I do not mean to suggest that when nearly a third of the black men who live in some states are barred from the franchise, we need not be concerned about the effects of their exclusion on black electoral power as a whole.[24] However, more is at stake here than formal access to the ballot box.[25] As I see it, for African Americans, franchise rights have never been purely or primarily instrumental. Those rights are also, and perhaps more fundamentally, *constitutive* of black political culture in positive and affirmative ways. The history of black civic publics in the United States suggests that participation in formal electoral "politics" has enabled African Americans to contest and redraw the very boundaries of what the dominant discourse has defined as "political."[26] Specifically, the African-American struggle for and exercise of voting rights have been important experiential building blocks for the construction of an alternative, oppositional black public sphere. The existence of a black "subaltern counterpublic" (Fraser 1997) has made it possible for this subordinated social group to create "parallel discursive arenas" and "invent and circulate *counter*discourses" that challenge the dominant discourse on race and empower African Americans to "formulate oppositional interpretations of their identities, interests and needs" (1997, 81). Over time, the participation of African Americans in this counterpublic sphere has given rise to a civic activist consciousness whose emergence has produced "a devastating critique of American political institutions and values as well as suggestions about theoretical and institutional alternatives" (Dawson 1994, 201). Black American engagement in mainstream "franchise politics" has been indispensable in creating a subaltern site for, and a subaltern set of institutions for facilitating, deliberation and discussion of a whole range of subjects that racialized stratification would otherwise shield from interrogation and contestation (Gregory 1994, 159).

In this post–civil rights era, some have doubted whether a black public sphere can even be said to exist in contemporary America (Dawson 1994, 197). Although reports of its death may be premature, the impact of ex-felon disenfranchisement laws on the political life of the black civic sphere should command the concern of democratic constitutionalists. As my colleague George Fletcher has noted, the basic question "is whether categorical divestment of voting rights introduces an impermissible element of caste into the American political system" (Fletcher 1999, 1895), in which African Americans increasingly constitute a discrete class of "abjected citizens" (Daniel 2000, 68). I seek to show that for African-American citizens, meaningful action in that system not only involves engagement in traditional, franchise-based politics; it also includes participation in the subaltern enclaves of oppositional discourse that permit members of the black public sphere to define and understand political issues, test political options, and organize effective political intervention. Felony disenfranchisement regimes quite literally block increasing numbers of African Americans from access to a political institution that has been crucial in creating and sustaining black civic activism and consciousness. From this perspective, we may rightly ask whether the vulnerable racial publics to which these men and women belong can perdure in the face of their prolonged, sometimes permanent exclusion from the voting booth.[27] Even if they do, there is sufficient reason to believe that the comparative strength and status of the black political sphere will be compromised for many decades to come. Again, what is at stake here is not a moral, but a political issue.

I have argued here for a political conception of racial justice that seeks a greater democratization of the power relations among racial publics in this country. Specifically, this democratic vision of racial justice defends the right of vulnerable racial publics to full and effective political participation in the institutions of American democracy. Further, it robustly supports and promotes the coalescence of organized enclaves of opposition that empower subaltern racial publics to criticize and contest the reigning understandings and practices of democracy. Can a constitutional democracy that takes these commitments seriously permit felony disenfranchisement to become a permanent part of its basic political structure or practices?

One might insist, with Randall Kennedy and others, that absent evidence of biased decision making, the disparate racial impact of these laws raises no problem under our current constitutional regime. This objection, however, misses the point. The critical position advanced here stands on a political norm of legitimacy, not the narrower norm of constitutionality. To take this normative shift and ask the properly *political* question about these laws is to answer it: viewed through a normative lens of political legitimacy, felony disenfranchisement laws are unjust because they deprive the African-American civic public of full and free access to one of the minimum conditions of collective democratic action. Moreover, this state of affairs harms "blacks as a collectivity" (Kennedy 1998, 376): on my account, the regime of voting rights divestment adversely affects the political possibilities of *all* African Americans,[28] including those "good" Negro citizens who meet "the established moral standards of white middle-class Americans" (1998, 17) and, as a formal matter, retain the right to vote.

A political analysis of the connections among the crack cocaine–power cocaine sentencing differential, felony disenfranchisement laws, and the structural debilitation of the black public sphere thus reveals the limits of racial moralism. In the final instance, racial moralism produces too narrow a vision of racial injustice and its remediation. The "politics" (such as it is) of "racial reputation" cannot possibly achieve the justice its advocates so desperately want from it: recognition of the equal moral personhood of black Americans provides no protection against the harm of unequal political citizenship.[29] As Leopardi once aptly put it, "[s]uch is ethics; and such is the extent to which moral beliefs have anything to do with actions" (Gilroy 2000, 54).

CONCLUSION

For much of the last century, the debate between the proponents of colorblindess and the defenders of race-consciousness has stood at the center of American public discourse on the question of racial justice. My effort in these pages has been to show that the underlying normative framework of this debate—what I have called racial moralism—may have reached the end of its term of service. Whatever one may think about its value in decades past, the language of racial moralism offers too limited a grammar for addressing the challenges of our racial future. Contesting this constricted moral vision, I have advanced a political understanding of racial justice whose conceptual resources more fully comport with the realities of racialized hierarchy and subordination in our own time.

More than a few readers may dispute the conception of race and racial politics defended here, not only in its particulars, but in its enabling premises. To them I can only say that I do not take such challenges as a threat to the political conception of racial justice-seeking. To the contrary, they are themselves a potential instance of the democratic politics I would endorse. A properly political vision of racial justice not only requires, but invites its own contestation. Finally, since the substance of the political conception of racial justice-seeking can only emerge in and through the actual practices of democracy, this essay has not attempted a detailed map of its institutional architecture. Rather, and more modestly, my purpose here has been to explore and defend a few elements of its basic design. In doing so, I hope to have shown how the twin notions of racial citizenship and racial civic publics might be used as a compass for steering our national conversation on race, politics, and justice beyond the boundaries of racial moralism, toward the more open frontier of multiracial democracy.

NOTES

1 Although this exploration of the political conception of racial justice is informed by the particular case of Americans of African descent, I do not mean to suggest that it has no application to other publics of color. I limit my discussion to African Americans for two reasons. First, considerations of space will not permit the careful comparative analysis that expansion of the argument beyond the African-American case would demand. Second, in many salient ways, the African-American experience has determined the structure and substance of racial formation in the United States. As Joe Feagin (Feagin 2000, 3) notes, "[n]o other racially oppressed group has been so central to the internal economic, political, and cultural structure and evolution of American society—or to the often obsessively racist ideology developed by white Americans over many generations."

2 T. Alexander Aleinikoff has argued that the contemporary proponents of color-blindness have taken this sentence out of context. Aleinikoff contends that, taken as a whole, the dissent from which this language has been wrenched is an attack not "on the use of racial classifications, but on a social system based on an ideology of white supremacy" (Aleinikoff 1992, 961).

3 Although Dworkin does not affirmatively develop the argument, the moral reading urged in *Freedom's Law* would appear to support the constitutionality of race-based affirmative action. However, one must infer this from Dworkin's argument, since his discussion of affirmative action focuses in the main on a critical discussion of the failure of one of its prominent critics (former Solicitor General Charles Fried) to produce a unifying moral principle that would establish the constitutional case against it. His other work suggests Dworkin would anchor the constitutional defense of race-based affirmative action in the moral norm of equal status and concern for all races. See his *A Matter of Principle* (Dworkin 1985, 293–315).

4 Lest I be misunderstood, I should perhaps make it clear that I do not view the terms "normative" and "moral" as synonyms. As I use it here, the moral conception is merely one form of normative argument regarding race, racism, and justice; it does not exhaust the field of normative thinking about racial justice-seeking. Indeed, my purpose in these pages is to recommend a political alternative to the moral conception that, on my account, provides a more precise and productive normative perspective for engaging questions of justice in our multiracial democracy. A thoughtful critical exploration of the distinction in another context is Waldron 2000.

5 It bears remarking that in this respect, the moral conception views justice as a problem of fair (racial) distribution. For criticisms of this distributive paradigm of justice see Young (1990, 15–38) and Shapiro (1999, 232).

6 As he has made clear elsewhere, Dworkin does not understand the norms of equal status and equal concern to mean that all racial groups are entitled to *equal treatment* under the law. Dworkin argues that the moral principles of equal status and equal concern embodied in the Fourteenth Amendment guarantee the right to "treatment as an equal," but not to "equal treatment" (Dworkin 1977, 227).

7 Readers of Dworkin and Gutmann may object to my description of these two scholars as moralists on questions of racial justice.Both, it might be said, take care to highlight the fact that the moral framework that informs their conception of racial justice is a "political" morality (see Dworkin 1996, 2; Appiah and Gutmann 1996, 107). The objection mistakes the thrust of my claims about Dworkin and Gutmann, which look beneath the precise language they use to uncover what I see as the basal logic that drives their argument. While I do not deny that the chief theoretical preoccupation of these two scholars is the public (and thus, in this limited sense, political) practice and justification of racial claims-making, I would still want to insist that Gutmann's

model of "fairness" and Dworkin's conception of "equal status and equal concern" both rest their principle of racial justice on moral foundations. Unlike the concept of "morality," Dworkin's and Gutmann's use of the term "political" is curiously elusive, without fixed propositional content. Very little in their argument appears to turn on its deployment; moreover, when the word is used, it has nothing at all to do with questions of power *as such*, and thus never goes (as it were) *all the way down*. Normatively, the defense Dworkin and Gutmann offer of race-conscious policy remains an essentially moral argument. Readers who doubt my characterization of Dworkin and Gutmann should note how quickly after its initial introduction "political morality" becomes simply "morality" (see, e.g., Dworkin 1996, 2; Appiah and Gutmann 1996, 108). To my mind, this casual, unreflective semantic slippage further supports my view that the normative fulcrum on which their arguments turn is moral rather than political in any complex sense.

8 I borrow this image from Jürgen Habermas's critique of the "ethical constriction of political discourse" (Habermas 1996, 23).

9 In discussing the *Brown* Court's attention to "the hurt of exclusion," Kenneth Karst emphasizes the fact that Chief Justice Warren, the author of the opinion, had regularly engaged his former driver in conversations about the latter's life as a black schoolchild in the South. Quoting Warren's onetime employee, Karst reports that these talks with his driver about "how the black man felt, how the black kid felt" were in great measure responsible for the opinion's focus on the "deep psychic harm" of racial segregation (Karst 1989, 18–19).

10 It bears remarking that the *Brown* Court remarks on the political functions of public school education even before it formally states the constitutional issue to be decided; the "psychic harms" theory on which the decision has traditionally been deemed to rest is introduced much later in the Court's opinion.

11 For an argument along similar lines (but with a different trajectory) see Aleinikoff (1992, 974).

12 For an extended normative defense of this connection see O'Neill (1996).

13 In this regard, I disagree with Charles Mills's implicit assertion that "racial polity" in the United States must always and only be a "white supremacist polity" (Mills 1999, 17, 31). That the two ideas have been closely identified in American political life ought not obscure the fact that these connections are historical, not inherent. As such, they are subject to change. Although it may be difficult for us to imagine such a future, a democratization of the relations among this country's diverse racial publics might well create the conditions for transforming the inherited meanings of race and forging a political society in which racial difference need not be or become a technology of racial domination. For a thoughtful defense of a democratic politics of difference see Kerchis and Young (1995). See also Gotanda (1995, 273).

14 Although I can only remark it here, one important historical example of the use of the citizenship idea to constitute a black civic public can be found in the Montgomery bus boycott. The Montgomery boycott is widely regarded as an inaugural moment in the consolidation of the modern African-American civil rights movement. Most accounts of the event (and the movement as a whole) have emphasized the moral language in which the boycott's leaders defended the campaign. However, in a famous speech at the Holt Street Baptist Church during the early days of the boycott, it was a political conception of African-American citizenship to which Martin Luther King Jr. appealed as the predicate ground of the assault on Montgomery's segregated bus system. King began his speech by noting that the boycott was anchored "first and foremost" in the fact that "we are American citizens—and we are determined to apply our citizenship—to the fullest of its means" (Branch 1988, 138–39). Needless to say, in calling attention to the role the language of citizenship played in the black civil rights movement, I do not mean to minimize the importance of moral language in mobilizing African Americans and their allies in the struggle against *de jure* segregation. For an account of how the civil rights movement staged "the conflict over segregation as a moral drama" see *Self-Rule: A Cultural History of American Democracy* (Wiebe 1995, 234).

15 Aleinikoff's stated project is to argue the thesis that "liberty" rather than "equality" is the central value defended in Harlan's dissent and, more fundamentally, in the Reconstruction Amendments as a whole (see Alienikoff 1992, 963–64).

16 Aleinikoff concedes earlier that "liberty is a capacious term open to any number of interpretations that support very different kinds of civil rights policies" (1992, 976).

17 Similarly, Kennedy wonders whether black communities are "hurt by prosecutions of pregnant women for using illicit drugs harmful to their unborn babies or helped by interventions which may at least plausibly deter conduct that will put black children at risk" (Kennedy 1998, 10)?

18 Kennedy borrows this term from Evelyn Brooks Higginbotham (1993). It bears remarking that for Kennedy, the "politics of respectability" is a normative ideal. By contrast, Higginbotham uses the concept critically and as an interpretive construct for understanding the history of the women's movement in the black Baptist Church in the late nineteenth and early twentieth centuries.

19 Strangely, Kennedy never tells us what it is that makes his urged campaign to garner racial respectability "political," even in the narrow sense of formal engagement with the state. Indeed, an interest in the state is nowhere to be found in his account of the "politics" of respectability. In this respect, Kennedy's proposal is the academic version of the spirit that animated the Million-Man March. Indeed, Kennedy describes the text of the pledge prepared for that gathering as a model effort to "uplift the racial reputation of African-American men" (1997, 18). For a historical account and critique of the "racial uplift" ideology Kennedy endorses, see Kevin Gaines's *Uplift the Race: Black Leadership, Politics, and Culture in the Twentieth Century* (Gaines 1996).

20 Kennedy notes that nationally, 92.6 percent of those sentenced for federal crack cocaine–related offenses in 1992 were African-American; a mere 4.7 percent of convicted crack cocaine offenders were white. By contrast, that same year, 45.2 percent of defendants convicted under the federal laws punishing powder cocaine–related crimes were white; 20.7 percent of those sentenced were African-American (Kennedy 1998, 364–65).

21 See generally *Washington v. Davis* (1976). Kennedy has elsewhere offered a more extended defense of this interpretation of the Equal Protection Clause (see Kennedy 1994).

22 The report offers comparably dire projections for black women. In the ten years from 1985 to 1995, the rate of female incarceration rose by 182 percent (as compared to an increase of 103 percent for men). Because black women are sentenced to jail and prison at a rate eight times higher than their white counterparts, the effects of increased incarceration on black women are obviously magnified (Fellner and Mauer 1998, 13).

23 One objection to the line of argument advanced here would deny that there are any relevant connections between the powder cocaine–crack cocaine sentencing differential on the one hand and felony disenfranchisement laws on the other. The factual premise of the objection is that the predicate of felony disenfranchisement laws is conviction, not length of imprisonment. However, this premise holds true only for jurisdictions that bar ex-felons from voting for life. The sentencing differential is far from irrelevant in states whose disenfranchisement laws are time-bound. Equalization of the prison terms for crack and powdercocaine would shorten the period during which offenders of color would be excluded from the franchise. Moreover, we should not underestimate the impact of the felon disenfranchisement regime on voting and vote-eligible members of racial civic publics, on whom it is not unreasonable to believe these laws have a dispiriting effect, contributing as they do to what I call the "political disorganization" of the oppositional counterpublics from which these offenders come, and to which the majority return. For a thoughtful critical account of how drug law enforcement contributes to the "social disorganization" of black and Latino communities see Meares 1998; see also Butler 1995.

24 Indeed, our concern should be heightened when the higher percentage of black ex-felons provides a pretext for surreptitiously purging duly registered African-American voters from voter registration rolls, as occurred in Florida during the last presidential election. See Herbert 2000.

25 This of course is not to say that the effects of ex-felon disenfranchisement may not pose serious problems under contemporary voting-rights jurisprudence. A discussion of these problems can be found in Harvey 1994.

26 For a discussion of the distinction between "politics" (*la politique*) and the "political" (*le politique*) see Claude Lefort's *Democracy and Political Theory* (Lefort 1988, 10–11, 216–18).

27 This is not to suggest that African-American convict-citizens have not created their own venues for political education and critical opinion formation within U.S. jails and prisons. They have done so, however, against enormous odds, and often in the face of systematic opposition by politicians and brutal repression by penal officials. It may well be that the repeal of felony disenfranchisement laws would enhance the prospects for more fully integrating black prisoners' developing critical perspective on race and the politics of incarceration into the deliberative discourses of the broader black public sphere.

28 Let me make plain what I am not claiming. Nothing in my description and defense of an African-American public sphere assumes a unitary black consciousness. I do not believe that all black citizens think or act alike, or that "*simply* being black or claiming African descent has been enough to produce racial unity through shared identity" (Outlaw 1995, 47–48). To the contrary, my use of the term "black civic *publics*" not only recognizes, but affirms disagreement and dissent as crucial, constructive features of African-American political life. Indeed, my pluralized conception of black political society would accord its members rights of partial or permanent exit. In this respect, I fully agree with Jane Mansbridge that the viability of "enclaves of resistance" is not undermined but enhanced when "some individuals immerse themselves in enclave life and thought while others span the spectrum between the enclave and the outside world" (Mansbridge 1996, 58). However, these exit rights necessarily presuppose the existence of a public sphere from which racial dissidents might exit.

Moreover, as I understand it, the notion of a "black civic public" denotes a common "political culture," not a common "racial culture" (Ford 2000). By way of a concrete example, consider the dynamics of black civic public life in the city in which I live, New York. Black people from the U.S. South, the Caribbean, Central and South America, Europe, and Africa have mobilized around an alternative, activist vision of racial justice in the urban polity. These black counterpublics have addressed issues from police brutality to environmental justice to the politics of race and representation in the city's cultural institutions. An oppositional black public presence in New York City has not required suppression of the myriad cultural (or class) differences among its constituent groups. This is because the political identity of these black urban counterpublics in no way entails the claim of a singular cultural identity. Rather, collective political action by black civic publics in New York City has stemmed from the recognition of a common location in the network of the city's racialized power relations.

29 A historical illustration of the point can be found in the disjunction between moral and political discourses that has characterized U.S. debates over the civic status of women. As Judith Shklar has noted, "[h]istorically the trouble has not been that Americans claimed that one had to be morally good to be a citizen. On the contrary, women particularly were said to be good more frequently than men, but they were not fit to be citizens" (Shklar 1991, 7).

REFERENCES

Aleinikoff, T. Alexander. 1992. "Re-reading Justice Harlan's Dissent in Plessy v. Ferguson: Freedom, Anti-racism, and Citizenship," 1992 *U. Ill. L. Rev.* 961–77.

Appiah, K. Anthony, and Amy Gutmann. 1996. *Color Conscious: The Political Morality of Race*. Princeton, N.J.: Princeton University Press.

Bansal, Preeta, and Derrick A. Bell. 1988. "The Republican Revival and Racial Politics," 97 *Yale L. J.* 1609–22.

Bell, Derrick A. 1995. "Racial Realism," in *Critical Race Theory: The Key Writings that Formed the Movement*, ed. K. Crenshaw, N. Gotanda, G. Peller, and K. Thomas. New York: The New Press.

Bickel, Alexander M. 1973. "Citizenship in the American Constitution," 15 *Ariz. L. Rev.* 369–87.

———. 1975. *The Morality of Consent*. New Haven, Conn.: Yale University Press.

Branch, Taylor. 1988. *Parting the Waters: America in the King Years 1954–1963*. New York: Touchstone.

Butler, Paul. 1995. "Racially Based Jury Nullification: Black Power in the Criminal Justice System," 105 *Yale L. J.* 677–725.

———. 1998. "(Color)Blind Faith: The Tragedy of Race, Crime and the Law," 111 *Harv. L. Rev.* 1270–88.

Chávez, Lydia. 1998. *The Color Bind: California's Battle to End Affirmative Action*. Berkeley: University of California Press.

Cole, David. 1999. *No Equal Justice: Race and Class in the American Criminal Justice System*. New York: The New Press.

Daniel, Jamie O. 2000. "Rituals of Disqualification: Competing Publics and Public Housing in Contemporary Chicago," in *Masses, Classes and the Public Sphere*, ed. M. Hill and W. Montag. New York: Verso.

Dawson, Michael C. 1994. "A Black Counterpublic: Economic Earthquakes, Racial Agenda(s), and Black Politics," 7 *Public Culture* 195–224.

DuBois, W.E.B. 1986. *Writings*. New York: The Library of America.

Dworkin, Ronald. 1977. *Taking Rights Seriously*. Cambridge: Harvard University Press.

———. 1985. *A Matter of Principle*. Cambridge: Harvard University Press.

———. 1996. *Freedom's Law: The Moral Reading of the American Constitution*. Cambridge: Harvard University Press.

Feagin, Joe R. 2000. *Racist America: Routes, Current Realities, and Future Reparations*. New York: Routledge.

Fellner, Jamie, and Mark Mauer. 1998. *Losing the Vote: The Impact of Felony Disenfranchisement Laws in the United States*. Washington, D.C.: The Sentencing Project.

Fletcher, George F. 1999. "Disenfranchisement as Punishment: Reflections on the Racial Uses of Infamia," 46 *U.C.L.A. L. Rev.* 1895–1906.

Ford, Richard T. 2000. "Race as Culture? Why Not?" 47 *U.C.L.A. L. Rev.* 1803–14.

Fraser, Nancy. 1997. *Justice Interruptus: Critical Reflections on the "Postsocialist" Condition*. New York: Routledge.

Gaines, Kevin K. 1996. *Uplifting the Race: Black Leadership, Politics and Culture in the Twentieth Century*. Chapel Hill: University of North Carolina Press.

Gilroy, Paul. 2000. *Against Race: Imagining Political Culture Beyond the Color Line*. Cambridge: Belknap Press of Harvard University Press.

Golenpaul, Ann, ed. 1997. *Information Please Almanac*. Boston: Houghton-Mifflin.

Gotanda, Neil. 1995. "A Critique of 'Our Constitution Is Color-Blind,'" in *Critical Race Theory: The Key Writings that Formed the Movement*, ed. K. Crenshaw, N. Gotanda, G. Peller, and K. Thomas. New York: The New Press.

Gregory, Steven. 1994. "Race, Identity and Political Activism: The Shifting Contours of the African American Public Sphere," 7 *Public Culture* 147–64.

Habermas, Jürgen. 1996. "Three Normative Models of Democracy," in *Democracy and Difference: Contesting the Boundaries of the Political*, ed. S. Benhabib. Princeton, N.J.: Princeton University Press.

Harvey, Alice E. 1994. "Comment: Ex-Felon Disenfranchisement and Its Influence on the Black Vote," 142 *U. Pa. L. Rev.* 1145–89.

Herbert, Bob. 2000. "Keep Them Out!," *New York Times*, 7 December 2000, A39.

Higginbotham, Evelyn B. 1993. *Righteous Discontent: The Women's Movement in the Black Baptist Church, 1880–1920*. Cambridge: Harvard University Press.

Honig, Bonnie. 1993. *Political Theory and the Displacement of Politics*. Ithaca, N.Y.: Cornell University Press.

Huling, Tracy, and Mark Mauer. 1995. *Young Black Americans and the Criminal Justice System: Five Years Later*. Washington, D.C.: The Sentencing Project.

Karst, Kenneth L. 1989. *Belonging to America: Equal Citizenship and the Constitution*. New Haven, Conn.: Yale University Press.

Kennedy, Randall. 1994. "The State, Criminal Law, and Racial Discrimination: A Comment," 107 *Harv. L. Rev.* 1255–78.

———. 1998. *Race, Crime, and the Law*. New York: Pantheon.

Kerchis, Cheryl Z., and Iris M. Young. 1995. "Social Movements and the Politics of Difference," in *Multiculturalism from the Margins: Non-Dominant Voices on Difference and Diversity*, ed. D.A. Harris. Westport, Conn.: Bergin and Garvey.

Lakoff, George. 1996. *Moral Politics*. Chicago: University of Chicago Press.

Lefort, Claude. 1988. *Democracy and Political Theory*. Minneapolis: University of Minnesota Press.

MacIntyre, Alasdair. 1981. *After Virtue*. Notre Dame, Ind.: University of Notre Dame Press.

Mamdani, Mahmood. 1996. *Citizen and Subject: Contemporary Africa and the Legacy of Late Colonialism*. Princeton, N.J.: Princeton University Press.

Mansbridge, Jane. 1996. "Using Power/Fighting Power: The Polity," in *Democracy and Difference: Contesting the Boundaries of the Political*, ed. S. Benhabib. Princeton, N.J.: Princeton University Press.

Marable, Manning. 1995. *Beyond Black and White: Transforming African-American Politics*. New York: Verso.

Mauer, Mark. 1997. *Intended and Unintended Consequences: State Racial Disparities in Imprisonment*. Washington, D.C.: The Sentencing Project.

Meares, Tracey L. 1998. "Social Disorganization and Drug Law Enforcement," 35 *Am. Crim. L. Rev.* 191–227.

Miller, Jerome G. 1996. *Search and Destroy: African-American Males in the Criminal Justice System*. New York: Cambridge University Press.

Mills, Charles W. 1999. "The Racial Polity," in *Racism and Philosophy*, ed. S.E. Babbit and S. Campbell. Ithaca, N.Y.: Cornell University Press.

Mouffe, Chantal. 1993a. "Democracy, Power and the 'Political,'" in *Democracy and Difference: Contesting the Boundaries of the Political*, ed. S. Benhabib. Princeton, N.J.: Princeton University Press.

———. 1993b. *The Return of the Political*. New York: Verso.

Omi, Michael, and Howard Winant. 1986. *Racial Formation in the United States: From the 1960s to the 1980s*. New York: Routledge.

O'Neill, Onora. 1996. *Towards Justice and Virtue: A Constructive Account of Practical Reasoning*. Cambridge: Cambridge University Press.

Outlaw, Lucius T. 1995. "Racial and Ethnic Complexities in American Life: Implica-

tions for African Americans," in *Multiculturalism from the Margins: Non-Dominant Voices on Difference and Diversity*, ed. D. A. Harris. Westport, Conn.: Bergin and Garvey.

Pitkin, Hannah F. 1972. *Wittgenstein and Justice*. Berkeley: University of California Press.

Posner, Richard A. 1974. "The DeFunis Case and the Constitutionality of Preferential Treatment of Racial Minorities," 1974 *Supreme Court Review* 1–32.

Schmitt, Carl. 1976. *The Concept of the Political*, trans. George Schwab. New Brunswick, N.J.: Rutgers University Press.

Shapiro, Ian. 1996. *Democracy's Place*. Ithaca, N.Y.: Cornell University Press.

———. 1999. *Democratic Justice*. New Haven, Conn.: Yale University Press.

Shklar, Judith N. 1991. *American Citizenship: The Quest for Inclusion*. Cambridge: Harvard University Press.

Small, Stephen. 1999. "The Contours of Racialization: Structures, Representations, and Resistance in the United States," in *Race, Identity, and Citizenship*, ed. R. Torres, L. Mirón, and J. Inda. Oxford: Blackwell.

Smith, Rogers M. 1997. *Civic Ideals: Conflicting Visions of Citizenship in U.S. History*. New Haven, Conn.: Yale University Press.

Thernstrom, Stephen, and Abigail Thernstrom. 1997. *America in Black and White: One Nation, Indivisible*. New York: Simon and Schuster.

Unger, Roberto M. 1997. *Politics: The Central Texts*. New York: Verso.

Waldron, Jeremy. 2000. "Ego-Bloated Hovel," 94 *Northwestern L. Rev.* 597–624.

Wiebe, Robert H. 1995. *Self-Rule: A Cultural History of American Democracy.* Chicago: University of Chicago Press.

Young, Iris M. 1990. *Justice and Politics of Difference*. Princeton, N.J.: Princeton University Press.

CASES CITED

Adarand Constructors, Inc. v. Pena, 515 U.S. 200 (1995).
Brown v. Board of Education, 347 U.S. 483 (1954).
City of Richmond v. J. A. Croson Co., 488 U.S. 469 (1989).
Dred Scott v. Sandford, 60 U.S. (19 How.) 393 (1837).
Hunter v. Underwood, 421 U.S. 222 (1985).
Loving v. Virginia, 388 U.S. 1 (1967).
Plessy v. Ferguson, 163 U.S. 537 (1896).
Regents of the University of California v. Bakke, 438 U.S. 265 (1978).
Washington v. Davis, 426 U.S. 229 (1976).

PART II
Law and the Constitution of Selves and Society

Visions of Self-Control

FASHIONING A LIBERAL APPROACH TO CRIME AND PUNISHMENT IN THE TWENTIETH CENTURY

Jonathan Simon

One might imagine a political history of crime in the United States during the twentieth century.[1] The landscape would be familiar to most legal scholars and social scientists. The century begins, from this perspective, with a series of new initiatives taken at the state and local levels, but promoted by the emerging national coalition we know as the Progressives, including most famously parole, probation, and the juvenile court (Rothman 1980). The Prohibition years of the 1920s and early 1930s crystallized this emerging national consciousness of crime as a governmental problem, producing the first large-scale national crime problem and the first national studies of criminal justice institutions (Pound 1930; Cleveland Survey of Criminal Justice 1922). Previously government investigations of criminal justice were dominated by concerns of partisan politics (Walker 1998, 152). The 1930s also witnessed the dawn of nearly a half century of Supreme Court intervention in state trial courts, aimed in large part at civil rights objectives.[2] In the 1950s and 1960s this expanded into what amounted to a revolution in criminal procedure.[3]

In the 1950s a national consensus coalesced favoring rehabilitation of offenders by means of a scientifically based penology. In the 1960s, violent crime reemerged as a national political problem, with alarming rises in violent crime reported to the police, a menace that merged with the growing specter of riots and assassinations (well summarized in the then-current expression "lawlessness"). In the 1970s and 1980s a national consciousness emerged about due process and equity in sentencing. This time legislatures and Congress took the lead, repudiating parts of the Progressive tradition of rehabilitation and scientific penology in the name of fairness. In the 1980s and 1990s, state and national political leaders committed themselves to an unprecedented expansion of the prison population, which they accomplished by toughening sentences for many crimes, especially drug and violent offenses (Caplow and Simon 1999; Mauer 1999; Currie 1998; Tonry 1995).

The historical register I want to work in is slightly different. It runs parallel to the conventional political history of crime, but the landmarks on this journey are somewhat less familiar. One might think of this as a history not of the political or legal response to crime but of the technologies of power (Foucault 2000, 332) by which crime has been made a pathway to power over and knowledge of the population. In this history, the early part of the twentieth century is marked by the emergence of the new social sciences, especially criminology and psychology, as rivals to law both as forms of expertise and as successful models of how to rationalize government. In Europe this led to open warring between lawyers and scientists over who would dominate the problem of crime. In the United States this conflict was largely resolved through a "great compromise" that left legal authorities in charge of the adjudication of guilt but opened much of the sentencing and punishment end of the system to the influence of the social sciences (Rothman 1980; Garland 1985; Green 1995). What facilitated the compromise was the emergence of the social as a space of research, problems, and practices, in between the political act of criminal conviction and the bureaucratic task of punishing.

The middle of the century saw the terms of the Great Compromise challenged by a popularization of the ideas of social determinism (could criminals meaningfully avoid crime?) and the success in the 1970s of civil rights lawsuits demanding judicial intervention in prison management (Feeley and Rubin 1998). The nature of the prison regime and its relationship to liberalism has since the 1960s become a greater challenge to the liberal state than it has been at any time since the Jacksonian era a century earlier. The spectacle of totalitarian regimes in Europe and their conduct between the 1920s and the 1950s played a complex role here. The use of coercive state agencies to perfect the dominance of party and state over civil society in Europe recast the conduct of American police departments, sheriffs, jails, and local courts, especially in the South, as a threat to democratic values. After World War II, the "crimes against humanity" of the German Nazi regime framed a somewhat different problem of liberal governance: how to produce bureaucracies capable of effectively managing mass society while holding the individuals who staff those bureaucracies accountable to norms of humanity (Cover 1986).

The 1950s through the 1980s saw the rise of competing forms of expertise intended to manage the large populations brought under formal state authority by the twentieth-century expansion of both penal and welfare functions of the state (Rothman 1980; Garland 1985). The first part of this period saw the dominance of a social psychological approach closely aligned with social democratic politics. Abnormal social conditions, not abnormal people, produced crime. Prisons sought to create "therapeutic community" and a proliferation of agencies offered normalizing treatment to the clients of the state (Jones 1953; Cohen 1985; Simon 1993a, 72–74). By the 1980s a different set of twentieth-century forms of expertise were gaining the upper hand, forms focused on operations research, systems engineering, and risk management (Feeley and Simon 1992 and 1994). Many aspects of these discourses, including statistical modeling of crime outcomes, emerged early in the century but for complex reasons remained secondary to social psychology–based strategies (Simon 1993a, 172). Rather than normalizing deviant individuals back into communities reinforced with governmental actors of all sorts, the new expertise sought to align itself with a regime of risk assessment, custody, and punishment (Young 1999).

A single essay could not adequately present either a political history or a history of political technologies, and certainly not both. In attempting to do some justice to the latter kind of history, I consider three examples that can be brought into focus in terms of both types of history. Because these are more or less chronologically situated accounts, it is tempting to read in them a story of an evolution in the strategies or rationalities of power. I believe it is more useful to see each of these stories as illustrating more or less available, more or less competitive programs for reforming penal institutions and practices. At different times during the century, and in different settings, different programs have been more or less influential. None of them is unique to penality; indeed, all represent aspects of the more general problem of the "self" and governance in twentieth-century liberal societies.

Liberal government in this sense seeks to govern people through rather than in spite of their freedom (Rose 1999), but the way in which that freedom is operationalized and acted upon varies. Starting at the end of the nineteenth century, in a variety of legal fields, the new social sciences began to exert an influence on legislatures and courts and to cast the social as both a problem for law and lawyers and a resource for solving problems (McEvoy 1995; Garth and Sterling 1998). Over the last four decades of the twentieth century the program was substantially reshaped as legal professionals tried to cope with the maturing and erosion of the social itself (Rose 1999; Simon 1999, 146–47).

The "juvenile court movement," as it was called in the first part of the twentieth century, exemplified what Roscoe Pound called "the strong social interest in the moral and social life of the individual" (1913, 311). For Pound, and for many other observers at this time, constructing forms of government capable of effectuating that interest was the top priority of progressive politics and science. Their optimism was based on a whole family of approaches to representing and intervening in crime and criminal justice. Historians of penality like David Rothman (1980) and David Garland (1985) have shed tremendous light on the complex array of discourses, experts, and institutions that fed into this reform movement that in the United States called itself Progressivism. But during Pound's era of influence many of these themes could be invoked (if not exactly summarized) in the idea, perhaps the slogan, of "socializing the law."

What this term meant is not altogether clear.[4] As Michael Willrich points out, "socializing the law" constituted an agenda of criticism of the dominant conception of law among elite lawyers, academics, and jurists (Willrich 1998). To socialize the law meant to bring in the things excluded by formalistic jurisprudence, even if that entailed removing many of the constraints due process had placed on the power of courts. But proponents of socialization had something positive in mind as well: the production of new kinds of knowledge about the social and biological origins of crime that would ultimately produce new modes of intervention quite apart from the punitive model of the prison. As a signal term among proponents of the progressive agenda in criminal justice policy, it provides an opening for us into the problems of fashioning a liberal approach to crime and punishment in the early twentieth century.

The law of homicide came into its own in the twentieth century, emerging as a far more important theme for legislation, policing, and academic scholarship than it had been in any previous period. The reshaping of the law of homicide throughout the the century would bring the problem of self-control into its own from out of the complex common-law background of "malice aforethought" (Dressler 2001, 503). Through the problem of homicide, twentieth-century judges and scholars reconstructed substantive criminal law more generally around the problem of a subject's capacity to control his or her "self." This allowed criminal law to escape the trap seemingly set by nineteenth-century developments in psychology and medicine. The underlying subject of control, the culpable subject invoked by modern criminal law, was not simply the "psychological" subject promoted by positivist criminology at the beginning of the twentieth century. Rather, it was the subject conceived as a rational risk taker and risk maker—a subject whose governance would call for an expertise informed by but not controlled by the human sciences as then conceived (Wechsler and Michael 1937; ALI 1985).

The maximum-security prison emerged in the twentieth century as a response not to crime, but to the prison itself and to the breakdown of the nineteenth century's penitentiary project. The problem of recidivism became a constitutive factor for the "new penology" that flourished at the end of the nineteenth century. This led to the promotion of reform schemes to reshape prison regimes along medical and psychological lines. Ironically, it also encouraged the construction of special security regimes to handle individuals who had been made more dangerous by the very failure of prisons to reform them. This reached its climax in the 1960s, when California simultaneously created both the most medically and psychologically oriented prison programs and developed the most systematic set of maximum-security principles yet employed. The "segregated housing unit" (or "shu" in prison parlance), a regime of near total isolation designed to cope with the emergence of radical prisoners and racialized prison gangs, built on techniques of "administrative segregation" developed early in the century (Rothman 1980), but intensified and extended them. The latest versions of the maximum-security strategy eliminate any effort at inculcating self-control in favor of a new hybrid target of the "prisoner in his cell," a machine/human organism or cyborg (Haraway 1991, 9). No doubt these institutions are structured by a large number of uniquely penal forces, but they also share a lot with very different settings like airports, massive shopping centers, and gated resort or residential communities.

A STRONG SOCIAL INTEREST IN THE MORAL AND SOCIAL LIFE OF THE INDIVIDUAL: THE JUVENILE COURT MOVEMENT AND THE SOCIALIZATION OF LAW

In Conyers, Georgia, a court hearing was conducted in August 1999 regarding whether a fifteen-year-old boy named T.J. Solomon, who had shot several classmates (one month after the far more deadly and more widely publicized student shooting at Columbine High School near Denver, Colorado), should be tried in juvenile or adult court. This kind of hearing has been a central issue for many defendants of juvenile age for several decades now, since the Supreme Court held in *Kent v. United States*[5] that due process required an adversarial hearing before the juvenile status of a defendant could be waived. *Kent* initiated a dramatic reduction in the autonomy of the juvenile court by the Supreme Court, which some noted scholars view as presaging and determining the general collapse of faith in the juvenile court idea in the last decade of the twentieth century (Feld 1999, 108). Whatever the case, a great deal is at stake for defendants facing the due process hearing mandated by *Kent*. Juvenile sanctions generally terminate at the age of twenty-one. For T.J. Solomon, even the harshest juvenile sanction could only last six years. The adult charges against him, in contrast, carried a maximum prison term of more than a hundred years.

Solomon is just one of a number of teenage killers who have recently come before the courts and the vast media sector devoted to crime coverage in the United States. As a result of a pair of Supreme Court decisions in the 1980s,[6] none of the young killers involved in the recent incidents has been sentenced to death (although the Columbine High school killers, Harris and Klebold, eighteen and seventeen respectively, would have been eligible had they not executed themselves). But many states now permit, and some require, juveniles as young as fourteen charged with violent crimes to be tried in adult court (Feld 1999, 190). As a result, most of the killers in the recent spate of high-school shootings are serving life sentences that offer little hope of ever leaving prison. Barry Loukaitis, who at age fourteen killed a teacher and two students in Moses Lake, Washington, is serving two life sentences. Luke Woodham, who at sixteen killed two students and wounded seven in Pearl, Mississippi, is serving three life sentences. Michael Carneal, who at fourteen killed three students and wounded five in Paducah, Kentucky, is serving life. In contrast, two students who at eleven and thirteen killed five people and wounded ten in Jonesboro, Arkansas, were adjudicated as juveniles and will be released when they reach the age of twenty-one.

Law in the Modern City

T. J. Solomon's lawyers argued that he was a suicidal and nearly psychotic young person. They put on the stand psychiatrists and psychologists who testified that they had examined T. J. and had found that he suffered from a mental illness and needed psychiatric hospitalization. Eyewitnesses to the shooting testified that he shot low and without seeming to aim. He did not pursue anyone (as the Columbine killers had), and without discharging the full load in his cartridge he ran out of the room, put a magnum pistol to his own head as if to commit suicide, and then immediately surrendered to an unarmed school administrator. In addition, the gun he had chosen from his father's collection was less lethal than others available to him there.

The prosecutor—hardened, some believe, by a series of deadly shootings in the United States during the summer of 1999—characterized the defendant as a calculating criminal whose neatly choreographed acts of mayhem required severe punishment. The prosecution emphasized the premeditated nature of the act, pointing to Solomon's apparent effort to mimic the Columbine killers. The trial judge ruled that Solomon's case should be heard in adult court, where instead of confinement until age twenty-one he would face a possible life sentence. In explaining his decision to ignore the extensive psychiatric testimony presented by the defense, the judge emphasized the willful and calculating quality of Solomon's act: "The fact that the child has attempted to copy a heinous, premeditated crime and showed such disrespect for the safety of others . . . makes the public's interest to treat him as an adult paramount to any interest of the individual child."[7] The judge was rather explicit that the public interest and the interest of T. J. Solomon as a fifteen-year-old in any kind of future as an individual were in conflict, a conflict the court resolved not only in the public's favor but in a way that accorded no weight to the juvenile's interest. Violent crimes like homicide and attempted homicide were often kept in adult court until after World War II. In the thirty years or so after the war practice was highly inconsistent both within and between jurisdictions. The most liberal states like New York kept most of their violent teenagers in juvenile court during the 1950s and 1960s. The result in *Solomon* is now typical of how juvenile violent crime is treated. The judge's reasoning indicates how far our contemporary thinking has departed from the model of the public interest associated with the origins of the juvenile court. At that time constructing problematic subjects as juveniles was identified with the public interest (even though it came with a loss of rights on the part of the offender) because it meant a host of preventive and remedial measures could be deployed.

Progressive penality emphasized the individual both as a complex site of knowledge (biology, psychology, sociology) and as an essential problem of social control. Roscoe Pound,[8] perhaps the most influential legal academic speaking to the problems of crime, punishment, and government in the early twentieth century, articulated this as the social interest in "the moral and social life of the individual."

> For there is a strong social interest in the moral and social life of the individual. If the will of the individual is subjected arbitrarily to the will of others because the means of protection are too cumbrous and expensive to be available for one of his means against an aggressive opponent who has the means or the inclination to resist, there is an injury to society at large. The most real grievance of the mass of the people against American law is not with respect to the rules of substantive law, but rather with respect to the enforcing machinery, which too often makes the best of rules nugatory in action. (1913, 315)

Pound had in mind primarily the civil rather than the criminal courts. He would spend most of his career obsessed with the need to modernize courts. In this article, titled "The Administration of Justice in the Modern City," Pound argued that American legal institutions were not capable of offering nearly the solicitude and care toward individual transactional interests promised by the theory of justice on which they were based. In particular, the great urban masses gathered by the rapid industrialization and immigration of the late nineteenth century were systematically deprived of any real opportunity to pursue their social lives as individuals in the absence of institutions capable of recognizing and treating them as such.

Pound was particularly focused on making civil litigation available to the masses through innovations like the small claims court (1913, 315). He was somewhat more circumspect about the juvenile court, which combined enormous power to resolve the problems afflicting individual urban families with virtually unreviewable discretion to impose its own vision of justice on the parties. Pound's oft-quoted dictum about the juvenile court is worth quoting again and in full.

> The powers of the court of Star Chamber were a bagatelle compared with those of American Juvenile Courts and Courts of Domestic Relations. If those courts chose to act arbitrarily and oppressively they could

> cause a revolution quite as easily as did the former. The powers which we are compelled to entrust to them call for the strongest judges we can put upon the bench. (1913, 322)

Pound quite explicitly positions himself as an enlightened member of the ruling class considering the fate of capitalist democracy in the great cities at the beginning of the twentieth century. He recognizes the potential working-class claim of injustice on the part of middle-class judges capable of imposing their own normative order as justice (a claim that would be explored more fully in the 1960s and 1970s—see, e.g., Platt 1977). From this perspective the juvenile court was a gamble. Its discretionary powers might serve to effectuate society's interest in the moral life of its working-class individuals, or to provoke the great masses of the cities toward open rebellion. His last line suggests that this is a reason to put the best lawyers on the bench, not a reason to abandon the experiment necessitated by the grave threat posed by the lower classes concentrating in American cities.[9]

If we expand Pound's notion of a social interest in the individual, one peculiarly posed by the conditions of life in the great cities at the beginning of the twentieth century, we find two quite different projects that can be identified with the juvenile court.

Surveillance of the Urban Poor at the Level of the Individual

The new courts and the clinics that grew alongside some of them in the most progressive cities like Chicago and New York expanded the capacity of established urban police forces to track deviant behavior at the individual level. The police, after all, collected only arrest reports. In the twentieth century juvenile clinics began to accumulate literally tens of thousands of files on young men and women deemed potentially delinquent or dependent. In many cases these files went well beyond reports of arrest circumstances to include detailed notes by social workers, psychologists, and probation officers on the juveniles and their families (Simon 1997). Proponents, like psychologist William Healey, the head of the first juvenile court psychological clinic in Chicago, believed that individual-level reports would produce an effective clinical course of treatment appropriate to the vast majority of delinquents (Rothman 1980). Whatever a science equipped with better theories and better computational equipment might have achieved, it is pretty clear that twentieth-century juvenile courts never fulfilled that function. It would be more productive to recognize these practices as having a kinship to the great file-producing machines of the Communist and Fascist regimes of the twentieth century, i.e., as a political technology capable of making a segment of the population visible as individuals. Less clear is what this political technology did.[10]

Preventing the Normative Conditions of the Immigrant Metropolis from Losing Its First-Generation Americans to Crime and the Prison System

Pound would have shared the conviction of many more recent commentators that the juvenile court movement reflected real concern by elites that the children of the immigrants would be lost to successful integration in the market economy and the political system. The parents were all right; they had been successfully reared in some normative order and had made the voluntary choice to immigrate. The children, however, could not look to their parents for clear lessons on being Americans, and the failures of community and school left delinquency as a negative organizer of a potentially anomic underclass.

How could the juvenile court change this outlook? The theoretical answer turned out to have little impact on practices outside a few of the most progressive court systems. Most juvenile court dispositions in the twentieth century amounted to either another chance with a promise to make a better start or incarceration in a place very much like a prison. In practice the juvenile court worked to prevent criminalization only by keeping the juvenile out of prison, but that is often where they were sent. In the decades after Pound, sociologists would experiment with direct efforts to influence or even organize juvenile groups. The results of that work have never been systematically studied.

The proponents of the juvenile court believed it would accomplish its goal by operating as a flexible mechanism of intervention to adjust those other institutions of society, the family, the school, and the community, to the individual problems of the deviant. The goal was to create a set of conditions under which troubled juveniles might become autonomous agents in the manner valorized by liberal economic principles. The early hope was placed on the juvenile judge him-or herself (and it was an early place in which women could exercise judicial power) to influence both the wayward juvenile and the communities that tolerated unwholesome conditions. It would take the Supreme Court's 1960s decisions imposing due process requirements to put that hope fully to rest (although it had clearly faded far earlier). Juvenile probation officers offered an independent and more enduring hope of a gender appropriate individual influence over the delinquent juvenile. In reality the record was largely one of failure, exemplified by the ready use of confinement as a response to persistent (even low-level) deviance.

A striking mid-twentieth-century example of this is the treatment young Lee Harvey Oswald received while a subject of the Bronx County Juvenile Court (Simon 1997). Oswald was arrested for persistent truancy and sent for a month of evaluation to the Home for Boys. He was ordered released under the supervision of John Carro, an ambitious young man who would rise to be an administrative assistant to Mayor Robert Wagner by the time of Oswald's moment in history. Carro took a tough stance on Oswald's truancy, which he blamed on Oswald's unconventional and confrontational mother, Marguerite Oswald. Carro filed a report at the time urging confinement for Oswald (whose only crime at that point was evading the compulsory education laws) based on Marguerite's failure to cooperate in his supervision of Lee. Carro predicted that the family situation, mainly deviant in its lack of gender role conformity, would lead to more serious crime. (He felt understandably vindicated after the assassination of President Kennedy.)[11]

The Socialization of Juvenile Court Procedure

Pound, and others in his generation, had a name for the kind of changes he imagined legal institutions needed to make in order to realize both aspects of the social interest in the individual lives of the urban poor. He referred to it as "socialization." "Demand for socialization of law, in America," he wrote, "has come almost wholly if not entirely from the city" (1913, 311). It is difficult now to recapture fully the sense in which Pound used this term, or its meaning in articles like Miriam Van Waters's "The Socialization of Juvenile Court Procedure" (1912) and Edward F. Waite's "How Far Can Court Procedure Be Socialized Without Impairing Individual Rights?" (1922). No institution was more strongly associated with this process than the juvenile court.

Van Waters, the first "referee" of the Juvenile Court of Los Angeles County,[12] opened her article with the remarkable proposition that "the usefulness of any human institution depends on the degree to which it is socialized" (1912, 61). The juvenile court, in her view, was the first legal institution to be socialized.

> Courts, for thousands of years, have been rendering decisions, but until the juvenile court with its clinics, its staff of experts, doctors, psychologists, psychiatrists, and social workers was established no one ever traced the actual result of a court decision in terms of human values. What becomes of the lives of individuals upon whom the courts pass judgment? What sum total of end results have we accumulated? No one knows. But the juvenile court is conceived in the spirit of the clinic; it is a kind of laboratory of human behavior. (Van Waters 1912, 61)

Van Waters's definition of socialization is notable in that it begins and ends with the juvenile court.

> Socialization—what do we mean by this term as applied to Juvenile Court procedure? I take it to mean the process by which the purpose and goal of the Juvenile Court is best attained, that method which best frees the spirit of the Juvenile Court and permits it to serve the social ideal it was created to express. (1912, 63)

This strikes us today as an unhelpful tautology. But it reflects the degree to which novel institutions and the political technologies they showcased were inextricably tied up with efforts to imagine more general ideas for reforming government more broadly.[13]

Far less enthusiastic was Edward F. Waite, a Minnesota trial judge and a frequent speaker on juvenile justice in the 1920s. Waite's vision was also grounded in an institutional ideal, but for him it was the general jurisdiction territorial court of the sort that he had conducted. From this perspective, socialization meant a loss of control on the part of individual subjects in law over their exposure to judicial power. In his article, "How Far Can Court Procedure Be Socialized without Impairing Individual Rights?" (1922),[14] Waite described "what is termed socialization" as a shift by the courts from ruling on disputes over private rights to "the performance of what are conceived to be community obligations" (1922, 339). Waite noted that from a lawyer's point of view the most important piece of this shift was the expanding police power of the state to secure the general welfare. Under the claim of helping, the state was empowered to bypass certain kinds of traditional legal safeguards on the power of individuals.

When comprehensively implemented to completely replace punitive justice with "parental" justice, Waite saw few if any constitutional limits on socialized law in juvenile court (1922, 339). If, however, "juvenile court" were just a name given to criminal courts for children, socialization would be a major constitutional imposition. Waite's basic position, close to the heart of the "great compromise" between criminal law and criminal science in the United States, was that a socialized penality is fine so long as it begins after the the defendant is convicted of violating a juvenile measure. "In criminal proceedings the child has, before conviction, all the legal rights of the child. Here the field of socialization is practically limited to treatment of the child after conviction" (1922, 346).

Pound's usage of socialization incorporates both the promise and the threat. Both proponents and opponents saw socialization as a program in action taking place in particular institutions rather than as a set of propositions. Seen in archaeological perspective from nearly a century later, the term seems mostly to gesture toward a set of technologies and discourses about conflict in the modern city. Socialization points to a set of ways to collect and distribute knowledge about the social circumstances of all parties to disputes; to enter the social context of the dispute into legal and political knowledge; and to allow that knowledge cumulatively to redirect the interventions of the court.

Individual Knowledge

Socialization would apply to the decisions in individual cases by freeing judges to hear any useful evidence that might illuminate the circumstances of the delinquent youth. As Van Waters argued, traditional courts operated according to rules of criminal evidence that obstructed the modern goals of crime suppression: "In a socialized Juvenile procedure no useful evidence should be excluded from the court. Each relevant fact should be admissible, but we should adhere closely to that body of the rules of evidence which applies the test to truth" (1912, 65).

Socialization of the law presumed that knowledge of individuals would move in circuits well beyond the specific. This archival function was exemplified by the Child Guidance Clinic that was opened alongside Chicago's pioneer juvenile court. William Healey, a leading psychologist of his day, directed the clinic and became a spokesperson for the project of collecting case histories of delinquents, through which the truth of crime would emerge.[15] His numerous books and articles profiled the stories of individual delinquents to highlight the complex interactions leading to delinquency. These narratives offered glimpses of an elusive truth of crime that promised to accumulate over time with the data in the archive of the Chicago clinic and others like it that would grow across the country.

Sociologist Ernest Burgess praised Healey's methods in glowing terms in a 1923 article in the *American Journal of Sociology*, the house organ of the influential Chicago school of sociology.

> In place of the method of general observation, theoretical speculation and the amassing of available statistical data [Healey] substituted the method of case study. This new technique wrought a revolution in criminology. The study of behavior was now placed upon an empirical, inductive basis. (Burgess 1973, 180)

Healey's complex lists of causal factors in delinquency provided a ready narrative for any case, and they seemed likely to yield deeper insights in time (Rothman 1980, 55).

Commensurately, socialized law would expand its remedial powers to effectuate the judgments that such an inquiry would often drive toward. Van Waters assumed that this would require a judiciary trained well beyond the law. "Socialization implies that judges and court officials are to be experts, experts with scientific training and specialists in the art of human relations" (1912, 69).

Community Knowledge

Socialization of law pointed to a new approach to constructing courts as remedial institutions, and indeed to new ways of conceiving the exercise of government power in courts. Foucault (1991, 103) characterized the "'governmentalization' of the state" as the process by which state institutions came to rationalize their rule as the "pastoral" one of fostering the health and well-being of their populations. The "socialization of the law" was one name given to this process of rationalization in the early twentieth century.

Socialized law would look beyond the interests of the parties to consider the problems of the whole community.

> Interests and obligations of the community, as well as the parties to the record, have come to be taken into account—not in every sort of court and every variety of proceeding, but in many. Legal forms and precedents have again and again given way to considerations of human welfare. (Waite 1923, 234)

Socialized law would also distribute knowledge to and of the community as part of its normalizing function. Van Waters described "social opinion" as the "driving force in socialization" (1912, 67). The juvenile court would become a clearinghouse for information about the delinquency problems in a community and a vehicle for mobilizing the existing resources of social control within the community.

Transformational Power

Socialized procedures remain incomplete as long as they rely only on the coercive management of the individual in the interest of social control. Truly socialized institutions must transform their subjects so that they understand themselves in terms of their social situation. Subjects themselves must become consumers of what socialized agencies produce. Thus, Van Waters noted, the court started off with a disadvantage not faced by medicine. "To the clinic the patient comes because he must. It is the business of the social worker to make him feel sick before hand; that is to say, the social seriousness of the situation should be established" (1912, 65).

Socialized law would have to forswear retributive justice. Otherwise the expanded police powers exercised by institutions like the juvenile courts would be an unprecedented retrenchment of civil liberties. Judge Waite's view—that stripping juveniles of the opportunity for a true adversarial hearing, with counsel, would violate the constitution—was vindicated more than forty years later by the Supreme Court's decision in *Gault v. Arizona*.[16]

Youth, Crime, and Threat: Socializing the Law as a Liberal Reform

Such a listing may remind us primarily of the degree to which this project has failed us. Rapid progress in individual-level scientific diagnosis and prediction did not take place. The entire strategy of collecting a mass of detailed observations in an open-ended classification system was doomed in an age without cheap methods of computation.[17] For our present purposes it is more interesting to consider the appeals of socialization as a strategy for constructing knowledge/power relations, in short as a political technology. First, Pound and his contemporaries heard in socialization a bit of what we now hear predominantly, i.e., its social-psychological meaning as a process through which an individual is brought to a conscious awareness of social expectations. We are familiar with the idea that the juvenile court is meant to be a court of socialization, i.e., a court aimed at bringing juveniles into awareness of social expectations. Even the poor, from this perspective, must be governed from a self at the center, a subject aware of its social obligations. This required technologies of the self that, as Van Waters suggests, could bring an individual to a consciousness of his or her own "sickness" from a social perspective.[18]

Second, for Pound and his contemporaries this idea applied to the law and the court just as much as to the delinquents on whom they would operate. To socialize law in this sense meant to make courts aware of and accountable to the norms and expectations of society. In place of courts that simply passed judgment on the flow of bodies brought before it, juvenile courts were expected to have an ongoing accountability for their judgments.

Third, Pound and others heard also the project of a science of social norms and the processes by which individuals become normalized in them. Socialization of law, in this sense, meant constructing a legal system that produced knowledge of the social as a collateral function of its tasks of judgment. The court's faculty of judgment, then, does not disappear into the human sciences (the fear of many at the turn of the century), but human science is expected to produce the flow of knowledge about both court and society that will make the former accountable to the latter.

The last decades of the twentieth century saw a dramatic set of changes in the juvenile court, the cumulative effects of which seem to have been to reverse the preceding history of that court. In the 1960s, as part of its larger reform of state criminal justice, the Supreme Court examined juvenile courts in a series of cases that sharply questioned the reality of the pastoral rhetoric enshrined in most juvenile statutes. In doing so the Court imposed many of the due process rights associated with the adult criminal process, including the right to counsel[19] and the "reasonable doubt" standard of proof.[20] Starting in the 1980s, popular concern about juvenile violence led many states to revise their original juvenile justice statutes to make public security a coequal concern with protecting the juvenile's rights and well-being. Most states have also made it far easier to move serious felonies out of juvenile court altogether, sometimes without any right to consideration by a juvenile court judge. Even within juvenile courts, however, the operant ethos is becoming increasingly punitive.

In his recent book, *Bad Kids* (1999), Barry Feld suggests that the class context that made the juvenile court meaningful, an industrializing society seeking to integrate the urban masses that concerned Pound and his contemporaries, has long since vanished. In its absence the juvenile court simply functions as a second-class justice system for a population composed overwhelmingly of minority youth whose future usefulness to the labor market has long been considered dubious. He has called forcefully for replacing the juvenile court with adjudication in normal criminal courts authorized to impose special juvenile sentences. But perhaps the question that needs discussing is not whether to have a juvenile court, but Pound's question of the social interest in the moral and social life of the individual and whether it is vindicated by the administration of justice in our twenty-first-century cities. Pound saw the modern city, with its large influx of immigrants and its industrial economy, as requiring new strategies to make possible the ideal of government by and through individuals. The socialization of law would produce a cycle of knowledge and power. Law itself would be reshaped by "social science and economics" (Pound 1913, 324). That in turn would make communities more governable within the broad framework of liberalism. We might take Pound's challenge to heart in our own time. How do our legal institutions perform at making the individual an effective and realistic relay of (self-)power and (self) knowledge at the end of the twentieth century in what we now describe as a postmodern city? These cities ironically are facing the largest influx of immigrants since the turn of the twentieth century. They also reflect the rise of a new economy that functions largely outside the structures of the unions and political organizations that had previously set some limits on its exploitation. In the midst of these challenges the tendency of courts to retreat to simplistic notions of accountability and responsibility are deeply reactionary.

The great obstacle Pound foresaw to this reconstruction was the political power of rural America, whose values in Pound's view remained in line with the eighteenth-century core of the common-law legal system. It was the city against the country in a battle over whether law would be socialized. At the end of the twentieth century it is still possible to identify features of the pattern Pound described. Gun control, for example, is supported overwhelmingly in urban areas (central cities plus suburbs) where the majority of the voters live. But the political system remains far more beholden to rural ideological support for gun ownership. But to a degree unforeseen by Pound, law in the contemporary United States is shaped by a suburban middle class that views the cities as sources of contagion and danger and the young inhabitants of those central cities as presumptively dangerous. As Feld argues, juvenile justice is overwhelmingly seen and operated as a control program for the urban underclass (1999). It is suburban voters who by and large have voted for the increasingly punitive tone with which these underclass youth are addressed in the justice system. Many of our systems of urban governance are endangered today by hostility on the part of suburban voters to treating inner-city residents as fellow citizens, and their readiness to use criminal law as a cudgel against the minority communities that are now the majority in many large central cities. It may be that our response to the largely underclass constituents of the juvenile court is more hostile today than that held by elites toward the ethnic working-class constituents of the early twentieth century (Feld 1999). It may also be that we are losing the clarity with which we once looked at adolescence as a distinct phase of life. But both of these changes may be less critical than the failure of the socialization of law.

Here we might recall the other twentieth-century meaning of "socialization", i.e., public takeover of private productive assets, as was done on occasion by some postwar European governments. This strategy has far fewer defenders today, even among the many who do not favor neoliberalism. Yet the collapse of faith in this strategy as a program for democratizing the economy has not by itself produced other programs for doing so. "Socialize the law" would be an almost incomprehensible slogan today. But that does not help us escape the burden of reconstructing liberalism in the face of many of the same forces that perturbed Pound's generation, i.e., immigration, growing economic inequality, and loss of faith in political institutions.

A RATIONALE OF THE LAW OF HOMICIDE: MODERNIZING THE SUBSTANTIVE CRIMINAL LAW FOR THE REGULATORY STATE

The twentieth century did not invent the law of homicide, but in many respects twentieth-century jurists and academic theorists remade that body of law. Beginning in the latter decades of the nineteenth century, academic criminal law scholars and judges in the United States[21] made the doctrinal anomalies of the law of homicide a problem of systemic irrationality in the law. The main complaint was that the central distinctions in the law of homicide, between first-and second-degree murder (capital or not), manslaughter (short or long sentence), and self-defense (acquittal), depended on a body of precedent with significant inconsistencies. Perhaps this academic discourse would have been less relevant had homicide not also become a problem for government at the state and national levels.

Prohibition

Prohibition led to a frightening spike in the murder rate. Firearms and violent tactics flourished in the illegal economies created in the large cities by the trade in alcohol. As with drugs today, the laws put in place to enforce Prohibition brought all kinds of new people into the criminal justice system, and with long sentences and growing use of the death penalty there was plenty of grist for the appellate courts. There a variety of progressive state supreme court justices, including Cardozo in New York, began to reshape doctrinal forms like "felony murder." Academics, especially the late Herbert Wechsler, began in the 1930s to take up this process of comprehensively reshaping the law of homicide and produced results in the form of legislation, model legislation, and judicial opinions during the 1950s and 1960s.

Abolition of Capital Punishment

Across Europe and the United States the beginning of the twentieth century saw the issue of abolition of capital punishment regain momentum. The struggles of the nineteenth century had seen the death penalty restricted to a few of the most life-threatening felonies. In the first half of the twentieth century debate moved to whether killers ought to receive the death penalty. After World War II, however, it seemed quite possible that the liberal democracies would abolish capital punishment altogether. While that has come to pass for Europe, there is little reason at the moment to think that Japan, and especially the United States will be merely late to adopt this norm. In the U.S. case capital punishment has established a stable supermajority of public support and an institutional structure capable and willing to carry out executions.[22]

In part as a result of the pressure to limit the death penalty, many of these societies, including both the United Kingdom and the United States, saw a reworking of the law of homicide along quite similar lines during the post–World War II period. The Homicide Act of 1957 in the United Kingdom made it possible, for the first time in English law, for juries to choose between the death penalty and life imprisonment for murder and greatly expanded the range of deliberate homicide cases in which a jury could consider a manslaughter conviction as an alternative to murder, resulting in sentences of as little as ten years or less (Elliott 1957). Most American jurisdictions already permitted juries to decide between death and life imprisonment. The American Law Institute's (1985) *Model Penal Code* expanded the applicability of manslaughter and restricted the reach of felony murder.

The constitutional reformulation of the American death penalty in the 1970s has given rise to another stage in the development of the law of homicide (Givelber 1994). Death-penalty trials have become the major venue in American justice for articulating the factors that aggravate and mitigate homicides (Simon and Spaulding 1999). Ironically, in a time of decreasing political support for a progressive and scientifically informed penology, the death penalty remains the last significant setting for the legal development of individualization and social context. Indeed, at a time when the law of sentencing has shifted toward mandatory sentences based on crime and criminal history factors, the Supreme Court has held that the Constitution protects the right of the defense to present individualized evidence to a jury considering the death penalty.[23] But the proliferation of law has led to a significant backlash of public opinion against courts and procedures. Pressure to speed up executions in the last decade of the century has led Congress for the first time in a century to make major retrenchments in the judicial review of the criminal process.[24]

The Problem of Mental Illness

A third way in which homicide became problematic was the law of mental illness, both as a full defense to murder and in mitigation of murder to manslaughter. Perhaps more than any other issue, this seemed to many observers of the struggle between criminal lawyers and the human sciences to be the site of a decisive battle. It was here that the clash between law and the clinical sciences was most heated. While analytically distinct, the psychological-biological subject of science passes closest to the vague moral and juridical subject of *mens rea*, intent, "malice aforethought," and the other terms through which we have conjured up the guilty essence of the criminal offender.

At the beginning of the century many saw this as the battle in which the social sciences would unseat law. Instead, it came to be solidly integrated into the apparatus of criminal law by mid-century without unseating the lawyers or judges. The psychological experts became creatures of the legal presentation. Lawyers, however, continued to be drawn to the capacity of insanity to motivate critical reflection on the constructs of the law of homicide. Insanity became a window into the problem of self-control. Under what conditions can people be expected to control themselves? It is still in the general field of mental illness that novel theories arise, from battered-woman syndrome to the influence of junk food on the capacity of a subject to control strong emotions.

A NEW DEAL FOR HOMICIDE: HERBERT WECHSLER AND THE RATIONALE OF THE LAW OF HOMICIDE

The career of Herbert Wechsler offers up a privileged window into the twentieth-century construction of criminal law as an intellectual as well as governmental project. In a life that spanned most of the century Wechsler became one of the leading intellectual forces in criminal law but also in constitutional law and especially the quintessentially twentieth-century topic, federal courts. Born in New York in 1909, and educated at City College of New York and Columbia Law School, Wechsler was on the younger end of that generation who came into law teaching—and later, government service—in the developmental years of the New Deal. Wechsler's work, initially in law review articles and then as chief reporter for the *Model Penal Code*, became the basis for the most influential approach to modernizing homicide law in the twentieth century. This project, the statutory results of which are very much our present, placed the problem of self-control at the very center of homicide, in a way that recast the complex array of behaviors sanctioned by various common-law doctrines.

As an assistant professor of law at Columbia, Wechsler published two articles in 1937 that laid out the case for a reconstruction of penal law as an essential part of the New Deal reconstruction of government. The more programmatic of the two, "A Caveat on Crime Control" (Wechsler 1937), was published in the *Journal of Criminal Law and Criminology*, long the voice of progressive reform in criminal law and criminal justice. Wechsler attacked the over-long reach of criminal justice experts (read social scientists) who claimed a capacity to differentiate among offenders. He also went after politicians, criticizing by name New York governor Herbert Lehman, Manhattan district attorney (later governor and Republican presidential nominee) Thomas Dewey, and FBI director J. Edgar Hoover, for paralleling the pretense of scientific expertise with the implication that the crime problem could be solved by a simple administrative will to power.

Wechsler felt that substantive criminal law, as the guiding force of the state's power to punish, could be rationalized and modernized a great deal, but not reduced to science. Instead, as an art of democratic government, criminal law required recourse to popular norms and judgment. Wechsler pointed to a renewed effort at codification and a new role for traditional legal notables (jurists and academics) as criminal law experts, and he did so in a way that took account of the claims of social science without entering into a contaminating alliance with them.

In the same year, Wechsler also published a two-part article in the *Columbia Law Review* with his colleague at Columbia, Jerome Michael, under the title "A Rationale of the Law of Homicide." The basic themes of "A Caveat on Crime Control" were all developed in far greater detail, and the pair added a massive apparatus of scholarly footnotes digesting criminal law decisions for U.S. and other common-law jurisdictions.[25] The article helped establish Wechsler as the emerging leader of American criminal law jurisprudence, and with the decline in Pound's influence and John Wigmore's death in 1943, as the leading figure in American legal education engaged in negotiating the boundaries between law and human science, criminal law and penal administration. In 1940, Wechsler and Michaels published their textbook, which became the template for virtually all model criminal law casebooks since.

At mid-century, Wechsler became Chief Reporter for the American Law Institute's *Model Penal Code (MPC)*, the work that sealed his fame as one of the authors of modern criminal law. In 1985, writing the foreword to the last twentieth-entury edition of the *Code*, Wechsler could count thirty-four states that had comprehensively revised their codes since 1960, all of them in at least substantial engagement with the *Code*. A few "more ambitious" states went a good deal further, adopting the central themes of the *Code* if not adopting it word for word. Other states borrowed from the Code in revising separately their statutes on rape and capital punishment.

Wechsler also influenced the model of what a twentieth-century criminal law professor should aspire to be. He was engaged with criminology and the other human sciences laying claim to the penal estate in the twentieth century, but he was not of them. Wechsler helped forge a model for relating law and social science that contributed to assuring the supremacy of legal knowledge and legal notables. More than any other figure, Wechsler shapes the basic settlement between law and social science in the context of New Deal reconstruction of government, a settlement that we very much still live with.

The basic outlines of the "great compromise" were already in place well before Wechsler. This compact gave to the law the problem of guilt, leaving the administration of punishment open to more or less great penetration by the social sciences. Few saw this as a stable situation (Green 1995, 1939). It could be defended as a compromise between traditional American values of liberty and the new capacities of expert government, or as a period of adjustment necessitated by the fact that the social sciences had not yet advanced to the point where they could absorb the full judgment function of criminal law. In his 1937 articles, Wechsler built on this compromise, codifying it and removing much of its appearance of irrationality in a way that increased the power and autonomy of criminal law.

While little in his position may have been totally original, his success stemmed from his ability to think through the logic of the great compromise as a problem of reconstructing government. In particular, Wechsler succeeded in articulating a liberal penality, with self-control as the objective of criminal law, but distinct from the project of socializing the law (exemplified by the juvenile court) and its contaminating collaboration with the social sciences. Many criminal law professors in the twentieth century were marginalized in the law-school world by the taint of having to engage the messy boundary between law, human science, and social welfare, and by the sheer intellectual cost of having to master texts in many other disciplines. Wechsler's career, however, extended to the very center of power within academic legal discourse, namely, to constitutional law and federal courts.

Similar ideas were being debated in Great Britain. But Wechsler's program offers us a revealing view because it so clearly links government, pedagogy, and research. This program was in large part codified in part I of the *MPC*. It remains the most influential approach to criminal law drafting in United States law.[26]

Criminal Law as Risk Management

Wechsler was certainly not the first to articulate the view that the main purpose of criminal law is the management of dangerous individuals. This "social defense" approach was widespread in Europe and the United States in the 1920s. What Wechsler did was interpolate risk taking as a calculable variable of blameworthiness between intentional acts of malice and devices for shifting blameworthiness onto individuals deemed threatening to the community. While others in the first third of the twentieth century assumed that dangerousness would ultimately yield to a psychological analysis of individual pathology, Wechsler focused on the larger structure of behavior and undesirable outcomes. The resulting expertise was not so much a science of dangerous individuals as a jurisprudence of risk.

To Wechsler criminal law should begin with the question of what behaviors we ought to repress and only then should move on to the problem of whom to punish and how. In addition to the undesirable behaviors themselves, criminal law must examine behaviors closely associated with those outcomes that can more effectively lead to prevention of crime. This opens up the prospects of science and policy aimed at social behavior management across a broad spectrum, of which common-law crimes are merely an archipelago of established peaks of disorder.[27]

> Since the end to be achieved is the protection of the public against human behavior that has undesirable consequences, the determination of what behavior to make criminal presents three issues: (1) what consequences of behavior is it desirable to prevent; (2) what behavior tends to produce these consequences, directly or indirectly, or serves to identify persons who are likely to engage in such behavior; (3) which of these forms of behavior can be prevented by the methods of the criminal law, without causing more harmful consequences than the prevention achieved is worth? (Wechsler 1937, 630)

Even a person's intent to kill is only important at certain points along the continuum of risk. One who hopes not to kill but subjects others to outrageous risks (Wechsler and Michael offer the example of derailing a passenger train) deserves little credit for not desiring the predictable deaths (Wechsler and Michael 1937, 1276). Only those who have limited their approach to very low risks should be seen as better risks themselves because they did not intend to kill.

But Wechsler is also concerned that risk-taking not be criminalized generally. Some behavior leading to undesirable outcomes may be valuable in its own right, or may be linked to other activities of value, or may not be susceptible to the main treatments of the penal sanction. His example is noteworthy in its concern for the prospect of escalating class conflict in the midst of the Great Depression.

> The danger here, be it noted, is not only that of corruption and abuse; it is the far more fundamental one, which criminologists often fail to note,

> that not all behavior which threatens violence or destruction of property is equally undesirable and some may not be undesirable at all. Labor unions make strikes probable and strikes involve a danger of violence, but this evil is totally incommensurate with the evil of abolishing labor unions or prohibiting strikes. A demonstration of unemployed may create a danger of riot but it may also be the efficient cause of a grant of relief that will prevent starvation. A similar point holds with regard to "racketeering," for a capitalist economy often posits difficulties in distinguishing "racketeering" activity from clever financing, the exploitation of new opportunities, shrewd competition or even aggressive labor leadership. (Wechsler 1937, 632)

Positivist criminology and psychology had besieged both classical utilitarian policy discourse and common-law construction of crimes. By establishing risk as a kind of twentieth-century alternative to Bentham's utility calculus, Wechsler fashioned a new kind of expertise for legal specialists. Law professors were not to play amateur sociologist or psychologist; rather, they were to produce a rigorous kind of reasoning about institutions that could take account of the social without being of it. Wechsler identified legal technique with skillful reasoning about risk taking of a sort not unlike that which today animates much that is productive in law and economics.

Criminal Law and Crime Repression: Wechsler's Version of the Great Compromise

As is well known, American criminal lawyers did far better than their European counterparts in turning away the thrust of their competitors in the human sciences during a struggle that began in the late nineteenth century with a burst of new claims for the application of positive scientific methods, modeled on biology and medicine, to the criminal law. The United Kingdom and the United States followed similar paths in enacting what Green (1995) calls the "great compromise" between criminal law and criminology, i.e., separating guilt and the administration of punishment. Of course, the terms of that compromise were highly contested and varied over time.

In Wechsler there is none of the optimism expressed at the start of the century that criminals as a class would soon be abolished through incapacitation, eugenics, and transfer to an expanded system of custodial mental health. Neither does he embrace the idea that prisons will realistically obtain to the quality of hospital clinics, educational institutions, or churches. Rather, he recognizes prison as severe punishment capable of achieving deterrent and incapacitative goals but only at the sacrifice of the well-being and the long-term prospects of the offender. Yet at the same time, in its very determined pragmatism, Wechsler's work offers a kind of optimism more far-reaching than that of the positive criminologists. Wechsler summed up the second set of problems fundamental to substantive criminal law as follows:

> The determination of what to do with persons who are convicted of crime therefore presents three issues: (1) what methods of treatment best serve the various possible ends of treatment; (2) to what extent are the various ends of treatment in harmony or in conflict with one another; (3) where they are in conflict, what is their relative importance. (Wechsler 1937, 631)

This framework was elaborated for more than fifty pages in "A Rationale, Part II." Consistent with the model of legal expertise sketched above, Wechsler and Michael show that you can make a lot of general inferences about how to order punishments without having any specific empirical information on their performance. Indeed, as in "A Caveat," Wechsler and Michael remain properly sober about the difficulty of combating crime. Yet neither article ever takes a stand on whether deterrence works, even for those not excluded by mental illness and other legally recognized excuses; whether any rehabilitative techniques work; or whether the incapacitation of offenders produces a net decline in crime sufficient to warrant its costs. Rather, having rejected retribution and embraced the trio of utilitarian approaches, the Wechsler approach was to find what later legal academics would think of as the Pareto optimal trade-off between them in different settings.

> The unwelcome truth may be that there is no genuine solution to the ultimate dilemmas of treatment, because there is no knowledge sufficient to guide a rational choice. Bentham's insight that the only choices to be made are choices among evils carries with it the conclusion that none can be made with conviction or satisfaction. (Wechsler 1937, 634)

The result is both brilliant and disturbing. It is brilliant, because Wechsler managed to separate once and for all the fate of substantive criminal law and the prestige of jurists from the inherently vulnerable project of positive criminology. If the success of criminal law depended on empirical knowledge of crime and the experimental techniques aimed at preventing it, it was a doomed enterprise. The project of collecting empirical data on crime and law enforcement was just beginning in the 1920s and 1930s and promised to be very costly. More importantly, there were no tried and tested methods to "correct" convicted criminals, no analogy to penicillin that could provide a spectacular example of what penological science could do. While earlier influential legal notables like Roscoe Pound endorsed the idea that criminal law would eventually become an empirical science, Wechsler rejected it without making common league with reactionary doctrinal formalists. Recalling in an oral history interview during the 1990s what he considered misguided ideas regarding penal reform that were circulating in the 1930s, Wechsler speculated that a *Model Penal Code* shaped by those principles would have been a disaster.

> For one thing, the notion was somehow that the reordering of criminal law involved a great empirical exercise. In other words, they needed millions and millions of dollars in order to study something that you were going to go out into the world and look at and count. I never got very clear on what it was that you were going to count and look at, but the techniques of sociology were going to be all conscripted—as though this was going to increase your insight as to whether forcible sexual intercourse is something that a good society should try to protect people against, whether you have to count something in order to know that. (Silber and Miller 1993, 869)

Wechsler, who entered Columbia Law School in the midst of its faculty wars over legal realism, envisioned a role for legal experts that would be neither subordinate to nor blind to the social sciences. In his oral history interview he laid his own claim to the most "vital and significant" part of the realist legacy:

> The part that focused not on more accurate empirical description, but on better normative determination. And there it was a matter of simply of displacing the closed system view, of recognizing legislative changes, of marshalling the facts that had a bearing on the wisdom of legislative choices. This is the common-sense approach—call it utilitarian, if you will—but when you get down to ultimate value choices, it doesn't help very much. (Silber and Miller 1993, 872)

On the surface Wechsler extended a hand of cooperation toward the human sciences. The entire second part of "A Rationale for the Law of Homicide" is given over to identifying those features of the offender as an individual that alter the dangerousness posed and should be taken into account in the sentencing. Yet the upshot of the piece is not to set up a permanent traffic between the rival discourses but to establish boundaries and limited zones of relevance, a kind of Berlin Wall behind which the Great Compromise could operate.

Not only did this preserve for legal expertise a unique role in an expanding knowledge base of governance; it constructed the subject of criminal law in a new way. In the place of the psychological subject of positive criminology, Wechsler constructed a subject capable of varying degrees of conscious risk taking. This new subject was a distinct improvement over the problematic subject of common law (monarchical after all), yet it remained at least relatively autonomous compared to the biological, psychological, and social subject of the positive human sciences. This new subject was not the simple pleasure maximizer of Benthamite utilitarianism, but a prudent manager of the risks he or she created and those of others around. In taking on this later role the subject escaped from being the mere product of social and psychological forces. The criminal as risk manager would also extend beyond the knowledge of the positive sciences of the criminal.

The Age of Public Opinion

On this model the legal thinker played a vital role in the circuitry of democracy. Projects like the Model Penal Code and the legislative reforms encouraged by it would clarify the value choices made long ago in the common law and now obscured by language and tradition.

> The important point is to be aware of what the value choices are, and so far as possible, to be able to articulate the reasons that lead to choosing A rather than B. Why? So that accurate statement can enable the next person to know whether he or she goes with you or against you. And in the end—in a democracy, of course—the voters will, if they're informed, be determinative, so that in that sense, the whole thing is utilitarian. (Silber and Miller 1993, 872)

Wechsler and Michaels's "Rationale of the Law of Homicide" presented an optimistic picture of the relationship between legal expertise and popular sentiment. The "core of popular demand is for some graduation of the severity of punitive treatment in accordance with the actual or probable results of crimes of various sorts and the characters of criminals of various sorts."[28] This lined up conveniently with the basic intuitions expressed by the law of homicide. Wechsler was confident that the fine-tuning of these essentially democratic intuitions with scientific research on the results would produce an order both democratic and stable.

While this maneuver has spared the prestige of law from the enormous decline that has been visited on penology, it has also contributed to a myopia about punishment that pervades American legal education, and through that perhaps to the failure of political discourse to confront the true costs of America's late-twentieth-century paroxysm of penal severity. In some form Wechsler's version of the great compromise is now taught to virtually all law students. It separates the rationalization of criminal law once and for all from any responsibility for the size or character of the penal system. How effective punishment will be in achieving the aims of the criminal law is never answered. It is presumed that proper legal management of substantive criminal law can and should be focused on maximizing the capacity of the system to repress crime within the limits of democratic norms.

It is of course deeply unfair to hold the Wechsler of the 1930s and 1940s responsible for the booming penal population in the United States at the end of the twentieth century. He viewed criminal law as playing a relatively modest role in the future of government. He saw his task as one of modernizing this archaic branch of government so that it would not be an embarrassment—or worse, an example—to a rapidly expanding national government. Indeed, his examples reveal that he anticipated that the growth of government would come in areas like labor and welfare and that the challenge would be to limit the appeal of the criminal law and particularly its harshest sanctions to an administrative state facing noncompliance of an ever greater scale.

> Assume that it is desirable to prevent the labor of children in industry and that it is therefore proposed to make the employment of children criminal. Compare the relative *disadvantages* which such action is likely to entail if the treatment prescribed for the offending employer is a fine commensurate with the profits derived from such employment and if it is a long term of imprisonment. (Wechsler 1937, 631 n. 2)

At a time when the New Deal was reconstructing government, Wechsler may well have concluded that in the long run many contemporary criminal populations and problems would be diverted into different kinds of regulatory settings. Prisons were expensive, and in the midst of an unparalleled economic crisis, the public's tolerance for severe repression was correspondingly limited. Modern government would tend away from criminal law as a solution.

> Man becomes good socially by being good individually and the general means to individual goodness are education, freedom from economic and physical handicaps, and the opportunity to function and be of service. . . . The most satisfactory method of crime prevention is the solution of the basic problems of government—the production and distribution of external goods, education and recreation. (Wechsler 1937, 636–37)

Wechsler also seems to have seen the penal establishment as less disturbing to democratic values in the United States than the police apparatus. Unlike prisons, which were bound by the decisions of judges and courts, police could turn their powers across many areas of society and had the flexibility to accomplish many ends.

> The proposals for universal finger-printing, more extensive powers of arrest, search and examination, simpler extradition procedure, broader ex-

> tradition rules or total abolition of extradition formalities raise dilemmas as serious as those presented by the substantive criminal law. Such measures may make it easier to catch criminals; they may also achieve other results ranging from the industrial blacklist and the shooting of wrongly suspected persons to the facilitation of a fascist coup d'etat. (Wechsler 1937, 635)[29]

But in consigning these problems to procedure rather than to substantive criminal law, Wechsler ignored something that now haunts us. The existence of a professional law enforcement and penal establishment creates a constant political pressure to expand the range of acts reachable by substantive criminal law in order to expand the terrain of police arrest and intervention generally. Indeed, Wechsler's substantive criminal law agenda would create doctrine peculiarly vulnerable to just the kind of arrest-driven expansion of the penal system we are now experiencing with drug crimes.

BLOOD IN MY EYE: THE VIEW FROM ADMINISTRATIVE SEGREGATION

Consider a scene from the last years of the twentieth century. In August 1999, a letter reached the *Miami Herald* from one of Florida's "super-maximum" security prison wings, at the Florida State Prison in Starke. The wing houses a number of death-row and other inmates classified as highly dangerous; prisoners are kept in near total isolation. The letter offered the following description and plea:

> The sounds of prisoners screaming in pain and of bodies being beaten keeps the inmates in the entire wing up all night. I can hear the officers forcibly take inmates from their cells. The wretched sound of fists and boots striking flesh are unmistakable as is the sound of some kind of weapon (a stick or a broom handle?) being used. They scream. They whimper. Then there is silence. Somebody needs to get the Feds in here. (Pens 1999)

Two days after the letter arrived, Frank Valdes, a death-row prisoner on the wing, died of severe blunt traumas. Inmates report that these traumas were delivered by a team of guards performing what is known in penitentiary talk at the end of the twentieth century as a "cell extraction."[30] The guards involved and others in a position to witness the events refused to cooperate with either the Florida Department of Law Enforcement or the FBI. Their lawyers acknowledge that Valdes, on death row for killing a prison guard, was not popular, but they deny that guards caused his death. Instead, they have offered the theory that Valdes repeatedly leaped to the floor from his upper bunk, in an apparent suicide attempt. Medical evidence suggests injuries incompatible with such falls, but likely caused by boots, including the virtual crushing of his testicles. When reporters were allowed onto the wing a day after Valdes's death, they found another prisoner whose broken jaw was finally receiving medical attention nine days after a similar beating.[31]

A quiet August momentarily broken by tales of horror coming from some penitentiary/prison is a scene that could be played out in virtually any decade in the twentieth century. Notwithstanding the promise of the prison to produce the humane and civilized reduction of the malefactor to submission (and perhaps much, much more), it has regularly handed its political masters deeply embarrassing contradictory evidence. As Foucault (1977) most famously pointed out, the capacity of the prison to reinvent its mission in more and more ambitious ways has coexisted with its seemingly constitutional inability to solve the most basic problems of social control.

Today's prisons may in fact be producing an impressively low level of violence given the unprecedented size of the penal population. But the severity of the violence reported out of some of our most contemporary prisons makes it impossible to talk about any real evolution here.[32] Rather, the struggle for control over not simply criminals, but people subjected to imprisonment, has proven one of the twentieth century's enduring problems of government. Thomas Dumm's (1987) *Democracy and Punishment* provides a compelling portrait of penology as a site for fashioning a republican model of social control (one useable across a wide variety of social situations) in the nineteenth century. The famous Jacksonian penitentiaries in Philadelphia and in Auburn, New York, offered in their rival versions of the consensus strategy of solitary confinement two different approaches to governing citizens in a post-monarchical society. Philadelphia's program of keeping the inmate confined to the cell virtually all the time, with work conducted in the cell, sought to produce capacities for self-government by deepening the interiority of the subject through transforming study and prayer. New York's congregate system, working inmates at collective (although silent) labor and then isolating them at night, modeled an alternative program based on disciplinary regimes of control over groups. Dumm argues that the decisive victory for the Auburn system signaled a shift in American democracy toward reliance on discipline.

At the end of the twentieth century some observers see the dead end of self-control as a penal objective and the birth of an explicit waste-management model (Robertson 1997). For these critics, the super-max prisons like Florida's X-wing show the prison returned to its most infantile and severe prescriptions (total isolation) coupled with a complete abandonment of any effort at useful transformation of the inmate. In the remainder of this section I trace one of the strongest examples of a twentieth-century effort to create a technology of self-control. Unlike the juvenile court movement, which was aimed at relatively low-level deviancy and delinquency, and the struggle to rationalize the law of homicide, which was aimed at extreme behavior but for the ordinary majority of the population, the prison as a tool of self-control in the twentieth century has been directed at those deemed most dangerous and irascible.

Maximum Security

If the prison has a distinctively twentieth-century form, it is probably not the brief flirtation with hospital-like prisons in the 1950s and 1960s (although at the time they seemed the culmination of a century of effort), but rather the maximum-security prison that grew out of the nineteenth-century penitentiaries once their Jacksonian imaginary no longer rationalized them. In the twentieth century, these stolid prisons built for serious custodial social control on a mass-market basis were built during periods of high tax revenues and fear of crime, especially the 1920s, the 1950s, and rather rapidly since the 1980s.

The Jacksonian penitentiaries described by Dumm (1987) and Rothman (1971) would not have been understood as maximum-security prisons. The penitentiaries envision a singular transformative role with respect to all serious malefactors. These places created their own kind of prison within a prison, the hole, where isolation, poor diet, and lack of light and amenities served as punishment for inmates whose recalcitrance passed some level of tolerance by the prison regime. Maximum security is rather a product of two developments that existed in the nineteenth century but ripened into major obsessions at the start of the twentieth century. The first was the rise of a visible and calculable problem of recidivism. For much of the nineteenth century it was possible to deny the magnitude of the portion of the prison population consisting of repeat players. How is the prison supposed to work on its own failures? By the late nineteenth century the recidivist had emerged as a criminal subject all its own. The second was the push to create more treatment-oriented, more specialized prisons for the subclasses of offenders that psychologists and social workers began to discern among the mass of the criminal class: inebriates, imbeciles, juvenile delinquents, sexualized girls. This necessarily hardens the content of the mass of those left who are residually defined as the less treatable, more dangerous.

By the time the sociology of the prison flourished beginning with the work of Donald Clemmer (1940) and Gresham Sykes (1952), and continuing into the 1970s (Jacobs 1977; Simon 2000), the term "maximum security" was well established to describe the regime of the large old (usually nineteenth-century) former penitentiaries that now coexisted with other newer, and often smaller prisons. The old mainline prisons generally had the tightest security and received recidivists and the most violent of first offenders. These were the prisons depicted by the "Big-House" movies made by Hollywood in the same decades. "Maximum security" as a name for a kind of prison points immediately to its reason for existence, i.e., to overcome the resistance of inmates to imprisonment.[33] Through the work of Cressey and Sykes, among many others, the resistance of inmate culture—what Cressey called the "prison community," and Sykes the "society of captives"—became a visible object of knowledge and intervention. Of course, much of what they did was to make visible the webs of accommodation that the prison had already created with its captive population, but by the 1950s and 1960s the education of prison administrators assured that this sociologically reflexive version of administrative accommodation was programmed more and more into the real thing.

In the 1920s, when Nathan Leopold (1957) began serving his *Life Plus 99 Years* sentence in the Illinois State Prison at Joliet (Stateville), control relied on the remnants of the old nineteenth-century congregate discipline established first in Auburn, New York. Inmates were required to move silently and in single file through all changes of shift and location. But these measures were falling into disuse. As revealed by both Clemmer for the prison of the 1930s and Sykes for the prison of the 1940s, a tolerable order inside the prison required corrupt accommodation of inmate culture in order to create inmate leaders and organization. As Charles Bright (1994) shows in his study of one of the greatest Big House prisons of all, the Southern Michigan State Prison at Jackson, from the 1920s to the 1950s, this cultural accommodation was also an economic accommodation in which prison rackets sustained the enforcement of norms in the prison society tolerable to the warders.

Although it is often romanticized for its solidarity-enhancing features, the Big House control strategy was also and perhaps primarily a program of self-control (Bright 1994). The regime of accommodation created not only inmate hierarchies but also inmate social structures with stable roles through which men could do time peacefully and preserve a functioning sense of ego continuity with their free lives before and after imprisonment. Bereft of a meaningful way to assure both these things, prisons degenerate into violent and chaotic worlds that cannot sustain any kind of meaningful discourse of modernity or civilization. But as attractive as the Big House–era prison is in many respects from the vantage of today,[34] its anchors in the broader economy and society are no longer available. Its relationship to the relatively hardy and progressive features of twentieth-century industrial labor divides us from it.

Closer in both time and possible relevance to our current moment is the period from 1950 through 1980, in which the high-water mark of investment in a real scientific base to rehabilitative prisons was reached, concurrently with the formation of a radical prisoner movement, spurring in response the most severe forms of maximum-security custody yet invented.

Direct Technologies of the Self

The Big House was a way of governing through self-control, but at a distance, through the web of inmate social structure. But the Big House era invented a technology of its own for taking direct management of self-control.

As Rothman points out (1980, 135), administrative segregation practice was invented right in the midst of the Progressive era's fascination with individualizing forms of knowledge, as a kind of dark side to the Progressive intent to be more flexible and open to the community. The term has a distinctly twentieth-century ring. "Administrative" reminds us that it could be ordered at the discretion of prison administration and was typically beyond at least the immediate review of courts or even parole boards. "Segregation" names the logic of separation, classification, and isolation.[35] This could be legitimately presented as reform because administrative segregation promised to wield this discretion to separate in a manner completely different from its nineteenth-century cousin, "the hole." Both were often responses to disciplinary violations of a serious sort, and they shared an emphasis on isolation. But the hole was supposed to be physically punitive (albeit in a more controlled manner than whipping) and relatively short-term. Administrative segregation, in contrast, was intended to accommodate long, possibly indefinite confinement (Rothman 1980, 152).

Over the course of the twentieth century administrative segregation served a variety of different real and imagined functions, primarily in the service of making the prison itself more manageable. Many early-twentieth-century observers expected it to become a model for eugenics, by permanently removing from the general population those who appeared to have the most intractable criminality. In the 1950s and 1960s administrative segregation was also supposed to permit intensive diagnosis and preliminary treatment. In California in that era, most prisoners spent their first weeks or months in so-called "adjustment centers" (or "ac" in prison terminology) where prison staff attempted to develop individualized treatment programs.

The major forms of rehabilitation in California's prisons in this era consisted of methods for instilling in prisoners specific modes of thinking and acting upon themselves as a self—in short, instilling "technologies of the self." These included group therapy of the sort depicted in an asylum setting in the 1975 movie *One Flew Over the Cuckoo's Nest*. Even for cynical prisoners, this meant an exercise in making up a self with narratives to satisfy the staff demand for participation, a demand backed up by parole boards and the indeterminate sentence system.[36]

A second technology that has been far less appreciated than the often-lampooned world of group therapy and may have been more effective in changing prisoners was reading and writing. Eric Cummins (1994) uncovers a remarkable history of success in which reading and writing came to be genuinely valorized by prisoners who invested time and energy in participating in the circulation of books and manuscripts. Cummins points out that in its heyday the San Quentin prison library held more than 38,000 volumes, the vast majority of them nonlegal. In contrast, in the 1990s the prison has held less than 10,000 volumes, the majority being legal materials (Cummins 1994, 28, 250).

The rehabilitative program, including the intensive version of the adjustment centers, encouraged convicts to read and to write. In the era before the telephone and television were accessible in prisons, both these activities were attractive to inmates. A third technology was the adjustment center itself. The adjustment center worked with this regime in two ways: to remove those whose disruptive behavior threatened these technologies; and to allow more intense and uninterrupted treatment.

It is in these spaces that Cummins (1994) traces the development of one of the more interesting moments in twentieth-century penality: the radical prisoners movement that flourished in California, especially the San Francisco Bay Area, between the 1950s and the 1970s. It was a moment when rehabilitation worked and paradoxically endangered the liberal state that had set it in motion.

George Jackson: The Convict as Writer and Revolutionary

In his life and his career in California's prisons, George Jackson encountered almost all of the possibilities and risks in this approach to self-control. His violent death and his writings played a real role in bringing down the rehabilitative penal regime (at least in influential California) and led to the era of the super-max prisons like Florida's X-wing. Jackson's treatment at San Quentin in the early 1970s modeled the shift we have experienced from administrative segregation as technology of the self to administrative segregation as a technology to destroy the self. In his short life Jackson passed through a remarkable series of careers: unsuccessful armed robber, inmate in Soledad and San Quentin prisons in California, field marshal in the military wing of the Black Panther Party, and the author of a best-selling collection of letters from prison with a foreword by the celebrated French writer and prisoner Jean Genet. Jackson died at thirty, on August 23, 1971, in a cinematic blaze of gunfire as he stepped out of the adjustment center at San Quentin, having spent seven of his eleven prison years in that and similar administrative segregation units. His final act, charging through a door from the adjustment center he and his followers had just seized into a prison yard overseen by what Jackson knew were dozens of correctional officers and state police officers, resembled nothing so much as the culminating scene of the 1969 film *Butch Cassidy and the Sundance Kid*.[37]

Jackson died so young that it is easy to assimilate him to the portrait of the young black man as criminal threat that has prevailed since the 1970s. In fact, however, he was born into a different time, in 1941. He did not start life in the kind of zones of hardened underclass poverty that have replaced the far more economically complex "ghettos" since the riots of the 1960s, and to which much of the contemporary prison population traces its roots. Rather, Jackson was born to a family of urban immigrant strivers in Chicago's near-west-side ghetto near Lake and Racine streets. Jackson's father, reared in the South, was a postal carrier.[38] Nonetheless, young George fell into the culture of criminality that for a variety of reasons was coming to dominate social and economic life in the ghetto by the mid-1960s.

In *Soledad Brother*, Jackson recounts being caught for the second of a pair of muggings when he was twelve and receiving only a beating by the police officer rather than an arrest (1994, 10). His father transferred to the seemingly more prosperous city of Los Angeles in the late 1950s in an effort to prevent George from being sucked into Chicago's criminal justice system. Still, at fifteen Jackson was busted for a burglary at Gold's department store on Central Avenue in the commercial heart of L.A.'s de facto segregated black belt. This time he was sent to a prison run by California's Youth Authority, where he encountered a regime of military drilling and physical culture not unlike the present-day boot camps (1994, 13).

Jackson's entry into the California adult prison system in 1960 at the age of eighteen (1994, 4), his failure to gain parole from prison, and his increasing entanglement in the dark side of the rehabilitative ideal's discretionary justice described everything that was dangerous about California's approach to punishment as self-control. Convicted along with two buddies of using a gun to rob a service station of seventy dollars, Jackson took a guilty plea on his public defender's assurance that he would receive only a short sentence in county jail. Instead, he was the only one of the three to receive a prison term. His sentence was typical of the sort that California handed out at the height of its rehabilitative phase: one year to life in prison. Like many of the other inmates around him, particularly African-American inmates, Jackson could not accept the subject position California's rehabilitative penology required inmates to take. His continued resistance, evidenced in disciplinary violations, kept him in administrative segregation and led to continued refusals on the part of California's Adult Authority (the parole board) to set even a tentative date for his release. In California the practice was that some time after the minimum, the Authority would set a target release date, to be followed by a specified number of additional years under parole supervision. Although it was typical for the Adult Authority to wait for a while beyond the minimum sentence before setting this presumptive date (and such dates were only presumptive in any event), Jackson served an extraordinary amount of time without such a date, i.e., without any clear expectation of when he might get out. The letters in *Soledad Brother*, mostly to Jackson's family, are poignant testimony of the sheer anxiety attending the movements of the mysterious and Kafkaesque Adult Authority. In one letter in 1967, for example, Jackson grimly notes his impending transfer to Folsom and comments on the logics of parole as seen by an inmate.

> It is a maximum security prison like this, so there will be no change in my fortunes. One prison is like the other, except perhaps the minimum

> security places in the southern part of the state where they have a less aggressive atmosphere where if one can get around the local constabulary, the chances for parole are greater. That is part of the reason that the guy who was arrested with me went home four years ago and I am still here. Right before I was forced into this situation in Soledad and sent here, he was sent to Chino. But his folks had money to pass around. (1994, 141)

Yet at other moments Jackson's letters reveal him caught up in the narrative of the parole process.

> No new [*sic*] problems. I've got six months clean now, since June 8. That is not much and surely not enough to satisfy my warders but by June of next year it will be twelve months clear. True! (1994, 150)

Cummins (1994) argues that Jackson was in many respects the fulfillment of the technologies of self-control that the rehabilitative prison had been promoting. Like Malcolm X and Eldridge Cleaver, his was the kind of conversion story that seemed to reveal precisely the power of such technologies as reading, writing, introspection, and dialogue about the failures of the self to achieve social cooperation (whether conducted in a Muslim study group or in a prison group therapy session). Unfortunately for both Jackson and the rehabilitative ideal, he was the system's worst nightmare: a black prisoner, empowered by the prison's technologies of the self to call for reappraisal of the very meaning of crime and a revolutionary attack on the state and its functionaries, especially the prison system, who was reaching a multiracial audience outside.

> I was 18 years old [when I came to prison]. I've been here ever since. I met Marx, Lenin, Trotsky, Engels, and Mao when I entered prison and they redeemed me. For the first four years I studied nothing but economics and military ideas. I met black guerrillas. . . . We attempted to transform the black criminal mentality into a black revolutionary mentality. (1994, 16)

The other side of George Jackson is as an embodiment of the administrative segregation units themselves and their increasing potential to be decoupled from any rehabilitative ambition. As Cummins (1994) suggests, Jackson's books, *Soledad Brother* and especially *Blood in My Eye*, were in a real sense products of the segregation machinery itself. Isolated from contact with the outside world, stressed by the almost constant noisemaking that goes on among prisoners undergoing psychological deterioration, Jackson's writing became more and more a prophecy, a dark prophecy that could only end in his rather spectacular death.

It does seem as if Jackson's ultimate involvement (as accused and/or actor) in homicide (of a Soledad guard beaten and thrown to his death off a tier in apparent reprisal for a violent inmate death), was required by the logic of his position. The more political he got, the less parole was ever going to be a possibility. The less parole became a possibility, the more the adjustment center's administrative segregation regime moved toward a self-destruction machine. The more he became a subject for the guards to destroy, the more Jackson had to be a killer. As a killer Jackson actually faced a mandatory death sentence set by statute for prisoners murdering guards. Most likely, the clearer it became to Jackson that he was going to die there, the more he must have been willing to court a spectacular death involving acts of lethal violence against the state.

CONCLUSION

Perhaps the first thing that ought to strike us about criminal law and punishment at the end of the twentieth century is that they are here at all, and thriving, especially in the early industrializing states of the North Atlantic, Europe, and Japan. The idea that criminal law and punishment would wither away, or more precisely, evolve into something altogether more modern, enjoyed a tremendous currency among thinkers throughout the political mainstream of these societies and seemed plausible as late as the 1970s.

Today it is evident that punishment is not going to wither away or evolve into something else. Prison systems, perhaps the most common mode of punishing serious crimes in these societies, are growing in almost all of them, and in the United States at levels that are nothing short of world-historic (Caplow and Simon 1998). Moreover, the belief that the prison itself must ultimately be remade as a kind of school, a kind of hospital, a kind of laboratory, so palpable to "expert" observers from the 1870s to the 1970s, has collapsed. Indeed, if they converge it is because in so many sectors of at least U.S. society, our schools and hospitals are becoming more like prisons.

Meanwhile, modern substantive criminal law moves along with this increasingly uncontrolled punishment system, changing just enough to convince us that it lives, providing perhaps a small measure of legitimation but little real rationality to that punishment system. One result, which we in the United States at least can hardly ignore, is the effect of penal expansion on historically disenfranchised minorities, especially African Americans. It is not too dramatic to say that the rediscovery of the Fourteenth Amendment, the second reconstruction, which may be the single most important occurrence in American law in the twentieth century, is palpably at risk in this development. This is especially ironic because the completion of reconstruction in criminal law has been one of the longest ongoing such efforts in this century.[39]

A second result, less often noted, but also important, has been a fundamental alteration of the relationship between expertise and government. In no other area of social welfare was the twentieth-century state more committed in theory to a scientific dimension of governance than in criminal law. The abandonment of this commitment is one of the most significant indicators of change in the rationalities of liberal government overall.[40] As Francis Allen recognized more than two decades ago, the decline of the rehabilitative ideal signaled a significant change in the cultural anchors of interventionist government. But with the perspective of another quarter century it is evident that it is not merely rehabilitative penology that has become problematic. That might have presaged merely another turn back toward deterrence and economic models of government that have indeed seemed to enjoy some political currency in recent years. But increasingly we are seeing the retreat of any substantive policy expertise in favor of managerialism and a postmodern pastiche of more or less populist gestures (Simon and Feeley 1995; Simon and Spaulding 1997).

The German sociologist Ulrich Beck has suggested that science (along with the nuclear family) served in the formative period of industrial society as a source of mystification as well as critical scrutiny, a way of preserving authority and shielding certain elements from the critical glare of modern consciousness (Beck 1992). To invoke science was to invoke an ethical foundation for government. The populist backlash against expert rationalities in criminal justice has been a privileged site for the larger process of struggle against an interventionist expert state that has gone on in the United States and other advanced liberal societies since the 1970s.

The end of the century is also witnessing a major reconfiguration of the relationship between knowledge and power in crime and punishment. Certain forms of expertise—those associated with social work and clinical psychology, both long thought central to the twentieth-century truth of crime—have come under increasing political pressure (Simon 1997). Meanwhile other forms of expertise—actuarial prediction, information systems management, genetics, and behavioral psychology, among others—have become more critical. Law as a regulator of crime and punishment has looked like a winner or at least a survivor of the twentieth century, but that may be an illusion of an over-narrow time frame. As a traditional source of truth, and one that has retained high cultural prestige, criminal law has continued to command attention. But its real ability to make either crime or the punishment system visible in ways that are ultimately productive for liberal democracy as currently constructed is in much greater doubt.

NOTES

1 The best such effort is Lawrence Friedman's recent one-volume history of crime and criminal justice in the United States (1993).

2 Powell v. Alabama, 287 U.S. 45 (1932); Brown v. Mississippi, 297 U.S. 278 (1936); Chambers v. Florida, 449 U.S. 560 (1938).

3 Mapp v. Ohio, 367 U.S. 643 (1961); Gideon v. Wainright, 372 U.S. 335 (1963); Miranda v. Arizona, 384 U.S. 436 (1966).

4 The term "socialization" has been used most commonly within the social sciences. The *Oxford English Dictionary* 2d Compact Edition, cites an 1846 article by Fourier in the *London Phalanx* describing the progress of human societies from "edenism," a primitive state, to "socialization," a fully developed cooperative state. Also illuminating is the following 1895 usage from Georg Simmel: "The investigation of the forces, forms, and development of socialization, of cooperation, of association of individuals, should be the single object of sociology as a special science."

5 383 U.S. 541 (1966).

6 Stanford v. Kentucky, 492 U.S. 279 (1989), holding that execution for a crime committed while sixteen years of age is not cruel and unusual punishment; Thompson v. Oklahoma, 487 U.S. 815 (1988), holding that execution for a crime committed while fifteen is.

7 James Pilcher (AP), "Adult Trial for Georgia Shooting Suspect," *The Arizona Republic*, 12 August 1999.

8 My reading of Pound's role is influenced by Thomas A. Green's (1995) groundbreaking article, "Freedom and Criminal Responsibility in the Age of Pound: An Essay on Criminal Justice."

9 Pound saw this weakness as part of the more general problem of governing urban America, i.e., the stranglehold of eighteenth-century legal thought on the imagination of jurisprudence. He openly criticized the courts for allowing far too much potential litigation to shift away into other forms of dispute resolution, including crime. The problem was to make the ideological construct of individual will formation truly operational for the mass of the urban working classes who lacked the personal resources to take their disputes through the archaic existing channels.

10 I discuss a haunting example of the uses of these files in my article, "Ghosts of the Disciplinary Machine: Lee Harvey Oswald, Life-History, and the Truth of Crime" (Simon 1997). When the Warren Commission investigated the backgrounds of Lee Harvey Oswald, the only suspect in the killing of President Kennedy, and Jack Ruby, the Dallas nightclub owner who murdered Oswald, they were able to draw on files of both men, produced in their youths by the juvenile justice institutions of New York and Chicago respectively (Oswald in the 1950s, Ruby in the 1920s). In both cases the files yielded lots of clinical descriptions that proved useful in the Commission's development of a largely psychological explanation for both crimes.

11 For Carro's account in the aftermath, see Donald Jackson, "The Evolution of an Assassin," *Life*, 21 February 1964, at 68A. Both the media and the Warren Commission gave considerable credence to the theory that Oswald's family problems as uncovered during his encounter with the juvenile court were the real cause of the crime (see Simon 1997, 86–94).

12 A referee was a lay worker associated with the court operating like a trustee in a civil case.

13 It is important to emphasize that penality was far from the only location for such exemplary practices. A striking example at more or less the same time as the juvenile court was workers' compensation (see Simon 1993; McEvoy 1995; Witt 2001).

14 The title seems to have been given to him in the form of a question he was to answer in an address to a conference on juvenile courts held under the joint auspices of the Federal Children's Bureau and the National Probation Association in Milwaukee in 1921.

15 For discussions of this case history approach see Rothman 1980, 54–56; Bennett 1981.

16 387 U.S. 1 (1967).

17 Recall that as late as the 1960s, computer runs required lots of expensive human labor in punching cards and running data.

18 I argue (Simon 1997, 111) that this worked for at least some subjects like the young Lee Harvey Oswald, who through their exposure to juvenile clinic examination came to see themselves as a problem in a new way. Oswald, who readily absorbed the clinic's message that de-

viance at any level is dangerous, wrote to his mother that he was intimidated by the youths in his custodial clinic who "smoke cigarettes and kill people." Unfortunately for the country, Oswald's ultimate effort to solve himself as a problem may have been his fatal gunshots on Dealey Plaza.

19 *In re* Gault, *supra* note 17.

20 *In re* Winship, 397 U.S. 358 (1970).

21 In ways I will not try to develop here, the reform of substantive criminal law in both the United States and the United Kingdom during the second half of the twentieth century has been substantially parallel.

22 A recent debate has opened up on the topic of wrongful execution, spurred on by a number of death-row inmates cleared after close calls with execution. It remains to be seen whether this will substantially alter the growing momentum toward actually using the death penalty. More executions took place in 1999 in the United States than at any time since the 1950s.

23 Lockett v. Ohio, 438 U.S. 586 (1978).

24 Anti-terrorism and Effective Death Penalty Act of 1996, Pub. L. no. 104–132, 110 Stat 1214 (1996).

25 So far I have not had time to explore Jerome Michaels' contribution to the project, but I assume it is quite important despite the fact that he was the junior author on the piece. His 1935 book with Mortimer J. Adler, *Crime, Law, and Science*, is an important source.

26 See, e.g., Estrich 1998, defending the *MPC*'s strategy of making reasonableness a central problem for the fact finder; Pillsbury 1998, defending the *MPC*'s approach to mens rea.

27 In this regard Wechsler anticipated by twenty years the shift of the social sciences themselves from the focus on abnormal individuals associated with clinical psychology to a focus on normal populations associated with the behavioral sciences (Laub and Sampson 1991).

28 At 1268.

29 "This is a point which peculiarly escapes those students of the crime who constantly contrast the modernity of the methods of the criminal and the antiquity of the 'legal obstacles' with which we surround those whom we expect to catch him." Id. One must assume that Wechsler wrote with deliberate irony in a journal largely devoted to celebrating modernization of police and the criminal justice apparatus generally.

30 A cell extraction looks something like a game of tackle football played with high-tech "nonlethal" weaponry on an 8-by-10 playing field against an unequipped and often psychotically debilitated opponent. See the accounts in Madrid v. Gomez, 889 F. Supp. 1146 (U.S. District Court, N.D. Cal. 1995).

31 Seven guards were eventually charged with second degree murder. See Cazares 2001, 1B. Retrial of the first three, held in prison-dominated Starke, Florida, resulted in aquittals.

32 There is reason to fear that the relatively low level of death and mayhem in American prisons (given their record populations) may be a product of the massive prison-building program of the 1980s and 1990s, and the even older judicial commitment to oversee prison conditions. The latter has been dealt a series of severe legal blows, especially the Prison Litigation Reform Act of 1996, which has destabilized prison consent decrees all over the country and put into question the ability of ordinary prisoners to bring their grievances to federal courts.

33 Historically, for those sent to a maximum-security prison, the only hope of transfer to a less severe regime was some consistent period without disciplinary violations, i.e., of nonresistance to the prison routine.

34 We cannot afford to ignore its deep racism. One should also be reminded of its inevitably regionalist bias. In parts of the former Confederacy, however, including states like Louisiana, the violence was sustained far longer, into the era of court-based reorganization in the 1970s.

35 In this sense it must have its origins in the common hermeneutic ground of racial segregation.

36 Vivid descriptions of group therapy in the California prisons during the early part of this era are in convict-turned-author Malcolm Braley's memoir, *On the Yard* (1967).

37 The 1967 film *Bonnie and Clyde* also comes to mind from that period. White radicals had to

go to Hollywood to live out fantasies of heroic death at the hands of the state. For black radicals like Jackson, the state apparatus was more than willing to play the part of fascist assassin. While the celebrity was equally real for a while, the consequences for the black radicals were unfortunately all too real as well. In my hometown of Chicago a few years earlier, Black Panther leader Fred Hampton was killed in more or less the same script by a hail of police bullets while somewhat less theatrically sleeping in his bed. The fusillade preceded the serving of a search warrant for weapons at the Panther apartment by State Attorney Edward Hanrahan and a special unit of police attached to his office.

38 Since Reconstruction, postal service employment has been an especially valued occupation within the African-American community.

39 The 1930s due process decisions involving African-American defendants in southern Jim Crow justice systems are among the earliest signs of an effective majority on the Supreme Court to effectuate aspects of the federal protection for civil rights promised in the Civil War Amendments. See cases cited *supra* note 3.

40 On liberalism as a rationality of government and its development during the twentieth century see Rose 1999.

REFERENCES

Allen, Francis. 1981. *The Decline of the Rehabilitative Ideal: Penal Policy and Social Purpose*. New Haven, Conn.: Yale University Press.

American Law Institute. 1985. *Model Penal Code and Commentaries*. Rev. ed. Philadelphia: American Law Institute.

Beck, Ulrich. 1992. *The Risk Society: Towards a New Modernity*, trans. Mark Ritter. London: Sage Publications.

Bennett, James. 1981. *Oral History and Delinquency: The Rhetoric of Criminology*. Chicago: University of Chicago Press.

Braly, Malcolm. 1967. *On the Yard*. London: Penguin Books.

Bright, Charles. 1994. *The Powers that Punish: Prison and Politics in the Era of the "Big House," 1920–1955*. Ann Arbor: University of Michigan Press.

Burgess, Ernest. 1973. "The Delinquent as a Person." 1923. In *Ernest W. Burgess: On Community, Family, and Delinquency*, ed. Donald Bogue. Chicago: University of Chicago Press.

Cazares, David. 2001. "Father Sues over His Son's Prison Slaying," *South Florida Sun-Sentinel*, 17 July, 1B.

Clemmer, Donald. 1940. *The Prison Community*. New York: Holt, Rinehart and Winston.

Cleveland Survey of Criminal Justice. 1922. *Criminal Justice in Cleveland*. Cleveland: Cleveland Foundation.

Cohen, Stanley. 1985. *Visions of Social Control: Crime, Punishment, and Classification*. Oxford: Polity Press.

Cover, Robert. 1986. "Violence and the Word," 98 *Yale Law Journal* 1601.

Cummins, Eric. 1994. *The Rise and Fall of California's Radical Prison Movement*. Stanford, Calif.: Stanford University Press.

Dressler, Joshua. 2001. *Understanding Criminal Law*. New York: Lexis Publishing.

Dumm, Thomas. 1987. *Democracy and Punishment: Disciplinary Origins of the United States*. Madison: University of Wisconsin Press.

Elliott, D.W. 1957. "The Homicide Act, 1957," 1957 *Criminal Law Review* 282–92.
Estrich, Susan. 1998. *Getting Away with Murder: How Politics Is Destroying the Criminal Justice System*. Cambridge: Harvard University Press.
Feeley, Malcolm M., and Edward Rubin. 1998. *Judicial Policy Making in the Modern State: How the Courts Reformed America's Prisons*. Cambridge: Cambridge University Press.
Feeley, Malcolm M., and Jonathan Simon. 1992. "The New Penology: Notes on the Emerging Strategy of Corrections and Its Implications," 30 *Criminology* 449–74.
———. 1994. "Actuarial Justice: Power/Knowledge in Contemporary Criminal Justice," in *The Future of Criminology*, ed. David Nelken, 173–201. London: Sage.
Feld, Barry. 1999. *Bad Kids: Race and the Transformation of the Juvenile Court*. New York: Oxford University Press.
Foucault, Michel. 1977. *Discipline & Punish: The Birth of the Prison*. New York: Pantheon.
———. 1991. "Governmentality," in *The Foucault Effect: Studies in Governmentality*, 87. Chicago: University of Chicago Press.
———. 2000. *Power: Vol. 3. Essential Works of Foucault 1954–1984*, ed. James D. Faubion. New York: New Press.
Friedman, Lawrence (1993) *Crime and Punishment in American History* (New York: Basic Books)
Garland, David. 1985. *Punishment & Welfare*. Brookfield, Vt.: Gower.
———. 1990. *Punishment and Modern Society*. Chicago: University of Chicago Press.
Garth, Bryant, and Joyce Sterling. 1998. "From Legal Realism to Law and Society: Reshaping Law for the Last Stages of the Social Activist State," 32 *Law & Society Review* 409–772.
Givelber, David. 1994. "The New Law of Murder," 69 *Indiana Law Journal* 375.
Green, Thomas. 1995. "Freedom and Criminal Responsibility in the Age of Pound: An Essay on Criminal Justice," 93 *Michigan Law Review* 1915–2053.
Haraway, Donna. 1991. *Simians, Cyborgs, and Women: The Reinvention of Nature*. New York: Routledge.
Jackson, George. 1971. *Blood in My Eye*. Baltimore: Black Classics Press.
———. 1994. *Soledad Brother: The Prison Letters of George Jackson*. 2d ed. Chicago: Lawrence Hill Books.
Jacobs, James B. 1977. *Stateville: The Penitentiary in Mass Society*. Chicago: University of Chicago Press.
Jones, Maxwell. 1953. *The Therapeutic Community: A New Treatment Method in Psychiatry*. New York: Basic Books.
Lane, Roger. 1997. *Murder in America: A History*. Columbus: Ohio State University Press.
Langan, Patrick A., and David P. Farrington. 1998. *Crime and Justice in the United States and in England and Wales, 1981–96*. Washington, D.C.: U.S. Department of Justice, Office of Justice Programs, Bureau of Justice Statistics.
Laub, John H., and Robert J. Sampson. 1991. "The Sutherland-Glueck Debate: On the Sociology of Criminology," 96 *American Journal of Sociology* 1402.
Leopold, Nathan. 1957. *Life Plus 99 Years*. New York: Doubleday.

Mauer, Marc. 1999. *Race to Incarcerate*. New York: The New Press.

McEvoy, Arthur F. 1995. "The Triangle Shirtwaist Factory Fire of 1911: Social Change, Industrial Accidents, and the Evolution of Common-Sense Causality," 20 *Law & Soc. Inquiry* 621.

Pens, Dan. 1999. "Insanity, Brutality and Fatality: Florida's X-Wing Marks the End of the Line," 10 *Prison Legal News* No. 10, 1–3.

Pillsbury, Samuel. 1998. *Judging Evil: Rethinking the Law of Murder and Manslaughter*. New York: New York University Press.

Platt, Anthony. 1977. *The Child Savers: The Invention of Delinquency*. Chicago: University of Chicago Press.

Pound, Roscoe. 1913. "The Administration of Justice in the Modern City," 26 *Harvard Law Review* 302.

———. 1930. *Criminal Justice in America*. New York: H. Holt and Co.

Robertson, James. 1997. "Houses of the Dead: Warehouse Prisons, Paradigm Change, and the Supreme Court," 34 *Houston Law Review* 1003–37.

Rose, Nikolas. 1999. *The Powers of Freedom: Reframing Political Thought*. Cambridge: Cambridge University Press, 1999.

Rose, Nikolas, and Peter Miller. 1992. "Political Power Beyond the State: Problematics of Government," 43 *British Journal of Sociology* 173–205.

Rothman, David J. 1971. *The Discovery of the Asylum: Order and Disorder in the New Republic*. Boston: Little, Brown.

———. 1980. *Conscience and Convenience: The Asylum and Its Alternatives in Progressive America*. Boston: Little, Brown.

Silber, Norman, and Geoffrey Miller. 1993. "Toward 'Neutral Principles' in the Law: Selections from the History of Herbert Wechsler," 93 *Columbia Law Review* 854–931.

Simon, Jonathan. 1993a. *Poor Discipline: Parole and the Social Control of the Underclass 1890–1990*. Chicago: University of Chicago Press.

———. 1993b. "For the Government of Its Servants: Law and Disciplinary Power in the Work Place, 1870–1906," 13 *Stud. L. Pol. & Soc'y* 105.

———. 1997. "Ghosts of the Disciplinary Machine: Lee Harvey Oswald, Life-History, and the Truth of Crime," 10 *Yale Journal of Law & the Humanities* 75–113.

———. 1999. "Law after Society," 24 *Law & Social Inquiry* 143–94.

———. 2000. "The 'Society of Captives' in the Era of Hyper-Incarceration," 4 *Theoretical Criminology* 285–308.

Simon, Jonathan, and Malcolm Feeley. 1995. "True Crime: The New Penology and Public Discourse on Crime," in *Punishment and Social Control: Essays in Honor of Sheldon Messinger*, ed. Thomas G. Blomberg and Stanley Cohen. New York: Aldine de Gruyter.

Simon, Jonathan, and Christina Spaulding. 1997. "Tokens of Our Esteem: Aggravating Factors in the Era of Deregulated Death Penalties," in *The Killing State: Capital Punishment in Law, Politics, and Culture*, ed. Austin Sarat, 81–114. New York: Oxford University Press.

Sykes, Gresham. 1958. *The Society of Captives: A Study of a Maximum Security Prison*. Princeton, N.J.: Princeton University Press.

Van Waters, Miriam. 1912. "The Socialization of Juvenile Court Procedure," 3 *Journal of Criminal Law and Criminology* 61–69.

Waite, Edward F. 1922. "How Far Can Court Procedure Be Socialized Without Impairing Individual Rights?" 12 *Journal of Criminal Law and Criminology* 339–47.
———. 1923. "The Outlook for the Juvenile Court," in *Annals of the American Academy of Political and Social Science*, 229–42. Philadelphia: A.L. Hummel for the American Academy of Political and Social Science.
Walker, Samuel. 1998. *Popular Justice: A History of American Criminal Justice*. 2d ed. New York: Oxford University Press.
Wechsler, Herbert. 1937. "A Caveat on Crime Control," 27 *Journal of Criminal Law and Criminology* 629–37.
Wechsler, Herbert, and Jerome Michael. 1937. "A Rationale of the Law of Homicide," parts I & II, 37 *Columbia Law Review* 701–61, 1261–1325.
Willrich, Michael. 1998. "The Two Percent Solution: Eugenic Jurisprudence and the Socialization of American Law, 1900–1930," 16 *Law & History Review* 63–111.
Witt, John Fabian. 2001. "Toward a New History of American Accident Law: Classical Tort Law and the Cooperative Firstparty Insurance Movement," 114 *Harvard Law Review* 690.
Young, Jock. 1999. "Cannibalism and Bulemia," 3 *Punishment & Society* 387–408.
Zimring, Franklin, and Gordon Hawkins. 1998. *Crime Is Not the Problem: Lethal Violence in America*. New York: Oxford University Press.

Twentieth-Century Legal Metaphors for Self and Society

Guyora Binder

STATUS TO CONTRACT

IF THE TWENTIETH CENTURY has been law's century, a century of unparalleled cultural preoccupation with legal arrangements, Henry Sumner Maine announced its advent with his famous formula that "the movement of the progressive societies has hitherto been a movement *from Status to Contract*" (Maine 1963). With this succinct definition of modernity, Maine envisioned a world in which the condition and relations of persons would no longer be received from tradition, but would be made—made by impulses of the will given form and effect by law.

The device by which this dazzling transformation would be wrought was the contract, a prophetic vision of a novel future that, with all the performative power of a magical incantation, made it so. Contract was a marvel of the industrial age, a machine for mass-producing changes, fashioning legal instruments for use in any enterprise. To be sure, contracting could change the face of society, launching ships, building cities, clearing forests, leveling mountains. But, Maine seemed to be saying, contract also altered society's mind, its soul. For it implied that society was no longer an organic growth, but a machine assembled from discrete parts—individual subjects.

The newer conception of society as an artificial construct of private contracts probably owes less to social contract theory than to changes in the practice of law and business. In a study of nineteenth-century thought on slavery, labor, and marriage, Amy Stanley concludes that "by the end of the civil war, leading publicists of contractualism had dismissed the social contract as a figment of philosophers' imagination, and instead hailed the ascendance of market conceptions of contract" (Stanley 1998, 12).

These market conceptions of contract were increasingly important in nineteenth-century American law. Grant Gilmore reasoned that "In a preindustrial society, contract liability . . . was not a matter of much importance. Blackstone devoted only a few pages to it. With the industrial revolution contract liability became all-important . . . and the first books on contracts appeared in England" (Gilmore 1977, 45). The common law had originally premised liability on faulty performance under the action of assumpsit rather than nonperformance of a verbal promise, and colonial American courts were more likely to analyze unconsummated transactions as the wrongful receipt of a benefit than as a broken promise (Teeven 1990, 166,177; Simpson 1979, 543).

By mid-century contracts had become important in American law, although perhaps not yet the idea of contract. Gilmore again: "In the pre-Langdellian era, no one thought of developing a theory of contract. . . . There were as many types of contracts as there were classes of people to enter into them: contracts of factors, brokers, auctioneers, executors and administrators, trustees, seamen, corporations, guardians, landlord and tenant—an on and on in a never-ending list" (Gilmore 1977, 45). Theophilus Parsons's important mid-century treatise organized the law of contract around particular industries and legal relationships. It reflected a social ontology of traditional trades, established institutions, entrenched elites, and yes, statuses (Parsons 1857). It was a Whig document that saw industries as discrete, entrenched, protected spheres of social activity, engines of an ordered, supervised progress toward a national telos. It did not conceive of all of society as a single market, generating uncharted growth and gratifying unchanneled desire. Yet it did see every sphere of social activity as an arena for contracting. Thus Parsons's treatise opens with the sweeping claim that "[t]he Law of Contracts, in its widest extent, may be regarded as including nearly all the law which regulates the relations of human life. Indeed, it may be looked upon as the basis of human society. . . . [F]or out of contracts, express or implied, declared or understood, grow all rights, all duties, all obligations, and all law" (Parsons 1857, 1).

If contract law became increasingly important in organizing business during the nineteenth century, it also became an increasingly salient idea in social reform. More than any other development, the dispute over slavery separated the ideas of contract and status in the popular mind and promoted the notion that a labor contract connoted jural equality. According to Stanley,

> the conflict over slavery infused the principles of self-ownership, consent, and exchange with new ideological urgency. As abolitionists asserted that the slave system was at war with fundamental contract rights, contract became the language of insurgent popular politics. . . . Abolitionism also reshaped the meaning of contract freedom by dissociating wage labor from relations of personal dependency while at the same time placing the contract between husband and wife at the forefront of the debate over slavery and freedom. (Stanley 1998, 17–18)

The Union victory and the abolition of slavery of course affirmed the contractualist vision of labor relations. Yet these events were linked to other political, economic, legal, and intellectual changes. The professionalization of law stood at the crossroads of many forces, reflecting a broader crisis and transformation in political authority. Before the Civil War lawyers had been not only political leaders but cultural icons, Ciceronian embodiments of a certain republican ideal of eloquence and prudential reason (Ferguson 1984; Kronman 1993). Lawyers had been deeply involved in efforts to preserve the republic by compromising the slavery question, and their failure had cast discredit on themselves and on the Constitution for which they purported to speak. After the Civil War and Reconstruction, Americans vested their national pride more in innovations in science and industry and less in their civic institutions. A newly scientific conception of law would allow lawyers to take their place in progressive society—but as academically trained scientific experts and technicians rather than as exemplars of civic literacy and eloquence. Although legal science and progressive social science are often seen as opponents, both were part of a larger progressive project of professionalizing governance.

While lawyers lost political and cultural credibility as statesmen, the social world on which much antebellum legal doctrine and ideology had depended began to crumble. The decline of independent artisanship as an economic sector, the growth of new industries, and the proliferation of new forms of enterprise made contracting a more salient and more flexible feature of social and economic life. More and more domains of life seemed subject to the unpredictability of market organization, and new atomistic descriptions of society became available. The most important were the Social Darwinist portrayal of society as a competition for survival and the classical liberal model of social life as an assemblage of clearly bounded spheres of liberty within which individuals could freely choose without affecting or being affected by others. Joseph Singer (1982) and Robert Gordon have presented this liberal ideal as the chief influence on the late-nineteenth-century legal scientists who reorganized the common law of civil liability around general theories of contract and tort. According to Gordon,

> The function of legal science was . . . to draw as clearly and sharply as possible the boundary lines beyond which the conduct of social actors would be sanctioned and behind which it would not. Legal science would thus create, as it were, combat zones of free conduct in which individuals might do as they willed without fear of legal reprisal, and it would specify the precise legal consequences of infringing on someone else's zone. (Gordon 1983)

Gordon's colleagues in the Critical Legal Studies movement produced a host of such descriptions of late-nineteenth-century academic legal thought as a "classical legal consciousness," linking comprehensive theories of private law to an individualist social ontology by means of a political program of classical liberalism (Kennedy 1980; Mensch 1982). For Gary Peller, the due process right of liberty of contract depended on the view that "a contract was a contract, whether for groceries, futures or employment because it was a universal form of association correlated with the transcendental subjectivity of the individual" (Peller 1985, 1217).

Brook Thomas argues that the idea of contract and the model of society as a continuous process of contracting were influential not only in legal thought, but in the wider culture of the Gilded Age (Thomas 1998). According to Thomas, the realist literature of late-nineteenth-century America was centrally concerned with the "promise" of contract to establish a rational, egalitarian society unmarred by such barriers to social mobility and humane social intercourse as received status and customary prejudice. This is to say not that realist literature celebrated market society, but that it reflected contractualism's social ontology of subjects who—perhaps naively—hoped to choose their social fate by forthrightly revealing their preferences. At the same time, by portraying the defeat of these expectations—the false promise of contractualism, if you will—realist works teach a lesson of accommodation to limits replicating the fundamental economic principle of scarcity that justifies the rationing of hopes and opportunities by price (Dimock 1990; Jameson 1981).

At a deeper level, the mimetic project of realism reflected the modernist scientific project of knowing subjectivity that Foucault portrayed as the aim of all the human sciences in the nineteenth century. Realist literature sought to create a virtual subjective experience for the reader and to reveal, through point of view or through clinical examination, the inner lives of individual characters. Thus, regardless of the particular stance it took toward markets and contracts, realist literature confirmed the ideas that society's true substance consisted of individual subjectivity and that the function of any written instrument was to represent that true substance as accurately and transparently as possible. It thereby affirmed the independence of subjective mental states and desires from the institutions and media of expression by which they might be represented, measured, known, and aggregated (Gagnier 1987; Jameson 1981; Binder and Weisberg 2000).

Contract, then, was a powerful trope at the century's turn, a metonymic representation of society as a dynamic field of competing and transacting wills. This modernist social ontology in turn entailed certain ideas about value and meaning. Value inhered not in some notion of objective reason to which subjective desire must bow, but in subjective desire itself. In political theory, legitimacy sprang from consent, whether of individuals or peoples. In legal theory, law was the will of the sovereign. In ethics, moral value was a function of the utility states of individuals or of the conditions—the rights and liberties—necessary for autonomous choice. In aesthetics, value was at least in part a function of the qualities of genius—imagination and deep emotion duly sublimated and presented for appreciation and contemplation.

A contract is not only an instrument conferring authority on the subjective desires of the parties. It is also a written instrument, a text. If society were a contract, not only should it value states of affairs in the way contracting parties do, but it should use language in the way contracting parties do. Language expresses subjective desire, and the way to understand or interpret language is to identify the subjective desire for which it stands. That is why it seemed sensible to treat literature—and, by analogy, other arts—as expressions of emotion. Indeed, some historians of the business of literature have argued for a close connection between the development of proprietary rights for authors and the romantic aesthetic of genius (Jaszi 1991; Woodmansee 1984).

While contract does not have the currency it once did as a metaphor for society, the general sense that modern American society is an artifact of law has not diminished. Over the course of the twentieth century, contract has been replaced by other legal metaphors for society in legal thought, social thought, and popular culture. Some of the newer legal metaphors I will touch on include interests, claims, process, institutions, and transactions. Just as we can read the metaphor of contract as a clue to turn-of-the-century ideas about meaning and value, we can read these newer legal metaphors as evidence of newer ways of thinking about meaning and value. These newer metaphors suggest a more impersonal ontology of social life, as a kind of discursive process, a social ontology organized around institutions, norms, and identities rather than around subjects and preferences. This social ontology entails a different discourse of value and justification that is more aesthetic than mimetic, organized by the aspiration to compose a social artifact rather than to represent an existing social reality. Taken together, the legal metaphors of claims, process, institutions, and transactions offer a redescription of society as a kind of discursive or semiotic process without any necessary origin or referent in subjective meaning.

FROM LIBERTIES TO INTERESTS

I begin with two legal metaphors: *interests* and *claims*. Over the course of the twentieth century, interests tended to replace liberties as a dominant legal metaphor for individual will. And more recently the notion of interest has morphed in the popular mind into something more like a claim, or argument, or story, or stratagem.

I propose that we consider both interests and claims as having the same sort of place in contemporary social thought that liberties did in classical liberalism. Thus, classical liberalism viewed society as composed of individual wills, each afforded a sphere of autonomy within which they could act without legal liability and without infringing on the spheres of others. This was a spatial model of rights, a sort of idealization of the social isolation of frontier living. Persons were imagined to be far enough apart to be able to engage in many pursuits without affecting one another. Their spheres of liberty did not interpenetrate or come into conflict. Relations among persons could be regulated by consensual contracts because people were free to avoid social relations entirely so long as they engaged merely in "self-regarding" acts.

If the formalist project of classical liberalism depended on a somewhat rustic vision of social life, its plausibility was increasingly challenged by developing urbanization, industrialization, transportation, and communication. The social effects of action seemed farther flung, just as people seemed closer together. Thus the formalist project of classical liberalism needed a good deal of explaining even in the nineteenth century. As Joseph Singer tells this story, the theorists of classical liberalism tended systematically to confuse rights (which imposed duties of facilitation or noninterference on others) and liberties (permitted acts that could be interfered with by others). By the early twentieth century, however, legal theorists had become conscious of the problem. According to Singer, such twentieth-century jurists as John Salmond, Wesley Hohfeld, and Walter Wheeler Cook

> refuted the proposition that there was a necessary logical connection between liberties and duties on others not to interfere with those liberties. . . . Hohfeld's . . . analysis represented the culmination of a long attack on the meta-theory of self-regarding acts as a means of describing and justifying the rules in force. The modern writers recognized the extent to which the legal system allows individuals to harm each other. . . . They asserted that legal liberties could not be justified by the fiction that they concerned self-regarding acts, but had to be justified by the policy conclusion that freedom to do the acts involved was more important than the good to be obtained by forbidding those acts in the interest of security. Whether to grant a liberty to do a specific set of acts began to be seen as a choice between competing interests and policies.
>
> Second, the modern analytical writers demonstrated that the legal system did not completely abolish the insecurity in the supposed state of nature. The economic realm of competition between competing businesses, between competing workers, and between capital and labor is a central component of the liberal legal system. . . . The legal system . . . merely provided rules to define the areas within which the war of all against all could rage as an integral part of life under the rule of law. (Singer 1982, 1056–57).

The analysis of liberties as interpenetrating spheres of potentially conflicting action, then, implied a new vision of society as an arena of struggle. Moreover, the basic units composing these arenas were no longer bounded individual wills. As Singer comments: "While the classical writers defined legal liberty as permission to do self-regarding acts, the modern writers redefined legal liberty as a relationship . . . that made others vulnerable to harm" (Singer 1982, 1056–57). There soon followed the legal realist redefinition of property as a social relation mediated by goods, and a delegation from the state of sovereignty or political authority (Singer 1993).

If property rights are understood to confer power, it follows that contractual bargaining is never truly equal and that all contractual consent is coerced through the exercise of superior bargaining power. Even supporters of laissez-faire markets came to recognize this. An example is the Supreme Court's 1915 *Coppage v. Kansas* decision striking down a Kansas "yellow-dog" statute that precluded employers from conditioning employment on nonmembership in a labor union. The *Coppage* Court asserted that unequal constraint was the inevitable and therefore legitimate result of combining liberty of contract with protection of property.

> No doubt, wherever the right of private property exists, there must be inequalities of fortune; and thus it naturally happens that parties negotiating about a contract are not equally unhampered by circumstances. This applies to all contracts, and not merely that between employer and employee. Indeed, a little reflection will show that wherever the right of private property and the right of free contract coexist, each party when contracting is more or less influenced by the question whether he has much property, or little, or none; for the contract is made to the very end that each may gain something that he needs or desires more urgently than that which he proposes to give in exchange. And, since it is self-evident that, unless all things are held in common, some persons must have more property than others, it is from the nature of things impossible to uphold freedom of contract and the right of private property without at the same time recognizing as legitimate those inequalities of fortune that are the necessary result of the exercise of those rights. (*Coppage v. Kansas*, 236 U.S. 1, 17 [1915])

This passage, explicitly justifying inequality and coercion as the inevitable consequences of liberty of contract, is far from the utopian vision of classical liberalism. And by invoking the alternative of holding all property in common, it implies a radically different social ontology, in which the vital interests of all persons overlap. The redefinition of markets as arenas of mutual coercion was of course developed further by Robert Hale and the early institutional economists (Fried 1998).

This is not yet a social ontology of claims, but something more like a social ontology of interests. In other words, the progressive and realist attack on classical liberalism was part of a movement of the popular mind from a libertarian to a more utilitarian conceptualization of commerce. This development presumably helped the Supreme Court come to see commercial regulation as a subject for legislative and administrative policy analysis rather than for constitutional analysis. In repackaging desire as interests or utility states rather than as liberties, progressive jurisprudence and legal realism tended to change the cultural meaning of law. No longer would law draw boundaries of moral legitimacy around desire, affirming its propriety within an actor's sphere of autonomy and its vulnerability to public judgment beyond that sphere. I am suggesting that there had been a certain homology between classical liberalism and Victorian morality, and that the assault on classical liberalism in political and legal theory at once freed the self from the rigid constraints of propriety and weakened the self's boundaries. Law would arbitrate between contending interests, rather than policing the boundaries of the self.

One implication was that economic regulation, including even the regulation of labor, was no longer an effort to define or protect individual liberty. It was an inherently speculative effort to promote welfare that might benefit some and harm others but that would vindicate the rights of none. Eventually, the language of interest-balancing became hegemonic in constitutional law, so that even rights of free speech became "speech interests" and the remediation of racial discrimination became a "compelling state interest." Fundamental rights were policy interests of particular gravity, to be weighed in the balance (Aleinikoff 1987).

In affirming a social ontology of contending interests, the legal realists helped prepare the way for the law and economics movement that has dominated legal thought—and shaped much public policy discussion—in the last quarter century. Consider Coase's 1960 article "The Problem of Social Cost," said to be the most cited law review article of all time. Here he argues against the use of regulation and tort liability to internalize external social costs of production by invoking a Hohfeldian picture of economic life as a network of conflictual social relations.

> The question is commonly thought of as one in which A inflicts harm on B and what has to be decided is: how should we restrain A? But this is wrong. We are dealing with a problem of a reciprocal nature. To avoid the harm to B would inflict harm on A. The real question that has to be decided is: should A be allowed to harm B or should B be allowed to harm A? The problem is to avoid the more serious harm. (Coase 1960)

Coase proceeds to argue that without transaction costs, the more serious harm will be avoided automatically by the smooth logic of price regardless of which party has a legal right to harm the other. While conceding that transaction costs will often prevent or impede bargaining between A and B, he denies that this necessarily justifies regulation, which generates costs and inefficiencies of its own. Finally, he argues that liability on the part of A alone will not internalize all external costs, since then B's contribution to his own harm (and so to A's liability) would not be recognized and internalized (Coase 1960, 32–34). Coase thereby renders concrete the delegitimizing implications of the realist analysis of legal entitlements. He conjures up a social world in which transaction costs prevent welfare-maximizing exchanges and thereby preclude everyone from using resources efficiently. In such a world, the magic of contract cannot justify private desire as a contribution to social welfare. Each individual is thrust forth from her own personal garden of Eden and must compete for the favor of the regulatory state by making spurious claims to serve society while scheming to cheat efficiency and impose external costs.

FROM INTERESTS TO CLAIMS

A social ontology of interests defines a moral wilderness that denies us the personal justification promised by classical liberalism's ontology of rights. In what began as and remains a puritanical society, this disenchantment of the law leaves Americans yearning for justification. This tension is one source of a newer legal theme in popular culture: that of claiming. By claiming, I mean the activity of representing one's self in public arenas as a grievant. To claim is often to advert to a right, but it involves a different relationship between personality and right than that contemplated by classical liberalism. To claim is not to act securely within a sphere of autonomy defined by rights, but to assert a right to redress. To claim is to project one's personality outward into an inherently unpredictable public space of controversy. The paradigm of claiming is the lawsuit, of course, but claiming goes on in other arenas besides courts: the street protest; the televised hearing; the press conference; the interview or "panel discussion"; the tell-all autobiography; the daytime TV talk show; the consciousness raising, recovery, or self-help group; the letter-to-the-editor; the employee grievance; the consumer complaint; the intra-office memo.

I draw this idea of claiming in part from an episode in late-twentieth-century sociology of law that we might call the civil litigation wars. This was the controversy that developed in the 1980s around the charge that America was an excessively litigious society. Since the charge was often invoked in support of proposals to reform tort and civil rights law by restricting damage awards and access to justice, it provoked a substantial investment of scholarly resources in efforts to minimize—or at least contextualize—American litigiousness. One of the contextualizing stratagems was to compare—or to insist on the need to compare—the amount of litigation to the amount of injury, or rights violation. Litigation was caused by relying on haphazard private enforcement to achieve social goals that could better be achieved by systematic regulation. Nevertheless, absent regulation, tort litigation was indispensable and should not be curtailed. In suggesting that Americans litigated only a fraction of the wrongs done them, the Civil Litigation Research Project drew attention to the cultural filters that defined and selected disputes, the cultural processes by which misfortunes were constructed as claims (Felstiner, Abel, and Sarat 1981).

While these scholars argued that considerable injustice was being acquiesced to by oppressed persons without the awareness, will, or resources to seek redress, their emphasis on the cultural construction of disputes suggested the somewhat different implication that injustice itself was a cultural construct. This implication resonated with the Hohfeldian–Coaesean view that all action initiated a chain reaction of external costs and benefits so that to recognize a right on the part of any one claimant was to injure others.

Avoiding judgment on whether Americans litigated too much or too little, Lawrence Friedman set out to explain the perception of rampant litigation by portraying late-twentieth-century America as a society saturated by law (Friedman 1985). Much of this, Friedman argues, was simply a function of modernization. The more we depend on strangers for goods and services, and the more complex and technical those goods and services become, the more we must rely on legal regulation rather than familiarity and trust to secure our health, welfare, and economic security. At the same time, Friedman argues, the more science, technology, and the regulatory state succeed in delivering security, the higher our expectations become.

Yet Americans are more law-obsessed than citizens of other modern states. Americans have many more lawyers per capita than any similar society, and it is tempting to see these lawyers as freelance bureaucrats regulating matters that would be left to officials elsewhere (Abel and Lewis 1989; Galanter 1987). We set our lawyers watching our government bureaucrats, and we have other lawyers designing, advising, and watching the private bureaucracies—business and nonprofit corporations—that handle most of our affairs. The American version of modernity has been shaped by a "due process revolution" that formalizes decision making not only in government but in private institutions as well.

American culture is characterized by a perhaps religiously inspired optimism about human nature and destiny that paradoxically nurtures grievances. Americans believe in the ever-present possibilities of redemption, resurrection, and luck. Thus, according to Friedman, they have come to embrace two vague "superprinciples" of justice: the principles of security and due process. Friedman's security principle is the expectation that "there shall be no calamity so great, so overwhelming"—other than criminality—"that it utterly and irrevocably ruins a person's life" (Friedman 1985, 72). Friedman's due process principle decrees that "no organization or institution of any size should be able to impair somebody's vital interests . . . without granting certain procedural rights" (1985, 81).

These two principles dictate that no misfortune can be met without a demand for a second chance, a hearing, an appeal. They frame what Friedman calls an expectation of "total justice," but that I would call an insatiable yearning for justification. Our pleadings remain shadowed by the realist insight that we cohabit a jural space with our correlatives. Except on TV lawyer shows, claims are negotiated, not tried. Even our longed-for day in court is more a fantasy than an expectation. Our claims gesture vaguely toward hypothetical remedies, but these are merely the referential meanings of our claims, which may be more significant as performances.

If the civic identity of the classical liberal citizen was coextensive with his liberties, our civic identities may now be coextensive with our claims. Yet our claims are less our expectations than our discursive possibilities, our strategic opportunities. We are the lawsuits we could bring, the controversies we could spark, the representations of ourselves—and others—that might interest the media. This seems to be how lawyers perceive themselves, if we are to credit Lawrence Joseph's fabulous book, *Lawyerland*, which allows us to listen in on a dozen manic, ironic, logorrheic New York City lawyers (Joseph 1997). Joseph's lawyers are, first of all, performances for hire. Each is a fully realized character, ready to soliloquize at the drop of a hat. They speak with staccato urgency, as if fully expecting to have no more than five seconds to get their point across and to impress their personality upon a tense situation before they are interrupted. They automatically register and catalogue pretense and malfeasance everywhere they look, a sea of strategic opportunities to object, expose, embarrass, or extort, most of which they leave unexploited—for the time being. These routine irregularities are no more and no less injustices than would be their exposure and redress. Their predictable availability for strategic exploitation is the constitutive condition of the lawyer's work, and of the working of the law. This has become a familiar portrayal of lawyering in fiction written by lawyers. Scott Turow's prosecutor is saved from an unjust murder conviction not by his innocence, but by his lawyer's implicit (and therefore legal) threat to uncover the judge's corruption in open court (Turow 1987). John Grisham's young lawyer escapes the clutches of his Mafia law firm, his homicidal clients, and the FBI, all without violating the sacred principle of attorney–client confidentiality, by building a racketeering case against his employers for the banal offense of overbilling (Grisham 1991).

While the profusion of lawyer novels, movies, and TV shows suggest that law is especially significant in our media culture, we should not overlook the converse possibility that pop culture has invaded law. Consider the way the Clarence Thomas hearings, the O. J. Simpson trial, and Kenneth Starr's investigation were all played to the media. Perhaps cultural media like TV have so conditioned our experience of discursive processes like legal representation that we now see them as entertainment, occasions for the portrayal of character and the crafting of fiction. Both legal claiming and artistic expression converge in a play for celebrity.

This is certainly how William Gaddis's law novel, *A Frolic of His Own*, portrays both law and literature. Virtually every character in the novel is entangled in lawsuits—mentioned in passing are two Japanese car manufacturers named Sosumi and Isuyu—and the novel opens with the statement that "in the next world you get justice, in this world you have the law" (Gaddis 1994, 11). We are later told that law is nothing but "language" (1994, 284), and the litigious characters include two creative artists. One is Oscar Crease, historian and amateur playwright, who is suing the Hollywood producers of a Civil War extravaganza for copyright infringement of his unpublished play about his grandfather, a Supreme Court justice. The other is R Szyrk, creator of a controversial public sculpture, who first sues to protect and preserve it from a hostile village government, and then, when it has become the valuable object of public controversy, sues to recover possession of it from the village, which now sees it as a valuable boon to tourism. These suits are presided over by Crease's father, a controversial nominee to the U.S. Court of Appeals. Thus all of these characters are engaged not only with the law but with the mass media as well. In a crucial passage, Oscar's sister characterizes his literary exploits as a separate frolic, an escape from the strictures of the law, but the whole weight of the story refutes this conception of art as an idyllic realm of self-expression. In this novel, art is more often a social act of claiming recognition, carried out in a public space where it inevitably collides with competing claims for recognition.

What will change in our conceptions of meaning and value, if we no longer populate the social world with sovereign individuals, asserting rights and interests? The shift from a social ontology of rights to a social ontology of interests suggests a corresponding shift from a libertarian to a utilitarian ethics. But the shift from a social ontology of interests to one of claims, performances, and stratagems seems to require a different approach altogether to ethical and political value. Ethics and politics become less a matter of appropriately weighing the concerns of individuals than of designing appropriate conditions for self-representation.

FROM PROPERTY TO PROCESS

"Due process" is mentioned in the Fifth and Fourteenth Amendments to the Constitution as a condition for the deprivation of life, liberty, and property and had by the start of the twentieth century become an important constraint on the public regulation of private property. The story of this period handed down by progressive critics of judicial review is that under the guise of process, courts prevented progressive regulation of property and of labor contracts so as to enforce a substantive vision of laissez faire. A more contemporary revisionist view, reflected in Bill Novak's contribution to this volume, is that the courts impeded little progressive legislation and legitimated much, as permissibly imposing health, safety, or moral regulation on property "affected with the public interest."

In the latter decades of the nineteenth century, judges began to express suspicions that progressive legislation reflected redistributive rather than health or safety motives (Hovenkamp 1991, 193–204; Horwitz 1977, 26, 29–30). Partly in response to judicial pressure, legislatures began to develop more systematic factual records to support their decisions. Increasingly, some form of hearing was seen as a condition of due process, warranting the reasonableness of regulation (Currie 1985; *Davidson v. New Orleans*, 96 U.S. 97, 105 [1878]; *Chicago, M & St. P Ry v. Minn.*, 134 U.S. 418, 457 [1890]). The period between the Civil War and the turn of the century witnessed a proliferation of investigative commissions and boards whose responsibilities involved proposing as well as implementing state legislation on such matters as railroads, insurance, corrections, charities, education, agriculture, and health (Brock 1984).

Janet Lindgren has shown how judicial review of regulatory legislation in New York state between 1870 and 1920 was more a matter of *informing* the legislative process than of frustrating or nullifying it (Lindgren 1983). Judicial enforcement of constitutional strictures on the form of special legislation pushed the legislature to seek more comprehensive and arguably fairer policy solutions to the various problems that attended industrialization (Lindgren 1983, 594–95). Due process review of legislation gave voice to interest groups that had been unheard in the initial legislative process; when these groups proved insubstantial, the legislation typically would be passed again, with some minor improvements in procedural fairness (Lindgren 1983, 599–604). But where litigation revealed that licensing laws arbitrarily excluded qualified participants from a trade, the legislature gave in (Lindgren 1983, 626–29). In the highly contested arena of labor relations, due process invalidation of protective labor legislation provoked constitutional amendments that chastened the New York Court of Appeals. At the same time, the threat of judicial review inspired the legislature to support its legislation with data.

Outside of New York and a few other states, historian William Brock notes a tremendous expansion of state regulation in the later decades of the nineteenth century, unimpeded by constitutional requirements of reasonableness and generality: "Judges sometimes expressed fears, but time and again they came back to the principle that only the law-making body could judge what means best served the public good" (Brock 1984, 61, 62–85). They did so because legislation was now supported by the efforts of inspectors and statisticians investigating mines, prisons, and poorhouses. Thus, due process review became one mechanism in a broad movement toward the professionalization of legislation in the decades after the Civil War. Reforms in Congressional procedure aimed at reducing the power of party divided decision-making authority among committees by subject matter; electoral reforms facilitated longer careers for effective and popular legislators and so promoted the development of expertise on those committees (Nelson 1982, 114–19; Smith and Deering 1984, 33; Katz and Sala 1996, 121–33). The result was a seniority system and a new role for the legislator as a career expert on certain policy problems (Smith and Deering 1984, 35). Due process review combined with such reforms to cast legislation as a much more rational and deliberative process than in the Jacksonian era. In defending progressive legislation against the presumption that common law adjudication brought to bear greater accumulated experience, Roscoe Pound argued that

> there is coming to be a science of legislation . . . modern statutes are not to be disposed of lightly as off-hand products of a crude desire to do something, but represent long and patient study by experts, careful consideration by conferences or congresses or associations, press discussions in which public opinion is focussed upon all important details, and hearings before legislative committees. (Pound 1908, 384)

Rather than seeing post-Reconstruction courts simply as antagonists to Progressive legislatures, we can count courts among the conditions for the emergence of legislative progressivism. On this view, Progressive-era courts and legislatures were engaged in a partly competitive and partly cooperative dialectical process, challenging one another to embody scientific rationality.

The development of new social scientific technologies of policy making made legislation and administration look more and more like structured processes of gathering and weighing information akin to judicial procedure. At the same time, scientists and philosophers developed a new picture of science as a continuous and fallibilist process of rational inquiry, research, and debate. It became possible to reconceive legal decision making as such an open-ended process of rational investigation and discussion. The term "process" acquired an association also with the routines of assembly-line manufacture. "Process" had become more than procedure: it was procedure without end, perhaps to no end.

For Benjamin Cardozo, the "judicial process" was a craft of policy making that depends on the creativity, circumspection, and discursive skill of the judge, who must intuit societal needs, harmonize them with received legal authority, and win for the results the attention, the understanding, and hopefully the support of the public (Cardozo 1921). For James Landis, *The Administrative Process* should involve an ongoing cooperative dialogue between federal regulators and regulated industries (Landis 1938). Alexander Bickel would later offer a similarly dialogic account of judicial review as a discursive process of articulating principle and placing it before the political branches and the public for judgment (Bickel 1962). According to this argument, judicial review was compatible with democracy because it could only temporarily check and question, but not finally obstruct majority will. It was part of a neverending "colloquy" among courts, political branches, and public.

Bickel's apologia for judicial review was emblematic of the postwar jurisprudential movement known as the "Legal Process" school, after the legal method teaching materials developed by Henry Hart and Albert Sacks at Harvard. Hart and Sacks treated legislation, administration, and adjudication as parts of a continuous process of gathering, processing, and restating information about societal needs and preferences. They analyzed most legal problems as questions of which institution was competent to decide what, according to what standard, and subject to what further procedures and standards of review. Thus law was a continuous process of allocating decision-making discretion, and every legal question was ultimately procedural. Our revisionist narrative about substantive due process described earlier is itself an example of legal process thought, indebted to Bickel.

Legal process thought eventually interacted with social movement lawyering to give rise to the "due process revolution" and thereby helped reshape expectations about government decision making in the wider culture. According to the conventional story, the great expansion of federal responsibility during the New Deal and World War II finally settled the question of the legitimacy of regulatory legislation. Yet the proliferation of administrative agencies raised new questions about the legitimacy of agency discretion, particularly in light of the mobilization of the American populace to fight "totalitarian enemies." After the war, the Administrative Procedure Act was passed to address these concerns by establishing a "notice and comment" process for rule making and a quasi-judicial hearing process for enforcement actions, in front of independent arbiters, designed to produce a judicially reviewable record. Judicial review and academic criticism of administrative decision making focused on the problem of ensuring administrative compliance with legislative goals.

By the 1960s, however, this "traditional model" of administrative law began to collapse under the pressure of litigation and widespread criticism. Critics charged that regulatory decision making was often "captured" by regulated industries, thereby frustrating legislative policy. At the same time, agencies distributing government benefits exercised a discretionary power over the recipients that, while not necessarily at odds with legislative policy, threatened civil liberty. Critics proposed to cure both problems by expanding the procedural rights of adversely affected interests to influence or contest administrative decisions both within the agency and in court. Under pressure from environmentalist, consumer, welfare rights, civil liberties, and other pressure groups, Congress and the courts adopted reforms that exemplified a new "pluralist" model of administrative process as a contest among competing interests rather than the pursuit of a public interest defined by the legislature (Stewart 1975; Rabin 1986). Public participation in formal proceedings became part of the experience of many more citizens and representatives of businesses, as the spirit of street protest was domesticated and institutionalized in the form of a culture of claiming.

One influential articulation of the due process critique of administrative law was Charles Reich's 1964 article, "The New Property." Drawing on legal realist ideas, Reich argued that an oft-overlooked implication of the increasing government role in managing the economy was the government's power to benefit, facilitate, and subsidize. Since government-controlled economic activity would inevitably benefit someone, a regulatory and activist state was by definition a welfare state. In such a welfare state, the distribution of wealth was always partly a creature of government policy, and the potential beneficiaries as well as the targets of government policy were affected interests. Indeed, the more of society's wealth that was subject to public control, the more dependent individual members of society might be on government largess. Thus, Reich argued, government benefits and subsidies were replacing private property as individual endowments; and this shift had disturbing implications for individual independence and civil liberty. If classical liberalism exalted property as a bulwark against state tyranny, the decline of private property promised a decline of individual liberty. Reich offered a litany of cases of crucial government benefits—professional licenses, broadcasting licenses, U.S. residence, passports, unemployment insurance, social security stipends—denied on political or moral grounds. The power to benefit became the power to regulate conscience.

And yet, acknowledging the realist critique of classical liberalism, Reich conceded that there was no returning to a Jeffersonian republic of independent producers and yeoman farmers. Industrialization and urbanization had rendered obsolete the ideal of independence shared by liberalism and republicanism and had revealed property to be a social relation:

> During the industrial revolution, when property was liberated from feudal restraints, philosophers hailed property as the basis of liberty, and argued that it must be free from the demands of government or society. But as private property grew, so did abuses resulting from its use. In a crowded world, a man's use of his property increasingly affected his neighbor, and one man's exercise of a right might seriously impair the rights of others. Property became power over others. . . . (Reich 1964, 772)

The "liberation" of property from feudalism had only temporarily created the liberal market society heralded by Maine. In American society after World

War II, some of the most economically important endowments were such "status" goods as jobs, professional memberships, franchises, pension and health benefits, and the like. To the extent that these status endowments were privileges held at the arbitrary sufferance of government or large corporations (or government subsidized and regulated corporations), society had returned to a kind of feudalism (Reich 1964, 770).

The only way to reconstruct a zone of autonomy was to construct a "new property"—legally protected entitlements to the new forms of wealth—that would limit government's power to regulate personality. Reich develops a remarkable rhetoric that translates both the threat to freedom and the necessary protections into process terms, so that property itself becomes nothing more than the procedural posture of a dispute:

> Property draws a circle around the activities of each private individual or organization. Within that circle, the owner has a greater degree of freedom than without. Outside, he must justify or explain his actions, and show his authority. Within, he is master, and the state must explain and justify any interference. It is as if property shifted the burden of proof; outside, the individual has the burden; inside, the burden is on government to demonstrate that something the owner wishes to do should not be done. (1964, 771)

From this procedural definition of property it follows that placing a greater burden on government to justify a policy gives a property right to anyone adversely affected. Due process rights to a hearing, a trial, or a reasoned explanation are all property, because they perform the function of property. For Reich, property is simply whatever institutional procedures we establish to construct and protect an autonomous self. Property "is not a natural right, but a deliberate construction of society. If such an institution did not exist, we would have to invent it to have the kind of society we wish." And indeed, Reich thought we had to reinvent it as due process (1964, 778).

This kind of redefinition of substantive entitlements as procedural rights and of individuality as a discursive position became a standard trope in late-twentieth-century political theory. The trope appeared in John Rawls's redefinition of the just social contract as the outcome of rationally constrained deliberation (Rawls 1971 and 1993). From Bruce Ackerman—originally an expert on environmental regulation—there followed a reformulation of social justice as the outcome of rationally constrained dialogue (Ackerman 1980). In Germany, Habermas redefined justice as a continuing discursive process of legitimation conforming to "ideal speech conditions" (Habermas 1984–1987). This theoretical convergence of the ideals of distributive justice and democratic process reflected the changing political culture of advanced industrial societies in the late twentieth century.

FROM PREFERENCES TO INSTITUTIONS

The last two decades of the twentieth century saw the rise to prominence of the concept of institutions in many disparate academic discourses. What does this term mean? And what does it have to do with law?

Roughly speaking, institutions are conventions that confer authority, value, or meaning by agreement, whether explicit or tacit. Law is an example of an institution that invests certain decision makers with formal authority. Citizens generally feel obliged to follow legal rules, even when they do not wish to or when they think the rule is wrong. Citizens feel obliged to accept and obey the actions of officials within certain spheres of competence regardless of whether they approve of those actions. They expect that others will do the same, and this expectation enters into their calculus of whether to acquiesce and obey. Thus the coercive force of law depends upon its institutional authority (Will the army obey orders to fire on the dissidents? Will the peasants answer the Sheriff of Nottingham's questions?). Other examples of institutional phenomena constructed by shared belief are religious piety, the value of money, the value (both aesthetic and economic) of art, and the meaning of language. Institutions are distinguishable from organizations, but organizations may require "institutionalization"—a shared commitment to their authority or value—to survive. Of course authority can also be legally established, thereby lending to the organization some of the institutional authority of the law.

Let us consider three definitions of institutions drawn from seminal works in each of three different fields. According to the organizational sociologist Richard Scott, "Institutions consist of cognitive, normative and regulative structures and activities that provide stability and meaning to social behavior" (Scott 1995, 33). Thus institutions include ideology, social norms, and rules backed by sanctions that conserve the conditions of their own survival. Institutions are perpetuated by communication, by social structures and organizations that impose roles, and by routines of procedure and practice. For the institutional economist Douglass North, "Institutions are the rules of the game in a society, or, more formally, are the humanly devised constraints that shape human action. In consequence they structure incentives in human exchange, whether political, social, or economic. . . . [I]nstitutions define and limit the set of choices of individuals. . . . They can be . . . formal constraints—such as rules that human beings devise—and informal constraints such as conventions and codes of behavior" (North 1990, 3–4). For the philosopher of language John Searle, institutions are practices constituted by systems of rules of the form "X counts as Y in context C" (Searle 1995, 28). In other words, institutions are practices constituted by the collective ascription of meaning. Linguistic meaning, monetary value, promissory obligation, official authority, and property are all important examples of "institutional facts" for Searle. An institution exists in large part by virtue of the fact that people believe it exists.

None of these conceptions of institutions are limited to legal institutions. Nevertheless, all seem to treat legal authority and legal rules as paradigmatic cases of social order to which other principles of social order—moral norms, group identities, even linguistic meaning—can be analogized.

The analogy between linguistic meaning and legal authority becomes less strange if we remember that we act in institutionally defined roles much of the time, particularly when we work with written language. Interpretation generally involves putting a text to use in some institutional context in a way that will be accepted by other participants as legitimate. Interpreters are disciplined by community norms. The production of texts for publication or general circulation is usually convention-bound as well. Authors produce texts for use in some institutional context and so endeavor to make the text recognizably useful. Consequently, they often have an interest in perpetuating the institutional conditions of relevance for their work. Because writing and reading are often governed by the same conventions and institutional purposes, methods of interpretation that focus on the subjective intent of authors or the subjective experience of readers are often indistinguishable in practice. And to the extent that it becomes unnecessary or cumbersome to distinguish the conventions governing the writing and reading of a given work, it becomes possible to talk about the formal characteristics or linguistic meaning of the work.

On this view formalist claims about textual meaning are ultimately underwritten by assumptions about the use of texts within institutional practices. This institutionalist take on textual meaning follows from the widely repeated pragmatist pronouncements that meaning is use and that the conventions governing use are historically contingent and often informally defined "language games" or practices (Wittgenstein 1958). While a stable institutional context may be governed by very predictable language games, authors may prepare texts for use in institutional contexts of unknown longevity and changing purposes. It is therefore possible for authorial and reader conventions to diverge. At the same time, the conventions of writing or reading may recognize this and obligate writers to expect and accept the conventions of later readers, or obligate readers to seek and defer to the expectations of authors. Indeed, the legal process theorist Charles Curtis developed a theory of legal meaning as the allocation of decision-making authority and of legal interpretation as the assignment of such authority (Curtis 1950). These issues of allocating interpretive authority are familiar to lawyers, of course, but they are built into many other practices of using written texts (Binder and Weisberg 2000; Binder 1995).

In thinking about linguistic meaning, an institutional focus shifts our attention from subjective intent to social context. The same shift occurs when we think about value in institutional terms. Subjective preference or desire gives way to social context. While neoclassical economics is premised on the idea that competition produces efficiency, institutional economics more or less begins with Coase's insight that property, contract, and competition will not magically produce efficient allocations because of transaction costs. Goods will often have to be allocated by some mixture of cooperation and coercion. Add to this that the definition and enforcement of property and contract rights are themselves costly public goods requiring cooperation or coercion to establish and maintain, and it becomes apparent that spaces for private consumer and investor choice can only exist within an elaborate structure of formal and informal institutions. To organize credible regimes of cooperation and coercion, these institutions must be able to maintain themselves over time, which means that they will have quirky histories and anachronistic legacies and will persist when they impede as well as when they serve efficiency.

While institutional economics begins with the dependence of efficiency on institutions, it does not end there. The ideal of efficiency presupposes some stable or determinate structure of private wants, an assumption the inevitability of powerful historically received institutions casts into doubt. Thus a major theme in "institutionalist" writing in the social sciences has been the possibility that, like meanings, preferences are "endogenous to institutions." This possibility may be inherent in the very idea of "preferences," which signifies the abandonment of the nineteenth-century utilitarian's aspiration to identify, aggregate, and promote cardinal utility. Twentieth-century economics is built on the behaviorist proposition that all we can hope to know about subjective wants—and perhaps all that subjective wants are—are the choices people make in particular transactional contexts. To substitute "preference" for "desire" or "utility" is a little like substituting "word choice" for "meaning" when we talk about language—which is more or less what the structuralist does. The economist, no less than the structuralist, should be seen a skeptic who smugly begs the question of subjective intent.

What does it mean to say that preferences are endogenous to institutions? In the context of consumer choice, this idea embraces "endowment" and "wealth effects"—in which the value of particular goods to particular consumers depends on the background distribution of entitlements (Kennedy 1981; Kelman 1979; Radin 1982). It means that goods and services can be valued for their use in certain collective practices, or for their association with certain statuses, or roles, or group identities. It means that some goods may have no market value, because they are valued in a way that precludes their commodification (Walzer 1983). All of these considerations are operative in explaining why, for example, there is virtually no market in slave or bound labor in the United States—no legal market, and hardly any black market (Steinfeld 1991; Binder 1996). In this instance and many others, formal legal rules, informal social norms, and cultural values work together to construct and stabilize the market actors who will transact and thereby manifest "preferences." Like corporations, the consumers and laborers who participate in markets are also institutions—legal and cultural constructs. They are, of course, natural persons with bodily needs and cravings and pleasures. But when they make market choices, they are acting within roles and carrying out institutional functions. The consumer preference is, in this sense, an institutional product.

The dependence of preferences on institutions is perhaps more apparent in the political context than in the economic context. The political philosopher Stephen Holmes argues that notions like "popular will" and "welfare" are incoherent without authoritative institutional definition. Holmes reasons that popular will is a pernicious fiction unless concretized in stable institutions. Without such institutions, the public will be represented by urban mobs in the centers of government. With all their limitations, competitive elections and public discussions are far more broadly representative than this kind of mobocracy. Yet, Holmes argues, both of these institutions "are highly artificial constructs, requiring patient acceptance of elaborate procedures, institutions, rules. . . . For a society with millions of citizens . . . there is no such thing as a collective choice outside of all prechosen procedures and institutions" (Holmes 1995, 9).

Holmes adverts here to the familiar paradox of social choice theory according to which no social choice mechanism can aggregate fixed individual preference-orderings of more than two alternatives into a coherent social preference-ordering (Arrow 1963). This paradox expresses the following intuitions: First, polities must choose from an infinitely large number of alternative possible futures. Second, choosing by vote requires a sequence of pairwise comparisons of alternatives or a system of weighting the preference-rankings of individual voters. Third, as the number of alternatives and voters increases, it becomes more likely that the winner of a pairwise comparison will depend on the order in which they are compared and that different ways of weighting the preference-rankings of individuals will yield different results (Kramer 1973). Social choice theorists add that voters aware of the preferences of other voters and of the procedure for aggregating them may strategically misreport their preferences. The upshot is that if we understand democratic politics to include agenda-setting as well as voting, its results seem to depend on luck or strategic manipulation rather than on voter preferences.

Yet this entire line of argument that social choice does not reflect individual preferences assumes these individual preferences exist independently of processes of social choice. Some critics of social choice theory reject this assumption. They argue that far from delegitimizing democratic social choice as unconnected to voter preferences, the voting paradox shows that democratic social choice develops individual preferences that could not otherwise exist. Such critics argue that political preferences are often based on the interests or moral commitments of the social groups with which voters identify or on the social roles voters assume. Political conflict is not always conflict between the coherent preferences of competing individuals or groups; sometimes political conflict occurs within individuals, and political debate helps resolve it through a process of "collective self-determination" (Hurley 1989).

Not all individual preferences are relevant to that process of collective self-determination, argue Richard Pildes and Elizabeth Anderson: "norms of democratic political interaction constrain the expression of preferences in political processes to those that can be justified by publicly acceptable reasons" (Pildes and Anderson 1990, 2201). In their view, politics is never about the private preferences of individuals. People can act politically only if they act through institutions:

> [B]ecause different decision procedures lead to different outcomes . . . social choice theorists argue that political outcomes are meaningless or cannot reflect a coherent collective will. But this view imagines a collective will already in existence, lying in wait for democratic institutions to discover. Before institutions are formed, however, no such collective will exists. Political institutions and decision procedures must create the conditions out of which, for the first time, a political community can forge for itself a collective will. . . . No uniquely "rational" institutional architecture exists for constructing that will. *Each* bundle of institutions and practices represents a *distinct* social constitution of the collective will. (1990, 2197–98)

Once we view political preferences as institutionally conditioned judgments about a collective good (whether of a polity or of an interest group), we see the voter less as a private person expressing subjective desire and more as a kind of office-holder carrying out an official function.

Broadly speaking, then, the new interest in "institutions" among social scientists reflects a growing sense that the preferences and interests that undergird rational choice analysis are interpretations of social identities and roles that are conditioned and even constituted by law. Indeed, one strand of institutionalism in legal scholarship focuses on the ways law can regulate behavior by influencing social norms and social meaning (Lessig 1998; Kahan 1997).

While the new institutionalism is largely an academic trend, such trends do not arise in a cultural vacuum. Part of the context for this development is the end of the cold war and the enhanced prestige of markets and elections in the second and third worlds. The challenge of moving beyond ideological slogans to define these institutions and get them working has brought home the extent to which they are artificial rather than natural and how much they depend on law and culture. Markets and elections take many different forms, and their stability may depend on other kinds of institutions such as courts, political parties, independent news media, financial institutions, professions and crafts, universities, private advocacy groups, and professional police forces (Cohen and Arato 1992). Thus the new institutionalism may be related to the wave of institutional innovation required in giving concrete meaning to a triumphant but vague ideology (Binder 1993). And the losers in the ideological battle have in some cases simply moved their struggle from the ideological to the institutional plane (Unger 1998).

FROM SELF-EXPRESSION TO TRANSACTION

The increasing cultural importance of the idea of process, and of the practice of claiming, suggest that we have come to see society more as a discursive forum than as the marketplace envisioned by Maine. But it might be more accurate to say that these two institutions—once seen as distinct and even antithetical—have begun to converge in the popular mind.

It was not always so. The romantic ideas of art and literature depended upon a sharp dichotomy between aesthetic and instrumental action. While this view of art and literature prevailed in America later than it did in England, it had become influential by the second half of the nineteenth century (Ferguson 1984). Art and commerce both came to be seen as manifestations of subjectivity, and we can compare literary works and legal instruments as textual representations of desire. But wills, contracts, and statutes were instrumental representations of desire, while poems and novels were aesthetic representations of desire, sublimations that transformed desire into an object of contemplative reflection. The aesthetic sensibility of romanticism was at once opposed to and bound up with the calculating, instrumental sensibility of commercial capitalism. Romantic art presented itself as a refuge from and a protest against utility that by its very existence bore witness to the human capacity to refashion rather than merely indulge the desiring self. Art also was a manifestation of genius, of the uniqueness of its creator. The work of art was a unique object, an objective correlative of the distinctive sensibility of its creator. By contrast, commerce aggregated disparate desires into the abstraction of price and flattened human creativity into the sameness of commodity production. Where art expressed the self, consumption indulged the self and commodity production alienated it (Binder and Weisberg 2000).

This pattern of thinking about the relation of art and commerce persisted into the twentieth-century era of modernism. Jane Tompkins has commented that "the imputation that a poem might break out of its self-containment and perform a service would disqualify it immediately from consideration as a work of art. The first requirement of art in the twentieth century is that it should do nothing" (Tompkins 1980). Nevertheless, Walter Benjamin's classic essay, "The Work of Art in the Age of Mechanical Reproduction," predicted that the mass production of images and decorative objects during the twentieth century would pose a crisis for the romantic conception of art as the presentation of authentic self-expression for aesthetic appreciation (Benjamin 1969, 217–52). By mid-century, formalist and structuralist critics had mounted a thoroughgoing attack on the ideal of authentic self-expression. The creative work was to be analyzed as a formal object, independent of the personality of its creator. Yet such criticism perpetuated a view of artworks as intrinsically significant objects, to be appreciated apart from any social purpose.

By the last decades of the twentieth century, however, the new interdisciplinary enterprises of Reception Theory, New Historicist criticism, and Cultural Studies reconceived art and literature as institutional practices of investment, production, and use that could be analogized and related to other institutional practices like commerce, government, and science (Fish 1989; Tompkins 1980; Greenblatt 1988; Thomas 1991; Bourdieu 1991). This more institutionalist picture of art and literature entailed a reinterpretation of artistic expression. Just as an institutionalist perspective redefined the instrumental practices of voting and transacting as role-performance rather than self-revelation, the new interdisciplinary criticism redefined the expressive practices of art and literature as role-performance, conditioned by generic conventions, political authority, and economic circumstance.

A striking theme in this new body of critical thought was the analogy of artistic and literary works to money. Benjamin had touched on this theme in noting that coins were among the earliest works of art to be mechanically produced. And as New Historicist Marc Shell demonstrated in *Money, Language, and Thought*, literary authors have long explored analogies between artifacts and coins, and later between words and paper money. *Faust*'s "Paper Money" scene is Goethe's critique of idealist philosophy (Shell 1982, 102). Commenting on the "Mississippi Bubble," Washington Irving wrote that "promissory notes, interchanged between scheming individuals, are liberally discounted at the banks, which became so many mints to coin words into cash; and as the supply of words is inexhaustible, it may readily be supposed what a vast amount of promissory capital is soon in circulation" (Shell 1982, 39). These examples gave voice to a much less sanguine view of promissory instruments than Maine would offer. According to this view, a commercial economy is a vast fiction, built on the pretense that all the paper money in circulation can be redeemed for gold.

We are told that paper money originated in medieval Europe when goldsmiths provided negotiable receipts for gold left with them on account. Realizing that not all these receipts were likely to be redeemed at once, some goldsmiths paid their debts by issuing extra receipts that were, essentially, nothing more than promises to pay. Paper money remained associated with private banking through much of the early history of the United States, as the federal government issued no bills between the Revolution and the Civil War. Banknotes varied considerably in reliability and negotiability and counterfeiting was rife. Thus a national paper currency was still a relatively new phenomenon at the end of the nineteenth century, and controversy raged about whether the new notes would be backed by gold, by gold and silver, or simply by legal fiat. Populists linked rural prosperity to easy credit and easy credit to plentiful money. And they shared with their goldbug opponents the faith that the money supply must depend on the amount of precious metals backing it. Thus the possibility of a disparity between paper money and tangible value was a source of intense anxiety in the "Gilded" Age.

New Historicist critic Walter Benn Michaels has documented the exploration of this anxiety in the naturalist literature of the period (Michaels 1987). Precious metals became emblems of naturalness or authenticity, while paper money stood for artifice and fiction. Thus the two features of self-expressive art romanticism had linked—authenticity and imagination—became antagonistic in naturalism. And the social experience that provoked this disengagement of artifice from personality was the abstraction of commerce, the gradual transformation of the business world of raw materials, commodities, and machines into a professional world of ideas and representations. Paper money was the ultimate symbol of this transformation of tangible goods into ideal abstractions that were nevertheless impersonal, unauthored, fungible. Turn-of-the-century *trompe l'oeil* painters like William Harnett and John Haberle achieved notoriety with their life-size paintings of bills and other printed documents, while the forger Jim the Penman was admired for his hand-drawn counterfeit bills, which, after his arrest, traded on the art market above their face value (Michaels 1987, 161).

Over the course of the twentieth century, the semiotic link between money and metal became increasingly attenuated, but it was only in the 1970s that the dollar was finally "freed" from the gold standard. Only in our lifetimes has it become apparent to all that monetary value is a function of the confiscatory and regulatory power of the sovereign state. And as Benjamin anticipated, one consequence of the mass production and circulation of ideas—for that is what financial instruments are—has been a transformation in our ideas about ideas. At the end of the twentieth century, we are less likely to see a negotiable instrument as a peculiar kind of artifact and more likely to see artifacts as peculiar kinds of negotiable instruments. We now have movies that spin off products that account for the bulk of their profitability—so that the last century's most distinctive art form has evolved into an extended commercial. And coincident with the liberation of money from its material referent in metal commodities, the world economy is supposed to have shed its burden of heavy machinery and ascended to the heaven of electronically transmitted information.

In sum, I am suggesting that the abstraction of commerce has changed our perception of the ideal, of meaning and value and culture, from a medium of authentic self-expression to a network through which unauthored electronic blips circulate as currency. Metaphors of circulation and economy abound in the writing of such postmodern social theorists as Foucault (1979), Lyotard (1988), and Bourdieu (1991). Yet even Searle, an avowed opponent of postmodernism, draws an analogy between language and money in *The Construction of Social Reality*. The fact that money can be made valuable by legal fiat is Searle's paradigm of institutionally constructed reality. He uses this familiar fact to acclimate his readers to the idea that meanings too are coined. In this spirit, New Historicist critics tend to see artistic creation as just a special case of the discursive function of transmitting information and transacting value. New Historicists tend to describe artistic production as a negotiation or transaction, and to focus on preromantic literature that was much less insistent on its autonomy from commercial or political interest (Greenblatt 1988; Gallagher 1994; Lynch 1998; Miller 1990). The result is a reinterpretation of the emergence of romantic art and literature not as the liberation of authentic personality, but as part of an institutional or disciplinary project of coining, negotiating, and circulating fictive characters.

These themes are all at play in the droll artwork—at once graphic and performative—of Stephen Boggs. Like the Gilded Age artists Harnett and Haberle, Boggs makes pictures of money. Of course, producing such images has a different significance today than it did then: the bills depicted are no longer themselves representations of something tangible, a certain weight of gold. Bills are today literally floating signifiers, referring to—that is, redeemable for—only other like signifiers. The Gilded Age *trompe l'oeil* artists played on then-current anxiety about paper money. Boggs, by contrast, awakens an inured audience to the fact that bills are artworks and significant documents. The context is different too, in that Boggs's performance comes after a century of abstract art. Boggs's audience is dazzled by the sheer effort of draftsmanship required to draw a bill by hand, and far from being received as avant garde, his work often seems to gratify nostalgia in his viewers for a departed craft economy. He also works in an era when the homely manufactured products and packages of recent generations have become collectible tokens of nostalgia.

But what most distinguishes Boggs's work from that of his predecessors is its performative aspect. He typically draws his bills in public, often in commercial establishments, before fascinated onlookers. Then—and this is the point—he offers them in payment for a good or service. Reactions of incredulity, outrage, amusement or delight are then followed by a debate over the meaning of value, or a negotiation over the value of meaning. The bargain is usually refused, and Boggs may "spend" days of effort trying to negotiate one of his bills, performing an audience-participation drama at each stop. Finally, the bill is accepted. Boggs demands change and a receipt, documenting the transaction. He then waits a day or two before contacting a dealer. The dealer alerts a collector who purchases the receipt, change, and the commodity purchased from Boggs, and then contacts the astonished holder of the bill, usually offering many times its face value. When all these elements of the transaction have been collected, the work of art—or at least its physical manifestation—is complete and may be exhibited or sold at a premium (Weschler 1999b; 1999a, 16–22).

Yet the performative aspect of the work doesn't end there. For Boggs's transactions arguably violate currency and forgery laws. He has been repeatedly arrested and prosecuted. During his English trial on the charge of making unauthorized "reproductions" of British pound notes, Boggs held up a fistful of British banknotes. "These are reproductions!" he expostulated. "These, by contrast," he continued, fanning out a stack of his own drawings, "are *originals*!" (Weschler 1999a, 52). An appreciative jury acquitted Boggs and his legal expenses were more than compensated for by the appreciative effect of the publicity on the market value of his work. Boggs has never yet been convicted, but he has suffered government seizure of some of his by now very valuable works and been forced to sue to recover them. He has so far run up $800,000 in legal bills, while the government is estimated to have spent several times that amount (Weschler 1999a, 53). To pay his legal fees, Boggs told writer Lawrence Weschler, he planned to produce eight one-hundred-thousand-dollar bills, prompting Weschler to comment:

> I suddenly realized that whether or not the Supreme Court agreed to entertain this particular suit of Boggs's—and if it did, no matter how it ruled—the loser was likely to go on mounting fresh challenges, ad infinitum, since this was that peculiar nightmare of a case in which both sides were in a position to go on covering all their costs simply by printing fresh money. (Weschler 1999a)

CASHING OUT

In these pages I have traced the emergence of a number of new legal metaphors for self and society. I have focused on the rise of a discourse of interests and process in legal theory and in the practice of legal disputing. And I have linked these ideas and practices to a new mode of conceiving and representing the self which I have called "claiming." I have emphasized new ways of thinking about economic and political choice as the playing of institutional roles rather than the expression of private preferences. And finally, I have explored a similarly institutional account of artistic creation as a kind of transaction and of art as a negotiable currency. What links these disparate metaphors together is the model of the self-possessed subject they leave behind, a model evoked by the convergent metaphors of contract, property, liberties, preferences, and self-expression.

Thus, changes in legal metaphors for self and society over the course of the twentieth century suggest that American culture has changed from a recognizably modern culture to one that may, following fashion, be called "postmodern." This transformation involves the declining cultural importance of personality as a source of meaning and value. It also involves a new awareness of institutions, roles, and representations. Where modernist social thought typically conceived law as a transparent medium representing a real social world of subjects, postmodern social thought more often imagines law as part of an institutional world that defines and enables the subjects it purports to represent.

Of course, my collection of legal metaphors is partial and selective. What I have most obviously left out is the most arresting legal metaphor in all of twentieth-century social thought: Foucault's trope that the enlightenment that invented the liberties also discovered the disciplines, and its corollary that in modernity the soul becomes the prison of the body. Foucault's conception of the rights-bearing, utility-maximizing, psychologically self-conscious, liberal individual as a construction of disciplinary institutions is graphically illustrated by his image of modern society as a panoptic penitentiary (Foucault 1979). This is perhaps the foundational trope of postmodern social theory, and it is above all a legal trope, linking contract, property, rights, interests, preferences, claims, and self-expressions to coercive institutions.

Because Foucault's prison metaphor is postmodernism's foundational metaphor, it is implicated in any contemporary redescription of subjectivity as the performance of a social role that is at once enabling and imprisoning. In this sense, the panopticon has not been absent from this essay, but present on every page.

In another sense, however, the prison has been absent from this litany of legal metaphors, absent in a way that courts misunderstanding. For the panoptic penitentiary is not merely a quaint product of Bentham's fussy imagination. It is a concrete reality upon which our society increasingly relies for a brutally direct social control that makes no pretense of discursive process or psychological persuasion. This essay has mostly traced the role of legal metaphors in contemporary perceptions of civil society. It has had little to say about the way our culture thinks about violence, which it thinks about all the time.

A common complaint against postmodernism is that it reduces society to discourse and thereby effaces the concrete power relations established by wealth and force. But such a postmodernism may accurately describe a society in which wealth consists increasingly in information and in which political and legal disputing increasingly concerns opportunities for self-expression. And it is a mistake to assume that a society thus devoted to discourse is necessarily a nonviolent society. For the Marxist critic Walter Benjamin, a society that industrialized the conditions of communication would be a mobilized society, and a mobilized society would be a violent society. If popular discourse deliberated the genuinely political questions of concrete power relations, Benjamin thought, the result would be revolutionary social change, imposed by force, if resisted by force. But Benjamin anticipated another scenario for twentieth-century history, a decadent substitute for democratic discourse, unleashing a different form of popular power:

> Fascism attempts to organize the newly created proletarian masses without affecting the property structure which the masses strive to eliminate. Fascism sees its salvation in giving these masses not their right, but a chance to express themselves. . . . The logical result of fascism is the introduction of aesthetics into political life. . . . All efforts to render politics aesthetic culminate in one thing: war. War and only war can set a goal for mass movements on the largest scale while respecting the traditional property system. (Benjamin 1969, 241)

In the twenty-first century, of course, the yearning to "eliminate the property structure" seems terribly quaint. I have suggested here that rather than opposing discursive process to "the property structure" we have come to see the property structure as a discursive process and property as a claim to information or ideas. With the elimination of the threat of socialism, the threat of fascism too will probably be confined to the industrializing semiperiphery. The "aestheticization" of public discourse that Benjamin feared is probably, for better or worse, an inevitable feature of postindustrial society. Nevertheless, Benjamin's larger point stands, and was reconfirmed late in the twentieth century in Robert Cover's essay "Violence and the Word" (Cover 1986). The massive violence of the kind we witnessed in the twentieth century requires collective action, mobilized and coordinated by discourse. Violence, like meaning, like money, is also an institutional product.

REFERENCES

Abel, Richard, and Philip S.C. Lewis. 1989. *Lawyers and Society: Comparative Theories*. Berkeley: University of California Press.

Ackerman, Bruce. 1980. *Social Justice in the Liberal State*. New Haven, Conn.: Yale University Press.

Aleinikoff, Alexander. 1987. "Constitutional Law in the Age of Balancing," 96 *Yale L. J.* 943.

Arrow, Kenneth. 1963. *Social Choice and Individual Values*. New York: Wiley.

Benjamin, Walter. 1969. *Illuminations*. New York: Schocken Books.

Bickel, Alexander. 1962. *The Least Dangerous Branch: The Supreme Court at the Bar of Politics*. Indianapolis, Ind.: Bobbs-Merrill.

Binder, Guyora. 1993. "Post-Totalitarian Politics," 91 *Mich. L. Rev.* 1491.

———. 1995. "Institutions and Linguistic Conventions: The Pragmatism of Lieber's Legal Hermeneutics," 16 *Cardozo L. Rev.* 2169.

———. 1996. "Critical Legal Studies," in *Companion to Philosophy of Law and Legal Theory*, ed. Dennis Patterson, 280. Oxford: Blackwell.

Binder, Guyora, and Robert Weisberg. 2000. *Literary Criticisms of Law*. Princeton, N.J.: Princeton University Press.

Bourdieu, Pierre. 1991. *Language and Symbolic Power*, ed. J.B. Thompson, trans. G. Raymond and M. Adamson. Cambridge: Harvard University Press.

Brock, William Ranulf. 1984. *Investigation and Responsibility: Public Responsibility in the United States, 1865–1900*. New York: Cambridge University Press.
Cardozo, Benjamin N. 1921. *The Nature of the Judicial Process*. New Haven, Conn.: Yale University Press.
Coase, Ronald. 1960. "The Problem of Social Cost," 3 *J. L. & E.* 1.
Cohen, Jean, and Andrew Arato. 1992. *Civil Society and Political Theory*. Cambridge: M.I.T. Press.
Cover, Robert. 1986. "Violence and the Word," 95 *Yale L. J.* 1601.
Currie, David P. 1985. "The Constitution in the Supreme Court: The Protection of Economic Interests 1889–1910," 52 *Univ. of Chicago Law Rev.* 324.
Curtis, Charles P. 1950. "A Better Theory of Legal Interpretation," 3 *Vand. L. Rev.* 407.
Dimock, Wai Chee. 1990. "The Economy of Pain: The Case of Howells," 9 *Raritan* 113.
Felstiner, William F., Richard L. Abel, and Austin Sarat. 1981. "The Emergence and Transformation of Disputes: Naming, Blaming, Claiming . . . ," 15 *Law & Society Rev.* 631.
Ferguson, Robert A. 1984. *Law and Letters in American Culture*. Cambridge: Harvard University Press.
Fish, Stanley. 1989. *Doing What Comes Naturally: Change Rhetoric and the Practice of Theory in Literary and Legal Studies*. Durham, N.C.: Duke University Press.
Foucault, Michel. 1979. *Discipline and Punish: The Birth of the Prison*, trans. Alan Sheridan. New York: Random House.
Fried, Barbara. 1998. *The Progressive Assault on Laissez-Faire: Robert Hale and the First Law and Economics Movement*. Cambridge: Harvard University Press.
Friedman, Lawrence M. 1985. *Total Justice*. New York: Russell Sage Foundation.
Gaddis, William. 1994. *A Frolic of His Own*. New York: Simon & Schuster.
Gagnier, Regenia. 1987. "Social Atoms: Working Class Autobiography, Subjectivity, and Gender," 30 *Victorian Studies* 335.
Galanter, Marc. 1987. "Adjudication, Litigation and Related Phenomena," 1987 *Law and the Social Sciences* 166.
Gallagher, Catherine. 1994. *Nobody's Story: The Vanishing Acts of Women Writers in the Marketplace 1670–1820*. Berkeley: University of California Press.
Gilmore, Grant. 1977. *The Ages of American Law*. New Haven, Conn.: Yale University Press.
Gordon, Robert W. 1983. "Legal Thought and Legal Practice in the Age of American Enterprise, 1870–1920," in *Professions and Professional Ideologies in America*, ed. Gerald L. Geison. Chapel Hill: University of North Carolina Press.
Greenblatt, Stephen. 1988. *Shakespearean Negotiations: The Circulation of Social Energy in Renaissance England*. Berkeley: University of California Press.
Grisham, John. 1991. *The Firm*. New York: Island Books.
Habermas, Juergen. 1984–1987. *The Theory of Communicative Action*. 2 vols. Trans. Thomas McCarthy. Boston: Beacon Press.
Holmes, Stephen. 1995. *Passions and Constraint: On the Theory of Liberal Democracy*. Chicago: University of Chicago Press.
Horwitz, Morton. 1977. *The Transformation of American Law, 1780–1860*. Cambridge: Harvard University Press.
House of Representatives of the State of Michigan. 1883. *Journal*.

Hovenkamp, Herbert. 1991. *Enterprise and American Law, 1836–1937*. Cambridge: Harvard University Press.

Hurley, S.L. 1989. *Natural Reasons: Personality and Polity*. New York: Oxford University Press.

Jameson, Frederic. 1981. *The Political Unconscious: Narrative as a Socially Symbolic Act*. Ithaca, N.Y.: Cornell University Press.

Jaszi, Peter. 1991. "Toward a Theory of Copyright: The Metamorphoses of Authorship," 1991 *Duke L. J.* 455.

Joseph, Lawrence. 1997. *Lawyerland: What Lawyers Talk About When They Talk About Law*. New York: Farrar, Straus & Giroux.

Kahan, Dan M. 1997. "Social Influence, Social Meaning and Deterrence," 83 *Va. L. Rev.* 349.

Katz, J.N., and B.R. Sala. 1996. "Careerism, Committee Assignments, and the Electoral Connection," 90 *Am. Pol. Sci. Rev.* no. 1 (March), 21–33.

Kelman, Marc. 1979. "Consumption Theory, Production Theory and Ideology in the Coase Theorem," 52 *S. Cal. L. Rev.* 669.

Kennedy, Duncan. 1980. "Toward an Historical Understanding of Legal Consciousness," 3 *Res. In L. & Soc.* 3.

———. 1981. "Cost-Benefit Analysis of Entitlement Problems: A Critique," 33 *Stan. L. Rev.* 387.

Kramer, Gerald H. 1973. "On a Class of Equilibrium Conditions for Majority Rule," 41 *Econometrica* 285–97

Kronman, Anthony T. 1993. *The Lost Lawyer: Failing Ideals of the Legal Profession*. Cambridge: Harvard University Press.

Landis, James McCauley. 1938. *The Administrative Process*. New Haven, Conn.: Yale University Press.

Lessig, Lawrence. 1995. "The Regulation of Social Meaning," 62 *U. Chi. L. Rev.* 591

———. 1998. "The New Chicago School," 27 *J. L. S.* 661.

Lindgren, Janet. 1983. "Beyond Cases: Reconsidering Judicial Review," 1983 *Wisconsin Law Review* 513.

Lynch, Deirdre Shauna. 1998. *The Economy of Character: Novels, Market Culture, and the Business of Inner Meaning*. Chicago: University of Chicago Press.

Lyotard, Jean-François. 1988. *The Postmodern Condition: A Report on Knowledge*, trans. G. Bennington and B. Massumi. Minneapolis: University of Minnesota Press.

Maine, Henry Sumner. 1963. *Ancient Law: Its Connection with the Early History of Society and Its Relation to Modern Ideas*. Boston: Beacon Press.

Mensch, Elizabeth. 1982. "The History of Mainstream Legal Thought," in *The Politics of Law: A Progressive Critique*, ed. David Kairys, 18. New York: Pantheon Books.

Michaels, Walter Benn. 1987. *The Gold Standard and the Logic of Naturalism: American Literature at the Turn of the Century*. Berkeley: University of California Press.

Miller, William Ian. 1990. *Blood-Taking and Peacemaking: Feud, Law & Society in Saga Iceland*. Chicago: University of Chicago Press.

Nelson, William E. 1982. *The Roots of American Bureaucracy 1830–1900*. Cambridge: Harvard University Press.

North, Douglass. 1990. *Institutions, Institutional Change and Economic Performance*. New York: Cambridge University Press.

Parsons, Theophilus. 1857. *The Law of Contracts*, 1st ed. Boston: Little, Brown.

Peller, Gary. 1985. "The Metaphysics of American Law," 73 *Cal. L. Rev.* 1151.
Pildes, Richard H., and Elizabeth S. Anderson. 1990. "Slinging Arrows at Democracy: Social Choice, Value Pluralism, and Democratic Politics," 90 *Col. L. Rev.* 2121.
Pound, Roscoe. 1908. "Common Law and Legislation," 21 *Harv. L. Rev.* 383.
Rabin, Robert. 1986. "Federal Regulation in Historical Perspective," 38 *Stan. L. Rev.* 1189.
Radin, Margaret Jane. 1982. "Property and Personhood," 34 *Stan. L. Rev.* 957.
Rawls, John. 1971. *A Theory of Justice*. Cambridge: Harvard University Press.
———. 1993. *Political Liberalism*. New York: Columbia University Press.
Reich, Charles. 1964. "The New Property," 73 *Yale L. J.* 733.
Scott, W. Richard. 1995. *Institutions and Organizations*. Thousand Oaks, Calif.: Sage Publications.
Searle, John. 1995. *The Construction of Social Reality*. New York: The Free Press.
Shell, Marc. 1982. *Money, Language and Thought: Literary and Philosophical Economics from the Medieval to the Modern Mind*. Berkeley: University of California Press.
Simpson, A.W.B. 1979. "The Horwitz Thesis and the History of Contracts," 46 *U. Chicago L. Rev.* 533.
Singer, Joseph. 1982. "Legal Rights Debate in Analytical Jurisprudence from Bentham to Hohfeld," 1982 *Wis. L. Rev.* 975.
———. 1993. *Property*. Boston: Little, Brown.
Smith, S. S., and C. J. Deering. 1984. *Committees in Congress*. Washington, D.C.: CQ Press.
Stanley, Amy Dru. 1998. *From Bondage to Contract: Wage Labor, Marriage, and the Market in the Age of Slave Emancipation*. Cambridge: Cambridge University Press.
Steinfeld, Robert J. 1991. *The Invention of Free Labor: The Employment Relation in English and American Law and Culture, 1350–1870*. Chapel Hill: University of North Carolina Press.
Stewart, Richard. 1975. "The Reformation of American Administrative Law," 88 *Harv. L. Rev.* 1167.
Thomas, Brook. 1991. *The New Historicism and Other Old-Fashioned Topics*. Princeton, N.J.: Princeton University Press.
———. 1998. *American Literary Realism and the Failed Promise of Contract*. Berkeley: University of California Press.
Teeven, Kevin M. 1990. *A History of the Anglo-American Common Law of Contract*. Westport, Conn.: Greenwood Press.
Tompkins, Jane P. 1980. "The Reader in History: The Changing Shape of Literary Response," in *Reader Response Criticism: From Formalism to Post-Structuralism*, ed. Jane P. Tompkins, 201. Baltimore: Johns Hopkins University Press.
Turow, Scott. 1987. *Presumed Innocent*. New York: Farrar, Straus & Giroux.
Unger, Roberto Mangabeira. 1998. *Democracy Realized: The Progressive Alternative*. New York: Verso.
Walzer, Michael. 1983. *Spheres of Justice: A Defense of Pluralism and Equality*. New York: Basic Books.
Weschler, Lawrence. 1999a. *Boggs: A Comedy of Values*. Chicago: University of Chicago Press.

———. 1999b. "A Contest of Values," *The New Yorker*, 10 May 1999, 52.

Wittgenstein, Ludwig. 1958. *Philosophical Investigations*, trans. G.E.M. Anscombe. New York: Macmillan.

Woodmansee, Martha. 1984. "The Genius and the Copyright: Economic and Legal Conditions for the Emergence of the 'Author,'" 17 *Eighteenth Century Studies* 425.

Citizenship, Agency, and the Dream of Time

Carol J. Greenhouse

TODAY, TALK OF "identity" easily neglects the term's recent manufacture and the local circumstances of its production. This makes it easy to ignore the emerging signs of its transformation. The semantic economy of the term "identity" in anthropology, cultural studies, and the human sciences involves a significant conceptual innovation that was specific to a particular time, place, and politics. Scholars and activists who are middle-aged today (trained before the mid-1980s) can probably remember when the current usage of "identity"—and its marvelously bold breadth and concision—was new. Roger Rouse dates social scientists' contemporary usage to the 1950s, noting its acceleration as a "generalizing" element of social science and popular discourse over the decade of the 1980s—"the most vivid idiomatic symptom of the anxieties and opportunities that the recent challenges to the old topographies of difference have brought about" (Rouse 1995, 381, and see n. 28). Those old topographies were American, and their challenges were felt in a particular way within the United States.

The recent emergence of "identity" as a keyword for sociolegal studies came at a historical moment when three simultaneous developments converged, each with its own effects on established methodologies and domains of inquiry in the human sciences. First, within the United States, a liberal rights discourse (the origins of which had been the legislative and judicial arenas of the civil rights movement in the 1950s and 1960s) developed a deepening schism between its formulation as a law-based regulatory move-

Earlier versions of various portions of the essay were presented to forums provided by Indiana University; Université Paris I; University of Tours; Université Paris X; the American Anthropological Association; the Paris committee of the French-American Foundation; the Ecole des Hautes Etudes en Sciences Sociales, Paris; and the Amherst College/American Bar Foundation conference on "Law 2000." I am deeply grateful to my hosts and colleagues in these contexts, with special thanks to Marianne Constable, Susan Coutin, Bryant Garth, Jean Heffer, Robert Ivie, Robert Kagan, Jean-Loup Amselle, Dominique Daniel, Austin Sarat, Jeff Wasserstrom, and, as always, Fred Aman.

ment and a market-based deregulatory movement. The corresponding effect in the human sciences was to expand the range of disciplines engaged with law and politics from political science and sociology primarily to anthropology, history, and more broadly the law and society movement. U.S. scholars' longstanding commitment to mapping the sources and effects of race- and class-based inequality under the law followed the rights-based movements of women and minorities to their broader milieux in contemporary American society and culture, expanding the contexts for cultural analysis along lines of solidarity with social movements and within an intellectual sphere no longer defined by the more strictly structural or organizational concerns of political science and sociology. Second, the demands of colonized peoples for citizenship, especially in Africa and Asia, expanded the terrain of these multidisciplinary engagements from a primary intellectual focus on the United States to a broader cross-national field. Third, more recently, the emergence of transnational movements—of business, markets, migrations, and new social movements—drew increasing attention to the potential parallels between the aspirations of cultural groups at home and abroad, and to the availability of the academy as a public sphere where such aspirations could be voiced. The expansion of the academy itself—both intellectually and in terms of the diversity of the professoriate and student population—is an integrally related development. "Identity" captures these indelible associations of cultural recognition and the social movements whose demands for recognition define the political space—a transnational space—around this new keyword.

Before scholars talked about "identity," there was not one word but many other words: race, class, sex (gender came later), ethnicity, culture, subculture, custom, colonialism, independence movements, new nations, developing countries, inequality, legal pluralism, and many others. "Identity" came belatedly to refer to all of these at once, encompassing (and refusing) the older, separate frames of reference and evoking their common stakes. As a term in usage in the United States, "identity" is specific to the post–civil rights era and the efforts of American scholars in that period to broaden the discourse of liberal pluralism past the nation-state, both as a gesture of recognition and as a question about the wellsprings of democracy's possible futures in the world at large. Indeed, my main suggestion in this essay is that the keyword "identity" in sociolegal studies is sustained by specific conditions of national citizenship produced in the United States in the late twentieth century and that those conditions are now passing.

IDENTITY AND CONSCIOUSNESS IN THE NATION

The theme of identity emerged as an issue for the human sciences in the United States at a historical moment when reformist and nationalist movements at home and abroad came to be imagined within a unified transnational legal field. This was essentially a liberal pluralist vision that emphasized identity groups and their potential for literal and figurative movement—in migration flows as well as in demands for rights (see Merry 1992 for a review of legal anthropology under the rubric of transnationalism). A transnational approach to the question of identity gave it two "faces" or "directions," so to speak—looking simultaneously to origins and futures, in the ways "difference" within states challenges "the nation" through new knowledges, social arrangements, and social demands (Bhabha 1994, chap. 8). Transnationalism is a question not just of origins and mobility, in other words, but also of the ways institutions become available to new publics (or fail to become available). Constructivist approaches have emerged along the horizon where cultural studies (including ethnography) and sociolegal studies address themselves to the cultural and political dynamics of the public sphere, in which large-scale institutions (the state, for example) are implicated in a wide range of private spheres well beyond their jurisdictions.

In the abstract, constructivist approaches automatically belong to neither the Right nor the Left. For classic liberals, constructivism lends itself to pluralism, individual choice, and a methodology of colorblindness, as solidarity is deconstructed to expose individual interests and choices. For critics, on the other hand, constructivism exposes key social categories and mainstream claims as elements of powerful interests, including the state's legitimation scenario. For these critics, identity is reconstructed in a field of antagonisms and displacements. Thus, the conundrums in the constructivist position are not at the level of abstract definitions, but in the question of which conditions, promises, and risks attach to actual public spheres. If one thinks about identity with constructivist tools, then, one should presuppose neither a field of inevitable solidarities and antagonisms nor a "nationalist historicism" in which "cultural histories coalesce" (Bhabha 1994, 152). Rather, constructivism commits one to an ethnographic project of considering the fields of encounter where these or other understandings operate as actual possibilities. Ethnography inevitably reveals these fields of action and interpretation as fragmentary, uneven, and unstable; these dynamics are objects of ethnographic inquiry in themselves. To borrow Joan Scott's cautionary phrase, "It is not a happy pluralism that we ought to invoke" (Scott 1988, 176).

We should not invoke a "happy pluralism" in part because the state, the nation, citizenship, and culture constitute different topographies of time (history/future), space (national/transnational), and contestation. Contemplating U.S. multiculturalism from a transnational perspective, Lisa Lowe evokes these positions in terms that link states and subjectivities:

> Cultural forms are not inherently "political," indeed in the modern nation-state, culture has been traditionally burdened to resolve what the

> political forms of the state cannot. Alternative cultural forms and practices do not offer havens of resolution but are rather often eloquent description of the ways in which the law, labor exploitation, racialization, and gendering work to prohibit alternatives. Some cultural forms succeed in making it possible to live and inhabit alternatives in the encounter with those prohibitions; some permit us to imagine what we have still yet to live. (Lowe 1998, 19)

Lowe's claim is intriguing, since it is first a comment not on the workings of politics, but on the temporality of politics—that is, the branchings of possible futures from the present. Lowe's appeal for alternatives suggests that cultural forms are inherently political—with the implication that the location of politics is not limited to established institutions or lines of power (on "political locations," see Gupta and Ferguson 1997). Her doubling of time and identity around the political conditions of the present and imaginable alternative forms of the future evokes W.E.B. Du Bois's "double-consciousness."

For Du Bois, time, space, and consciousness meet at the horizon of the "color-line": "The problem of the twentieth century is the problem of the color-line,—the relation of the darker to the lighter races of men in Asia and Africa, in America and the islands of the sea" (1990 [1903], 16). Coming early in the book, this passage offers a concise depiction of a temporal axis (middle passage, enslavement, emancipation, struggle against racism and poverty, even "the twentieth century") in relation to a spatial axis ("Asia, Africa, America and the islands of the sea"). The color-line is the intersection of these two planes, and together, they form the matrix of "double-consciousness"—the "gifted . . . second-sight" that permits self-consciousness through "the eyes of others" (Du Bois 1990 [1903], 8–9).

Importantly, double consciousness, for Du Bois, is not an *attribute* of the people to whom he refers as "the Negro" but a *relation* formed in what Nahum Chandler later calls the "vortex" of "the double articulation since the 16th century of the history of slavery . . . in the Americas and the Caribbean and the emergence of a global practice of racial distinction" (Chandler 1996, 78–79). Conceived in this way, "identity" is always implicitly a reference to the nation-state in a global context. As Chandler explains, what is at stake in Du Bois's concept of double consciousness is not the identity of "the Negro" but the "schema of [a] discourse" that precludes the production of "a non-essentialist discourse" of identity in relation to the nation:

> There is not now nor has there ever been a free zone or quiet place from which the discourse of Africanist scholars [including Du Bois, among others] would issue. . . . It emerges in a cacophony of enunciations that marks the inception of discourses of the "African" and the "Negro" in the modern period. . . . At the core of this cacophony was a question

> about identity. On the surface, its proclaimed face, it was a discourse about the status of the Negro (political, legal, moral, philosophical, literary, theological, etc.) subject. On its other and hidden face, the presumptive answer to which served as a ground, organizing in a hierarchy the schema of this discourse, and determining the elaboration of this general question, was a question about the status of the European (and subsequently "White") subject. (Chandler 1996, 79–80; note omitted)

The keyword "identity" names this temporal/spatial juncture within social relationships.

Indeed, the modern nation emerges with the very possibility of disavowing such contradictions (most importantly under the rubric of citizenship); postmodernity makes such disavowals problematic to the extent that citizenship is conceptually and pragmatically complicated by its extensions into transnational social fields (see, for example, Coutin 1999, Ong 1999). John and Jean Comaroff associate a transformation in the fields of identity specifically with the global rise of neoliberal capitalism: "The geographically localized, nationally bounded conception of society and culture, of a homogeneous imagined community, is at once compromised, pluralized, problematized. So, concomitantly, is the nature of identity: no longer contained neatly in citizenship, in the modernist subject, it is 'free' to redefine itself along any number of axes of being in the world" (Comaroff and Comaroff 1999, 15). This is something of the context in which Chandler calls for a continual "desedimentation" (1996, 80) of the discourse of double consciousness as a means of ongoing cultural critique. Given this history of the present and future, "identity" may appropriately be taken to imply the discursive centrality of rights-based struggle to collective self-recognition within the U.S. national timespace. Identity, in other words, is a form of agency both in its tacit acknowledgment of personal association and (with) social movements (see Bhabha 1998) and in its singularization of transnational timespace under the rubric of specific institutions and political practices in relation to the state. My purpose here is to emphasize that the notion of identity as agency implies a historically specific reference to particular experiences and political struggles conceived in relation to nation-states.

Is there a temporality for a diasporic democracy that does not subscribe to nationalism's *a priori* vision of homogeneity or "happy pluralism" as the future of the nation? In what follows, I reflect on this question in two main registers. First, drawing especially from Hannah Arendt and Alexis de Tocqueville, I develop the notion of "empirical citizenship"—"empirical" to evoke a contrast with Marx's "abstract citizenship" as well as to conjure the prospects for ethnographers and others who seek domains of inquiry in contemporary transnationalism. Empirical citizenship is my term for people's capacity for identifying with others and making this the basis of their demands on the state—whether these other projects be transnational or outside the discourse of "the nation" altogether. These are highly substantive gestures. Moreover, people's needs, uses, and aspirations for agency and partnership are by no means monopolized by the symbolism of belonging to a nation or by the liberal discourse of rights.

The second essay's register is more concrete, involving a brief chronicle of recent events in the town where I live. These are not ethnographic field notes; they are not part of a formal study. I relate them here because they left me convinced of the need to rethink "identity" and its "alternatives" (to borrow Lisa Lowe's word) in relation to possible renovation of the public sphere as a site of assembly, attentiveness, and political agency. Ultimately, I suggest that these other realms of citizenship should be taken seriously as sources of whatever will come after "identity." Part of that project involves acknowledging the extent to which identity fuses the temporality of the nation to the institutional practices of the state, making temporality a useful point of departure toward the larger question of how citizenship might figure in whatever democracy is becoming.

WON-JOON YOON, 1972–1999

On the Fourth of July, 1999, in Bloomington, Indiana, Won-Joon Yoon was murdered by gunshot as he walked across the lawn of the Korean Methodist Church on his way to Sunday morning worship. He was twenty-six. Born and raised in Seoul, Korea, he had been in Bloomington just a few weeks, awaiting the beginning of his first year in the doctoral program of the Economics Department at Indiana University. The church is across the street from the main campus. He was killed by Benjamin Smith, also an IU student, recently transferred from the University of Illinois. These young men were unknown to each other. Before the day was out, it was clear that Won-Joon Yoon had been killed by the same person who had killed Ricky Byrdsong in Skokie, Illinois, and wounded nine others in and around Chicago the day before. Smith kept his guns in the front seat of his car. His drive-by targets were African Americans, Asian Americans, Asians, and orthodox Jews—all men. After the attack on Third Street on Sunday morning, the police chased him down on a highway heading west; as they closed in, he killed himself. It turned out that his name and his links to hate groups were already known. The previous summer, he had leafleted cars and lawns in the neighborhoods near the university with racist tracts. These had inspired a collective response under the banner of a group called "Bloomington United," led by the campus ministries. Bloomington United led the community response once again in the aftermath of this killing. Eight days after Won-Joon Yoon's death, Bloomington residents gathered in the university's concert hall to pay their—our—respects to him "and all human beings who have been victims of crimes of hate" (Bloomington United 1999)—to pray, to promise solidarity with the victims and their families (his family was present), and to talk frankly about racism—some of it very close to home. The director of the Asian Cultural Center spoke of the local landscape and of students' "folklore of fear" as an invisible supplement to the local maps and guidebooks. The attorney general of the United States spoke; the president of the United States sent a message (via messenger). The mayor of Bloomington spoke. Most of the campus advocacy groups were represented on the dais; some of their representatives spoke. The ministers and rabbi who led Bloomington United spoke; so did the chancellor of the Bloomington campus. Won-Joon Yoon's cousin gave an elegy; and, unexpectedly, at the end, his father went to the stage, to recite from memory (in English) the Twenty-third Psalm. He performed it as an exhortation, arms raised high. At the center of the stage, the stone urn containing Won-Joon Yoon's ashes stood between two thick candles on a pedestal next to the podium; his picture—smiling—filled the background. At the end, the candles were taken away to light others, and a minister carried the urn to the head of what became a vast procession. There was a candlelight march; thousands of people—far more than the already many the hall could accommodate, far more than there were candles—filled the streets and walked the few blocks from the arts center to the church in silence. Over the meter of our footsteps, someone sang, alone, "We shall overcome." At the church, the lieutenant governor spoke; the minister offered prayers of rededication. Then everyone dispersed.

In the week between the killing and the community gathering, my impression was that there was not much talk of hope, and this made any talk difficult. Anything unrelated to the events, as we called the murder, felt like an obscene forgetting; yet to dwell on the shooting was to extend the violence. Mostly, the atmosphere was one of stillness. It was summer, and some of the silence could pass for tranquility, but for the small white cross planted on the church lawn that sprouted bouquets of flowers wrapped in cellophane and ribbon. Later—after the gathering—one could talk again, "we" having been reconstituted somewhere in the performance of the future tense, and in the present, in the concreteness of our collective presence. One could speak of Won-Joon Yoon again; one could not speak of him. There were other stories, some related to his; other testimonies; and eventually other subjects.

This is not a chronicle with a plot line; the salience of these events was not—is not—their sequence. If anything, the week between the killing and the gathering was an un-time. Still, the fact that *this* gathering was a response to *this* killing gave it the form of a resolution, a stage in a process *in time*—specifically, by virtue of the officials present on the platform, in the time of the nation. By this I mean that the event was legible—its form could be said to have an intended effect—in relation to the long national history that made combating race hatred a public commitment, expressed in part in the long history of antiracist struggle through federal law, and in idioms (prayers, songs, speeches, assemblies) with their own aesthetic, social, and political histories. The community gathering borrowed its forms from that long strand in the national story: its rhetorical framework came from the civil rights movement; the represented groups were advocacy groups that are the modern local legacy of federal civil rights enforcement. The gathering was not ours alone, therefore; it also belonged to all those other occasions. The march was not ours alone, or just for that night; it was also—as that lone singer reminded us—a road that had been built and traveled by others.

Inevitably, the rites heightened this sense of disparity between the constancy of civil rights struggle, the durability of the public sphere (the nation, the state, the town, and the university), and the brevity and individuality of Won-Joon Yoon's life. The public officials' messages were about law, law enforcement, and citizenship, among other things; but they—like everyone else—remembered to pronounce Won-Joon Yoon's name, and to imagine the direction of his lost life. No one made him "a victim"—he remained, always, a single person with a name, a face, faith, friends, and family. The president's message promised legislation (the Anti–Hate Crimes Act), but there was no canned hope in that promise or in any other address. If there was hope in the room, it did not flow from the podium, but from the fact of the assembly. To borrow Homi Bhabha's words from another context, the federal presence allowed us to imagine ourselves as a plebiscite, sharing some of our work of memory and redemption with (as) the nation, entering together into the risks of consolation:

> The anteriority of the nation, signified in the will to forget, entirely changes our understanding of the pastness of the past, and the synchronous present of the will to nationhood. We are in a discursive space similar to that moment of unisonance in [Benedict] Anderson's argument [in *Imagined Communities*] when the homogeneous empty time of the nation's "meanwhile" is cut across by the ghostly simultaneity of a temporality of doubling. To be obliged to forget—in the construction of the national present—is not a question of historical memory; it is the construction of a discourse on society that *performs* the problem of totalizing the people and unifying the national will. That strange time—forgetting to remember—is a place of "partial identification" inscribed in the daily plebiscite which represents the performative discourse of the people. (Bhabha 1994, 160–61)

But "the will to nationhood" does not "circulate in the same temporality as the desire of the daily plebiscite" (1994, 160). The nation we allowed into our choreography that night was—in the instant—at once a sharp yearning for contact (this stranger's life), a revitalizing irony (this death in this peaceful community), and a long glance outward (this nation among others). Sometimes, registering the incommensurable is called "consolation." Bhabha writes from another context but his words are apt here: "It is from this incommensurability in the midst of the everyday that the nation speaks its disjunctive narrative. From the margins of modernity, at the insurmountable extremes of storytelling, we encounter the question of cultural difference as the perplexity of living and writing the nation" (1994, 161).

What was the time of that night, when a candid confession of grief and mystery was more welcome than promises of security, and one could begin to contemplate without shame the sense of being comforted? What was the time of that night, when "the question of cultural difference as the perplexity of living and writing the nation" was so vivid? How shall that night be arranged alongside others?—what notions of identity and agency unfold from that night's complications?

NEITHER HISTORY NOR NATURE

"In the situation of radical world-alienation, neither history nor nature is at all conceivable," Hannah Arendt wrote (1968, 89). The context is "The Concept of History," her essay on action and meaning. Meaning, she observes, is never decided by action; it is settled afterwards, post hoc; agency is inevitably a retroactive assessment of causality—an artifact of the requirements of narrating causality (1968, 75–82, esp. 77; see also Bhabha 1994, 190). Bhabha refers to this "break" between the "development" of history and "historical discourse" as a "time-lag—the temporal break in representation" (1994, 191); however, it is important to specify that Arendt does not encompass agency altogether in her critique of "making history" (her evocation of Marx), but only the necessity of a connection between agency and history in the Marxian sense. This opens the possibility of other histories, other temporalities.

In *The Human Condition*, Arendt (1998, 175–247) specifies a variety of conditions under which agency and history might be either connected or disjoint. Agency is contingent on the political sphere, and Arendt enumerates specific conditions of access, audience, and acknowledgment. Agency is no synonym for individuality or action in the conventional sense of deeds, then; it rather rests on the fact of what Arendt consistently calls "plurality" (see 1998, 176). She evokes these conditions as the essence of freedom—a freedom so available, and so valuable, that she compares it to "a second birth":

> With word and deed we insert ourselves into the human world, and this insertion is like a second birth, in which we confirm and take upon our-

> selves the naked fact of our original physical appearance. . . . Its impulse springs from the beginning which came into the world when we were born and to which we respond by beginning something new on our own initiative. (1998, 176–77)

But when the conditions of agency—self-disclosure in one's public speech and acts—are not met, when the agent has no name, Arendt sees instead the makings of a second death:

> Without the disclosure of the agent in the act, action loses its specific character and becomes one form of achievement among others. It is then indeed no less a means to an end than making is a means to produce an object. This happens whenever human togetherness is lost, that is, when people are only for or against other people, as for instance in modern warfare. . . . Action without a name, a "who" attached to it, is meaningless, whereas an art work retains its relevance whether or not we know the master's name. The monuments to the "Unknown Soldier" after World War I bear testimony to the then still existing need for glorification, for finding a "who," an identifiable somebody whom four years of mass slaughter should have revealed. The frustration of this wish and the unwillingness to resign oneself to the brutal fact that the agent of the war was actually nobody inspired the erection of the monuments to the "unknown," to all those whom the war had failed to make known and had robbed thereby, not of their achievement, but of their human dignity. (1998, 180–81)

Perhaps because Arendt herself uses a single lifetime as synecdoche in her argument, Bhabha (1994) refers to the "temporal break in representation." However, it is important to note that the temporality with which Arendt contemplates agency and personal vulnerability to social erasure is not unidirectional (as representation necessarily is). One cannot "make history," nor can one make oneself, she argues, but under some circumstances one can reveal oneself (to oneself and others)—or under other circumstances be subject to violent erasure from the collective memory. There is an enduring dignity for an artist in an unsigned work of art because it remains art, she asserts, in a way that nameless war dead are lost utterly, more than dead (Arendt 1998, 180). In context, through this assertion she performs a calculated reversal of the conventional weighting of actions over words, weapons over flesh.

There is temporality in agency in this sense, to the extent that agency originates in the bond between speaker and listeners, in the attention of audiences, in the durability of beauty, in personal and collective memory, and in the meaning post hoc narrative accords to an individual. Temporality inheres in the generative split between action and agency—that is, between an act and its meaning—but not because these are in some sense sequential. Rather, they are the experiential dimensions of relevance. Everywhere, officializations of time bridge and conceal the temporalities inherent in agency and its varieties (Greenhouse 1996). And temporality can be extinguished by violence (Arendt 1998, 180–81, and see also 50–51).

For Arendt, the temporality in agency begins in speech and acts recognizably one's own, but it does not end there. Arendt makes time the narrative conjunction of personal expression and public acknowledgment—but the name she gives this conjuncture is "identity": "The unchangeable identity of the person, though disclosing itself intangibly in act and speech, becomes tangible only in the story of the actor's and speaker's life; but as such it can be known, that is, grasped as a palpable entity only after it has come to its end" (1998, 193). Identity is contingent on the assessments and acknowledgments of others; in this sense, identity is the active principle of agency. One does not "make" the meaning of one's own life (1998, 193–94), except in the individualist's delusions.[1]

Arendt's discussion dwells on ideals she associates with classical Greece, but it is not a study of Greece. Her classical references serve primarily as tropes with which to substantiate her evocation of modern disenchantments, to mark them as modern. Thus, when she states that the space of the polis was defined by laws, she is asserting the failure of modern law to provide safety: "To them, the laws, like the wall around the city, were not the results of action [agency in the sense just described] but products of making. Before men began to act, a definite space had to be secured and a structure built where all subsequent actions could take place, the space being the public realm of the *polis* and its structure the law; legislator and architect belonged in the same category" (Arendt 1998, 194–95). Within the space of the law, agency, identity, and politics form a single constellation of possibilities; they are—for Arendt—different modalities of a potentiating and always plural humanity, confirming them as the essence and empirical reality of *time*. Arendt's dream of time is a particular dream of citizenship.

For Arendt, humanity's "plurality" is the precondition of political life within the nation. Reflecting on a related question, Bhabha suggests that "nationness" is to be found in the emergence and negotiation of "interstices—the overlap and displacement of domains of difference" (1994, 2). Arendt, too, places citizenship at the core of her reflections on identity and agency, in that the polis was restricted to citizens. What interests me in these formulations is the concreteness, or sitedness, of citizenship—as being not first or immediately a location in the symbolic order of the nation-state, but a nexus of communication in specific contexts.

The community service for Won-Joon Yoon was officially called "a community gathering to heal and unite." The nineteen speakers that night, speaking of Won-Joon Yoon, offered no consolation in the form of references to his achievements, or to the ennobling resonances of his short life in the archive of time. Instead, the night unfolded around the repetition of his name, the picture of his handsome smiling face, his very material absence (his ashes, his eyeglasses, his Bible, his family and friends). The meaning of his life—his family and friends will know. The meaning of his death became the public charge that night; it was the concreteness of that charge, and the reality of our chosen and overlapping associations, that allowed one to think the future from that moment, and to speak plausibly of beginnings.

NARRATION AND THE NATION

Historian Mary Ryan draws on Arendt's writing on citizenship to specify cities and public life as "the empirical center of the history of democracy peculiar to the United States" (Ryan 1997, 8)—a discovery for which she gives credit to Alexis de Tocqueville. For Tocqueville, the fact of an empirical federal center within the abstraction of the federal system made very tangible a set of contradictions and risks in U.S. democracy, and today those remain relevant to the problematic search for a temporality appropriate to contemporary struggles for justice. Arendt turns often to Tocqueville, largely for his analysis of the American Revolution and the character of U.S. democracy. *Democracy in America* is both specific and concrete in terms quite parallel to Arendt's sketches of the polis—but it is also different in at least three ways that are relevant to this discussion. First, Tocqueville portrays Americans as individualists. Second, their sphere of meaning making is not the political sphere alone, but also the market—to which the political sphere is thereby fused. And third, Tocqueville is concerned with the limits of U.S. democracy, specifically as revealed by the condition of Indians and slaves. These three issues are related, but it is especially the last of these that is important to the present discussion.

Importantly, individualism arises in Tocqueville's analysis as an attitude, an orientation, an identification with society, predicated on state citizenship.[2] It is an identification of the self with the state—not membership as such. Thus, citizenship is much more than a legal status—and even more than eligibility to participate in the polis as an equal. But the association of self and state brings into proximity two incomparable subjects, representing them as if they were two elements of a single entity distinguishable mainly by their obvious differences of scale. Importantly, this representation of scale can be misleading. Further, the association of incommensurate subjects obviates a demography of the empirical nation; the personal association of self and state and the symbolic and material work required to sustain it as an identity relation *are* "the nation." In other words, "the nation" in this sense is not hyphenated to the state, but—from an empirical standpoint—to the self.

Individualism gives citizenship a person's face and form, and perhaps it seems obvious that citizenship should be figured in this way. But this is a figuration, an image—not demography. Citizenship becomes empirical—if it does become empirical—through the claims of actual persons from within their self-identity as citizens: what they ask the state's agents to do for them, or what they demand from the state so that they can act on their own or others' behalf.[3] This empirical dimension of citizenship makes citizenship crucial to survival under some circumstances, or to mobility, or simply satisfaction, even pleasure. Legal citizenship (the symbolic order of the citizen from the state's side) does not account for the significance of citizenship as a crucial dimension of personal experience. Those realms of significance take the state into spheres of activity far beyond its own jurisdictions, technically speaking, in the lives of individuals and the collective purposes of groups.

As a topic for social theory, discussion of citizenship tends to focus on the state's according of rights to citizens as a matter of law (e.g., Kymlicka 1995; Toniatti 1995; Turner 1993; Yeates 1996) and on acknowledgments, through citizenship, of particularities within national identity conceptualized in collective terms (van Steenbergen 1994; Shapiro and Kymlicka 1997; and Habermas 1995). Tocqueville's discussion of individualism is fascinating and relevant today because he begins the question of citizenship on the *other side* of that legal relation, that is, at the point where an actual person embraces the "artificial person" (Marx 1975 [1843]: 98) created by the state as his or her personal warrant. Not everyone can do this. Furthermore, viewed from that "other side" citizenship turns out to be a different relation altogether. In theory, citizenship confirms an individual's relevance in (and to) the state through rights and duties; however, in practice, it is first and foremost a form of charisma.[4]

Citizenship is two-sided, then, and its two sides are inevitably incommensurable. Concretely, the state's legal regulation of society derives from something other than the individualist's identification with the state through his or her personal actions; the one involves effective bureaucratic measures (including persuasion and coercion), while the other involves private needs and wants and subjective worlds of meaning.[5] This means that there is an ethnographic question to be asked about citizenship, regarding whether and how people incorporate the state into their own self-understandings and agency.

Recent ethnographic studies in the United States offer numerous examples of people's needs for and uses of citizenship to forge bonds *through* the state, or *in front of* the state, but not necessarily *to* the state. These studies confirm the multisitedness and fluidity of empirical citizenship, as the following examples illustrate.

In *Black Corona*, Steven Gregory (1998) considers grassroots activism in a neighborhood of New York City that borders La Guardia Airport. Part of the book details a property dispute between local residents and a variety of public and private entities associated with the development of the airport. The neighbors—mostly African Americans—organize to oppose the airport's expansion into their community. As citizens and under so-called "sunshine laws" that guarantee public access to certain government proceedings, they have the right to receive information about, observe, and participate in the decision-making processes that affect their property; however, they also face procedural obstacles, in part because the agencies involved are not exclusively public—they also include corporations. The residents' effort borrows something of its organization and rights discourse from the civil rights movements of the 1950s and 1960s—which focused on legal rights precisely because constitutional doctrines of citizenship provided a basis for remedies where the private sector would not. Their mobilization highlights the extent to which the expansion of the private sector displaces some of the arenas, but not the substance, of citizen action.

Susan Coutin's ethnographic work with Salvadorans in the United States illustrates other dimensions of the substance of citizenship (Coutin 1999, 2000, 2001). Salvadorans who escape from terror in their home country and arrive in the United States without papers must present themselves to officials of the United States Immigration and Naturalization Service to apply for refugee status. They have the right to an interview at which they are allowed to present evidence of personal danger at home. Refugee status is an individual status, however, and they must be able to prove that they were personally threatened; it is not enough to show that one's closest friends disappeared in the night (Coutin 2001). Refugee status, like citizenship status (Coutin 1999), allows individuals to recover their social bonds and—literally and figuratively—to rejoin their community in El Salvador and in the United States.

Aihwa Ong's (1999) study of "flexible citizenship" includes many examples of contemporary reworkings of citizenship as a modality of transnationalism. One vignette involves a woman from Hong Kong who has made a large fortune as a transnational developer and who purchased a home in an elite neighborhood of San Francisco. When she began architectural modifications that would have added a third story to her house, her neighbors objected, addressing their objections—as is their right as citizens—to the city zoning board. At first, their objections were on the grounds that the higher elevation of the modified roof line would block the scenic vista from their own properties. But tensions flared when one of her neighbors said publicly: "We don't want another Chinatown here." Eventually, city officials apologized to the homeowner, but—enraged—she donated her house to the homeless of San Francisco with the stipulation that no Chinese should be sheltered there—a double insult to her neighbors since there are no Chinese among San Francisco's homeless population (Ong 1999, 102–3).

Barbara Yngvesson (1997) writes about adoption, including a moving account of her personal experience that she presents among other testimonies gathered in interviews. She describes how she and her husband, living in Massachusetts, learned of a woman in California—the birth mother of their younger son, Finn—anxious to place the baby with an adoptive family. The birth mother wanted to bring her baby to the couple personally. This poses both cultural and legal problems, since while the culture puts motherhood beyond the law, adoption requires state action—it cannot be private. Accordingly, Massachusetts law prohibits the direct transfer of a child from birth parents to adoptive parents. The plan for the process in this case involved separate rooms, in which each family would be represented by a lawyer who would pass the baby between them, taking him from his birth parents and placing him in the arms of his adoptive parents. But when the time came, they arranged to be together in a "complex ceremony of severance and joining" (1997, 35) that they improvised to respond to the legalities involved but also to suit their own sense of the occasion. Thus, "the legal moment that was to separate Finn 'irrevocably' from his mother and join him . . . to us . . . became inseparable from an 'illegal moment,' an outlaw time in which we violated Massachusetts adoption law, agreeing that this was not only a transaction between a birthmother and the state, and between potential adoptive parents and the state, but that it was also, in Finn's birthfather's words, a 'parent-to-parent matter' " (1997, 35). In the event, the bonds of citizenship were appropriated—as the substance of ceremony—by the parents and the others present, and reformulated as enduring connections between the Yngvessons and their younger son's birth parents.

These are just moments from much longer stories, and there are many more such stories—of collective action, individual survival, "transnational belonging" (Susan Coutin's phrase), and family life. I choose these because they give some sense of the way "citizenship" juxtaposes domains of life that are ordinarily imagined as separate, differentiated by scale, location, or interest. My main point is that citizenship is not merely the architecture of the state or an abstract sense of belonging to a nation, but a medium—more accurately, a range of media—of social action and active social connection. I make this point cautiously and provisionally with the United States in mind—since law has long doubled as an everyday language among the American middle class (see Bowman and Mertz 1996; Engel and Munger 1996; Ewick and Silbey 1998; Greenhouse 1986; Greenhouse, Yngvesson and Engel 1994; Kourilsky-Augeven 1997; Merry 1990; Yngvesson 1993). But it would seem that citizenship is as much a matter of "the loci of the heart" as it is of law.[6] These two "faces" of citizenship do not necessarily mirror each other, making it all the more important to understand how individuals' needs for citizenship stem from their desires (tangible and intangible) and their personal sense of responsibility and dignity in their relations with other people, as well as how these are (or are not) recognized by the state through citizenship.

While the public discourse of citizenship emphasizes membership and belonging to a nation, empirical citizenship is about belonging or not belonging in one's own life. The public discourse (including academic discourse) stresses that citizenship is a vital cultural literacy for individual men and women whose status as consumers or creditors, employees or employers, and taxpayers, among other things, devolves from their rights as citizens. This is arguably true. But empirical citizenship also reveals the centrality of citizenship to living one's chosen ties to others. Perhaps the most striking ethnographic finding in this area is the extent to which people call on citizenship for more collective purposes. Referring once again to the examples cited earlier: Modern immigrants want citizenship precisely so that they can have the freedom to visit home. Reuniting families, or nurturing adoptive families, often means adjustments to citizenship. Ethnographic studies of citizenship suggest that in practice citizenship is deeply important to people; however, its importance is felt in terms quite other than the symbolic order implied in the public discourse. In practice, citizenship is less about the exclusive sense of belonging to a particular state than it is about securing the autonomy necessary for maintaining multiple commitments, sometimes in multiple locations—as if the world were without borders and citizenship were the key to mobility.

These examples (and others we might consider) suggest that while the state treats citizens as units in an administrative arithmetic, the person's embrace of citizenship as his or her own involves an entirely different set of issues—potentially not referring to administration and by no means necessarily limited to or contained by the nation-state. The citizen looks not so much up to the state as inward, and outward, to other people. The image of the self as citizen makes the state integral to the constitution of the person and draws the idea of legality directly into the personal subjective realm—as desire, pleasure, pride, pragmatism, fear, shame, and terror (among other possibilities) in a host of public and private settings. As William Maurer writes: "We cannot view the kinds of individual persons constructed in modern worlds as separate from the kinds of states they inhabit and construct, and which at the same time inhabit and construct their personhood" (1998, 6). Quite apart from what citizenship means in the legal and political *organization* of the state, then, citizenship makes a place—albeit a highly ambiguous place—for the state in the subjective and emotional lives of ordinary people, in relation to the question of who they are to themselves and to others. Individualism, as drawn by Tocqueville, encompasses this contradictory gap at the center of citizenship; I believe this is why Tocqueville refers to individualism as a defect of reason.[7] An individualist is always simultaneously inside and outside the community, simultaneously performing for it and judging the performances as part of the audience.[8] Empirical citizenship, then, originates in both the discourse of rights and the reality of desire (purposive action in the broadest possible sense), suffusing the one with the other, surpassing the time and terrain of the nation.

CONDITIONS AND CONTRADICTIONS

In the state's mythic space of contradiction, law and life of necessity include some element of fantasy with respect to each other (Žižek 1996a, 112–18). In citizenship's "space of symbolization" (borrowing Žižek's phrase again) desire—which I mean here as a broad reference to conscious needs and wants—maintains a vital and revitalizing link between the symbolic form of the citizen and the empirical reality of the person, and locates that connection centrally within the empirical individual (Dolar 1996, 27). I draw on the language of psychoanalysis here, since it lends itself to the task of exploring how the incommensurabilities within citizenship yield problems of narrative; however, this is not a psychoanalytic argument about individuals. It is an argument about the capacity of a powerful public discourse to obscure its contradictions, limits, and alternatives—with consequent challenges to personal and collective experience. Arendt, more concerned with the equality of members of the polis than with its criteria of membership, seems not to have considered that the desire for membership is also a potent form of desire—or that desire (for equality, for example) is a form of agency not necessarily enabled by the law's sheltering walls.[9] In the aftermath of enforced school integration in Little Rock, Arkansas, for example, she wrote critically of the Supreme Court's intervention in what she regarded as a private area of concern (children's education).

Tocqueville understood well the contradictions and concreteness of desire within the frameworks of citizenship: the production and consumption of wealth, as literal investments of physical energy, are important themes of his study. In *Democracy in America*, it is not the analysis of individualism that carries the burden of his argument, but his chapter linking the subjects of racism, commerce, and federalism.[10] Tocqueville presents the reality of enslavement and the illusory freedom of Indians living outside the American democracy as social realities arising from the specific political conflicts over federalism in the United States.

Importantly, these margins are not just at the nation's borders, though as recent ethnography in the United States has made clear, the national borders figure importantly in the symbolic orders of citizenship (Chock 1998; Coutin 2000; Urciuoli 1999). Today, well inside those borders, the practical realities of federalism remain integrally tied to the social judgments and allocations of resources that make inner cities frontiers as well (Davis 1992, chap. 5; Greenhouse 1998; Herbert 1997). No less than in Tocqueville's times, perhaps, the modern cross-currents of federalism and globalization are integral to social status and social judgment. The tensions between states and the federal government continue to be integral to the pragmatics of citizenship today, and similarly occasion deep emotion—for example, in public debates over immigration and welfare, over abortion, or (in an earlier period) over integration, or (even earlier) over abolition and "Indian removal."

"The nation" of the United States is not any one model of federalism, but all such possibilities together with whatever is at stake in the differences among them. From an empirical standpoint, therefore, the nation cannot contain difference (as the public discourse claims), but only the opposite—it can only confirm its own incompleteness. This is the context in which empirical citizenship's openness beyond the nation is significant. For example, from this standpoint—as in the community gathering—it is possible to imagine a citizenship that would suspend the difference between national and foreign (and for this reason I think it is unlikely that "identity" would be the keyword of that movement).

CONCLUSION

I began by suggesting that the modern usage of "identity" is precoded with the specific struggles and aspirations for social justice in the United States. It is a distinctly twentieth-century term, fusing political and psychological frameworks of association, and situating these squarely within a liberal pluralist framework. In the twenty-first century, these fusions and situations are unsettled by the very uses people have made of their citizenship within and across borders. This is the context in which I suggest that while the symbolic (and legal) order of citizenship might seem to be about categories and conditions of membership, "empirical citizenship" (as I have termed it in this essay) entails a much broader and more flexible register of agency, purpose, and partnership. In referring to "empirical citizenship," my purpose is not to contrast a "believed in" world to the world of practice, or to claim a particular American attitude toward citizenship. Rather, it is to suggest that temporality—the very relation of past, present, and future—is implicated in democracy's future, as citizenship reveals—always partially—the manifold agencies and identifications people bring to or take away from neoliberalism's shape-shifting the public sphere.

In this essay, my experiment has been to reconfigure some key terms of social analysis—identity, agency, citizenship—as temporalities rather than structural positions, for the sake of widening our grasp (as ethnographers and socio-legal scholars) of the contemporary scenarios where states are being refashioned. By virtue of their empirical character, Arendt's key terms—identity and agency—lent themselves well to this project, although her reflections on the polis stop short of questions of membership and inclusiveness. Accordingly, I turned to one of her own key sources—Tocqueville's analysis of American democracy. Tocqueville's analysis is also highly empirical, in its fashion, and more alert to contradiction as an animating aspect of personal and political experience. His analysis of individualism, and even more so his reflections on democracy's risks and federal frailties, led me to consider citizenship in the United States as a highly subjective and intrinsically fragmenting—but also empirical—association of self and state. The dimensions and consequences of that association tend to be taken for granted in American public discourse (including much scholarship). This means that the specificities of the U.S. state have not registered as ethnographic objects. Specifically, and more importantly, it has meant that difference is readily mistaken for a question of demography, rather than as a question of how anyone's political subject position is constituted in relation to the state. From this perspective, the presence of state officials was not simply the luster of that July night, but part of a collective effort on the part of several thousand people to claim for themselves the preconditions of political agency by bearing witness to each other's presence in a sphere marked as public, political, and even historic by the presence of those officials. And from this perspective, it does not matter that we do not know what the sequels of that gathering may turn out to be, or where we should look for them, or when. Not knowing now poses no immediate limit to the possibilities; instead it points to the timeliness of addressing ourselves to the task of reassessing the conventional usages of certain terms in the lexicon of social analysis: citizen, nation, and power (among others). Along these lines, what matters especially is some reconceptualization of temporality and agency so that we can be prepared to recognize what time this will turn out to have been.[11]

To conclude more concretely, and to answer a question some readers may have in mind: yes, this would have been a different essay if that summer had been different. Writing about identity, the essay I began before those events would have been more one-sided, focused on the ways biopower and desire reproduce the historical conditions by which the state can be turned to particular purposes. That would have left "identity" more or less constant, as an analytic rubric of need or interest—in relation to income disparities, for example, together with the criminalization of the poor and nonwhite, and an ominous politics of the body and national borders. The shape of whatever those reflections might have been had to shift when I realized that I could not write that without seeming to have undertaken an explanation of Won-Joon Yoon's killing. My effort instead has been to acknowledge both the outrage of his death and the mysterious power of public assembly to concretize the possibility of positive change, while rejecting—please—a temporality that would compel one to conclude that he died *for us.*

NOTES

1 Arendt's conditions are stringent, especially in contrast to the more usual social science formulation of agency influenced by Anthony Giddens, for whom agency is purposive action as well as the intended or unintended effects of people's acts (Giddens 1979, chap. 2). Perhaps because of its universalism, Giddens's formulation of agency is the more familiar one in the human sciences today (see, e.g., Castells 1997, 6–12). Arendt's usage is more demanding in terms of its preconditions; it is strikingly narrow in its specific reference to a concrete political sphere (Arendt 1998, chap. 2, esp. 22–28)—to emphasize that the conditions for agency are met only where (she might say "when"—it is a temporal issue) there is a public commitment to making political institutions available and responsive to the self-disclosing expressions of individuals (see also Arendt 1965, 32; and Williams 1997).

2 *Democracy in America* is a study of democratic myths and contradictions, and the book is organized in precisely this way. Volume 1 is about federal and local institutional structures: the Constitution, the mechanics of democratic government, and the institutions of everyday public life, including political life. These are mythic structures—that is, a social and political grammar with real effects and stakes. Volume 2 is about the implications of democracy for daily life—ordinary people's efforts to make their democracy into a matter of daily living, the subjective side of democracy for individuals, families, communities, and the nation.

It is in volume 2 that Tocqueville uses his invented word, "individualism," for the sake of describing the liberal subjectivity he associates with modern democracies (1945, 2.2.104; see also 1.iv n. 1).

3 Marx's critique of Hegel's Doctrine of the State emphasizes the difference between these two existences (Marx 1975 [1843], 98–99) that individualism merges.

4 The implication of individualism as Tocqueville defines it (and as contemporary ethnographers have rediscovered it—see especially Varenne 1977 and 1986) is that American citizenship redistributes a charismatic identification of self and state borrowed from kingship. Individualism rests on the presumption of citizenship (i.e., kingship) by birth, thereby providing the symbolic tools for fashioning state authority as if it were natural and unmediated (see Marx 1975 [1843], 99). As Iris Marion Young observes, a distinction between the individual and the universal is itself universalizing (Young 1995; see also Laclau 1996). This absent mediation (of the already universal) is the object of Tocqueville's evident fascination with the American view that political authority should be based on public opinion (1945, 1.409–10). Both of these symbolic messages—reallocating sovereignty to individuals, and making state authority "real" (in a symbolic sense) by deriving it without mediation from "the people"—remain important to any plausible reading of the contemporary political landscape of the United States.

5 On the inevitability that political identities involve a symbolic "gap," see Laclau and Zac 1994. Laclau and Zac view the problem of incommensurability as arising from "the originary split constitutive of all representation" (1994, 15). My own interest is in the nonreciprocity of identities within the American state, i.e., a specific political gap, rather than a generic symbolic gap. See also Laclau's discussion (1996, esp. 46–52) of the universal and the particular.

6 I borrow this phrase from Elizabeth Mertz's "Legal Loci and Places in the Heart" (1994).

7 Bhabha (1994, 163) also notes the transgressive aspect of a concept of difference that cannot "add up," but only "add to."

8 The tensions arising from this hypersubstitutability of citizenship's subject and object can expand to any scale without altering its basic form: in the midwestern town he called Appleton, Varenne found that individualism "works" among friends and within households, voluntary asso-

ciations, civic organizations, churches, and municipal government (Varenne 1977 and 1984). He explored numerous situations in which people regard (and act on) their own individuality in generic terms, "embracing freely an imposed state of things" (to borrow Žižek's phrase again)—for example, committing themselves to life choices from the more or less fixed menus they associate with social roles (as daughter, wife, friend, and so forth; see also Greenhouse 1986). This makes the community—as a perceived social space—predominantly "horizontal" (Varenne 1977, 150–59; see also Bhabha 1994, 141), as if it were a sum of parts fitted together, individuals into their types within an overall division of labor (in the broad Durkheimian sense), and (I would add) within an open-ended social geography that can be either literal or figurative. But this horizontality—the "fused horizon" to which Bhabha (1998) refers critically as a misreading of multiculturality (see Taylor 1994). It is not, in fact, immediately or automatically a charter for pluralism; I will return to this point later.

9 In the aftermath of enforced school integration in Little Rock, Arkansas, she wrote critically of the U.S. Supreme Court's intervention in what she regarded as a private area of concern (children's education):

> The American Republic is based on the equality of all citizens, and while equality before the law has become an inalienable principle of all modern constitutional government, equality as such is of greater importance in the political life of a republic than in any other form of government. The point at stake, therefore, is not the well-being of the Negro population alone, but, at least in the long run, the survival of the Republic. (Arendt 1959, 47)

In this same passage, she reflects on Tocqueville's assessment of the discursive centrality of equality in the American politics he knew:

> Tocqueville saw over a century ago that equality of opportunity and condition, as well as equality of rights, constituted the basic "law" of American democracy, and he predicted that the dilemmas and perplexities inherent in the principle of equality might one day become the most dangerous challenge to the American way of life. In its all-comprehensive, typically American form, equality possesses an enormous power to equalize what by nature and origin is different—and it is only due to this power that the country has been able to retain its fundamental identity against the waves of immigrants who have always flooded its shores. But the principle of equality, even in its American form, is not omnipotent. . . . (Arendt 1959, 47–48)

10 Indeed, if there is a fulcrum to *Democracy in America*, where it might be said that all preceding is introduction and all following is development, it is the final chapter of the first volume, at the literal middle of the work. The chapter, titled "The Present and Probable Future Condition of the Three Races that Inhabit the Territory of the United States," contains more than 25 percent of the pages of the first volume. Structurally, too, it links the two halves of the work—the first volume on institutions, the second volume on democratic myths and experiences—with an analysis of the relationship among the themes of race, commerce, and federalism.

Importantly, in Tocqueville's analysis, individualism (as a social structure built around self-interest within a national space) endows commodities and material desires with nationalist meaning, making these into elements of the experiential machinery of federal power and providing federal power with some of its extraordinary flexibility and concreteness. In experiential terms, as Tocqueville goes on to suggest, the federal movement takes capital as its engine, the body as its vehicle, "community reason" as its cargo (1945, 1.409); its sites of exchange encode the country's celebrated surfaces (Baudrillard 1988) with hidden presences and lines of jurisdiction. The mobility of capital and the individual body answer to the fundamental ambiguity of federalism—that is, the ambiguity of sovereignty (as between the federal government and states). It is interesting to register Tocqueville's absorption in the fact that the *constitutional* ambiguities of federalism define a *subjective* problem for individuals—and a subjective problem that demands personal resolution. Specifically, Tocqueville sees the subjective crisis of federalism as a split in every citizen's identity, making moot the ordinary distinction between "here" and "there." Commerce restores the dimensions of time and space to the nation where federalism complicates them or seems to cancel them outright. Indeed, commerce, from Tocqueville's point of view, seems to provide the means for a resolution to the subjective crisis of federalism. Importantly, he regards commerce not just as a means of accumulating capital, but also as a means of concretizing the self—that is, the mobility and energy of the empirical person—within the state. The nation has empirical meaning within the framework Tocqueville maps out only to the extent that commerce—like a royal progress—traverses its territory on the legs and backs of its citizens. By their expenditures of energy, they fill in that territory, making it and its boundaries real.

"The Condition of the Three Races" is Tocqueville's description of U.S. democracy's most telling contradiction and an object lesson in its most profound risks. Tocqueville shows us what lies beyond inclusion and exclusion, beyond the state's mobile boundary, mobilized by difference. But the margins are made at the center. Importantly, Tocqueville considers "the three races" as three distinct and interrelated political *situations* (see Berlant 1991).

Then (and now), federalism was in a state of dynamic tension between states' rights and a strong federal government. Tocqueville rues what he regards as Andrew Jackson's tactics for strengthening the central government at the expense of federalism by offering special privileges to the strong states' rights states (1945, 1.431–32). He is not explicit, but we might imagine that the privileges Tocqueville had in mind included the expulsion of the Creeks and Cherokees from Georgia and concessions to slave-holding states. The stronger the central government, the greater the resistance, pressing not inward toward the center but outward against these margins; thus, there was a practical politics that extended the precariousness of the federal government to the situation of Indians and slaves. But crucially, Tocqueville's discussion of Indians and slaves focuses not on the sole fact that they are outside the democracy, but that they were pushed outside by democratic means.

11 All of these questions occasioned lively debate at the conference—with special thanks to Jon Simon, Robert Gordon, Marianne Constable, and Marc Poirier.

REFERENCES

Arendt, Hannah. 1959. "Reflections on Little Rock," 6 *Dissent* no. 1, 45–56.

———. 1965. *On Revolution*. New York: Viking Press.

———. 1968. *Men in Dark Times*. New York: Harcourt, Brace and World.

———. 1977. *Between Past and Future*. Enlarged ed. Harmondsworth, U.K.: Penguin.

———. 1998. *The Human Condition*. 2d ed. Chicago: University of Chicago Press.

Baudrillard, Jean. 1988. America. Trans. Chris Turner. London: Verso.

Berlant, Lauren. 1991. "National Brands/National Body: *Imitation of Life*." In *Comparative American Identities: Race, Sex and Nationality in the Modern Text*, ed. H. Spillers, 110–40. New York: Routledge.

Bhabha, Homi. 1994. *The Location of Culture*. New York: Routledge.

———. 1998. "Anxiety in the Midst of Difference," 21 *Political and Legal Anthropology Review* no. 1, 123–37.

Bloomington United. 1999. A Community Gathering to Heal and Unite (Program). July 12, 1999, Bloomington, Indiana. On file with author.

Bowman, Cynthia Grant, and Elizabeth Mertz. 1996. "A Dangerous Direction: Legal Intervention in Sexual Abuse Survivor Therapy," 109 *Harvard Law Review* no. 3, 551–639.

Brah, Avtar. 1996. *Cartographies of Diaspora: Contesting Identities*. London: Routledge.

Canovan, Margaret. 1998. "Introduction." In Hannah Arendt, *The Human Condition*, 2d ed., vii–xx. Chicago: University of Chicago Press.

Castells, Manuel. 1997. *The Information Age: Economy, Society and Culture,* vol. 2: *The Power of Identity*. Oxford: Blackwell Publishers.

Chandler, Nahum. 1996. "The Economy of Desedimentation: W.E.B. DuBois and the discourses of the Negro," 19 *Callaloo* no. 1, 78–93.

Chock, Phyllis. 1991. "The Irony of Stereotypes: Towards an Anthropology of Ethnicity," 2 *Cultural Anthropology* 347–68.

———. 1998. "Porous Borders: Discourses of Difference in Congressional Hearings on Immigration." In *Democracy and Ethnography: Constructing Identities in Multicultural Liberal States,* ed. C. Greenhouse, 143–62. Albany: State University of New York Press.

Comaroff, Jean, and John L. Comaroff. 1991. *Of Revelation and Revolution, vol. 1: Christianity, Colonialism, and Consciousness in South Africa*. Chicago: University of Chicago Press.

———. 1997. *Of Revelation and Revolution, vol. 2: The Dialectics of Modernity on a South African Frontier*. Chicago: University of Chicago Press.

Comaroff, John L. 1996. "Ethnicity, Nationalism, and the Politics of Difference in an Age of Revolution." In *The Politics of Difference: Ethnic Premises in a World of Power*, ed. E. Wilmsen and P. McAllister, 162–83. Chicago: University of Chicago Press.

Comaroff, John L., and Jean Comaroff. 1992. *Ethnography and the Historical Imagination*. Boulder, Colo.: Westview Press.

———. 1999. "Introduction." In *Civil Society and the Political Imagination in Africa,* ed. John Comaroff and Jean Comaroff, 1–43. Chicago: University of Chicago Press.

Coutin, Susan. 1999. "Citizenship and Clandestinity among Salvadoran Immigrants," 22 *Political and Legal Anthropology Review* no. 2, 53–63.

———. 2000. *Legalizing Moves: Salvadoran Immigrants' Struggle for U.S. Residency.* Ann Arbor: University of Michigan Press.

———. 2001. "The Oppressed, the Suspect, and the Citizen: Subjectivity in Competing Accounts of Political Violence," 26 *Law and Social Inquiry* no. 1, 63–94.

Davis, Mike. 1992. *City of Quartz*. New York: Vintage Books.

Dolar, Mladen. 1996. "The Object Voice." In *Gaze and Voice as Love Objects*, ed. R. Salecl and S. Žižek, 7–31. Durham, N.C.: Duke University Press.

Du Bois, W.E.B. 1990 [1903]. *The Souls of Black Folk*. New York: Vintage Books.

Engel, David, and Frank Munger. 1996. "Rights, Remembrance, and the Reconciliation of Difference." 30 *Law & Society Review* no. 1, 7–53.

Ewick, Patricia, and Susan Silbey. 1998. *The Common Place of Law*. Chicago: University of Chicago Press.

Fanon, Frantz. 1986. *Black Skin, White Masks*. London: Pluto.

Giddens, Anthony. 1979. *Central Problems in Social Theory: Action, Structure and Contradiction in Social Analysis*. Berkeley: University of California Press.

Greenhouse, Carol J. 1986. *Praying for Justice: Faith, Order and Community in an American Town*. Ithaca, N.Y.: Cornell University Press.

———. 1996. *A Moment's Notice: Time Politics across Cultures*. Ithaca, N.Y.: Cornell University Press.

———. 1998. "Figuring the Future: Temporality and Agency in Ethnographic Problems of Scale." In *Power and Justice in Sociolegal Studies,* ed. A. Sarat and B. Garth, 108–35. Evanston, Ill.: Northwestern University Press and American Bar Foundation.

Greenhouse, Carol, and Davydd J. Greenwood. 1998. "Introduction: The Ethnography of Democracy and Difference." In *Democracy and Ethnography: Constructing Identities in Multicultural Liberal States*, ed. C. Greenhouse, 1–24. Albany: SUNY Press.

Greenhouse, Carol, Barbara Yngvesson, and David Engel. 1994. *Law and Community in Three American Towns*. Ithaca, N.Y.: Cornell University Press.

Gregory, Steven. 1998. *Black Corona: Race and the Politics of Place in an Urban Community*. Princeton, N.J.: Princeton University Press.

Gupta, Akhil, and James Ferguson. 1997. "Discipline and Practice: 'The Field' as Site, Method, and Location in Anthropology." In *Anthropological Locations: Boundaries and Grounds of a Field Science,* ed. A. Gupta and J. Ferguson, 1–46. Berkeley: University of California Press.

Habermas, Jürgen. 1995. "Citizenship and National Identity: Some Reflections in the Future of Europe." In *Theorizing Citizenship*, ed. R. Beiner, 255–81. Albany: SUNY Press.

Herbert, Steve. 1997. *Policing Space*. Minneapolis: University of Minnesota Press.

Kourilsky-Augeven, Chantal, ed. 1997. *Socialisation juridique et conscience de droit*. Paris: Librairie Générale de Droit et de Jurisprudence.

Kymlicka, Will. 1995. *Multicultural Citizenship: A Liberal Theory of Minority Rights*. Oxford: Clarendon Press.

Laclau, Ernesto. 1996. "Universalism, Particularism, and the Question of Identity." In *The Politics of Difference: Ethnic Premises in a World of Power*, ed. E. Wilmsen and P. McAllister, 45–58. Chicago: University of Chicago Press.

Laclau, Ernesto, and Lilian Zac. 1994. "Minding the Gap: The Subject of Politics." In *The Making of Political Identities*, ed. E. Laclau, 11–39. London: Verso.

Lowe, Lisa. 1998. "The Power of Culture," 1 *Journal of Asian American Studies* no. 1, 5–29.

Marx, Karl. 1975 [1843]. "Critique of Hegel's Doctrine of the State." In *Karl Marx, Early Writings*, trans. Rodney Livingstone and Gregor Benton. Harmondsworth, U.K.: Penguin Books.

Maurer, William. 1998. "Cyberspatial Sovereignties: Offshore Finance, Digital Cash, and the Limits of Liberalism," 5 *Indiana Journal of Global Legal Studies* no. 2, 493–519.

Merry, Sally Engle. 1990. *Getting Justice and Getting Even*. Chicago: University of Chicago Press.

———. 1992. "Anthropology, Law, and Transnational Processes," 21 *Annual Review of Anthropology* 347–369.

Mertz, Elizabeth. 1994. "Legal Loci and Places in the Heart: Community and Identity in Sociolegal Studies," 28 *Law & Society Review* 971–92.

———. 2002. "The Perfidy of Gaze and the Pain of Uncertainty: Anthropological Theory and the Search for Closure." In *Everyday Life in Unstable Places*, ed. C. Greenhouse, E. Mertz, and K. Warren. Durham, N.C.: Duke University Press.

Ong, Aihwa. 1999. *Flexible Citizenship: The Cultural Logics of Transnationality*. Durham, N.C.: Duke University Press.

Rouse, Roger. 1995. "Thinking through Transnationalism: Notes on the Cultural Politics of Class Relations in the Contemporary United States," 7 *Public Culture* 353–402.

Ryan, Mary P. 1997. *Civic Wars: Democracy and Public Life in the American City during the 19th Century*. Berkeley: University of California Press.

Salecl, Renata, and Slavoj Žižek, eds. 1996. *Gaze and Voice as Love Objects*. Durham, N.C.: Duke University Press.

Scott, Joan Wallach. 1988. "The Sears Case." In J. Scott, *Gender and the Politics of History*, 167–77. New York: Columbia University Press.

Shapiro, Ian, and Will Kymlicka, eds. 1997. *Ethnicity and Group Rights* (*Nomos* xxxix). New York: New York University Press.

Singh, Nikhil Pal. 1998. "Culture/Wars: Recoding Empire in an Age of Democracy," 50 *American Quarterly* no. 3, 471–522.

Taylor, Charles. 1994. "The Politics of Recognition." In *Multiculturalism: Examining the Politics of Recognition*, ed. A. Gutman, 25–73. Princeton, N.J.: Princeton University Press.

Tocqueville, Alexis de. 1945. *Democracy in America*. 2 vols. Trans. Henry Reeve, rev. Francis Bowen, ed. Phillips Bradley. New York: Vintage Books.

Toniatti, Roberto. 1995. "Minorities and Protected Minorities: Constitutional Models Compared." In *Citizenship and Rights in Multicultural Societies*, ed. M. Dunne and T. Bonazzi, 195–219. Keele: Keele University Press.

Turner, Bryan S. 1993. "Contemporary Problems in the Theory of Citizenship." In *Citizenship and Social Theory*, ed. B.S. Turner, 1–18. London: Sage.

Urciuoli, Bonnie. 1998. "Acceptable Difference: The Cultural Evolution of the Model Ethnic American Citizen." In *Ethnography and Democracy: Constructing Identities in Multicultural Liberal States*, ed. C. Greenhouse, 178–95. Albany: SUNY Press.

van Steenbergen, Bart, ed. 1994. *The Condition of Citizenship*. London: Sage.

Varenne, Hervé. 1977. *Americans Together: Structured Diversity in a Midwestern Town*. New York: Teachers College Press.

———. 1984. "Collective Representation in American Anthropological Conversations: Individual and Culture," 25 Current Anthropology 281–300.

———. 1986. "Drop in Anytime: Community and Authenticity in American Everyday Life." In Symbolizing America, ed. H. Varenne, 209–28. Lincoln: University of Nebraska Press.

———. 1998. "Diversity as American Cultural Category." In *Democracy and Ethnography: Constructing Identities in Multicultural Liberal States*, ed. C. Greenhouse, 27–49. Albany: SUNY Press.

Von Eschen, Penny M. 1997. *Race against Empire: Black Americans and Anticolonialism, 1937–1957*. Ithaca, N.Y.: Cornell University Press.

Wagoner, Paula L. 1997. "Surveying Justice: The Problematics of Overlapping Jurisdictions in Indian Country," 33 *Droit et Cultures* no. 1, 21–52.

Williams, Susan H. 1997. "A Feminist Reassessment of Civil Society," 72 *Indiana Law Journal* no. 2, 417–62.

Yeates, Nicola. 1996. "Appeals to Citizenship in the Unification of Europe: The Political and Social Context of the EC's Third Programme to Combat Poverty." In *Citizenship, Human Rights and Minorities: Rethinking Social Control in the New Europe*, ed. V. Ruggiero. XX conference of the European Group for the Study of Deviance and Social Control. Athens/Komotini: Ant. N. Sakkoulas Publishers.

Yngvesson, Barbara. 1993. *Virtuous Citizens, Disruptive Subjects*. New York: Routledge.

———. 1997. "Negotiating Motherhood: Identity and Difference in 'Open' Adoptions," 31 *Law and Society Review* no. 1, 31–80.

Young, Iris Marion. 1995. "Polity and Group Difference: A Critique of the Ideal of Universal Citizenship." In *Theorizing Citizenship*, ed. R. Beiner, 175–207. Albany: SUNY Press.

Žižek, Slavoj. 1996a. " 'I Hear You with My Eyes'; or, The Invisible Master." In *Gaze and Voice as Love Objects*, ed. R. Salecl and S. Žižek, 90–126. Durham, N.C.: Duke University Press.

———. 1996b. "There Is No Sexual Relationship." In *Gaze and Voice as Love Objects*, ed. R. Salecl and S. Žižek, 209–49. Durham, N.C.: Duke University Press.

PART III
Regulatory Processes in Society and Economy

The Rhetoric of Community

CIVIL SOCIETY AND THE LEGAL ORDER

Marianne Constable

THE PAST DECADE OR SO has seen a resurgence of concern about and appeals to "civil society" in American political and social theoretical discussion. Influenced in part by events in eastern Europe, such discussion has intersected with homegrown American communitarian critiques of liberalism and has resulted in various calls and strategies for "civic renewal" and/or greater "community." Civility and trust are all the rage: from the critique of rights talk to attempts to regulate campus hate speech or even, as recently reported, to rein in bad off-campus student behavior by issuing instructions about trash and late-night noise (Goldberg 1999, A7); from the latest pronouncements about confidence in the institutions of federal government to proposals for "shaming" offenders (COSSA 1999b, 5–7; *Communitarian Update* 1999; Etzioni 1999).[1]

Against the background of such discussions, this chapter looks at the place of community, its relation to the legal order, and its entanglement in issues of civil society in the late-twentieth-century United States. The chapter's main focus is on how large-scale agencies that increasingly administer everyday life already and actually govern in part through what might be called "practices of community." In a paper on "Civilizing Civil Society," the sociologist Philip Selznick claims that "In a democracy[,] government is the instrument of the community, subject to sustained and unfettered criticism, accountable to popular will" (Selznick 1998, 26). By contrast, this chapter aims to show how, in the United States, community is often an instrument of government, a tactic for the rhetorical construction of a public that partakes in a particular dynamic of expertise and accountability that stands in complicated relations to aspirations of democracy and the rule of law.

The author thanks Olga Kotlyarevskaya for research assistance and Alan Comnes, Jack Tweedie, the editors, reviewers, and Law 2000 participants for helpful comments.

Mary Ann Glendon argued in *Rights Talk* ten years ago that rights-laden American political and legal discourse risked trivializing core democratic values. She suggested that the potential for renewal of impoverished American political discourse lay in a return of sorts to the language of "freedom and responsibility, individual and community, present and future" that she still found occurring "around the kitchen table, in the neighborhood, the workplace, in religious groups, and in various other communities of memory and mutual aid" (Glendon 1991, 174).

Today, "community talk" has certainly entered American legal and political discourse. One hears of the campus community, the black community, the gay community, the disabled community, the business community, the community of biomedical researchers, the local community, communities of users, of service providers, and so on. "Community" has not only entered the discourse; community involvement has become part of the practices of administrative agencies in such a way that community expertise is entwined with the social scientific expertise on which such agencies rely. The conjunction of social expertise and the civil values that community is taken to represent correspond to an expanded civil society in which—in the name of responsibility and community—government inserts itself into the numerous activities of everyday life that are represented precisely by what goes on "around the kitchen table."

The first section of the chapter looks briefly at community talk, suggesting the pervasiveness and ubiquity of multiple senses of community currently in circulation. The second section turns to the changing roles of social science expertise in administrative agencies from the 1970s through the 1990s and shows how current practices both encourage clients or beneficiaries of particular programs to become responsible community members and promote particular interactions between citizens and agencies. The third section shows how the engagement of community members as local experts in information-gathering and representational practices helps constitute communities of "service users." The last section touches on the implications for understanding contemporary issues of law and democratic accountability of the new politics of association—a governmental dynamic in which community members are represented as local or citizen experts who, in the name of responsibility and responsiveness, cooperate with and provide information to policy and social science experts whose goal is managing the public order.

COMMUNITY TALK

In a recent newsletter, the Consortium of Social Science Associations (COSSA) reported on a conference, sponsored by the National Academy of Sciences Commission on Social and Behavioral Sciences and Education, on "Racial Trends in the U.S." At that conference Christopher Edley, Harvard University law professor and Special Consultant to the President on the Race Initiative,

> suggested a vision of racial and ethnic justice that would create a society with "no evidence of the legacy of slavery," and a nation that would celebrate diversity rather than merely "tolerate it." He proposed two tracks that would get us there. First, an "opportunity agenda" that would stress educational achievement, community security and criminal justice, economic security and development, and civil rights enforcement. Second a "community track" that would build a moral and political consensus to "understand community." Edley challenged social scientists to conduct research that would equal the effort of the biomedical research community's focus on comprehending the AIDS epidemic. (COSSA 1998a, 5)

Each of the four references to community in Edley's "vision of racial and ethnic justice" invokes a different—although at times overlapping—sense of community. The reference to "community security and criminal justice" under Edley's "opportunity agenda" suggests the safety and security of those who live in *neighborhoods*. The "community track," distinguished from the "opportunity agenda," suggests that attention be paid not only to individual and civil rights and needs but to *collective or group identities*. The communities that constitute those identities are somehow *subject to "moral-political consensus."* Finally, social scientists themselves are constituted as a *research community* analogous to that of biomedical researchers.

In several ways, Edley's statement articulates, in the language of the 1990s, concerns that had persisted throughout the twentieth century. Edley's desire to move beyond toleration of differences and to celebrate "diversity" is certainly not the language or approach to the "nation" of the early 1900s (Constable 1996). And yet American concern—even anxiety—about differences, about the relation of the many to the one, about the fragmentation or unity of its civic life, does pervade the century. Harold J. Laski, for instance, in 1917, asked: "How far and in what way, is our society one? how far is there an interest of the whole, a monistic interest, which transcends the interests of the many who compose that whole?" (Laski 1917, cited in Rodgers 1987, 197). Laski himself then proposed the devolution of democracy to the workplace and the neighborhood. But Laski was not heeded until after the First World War, writes Daniel Rodgers. During the 1920s, political scientists began to scrutinize voter apathy, the decline of parties, and the techniques of new-style pressure groups. By the late 1930s, Rodgers argues, "pressure groups" had become the new democratic unit, the essential "watchdog" of society. From the 1940s to the 1960s, "interest groups," resentful of "the concentration of private and public power in even more distant, bureaucratic forms," multiplied rights claims on behalf of women, gays, children, ethnic group members, urban dwellers, consumers, welfare recipients, humans, defendants, and prisoners (Rodgers 1987). Out of this multiplicity of interest groups emerged the multiplicity of communities that in the 1990s allowed Edley to invoke neighborhood community, collective or group identity, and research community in a vision of racial and ethnic justice "that would create" a nation to which Edley aspires. If the neighborhood community is now a site of contestation over security, identity, and rights, and if the national community is a site of contestation over morality and difference, the research community provides the expert knowledge needed to inform the policy that will enable society and nation to reach "moral and political consensus" beyond mere toleration of difference.

Turning as Edley does to the social researcher for expertise concerning just social policies is not new either. Indeed, the twentieth-century history of the American legal order is commonly taken to be a story of the rise of the regulatory state or of administrative agencies largely dependent on the authority of social science expertise. (Theodore Lowi [1979, 115] lists forty federal regulatory laws and programs enacted between 1969 and 1976 alone. These range from toy safety, egg product inspection, boat safety, noise control, consumer leasing, toxic substances, and safe drinking water to clean air, water pollution control, economic stabilization, flood disaster protection, atomic energy, and more. A huge literature exists on the growth, possibilities, and pathologies of the regulatory welfare state and its expertise; see Selznick 1949 and 1957; Davis 1969; McConnell 1970; Reich 1964; Nonet 1969; Stewart 1975; Nonet and Selznick 1978; Bardach and Kagan 1982; Heclo 1977; Kagan 1978; Mashaw 1983; Melnick 1983 and 1999; and others.) The multiple and conjoined usages of "community" in Edley's plan, however, point to the emergence of a particular form of social policy and social expertise that appears most starkly only at the end of the twentieth century.

Since the 1970s, transformations have occurred in administrative agencies. In the last twenty-five years or so, non-strictly-state institutions and organizations—including private and for-profit groups—have come to exercise and manage functions and tasks that earlier in the century had come to be associated with federal or state governance (examples: insurance companies, health maintenance organizations and managed-care providers, charter school programs, credit-checking outfits, private security companies, private prisons, partnerships between volunteer organizations and local governments, and so forth). The encroachment of market institutions into what had formerly been conceived as exclusive domains of state or private concern suggests an expansion of the "sphere of social interaction between economy and state" of "civil society" (Cohen and Arato 1992, ix).[2]

Challenges to public agency monopoly of particular governmental functions have not meant the disestablishment of state agencies nor the demise of expertise. Rather, the challenges to large state agencies that have occurred continuously since at least the 1970s have led to the transformation of expertise and to the production of a new kind of expertise in which two tracks, that of community member and that of social researcher, converge. The adoption—by state agencies, quasi-public organizations, and private parties alike—of the techniques of management, accounting, and evaluation that characterize market enterprises has meant that expertise no longer simply belongs to the social researchers, planners, and efficiency experts, who are held accountable to professional norms and external goals. Expertise belongs concurrently to the citizen—a citizen trained to community responsibility and appealed to, as responsible community member and local expert, to participate in government that increasingly administers what may loosely be termed the activities of everyday life—working, eating and drinking, learning, resting and recreating, traveling, reading, watching television, driving, and so forth.[3]

PRACTICES OF EXPERTISE AND PARTICIPATION

As we have learned from Michel Foucault and others, particular social projects—the leper colony, the plague city, the Panopticon—carry with them their own "political dreams" (Foucault 1979a, 198). In the 1990s, the empowered community member emerges as the political dream of the projects of administrative agencies—and further, lends him- or herself to projects promoting the privatization of formerly public functions. A conjunction of particular ideological political concerns for security and democracy (identified by Foucault in his work on governmentality [1979b] and described further in the works of Thomas L. Dumm [1999], Nikolas Rose [1999], Barbara Cruikshank [1999], Jonathan Simon [1999, 2000], Mariana Valverde *et al.* [1999], and others [Burchell, Gordon, and Miller 1991]), and the growing significance to governance of the non-therapeutic social sciences (Power 1990), contribute to the appeal empowerment holds as political dream, political tool, and political project.

As the expertise of the therapeutic professions (the human sciences to which Foucault points—public medicine, psychology, social welfare city planning, and so forth) has given way to that of experts in the fields of financial planning, management, administration, and public accounting,[4] the latter rely increasingly for their "substance" on local knowledge, the input of the democratic citizen or local community member. The accounting and auditing fields hold out a common vocabulary for moving between public and private, state and market concerns. They offer the tools for organizing and evaluating data in otherwise ostensibly incompatible registers by allowing the translation of data into the transparency and visibility of the ledger book or the account sheet. As they do so, they displace what were formerly the domains of the therapeutic professions.

The experience of Health and Human Services (HHS) highlights the sorts of changes in administration that occurred from the 1970s through the 1990s. In the 1970s, HHS shifted from an older professional model of evaluation and review to a new Quality Control (QC) model. Each model corresponds to particular visions of agency decision making and of the agency's beneficiaries. The 1970s saw the social work professional give way on the front line to the clerk and at higher administrative levels to the technocratic manager with a background in business administration (Simon 1983, 1216). Relations between worker and claimant changed as interactions became formalized and routine.

William Simon describes how, under the older (pre-1970s) HHS regime, supervisors reviewed written case records and consulted with caseworkers, who were encouraged to participate actively and to respond to the supervisors' comments. The relationship was "a collegial one between professionals, albeit professionals of unequal experience and authority. . . . The goal was an informal consensus regarding the appropriate disposition of the case" (1983, 1206). Simon acknowledges in part that this goal was not always met (1983; Handler 1983). Supervision was supplemented by procedures including a federal audit, in which the records of a sample of the caseload would be examined; the federal share of improper payments in the reviewed cases would not be reimbursed. When patterns of mistakes or lawlessness emerged, HHS would press states to change their policies, often in major areas, and to instruct their workers accordingly (Simon 1983, 1207).

The replacement of the federal audit with Quality Control (QC) in the 1970s coincided with and was stimulated, at least in part, by the rise of the welfare rights movement in the 1960s. QC aimed at catching "errors" of overinclusion, which the rights movement, culminating in *Goldberg v. Kelley* and the right to a pre-termination fair hearing, made more difficult to correct. QC involved three differences in procedures:

> First, [the new procedures] use statistical methods to designate the sample of cases for review and to derive from the reviews an estimate of the total number of the state's cases and the total amount of its payments in "error."
>
> Second, since 1973, these estimates have been backed by "fiscal sanctions" in the form of withheld federal reimbursement for a portion of the estimated erroneous payments in the entire caseload, not just the cases reviewed.
>
> Third, Quality Control involves a more intensive and detailed review of the sample cases than the old procedures. In response to the federal system, the states have developed their own supplementary quality control processes, which make similar but less intensive reviews of larger samples of cases. These supplementary reviews are designed to lower error rates in advance of the federal reviews. (1983, 1207)

Simon argues that the new QC propagated a "question-begging rhetoric of 'error' to promote reforms that often could not survive reflective analysis"

(1208). Many of the "errors" reflected disagreements between reviewers and initial decision makers about ambiguous norms or evidence. Some errors occurred because reviewers used different, more time-consuming or more expensive, procedures than the initial decision maker; errors were found to decrease as reviewers' caseloads went up. Some errors were procedural and when remedied did not affect the grant or provide benefits to the program. Finally, Simon claims, the QC regime ignored the distinction between these errors and more serious ones. QC thus reinforced the trend toward formalization of eligibility norms, intensified organizational hierarchy, increased documentation requirements, and shifted costs toward recipients (1210–12).

During the same period, Simon writes, social work professionalism lost ground as an ideal: "Congress turned away from counseling toward economic approaches (financial incentives and work requirements) to fostering recipient self-support" (Simon 1983, 1215). Social workers and caseworkers were replaced with "eligibility technicians" or "income maintenance workers" (1215). According to Simon, the reforms "seem to have reduced the claimant's experience of oppressive and punitive moralism, of invasion of privacy, and of dependence on idiosyncratic personal favor . . . [but] they also . . . reduced their experience of trust and personal care and have increased their experience of bewilderment and opacity" (1221).

The 1990s see welfare transformed once again—to a decentralized block grant system whose challenge is not only to make recipients economically self-supporting but also to engage them in "community." The Personal Responsibility and Work Opportunity Reconciliation Act of 1996 replaced Aid to Families with Dependent Children (AFDC) with Temporary Assistance to Needy Families (TANF) block grants to the states. The act imposes time limits on welfare benefits, requires recipients to go to work, and increases the role of the states in determining and providing benefits. The act aims not only at "work opportunity," but also "personal responsibility." It stresses the importance of having some sort of "community work experience" and states that "responsible fatherhood and motherhood" are key to marriage as the "foundation of a successful society" in which the interests of children come first. The most recent state welfare program innovations include cooperative programs for child care and transportation for workfare beneficiaries, many of which are worked out via state and local partnerships.

The long-term effects of TANF remain to be seen. At least one study suggests that welfare officials in Maryland claim credit for client compliance rates and lifestyle changes that actually correlate to documentation rates of already occurring behavior (Wilson, Stoker, and McGrath 1998). What the study calls TANF's "paternalistic reforms" serve to "organize" the client (1998, 484, 485).

The point here is not to criticize what some have called the thin and ill-defined conception of "community values" used to justify the work requirements of the act (Alstott 1999) nor even to articulate objections to welfare agencies taking on the role of "moral tutors" (Wilson, Stoker, and McGrath 1998). The point, rather, is to emphasize that a new rhetoric of personal responsibility and participation in community and the desirability of community-state partnerships is specifically invoked and valorized in the 1990s version of aid to the poor.

Such rhetoric is not without consequence. Despite its goal of financial independence, the latest system of aid to the poor cannot be reduced to an "economic" approach to self-support. Neither does it mark a return to an older therapeutic model nor to a rights-based system. Its emphasis on goals of personal responsibility and civic competence suggests a family resemblance to many other community-oriented programs—Neighborhood Watch campaigns, community arbitration boards, emergency and disaster preparedness programs, community health centers, and city or regional planning for public facilities. These programs too rely on detailed information gathered through extensive documentation from those who are to be served. The programs often cite empowerment as a secondary goal. And they also require "partnering" between "community" and agency for the integration of good citizen-worker-residents into a civic life that will be fostered by healthy or safe social and civic environments.

The epitome of such partnering is encountered in the "emerging field" of "community justice" (Karp 1998). Community justice may include "a wide array of programs, and 'community-based initiatives,' including community policing, 'weed and seed,' neighborhood revitalization, drug courts, community corrections, community courts and neighborhood prosecution and defense units, prevention and diversion programs, restitution, community service, victim services, and dispute and conflict resolution efforts in schools and neighborhood organizations" (Bazemore 1998, 330, citing NIJ 1996). Citizens may be involved in these programs in a variety of ways. One study describes four models of citizen decision making in neighborhood sanctioning—"circle sentencing," "family group conferencing," "reparative probation," and "victim/offender mediation" (Bazemore 1998). While these models make use of different conceptions of community, they ostensibly share an informal nonadversarial approach to sanctioning that is presented as a community-based alternative to court sanctioning. As alternatives to formal processes, however, they necessarily require community decision makers to maintain a relation to the formal system, whether to a judge, prosecutor, or court official with whom they share decision making and authority, or to police and probation officers who are responsible for monitoring and enforcing the program.

In the context of the community justice movement, scholars compare a traditional model of crime and order to the community model. The former "system of justice performs as a professional service system of state agents who work in response to criminal events . . . [and are] accountable for a set of professional standards that apply uniformly to all who are engaged in the practice of justice." The community model, by contrast, "involves professionals who work in response to problems articulated by citizens. . . . Because of the heavy dosage of citizen input and activity in the latter model, professional effort tends to be judged on the basis of citizen satisfaction with justice services" (Clear and Karp 1998, 20–21).

In the community model, the citizen takes the place of the colleague or fellow professional in judging performance. But citizen input does more than simply establish a gauge—satisfaction with services delivered—by which to judge professionals' performance. Policy makers also use citizen concerns and desires to determine what problems to address and to develop strategies. The success of those strategies will in turn depend on the evaluations of citizens, as interpreted by a new breed of social analysts who specialize less in substance than in the efficiency of planning, administration, and budgets.

Consider performance-based rate-making in utilities regulation, for instance. Such an approach ostensibly gives utilities incentives to control costs without cutting quality, since utilities can get bonuses if, for instance, they receive 80 percent satisfaction on customer surveys. If standards of satisfaction are not met, the utility may have to give the customer a rebate. Utilities regulators set objective standards for performance, but qualitative issues such as determination and evaluation of customer satisfaction are increasingly carried out by social researchers whose (private) firms can keep up with measures that change over time and can generate statistical comparisons using data from other utility companies. Again, the point of this example is not to argue against such a system (although winter 2000–01 utility rates may give one pause). Rather, it is to suggest how this scheme differs from the reliance twenty years ago, say, on watchdog groups of customers and rate payers such as TURN. The current system relies on the circulation of information between customers, the regulator, a (public or private) utility, and the research company.

In his work on community policing in Australia, Patrick O'Malley points to the emergence of what he calls a "neo-liberal community" that is characterized by its vision of enterprising and responsible individuals and organizations. O'Malley argues that as the model of the commercial enterprise displaces a statist welfare model of policing, the neoliberal community, through input and partnership, becomes an aspect of government rather than simply the site of delivery of social interventions (O'Malley 1999). As in community policing, so too, one might argue, in the new welfare and in utilities regulation. Community partners with agency such that a program's beneficiaries become more than mere recipients. Instead, they are the members-in-training and/or the participant-members of the new community-agency partnership in government.

A MEMBER OF THE COMMUNITY

While ideals of responsibility and duty to one's fellows have always been associated with community, conceptions of community may change. Conventional political theory would have it that American citizens vote, serve on juries, and contribute to public discussion. The community member of the late twentieth and early twenty-first century may still hold these so-called obligations, but they take on a different cast when the community member or citizen is represented in different ways (Constable 1994).

Although the U.S. Constitution nowhere mentions "democracy," it lays out the structure of a representative government. Article I, Section 2 calls for the apportionment of representatives and direct taxes "among the several States . . . according to their respective Numbers." Since 1787, not only the budget, but also the functions of what is now the multi-billion-dollar industry of the census, have apparently grown. In an essay written in 1985, an official of the Census Bureau identifies three functions of the census (Robey 1989, 5, citing Clemence 1985). The first two are straightforward. The first concerns juridical matters of sovereignty and federalism: "to settle disputes between large and small states about the distribution of power, and to promote a core principle of political democracy that such power must be redistributed periodically and peacefully." The second incorporates, in Foucault's terms, governmental matters: it involves the "quest for knowledge, fulfilled by the 10–year statistical portrait of the people and the economy." Such a portrait—"a source of pride for an expanding nation," according to the author—is both a depiction of the civic whole and "a description of problems to which American ingenuity could be applied"—a representation of the problems of governing a population (Robey 1989, 5, citing Clemence 1985).[5]

The essay also lists a third function that it claims "comes of age" in the 1980 census:

> the social value of participating in the census, not just as respondents to questionnaires, but as stakeholders influencing the rules of the enterprise before it begins, becoming involved in the operation, and even in helping to validate the usefulness of census results. (Robey 1989, 5, citing Clemence 1985)

What the author calls the "value of participating . . . as stakeholders" points precisely to the insertion of a particular understanding of community and civic life into what had already been established as a largely social scientific and governmental enterprise.

Several new census programs refine the meaning of community and develop the participation of "stakeholders." The new American Community Survey

(ACS), for instance, will provide annually updated information that the agency claims will eventually eliminate the need for a long form in the decennial census. ACS intends

> to provide data users with more timely information on the nation's communities. . . . Whereas the long-form provides a snapshot of where the country is, the ACS . . . will provide a "video." Specifically, the Bureau and policymakers will be able to see societal changes as they are occurring and, thus, plan accordingly. Specifically, the Bureau plans from time to time to add specialized questionnaires or supplements to collect new information and identify special populations or societal conditions. (COSSA 1998c, 6)

The 2000 census also includes an initiative called America Counts Today (ACT). In part a response to the Supreme Court ruling that sampling may not be used in enumeration of the population for purposes of reapportionment (though the Court left open its use for other purposes), ACT is meant "to increase local community involvement and count everyone in the next census." It comprises several proposals, including increased advertising and the use of Americorps participants to assist the Census Bureau in conducting the count (COSSA 1999a, 4).

The rhetoric of community member as stakeholder in enterprises of government is pushed even further in matters of health, where government conversely becomes a stakeholder in the community member's health. The second of the Department of Health and Human Services' six goals for "Healthy People 2010," for instance, is "Promoting personal responsibility for health lifestyles and behavior" (COSSA 1998b, 21).

The community member's responsibility emerges at a grander level, too. President Clinton in 1997 established an "Advisory Commission on Consumer Protection and Quality in the Health Care Industry." According to one commentator, its task was "to reform 'managed care,' to domesticate it, to make it safe and as worthy of the public trust as its defenders contend it already is." Clinton asked thirty-four "citizen-experts to draft a 'bill of rights' protecting Americans from the corporations insuring their health." Creation of this panel followed widespread dissatisfaction with managed health care and health maintenance organizations (HMOs). The problems with the medical profession that HMOs were meant to address have given way to problems with the very "health care providers" that have replaced doctors, nurses, and medical assistants. Former patients have become "health care consumers" in Clinton's terms, asked to take responsibility for declaring their rights (Sprinkle 1997, 13).

In Britain, a similar concern has emerged for the role—and name—of "patient." According to the *New York Times*:

> The chief executive of the King's Fund, an influential British health charity and research organization, says it is high time to abolish the word "patient."
>
> . . . But if "patient" has to go, what word should replace it?
>
> . . . Rabbi Neuberger considered but rejected "client," which she thought made health care delivery sound like a purely financial transaction. . . .
>
> "Consumer" also struck her as wrong, conjuring an image of the "constant ingestion of pills and potions." She finally settled for "user," a word that "despite its lack of elegance," conveys action rather than passive acceptance, confidence rather than bewilderment, power rather than dependency. "It could even suggest an equalization of status between health professional and service user that is nearer the climate in which modern health services should be provided," she declared. (Zuger 1999)

If Clinton is behind the curve on the terminology of consumers and users, the technique he uses—citizen-experts—is nevertheless one of widespread currency. Communities of service users band together to press for what they need, about which they are considered best and local experts.

Clinton actually calls on these citizen-experts to articulate not needs but "rights," a locution commonly associated with liberalism's so-called autonomous individuals rather than with their socially encumbered brethren. But Clinton's citizen-expert is not quite the individual of classical liberalism. Rather, the citizen-expert is a *user* of *services*, the proper correlate to a service *provider* (as "consumer" is, properly, to "producer").

The user of services suggests a particular analysis or image. While the British "user" conveys "action," "confidence," "power," rather than passivity, "bewilderment," "dependency," it has been argued that in the context of library and computer technology, the term "user" reminds us of the absence of perfect freedom, since "all of these choices are given by the technical structures designed by the programmer" or server (Lyman 1996, 7). (In an era of digital expansion and shrinking library support, administrators and librarians call on scholars at research libraries to fill out surveys concerning their preferences for the distribution of scarce resources and to serve on joint faculty-administrative task forces, which processes ultimately legitimate "difficult administrative decisions." No longer reader nor patron, neither strictly empowered citizen nor simple tool of legitimation, the library services user may actually epitomize the contemporary subject [Constable 2000]).

In the context of social policies and expertise about human services, "user" warrants close examination. The user seems to be the offspring of the "rational actor" and the "consumer." While the "rational actor" assumed by policy makers is too abstract and ethereal, too ungrounded in the things of the world, to serve as a model citizen, the market "consumer" is too undiscriminating and materially oriented to be taken seriously as an expert. The "service user," an heir to both, offers compensation, so to speak, for the shortcomings of rational choice and marketing theory. The "user" combines the techniques of cost-benefit analysis and concern for economic efficiency with utilitarian calculations as to satisfactions—in a new civic form. The user manipulates the things of this world, yet distinguishes between needs and desires. The user draws on experience of these needs to contribute to representations of the public or publics (in user surveys, for instance). And more importantly, as citizen-expert, the user engages with others within given structures. Indeed, as an entity already situated in relations and dependencies with others, the service user—like all members of contemporary society—engages in a particular politics of association.

THE NEW POLITICS OF ASSOCIATION

The previous sections suggest that the rhetoric of community is not reducible to an exhortation to civility nor to a call for shifting the vocabulary of political disagreement from a terrain of legal rights to one of moral responsibility, as some communitarians would have it. Rather, as currently deployed, discourses of community accompany everyday practices of legal institutions that contribute to representations of a public that are themselves put to use to promote the civic health of the community and its members. The community member, serving simultaneously as local expert and responsible citizen, supplements the knowledge of social science experts employed by agencies—both public and private—that it entrusts with maintaining the social order.

Citizens disclose information about themselves, their concerns, their neighbors, and their neighborhood, to promote public safety, health, and welfare. They register to take tests, learn interactively and give feedback so that they themselves and future generations of test takers, interactive learners, and ballot punchers will be more ably served by colleges, banks, museums, departments of motor vehicles, election boards, and so forth. They constitute the targets of opinion polls and of surveys of customer preferences and consumer satisfaction, the profiles of demographics and the more recent "psychographics" of media research services. Through the strategies of social science and mass media in which they partake, they are constituted as the public that in turn becomes the basis for local and national policies as well as for less ostensibly political measures such as dietary recommendations, for instance, which by law will be disseminated via the market.

What are the implications of this cycle of interpenetration of community, economy, and society for issues of law and politics?

Such a dynamic raises questions as to the meaning of democracy. On the one hand, what could be more democratic than an engaged citizenry that is fully integrated into the management of its own affairs? The local or town meeting has long been considered an avenue for accessing a grander or larger civic competence and civic life. That communities not only are called on but demand to be inserted into processes of government suggests that ideals of participation and representation that once were associated with a greater (and often exclusionary) whole, however mythical or imagined—the nation, civilization—are now enacted in a multiplicity of sites. Community today thus appears to serve less as a model of the social order writ large (recall the distinctions between and the commonality of the great unities, *Gemeinschaft* and *Gesellschaft*) than as local political power.

And yet it remains in question whether today's "community" does not divide and multiply less than equally. In the 1960s and 1970s, so-called marginal and/or dependent subpopulations (the poor, the insane, convicts) were made the subjects and objects of disciplinary and governmental techniques that owed much to the human sciences and were deployed by state agencies and other institutions (Dumm 1987; Simon 1993). In the 1990s, even those who belong to what would formerly have been thought of as the mainstream have become members of communities or groups whose interests ostensibly threaten to become marginalized. As these groups/communities become the empowered partners of a variety of public, quasi-public, and private institutions that deploy the very concepts of civility and community to identify, address, and engage them in producing a public order, the consonance of that order with democratic aspirations to "freedom and responsibility" may urge us to rethink our terms. If, in a democracy, community subjects government to "sustained and unfettered criticism," what is one to make of a situation in which public discourse sustains not criticism but government? What becomes of the accountability of government to the public will when quasi-public/quasi-private government generates that will?

To some extent, this question returns us to the study of administrative law, where the modern incarnation of the issues surrounding the possibility of a government ruled by laws and not by men plays itself out. The move to community-agency partnerships discussed above is paralleled in areas such as civil rights, worker safety, environmental health, by growing emphasis on corporate self-regulation and the problems and opportunities it presents (Edelman, Abraham, and Erlanger 1992; Espeland 2000; Weber 1998; Rees 1988 and 1994). In what sense is the corporation, already legally declared a "person," a community member? Joseph Rees argues persuasively in his sophisticated study of the aftermath of Three Mile Island that it is time that "the idea of community—and communitarian regulation" be taken seriously, even in a technological society dominated by large-scale organizations. Conversely, this chapter suggests that it is time that those who would espouse the idea of community as balance to an excess of rights take seriously—as does Rees—the practices and everyday interactions of large-scale organizations that make up the legal order of a complex technological society.

They will find that the old dichotomies of community vs. rights, of public vs. private, of social order vs. individual autonomy, no longer suffice. The new communities are not the now-mythic singular civic community. Neither are they interest groups. Rather, "community" covers a range and multiplicity of groups, of associational and representational practices, of organizations and patterns of relations. Invocations of community empowerment and of the civic competence, duty, and responsibility of community members combine with the latest strategies of social research and efficiency experts to form particular practices of expertise and to justify their insertion into a variety of processes of governing.

Whether justice is found in any instance of course depends on particulars. Rhetoric, however, may be more general. Deployment of the rhetoric of community in the legal order of the late twentieth century suggests that community, somewhat like the family before it (as Foucault argued), rather than being the model for civic or public life, is in danger of becoming an element internal to an ostensibly social-scientifically ascertainable population, an instrument for the government of public order.

When Americans sit around their kitchen tables—alone or with others in their households—filling out warranties and surveys, opening up or throwing out junk mail, reading the backs of cereal boxes for minimum Recommended Daily Allowances, they too are engaged at a local level in administration of government. As members of the American public, they are participating in the practices and dialogues of late-twentieth-century "civil society."

NOTES

1 An article on "American's [*sic*] Trust (or Lack of) in Government Institutions" in COSSA's *Washington Update* (1999a, 5–7) reports on three presentations in a 1999 seminar. One shows that the public has lost confidence in the institutions of federal government in the last thirty years; one suggests that public distrust of government institutions is a result of structural problems reported by the media, rather than a result of the media itself; one shows a decline in young people's participation or intention to participate in politics, although they are participating in other community affairs. The latter suggests also that the problem is being recognized by those who are making efforts to "reinvigorate the field of civic education."

Compare "America's Civic Health Improving," an article that appeared less than a month later in *The Communitarian Update* (1999), reporting on a National Commission on Civic Renewal announcement that the Index of National Civic Health, "a composite of measurements of political participation, trust, strength of the family, group membership, and personal security," which has been monitored since 1974, indicates gains in all categories between 1994 and 1997 (as compared to drops in all categories from 1984 to 1994). (The same issue advertises "Back to the Pillory?" by Amitai Etzioni: "Etzioni examines whether shaming might be useful in our criminal justices system.")

2 "Civil society" has been defined in many ways (Krygier 1997), and the number of books and

articles on American civil society and the quandary of community proliferates. The gist of such works varies: many are concerned about "loss" of community in the face of overwhelming rights talk (Glendon 1991), an impossible liberalism (Sandel 1998), or a pervasive individualism (Bellah et al. 1985); others would focus on the "paradoxes" of community (Greenhouse, Yngvesson, and Engel (1994); still others locate concern for a particular sort of community or civil society in morality (Selznick 1992), religion, the history of political thought (Cohen and Arato 1992), the availability of particular sorts of political speech (Rodgers 1987), or even fanaticism (Colas 1997). Despite their differences, these works all exhibit a concern for association and for a public participation that, however defined, is reducible neither to state action nor to the activity of the market.

One working definition of civil society, for instance, presents it as "a sphere of social interaction between economy and state, composed above all of the intimate sphere (especially the family), the sphere of associations (especially voluntary associations), social movements, and forms of public communication." The authors add that this conception is to be thought of both in terms of "juridical protections of the private sphere that are inevitably dependent on state legislation" and in terms of "extrapolitical movements and forms of pressure on the state itself" (Cohen and Arato 1992, ix, 605 n. 2).

3 The public entities alone concerned with these activities make up an alphabet soup. They include: working—OSHA, SSA; eating—FDA; drinking—ATF, local liquor laws, Surgeon General; learning—local school boards to Department of Education; resting and recreating—Consumer Protection agency, bicycle helmet laws, National Park Service, Environmental Protection Agency; traveling—INS, Customs, FAA; television and radio—FTC; driving—NHA, Highway Patrol, DMV, seat belt laws. Quasi-public and private organizations are of course also involved in promoting and structuring these activities.

4 The extension at least of accounting, beyond the firm and even beyond tax and government accounting into other spaces of public concern, was not unintentional: a concerted effort was made by the American Institute of Certified Public Accountants to deal with public relations and to increase the public service of its members (Carey 1970).

5 Informational materials released around the 1990 census show literally hundreds of references in the U.S. Code (1986) to census data. Data were used regarding affirmative action plan guidelines, food stamp regulations, home mortgage lending patterns, credit needs in particular neighborhoods, state redistricting plans, minority businesses, government contracts, illness, scientific and technical personnel availability, and so forth. The 1990 *Census ABC's: Applications in Business and Community* suggest that data can be used for selecting the best location for a store, planning a job training program, estimating need for home health care and support services, assessing the need for a reverse mortgage program, selecting merchandise lines of the right price level for a store, setting fundraising goals by neighborhood for house-to-house canvassers (U.S. Bureau of the Census 1990, 4). The document explains the use of data for locating a playground, planning adult literacy and ESL programs, securing a loan for a car wash, increasing newspaper circulation, and so forth.

REFERENCES

Alstott, Anne. 1999. "Work v. Freedom," 108 *Yale Law Journal* 967–1058.

Bardach, Eugene, and Robert A. Kagan. 1982. *Going by the Book: The Problem of Regulatory Unreasonableness.* Philadelphia: Temple University Press.

Bazemore, Gordon. 1998. "The 'Community' in Community Justice: Issues, Themes, and Questions for the New Neighborhood Sanctioning Models." In *Community Justice: An Emerging Field*, ed. David R. Karp. Lanham, Md.: Rowman & Littlefield.

Bellah, Robert N., et al. 1985. *Habits of the Heart: Individualism and Commitment in American Life*. Berkeley: University of California Press.

Burchell, Gordon, Colin Gordon, and Peter Miller, eds. 1991. *The Foucault Effect: Studies in Governmentality*. Chicago: University of Chicago Press.

Carey, John L. 1970. *The Rise of the Accounting Profession to Responsibility and Authority: 1937–1969*. New York: AICPA.

Clear, Todd R., and David R. Karp. 1998. "The Community Justice Movement." In *Community Justice: An Emerging Field*, ed. David R. Karp. Lanham, Md.: Rowman & Littlefield.

Clemence, Theodore G. 1985. "Historical Perspectives on the Decennial Census." 2 *Government Information Quarterly* no. 2, Special Issue: Symposium on the Decennial Census (November 1985), 355–68. [Cited in Robey 1989.]

Cohen, Jean, and Andrew Arato. 1992. *Civil Society and Political Theory*. Cambridge: MIT Press.

Colas, Dominique. 1997. *Civil Society and Fanaticism: Conjoined Histories*. Stanford, Calif.: Stanford University Press.

Communitarian Update. 1999. No. 21 (September 3).

Constable, Marianne. 1994. *The Law of the Other: The Mixed Jury and Changing Conceptions of Citizenship, Law and Knowledge*. Chicago: University of Chicago Press.

———. 1996. "The Regents on Race and Diversity: Reflections and Representations," 55 *representations* 92–97.

———. 2000. "The University Library at the Turn of the Century," 4 *Chronicle of the University of California* 138-156.

COSSA. 1998a. 17 *Washington Update* (October 26).

———. 1998b. 17 *Washington Update* (November 23).

———. 1998c. 17 *Washington Update* (June 15).

———. 1999a. 18 *Washington Update* (February 8).

———. 1999b. 18 *Washington Update* (August 9).

Cruikshank, Barbara. 1999. *The Will to Empower: Democratic Citizens and Other Subjects*. Ithaca, N.Y.: Cornell University Press.

Davis, Kenneth Culp. 1969. *Discretionary Justice: A Preliminary Inquiry*. Baton Rouge: Louisiana State University Press.

Dumm, Thomas L. 1987. *Democracy and Punishment: Disciplinary Origins of the United States*. Madison: University of Wisconsin Press.

———. 1999. *A Politics of the Ordinary*. New York: New York University Press.

Edelman, Lauren B., Steven E. Abraham, and Howard Erlanger. 1992. "Professional Construction of Law: The Inflated Threat of Wrongful Discharge," 27 *Law and Society Review* 497–534.

Espeland, Wendy Nelson. 2000. "Bureaucratizing Democracy, Democratizing Bureaucracy," 25 *Law & Social Inquiry* 1077–1109.

Etzioni, Amitai. 1998. "Community Justice in a Communitarian Perspective." In *Community Justice: An Emerging Field*, ed. David R. Karp. Lanham, Md.: Rowman & Littlefield.

Foucault, Michel. 1979a. *Discipline and Punish*. New York: Vintage Books.

———. 1979b. "Governmentality," 6 *Ideology and Consciousness* 5–21.

Glendon, Mary Ann. 1991. *Rights Talk: The Impoverishment of Political Discourse*. New York: Free Press.

Goldberg, Carey. 1999. "Moving Madness Holiday in Nation's College Capital," *New York Times*, 4 August, A7.

Greenhouse, Carol J., Barbara Yngvesson, and David Engel. 1994. *Law and Community in Three American Towns*. Ithaca, N.Y.: Cornell University Press.

Handler, Joel F. 1983. "Discretion in Social Welfare: The Uneasy Position in the Rule of Law," 92 *Yale Law Journal* 1270.

Heclo, Hugh. 1977. *A Government of Strangers: Executive Politics in Washington*. Washington, D.C.: Brookings Institute.

Kagan, Robert A. 1978. *Regulatory Justice: Implementing a Wage-Price Freeze*. New York: Russell Sage Foundation.

Karp, David. 1998. *Community Justice: An Emerging Field*. Lanham, Md.: Rowman & Littlefield.

Krygier, Martin. 1997. *Between Hope and Fear: Hybrid Thoughts on Public Values*. Sydney: ABC Books.

Laski, Harold J. 1917. *Studies in the Problem of Sovereignty*. New Haven, Conn.: Yale University Press.

Lowi, Theodore. 1979. *The End of Liberalism*. 2d ed. New York: W. W. Norton.

Lyman, Peter. 1996. "What Is a Digital library? Technology, Intellectual Property, and the Public Interest," 125 *Daedalus* (fall) 1–33.

Mashaw, Jerry L. 1983. *Bureaucratic Justice: Administrative Law from an Internal Perspective*. New Haven, Conn.: Yale University Press.

McConnell, Grant. 1970. *Private Power and American Democracy*. New York: Vintage Books.

Melnick, R. Shep. 1983. *Regulation and the Courts: The Case of the Clean Air Act*. Washington, D.C.: Brookings Institute.

———. 1999. *Taking Stock: American Government in the Twentieth Century*. Cambridge and New York: Woodrow Wilson Center and Cambridge University Press.

National Institute of Justice. 1996. *Communities: Mobilizing Against Crime*. Washington, D.C.: National Institute of Justice.

O'Malley, Pat. 1999. "Neo-Liberal Police: 'Partnership Policing' and the 'Empowered Community.'" Paper presented at Law and Society Association Summer Legal Institute, Rutgers, New Jersey.

Nonet, Philippe. 1969. *Administrative Justice: Advocacy and Change in a Government Agency*. New York: Russell Sage Foundation.

Nonet, Philippe, and Philip Selznick. 1978. *Law and Society in Transition: Toward Responsive Law*. New York: Octagon Books.

Power, Michael. 1990. *The Audit Society: Rituals of Verification*. Oxford: Oxford University Press.

Rees, Joseph V. 1988. *Reforming the Workplace: A Study of Self-Regulation in Occupational Safety*. Philadelphia: University of Pennsylvania Press.

———. 1994. *Hostages of Each Other: The Transformation of Nuclear Safety since Three Mile Island*. Chicago: University of Chicago Press.

Reich, Charles. 1964. "The New Property," 73 *Yale Law Journal* 733–87.

Robey, Bryant. 1989. "Two Hundred Years and Counting: The 1990 Census," 44 *Population Bulletin* (Population Reference Bureau).

Rodgers, Daniel T. 1987. *Contested Truths: Keywords in American Politics since Independence*. New York: Basic Books.

Rose, Nikolas. 1999. *Powers of Freedom: Reframing Political Thought.* Cambridge: Cambridge University Press.

Sandel, Michael. 1998. *Liberalism and the Limits of Justice.* 2d ed. Cambridge: Cambridge University Press.

Selznick, Philip. 1949. *TVA and the Grass Roots: A Study in the Sociology of Formal Organization.* Berkeley: University of California Press.

———. 1957. *Leadership in Administration: A Sociological Interpretation.* New York: Harper and Row.

———. 1992. *The Moral Commonwealth: Social Theory and the Promise of Community.* Berkeley: University of California Press.

———. 1998. "Civilizing Civil Society." Paper presented at Center for the Study of Law and Society, Berkeley, California, September 14. Originally prepared for "Expert Seminar" on Individualism, Civil Society, and Civil Religion, Vrije Universiteit, Amsterdam, February 3–6, 1998.

Simon, Jonathan. 1993. *Poor Discipline: Parole and the Social Control of the Urban Underclass, 1890–1990.* Chicago: University of Chicago Press.

———. 1999. "On Their Own: Delinquency Without Society," 47 *Kansas Law Review* 1–19.

———. 2000. "Megan's Law: Crime and Democracy in Late Modern America," 25 *Law & Social Inquiry* 1111–50.

Simon, William H. 1983. "Legality, Bureaucracy, and Class in the Welfare System," 92 *Yale Law Journal* 1198–1269.

Sprinkle, Robert Hunt. 1997. "Corporatism in Question: A Note on Managed Care," 17 *Report from the Institute for Philosophy and Public Policy* 13–17.

Stewart, Richard B. 1975. "The Reformation of American Administrative Law," 88 *Harvard Law Review* 1667–1813.

Sunstein, Cass. 1990. *After the Rights Revolution: Reconceiving the Administrative State.* Cambridge: Harvard University Press.

United States Bureau of the Census. 1990. *Census ABC's: Applications in Business and Community.* Washington, D.C.: U.S. Government Printing Office.

Valverde, Mariana, Ron Levi, Clifford Shearing, Mary Condon, and Pat O'Malley. 1999. *Democracy in Governance: A Socio-Legal Framework.* A Report for the Law Commission of Canada on Law and Governance Relationships. Ottawa, Ont.: Law Commission.

Weber, Edward P. 1998. *Pluralism by the Rules: Conflict and Cooperation in Environmental Regulation.* Washington, D.C.: Georgetown University Press.

Wilson, Laura A., Robert P. Stoker, and Dennis McGrath. 1998. "Welfare Bureaus as Moral Tutors: What Do Clients Learn from Paternalistic Welfare Reforms?" 80 *Social Science Quarterly* 473–86.

Zuger, Abigail, M.D. 1999. "Essay: Patient Suffers from Connotations," *New York Times,* 31 August, D5.

Law and the Corporation

Morton Keller

THE LARGE BUSINESS corporation has a well-established place in the American imagination as a sinister repository of private power. That fear rests on the widespread popular belief that aggregations of private economic power pose a public threat, and that special privileges and prerogatives have no place in a democratic republic. But there is an equally long-held American view that the best way to assure economic success is to encourage efficient, productive private enterprise. If that means big business capable of providing cheap goods and services on a large scale, then so be it. The result: a persisting, never resolved tension between the desires for a fair field and no favor and (to sustain the metaphor) for a field ploughed, sown, and harvested as quickly and as productively as possible. From the nation's earliest days to our own time, that conflict has shaped American corporation law.

I

The Supreme Court of the early-nineteenth-century Marshall-Taney era had an outsized interest in the powers and limits of the chartered corporation. But a rapidly changing economy and the rise of a distinctively American creed of democratic nationalism substantially changed the character of that interest. John Marshall and his Court sought to assure the sanctity (and thus the potential) of chartered bodies by bringing them under the protection of the Constitution's Commerce Clause in *Dartmouth College v. Woodward* (1819). Just as Alexander Hamilton linked the success of the new nation to fiscal responsibility, so Marshall and his colleagues subscribed to the mercantilist view that the inviolability of a charter was the best guarantee of economic growth. But by the 1830s, popular attitudes and economic necessity had substantially weakened that belief. Roger B. Taney's decision in *Charles River Bridge* v. *Warren* (1837) cleared the way to a less protective view of corporate charters, thus making room for new enterprise. The corporation came to be seen as a legal fiction created by the state, rather than as the coequal contractual party of the Marshall era (Hovenkamp 1991, parts I and II; Keller 1997, 58–59).

During the early and mid-nineteenth century, a number of states enacted laws designed to make incorporation as cheap and easy as possible. The democratization of what once had been an instrument of privilege turned the corporation into a business instrument more widely used in the United States than anywhere else in the Western world. But while incorporation had been made accessible to large numbers of would-be entrepreneurs, corporations remained very much the creatures of the states that chartered them. It was common for corporate charters to include a reserve clause empowering the legislature to amend it at any time. If companies engaged in activities that went beyond what was specifically prescribed in their charters, the courts might well void them as *ultra vires*. If firms did business in states beyond the one that chartered them, the courts treated them as "foreign corporations," subject with few constraints to the regulation of those other commonwealths. And side by side with the growth of free incorporation there rose the concept of the states' "police power": a capacity to regulate the safety, health, morals, and welfare of its people that could, and often did, justify a wide range of state and municipal regulation (Horwitz 1992, chap. 3; Hovenkamp 1988; Novak 1996).

This, in sum, was the ambiguous legal state of the corporation before the rise of big business in the late nineteenth and early twentieth centuries. The impact of that rise was qualitative as well as quantitative. Not only in its scale, but in its power relative to workers, suppliers, competitors, customers, and the general public, and in its capacity to influence politics, law, and government, the large corporation came to be widely viewed as the most fearsome threat to the republic since slavery and secession. At the same time, these new enterprises were demonstrating stunning productivity and price-lowering capacity.

The legal and judicial response to the rise of big business is one of the great stories of adaptation to new conditions in the history of American law. Over the course of the half century from 1870 to 1920, a complex new framework of corporation law, both private and public, took form. The traditional interpretation of this development saw it in near-conspiratorial terms. Subservient legislators, judges, and attorneys crafted a set of rules that shielded large corporations from unwanted regulation or taxation and empowered them to deal cavalierly with their workforce, lesser competitors, and the public. But in recent times there has emerged a more nuanced view of what happened, one that takes note of the degree to which old assumptions about the corporation and the dual desires to foster and control it shaped the legal-legislative response.

The most profound legal change was the shift from the view of the corporation as an artificial creation of the state to the view that it had many of the attributes of citizenship as defined in the Fourteenth Amendment—that, indeed, it had a kind of legal "personhood." Works such as Ernst Freund's *The Legal Nature of the Corporation* (1897) gave a theoretical gloss to the view that a corporation was a natural and not an artificial entity, and as such had a personality recognizable in law.

The courts were not quick to agree. The older notion, dating from the Taney years, that the corporation was an "artificial being" serving an aggregation "of individuals united for some legitimate business" (Justice Stephen Field's words) stubbornly persisted. Indeed, the decision in *Santa Clara County v. Southern Pacific Railroad Co.* (1886), which famously declared that corporations were persons within the meaning of the Fourteenth Amendment, was based on the belief that the corporation was the agent of its stockholders, not on the view that it was a separate legal entity. But it helped clear the way to ultimate judicial acceptance of the concept of corporate personality (Hovenkamp 1991, part IV; Horwitz 1992, chap. 3).

As that concept began to take hold around the turn of the century, the controlling doctrines of American corporate law changed. The *ultra vires* constraint on corporate activity, which depended on the assumption that the corporation was the creature of the state that chartered it, began its long legal journey to virtual irrelevance (if the corporation is a "real" and not an "artificial" person, then it should not be so constrained). The power of states to impose restrictions on out-of-state corporations also declined (if the corporation is a "citizen," then it should not be subject to such restraints) (Hovenkamp 1988, 1643; Horwitz 1992, 89; Keller 1977, 431–38).

This legal transformation was closely related to the rise of consolidated national corporations. The new big business had to make its way in a legal environment dominated by a state corporation law that favored local enterprise. The problems this posed were overcome by two major innovations in the legal framework of big business: the trust and the holding company.

The sequence is a familiar one. In the late 1870s, John D. Rockefeller's attorney, Samuel C. T. Dodd, adapted the venerable legal instrument of the trust to enable Standard Oil to absorb competitors. That firm's Ohio charter forbade it from holding stock in other companies. It got around that obstacle by turning itself into a trust and issuing trust certificates in return for the securities of the companies it took over. The market-controlling potential of the trust made it a conspicuous object of public concern (though in actuality less than a dozen such instruments were created). A number of states passed antitrust laws, and in 1890 the Sherman Antitrust Act swept through Congress. Meanwhile James B. Dill, another creative corporation lawyer, came up with a new device: the holding company, a corporation whose sole reason for being was to possess the stock of other corporations. (It was some time after this that Finley Peter Dunne's Mr. Dooley observed that what looks like a stone wall to the ordinary man is a triumphal arch to the lawyer) (Boorstin 1973, 414–20; Keller 1990, 87–88).

Holding companies confronted the same obstacle that the trust was designed to overcome: state laws that prohibited a corporation from holding the stock of other firms. The answer: get a state or two to ease that restriction, and then let interstate competition for the fees of their chartered companies do the rest. That in fact is what happened. Delaware and then New Jersey obligingly changed their laws and quickly became the home of many of America's largest corporations (organized as holding companies). These and other states competed to make their corporation laws maximally attractive and minimally intrusive. Thus Massachusetts revised its corporation laws in 1903 to accord with the "modern . . . theory . . . that an ordinary business corporation should be allowed to do anything that an individual may do" (Grandy 1993; Keller 1990, 88).

The most significant government response to the rise of big business was a system of oversight that came under the generic label of "antitrust." This regulatory approach was steeped in nineteenth-century economic beliefs. Its major purposes were to block cartels and their price-fixing ways and to prevent mergers that raised the specter of monopoly: in short, to preserve the liberal ideal of a level playing field of competing units. Government ownership and operation of railroads and public utilities had advocates. But they had little chance in an American political system deeply distrustful of strong national government and subject to the financial inducements of corporate interests (Keller 1990, 88–89).

The rise of large interstate railroad companies led to the first federal regulatory agency, the Interstate Commerce Commission, in 1887. The ICC was not a great leap forward in the administrative state, but rather "a new court" whose task, according to Thomas M. Cooley, the commission's first chairman, was "to lay the foundations of a new body of American law." The ICC's powers at first were limited to assuring that railroads did not engage in such unacceptable practices as rebating (just as sheriffs in late medieval England were statutorily empowered to make sure that the local miller or innkeeper did not violate common law or custom) (Keller 1977, 429).

The regulatory reaction to the rise of big business in general was hardly more cutting-edge. The Sherman Antitrust Act of 1890 outlawed "every contract, combination in the form of trust or otherwise, or conspiracy in restraint of trade or commerce." Its assumptions as to what was wrong, and what should be done about it, reflected old common-law (and early American) conceptions far more than it did the structural, economic, and social realities of the new big business. The Sherman Act was designed to serve the interests of competing enterprises, not consumers, and not labor (some of whose practices the courts soon brought under the rubric of illegal restraint of trade). It left enforcement to the Department of Justice and interpretation to the courts. And just as turn-of-the-century proposals for federal ownership and operation of the railroads fell on fallow ground, so did proposals for the federal chartering of corporations, or for a federal police power, or for an Interstate Trade Commission (Letwin 1965; Keller 1977, 434–36; Urofsky 1982).

Regulation so steeped in the past soon came under attack, and changes were made during the Progressive period of the early twentieth century. An antitrust division was created in the Department of Justice to strengthen Sherman Act enforcement; a Bureau of Corporations was in some vague way supposed to add to the federal government's supervisory clout. The ICC, buffeted by assertive federal courts and large shippers, got a boost when the Hepburn Act of 1906 gave it rate-setting powers. The Mann-Elkins Act of 1910 established a Commerce Court to review the ICC's rate and other findings. And in 1914 the Clayton Antitrust Act and a federal regulatory agency, the Federal Trade Commission, promised more muscular regulation of big business (Keller 1990, chaps. 2, 3).

In less than two decades an extensive infrastructure of administrative and judicial oversight had been created in response to the rise of large corporations. What was its effect? Resuscitation of the endangered world of small, free, competitive enterprise? More closely state-supervised large enterprises? A new kind of administrative supervision and a redefinition of American corporation law?

Hardly. Consider the century-long, recurrently unhappy saga of the Interstate Commerce Commission. At first it was hamstrung by judicial decisions that constrained its rate-fixing and other powers. Nor could the Commerce Court of 1910 make its way in the face of the hostility of the Supreme Court. Congress ended that lame, ill-fated experiment in 1913. In the same year the legislature ordered the ICC to undertake a full-scale valuation of the railroads' assets—roadbeds, rolling stock, the works—in order to develop a sound economic basis for a viable rate system. The result? A program of asset valuation that cost about $100 million, lasted for a decade, and finally slid into deserved obscurity—a splendid instance of the regulatory equivalent of emptying the sea with a slotted spoon. Meanwhile, ICC rate-making had the perverse effect of impairing, even more than their often inept managements were able to do, the railroads' ability to compete with the new technologies of motor and later air transport. It was more than a symbolic act when in 1996 Congress abolished the Interstate Commerce Commission (Keller 1990, 49–54; Martin 1971).

The experience of antitrust law was more complex. After an initial stage of judicial tooth-pulling very much like the federal courts' initial reaction to the Interstate Commerce Commission, the Supreme Court in its landmark *Northern Securities Co. v. U.S.* (1904) and *Standard Oil Co. v. U.S.* (1911) and *U.S. v. American Tobacco Co.* (1911) decisions restored some bite to antitrust law. *Northern Securities* made it possible to believe that there might be some legal bounds to corporate consolidation, and *Standard Oil* and *American Tobacco* actually ordered the breaking up of two massive holding companies.

But it is difficult to argue that law and regulation had more than marginal consequences for big business in early-twentieth-century America. True, the courts did call a halt to especially egregious applications of market control, as in the cases of Standard Oil, American Tobacco, and the movie producers' association in the 1920s. They continued to be hostile to cartel-like pricing and other agreements. But that only encouraged companies to seek market control through formal combination. And the Federal Trade Commission, which devoted itself almost exclusively to the relatively marginal corporate abuse of false and misleading advertising, offered little in the way of toughened administrative regulation.

The character of corporate America was more strongly shaped by the corrosive force of new technologies, products, and market conditions. Standard Oil's stranglehold on American oil and gasoline production and distribution certainly was affected when the Supreme Court's "rule of reason" decision broke it up into separate companies. But the sudden opening up of new oil fields in Oklahoma, Texas, and California, and the consequent rise of a flock of new, powerful companies—Gulf, Texaco, Shell—did far more to shape the future of the American oil business. Much the same could be said of the impact on United States Steel of the development of aluminum and plastics, and the impact of cars and trucks on the railroads (Keller 1990, chaps. 3, 4).

The pallid record of ICC and Sherman Act enforcement is eloquent testimony to the secure place of the large corporation in the twentieth-century American economy. A major contributing factor, of course, was the capacity of corporations to take care of themselves. The "capture" of regulatory agencies, legislatures, and courts by corporate interests is the persistent theme of a string of critics of corporate power in the twentieth century, running from Samuel J. Untermyer and Louis D. Brandeis to Ralph Nader.

But the general inability to stay the progress of corporate bigness was due to more than corporate clout. Another source of strength was the American public's ambivalent attitude toward size and success and its taste for large supplies of cheap goods and services. Beyond this lies the entrenched legal standing of the corporation: a reflection of its importance as an economic instrument and of the degree to which American law protects whoever (or whatever) has secured the status of a well-defined legal entity. It should be noted, too, that in this century as in the last, incorporation extends far beyond big business. In 1995 about 4.5 million corporations filed tax forms. So even if much of the nation's economic power is lodged in a relatively short list of giant companies, the corporate form itself is distributed widely enough (among small businessmen, farmers, etc.) to secure its general acceptance.

II

During and after the 1930s, American corporation law and regulation underwent substantial change. Adolph A. Berle and Gardiner C. Means's *The Modern Corporation and Private Property* (1932) epitomized the changes under way. Their book took a clear-eyed look not at the old issue of the legal nature of big business, but at the way it actually functioned. Instead of equating the corporation with a person, they equated it with the state. The corporation too was a bureaucratically administered institution with dangerously large resources of money and influence, run by managers less and less responsible to their stockholders (the equivalent of voters). The separation of ownership from management Berle and Means so persuasively described did much to erode the reigning legal paradigm of corporate personality.

Thurman Arnold's *Folklore of Capitalism* (1937) added an anthropological take on big business, further divesting it of the attributes of personhood. And it consigned small competitive capitalism—the reason for being of antitrust—to the realms of history and myth. (That view led to some embarrassment when Franklin Roosevelt appointed Arnold to head the Justice Department's antitrust division. But he adapted well enough, which suggests that history, and myth, have an authority of their own.)

At the same time, the New Deal produced a body of federal laws that put a policy gloss on the ruminations of Berle, Means, and Arnold. This included the securities regulation of the Securities Exchange Act and the Securities Exchange Commission (SEC); the price-and-production limits of the National Recovery Administration (NRA) codes; government aid to industrial unionization through NRA's section 7a and the National Labor Relations Act; the Robinson-Patman anti–price discrimination act of 1936, aimed at price-cutting chain and discount stores; the Public Utilities Holding Companies Act of 1935, empowering the SEC to break up electric utility monopolies; and the elevated corporation taxes of the Revenue Act of 1935.

But the New Deal paid less attention to corporate structure and monopolistic behavior as such than did its Progressive forerunner. The major attempt at structural reform was the Temporary National Economic Committee (TNEC) of 1938–1940. But this committee's proposals for disaggregating corporate power were lost in the swirl of wartime mobilization and postwar boom. Instead, New Deal corporation policy dealt with specific problems—shady stock practices, unemployment and low wages, obstacles to unionization, overproduction and underconsumption—and on expanding the capacity of the federal government to set things right. Shareholders and labor came in for greater protection, as did that old favorite, the small competitor. Consumers remained odd men (and women) out.

As radical critics bitterly observed, and as anti–New Deal businessmen failed to notice, this left the structure of big business essentially unchanged (though subject, it is true, to considerably more regulation). The payoff in this Faustian bargain came during and after World War II. With large profit incentives dangled before it, American big business rapidly mobilized to meet the production demands of war and then the consumer demands of the postwar decades (Hawley 1966; 1975, 50–82).

From the vantage point of 2000, it appears that the regulatory and legal relation of the state to the corporation has not greatly changed in its essentials since the 1930s. No major new regulatory agencies aimed specifically at corporations have been created, and corporate legislation has modified rather than transformed existing law. Examples: the Taft-Hartley labor law of 1946, which undid some of the union gains of the New Deal years; and the Williams Act of 1968, which updated the Securities Act of 1934 to cover tender offers.

Nor, compared to the first half of the century, has much attention been paid in recent decades to the nature of the corporation: "The corporation as a legal institution ceased to be of interest." Antitrust and other regulatory policies came increasingly under the sway of neoclassical economic analysis and organization theory. And the courts continued to support federal deference to state corporation law in matters concerning the internal governance of companies (Mark 1987, 1441; Hovenkamp 1988, 1688–89; *Burks v. Lasker* [1979]).

Discontent with the particularism of state regulation and its supposed susceptibility to corporate capture, conspicuous in the early years of the century, surfaced again after the 1960s. A number of law professors petitioned in 1976 for that old panacea, federal incorporation. SEC chairman William Cary made a splash with a 1974 *Yale Law Journal* article arguing that the interests of shareholders were endangered by states eager to reap the benefits of corporate chartering fees. To lure corporate managers, they engaged in a "race to the bottom" of lax regulation, thereby fostering corruption and incompetence. But strong evidence that this was so proved hard to come by. And the now regnant tendency to link corporate legal and regulatory policy to market economics came into play. Critics argued that competitive pressure among corporate managers to reward, and thus to attract, stockholders meant that there could just as well be a "race to the top," in which states sought to establish optimally efficient legal conditions for doing a profitable business (Romano 1993, 9; Cary 1974, 663–705; Winter 1978; Easterbrook 1983, 23–50; Romano 1987, 709–57; Fischel 1982).

Ralph Nader has for some decades been perhaps the most conspicuous critic of large corporations, advocating stricter federal controls over their products (as in the case of auto emissions), punitive class action tort litigation, and alterations in corporate governance such as public directors and federal incorporation. Another post-1950 strand of criticism has been concern, stretching from *The Man in the Gray Flannel Suit* to the Dilbert cartoon strip, over the dehumanizing consequences of the corporate office environment. In tone this echoes an earlier dismay over the even more debilitating consequences of the factory assembly line. But there is no sense that legislation can do much about white-collar corporate *angst*, compared to the hours and working conditions of blue-collar employees (Nader 1976).

Schemes to tame the modern corporation flit in and out. One of them holds that Congress should encourage socially responsible corporate behavior by establishing "altruistic capitalism" as a legal standard for corporate conduct. It could do so by requiring large corporations to draw two thirds of their directors from a "National Directors' Corps," "an elite group made up of experienced business and professional people committed to promoting altruistic capitalism." But even this proposal blunts its edge by requiring corporations to "strike a reasonable balance" between profits and the avoidance of undesirable social consequences. The American Law Institute's *Restatement of Principles of Corporate Governance*, which appeared in final form in 1994, sought to add ethical and public interest considerations to the traditional stress on profits and shareholders—with what impact is still uncertain, though the outcome of other ALI restatements suggests that no one should raise their hopes too high (Weiss 1980, 345, 418–34; American Law Institute 1994; Pejovich 1984).

One attempt to redefine modern corporation law proposes that the firm be viewed as a "nexus of contracts," a legal entity that is not a creation of the state or a person/citizen, but a set of contractual relationships: between owner/stockholders and managers, between management and workers. That concept fits well with the currently prevailing tendency to discuss the efficiency or inefficiency of corporate regulation in terms of neoclassical economic theory. Given the free-market orientation of this approach, the conclusion usually is on the side of regulation's inefficiency (Fama 1980; Posner 1973; Easterbrook and Fischel 1991; Winter 1978).

There have also been efforts to redefine the legal character of the corporation in ways that support a more collectivist approach. The concept of corporate "stakeholders," including not only stockholders and managers but employees, customers, and the general public, is an example of this. At the twentieth century's end there was talk of a "team production" approach to corporate law. This sought to replace the regnant view that the only responsibility of company directors (the firm's agents) was to maximize the return to shareholders (the firm's principals). Instead, it proposed that the value of the firm lies in the cooperative efforts—the team production—of managers, workers, and stockholders, and that directors are responsible to all of these parties (Hutton 1999; Blair and Stout 1999, 743–50; Bebchuck 1989).

Antitrust remains the most conspicuous form of corporate regulation. But it cannot be said that the issues (and outcomes) of antitrust in the late twentieth century differ significantly from those of earlier years. From *Standard Oil* and *American Tobacco* to the IBM, AT&T, Intel, and Microsoft cases of recent decades, from Brandeis and Holmes to Nader and Bork, the interplay of results (and nonresults), of conflicting issues and ideas, has been strikingly consistent. Since 1950, as before, the vigor of government antitrust suits and judicial responses has varied according to the inclinations of presidents, attorneys general and other enforcers, and judges. Enforcement slackened in the 1950s and 1980s, picked up in the 1960s and 1990s. Michael Pertschuk enlivened (some would say over-enlivened) the FTC in the 1960s; Arthur Levitt re-energized the SEC and Robert Pitofsky the FTC in the 1990s (Bork 1978).

In part this reflects the recurrent character of corporate mergers and consolidations and the inherent difficulty of regulating them. The conglomeration movement of the 1960s was brought down by its own inefficiencies, before the cumbersome machinery of antitrust could be brought to bear on it. (By 1977, about a third of the businesses acquired in the merger wave had been divested.) Between January 1984 and July 1985, 398 of the nation's 850 largest firms were restructured to avoid hostile takeovers—to the silence of a notably nonbarking regulatory watchdog. The experiences of IBM, AT&T, and most recently Microsoft strongly suggest that market control is as subject today to the vagaries of technological and other sources of economic change as it was in the days of Standard Oil, United States Steel, and the major railroad lines (Grandy 1993, 3–5).

The early-twentieth-century "rule of reason" in antitrust cases has been substantially replaced in judicial thinking by sophisticated economic analysis. But the underlying assumption behind antitrust in action—that big business is to be judged on the basis of its actual behavior and economic consequences, rather than by abstractions such as the nature of the corporation or "the curse of bigness"—remains alive and well.

The most notable late-twentieth-century twist to the antitrust impulse of the early twentieth century has been the effort to subject corporate political and public relations spending to government control: "First Amendment Antitrust." There is an eerie similarity between the debate a century ago over corporations' economic power and how to contain it, and the current controversy over their political power and how to contain it.

Restrictions on corporate campaign contributions date from the Tillman Act of 1907. The most significant recent regulatory effort by the federal government was the Federal Election Campaign Act (FECA) of 1971—the Sherman Act of First Amendment antitrust—and the Federal Election Commission (FEC)—its FTC. The analogy is not inappropriate: "The FECA was based on the idea that controls are needed to prevent powerful economic forces from warping the electoral [as, earlier, the economic] process." To pursue the metaphor: the FECA provision allowing corporations to donate funds to supposedly independent units—"ideological nonprofits" or Political Action Committees—has had as unexpected (and, for many, as undesired) an effect as the spur the Sherman Antitrust Act gave to the creation of holding companies (Vandegrift 1980, 469).

The courts' interpretation of First Amendment antitrust has been as variable as their treatment of economic antitrust. The Supreme Court in 1906 thought that corporations were protected by the Fourth Amendment's prohibition of unreasonable searches and seizures, but it refused to extend that protection to the Fifth Amendment right against self-incrimination. In 1942 the Court decided that the First Amendment did not block the regulation of commercial advertising. But the relationship of "commercial speech" to "political speech" remains complex and unclear. False and misleading statements about a product can constitute (as the FTC has long held) a conspiracy in restraint of trade. But in itself commercial speech can convey useful price and quality information to consumers (*Hale v. Henkel* [1906]; *Valentine v. Chrestensen* [1942]; Ross 1985, 445–69).

During the 1970s, the right of corporations to engage in political speech was broadly upheld. In *Buckley v. Valeo* (1976) the Court defanged FECA restrictions on corporate political spending as effectively as *E. C. Knight*, the Sugar Trust Case, had weakened the Sherman Act more than a century ago. And in *First National Bank v. Belotti* (1978), a Court majority extended a company's right to political expression even if it had no direct economic interest in the issue at stake. State control of speech, it argued, was in and of itself a suspect activity; and there was no evidence in this instance that corporate influence on Massachusetts politics was so outsized. Among the dissenters was Justice William Rehnquist, in strange bedfellowship with colleagues Thurgood Marshall, William Douglas, and William Brennan. The latter three wanted limits on corporate spending to level the political playing field; Rehnquist was concerned to safeguard the power of the states in a federal system of government. Similarly complex crosscurrents were common in early-twentieth-century economic antitrust decisions.

The *Belotti* decision stirred up one of those law review controversies that reflects the state of mind of the legal academy as much as it does the real world of law and regulation. *Belotti's* stark restatement of the liberal view of civil liberties as embodied in Holmes's "marketplace of ideas" metaphor was a red flag to the legal Left. Analogizing corporate speech to the speech of individuals not only pumped new life into the corporation-as-person legal fiction; it antagonized those who inclined to the view that "democratic capitalism" is "a contradiction in terms" (Cole 1991, 271; Patton and Bartlett 1981; Bolton 1980).

The effort to regulate corporate political spending got a boost from *Austin v. Michigan Chamber of Commerce* (1990), which appeared to open the door to substantive enforcement of First Amendment antitrust. The majority argued that there was a compelling state interest in stopping the corruption of the political process by "huge corporate treasuries." It distinguished the state Chamber of Commerce from incorporated advocacy groups on the ground that the former was not primarily in the business of influencing public debate.

Dissenting Justice Antonin Scalia acidly criticized the majority for condoning a state's constraint on political speech: "the Court today endorses the principle that too much speech is an evil that the democratic majority can proscribe." But an advocate of First Amendment antitrust argued that to endorse corporate freedom of speech today was equivalent to arguing for corporate liberty of contract a century ago. "[W]e must," he said, "empower government to minimize the threats to freedom of speech rights posed by private concentrations of wealth." The analogy of late-twentieth-century First Amendment antitrust with late-nineteenth-century economic antitrust is, it appears, complete (*Austin* at 669, 679).

But it seems likely that it will be as difficult to regulate corporations' political activity as it was to regulate their economic activity. As in the case of economic antitrust, "a complex, technical, and often illogical system regulating corporate political activity" has emerged. The FEC's opinions on acceptable and unacceptable political expenditure echo the sinuosities of the courts' treatment of economic antitrust. Should distinctions be made between commercial and "nonprofit ideological corporations," between corporate and union engagement in politics? Will it become necessary to distinguish between "good" and "bad" corporate political expenditures, as was done with the business practices of holding companies a century ago? May we expect soon a "rule of reason" standard for judging what is acceptable corporate political expression (Vandegrift 1980, 469; Cole 1991, 255–56, 262)?

This is not to say that the legal situation of American corporations has remained static over the course of the late twentieth century. As in the past, change has come from unexpected sources. One is the growth of environmental and workplace regulation, not necessarily directed at corporations as such but profoundly affecting them. Another is the explosion of product liability suits. A third has been the internationalization of business in all its aspects: ownership, management, production, markets.

The most substantial changes in the regulation of late-twentieth-century American corporations have had little to do with their structure, size, and economic power *per se*, the prime concerns of the early-twentieth-century regulatory movement. Instead they have come from what once would have been regarded as externalities: the social consequences of corporate activity. During the 1960s and 1970s, legislation established new regulatory regimes policing pollution and the environment (twenty-seven major laws between 1970 and 1990), worker safety, health care and pension plans, and racial or gender discrimination in the workplace. These laws added up to a significant tightening of the regulatory environment of large corporations. They have also had unanticipated and controversial consequences, as in the cases of automobile pollution controls and affirmative action: very much in the American regulatory grain (Weiss 1980, 347–48, 393–404).

Comparably important has been the so-called liability explosion. After the Civil War, punitive damage was eliminated from tort cases brought against corporations, on the ground that this constituted an improper mix of the functions of public and private law. But over the course of the twentieth century, judges substantially reduced the need to show negligence as a requirement of fault, established a broad definition of implied warranty, and enabled users and bystanders once thought well outside the reasonable sphere of tort actions to collect damages.

Year after year, multimillion—now multibillion—dollar judgments, in which punitive damages greatly outstrip compensatory ones, have been part of the American legal scene. Class action suits—against asbestos, chemical, and other industrial firms; against automobile and cigarette manufacturers—are in effect a major new regulatory instrument. True, compensation is commonly scaled back on appeal, and awards vastly benefiting individual parties and trial lawyers hardly constitute an equitable redistribution of corporate wealth. But there is no denying the impact of the liability explosion on companies' safety and warranty practices (Huber 1988).

There is another significant dimension to the evolving legal status of the corporation that may turn out to be the most important of all: the increasingly international character of corporate ownership and operation. Firms come into contact not only with a number of national legal systems, but with international bodies such as the International Labor Organization and the World Trade Organization, as well as with nongovernmental organizations concerned with health, environmental, labor, and other issues. Just as the rise of the national corporation in the late nineteenth century gave a new character to corporation law, the fact that more and more large corporations are transnational in their ownership, structure, and operations has had a major impact on their legal and regulatory milieu. Problems of taxation, intellectual property, and antitrust have already arisen. Half of the mergers investigated by the FTC today are international in character.

The legal implications of this transnational corporate environment are perhaps most evident in the European Community (EC). American companies have for some time been establishing wholly owned subsidiaries in Europe to manufacture, distribute, and license products, and European companies have been doing the same in the United States. Increasingly complex stock acquisition practices are designed to circumvent antimerger regulations, thus further obscuring the already murky issues of ownership and responsibility in a multinational corporate world.

American companies doing business in Europe face not only a variety of national legal systems, but an EC "competition law" that resembles but also differs from that of the United States. It is run by a European Commission and a European Court of Justice: a full-fledged judicial and administrative structure. The EC is not a national or international body in the traditional sense, yet it has sovereign jurisdiction over foreign companies doing business in its market. Indeed, the reach of the European Court extends beyond European subsidiaries to American parent companies.

In many ways the EC's authority over large enterprise is similar to that of the American government. Article 85 of the 1958 European Economic Community Treaty echoes section 1 of the Sherman Act in prohibiting anticompetitive conduct. Article 86 echoes the Sherman Act's section 2 by focusing on monopoly power and its abuse. Like the Clayton Act, the EEC Treaty prohibits specific acts such as price fixing, product or production limits, and market sharing.

Given the stronger administrative tradition in European law, it is not surprising that the Commission can issue injunctions and levy fines without having to go through the legal procedures required by the Sherman and Clayton Acts. Firms, too, have greater recourse to administrative relief. If it can be shown that product improvement or consumer benefit would result from the trade practice at issue, then an exemption from Article 85 can be granted: an administrative rather than a judicial rule of reason (Williams 1987, 517–35; Romano 1993, 128f).

The potential for conflict over jurisdiction, procedural and substantive rules, and divergent legal-judicial cultures might well seem limitless. It appears that American courts are less inclined than their European counterparts to take into account the citizenship of parties to a suit, and (presumably a reflection of their domestic experience) they are more sensitive to issues of comity.

Does the legal-regulatory response to the rise of the national corporation in America at the beginning of the twentieth century provide any useful guideposts for dealing with the transnational corporation at the beginning of the twenty-first? The international character of contemporary big business appears to make taxation and other regulatory avoidance easier. The regulatory and legal response so far rests more on a growing coordination among national enforcement bodies, and on bilateral agreements, than on the development of regulatory bodies. The lack of a supranational authority comparable to the U.S. federal government has fostered alternative modes of dispute resolution. One of these is arbitration. Companies find it less costly and inefficient to turn to arbitration, especially in clashes over such knotty issues as intellectual property.[1]

What of the future of American corporation law? There is little reason to think that antitrust will undergo a sea change. The similarities that link the Microsoft case today to the major antitrust actions of the early twentieth century are far more compelling than the differences. But there are problems that, while not new in themselves, have taken on disturbing dimensions in recent years and may call for innovative regulatory or legal remedies. The internationalization of the corporation, the problems of intellectual property posed by the computer revolution, and oversized executive compensation may be expected to produce increasing conflict, demands for amelioration, and—as night follows day—a search for legislative, administrative, and judicial solutions. What these solutions might be are, thankfully, beyond the remit of the historian. But that the old tension between the fear of corporate power and the desire for corporate efficiency will continue is as certain as anything can be (Roe 2000).

NOTE

1 Interview with former FTC chairman Robert Pitofsky.

REFERENCES

American Law Institute. 1994. *Principles of Corporate Governance: Analysis and Recommendations*. 2 vols. St. Paul, Minn.: ALI Publishers.

Arnold, Thurman W. 1937. *The Folklore of Capitalism*. New Haven, Conn.: Yale University Press.

Bebchuck, Lucian A. 1989. "The Debate on Contractual Freedom in Corporate Law," 89 *Columbia Law Review* 1395–1415.

Berle, Adolf A. Jr., and Gardiner C. Means. 1932. *The Modern Corporation and Private Property*. New York: Macmillan.

Blair, Margaret M., and Lynn A. Stout. 1999. "Team Production in Business Organizations: An Introduction," 24 *Journal of Corporation Law* (summer) 743–50.

Bolton, John R. 1980. "Constitutional Limitations on Restricting Corporate and Union Political Speech," 22 *Arizona Law Review* 373–416.

Bork, Robert H. 1978. *The Antitrust Paradox: A Policy at War with Itself*. New York: Basic Books.

Boorstin, Daniel. 1973. *The Americans: The Democratic Experience*. New York: Random House.

Cary, William L. 1974. "Federalism and Corporate Law: Reflections upon Delaware," 83 *Yale Law Journal* 663–705.

Cole, David. 1991. "First Amendment Antitrust: The End of Laissez-Faire in Campaign Finance," 9 *Yale Law and Society Review* 236–78.

Easterbrook, Frank H. 1983. "Antitrust and the Economics of Federalism," 26 *Journal of Law and Economics* 23–50.

Easterbrook, Frank H., and Daniel R. Fischel. 1991. *The Economic Structure of Corporate Law*. Cambridge: Harvard University Press.

Fama, Eugene P. 1980. "Agency Problems and the Theory of the Firm," 99 *Journal of Political Economy* 288–307.

Fischel, Daniel R. 1982. "The 'Race to the Bottom' Revisited: Reflections on Recent Developments in Delaware's Corporation Law," 76 *Northwestern University Law Review* 913–45.

Freund, Ernst. 1897. *The Legal Nature of the Corporation*. Chicago: University of Chicago Press.

Grandy, Christopher. 1993. *New Jersey and the Fiscal Origins of Modern American Corporation Law*. New York: Garland.

Hawley, Ellis. 1966. *The New Deal and the Problem of Monopoly*. Princeton, N.J.: Princeton University Press.

——. 1975. "The New Deal and Business." In *The New Deal: The National Level*, ed. John Braeman et al. Columbus: Ohio State University Press.

Horwitz, Morton J. 1992. *The Transformation of American Law 1870–1960*. Cambridge: Harvard University Press.

Hovenkamp, Herbert. 1988. "The Classical Corporation in American Legal Thought," 76 *Georgetown Law Journal* 1593–1689.

——. 1991. *Enterprise and American Law 1836–1937*. Cambridge: Harvard University Press.

Huber, Peter H. 1988. *Liability: The Legal Revolution and Its Consequences*. New York: Basic Books.

Hutton, Will. 1999. *The Stakeholding Society: Writings on Politics and Economics.* London: Blackwell.

Keller, Morton. 1977. *Affairs of State: Public Life in Late Nineteenth Century America.* Cambridge: Harvard University Press.

——. 1990. *Regulating a New Economy: Public Policy and Economic Change in America, 1900–1933.* Cambridge: Harvard University Press.

——. 1997. "The Making of the Modern Corporation," *Wilson Quarterly* (autumn) 57–69.

Letwin, William. 1965. *Law and Economic Policy in America.* New York: Random House.

Mark, Gregory A. 1987. "The Personification of the Business Corporation in American Law," 54 *University of Chicago Law Review* 1441–83.

Martin, Albro. 1971. *Enterprise Denied: Origins of the Decline of American Railroads, 1897–1917.* New York: Columbia University Press.

Nader, Ralph et al. 1976. *Taming the Giant Corporation.* New York: W. W. Norton.

Novak, William J. 1996. *The People's Welfare: Law and Regulation in Nineteenth-Century America.* Chapel Hill: University of North Carolina Press.

Patton, William, and Randall Bartlett. 1981. "Corporate 'Persons' and Freedom of Speech: The Political Impact of Legal Methodology," 1981 *Wisconsin Law Review* 494–512.

Pejovich, Steve. 1984. "Corporate Democracy: An Economist's Critique of Proposals for Corporate Governance and Structure." Washington: Washington Legal Foundation.

Posner, Richard A. 1973. *Antitrust Law: An Economic Perspective.* Chicago: University of Chicago Press.

Roe, Mark J. 2000. "Political Preconditions to Separating Ownership from Corporate Control," 53 *Stanford Law Review* 539–606.

Romano, Roberta. 1987. "The State Competition Debate: Corporate Law," 9 *Cardozo Law Review* 709–57.

——. 1993. *The Genius of American Corporate Law.* Washington, D.C.: American Enterprise Institute.

Ross, Susan L. 1985. "Corporate Speech on Political Issues: The First Amendment in Conflict with Democratic Ideals?" 1985 *University of Illinois Law Review* 445–69.

Urofsky, Melvin I. 1982. "Proposed Federal Incorporation in the Progressive Era," 26 *American Journal of Legal History* 160–83.

Vandegrift, Benjamin M. 1980. "The Corporate Political Action Committee," 55 *New York University Law Review* 422–71.

Weiss, Elliott J. 1980. "Social Regulation of Business Activity: Reforming the Corporate Governance System to Resolve an Institutional Impasse," 28 *UCLA Law Review* 343–437.

Williams, Marcus D. 1987. "European Antitrust Law and Its Application to American Corporations and their Subsidiaries," 9 *Whittier Law Review* 517–35.

Winter, Ralph K. 1978. *Government and the Corporation.* Washington, D.C.: American Enterprise Institute Press.

CASES CITED

Austin v. Michigan Chamber of Commerce, 494 U.S. 652 (1990).
Buckley v. Valeo, 424 U.S. 1 (1976).
Burks v. Lasker, 441 U.S. 471 (1979).
Charles River Bridge v. Warren, 36 U.S. 420 (1837).
Dartmouth College v. Woodward, 17 U.S. 179 (1819).
First National Bank v. Belotti, 435 U.S. 765 (1978).
Hale v. Henkel, 201 U.S. 43 (1906).
Northern Securities Co. v. U.S., 193 U.S. 197 (1904).
Santa Clara County v. Southern Pacific Railroad Co., 118 U.S. 394 (1886).
Standard Oil Co. v. U.S., 221 U.S. 1 (1911).
U.S. v. American Tobacco Co., 221 U.S. 106 (1911).
Valentine v. Chrestensen, 316 U.S. 52 (1942).

The Legal Origins of the Modern American State

William J. Novak

The transformation of the State is also the transformation of its Law.
—Léon Duguit

BETWEEN 1877 AND 1937 (between the formal end of Reconstruction and the formal constitutional ratification of the New Deal), the American system of governance was transformed, with momentous implications for twentieth-century social and economic life. Nineteenth-century traditions of self-government and local citizenship were replaced by a modern approach to positive statecraft, individual rights, and social welfare that is still very much with us today. The last such formative transformation in the structure of American public life, in the late eighteenth century, was dubbed by Gordon Wood "The Creation of the American Republic" (Wood 1969). The late-nineteenth and early-twentieth-century revolution in governance is best characterized as "The Creation of the American Liberal State."

By "The Creation of the American Liberal State" I mean to suggest that the period from 1877 to 1937 was not just an "age of reform" or a "response to industrialism" or a "search for order" (Hofstadter 1955; Hays 1957; Wiebe 1967). Rather, it was an era marked by the specific and unambiguous emergence of a new regime of American governance—the modern liberal state. Nineteenth-century patterns of social governance and local economic regulation—what I have described elsewhere (Novak 1996) as "the well-regulated society"—were displaced by a decisive twentieth-century reconfiguration of the relationship between state, capitalism, and population in the United States. A central nation-state consolidated around new positive and political conceptions of sovereignty and administration radically extended its reach into American economy and society. In the social sphere, new forms of cultural policing and social policymaking transformed the relationship of state and society. Social welfare emerged as a new object of a national administration increasingly committed to guaranteeing social rights and managing and insuring its population. In the economic sphere, the relationship of government and business underwent a similar restructuring. The state regulation of monopoly capital and mass production and consumption ushered in a new understanding of the interdependence of statecraft and economic growth and a new political-economic vision of planning and managed capitalism. Together these changes contributed to a portentous restructuring of American liberalism and democratic governance that arguably is the most significant legal-governmental development of the twentieth century.

Of course, this transformation in American governance and the creation of a modern administrative state in the United States has not escaped the notice of historians, social scientists, and legal scholars. Indeed, as Dorothy Ross (1991), Daniel Rodgers (1998), and James Kloppenberg (1986) have most recently reminded us, the very origins of modern social-scientific inquiry in the United States were wholly coincident with and participatory in the construction of the new state-centered socioeconomic policies of the Progressive era (Haskell 1977; Furner 1975; Lacey and Furner 1993). By mid-century, the theme of the relationship between American capitalism and democracy on the one hand and new forms of state organization on the other consumed innumerable liberal commentaries, from Thurman Arnold's *Folklore of Capitalism* (1937) to Karl Mannheim's *Freedom, Power, and Democratic Planning* (1950) to John Kenneth Galbraith's *New Industrial State* (1967). More recently under the rallying cry "Bringing the State Back In," new institutional sociologists and political scientists like Theda Skocpol (1992) and Stephen Skowronek (1982) have recentered attention on the transformations in the political structure and socioeconomic policies of the emerging American welfare state (Evans, Rueschemeyer, and Skocpol 1985). In the field of American history, such concerns did not need to be brought "back in," because they remained a staple of twentieth-century political history through the work of scholars like William Leuchtenburg (1963), Morton Keller (1977 and 1990), Barry Karl (1983), Ellis Hawley (1966), and Louis Galambos (1970). Even after the dramatic shift to social and cultural historical methodologies in the 1970s, historians of American labor, gender, and race relations have maintained a focus on the policies and social consequences of the creation of a twentieth-century American welfare state. Whether examining the tortuous emergence of New Deal labor regulations, the maternalist origins of welfare policy, or the racially constructed hierarchies of modern social services, social and cultural historians continue to expand our understanding of the multivalent social and political components of the American version of a social welfare state (Lichtenstein and Harris 1993; Gordon 1990; Katz 1993).

But within the rapidly expanding social-scientific literature on the emergence of a modern state in America, there lurks a consistent and curious interpretive deficiency. That deficiency concerns the role of *law* in that governmental transformation. Overwhelmingly, and with few exceptions, the rule of law is portrayed throughout the synthetic literature as something of an obstruction, a brake, an inertial force, a structural impediment, an ideological hindrance, an exceptionalist constitutional barrier to the development of a modern regulatory and administrative welfare state in the United States. From the first treatises of Progressive social science to the newest institutional studies, law, courts, and judges are represented continuously as great bogeymen of liberal reform—agents of an exceptionalist and backward-looking American jurisprudential tradition that regularly frustrated modern welfare statebuilding efforts. This chapter is an attempt to challenge (indeed, reverse) that pervasive mischaracterization.

The thesis that American law has operated as a negative check on the development of a modern bureaucratic welfare state in the United States is flawed in two respects. First, it neglects the important creative and constitutive (what some have called the *juris-generative*) role of law in the creation of the modern American state. For more than a century, historical and sociological jurisprudence has tried to move our conception of law beyond a negative and transcendental "series of Thou Shalt Nots addressed to power holders" toward a more positive and realistic conception of law as "the application of politically organized compulsion upon men's wills."[1] Such an active and constructive understanding of law downplays the significance of occasional tabloid constitutional cases like the *Slaughterhouse Cases, In Re Debs, Lochner v. New York*, and *Schechter Poultry*. Instead it emphasizes the massive amount of everyday lawmaking (judicial, legislative, and administrative) and the structural sociolegal changes accruing beneath surface political-constitutional skirmishes.[2] For example, in the arena of public law (the arena most susceptible to charges of welfare state obstructionism), this chapter introduces some of the new legal definitions of Union, national citizenship, constitutionalism, the state, sovereignty, positive law, legislation, federal police power, and administrative law without which it is difficult to contemplate the rise of any kind of welfare state in the United States. Such definitions embodied legal transformations of the first order that constituted the modern American state. The countless changes in private law (property, contract, tort, corporation law, commercial law, insurance law, etc.) that aided and abetted the creation of the American liberal state must also be factored into our story of modern political development. The failure to account for this positive (as opposed to negative) role of law in the construction of a central regulatory welfare state raises serious questions about our understanding of basic mechanisms of twentieth-century political-institutional change.

The second flaw in this "lag-and-drag" interpretation of the role of law in modern state-building is the way it distorts our characterizations of historical changes in American liberalism. For the negative legalism that is seen as obstructing twentieth-century social democracy is often identified as the residuum of a nineteenth-century jurisprudential tradition of natural law and individual rights that is out of step with the needs of a modern economy and society. The obstructionist interpretation of law and the welfare state, in other words, comes with a historical account of American political change. That account is dominated by the notion of a wholesale shift in the nature of liberalism from the nineteenth to the twentieth century—a shift precipitated by the rise of industrial and corporate capitalism. Whether characterized in A.V. Dicey's (1914) terms as a shift from individualism to collectivism or in Roscoe Pound's (1909) notion of a move from negative liberty to positive liberty or in John Dewey's (1935) ideas about the progression from old to new liberalism, this interpretation emphasizes the great transformation from nineteenth-century laissez-faire to the twentieth-century general welfare state. Particular political and intellectual attention is paid to the fierce turn-of-the-century battles that accompanied the transition: e.g., battles between conservative reaction and liberal progressivism in politics and between classical legal thought and legal realism in jurisprudence.

The myths of nineteenth-century laissez-faire, possessive individualism, and vested rights have been the targets of repeated critiques by legal historians since the breakthrough historical-sociological work of Willard Hurst (1956; Handlin and Handlin 1947; Hartz 1948; Lively 1955; Scheiber 1972; Novak 1996). Unfortunately, not as much critical legal attention has focused on the other half of the omnipresent laissez-faire/welfare state, individualism/collectivism, negative liberty/positive liberty formula—the role of law in the creation of a twentieth-century welfare state. This chapter looks into that other hand clapping: first, by investigating the origins and objectives of the persistent Progressive critique of law versus the state; second, by confronting that critique with rather obvious evidence of law's ubiquitous and positive role in welfare-state development (particularly in the transformative field of public law); and third, by suggesting the degree to which a fuller account of legal change in this crucial period of governmental development alters our perception of the evolution of American liberalism.

The formative period from 1877 to 1937 in United States history was not about a simple shift from laissez-faire individualism to interventionist statecraft, from a bourgeois *Rechtstaat* to a modern welfare state. Nor was it about a polarized battle between a backward-looking liberal rule of law and a forward-looking social-democratic welfare politics. Rather, the story was one of the mutual reconstitution of a jural *and* a welfare state, of liberalism *and* social welfare, of the rule of law *and* modern political administration—the synthetic story of the creation of a decidedly new liberal constitutional state.

But clearing the path for such a symbiotic understanding of the relationship of twentieth-century legal and state development first requires a reckoning with a powerful old paradigm—the legacy of *Lochner*—the idea of "legal orthodoxy" and the persistent Progressive conviction that higher law obstructed the people's welfare state. For the intellectual constructions of laissez-faire vs.

the welfare state and the rule of law vs. social-democratic politics were very much the products of the fierce political, economic, and constitutional battles that greeted the arrival of the twentieth century. And though they have dominated our understanding of law and statecraft for the last hundred years, they now mask more than they reveal. Laissez-faire vs. the welfare state; law vs. the state; negative vs. positive liberty; and individual rights vs. collective goods are basically turn-of-the-century ideological constructions that continue to obscure more significant systemic and structural changes in the modern American governmental regime. We should resist carrying over such constructions into our analyses of law and modern political economy as we open a new century.

INVENTING THE *LOCHNER* COURT: THE PROGRESSIVE DISCOVERY THAT LAW OBSTRUCTS POLITICS

It is easy amid the rapid shifts in contemporary intellectual fashion to forget the long and pervasive hold of "progressive historiography" on American thought during the first half of the twentieth century (Hofstadter 1968; Benson 1960; Horwitz 1984). From the turn of the century through the late New Deal, American political and economic development was interpreted primarily through the filter of intellectual categories developed in contests over Progressive reform in the early twentieth century. The essence of Progressive historiography was a remarkably simple understanding of the dynamics of historical change that stressed the determinative role of foundational socioeconomic conflict (often portrayed in a crude and normatively charged good fellow/bad fellow dialectic: e.g., the people vs. the interests, agriculture vs. commerce, democracy vs. capitalism). In the muckraking context of the turn of the century, such categories reflected the sense that the United States was riven with a basic class conflict that pitted the private economic interests of industrial robber barons against the public goods of democratic legislators seeking to curb the excesses of unregulated capitalism. Such stark normative juxtapositions of private and public, individual and democracy, self-interest and benevolence in the hands of provocative writers like Vernon Parrington and Charles Beard produced a powerful paradigm for thinking about the relationship of capitalism and the state in the United States. As Vernon Parrington summarized: "A lawless and unregulated individualism was destroying democracy. Government was becoming the mouthpiece and the agent of property interests. Something had gone wrong with the democratic plans and it was time for the friends of democracy to take stock of the situation" (Parrington 1930, ix). Progressive history provided a usable past—a great morality play—with which to promote the cause of reform legislation in the early twentieth century.

At the heart of the Progressive paradigm was a comparably simple understanding of the role of law in this great political contest. Parrington characterizes it as the Progressive "distrust of the judicial exercise of sovereign powers." As he put it, "Discovering when it attempted to regulate business that its hands were tied by judicial decrees, the democracy began to question the reasons for the bonds that constrained its will" (1930, xii).[3] For many Progressives, that was the basic story: the socioeconomic inequities of industrialization galvanized a mass of democratic reform legislation that was in turn frustrated by legal and judicial obstructionism. Law and the courts became, in Max Lerner's (1933, 672) words, "one of the great American ogres, part of the demonology of liberal and radical thought."

Charles Beard was the fountainhead for the Progressive critique of law. Beard's *Economic Interpretation of the Constitution* (1913) served as a thinly veiled critique of the U.S. Supreme Court. His historical analysis of the Constitution as an instrument through which specific economic interests of the founding generation were secured fit all too easily with a Progressive interpretation of a Supreme Court suspected of reading class interests into American constitutional law. In his *Contemporary American History, 1877–1913* (1914, 54), Beard was more explicit. In a section titled "Writing Laissez-Faire into the Constitution," Beard described a "new senatorial philosophy" that emerged in the late nineteenth century epitomized by Roscoe Conkling, corporate lawyer. That philosophy exalted personal private property rights and vigorously opposed the efforts of state legislatures to regulate property, franchises, and corporate privileges. According to Beard, Mr. Conkling's "group" actively sought a new jurisprudence—"some juristic process for translating laissez-faire into a real restraining force." In the development of Fourteenth Amendment constitutionalism, Conkling's army found a potent weapon to secure "federal judicial supremacy for the defense of corporations and business enterprises everywhere." As evidence for his thesis, Beard devised an oft-cited litany of the malevolent cases through which laissez-faire was written into the Constitution by a pro-business, anti-regulatory Supreme Court. Beard reached the constitutional pinnacle of this era, *Lochner v. New York* (1905), with the same conclusion articulated in Justice Holmes's dissent—American courts were guilty of deciding cases upon a social theory and economic interests out of synch with the democratic majority and the public welfare. Thus the idea of "Lochnerism"—of the invention of laissez-faire constitutionalism by an activist, economically interested Supreme Court to bolster the conservative status quo against the regulatory, social-welfare initiatives of Progressive reform—received one of its earliest statements.

But Charles Beard did not invent the Progressive critique of law single-handedly. Rather, legions of reformers, scholars, and publicists mounted an unprecedented campaign against the power of American courts and judges that continued into the 1960s (well after other parts of the Progressive paradigm expired) and that still resonates in legal-political scholarship to this day. In the early twentieth century, Beard was joined in his crusade by Louis Boudin (1932), J. Allen Smith (1930), Edward Corwin (1938), Frank Goodnow (1911), Gustavus Myers (1912), and others whose very titles reflected the main lines of the Progressive critique of law: *Government by Judiciary; The Growth and Decadence of Constitutional Government; Court over Constitution; Social Reform and the Constitution.* Frank Goodnow (1911, v) opened his investigation with a straightforward statement of Progressive purpose: "To ascertain, from an examination of the decisions of our courts . . . to what extent the Constitution of the United States in its present form is a bar to the adoption of the most important social reform measures which have been made parts of the reform program of the most progressive peoples of the present day." J. Allen Smith (1930, vii) more aggressively attacked the immanent "reactionary" spirit of U.S. constitutional law—"its inherent opposition to democracy, the obstacles which it has placed in the way of majority rule." Louis Boudin (1932, viii) began *Government by Judiciary* with a typical, foreordained acerbic conclusion: "We are ruled by *dead Men* . . . generations of dead judges." As if to seal the fate of the possibilities for law in the eyes of Progressives, to this critique of economic interest, conservative reaction, and antistatism was added the nebulous and damaging charge of the revival of natural law. Progressives like Pound (1909, 457, 460, 464) and Corwin (1955) honed the critique that lawyers and judges were trapped in anachronistic "eighteenth century theories of natural law" developed in the "high tide of individualistic ethics and economics" exaggerating "the importance of property and of contract." Law was thus not only obstructionist, but decidedly backward-looking, cloaked in the ancient metaphysics of the vaguely theocratic language of natural law (Haines 1930; Wright 1931; Fine 1956).

The confrontation between Franklin Roosevelt's New Deal legislation and Supreme Court constitutional review breathed new life into the Progressive critique of law. In 1938 Benjamin Twiss began his *Lawyers and the Constitution: How Laissez Faire Came to the Supreme Court* (1942) as a direct response to the "revolution of 1937" and as a direct attack on the "Four Horsemen" of anti–New Deal judicial apocalypse: Justices Van Devanter, McReynolds, Sutherland, and Butler. Twiss's story about law and the New Deal redeployed the stock figures and simple morals of a mature Progressive historiography. Citing Beard, Boudin, Corwin, Goodnow Holmes, Myers, Pound, and Veblen, Twiss began, "Americans are today beginning to learn that judicial decisions are not babies brought by constitutional storks but are born out of the travail of economic circumstance." Pushing Beard's economic interpretation almost to the point of self-caricature, Twiss portrayed a self-interested capitalist bench and bar brimming with lawyers like Joseph Hodges Choate—so "effectively quarantined from the Great Unwashed" that "his words virtually smelled of soap" (1942, 114, 260). From 1870 through 1937, lawyers like Choate amounted to "an inner council containing and representing the intelligence of . . . the dominant economic class" whose jurisprudential preoccupation was the elaboration of new doctrines (e.g., implied constitutional limitations,[4] dual federalism, liberty of contract, substantive due process) to protect established business interests and to eviscerate Progressive and New Deal reform initiatives.

Though other aspects of Progressive history suffered intense critical assaults in the 1950s and 1960s, the Progressive critique of law continued to flourish as historians like Clyde Jacobs (1954), Arnold Paul (1960), and Sidney Fine (1956) embellished the simple story line of Beard and Twiss. Jacobs emphasized the roles of treatise writers like Thomas Cooley, Christopher Tiedeman, and John Dillon in forging the laissez-faire doctrines of liberty of contract and the public purpose maxim restricting the taxing and spending powers of state and local governments. In the aptly titled *Conservative Crisis and the Rule of Law*, Arnold Paul examined battles over antitrust, labor law, and the income tax in coming to the familiar Progressive conclusion that turn-of-the-century economic conflict transformed the American judiciary into the principal bulwark of capitalist conservatism. But perhaps most significant for extending the Progressive critique of law beyond the New Deal was Sidney Fine's historical popularization of the idea of a great intellectual transformation. In a key chapter of his *Laissez Faire and the General-Welfare State* titled "Laissez Faire Becomes the Law of the Land," Fine synthesized the great mass of Progressive constitutional historiography (including the controversial charge of "the revival of natural law") in reaching the powerful conclusion that "it was in the courts that the idea of laissez faire won its greatest victory . . . establishing the courts as the ultimate censors of virtually all forms of social and economic legislation." Fine celebrated the victory of the general-welfare state over laissez-faire by the time of Harry Truman's Fair Deal and extended the Progressives' negative opinion of the role of law in that process: "The judiciary placed itself between the public and what the public needed and helped to protect individuals who did not need protection against society, which did need it" (1956, 126, 164).

Historians and social scientists have long since rejected many aspects of the Progressive synthesis—its economic reductionism, its instrumentalist treatment of ideas, its dichotomous conception of socioeconomic interest and conflict, its explicit moralizing, its presentist political partisanship, and its simple good fellow/bad fellow dialectic. As Richard Hofstadter argued, one of the key developments in social scientific thought since the 1950s was "the rediscovery of complexity in American history" as "an engaging and moving simplicity, accessible to the casual reader of history, [gave] way to a new awareness of the multiplicity of forces." Admitting the attraction of the simple schemas of progressive history, Hofstadter contended, "we [could] hardly continue to believe in them" (1968, 442). But despite the general disenchantment with Progressive categories, the influence of the Progressive critique of *law* persists.

Though the techniques of modern American legal history were first honed by Willard Hurst and others in search of the legal roots of modern economic and administrative policy, of late legal history has returned to variations on a neo-Progressive theme. Morton Horwitz, the most influential of Hurst's successors, has quite consciously reinvigorated one of the Progressives' oldest and most powerful legal theses—the idea of *law as politics*. In 1933, Max Lerner summed up the Progressive legal project: "At the heart of these polemics is the recognition that the real meaning of the Court is to be found in the political rather than the legal realm, and that its concern is more significantly with power politics than with judicial technology" (1933, 669). Though Horwitz's *Transformation of American Law* (1977 and 1992) paid more attention to doctrinal technology and private law than any of the Progressives did, his underlying objective in those volumes remained the same—to unveil the distinct politics of American law. Those politics echoed the Progressive critique: the American rule of law as calculatingly anti-democratic, economically conservative, and anti-redistributive—a hindrance to social-democratic or radical politics. Similarly, in the well-developed field of labor law, the Progressive theme of American law obstructing and constricting a more radical form of social-democratic politics has become something of a mantra. Starting with "Tocqueville's emphasis on the powers of the American legal and judicial elite over against society's 'democratic element,'" William Forbath has influentially argued for the "constitutive power of law" in narrowing the ambitions of the American labor movement. As Forbath concluded, "Labor's law-inspired laissez-faire rights rhetoric imported some of the liberal legal order's key assumptions about the uses and limits of state power. Thus it helped to recast many of labor's aspirations for reform and redistribution as not fit to be addressed to the state and polity" (1991, x, 169–71).[5]

But while the critical legal studies movement (Kairys 1982) has been particularly adroit in expropriating the Progressive themes of law as politics and law as an obstacle to social democracy, the more general theme of a fundamental turn-of-the-century shift from legal orthodoxy to Progressive reform has pervaded histories of all ideological tenors. Herbert Hovenkamp's law-and-economics tale of the rise and fall of nineteenth-century legal classicism perfectly complemented Sidney Fine. Hovenkamp's conclusion that "American constitutional law came to be built on the political economy of an unreconstructed Adam Smith" (i.e., hostile to state regulation and committed to wealth maximization, laissez-faire, private rights, and the virtues of self-interest) was classically Progressive (1991, 69). The disproportionate amount of attention devoted to legal realism and its critique of classical legal thought in twentieth-century legal history has directly extended Progressive themes (e.g., Hull 1997; Kalman 1986; Schlegel 1995; Twining 1973). The field of constitutional history, recently revived through the contributions of Jack Rakove (1996), Akhil Amar (1998), and Bruce Ackerman (1991), has basically returned to the classic interpretive framework and chronology of the Progressive scholar Edward S. Corwin, with his focus on three great constitutional moments (1787, 1868, and 1937) and his emphasis on three overarching themes: the origins of constitutional review, the content of constitutional rights, and Lochnerism and its New Deal repudiation.

But legal and constitutional historians have not been alone in the continued propagation of Progressive priorities. American political scientists and historical sociologists have assembled a portrait of a long and complex American state-building process that contrasts with the episodic and exceptionalist chronologies of some constitutional history. By examining the rise of the American welfare state and the development of American political organization in the broader context of Western socioeconomic and political modernization (à la Marx, Weber, Durkheim, and their progeny), scholars like Theda Skocpol (1992), Stephen Skowronek (1982), and Daniel Rodgers (1998) have increased our understanding of the range of variables and the transatlantic forces driving the expansion of the American polity in the early twentieth century. They have made certain aspects of the Progressive synthesis increasingly untenable: e.g., the harsh dichotomy of laissez-faire and welfare state, the overdetermined force of economic interest, and the causal personification of "reaction" and "democracy." But unfortunately, they have embraced Progressive legal history with enthusiasm. For front and center in the best new works on modern American state and political development is the classic Progressive trope: law as obstruction.[6]

Stephen Skowronek re-energized the historical study of American political development in political science with his influential thesis describing the nineteenth-century American polity as a wholly operational "state of courts and parties." Skowronek's argument about the actual local and functional use of nineteenth-century legal-political power was an important repudiation of naive Progressive ideas about laissez-faire. More problematic and more Progressive, however, was his conclusion that it was this very legalism of the early American state that frustrated twentieth-century reform efforts to build a more modern, national apparatus. One of the main reasons for "the limits of America's achievement in regenerating the state through political reform" for Skowronek was the "outmoded judicial discipline" created by "the constancy of the Constitution of 1789." As he concluded, "Forged in the wake of a liberal revolt against the state, the American Constitution has always been awkward and incomplete as an organization of state power" (1982, 287).

Similarly, Theda Skocpol, who perhaps more than any other scholar has expanded the depth and breadth of our understanding of the rise of a modern American social-welfare state, has also isolated the rule of law primarily as a constraint, forcing American reform in an exceptionalist maternalist direction (as opposed to the more paternalist workingmen's policies of European nations). Drawing directly on the secondary interpretations of Forbath and Skowronek (as well as Paul and Horwitz), Skocpol has argued that "repeated experiences with a court-dominated state around the turn of the century" deterred trade unionists from advocating the kinds of comprehensive social insurance and labor regulations behind the more centralized, bureaucratic social-welfare states of western Europe (1992, 227).[7] Law functioned as "hindrance" as well in Daniel Rodgers's comparative examination of the origins of modern social policy. In assessing the reasons for the limits of urban planning in early twentieth-century America, Rodgers pointed his finger directly at "the peculiarities of the law in the United States," what Thomas Adams called "the practically cast-iron Constitution" that "hemmed in American urban reformers in ways no progressives elsewhere experienced" (1998, 201). Thus, despite the progress of recent political history and political science in deepening our understanding of the emergence of a modern American welfare state, when it comes to the issue of law and constitutionalism we have not moved far past the original observations of the Progressives themselves. Like H. G. Wells, we continue to stress (and blame) the exceptional antistatist predilections of constitutional limitations for the peculiar structures and weaknesses of the American version of a modern polity. As Wells summarized, "America is pure eighteenth century. They took the economic conventions that were modern and progressive at the end of the eighteenth century and stamped them into the Constitution as if they meant to stamp them there for all time."[8]

Mark Twain once quipped that "though history may not repeat itself, it often rhymes." And indeed, when the topic is law and the creation of a modern social welfare state in the United States, historians and social scientists seem to speak in metrical verse. Since the early twentieth century, law has been characterized primarily as an obstruction to social-democratic political aspiration and as a principal reason for the exceptionalist trajectory of twentieth-century American state development. American Progressives felt that their legislative agenda was threatened by a Supreme Court and by American jurisprudential traditions hostile to regulation, redistribution, and reform. In response they assembled a powerful and polemical assault on American constitutionalism. The main elements of that critique resonate today in familiar phrases that furtively import the seemingly self-evident Progressive indictment into late twentieth-century analyses: government by injunction, government by judiciary, laissez-faire constitutionalism, legal (or Langdellian) orthodoxy, substantive due process, liberty of contract, the revival of natural law theory, classical legal thought, Holmes and Brandeis dissenting, the Four Horsemen, the revolution of 1937. The specter of "The *Lochner* Court" thus continues to loom large in analyses of the limits on American state-building. Why no socialism in America? Why no social rights? Why no social-democratic welfare state? Why no fundamental redistribution of wealth? The chief culprit, in classic neo-Progressive style, remains . . . the American rule of law.

THE TRANSFORMATION OF AMERICAN PUBLIC LAW

I don't buy it. In fact, the rest of this chapter advances a thesis almost directly antithetical to the Progressive critique of law. Far from being an obstruction or hindrance to the formation of a modern social-welfare state, American law, *especially* American *public* law, was in fact a font of creative energy—of legal ideas, institutions, and practices—that was absolutely crucial to the creation of a new regime of centralized, administrative, regulatory governance in the United States. Behind the Progressive mythology of negative laissez-faire constitutionalism lies an alternative story of law's positive force in producing a modern state in America. And contrary to oddly influential European proclamations of the weakness and incompleteness of that state, the obvious empirical reality is that the story of the twentieth-century American state is about the creation of a most powerful geopolitical entity. That entity, which has wielded staggering global influence in the twentieth century, was patently not the simple outgrowth of possessive individualism or of the protection of private rights of property and contract or of a governmental willingness to "leave alone." It was the product of a continuous and energetic process of state-building from 1776 through the Second World War (of the establishment of basic governing institutions, of the acquisition and distribution of new territory, of the promotion of national and international commerce, of the development of a powerful national defense, of the achievement of a regularized yet flexible national legal system, and of the growth of aggressive policies of police, regulation, administration, and redistribution) that should replace our parochial obsession with *Marbury, Lochner*, Field, Holmes, and the revolution of 1937 as the main story of American constitutional history. For the powerful twentieth-century geopolitical entity that is the American nation-state was distinctly the product of law—of a surprisingly effective common-law tradition, of important civil law conceptions of private right and public legislation, and of a constitutional law that (contrary to the Progressive critique) embraced change. Without this flexible, regularizing, and nationalizing force of law, it is difficult to imagine the diverse, divided, sectionalized, and conflicted population of the United States achieving anything like a modern state, let alone one of the most powerful in the world. Contrary to the opinions of its many critics, the many-sided legality of the American polity was not a weakness, but the key to its distinctive strength.

There are several places from which we might begin an effort to recapture the story of the positive force of law in modern American statebuilding. One is the nineteenth century. Though Progressives liked to posit a nineteenth century of laissez-faire, negative liberty, and old liberalism, legal histories of the period tell a different story—a tale of law crucially deployed in the creation of a national state and economy.[9] One of the most common themes in American constitutionalism, after all, is the central role of the Marshall Court in forging the legal prerequisites for a strong national commercial union through opinions like *Fletcher v. Peck, Dartmouth College, McCulloch v. Maryland*, and *Gibbons v. Ogden* (Beveridge 1916–1919; Corwin 1919; Newmyer 1986; White 1990). The instrumentality of American private law in creating and regulating the conditions for the growth of a national economy has been agreed to by scholars as ideologically different as Willard Hurst and Morton Horwitz (Hurst 1956; Horwitz 1977; Friedman 1973). And the so-called "commonwealth historians" have definitively demonstrated the active role of the nineteenth-century state through law in establishing, promoting, and regulating the nation's socioeconomic infrastructure through public works, subsidization, corporate charters, public lands policies, eminent domain, mixed enterprises, and the police power (Handlin and Handlin 1947; Hartz 1948; Lively 1955; Scheiber 1972; Novak 1996). With this established picture of the prolific role of law in nineteenth-century statebuilding and economic growth, do we really believe that somewhere in the late nineteenth century American law reversed course—that in a moment of conservative and class crisis it froze into a sclerotic, anachronistic, formalist impediment to modern political and economic development?

Of course not. And the second place to begin reconstructive work is the scholarship of a handful of legal historians who over the years have taken direct aim at that Progressive-era fantasy. In the 1960s and 1970s, Alan Jones and Charles McCurdy began to suggest that the Progressive indictment of laissez-faire constitutionalism was skewed. Jones (1967) carefully examined the legal career of the Progressive villain Thomas Cooley and discovered him to be not only the first head of the Interstate Commerce Commission but also something of a Jacksonian democrat with a special fondness for common-law statutory interpretation.[10] McCurdy's extensive inquiries (1975 and 1979) into the jurisprudence of that other Progressive antagonist, Stephen Field, established that he was neither a "handmaiden for 'business needs'" nor the product of "the Gilded Age with its Great Barbecue for the Robber Barons and for the rest—'let the public be damned.'"[11] More recently historians like Daniel Ernst (1995), Howard Gillman (1993), and Barry Cushman (1998) have taken these early threads of revision and have begun to weave a different pattern of generalizations about law and reform. Taking seriously the complexities of this era's labor law, its opposition to class legislation, and the quite early expansion of commerce clause jurisprudence, these historians have criticized Progressive notions of "government by injunction," "laissez-faire constitutionalism," and the "constitutional revolution of the New Deal."

But the most intriguing of all these revisionists was actually a Progressive himself—Charles Warren. One of the best legal historians of the early twentieth century, Warren challenged the Progressive interpretation of the turn-of-the-century Supreme Court before the ink was dry. In 1913, he penned two important articles (1913a, 294; 1913b, 667) that challenged the contemporary indictments that the Court was guilty of "judicial oligarchy" and "usurpation" in overturning "social justice" legislation "based on the individualist theories of a century ago." Curious about the representativeness of the omnipresent citation to *Lochner v. New York* in the Progressive critique of law, Warren undertook a comprehensive survey of the constitutional fate of state regulatory legislation between 1887 and 1911. Organizing his findings according to constitutional objection—due process (social justice); due process (private property); obligation of contract; and commerce clause—Warren found that of 560 Fourteenth Amendment cases, only three state laws relating to social justice were overturned (including *Lochner*); an additional thirty-four laws relating to private property were turned back primarily on taxation or eminent domain grounds. Of 302 cases decided upon the more established grounds of contract and interstate commerce, only thirty-six general state social and economic regulations were declared unconstitutional. The overwhelming majority of state regulatory laws in Warren's catalogue were upheld by the U.S. Supreme Court: "anti-lottery laws; anti-trust and corporate monopoly laws; liquor laws; food, game, oleomargarine and other inspection laws; regulation of banks, telegraph and insurance companies; cattle, health and quarantine laws; regulation of business and property of water, gas, electric light, railroad (other than interstate trains) and other public service corporations; negro-segregation laws; labor laws; laws as to navigation, marine liens, ferries, bridges, etc., pilots, harbors and immigration" (Warren 1913b, 695). Warren's survey perfectly grasped one important, immutable fact about the constitutional jurisprudence of the turn of the century that eluded other Progressives—this was an era of unprecedented expansion of state (and federal) police power.

Warren's survey also suggests a third place from which to begin revising Progressive preconceptions about law and modern statebuilding—the simple empirical reality of the explosion of law in the early twentieth century. Any researcher moving from the manageable world of pre–Civil War jurisprudence into the wholly unwieldy terrain of early-twentieth-century law can testify to the overwhelming increase in the sheer quantity and diversity of law. According to some measures, by the late 1920s Americans were being subject to some 23,000 new federal and state statutes biennially. New York State alone passed some 1,595 statutes during 1928–29 (Fuchs 1930). According to the U.S. Attorney General's Reports, the total amount of federal litigation in the United States rose from 47,553 cases in 1911 to 196,953 cases by 1930 (Clark and Douglas 1933, 1450). Whereas the United States Supreme Court had only 253 cases pending before it in 1850, as early as 1890 the docket had swollen to an unmanageable 1,800 appellate cases (Frankfurter and Landis 1927, 60, 86). The number of lawyers in the United States grew from an estimated 39,000 in 1870 to 161,000 by 1930; and as one might expect, the number of degree-granting law schools with a three-year course of study grew from seven in 1890 to more than 170 in 1931 (Clark and Douglas 1933, 1481, 1486–87). By any quantitative measure, the period from 1877 to 1937 was the real "formative era of American law." But beyond quantification, legal thought and legal policymaking pervaded the social, economic, and political transformations of the late nineteenth and early twentieth centuries. Those years marked the emergence of a new sociological jurisprudence emphasizing the close interconnections of law and society (Pound 1911–12). And despite the pervasive Progressive lament about legal obstructionism, law played a most prominent role in Progressive socioeconomic policymaking. Reformers from Grace Abbott to Woodrow Wilson enthusiastically endorsed and wielded law's positive reconstructive power—what E. A. Ross dubbed "the most specialized and highly finished engine of control employed by society" (Ross 1969 [1901], 106). Behind the highly visible antilegal polemics of Beard, Smith, Myers, and Boudin, another group of reformers including John Commons (1924), Richard Ely (1914), and Ernst Freund (1904) worked on a much more sophisticated analysis of the relationship of law and economic and political modernization in which jurists played crucial creative roles.

And that is the fourth and final perspective helpful in generating an alternative understanding of the role of law in modern statebuilding—the perspective afforded by legal and social theory. Without launching a prolonged theoretical digression, it is worth noting that the critical period in modern American state formation, 1877 to 1937, was simultaneously the great creative era in sociolegal thought. Far more significant than the overemphasized legal realist deconstruction of classical legal thought was the emergence of a powerful new school of sociolegal thinkers working on the direct correlation between modern legal and socioeconomic change: Emile Durkheim, Max Weber, Eugen Ehrlich, Léon Duguit, and Roscoe Pound. In contrast to the American Progressive critique, these thinkers stressed the degree to which law was absolutely central in creating and understanding the transformations in economy, society, and polity that gripped all Western nations in the late nineteenth and early twentieth centuries. Artfully mixing methods of the new sociology of Comte and Spencer and the historical jurisprudence of Maine and Vinogradoff, Durkheim proved that "one needs only cast an eye over our legal codes" to gain insight into modern social change and the shift from mechanical to organic solidarity (1984, 101). Particularly significant for understanding law and the modern state was Durkheim's challenge to Spencer and Tönnies that the growth of contract and statecraft were *directly* rather than inversely related, i.e., that state regulation *increased* with the growth of modern individualism and organic solidarity.[12] Extending further the sociological correspondence between modern law and political economy, Weber placed formal legal rationalization, from the reception of Roman law to the emergence of new forms of administrative-bureaucratic authority, at the very heart of the story of the development of modern state and economy (Weber 1978). But it was perhaps Duguit (1919) who provided the most direct focus on the specific transformations in public law on which new twentieth-century states were being built: transformations in public legal conceptions of contract, corporation, office-holding, legislation, administration, and sovereignty. More recently, legal theorists as diverse as Franz Neumann, Otto Kirchheimer (Scheuerman 1996), Jürgen Habermas (1996), and Gunther Teubner (1987 and 1988) have continued in-depth theoretical explorations of the important linkages between law, liberalism, organized capitalism, and modern forms of state development. History should be no slave to theory, but critical legal-theoretical insights like these are very helpful in widening the interpretive frame within which to approach law and the creation of the modern American liberal state.

With insights garnered from these four literatures and perspectives, it is possible to begin rethinking the relationship between law and modern state formation in the United States. Such interpretive avenues hint that beyond the Progressive critique of law in modern American society lies a different structural, causal, and normative story about law and twentieth-century state-building that needs to be fleshed out. From these hints, I assert that at bottom the creation of the American liberal state involved a foundational *legal* revolution of a scope unprecedented in American history—the transformation of American public law. That revolution creatively destroyed nineteenth-century patterns and institutions of legal rule and constructed in their place a newly juridified constitutional state. Three overarching features separated this transformation of American public law from nineteenth-century experience and altered the relationship of law and American society and economy: (a) the centralization of power, (b) the individualization of right, and (c) the rationalization and constitutionalization of American law.

The themes of central power and individual liberty define modern liberal statecraft. The essence of the governmental regime established in early-twentieth-century America was the *simultaneous* centralization of new state powers and the individualization of new private rights. Nineteenth-century understandings of associative citizenship in a confederated republic were supplanted by a new articulation of the rights of individual subjects in a nation-state.

On the public powers side of the equation, political scientists honed new theories of the central state and its sovereign powers while jurists invented constitutional room for new federal administrative and police powers. Economic policy was an obvious site for governmental centralization with such bureaucratic innovations as the Interstate Commerce Commission, the Federal Trade Commission, and the National Labor Relations Board. But public morals and health policies witnessed a similar trend with federal legislation like the Narcotic Drug Act, the Mann Act, and the Volstead Act and national administrative inventions like the National Public Health Service, the Food and Drug Administration, and the Children's Bureau of the Social Security Administration. The result of these and innumerable other federal experiments was a revolutionary shift upward in American political decision-making power (Hays 1980). A national administrative regulatory state overcame nineteenth-century local preferences and common-law limitations and assumed new comprehensive responsibilities for regulating business, maintaining infrastructure, providing social services, preventing risk, and planning for a national economy and population.

This centralization of power was complemented by a distinct individualization of the notion of right. Though most of the public initiatives of the nascent American welfare state were accompanied by a legitimating rhetoric of "socialization" (e.g., languages of social control, social organization, social reform, and social rights),[13] one should not be fooled about the general direction of change in the definition of liberal rights. In contrast to the positive and relative conception prevalent during the nineteenth century of rights *within* a community, the American liberal state entailed a more negative and individual definition of rights *against* a nation-state (though not at all *against* state-building). The experiments in collectivism and nationalism in this period were rooted in a new individualism that separated the rights-bearing citizen from intermediate loyalties of family, church, and locality. An expanded zone of private protection and individual autonomy was *quid pro quo* for the radical extension of state power in this period. Such negative individual liberties and civil rights ultimately were not opposed to the general process of welfare state-building; on the contrary, they integrated individual citizens with the national socioeconomic ambitions of the new state. Particular examples of this phenomenon include the invention of a new legal conception of privacy in this period, featuring a prominent concern for the protection of personality and personhood, and the postbellum transformation of the notion of civil rights from freedperson's guarantee to corporate bill of rights to civil liberties to the social rights of the early American welfare state. Such rights were an indispensable part of the new balance struck in the pursuit of public order and the protection of private liberty by the American liberal state.

A heightened separation of more capacious understandings of public power and private right was a hallmark of the liberal state, and the constitutionalization of American law played a key role in constructively mediating these seemingly antagonistic tendencies. Constitutional law replaced the common law in this period as the final authority on the legitimacy of exertions of state power and expressions of individual right. The significance of constitutionalization for modern civil rights is well documented. But three other crucial elements of legal-constitutional development have been comparatively neglected in histories of the late nineteenth and early twentieth centuries: legal positivism, administrative law, and federal police power. It is impossible for me to imagine four more important prerequisites for modern social-welfare statebuilding than the creation of a national constitutional law, the new understanding of public law as legislative fiat, the legal invention of a fourth bureaucratic branch of government, and the radical expansion of national social and economic police powers. Yet despite all the new attention to social science, economic organization, and social-welfare policy in this period, we have fairly little understanding of this foundational legal revolution.

But though the centralization of power, the individualization of right, and the constitutionalization of law capture the general direction of legal-political change in early-twentieth-century America, a full appreciation of the transformation of American public law requires an outline of some of the more specific changes in legal doctrine and practice that buttressed the creation of a new American state. Though an elaborate exposition of doctrine and especially practice is beyond the bounds of this chapter, it is possible to introduce four sets of jurisprudential innovations that underwrote modern state development in the United States: (a) the new legal definitions of state and sovereignty represented in the work of J. W. Burgess; (b) the new conceptions of constitutional and positive law captured in the important treatises of W. W. Willoughby; (c) the expansion of legislation and police power symbolized by the work of Ernst Freund; and (d) the invention of a centralizing administrative law as articulated by Frank Goodnow.[14]

One of the most important legal-political theoretical developments of the late nineteenth and early twentieth centuries was a fundamental rethinking of the nature of the state and state power. As part of a much broader reexamination of group identity generally, theorists of the period vigorously pursued new ideas about the nature of corporation, association, and state that challenged purely individualist or contractual conceptions of group organization. And though this extraordinary conversation was carried on by political scientists, sociologists, and historians as well as jurists, it was a distinctly legal discussion. The legal personality and the legal authority of groups was the key question, and the legal personality and authority of the state was its highest form (Gierke 1900; Maitland 1968; Laski 1917).

Legal and constitutional scholars first began fundamentally rethinking the nature of the American nation-state during the Civil War. The immediate post–Civil War period was flooded with treatises that drew on and carried forward the nationalist oratory of Webster and Lincoln, advocating a strong nationalist theory of the state and a constitutional defense of the Union. Sidney George Fisher (1862), J. A. Jameson (1867), Orestes Brownson (1866), John C. Hurd (1881), and others downplayed the original significance of compact, contract, states' rights, and constitution in the creation of state authority and defended the overriding prerogatives of nation, Union, and national government. As Fisher wrote in the heat of battle: "If the Union and the government cannot be saved out of this terrible shock of war constitutionally, a Union and a government must be saved unconstitutionally" (1862, 199). Hurd went even further, arguing that all antebellum attempts to derive the nature of sovereignty from constitutional standards were futile: "Sovereignty cannot be an attribute of law, because, by the nature of things, law must proceed from sovereignty. By the preexistence of a sovereignty, law becomes possible" (1881, 97). As Charles Merriam (1915, 296) summarized, "In the new national school, the tendency was to disregard the doctrine of the social contract, and to emphasize strongly the instinctive forces whose action and interaction produces a state" (Frederickson 1965; Keller 1977).

By the turn of the century, these crisis-induced reconsiderations of nation-state and sovereignty grew into the foundations of a new political science and jurisprudence. Drawing on European state theories, Theodore Woolsey (1878), John W. Burgess (1890), Woodrow Wilson (1890), and W.W. Willoughby (1896) moved American conceptions of state, sovereignty, and public law well beyond the nineteenth-century understandings captured by Alexis de Tocqueville and Francis Lieber. Whereas Tocqueville and Lieber oriented their inquiries around concepts of local authority and self-government, Woolsey, Burgess, Wilson, and Willoughby explicitly emphasized the nation-state and its encompassing sovereign powers. All began like Wilson's aptly titled *The State* (1890), with explicit critiques of divine, social contract and natural law theories of the state. They then typically followed Burgess in his new delineation of the relationship of state and sovereignty: "The essence of the state is everywhere, and at all times, one and the same, viz; sovereignty" (1890, I.74). "However confederate in character the Union may have been at the time of its creation," Willoughby declared about political development in the United States, "the transformation to a Federal State was effected." The essence of that state was not compact or natural rights or constitutional limitations, but sovereignty—that power that was "the source of all law" but "not itself founded upon law" (Willoughby 1904, 33).

Part and parcel of this positivist redefinition of state and sovereignty was a similar rethinking of the nature of law—constitutional law and positive law. Despite progressive claims of the revival of natural-law thinking or the rise of legal orthodoxy, far more significant for turn-of-the-century jurisprudence was the thoroughgoing constitutionalization of American law and the growing influence of analytical jurisprudence. Constitutionalization was directly linked to the growth of the American state; new conceptions of positive law underscored the influence of new legal ideas of sovereignty.

As suggested above, federal constitutional law displaced local common law as the preeminent legality in post–Civil War America. The postwar constitutional amendments further nationalized American law and precipitated a veritable cult of constitutionalism in the late nineteenth century. The consequences were legion as area after area of American law formerly left to a wide variety of local, state, and common-law interpretations came under the purview of the United States Supreme Court and its definitive renderings of the national boundaries between private and public right and state and federal power. The state police power, for example, was thoroughly constitutionalized in the late nineteenth and early twentieth centuries as age-old regulatory issues were reframed in a national context in *Munn v. Illinois* (1877), *Mugler v. Kansas* (1887), *Budd v. New York* (1892), and hundreds of other Supreme Court cases.[15] The modern state articulated by Woolsey, Burgess, and Wilson required a clearer national standard for delimiting private right and public power than the customary and hermeneutic standards of the common-law tradition. Constitutional law provided an ideal mechanism for promoting the simultaneous expansion of individual rights and governmental power that characterized the modern liberal state.

The themes of state, sovereignty, and positive constitutional law came together in the synthetic constitutional treatises of W. W. Willoughby (1896, 1904, 1910, and 1924; Mathews and Hart 1937). Willoughby joined the new theories of the state to a historical reinterpretation of U.S. constitutional law that laid the groundwork for twentieth-century public law. At the heart of Willoughby's system was the endorsement of analytical jurisprudence and a positivist conception of law as the command of a sovereign. In contrast to antebellum jurists who regularly rejected a Blackstonian or utilitarian argument for the force of law, Willoughby drew the nature of state sovereignty and all subsequent delineations of governing power from a strict "conception of law as wholly a product of the State's will" (1896, 180).[16] In this way, early-nineteenth-century concerns with custom, local self-government, compact, and common law gave way to a new emphasis on the positive constitutional powers of a central state. This more realistic and positivistic conception of law and sovereignty lay at the heart of the constitutional expansion of American governing power in the twentieth century.

The third important category of doctrinal change that made up this transformation of American public law concerned legislation—the nature of statute law and the extent of the police powers of state and federal legislatures to regulate in the public interest. Though we are all positivists now to the extent that we understand by the legislative power the plenary authority of the state to pass laws, the emergence of an omnibus legislative power distinct from a judicial one is a much thornier historical problem, as suggested by the work of Charles McIlwain (1910 and 1947).[17] In pre–Civil War America, the line between statute and common law (and between legislature and court) was often quite murky, as indicated by the prevalence of private legislation as well as the defining role of the common law of nuisance in the antebellum police power. "What was legislation in the nineteenth century?" remains one of the unresolved questions in American legal history. In the post–Civil War period, however, two things sharpened the distinction between law and politics: the comprehensive legislative experiments of the 1840s and 1850s (prohibition, police reform, married women's property acts, Field codes, and general incorporation laws); and the clearer scope given to the judicial power through the treatise-writing of Theodore Sedgwick (1857) and Thomas Cooley (1868).

Like definitions of state, sovereignty, law, and constitution, conceptions of legislative power grew clearer and more realistic as radical legislative initiatives proliferated between 1877 and 1937. The best example was the police power that became an explicit constitutional doctrine after the Civil War, trading in its ambiguous origins in common and police law for Ernst Freund's positivist and Progressive definition as the legislative "power of promoting the public welfare by restraining and regulating the use of liberty and property" (Freund 1904, iii). Lewis Hockheimer echoed Wilson and Willoughby: "The police power is the inherent plenary power of a State . . . to prescribe regulations to preserve and promote the public safety, health, and morals, and to prohibit all things hurtful to the comfort and welfare of society" (1897, 158). Contrary to the Progressive critique of restraint, the police power exploded in the early twentieth century. Statute books swelled, case numbers rose exponentially, and treatises and law review articles proliferated. A new forcefulness and resourcefulness crept into discussions of the police power as Progressives expanded the scale and scope of American legislative power, calling for the police power to be "more freely exercised and private property more freely controlled to meet the needs of the changed conditions of society." Some Progressives saw in the police power "almost unlimited opportunities for adopting whatever legislation the augmenting demands of social pioneers may require" (Brace 1886, 341; Ramage 1902, 698). And as Charles Warren hinted, despite the singular power of *Lochner v. New York*, an overwhelming number of cases embraced a more affirmative, open-ended use of the police power. Less time was spent legitimating the police power or sketching its roots in common or civil law as judges placed greater emphasis on the doctrine's capacity to directly promote the public good rather than merely protect or preserve it. In *Bacon v. Walker* (204 U.S. 311, 318 [1907]), the United States Supreme Court declared that the police power "is not confined . . . to the suppression of what is offensive, disorderly or unsanitary. It extends to so dealing with the conditions which exist in the State as to bring out of them the greatest welfare of its people" (Reznick 1978, 31–32).

But perhaps the most important development in the expansion of legislative and police power between 1877 and 1937 was the invention of a federal police power—the extraconstitutional centralization of general welfare lawmaking in the United States. In *United States v. DeWitt* (9 Wall. 41, U.S. [1870]), the U.S. Supreme Court adopted the clear antebellum constitutional consensus that the police power was explicitly a state rather than a federal power. The powers of the federal government were constitutionally enumerated, delegated, and limited—Congress wielded nothing analogous to the general plenary police authority of the state legislatures to regulate liberty and property in the public interest. Of course, one of the great stories of the period after 1870 is about Congress securing that power *de facto* if not *de jure* through its commerce, taxing, and postal powers. As Charles Evans Hughes told the American Bar Association in 1918, the most significant recent decisions of the Supreme Court involved "the extended application of the doctrine that federal rules governing interstate commerce may have the quality of police regulations" (Hughes 1918, 93–94). In the areas of business, labor, transportation, morals, health, safety, and education, powers and issues that were once the exclusive domain of state and local governments moved up into the purview of the national government in one of the most significant expropriations of political power in American history. And as Ernst Freund argued in 1920, the role of law and the judiciary in that expropriation was pivotal: "The consolidation of our own nation has proved our allotment of federal powers to be increasingly inadequate; and had it not been aided by *liberal* judicial construction, our situation would be unbearable" (Freund 1920, 181; Thompson 1923, 10). From *U.S. v. DeWitt* (1870) to *Hammer v. Dagenhart* (247 U.S. 251 [1918]) to *United States v. Darby* (312 U.S. 100 [1941]), American courts fashioned legal doctrine to accommodate a society looking more and more to the federal government for regulatory solutions.

Despite this dramatic revolution in legislative power, one might argue that an even bigger transformation in American law from 1877 to 1937 concerned changes in administrative authority. As Ted Lowi noted, "The modern method of social control involves the application of rationality to social relations. . . . Rationality applied to social control is administration. Administration may indeed be the *sine qua non* of modernity" (Lowi 1979, 21). Herbert Croly was equally insistent about the centrality of administration to Progressivism: "The progressive democracy is bound to be as much interested in efficient administration as it is in reconstructive legislation. . . . Its future as the expression of a permanent public interest is tied absolutely to an increase of executive authority and responsibility" (Croly 1912, 132). Accordingly, political scientists and theorists have spent a great deal of time charting the rise of administrative organization and bureaucracy in the early-twentieth-century United States (Rohr 1986; Cook 1996; Stillman 1998). But less attention has been devoted to the legal causes and consequences of that transformation. Two chief areas of legal innovation were: (a) a reconceptualization of the relationship of office-holding (Orren 1997) and self-government; and (b) the problem of the constitutional separation of powers. Like the common law generally, nineteenth-century conceptions of the legal nature of office-holding and administration assumed the kind of general continuity between ruler and ruled, office-holder and citizen, implied in the nature of local self-government. In contrast, modern administrative law and theory posited a foundational separation between the professional office-holder and the political life of the citizenry—a separation of ownership from control of the American polity.[18] Woodrow Wilson aristocratically justified the idea of administrative discretion and the limits of public opinion on modern bureaucracy: "Self-government does not consist in having a hand in everything, any more than housekeeping consists necessarily in cooking dinner with one's own hands. The cook must be trusted with a large discretion as to the management of the fires and the ovens" (1887, 213; 1908, 197; Waldo 1948, 104–55). But even more subject to change than nineteenth-century conceptions of local self-government was the constitutional doctrine of the separation of powers. The American system of divided and mixed government counterbalancing executive, legislative, and judicial as well as state and federal authority, posed a challenge for administrative reformers seeking to centralize administrative power in the hands of the executive. In short, the administrative revolution was not just a revolution in governmental organization; it entailed a decided transformation in American public law.

The career of Frank J. Goodnow embodied that transformation. In his pioneering casebooks and treatises on administration (1893, 1905, and 1906), Goodnow laid the groundwork for the jurisprudential transition from nineteenth-century conceptions of the powers and duties of office-holders to modern administrative law. In *Social Reform and the Constitution* (1911), Goodnow attempted to create jurisprudential room for the expansion of administrative power through a critique of an overly rigid constitutional understanding of federalism and the separation of powers. The tendency to emphasize the rights of states and individuals, he argued, "has resulted in a constitutional tradition which is apt not to accord to the federal government powers which it unquestionably ought to have the constitutional right to exercise." Goodnow called on courts to continue "to abandon certainly the strict application of the principle of the separation of powers whenever the demand for administrative efficiency would seem to make such action desirable" (1911, 11, 221). In *Politics and Administration* (1900), he went so far as to attempt to reduce the morass of the traditional American constitutional system to two primary functions: "the will of the state [politics] and the execution of that will [administration]." In direct opposition to nineteenth-century common-law notions of customary, participatory, and local self-government, Goodnow advocated a centralized and professionalized bureaucratic corps insulated from popular politics:

> The fact is . . . that there is a large part of administration which is unconnected with politics, which should be relieved very largely, if not altogether, from the control of political bodies. It is unconnected with pol-

> itics because it embraces fields of semi-scientific, quasi-judicial and quasi-business or commercial activity—work which has little if any influence on the expression of the true state will. (Goodnow 1900, 22, 85–86)

Though the struggle over administration and administrative law in the twentieth-century United States is one of the more complex and ongoing developments to unpack historically, Goodnow's early work captured the general thrust of Progressive legal innovation. In many ways, his initiatives in administrative law were the capstone of the changing conceptions of state, sovereignty, law, and legislation that began with the Civil War.

Together, the three broad tendencies of the centralization of power, the individualization of right, and the constitutionalization of law, coupled with these more particular changes in legal conceptions of the state, sovereignty, positive law, legislation, and administration, constitute what I refer to as the transformation of American public law. That legal transformation was central to the creation of a modern administrative welfare state in the United States. The fundamentally legal nature of that transformation should force us to revise the long-held Progressive idea of law as primarily an obstruction to statebuilding and social democracy in America. More significantly, the transformation of public law makes problematic some popular shortcuts explaining American political change from the nineteenth to the twentieth century: e.g., laissez-faire to the general-welfare state; negative to positive liberty; old to new liberalism. For the transformation of public law suggests that below surface generalizations about moving from individualism to collectivism lie deeper changes and more complex evolutions in governmental theory and practice—changes in conceptions of law, sovereignty, police, legislation, and administration.

CONCLUSION

One simple way to sum up the primary objective of this essay might be the slogan "bringing the *law* back in" to the story of modern American statebuilding. And such an emphasis on law has much to recommend it. Law's propensity for generalization and synthesis is one of its main attributes, a fact diversely illustrated by the legal-historical roots of Weber's modern theoretical synthesis as well as by the recent proliferation of legal scholars as public intellectuals. Of the *constitutive* capaciousness of law, Pierre Bourdieu commented: "The law is the quintessential form of 'active' discourse, able by its own operation to produce its effects. It would not be excessive to say that it *creates* the social world" (1987, 839). Law's location at the nexus of the private and the public, of ideas and actions, of the individual and the collective, of the socioeconomic and the political, of violence and the word make it an excellent vehicle for reintegrating the disparate intellectual, political, cultural, and economic issues that currently preoccupy a sprawling monographic literature.

But a renewed focus on the positive role of law in modern social and economic policymaking involves more than providing a supplemental variable—a richer, more complete historical story. Rather, I have argued that the incorporation of law changes the story fundamentally. First, a focus on law disrupts the master trope of the shift from laissez-faire to the general-welfare state in the United States. Though bolstered by state modernization theories and Franco-Germanic models of political development that highlight the "on-off" absence or presence of national sovereignty and central bureaucratic capacity, law introduces a more complex, conflicted, and long-term story of the evolution of police, administrative, and constitutional powers that is irreducible to our politically charged, overdetermined metanarratives about shifts from statelessness to statebuilding; negative to positive liberty; old to new liberalism; or individualism to collectivism. The legal story simply does not break down around such routine binaries.

Secondly, a fuller study of law should put to rest the currently widespread invocation of an exceptionalist American legal tradition as primarily a restraint, a limit, a check on Progressive state-building efforts (i.e., the persistent notion of law as an ogre frustrating liberal reform). Beyond the ubiquitously invoked unholy trinity of laissez-faire constitutional cases *E. C. Knight, In Re Debs*, and *Lochner v. New York* lies a largely unstudied, untapped mass of police, regulatory, administrative, corporation, utility, tax, eminent domain, health, insurance, telecommunications, monetary, and fiscal law that plays a crucial creative role in building the American liberal state. Statebuilding is about much more than institutions and political mobilization. It involves a substantive *legal* project deeply embedded in everyday private as well as public economic and social policymaking.

Finally, and perhaps most importantly, law introduces directly into the heart of the story of the creation of modern governance a normative set of questions about liberalism, rule, self-government, and democracy in a national regulatory welfare-state regime. The redefinition of American liberalism around a more negative and individualistic understanding of private right displaced an earlier rights tradition focused on participation and the possibility of self-government by a mutually regulating citizenry. The reorganization and centralization of public power in the liberal state made such acts of truly popular sovereignty difficult. The revolutionary constitutional invention of administration undermined it altogether, replacing a representative and legislative model of democracy with a practice of rulemaking by insulated and specialized bureaucratic experts. Mass producerist and consumerist economic policies coupled with compensatory social-welfare provisions and national risk management seem to have made democratic practice an anachronism.

Legal thinkers as diverse as Francis Lieber, Otto von Gierke, A. V. Dicey, Paul Vinogradoff, James Bryce, and Roscoe Pound have worried about this problem—the fate of a democratic, liberal rule of law in a centralized and rationalized nation-state—since the middle of the nineteenth century. Their concerns were shared by social and political philosophers like Tocqueville, Mill, and Dewey. Social theorists have identified a principal role for the transformation of law in the problems and possibilities of modern economy and society, from Weber's initial preoccupation with legal rationalization to Jürgen Habermas's and Gunther Teubner's more recent focus on the "juridification of modern social life." As Teubner most recently summed up this concern, "Law, when used as a control medium of the welfare state, has at its disposal modes of functioning, criteria of rationality, and forms of organization which are not appropriate to the 'life-world' structures of the regulated social areas and which therefore either fail to achieve the desired results or do so at the cost of destroying these structures" (1987, 4). The modernization of polity and economy through law came with important costs and foregone alternatives. Nineteenth-century conceptions of law, community, and self-government were creatively destroyed in the process of building the modern American liberal state. Such complex causation and sometimes unintended consequences should be considered carefully before we resort to simple normative shibboleths about the obstructionism of law or the natural and inevitable evolution from laissez-faire to the general-welfare state.

NOTES

1 This is a vast literature (some of which is discussed below), encompassing historical jurisprudence, sociological jurisprudence, legal realism, and critical legal studies. These particular renderings of the agenda are from Willard Hurst (1971, 228; 1964, 109). Hurst is also the author of one of the best calls for an integration of legal and political history:

> In deciding what to include as "law" I do not find it profitable to distinguish "law" from "government" or from "policy." The heart of the matter is that we formed organizations for collective action characterized by their own distinctive bases of legitimacy. . . . In order to see law in its relations to society as a whole, one must appraise all formal and informal aspects of political organized power—observe the functions of all legal agencies (legislative, executive, administrative, or judicial) and take account of the interplay of such agencies with voters and nonvoters, lobbyists and interest groups, politicians and political parties. This definition overruns traditional boundaries dividing study of law from study of political history, political science, and sociology.

For a fuller discussion see Novak 2000, 114.

2 *Slaughterhouse Cases*, 83 U.S. 36 (1872); *In Re Debs*, 158 U.S. 564 (1895); *Lochner v. New York*, 198 U.S. 45 (1905); *Schechter Poultry Co. v. United States*, 295 U.S. 495 (1935).

3 Note the "moralizing anthropomorphism of Democracy." As Max Lerner noted, part of the powerful attraction of the Progressive paradigm was that it allowed for the "personal identification of villainry" and, of course, goodness (Lerner 1933, 677).

4 Twiss was particularly intrigued with the formative role of Thomas McIntyre Cooley and his influential treatise, *Constitutional Limitations* (1868). Ignoring his regulatory work for the Interstate Commerce Commission, Twiss portrayed Cooley as a staunch conservative ideologue who "made up many of the principles out of his own head" and *Constitutional Limitations* as "a direct counter to the appearance a year earlier of Karl Marx's *Das Kapital*" (Twiss 1942, 18, 33).

5 Though Forbath's emphasis on legal ideas and the shaping of labor consciousness contrasts with Progressives' more direct emphasis on economic interest, his basic story about the force and direction of *law* is almost classically Progressive: "During the decades bracketing the turn of the century, courts exacted from labor many key strategic and ideological accommodations, changing trade unionists' views of what was possible and desirable in politics and industry. Judicial review and administration of labor legislation helped make broad legal reforms seem futile. Similarly, the courts' harshly repressive law of industrial conflict helped make broad, inclusive unionism seem too costly and a more cautious, narrower unionism essential" (1991, 6–7). Of course, not all of the new labor legal history follows Forbath's classic Progressive story (see for example Tomlins 1985; Ernst 1995; Tomlins and King 1992).

6 I am, of course, deeply indebted to this political science/political history literature and proceed cautiously with this critique. For if there's one thing the "Bringing the State Back In" revolution has accomplished in the capable hands of Skocpol and Skowronek (not to mention those working so ably on the American state before it was "brought back in," e.g., Morton Keller, Barry Karl, Ellis Hawley, Thomas McCraw, and Martin Sklar, among others), it has been the decentering of the New Deal and the recentering of attention on the transformative changes in the political structure and socioeconomic policies of the emerging American administrative welfare state in the critical period after 1877 and before the shift in the late New Deal that Alan Brinkley provocatively dubs "the end of reform." Still, one of the central defects of current state-centered approaches to this governmental revolution is the neglect or oversimplification of the pivotal role of law. While the state-centered paradigm has successfully challenged functionalist and instrumentalist conceptions of the state as merely an arena for social, cultural, and economic conflict and established the relative autonomy of the state as an independent historical actor, most of these interpretations have not moved beyond an instrumentalist conception of the role of the rule of law in American state-building. Where they see the historical problem of the building of an American administrative welfare state as primarily a problem of political and institutional organization and mobilization, I would like to suggest that modern American state-building looks quite different from the perspective of the problem of law and legal legitimation.

7 Skocpol's thin reading of American legal history is a real weakness in an otherwise brilliant investigation into American statecraft. Skocpol begins with Tocqueville's well-known observations about the power of bench and bar: "There is hardly a political question in the United States which does not sooner or later turn into a judicial one." Then, after a passing reference to *Marbury v. Madison*, she sums up nineteenth-century legal development this way:

> Private property rights and norms of market behavior were instrumentally adjusted to the needs of an entrepreneurial and rapidly growing capitalist economy. To limit the activities of labor unions, the courts used conspiracy doctrines, and then contract and equal-protection doctrines and interpretations of anti-trust laws. In spheres from the economy to the family, U.S. courts sought to maintain the boundaries of public versus private authority in American democracy. . . . Arnold Paul has summed up late-nineteenth-century legal developments as 'a massive judicial entry into the socioeconomic scene' effecting 'a conservative-oriented revolution' in the name of concentrated private property" (1992, 69–70).

8 Quoted in Rodgers 1998, 207. The thesis of the "inertial force" of law on American state-building extends right up to the present. In their excellent work on contemporary regulatory policy in the United States, Richard Harris and Sidney Milkis (1996) adopt an almost classically progressive position and chronology, arguing that "the constitution[al] foundations of the American political system generate powerful inertial forces that must be overcome if a qualitative shift in regulation is to be accomplished." They argue that the constitutional "bias against big govern-

ment has been one of the most serious obstacles faced by advocates of regulatory regime change in the twentieth century, and in a sense the history of American regulatory politics since the Progressive Era has been the history of the erosion of that bias" (1996, 34).

9 Here Stephen Skowronek's thesis about the power of nineteenth-century courts and parties is right on the mark: "The early American state maintained an integrated legal order on a continental scale; it fought wars, expropriated Indians, secured new territories, carried on relations with other states, and aided economic development" (1982, 19).

10 Jones criticized the Progressives for assuming that legislative initiatives and regulation were a priori public goods and that obstructions to legislative power must thus be the product of economic self-interest. Jones battled this misinterpretation by uncovering Cooley's creative impulse not in an alliance with economic interests but in a Jacksonian ideological persuasion that battled class privilege and concentrated economic power.

11 McCurdy located the key to Field instead in the issue of legal legitimacy and the constitutional necessity of generating lasting rules for separating public and private spheres. McCurdy insisted that Field's legal ideas were not subservient to economic interests. Field used his rigorous separation of public and private to squelch internal improvement bonds and to divest corporations of tax exemptions, lottery rights, and special grants. He upheld state legislation that prohibited certain businesses as detrimental to the public interest, that prescribed standards of fitness for lawyers and doctors, and that required railroads to erect cattle guards and grade crossings at their own expense. Also see Benedict 1985.

12 For a brief but excellent discussion of this point that also includes a fine English introduction to the work of Léon Duguit and Maurice Hauriou, see H. S. Jones 1993, 154–59.

13 For a provocative analysis of the "socialization of law," see Willrich 1998.

14 It is almost impossible to appreciate the full significance and reach of this transformation in public law without exploring the degree to which these legal ideas are put into actual practice in twentieth-century economic and social policymaking. But that inquiry requires a monograph, not an article. My hope is that the shortcuts provided by the synthetic works of Burgess, Willoughby, Freund, and Goodnow give at least a rough sense of the character and scope of this legal revolution.

15 *Munn v. Illinois*, 94 U.S. 118 (1877); *Mugler v. Kansas*, 123 U.S. 623 (1887); *Budd v. New York*, 143 U.S. 517 (1892).

16 Also see Woodrow Wilson's similar (but more qualified) endorsement of an analytical account of sovereignty in *The State* (1890, 634–35). Wilson struggled to mesh sovereignty, positive law, and constitutionalism in his definition of law as "the command of an authorized public organ, acting within the sphere of its competence. What organs are authorized, and what is the sphere of their competence, is of course determined by the organic law of the state; and *this* law is the direct command of the sovereign."

17 Also see Gough 1955; Pocock 1957. For a recent attempt to wrestle with this problem in an American context see Desan 1998.

18 For the classic statement of the same theme with respect to the administration of the private business corporation see Berle and Means 1932. As suggested in the discussion of state sovereignty, the parallels in debates about what is happening to the corporation and what is happening to the state are extraordinary.

REFERENCES

Ackerman, Bruce A. 1991. *We the People, volume 1: Foundations*. Cambridge: Harvard University Press.

Amar, Akhil Reed. 1998. *The Bill of Rights: Creation and Reconstruction*. New Haven, Conn.: Yale University Press.

Arnold, Thurman W. 1937. *The Folklore of Capitalism.* New Haven, Conn.: Yale University Press.

Beard, Charles A. 1913. *An Economic Interpretation of the Constitution of the United States.* New York: Macmillan.

———. 1914. *Contemporary American History, 1877–1913.* New York: Macmillan.

Benedict, Michael Les. 1985. "Laissez-Faire and Liberty: A Re-Evaluation of the Meaning and Origins of Laissez-Faire Constitutionalism," 3 *Law and History Review* 293–331.

Benson, Lee. 1960. *Turner and Beard: American Historical Writing Reconsidered.* Glencoe, Ill.: Free Press.

Berle, Adolf A., and Gardiner C. Means. 1932. *The Modern Corporation and Private Property.* New York: Macmillan.

Beveridge, Albert J. 1916–1919. *The Life of John Marshall.* 4 vols. Boston: Houghton Mifflin Company.

Boudin, Louis B. 1932. *Government by Judiciary.* 2 vols. New York: William Godwin, Inc.

Bourdieu, Pierre. 1987. "The Force of Law: Toward a Sociology of the Juridical Field," 38 *Hastings Law Journal* 805–53.

Brace, Harrison H. 1886. "To What Extent May Government in the Exercise of Its Police Power, Take, Destroy or Damage Private Property Without Giving Compensation Therefor?" 18 *Chicago Legal News* 339–41.

Brinkley, Alan. 1995. *The End of Reform: New Deal Liberalism in Recession and War.* New York: Alfred A. Knopf.

Brownson, Orestes A. 1866. *The American Republic: Its Constitution, Tendencies, and Destiny.* New York: P. O'Shae.

Burgess, John W. 1890. *Political Science and Comparative Constitutional Law.* 2 vols. Boston: Ginn & Company.

Clark, Charles E., and William O. Douglas. 1933. "Law and Legal Institutions." In President's Research Committee on Social Trends, *Recent Social Trends in the United States*, one-volume edition, 1430–88. New York: McGraw-Hill Book Company.

Commons, John R. 1924. *Legal Foundations of Capitalism.* New York: Macmillan.

Cook, Brian J. 1996. *Bureaucracy and Self-Government: Reconsidering the Role of Public Administration in American Politics.* Baltimore: Johns Hopkins University Press.

Cooley, Thomas M. 1868. *A Treatise on the Constitutional Limitations Which Rest upon the Legislative Power of the State of the American Union.* Boston: Little, Brown.

Corwin, Edward S. 1919. *John Marshall and the Constitution.* New Haven, Conn.: Yale University Press.

———. 1938. *Court over Constitution: A Study of Judicial Review as an Instrument of Popular Government.* New York: P. Smith.

———. 1955. *The "Higher Law" Background of American Constitutional Law.* Ithaca, N.Y.: Cornell University Press.

Croly, Herbert. 1912. "State Political Reorganization," 6 *American Political Science Review* 122–36.

Cushman, Barry. 1998. *Rethinking the New Deal Court: The Structure of a Constitutional Revolution.* New York: Oxford University Press.

Desan, Christine A. 1998. "The Constitutional Commitment to Legislative Adjudication in the Early American Tradition," 111 *Harvard Law Review* 1381–1503.

Dewey, John. 1935. *Liberalism and Social Action.* In John Dewey, *The Later Works, 1925–1953*, ed. Jo Ann Boydston, vol. 11. Carbondale: Southern Illinois University Press.

Dicey, A.V. 1914. *Lectures on the Relation between Law & Public Opinion in England during the Nineteenth Century.* London: Macmillan.

Duguit, Léon. 1917. "Law and the State," 31 *Harvard Law Review* 1–185.

———. 1919. *Law in the Modern State*, trans. Frida and Harold Laski. London: George Allen & Unwin.

Durkheim, Emile. 1984. *The Division of Labor in Society*, ed. Lewis A. Coser. New York: Free Press.

Ely, Richard T. 1914. *Property and Contract in Their Relations to the Distribution of Wealth.* New York: Macmillan.

Ernst, Daniel R. 1995. *Lawyers against Labor: From Individual Rights to Corporate Liberalism.* Urbana: University of Illinois Press.

Evans, Peter B., Dietrich Rueschemeyer, and Theda Skocpol, eds. 1985. *Bringing the State Back In.* New York: Cambridge University Press.

Fine, Sidney. 1956. *Laissez Faire and the General-Welfare State: A Study of Conflict in American Thought, 1865–1901.* Ann Arbor: University of Michigan Press.

Fisher, Sidney George. 1862. *The Trial of the Constitution.* Philadelphia: J.B. Lippincott.

Forbath, William E. 1991. *Law and the Shaping of the American Labor Movement.* Cambridge: Harvard University Press.

Frankfurter, Felix, and James M. Landis. 1927. *The Business of the Supreme Court: A Study in the Federal Judicial System.* New York: Macmillan.

Frederickson, George M. 1965. *The Inner Civil War: Northern Intellectuals and the Crisis of the Union.* New York: Harper & Row.

Freund, Ernst. 1904. *The Police Power: Public Policy and Constitutional Rights.* Chicago: Callaghan & Company.

———. 1920. "The New German Constitution," 35 *Political Science Quarterly* 177–203.

Friedman, Lawrence M. 1973. *A History of American Law.* New York: Simon and Schuster.

Fuchs, Ralph F. 1930. "The Quantity of Regulatory Legislation," 16 *St. Louis Law Review* 51–55.

Furner, Mary O. 1975. *Advocacy and Objectivity: A Crisis in the Professionalization of American Social Science, 1865–1905.* Lexington: University Press of Kentucky.

Furner, Mary O., and Barry Supple, eds. 1990. *The State and Economic Knowledge: The American and British Experiences.* New York: Cambridge University Press.

Galambos, Louis. 1970. "The Emerging Organizational Synthesis in Modern American History," 44 *Business History Review* 279–90.

Galbraith, John Kenneth. 1967. *The New Industrial State.* Boston: Houghton Mifflin Company.

Gierke, Otto. 1900. *Political Theories of the Middle Age*, trans. Frederic William Maitland. Cambridge: Cambridge University Press.

Gillman, Howard. 1993. *The Constitution Besieged: The Rise and Demise of Lochner Era Police Powers Jurisprudence.* Durham, N.C.: Duke University Press.

Goodnow, Frank J. 1893. *Comparative Administrative Law.* New York: G.P. Putnam.

———. 1900. *Politics and Administration.* New York: Macmillan.

———. 1905. *Principles of the Administrative Law of the United States.* New York: G.P. Putnam.

———. 1906. *Selected Cases on Government and Administration.* Chicago: Callaghan and Company.

———. 1911. *Social Reform and the Constitution.* New York: Macmillan.

Gordon, Linda, ed. 1990. *Women, the State and Welfare.* Madison: University of Wisconsin Press.

Gough, J.W. 1955. *Fundamental Law in English Constitutional History.* Oxford: Clarendon Press.

Habermas, Jürgen. 1996. *Between Facts and Norms: Contributions to a Discourse Theory of Law and Democracy*, trans. William Rehg. Cambridge: MIT Press.

Haines, Charles Grove. 1930. *The Revival of Natural Law Concepts.* Cambridge: Harvard University Press.

Handlin, Oscar, and Mary Flug Handlin. 1947. *Commonwealth: A Study of the Role of Government in the American Economy: Massachusetts, 1774–1861.* Cambridge: Harvard University Press.

Harris, Richard A., and Sidney M. Milkis. 1996. *The Politics of Regulatory Change: A Tale of Two Agencies.* 2d ed. New York: Oxford University Press.

Hartz, Louis. 1948. *Economic Policy and Democratic Thought: Pennsylvania, 1776–1860.* Cambridge: Harvard University Press.

Haskell, Thomas. 1977. *The Emergence of Professional Social Science: The American Social Science Association and the Nineteenth Century Crisis of Authority.* Urbana: University of Illinois Press.

Hawley, Ellis. 1966. *The New Deal and the Problem of Monopoly.* Princeton, N.J.: Princeton University Press.

Hays, Samuel P. 1957. *The Response to Industrialism, 1885–1914.* Chicago: University of Chicago Press.

———. 1980. *American Political History as Social Analysis.* Knoxville: University of Tennessee Press.

Hockheimer, Lewis. 1897. "Police Power," 44 *Central Law Journal* 158–62.

Hofstadter, Richard. 1955. *The Age of Reform: From Bryan to FDR.* New York: Alfred A. Knopf.

———. 1968. *The Progressive Historians: Turner, Beard, Parrington.* Chicago: University of Chicago Press.

Horwitz, Morton J. 1977. *The Transformation of American Law, 1780–1860.* Cambridge: Harvard University Press.

———. 1984. "Progressive Legal Historiography," 63 *Oregon Law Review* 679–87.

———. 1992. *The Transformation of American Law, 1870–1960: The Crisis of Legal Orthodoxy.* New York: Oxford University Press.

Hovenkamp, Herbert. 1991. *Enterprise and American Law, 1836–1937.* Cambridge: Harvard University Press.

Hughes, Charles Evans. 1918. "New Phases of National Development," 4 *American Bar Association Journal* 92–110.

Hull, N.E.H. 1997. *Roscoe Pound and Karl Llewellyn: Searching for an American Jurisprudence.* Chicago: University of Chicago Press.

Hurd, John C. 1881. *The Theory of Our National Existence, as Shown by the Action of the Government of the United States since 1861*. Boston: Little, Brown.

Hurst, James Willard. 1956. *Law and the Conditions of Freedom*. Madison: University of Wisconsin Press.

———. 1964. *Justice Holmes on Legal History*. New York: Macmillan.

———. 1971. "Problems of Legitimacy in the Contemporary Legal Order," 24 *Oklahoma Law Review* 224–38.

Jacobs, Clyde E. 1954. *Law Writers and the Courts: The Influence of Thomas M. Cooley, Christopher G. Tiedeman, and John F. Dillon upon American Constitutional Law*. Berkeley: University of California Press.

Jameson, John Alexander. 1867. *The Constitutional Convention*. New York: C. Scribner & Company.

Jones, Alan. 1967. "Thomas M. Cooley and 'Laissez-Faire Constitutionalism': A Reconsideration," 53 *Journal of American History* 751–71.

Jones, H.S. 1993. *The French State in Question: Public Law and Political Argument in the Third Republic*. Cambridge: Cambridge University Press.

Kairys, David, ed. 1982. *The Politics of Law: A Progressive Critique*. New York: Pantheon Books.

Kalman, Laura. 1986. *Legal Realism at Yale, 1927–1960*. Chapel Hill: University of North Carolina Press.

Karl, Barry. 1983. *The Uneasy State: The United States from 1915 to 1945*. Chicago: University of Chicago Press.

Katz, Michael B., ed. 1993. *The "Underclass" Debate: Views from History*. Princeton, N.J.: Princeton University Press.

Keller, Morton. 1977. *Affairs of State: Public Life in Late Nineteenth Century America*. Cambridge: Harvard University Press.

———. 1990. *Regulating a New Economy: Public Policy and Economic Change in America, 1900–1933*. Cambridge: Harvard University Press.

Kloppenberg, James T. 1986. *Uncertain Victory: Social Democracy and Progressivism in European and American Thought, 1870–1920*. New York: Oxford University Press.

Lacey, Michael J., and Mary O. Furner, eds. 1993. *The State and Social Investigation in Britain and the United States*. New York: Cambridge University Press.

Laski, Harold J. 1917. *Studies in the Problem of Sovereignty*. New Haven, Conn.: Yale University Press.

Lerner, Max. 1933. "The Supreme Court and American Capitalism," 42 *Yale Law Journal* 668–701.

Leuchtenburg, William E. 1963. *Franklin D. Roosevelt and the New Deal, 1932–1940*. New York: Harper & Row.

Lichtenstein, Nelson, and Howell John Harris, eds. 1993. *Industrial Democracy in America: The Ambiguous Promise*. New York: Cambridge University Press.

Lively, Robert A. 1955. "The American System: A Review Article," 29 *Business History Review* 81–96.

Lowi, Theodore J. 1979. *The End of Liberalism: The Second Republic of the United States*. 2d ed. New York: W.W. Norton.

Maitland, Frederic William. 1968. *Selected Essays*, ed. H.D. Hazeltine, G. Lapsley, and P.H. Winfield. Freeport, N.Y.: Books for Libraries Press.

Mannheim, Karl. 1950. *Freedom, Power, and Democratic Planning*. New York: Oxford University Press.

Mathews, John Mabry, and James Hart, eds. 1937. *Essays in Political Science in Honor of Westel Woodbury Willoughby.* Baltimore: Johns Hopkins University Press.

McCurdy, Charles W. 1975. "Justice Field and the Jurisprudence of Government-Business Relations: Some Parameters of 'Laissez-faire' Constitutionalism, 1863–1897," 61 *Journal of American History* 970–1005.

———. 1979. "The *Knight* Sugar Decision of 1895 and the Modernization of American Corporation Law, 1869–1903," 53 *Business History Review* 304–42.

McIlwain, Charles Howard. 1910. *The High Court of Parliament and Its Supremacy: An Historical Essay on the Boundaries between Legislation and Adjudication in England.* New Haven, Conn.: Yale University Press.

———. 1947. *Constitutionalism: Ancient and Modern.* Ithaca: Cornell University Press.

Merriam, C. Edward. 1915. *A History of American Political Theories.* New York: Macmillan.

Myers, Gustavus. 1912. *The History of the Supreme Court of the United States.* Chicago: C.H. Kerr & Company.

Newmyer, R. Kent. 1986. *The Supreme Court under Marshall and Taney.* Arlington Heights, Ill.: Harlan Davidson.

Novak, William J. 1996. *The People's Welfare: Law and Regulation in Nineteenth-Century America.* Chapel Hill: University of North Carolina Press.

———. 2000. "Law, Capitalism and the Liberal State: The Historical Sociology of James Willard Hurst," 18 *Law and History Review* 97–145.

Orren, Karen. 1997. "The Work of Government: Recovering the Discourse of Office in *Marbury v. Madison.*" Unpublished manuscript.

Parrington, Vernon L. 1930. "Introduction." In J. Allen Smith, *The Growth and Decadence of Constitutional Government,* ix–xvii. New York: Henry Holt & Co.

Paul, Arnold M. 1960. *Conservative Crisis and the Rule of Law: Attitudes of Bar and Bench, 1887–1895.* Ithaca, N.Y.: Cornell University Press.

Pocock, J.G.A. 1957. *The Ancient Constitution and the Feudal Law: A Study of English Historical Thought in the Seventeenth Century.* Cambridge: Cambridge University Press.

Pound, Roscoe. 1909. "Liberty of Contract," 18 *Yale Law Journal* 454–87.

———. 1911–12. "Scope and Purpose of Sociological Jurisprudence," 24 *Harvard Law Review* 591–619; 25:140–68, 489–516.

Purcell, Edward. 1973. *The Crisis of Democratic Theory: Scientific Naturalism and the Problem of Value.* Lexington: University Press of Kentucky.

Rakove, Jack N. 1996. *Original Meanings: Politics and Ideas in the Making of the Constitution.* New York: Alfred A. Knopf.

Ramage, B.J. 1902. "Social Progress and the Police Power of a State," 36 *American Law Review* 681–99.

Reznick, Scott M. 1978. "Empiricism and the Principle of Conditions in the Evolution of the Police Power: A Model for Definitional Scrutiny," 1978 *Washington University Law Quarterly* 1–92.

Rodgers, Daniel T. 1998. *Atlantic Crossings: Social Politics in a Progressive Age.* Cambridge: Harvard University Press.

Rohr, John A. 1986. *To Run a Constitution: The Legitimacy of the Administrative State.* Lawrence: University of Kansas Press.

Ross, Dorothy. 1991. *The Origins of American Social Science.* New York: Cambridge University Press.

Ross, Edward Alsworth. 1969 [1901]. *Social Control: A Survey of the Foundations of Order.* Cleveland, Ohio: Press of Case Western Reserve University.

Rueschemeyer, Dietrich, and Theda Skocpol, eds. 1996. *States, Social Knowledge, and the Origins of Modern Social Policies.* Princeton, N.J.: Princeton University Press.

Scheiber, Harry N. 1972. "Government and the Economy: Studies of the 'Commonwealth' Policy in Nineteenth-Century America," 3 *Journal of Interdisciplinary History* 135–51.

Scheuerman, William E., ed. 1996. *The Rule of Law under Siege: Selected Essays of Franz L. Neumann and Otto Kirchheimer.* Berkeley: University of California Press.

Schlegel, John Henry. 1995. *American Legal Realism and Empirical Social Science.* Chapel Hill: University of North Carolina Press.

Sedgwick, Theodore. 1857. *A Treatise on the Rules which Govern the Interpretation and Application of Statutory and Constitutional Law.* New York: J.S. Voorhis.

Skocpol, Theda. 1992. *Protecting Soldiers and Mothers: The Political Origins of Social Policy in the United States.* Cambridge: Harvard University Press.

Skowronek, Stephen. 1982. *Building a New American State: The Expansion of National Administrative Capacities, 1877–1920.* New York: Cambridge University Press.

Smith, J. Allen. 1930. *The Growth and Decadence of Constitutional Government.* New York: Henry Holt and Co.

Stillman, Richard J. II. 1998. *Creating the American State: The Moral Reformers and the Modern Administrative World They Made.* Tuscaloosa: University of Alabama Press.

Teubner, Gunther, ed. 1987. *Juridification of Social Spheres: A Comparative Analysis in the Areas of Labor, Corporate, Antitrust and Social Welfare Law.* Berlin: Walter de Gruyter.

———. 1988. *Dilemmas of Law in the Welfare State.* Berlin: Walter de Gruyter.

Thompson, Walter. 1923. *Federal Centralization: A Study and Criticism of the Expanding Scope of Congressional Legislation.* New York: Harcourt, Brace and Company.

Tomlins, Christopher L. 1985. *The State and the Unions: Labor Relations, Law, and the Organized Labor Movement in America, 1880–1960.* New York: Cambridge University Press.

Tomlins, Christopher L., and Andrew J. King, eds. 1992. *Labor Law in America: Historical and Critical Essays.* Baltimore: Johns Hopkins University Press.

Twining, William L. 1973. *Karl Llewellyn and the Realist Movement.* London: Weidenfeld and Nicolson.

Twiss, Benjamin R. 1942. *Lawyers and the Constitution: How Laissez Faire Came to the Supreme Court.* Princeton, N.J.: Princeton University Press.

Veblen, Thorstein. 1904. "Business Principles in Law and Politics." In *Theory of Business Enterprise.* New York: Charles Scribner's Sons.

Waldo, Dwight. 1948. *The Administrative State: A Study of the Political Theory of American Public Administration.* New York: Ronald Press Company.

Warren, Charles. 1913a. "The Progressiveness of the United States Supreme Court," 13 *Columbia Law Review* 294–313.

———. 1913b. "A Bulwark to the State Police Power—The United States Supreme Court," 13 *Columbia Law Review* 667–95.

Weber, Max. 1978. *Economy and Society*, ed. Guenther Roth and Claus Wittich. 2 vols. Berkeley: University of California Press.

White, G. Edward. 1990. *The Marshall Court and Cultural Change, 1815–1835.* New York: Oxford University Press.

Wiebe, Robert H. 1967. *The Search for Order, 1877–1920.* New York: Hill & Wang.

Willoughby, Westel Woodbury. 1896. *An Examination of the Nature of the State: A Study in Political Philosophy.* New York: Macmillan.

———. 1904. *The American Constitutional System: An Introduction to the Study of the American State.* New York: Century Company.

———. 1910. *The Constitutional Law of the United States.* 2 vols. New York: Baker, Voorhis & Company.

———. 1924. *The Fundamental Concepts of Public Law.* New York: Macmillan.

Willrich, Michael. 1998. "The Two Percent Solution: Eugenic Jurisprudence and the Socialization of American Law, 1900–1930," 16 *Law and History Review* 63–111.

Wilson, Woodrow. 1887. "The Study of Administration," 2 *Political Science Quarterly* 197–222.

———. 1890. *The State: Elements of Historical and Practical Politics.* Boston: D.C. Heath.

———. 1908. *Constitutional Government in the United States.* New York: Columbia University Press.

Wood, Gordon S. 1969. *The Creation of the American Republic, 1776–1787.* Chapel Hill: University of North Carolina Press.

Woolsey, Theodore D. 1878. *Political Science; or, The State Theoretically and Practically Considered.* 2 vols. New York: Scribner, Armstrong & Company.

Wright, Benjamin Fletcher Jr. 1931. *American Interpretations of Natural Law: A Study in the History of Political Thought.* Cambridge: Harvard University Press.

PART IV
Law, Lawyers, and the Marketing of Law

The Legal Profession

Robert W. Gordon

INTRODUCTION: A TROUBLED PROFESSION

AT THE TWENTIETH CENTURY'S end, legal business is booming—at least in some sectors of practice. Since 1975 there has been a huge increase in the numbers of law school graduates, in big-firm corporate-law practice in both domestic and foreign markets, in incomes at the top, in lucrative plaintiffs' class action practice, even in nonprofit "public-interest" lawyers. American law firms and styles of business lawyering are spreading over the globe. Yet the profession is suffering from a crisis of morale, identity, and reputation. Public regard for lawyers—always ambivalent—is low; by most measures a majority of lawyers are disaffected with their work; bar groups agonize over dangers they perceive to "professionalism"—hyper-adversarialism, incivility, ethical corner-cutting, and greed (see, e.g., ABA Commission on Professionalism 1986).

As in the national economy, the benefits of prosperity are very unevenly spread over a stratified and fragmented profession. At the apex of large-firm corporate practice, partners earn from $500,000 to more than $3 million a year. At the bottom end of public and charity-funded legal services, criminal defense, and the small-firm and solo practitioners who serve most clients, lawyers earn between $20,000 and $40,000, if they find legal jobs at all. Law school graduates in the lower tier are rightly worried about unemployment and obsolescence, as they face competition from franchised law firms producing discounted standardized services and from computer software and on-line legal-services programs. Law school applications at all levels, but especially in the lower tiers, have been dropping for a decade.

Even in the booming top tier, leading lawyers lament the decline from a golden age of independent-minded "lawyer-statesmen" who served the public interest as well as their clients to a present of ruthless and unethical "hired guns" and narrow specialists who think only of making money (see, e.g., Linowitz 1994). Others—especially the new generation of big-firm partners and trial lawyers—dispute this story of decline, arguing that "golden age" professionalism protected the economic and status interests of a snobbish cartel, and that today's more market-driven and socially inclusive profession delivers more efficient and higher-quality service to a wider range of clients (see, e.g., Posner 1998). Even big-firm lawyers, however, worry about increasing competition from accountants and financial consultants and about losing their autonomy—control over markets, terms of service and payment, authority, and working conditions—to house counsel, insurance companies, regulatory agencies, and other outside monitors and regulators. Corporate defense lawyers fiercely criticize the plaintiff's bar for manufacturing "meritless" lawsuits; plaintiffs' lawyers criticize their opponents for obstruction and delay. Meanwhile huge potential clienteles go unserved or underserved: most people who need legal services, if not among the few financed by insurance, contingent fees, statutory fee awards, or public subsidies, cannot find competent legal service at affordable prices.

A hundred years ago, lawyers sounded similar contradictory themes of decline and opening opportunity. Law, said bar leaders, was declining from a "profession to a business." Lawyers, they claimed, who once acted in the interests of the whole community were becoming subordinated to the narrow interests of specific clienteles, especially large corporations, and were in danger of losing their independence. Competition from title insurers and accountants was eroding legal livelihoods. The bar was becoming "overcrowded," and its standards were falling. A new plaintiffs' bar of mostly immigrant "ambulance chasers" was accused of cheapening the profession's ethics and multiplying "strike" suits. Yet then as now, other lawyers saw all these trends as signs of progress, of a bar adapting to modern conditions, adopting efficient business practices, and serving new clienteles; while not always progressive, such change was considered inevitable. And then as now, a small but significant handful of lawyers sought careers that would reconnect their profession's practices with its ideals of serving justice, the rule of law, and the public good.

At mid-century Willard Hurst took stock of the profession in his classic *Growth of American Law* (Hurst 1950). He found many of the complaints exaggerated. Lawyers were still a dynamic force in American society, serving valuable social functions as "social inventors"—architects of novel forms of private business structures and relations and of public regulatory laws and institutions—as mediators of social conflict, and as reformers of the quality and ethics of their profession. But Hurst also judged mid-twentieth-century lawyers, in contrast to founding-generation lawyers like Alexander Hamilton and John Marshall, as cautious, timid, and narrow, as either "technicians" unconcerned with the larger ends of law and policy or "partisans," unthinking extensions of clients' values and ends. He looked to two developments to rescue the profession from its narrowness: the expanding role of advisor to business interests who must take account of the policy purposes expressed in new forms of legislation and regulation, and the extension of cost-effective services to hitherto unserved clienteles. What follows builds on Hurst's pioneering work of historical analysis and critical scrutiny, brings the story up to date, and assesses the ironic fate of his hopes for the profession's future.

A SURVEY OVERVIEW OF THE PROFESSION

General Characteristics

Over the century some general structural features of the profession remained fairly stable, and distinguished the American legal profession from those in other societies and from its co-equal profession, medicine.

The American profession of law is formally a unified profession. Unlike European professions, the American has no distinct career paths for private lawyers and public lawyers such as judges, prosecutors, and bureaucrats; nor does it have distinct branches of practice such as the English divisions between barristers and solicitors or the French (until very recent consolidations) among *avocats, avoués, conseils juridiques,* and *notaires.* U.S. judges, prosecutors, and lawyers of the senior bureaucracy are appointed (or, as in the case of most state judges and district attorneys, elected) from the ranks of ordinary practitioners. Control over licensing, rules of practice, and discipline does not reside with the national government; rather, it is delegated to state bar associations and state courts. Control over entry and training is split between the state bar associations, which administer bar exams and prescribe minimal educational requirements, and the law schools, which admit, sort, train, and certify students for legal careers. Education is postgraduate, rather than (as in most countries) undergraduate.

Though formally a single profession, law is de facto many professions, fragmented and stratified into groups of lawyers with very different social origins, education and skills, social prestige, and practice tasks. A rough rule of thumb is that rank in the prestige hierarchy and (mostly) income depend on who one's clients are and where one went to law school. For most of the century the highest-status lawyers have been partners in large big-city law firms doing specialized work for corporations; nearly all of them have been top graduates of a handful of elite university law schools.[1] Before 1975 this elite was almost entirely white, male, and Protestant (except for a few Jewish firms that served Jewish banking and business clients); it has since opened to admit Jews and Catholics and—though promotion policies filter out most of these before partnership—women, blacks, Latinos, and very recently Asian Americans. The lowest-status lawyers have throughout been those who practiced on their own or in small partnerships representing individuals in trouble and without much money—small debtors and consumers, tenants facing eviction, people accused of crimes, personal injury victims, family members in conflict.

The middle tier does miscellaneous legal work for middle-class individuals—personal injury, real estate closings, estate planning, divorce—and for small businesses. Prestige, as the 1982 Chicago bar study put it, varies with distance from ordinary human suffering (Heinz and Laumann 1982). Prestige also correlates with social origins. The upper tier has consisted mostly of the children of businessmen and professionals; lawyers in the lower tier were for most of the century likely to be of recent immigrant origins and to have gone to law school at night or part-time (Carlin 1962).

Most of the work American lawyers do is for private clients, and their ethical orientation is toward those clienteles. Though this proportion has been declining sharply in the last half-century (from almost 90 percent in 1948 to 65 percent now), most lawyers are in self-employed private practice; in sole proprietorships, partnerships or professional corporations; or in in-house positions with corporate clients. Theorists of the professions (Osiel 1989; Krause 1996) suggest that lawyers everywhere orient themselves toward the social sectors most likely to further their privileges and power. In most societies that sector is the state; in some (like England and France until very recently, and Germany episodically) it is the organized profession itself. In the United States it is private clients, especially business clients. The dominant ideology of the American bar is libertarian. Though in fact most lawyers avoid criminal defense practice, and its prestige is low, they hold up the model of criminal defense as the paradigm of what they do: the aggressive protection of private rights against an overreaching state. Their driving ethics are those of zealous advocacy: their job is to help clients pursue their freely chosen projects within the limits of the law and to push for interpretations and applications of law that bend those limits in their clients' favor. Like lawyers in every legal system, they necessarily also have some duties to third parties, the courts, and the integrity of the substantive and procedural rules of the justice system; but they construe these other duties very narrowly.

Two other structural features of law practice contribute to its client, especially business client, orientation. One is that unlike European lawyers, American lawyers have mostly not tried to mark off distinct boundaries between business jobs and legal jobs, except when they are trying to repel competitors. Jacksonian hostility to professional privileges destroyed incipient legal guild organizations in the early nineteenth century (though the guilds were gradually rebuilt beginning in the 1870s) and got lawyers used to doing business alongside legal jobs. Lower-tier lawyers have always survived by doing a little real estate or land speculation or insurance or collection work on the side; upper-tier lawyers do business and financial consulting. Lawyers move easily from law practice to investment banking or to entrepreneurship, from in-house counsel's offices to executive positions, from law firms to accounting or financial-consulting firms. American business lawyers see their job not just as representing clients in court or rendering legal opinions, but as facilitating their clients' business plans, helping them design structures and transactions so as to steer them through mazes of regulations and minefields of liability. They tend to see themselves as extensions and technical instruments of their clients' projects, agents who "grease the wheels" of American capitalism, rather than as an independent estate with independent functions.

Second and more important, lawyers look primarily to clients to pay their fees. In this they differ fundamentally from physicians, who since the 1930s have been mostly cut loose from direct patient funding and have come to rely instead on a combination of insurance paid by employers out of wages; religious and private philanthropic grants to charitable hospitals; and what has gradually grown into an enormous taxpayer-funded state sector (almost 45 percent of all health care costs) that subsidizes health research and training of physicians and pays for medical treatment of veterans, military personnel, the elderly, the disabled, and the poor. Health care in the last decade has been evolving toward more for-profit forms of delivery, but these are still largely paid for by employer-financed insurance, and the state sector continues to expand. About 15 percent of the population has no medical insurance but is still eligible for free public emergency treatment.

Legal services by contrast are still where physicians' services were before the 1930s: mostly fee-for-service paid by clients out of pocket. Under the "American rule" of litigation expenses, each party generally pays his own legal expenses, whether he wins or loses. Some modifications qualify this pay-as-you-go regime. Unlike many other legal systems, the United States allows contingency-fee contracts whereby a civil plaintiff's lawyer who wins gets to keep 30–40 percent of the damages assessed against the losing party in litigation, but nothing if he loses. In civil rights litigation and shareholders' ("derivative") suits against their own corporations winning plaintiffs' lawyers are entitled by statute to recover attorneys' fees from defendants. There is remarkably little risk-pooling: liability insurance covers the cost of legal services for individuals as a byproduct of insurance against risks of common accidents (auto and homeowner's liability policies) and professional malpractice liability, and against liability of corporations who don't self-insure and their directors and officers. Except for a few plans sponsored by unions, there is almost no prepaid group legal insurance comparable to medical HMO plans, and almost no employer-paid legal insurance. Since the 1860s a tiny charitable sector has funded Legal Aid Societies to serve the poor; these have been supplemented by voluntary pro bono services contributed by the private bar, and since the 1960s by a public sector of state-funded criminal-defender programs and federally funded civil legal services offices serving poor clienteles. The basic overhead costs of the legal system—courts, judges, prosecutors and courtroom personnel, administrative agencies and their enforcement arms—are of course also socialized. But the public and nonprofit sectors of legal services for private persons, compared to for-profit fee-for-service law, remain tiny (around 3 percent of all lawyers), and the relative share of publicly funded services is declining.

For lawyers serving powerful and sophisticated business clients, the formal ethic of loyal service to client tends also to be the reality. Business clients often complain that their lawyers manufacture unnecessary work and overbill for their services; but the strongest public critiques of corporate lawyers have been that they are far too compliant with what clients want, employing their skills to subvert and maneuver around the framework of law and regulation that is supposed to constrain their clients' conduct. In the lower reaches of the bar, where clients are less sophisticated and can pay only low fees, or where the lawyer will be paid a contingent-fee award out of the proceeds of judgment or settlement, the complaints are that lawyers unduly dominate their clients, keep them uninformed, control decisions over basic objectives as well as strategy, and invest only as much effort in each client's case as will generate a return (see, e.g., Rosenthal 1974). In practices whose economics favor high volume and turnover, the lawyer will be tempted to allocate his time and effort to the cases in his portfolio with potential big-award returns and to skimp on the others. The lawyers in "mass tort class actions," who sue on behalf of hundreds or thousands of plaintiffs injured by the same product, such as asbestos or pharmaceutical products, rarely get to know their clients at all; such lawyers run their cases as they see fit and are virtually unaccountable to the people they represent (Coffee 1995; Weinstein 1995). Thus the paradoxical condition of a profession whose status is determined by its clients is that practitioners in its lower echelon have more independence from clients and more autonomy in setting the conditions of their work, and those in the higher echelons have less of both (Heinz and Laumann 1982, 353–89).

Some Basic Historical Trends

So far I've been talking about relatively stable features of the profession. Let me now sketch some of the major changes.

Numbers

The total number of lawyers has increased dramatically, from 109,000 in 1900 (or one lawyer for every 700 people) to nearly a million in 1999 (one for every 320 people). The increase has been steady except during World War II, and has been especially rapid since the 1970s, when law schools nearly doubled their enrollments to admit new groups of women applicants.

Ethnic/Gender Composition

The bar in 1900 was with token exceptions exclusively white and male. There were about 1,000 women lawyers in the entire country and about 730 black lawyers. Many schools refused to admit women as students (Harvard held out until 1950); no southern school would admit blacks. Ten states would still not admit women to practice. The ABA would not admit blacks to membership until 1948 (see generally Smith 1993). Antidiscrimination laws and affirmative action combined to produce a huge increase in black enrollments in law schools, from 2,000 in 1969 to 6,000 in 1985 (Abel 1989, table 30). Since then, however, there has been a slight decline; and black lawyers are strikingly underrepresented in law firms, making up 3.3 percent of associates in 1996 and only 1.7 percent of partners (Wilkins and Gulati 1996). The biggest change is in the profession's acceptance of women. Between 1967 and 1983, enrollment of women at ABA-approved law schools rose 1,650 percent, from 4.5 to 37.7 percent of the total (Abel 1989, 91); it has since risen to and stabilized at about 43 percent. Some combination of continuing discrimination and the brutal time demands of corporate practice have kept law-firm partner ranks predominantly male—around 85 percent or more in most firms. Women are better represented (around 25 percent) in prosecutors', government, and house counsels' offices, and among law teachers (see generally Epstein 1993; Drachman 1997).

Distribution of Lawyers over Practice Sectors

The most dramatic changes are in the growth of the large law-firm sector, and the growth of individual firms, on the one hand; and the decline in solo practice on the other. In 1900 a "large firm"—so large contemporaries called it a "law factory"—had 11 lawyers. Houston's Vinson & Elkins is typical. Like other big firms, V&E expanded geometrically in the boom legal market of the 1970s and 1980s. By the late 1970s the firm had 286 lawyers; by the 1990s it had 500. More and more business came in from increasing state and federal regulation, and V&E lawyers began to specialize in energy, environmental, patent, admiralty, and municipal bond law, and in antitrust, securities, and mass tort litigation, as well as its old fields of oil, gas, banking, and insurance. V&E opened branch offices in Dallas, Austin, Washington, London, and even Moscow. In 1993 it grossed $202 million and returned a profit per partner of $426,000 (Hyman 1998).

In the last half century the proportion of lawyers in "private practice" has declined significantly, from 89.2 percent in 1948 to about 68.3 percent in 1988. In that category the biggest decline is in "solo practice"—61.2 to 33.2 percent. Where have the lawyers gone? Primarily to "private employment" (as in-house employees of business—up from 3.2 percent in 1948 to 10 percent in 1988) and governments. Federal government employment of lawyers, as a proportion of all lawyers, is less than it was in the 1950s and 1960s (down from 5–6 percent to 3.7 percent), but state government employment of lawyers is up (from 1.8 percent in 1950 to 5.3 percent). A few more have become law teachers, up from 0.6 percent in 1951 to 1 percent in 1988 (Abel 1989).

The most striking finding of the most detailed study of allocation of lawyers' effort, the 1975 study of the Chicago bar, now being redone for the 1990s, is that in 1975 the share of legal effort, lawyers' time, going to corporate matters was 53 percent, and the share going to individual "personal plight" clients was 21 percent. In 1995 the share of effort going to corporate clients had increased to 61 percent, while effort to personal plight clients went down to 16 percent (Heinz et al. 1998, 762–70).

Specialization

Lawyers' work has become much more specialized. The leaders of the bar in 1900 were still mostly generalists, men who made their mark as trial lawyers trying a medley of civil and criminal cases such as wills, divorces, libels, and murders, as constitutional lawyers arguing before the Supreme Court, and as general business advisers. Already, however, the bar was beginning to specialize by clienteles: the upper bar represented corporate defendants (railroad and streetcar companies) in personal-injury tort suits; the lower bar represented plaintiffs. Until the 1930s lawyers in general corporate practice might still represent labor organizations; but after the Wagner Act brought into being a regular labor bar, lawyers represented either labor or management and almost never crossed the line. The growth of the regulatory state, with its arcana of complex technical administrative rules, doomed the generalist in corporate practice: a lawyer could spend a lifetime mastering a few sections of the corporate tax code and keeping up with new amendments and regulations. Fields such as prosecution and patents were already specialized by 1900; labor, tax, patents, antitrust, oil and gas, and securities were highly specialized by mid-century. In the late 1970s, 22 percent of Chicago lawyers worked in only one field, and 70 percent considered themselves specialists; by the late 1980s, 32 percent said they worked in only one field (Heinz et al. 1998). But solo and small practitioners still engage in a general family practice, except for criminal defense and personal-injury lawyers.

The "Professional Projects"

The historian of professions usually begins with an ideal picture of what a profession aspires to be, then describes how his or her profession achieved, or failed to achieve, the conditions of a successful "professional project." Past theorists of the professions stressed the projects of raising standards and quality of education, selection, ethics, competence, and discipline; of protecting professional ideals of service and reward in honor among peers rather than money; of the independence of professionals from nonprofessional outside controls; of autonomy in setting the conditions of work; and finally of promoting public goods such as the rule of law, the improvement of the legal system, and access to justice for the indigent and underserved. More recently, critical theorists (Auerbach 1976; Larson 1977; Abel 1989; Posner 1998) of professionalism—an interesting convergence of neoclassical economists and left-leaning sociologists—stress instead the professional project of "market control"—the bar's attempts to restrict competition among lawyers and from non-lawyers, to limit routes of access and police ethics of upstart groups, to create demand for and control supply of market for services, and to mystify their knowledge to gain authority over the laity. Both sets of theorists tend to focus attention on professional associations: in law's case, primarily the organized bar. This is not my main focus here, but this tradition of work in the sociology of professions, dominated in the study of lawyers by Richard Abel (see especially Abel 1989), is fundamental, and I will briefly indicate some of its findings.

Raising Standards, Restricting Entry

The bar's main collective "projects" were those of raising education and entry requirements, promoting law schools and administering bar exams, getting leverage over selection of judges, and institutionalizing disciplinary machinery. The bar elite had some success in regulating terms of entry by imposing examination requirements and standardizing requirements and content of education, restricting competition; but it fell well short of its ambitions to attain the level of control achieved by physicians: to restrict the production of professionals to a few approved schools. The bar was unable to shut down night schools between 1900 and 1930 and thus failed to close off access to immigrant and upwardly mobile lawyers. Its greatest successes in restricting supply came in the late 1930s, when more than 60 percent of all law students were in ABA-approved schools and all but eight states required at least two years of college (Stevens 1983). But by relying on educational credentials as the main entry barrier, the bar partly undid its own restrictive project. By the time it succeeded in almost universalizing college degree requirements, after World War II, college and postgraduate education were considerably more accessible.

Since their inception the bar associations have also promoted merit selection of judges, in conflict with political party machines that have preferred to keep judgeships as patronage rewards for loyal party service. This project has met with some success. Appointment or (as in most state systems) election to judgeships remains, with only occasional exceptions made for conspicuously able jurists, a reward for the politically well-connected. But bar associations have pervasively inserted themselves as official filters or influential endorsers of candidates in state and federal procedures for nominating judges. Their influence has tended to be conservative—prosecutors and corporate lawyers, for example, rather than criminal defense, plaintiffs' personal-injury, or labor lawyers, are overwhelmingly favored for federal judgeships—but with probably generally beneficial effects on competence and honesty (Hurst 1950, 141–46; Halliday 1987). Unfortunately, in recent years segments of the bar—usually trial lawyers representing plaintiffs on one side, and lawyers representing corporate defendants and insurers on the other—have turned some state judicial electoral contests into the rawest kind of interest-group politics, funneling campaign contributions to candidates to purge the bench of judges who issue rulings unfavorable to their clients and causes.

Protection from Competition

State bars also put in place an impressive array of arrangements that restricted competition among lawyers and between lawyers and other professions, but these too met with uneven success. Starting in the 1920s "unauthorized practice committees" fought fierce turf battles with encroaching neighbors—accountants giving tax advice, "administrative" specialists handling cases before agencies, title insurers and real-estate brokers handling property sale closings—with mixed success, often resulting in treaties marking off boundaries of legal work or allowing peaceful coexistence (Hurst 1950, 320–21; Rhode 1981). The bar's favorite internal restrictive practices—bans on advertising and minimum fee schedules—were struck down by the Supreme Court in the 1970s as violations of the antitrust laws and the First Amendment (*Goldfarb v. Virginia State Bar* [1975]; *Bates v. State Bar of Arizona* [1977]). Court decisions favorable to civil rights legal organizations and threats of antitrust enforcement persuaded the bar to end its hostility to group legal-service plans with "closed" panels of lawyers (the legal equivalent of HMOs). The bar has enjoined or prosecuted competition from lay providers of such services as divorce advice, even in markets that lawyers don't serve (Rhode 1981). But the flow of lay services in the form of advice books, do-it-yourself manuals, form books, and computer software programs has become a deluge no bar group can stop. The most formidable challenge to the professional monopoly now comes from accounting firms. These firms are coming to dominate corporate financial and tax transactional practice in Europe. In the United States they already employ some five thousand professionals, trained as lawyers but not claiming to practice law and unregulated by the bar, to find tax advantages for clients, and are they seeking to overturn the bar's long-standing prohibitions against lawyers as such practicing in organizations run by non-lawyers or shareholders (ABA Commission on Multi-Disciplinary Practice 1999).

Self-Regulation

Where the "professional project" has most conspicuously failed is where professions are supposed to be strongest but are predictably weakest: self-regulation—monitoring competence, disciplining deviants, instilling and reinforcing internalized systems of ethics and restraint. The first bar associations were founded by elites in the 1870s (Association of the Bar of the City of New York, 1870; American Bar Association, 1878) with the hope of enforcing ethical standards even against elite lawyers who were perceived as stretching the rules too far for the benefit of corporate clients (Powell 1988). But bar associations were soon turned into organs whereby the elites scapegoated lower-tier immigrant-ethnic personal-injury lawyers for offenses like soliciting clients and ambulance-chasing and ignored their own failings (Carlin 1966). As the bar associations gradually opened up to lower-tier lawyers, they lost the will to sanction any but the grossest misconduct, such as lawyers' theft of clients' funds. Yet to enforce even these minimal duties to clients, the bar set up disciplinary machinery so inert, unresponsive, underfunded, and self-serving that more than 90 percent of complaints were routinely disposed of with little or no investigation. Lawyers were and still are rarely disbarred for any reason other than felony conviction and theft of clients' money. Perhaps most astonishing, a profession whose main reason for being is that lay clients can't reliably evaluate the quality of services has never developed any institution for monitoring competence after the initial bar exam. Lawyers practicing in firms, like doctors in hospitals, are under some degree of collegial and hierarchical supervision (though this tends to be very loose once the lawyer is a partner, especially if he is a big business-getter); lawyers on their own are subject to none (see generally Rhode 1994; Wilkins 1992).

Not surprisingly, then, over the last half century the professional associations have gradually been losing control of discipline to external regulators: to judges, to new full-time disciplinary bureaucracies, to regulatory agencies such as the Internal Revenue Service and the Securities and Exchange Commission (which regulate by conditioning the right to practice before them), and to new legislative controls such as consumer-protection laws requiring standardized contract terms and disclosure to clients, malpractice actions, and insurers against malpractice and other risks trying to reduce the risks of lawyers' incompetence and misconduct (Powell 1986; Wilkins 1992). Malpractice claims doubled in the seven years between 1979 and 1986, and the average settlement went from $3,000 to $45,000 (Ramos 1994). The practice of law, almost completely unregulated in 1900, is now hedged about by thickets of rules, some with effective sanctions behind them. As a result, lawyers, especially those in the upper tier, are probably much more compliant with ethical obligations than in the old days. But ethics has come to mean simply following rules imposed by others.

Independence

The story of lawyers' loss of collective control over discipline is part of a more general story of decline in their independence and ability to control the conditions of their work, a trend common to all the professions in the late twentieth century (see Brint 1994; Krause 1996; Derber 1982). The elite of corporate lawyers, after a prolonged and agonized internal struggle, surrendered its claims to be an independent third force standing above the clash of ordinary interest groups such as capital and labor early in the century, as it embraced the role of provider of specialized technical services to and lobbyist for business interests. Though increasingly servants rather than independent counselors of business clients, corporate firms until around 1970 were able to form long-term relationships with clients that allowed firm partners considerable autonomy in allocating their time and structuring their work. Since then, however, many lawyers, like doctors, have lost much of their residual discretion to determine the terms, pace, and quality of their work, as they have been reclassified as subordinates within bureaucratic hierarchies. An especially harried group are insurance defense lawyers, who now have to process their cases according to rigid standardized protocols dictated by their employers or are governed by detailed contract terms imposed by clients or insurers. Even lawyers at the top of the hierarchy, like partners in large firms, have to submit to close monitoring by clients who specify budget caps, modes of travel (coach, increasingly), and allocation of associates to their case. The inside corporate lawyers who hire them have to justify their legal budgets to their chief financial officers. Time billing, introduced in the 1940s as an internal accounting device for allocating costs among cases and clients, has become a Taylorist instrument for monitoring and increasing lawyer work output. Meanwhile, in the lower tiers of practice, cost-cutting franchised law offices are crowding many lawyers out of practice and enforcing a strict work discipline on those who remain by standardizing forms, transactions, and caseloads and enforcing strict time accounting (Seron 1996; Van Hoy 1997).

Increasing Access: The Persistent Problems of Privatized Provision of a Public Good

In a liberal society, justice is a universal public good. All persons of full legal capacity are equal under the law; all have the same rights and are subject to the same obligations; each may call upon the legal system for the same benefits and protections—enforcement of contracts, protection from crimes and civil wrongs, defense against unfounded prosecutions, civil actions, and regulatory impositions—and is subject to the same taxes, regulations, restrictions, and conditions.

That is the theory. In practice, of course, the ability to enforce rights varies enormously with command of access to the legal and political systems. Access is mediated through professional intermediaries, gatekeepers and expediters with special contacts, inside knowledge of personnel and procedural custom, and specialized expertise in the arcana of the justice systems and the regulatory state. Lawyers are not the only such intermediaries, but in our society they are the most important.

Three basic structural features of the legal system, acting together, tend to widen the gulf between the liberal ideal of equal access and the reality of very unequal access: (a) Lawyer's services, as we've seen, are largely delivered through private markets and financed directly by clients. (b) Lawyers' ethics in our system give a very high priority to the service of client interests and much lower priority to furthering the public purposes of the legal system. (c) The procedures lawyers favor for the resolution of disputes, the making and applying of administrative rules, and even the structuring of transactions tend to be complex, expensive, and adversarial. These three mutually reinforcing basic characteristics of our system tend to skew the delivery of access and favorable outcomes heavily in favor of well-funded, repeat-playing interests (see generally Galanter 1974; Kagan 1994).[2]

For practical purposes, access to law is for the most part not an entitlement but a private consumption good, which you can get as much of, but only as much, as you pay for. Average hourly rates for lawyers were $180 in 1998; for partners in large firms $250; for lead partners $385. The market for law is dominated—in dollar volume and in hours of lawyer effort—by services to large businesses and wealthy individuals, and to plaintiffs who can recover legal fees by suing them. Legal institutions and procedures tend to develop in shapes distended by the interests of their most frequent and influential users, lawyers who can send hourly bills to high-end clients—elaborate bodies of legal principles, rules, exceptions, and qualifications; long drawn-out adversary procedures such as civil discovery or trial-type administrative hearings; labyrinthine mazes of technical regulations; forms such as those for securities and tax filings that are unfathomable to the untutored mind.[3]

The system of adversary ethics also raises the costs of lawyering. It requires lawyers for all sides to bear the (often duplicative) expenses of their own factual investigations and consulting expert witnesses. It not only licenses but exalts as the lawyer's highest role morality maneuvering for strategic advantage, partisan presentation of facts and law, and the attempt to discredit even evidence known to be truthful offered by the other side. All of this requires time-consuming and expensive counterstratagems, which, ultimately, clients must pay for.

Such processes are far too expensive for ordinary clients, who are thus shut out of them altogether (unless they promise to yield a supernormal contingent fee) or are relegated to the K-mart counter of heavily discounted cheap justice (see generally Hadfield 2000). A recent study of personal-injury claims found that about a fifth of injured claimants who went so far as to consult lawyers were turned away because their case was not worth enough; other studies confirm the same pattern for medical malpractice and other torts, that small claims never reach the legal system at all (Hensler 1991; Weiler 1991). The full-scale criminal trial, with its magnificent regalia of constitutional protections, has been priced out of the range of all but very rich defendants (business white-collar, drug, and organized criminals). The problems of differential access are naturally most glaring in situations of conflict, when people without much money for lawyers confront well-funded opponents heavily brigaded with lawyers. In such situations many people avoid lawyers altogether: in 1990 52 percent of divorcing families got their divorces without lawyers; in 88 percent of litigated divorce cases, at least one party was unrepresented or defaulted.

Justice may in theory be a universal public good, but in practice willingness to pay for other people's legal problems is low. Either the people are unsympathetic or their legal problems are seen as avoidable or better left unrelieved. Law has to a large extent been perceived as an optional consumption good (like cosmetic surgery), or worse, as a resource for oppression of others and evasion of just obligations or punishments. Litigation may be necessary to protect one's rights, but actually engaging in it is often culturally disparaged and deplored as antisocial and wasteful. Subsidies, it is feared, will invite moral hazard, as the least deserving will jam the system with false and trivial claims and expenses. The habitual legal problems of the poor are particularly unsympathetic as objects of charitable care or public subsidy: they are suspects needing defense in criminal cases, tenants resisting eviction, debtors resisting collection, spouses wanting divorces, welfare claimants, or illegal immigrants.

In our legal traditions, no rights are more centrally enshrined than the rights of the criminally accused. The rights to jury trial, counsel, bail, speedy trial, habeas corpus, confrontation with accusers, freedom from coerced confessions, and illegal invasions of privacy are the principal subjects of our state and federal Bills of Rights, the original "rights of free-born Englishmen." But the reality is that, with the exception of top-level white-collar defense and a handful of highly professional Public Defender offices, criminal defense practice is degraded and despised, at the bottom of the prestige hierarchy—a plea-bargaining bazaar carried on in the shabbiest of public buildings. Before the "Rights Revolution" pioneered by Warren Court decisions of the 1960s, the ordinary mass of people suspected, accused, and convicted of crimes either pawned what possessions they had to buy a plea-bargaining agent, or, if too poor (as most were) even for that, depended on casual charity—the random draw of court-assigned counsel—or disappeared from the legal profession's view altogether (see, e.g., Friedman and Percival 1981, 56–66; Moley 1930).

Lawyers' livings depend on cultivating good business relations with clients and collegial relations with judges, regulators, and court personnel; inevitably, many groups of lawyers (though not all) do come to identify with the people they habitually represent and adopt their point of view. Such dependencies set severe limits on accepting even paying clients if their causes are unpopular or their interests are adverse to regular clienteles. The leading railroads would give free passes or pay retainers to all the able lawyers in towns along their lines to prevent their taking on clients injured in railroad accidents (Thomas 1999, 247–59). In most of the Jim Crow South a white lawyer would only be available to represent a black criminal defendant if appointed by a court; even then, if the crime charged had a white victim, and especially if it were rape, the defense had to be perfunctory. White lawyers could not take on civil rights cases for blacks without risking loss of all their clients (Silver 1964). During the Red Scare of the 1950s, several bar associations passed resolutions discouraging or even forbidding members to represent Communists. Other associations admirably affirmed the principle that every person, however vile, deserved representation but in practice did nothing to assure lawyers would be provided for Communists; and usually they were not (Auerbach 1976, 231–62).

All legal systems have to mediate the inevitable conflicts between lawyers' private obligations to further their clients' interests and their public obligations to maintain the integrity of the legal framework. These conflicts are most intense in an adversary justice system where lawyers themselves, instead of supposedly unbiased officials, are charged with developing facts in litigation.

As I have noted, the American system is unusual in the degree to which it has come to stress the primacy of duties to clients over duties to the framework. In the nineteenth century, standard ethics manuals advised lawyers to be satisfied of the likely merits of clients' causes before instigating suits, to be scrupulous in arguing law and facts to tribunals, and to reach an independent view, not the client's view, of the demands of the governing law. (How many lawyers actually acted on this advice? Hard to say.) The first ABA ethics code also stressed the lawyer's fidelity to the public purposes of the legal system as well as to clients (ABA 1908). Since then every revision of the codes has moved them further away from the obligation to balance clients' interests against obligations to the legal system, toward almost exclusive duties of loyalty, confidentiality, and zealous advocacy to clients. The lawyer must press in his client's favor every plausibly arguable construction of the law and the known facts. He has almost no affirmative duties to assist adversaries, tribunals, or regulatory agencies to gather facts; to restrain clients from perjury or fraud; or to urge his clients to comply with laws or regulations (see ABA 1983).

For most of the profession's history increasing access to lawyers relied on the sporadic efforts of a few maverick reformers such as the Boston lawyer Reginald Heber Smith. The organized bar fiercely resisted any means of delivery of legal services other than fee for services paid out of pocket, and the great mass of lawyers was indifferent. Since the 1970s, however, the bar has overcome its historical resistance and supported institutionalized commitments to some level of low-fee or no-fee services.

Throughout the century some states have assigned court-appointed counsel to criminal defense or to brief and argue appeals *in forma pauperis;* except in the rare localities where a professional service has been created to handle these cases, however, such assignments have tended to fall upon the most marginal courthouse loiterers, those unable to attract clients by other means. Free lawyers for criminal defendants were not required at all in many states until the Supreme Court's decision in *Gideon v. Wainwright* (1963), and are still not provided for the post-conviction remedies that are the best practical hope for the wrongfully convicted or unfairly treated. Criminal defender programs are funded stingily out of the fear that suspects will manipulate the system to escape just punishment. In some states even a lawyer representing a defendant facing the death penalty will get a maximum of $500 to take the case. The quality of representation is often abysmal; yet courts will not reverse convictions for "ineffective assistance of counsel" even if the defense lawyer was visibly incompetent, drunk, drugged, or even fast asleep for most of the trial.

As with criminal, so with civil practice for the poor. Elite lawyers in major cities founded Legal Aid societies in the early part of the century with the usual Progressive mixture of philanthropic and social-control motives: to help give access to justice to the poor, to discourage disfavored claims, and to displace immigrant legal-aid societies that were considered over-aggressive in bringing personal-injury suits. Legal Aid programs traditionally refused to take divorces, bankruptcies, or personal-injury accident cases and insisted on conciliatory rather than adversary approaches to eviction and debt collection (Maguire 1928; Grossberg 1997). Bar regulations have contributed to the problem of unequal access—by resisting the contingent fee (still not allowed in criminal cases and divorces) and, until recently, group legal services; and especially by preventing entry by competing non-lawyers or paraprofessionals into markets monopolized by lawyers—even markets lawyers leave unserved.

Like organized medicine, organized law battled fiercely against government-funded services, fearing the controls that would come with them, until 1965, when the ABA switched to strong and effective support for the federally funded legal service programs initiated as part of President Lyndon Johnson's War on Poverty. Abel has suggested that local bars started supporting subsidized legal services when they realized that more lawyers for the poor would require more lawyers for those they were in conflict with (Abel 1989, 133); whatever their motives, bar groups at all levels have become staunch defenders of legal services. Such programs have been embattled from their beginnings, when Governor Reagan of California tried to shut down legal services offices that successfully brought class actions to recover withheld welfare benefits and gave legal aid to Cesar Chavez's farmworkers' movement (Johnson 1974; Stumpf 1975); as president, Reagan failed to eliminate but succeeded in weakening the program. Congress has cut funding for the program and prohibited federally funded legal-services lawyers from taking on class actions, representing immigrants, helping union movements, or suing for welfare benefits.

Recently some bar leaders have proposed making membership in the profession conditional on agreement to give a minimum number of hours (the ABA recommends fifty) per year of free service to poor clients, but the rank-and-file of the bar generally (and strenuously) resist mandatory pro bono. The ABA has also played a constructive role in trying to lower costs of service to moderate-means clients and to help small and solo lawyers modernize their practices to make them more profitable.

"Legal needs" are an artifact not only of cultural expectations about what kinds of misfortune deserve legal redress, but also of what the state through law, and the bar through its attempts to define the scope of its monopoly, define as problems requiring lawyers. Whatever is legalized can be delegalized, or at least deprofessionalized. The aim of worker's compensation programs in various states beginning around 1910 was to remove industrial accidents from the tort claims system and regulate them instead with a low-cost simplified administrative process, staffed by non-lawyer administrators (Friedman and Ladinsky 1967). This system was quickly reprofessionalized and clients came to be represented by a specialty Workers Compensation bar (Nonet 1969). Similar reforms are now widely proposed for many other kinds of torts—mass toxic torts, medical malpractice—but are strenuously resisted by the tort plaintiff's bar. Bar groups helped create small-claims courts in major cities where self-represented lay plaintiffs could collect small debts; the major users of these services, however, turned out to be landlords and consumer creditors. The bar ceded authority over tax advice to non-lawyers such as the H&R Block franchises that fill in tax forms and give out tax advice (of very uneven quality) to ordinary taxpayers. The delegalization of divorce by removing the need for parties to prove "fault" has simplified uncontested divorce proceedings so far as to make per se representation realistic, as has the proliferation of do-it-yourself legal form kits, recently improved by being marketed as computer software.[4]

LAWYERS' ROLES IN SOCIETY

Like Hurst's classic study in 1950, the primary aim of my study is to describe the practice tasks and social roles of different segments of the bar, to ask what jobs lawyers have done and for whose benefit.

The Upper Echelon: The Corporate Elite and Its Social Tasks

Before 1900 the lawyers ranked by the public and their peers at the top of their profession were rarely exclusively or full-time "corporate lawyers." A successful lawyer had important business clients: railroads, financial institutions, insurance companies, and industrial firms. He was also a courtroom lawyer who tried murders, divorces, and will contests as well as commercial cases; who argued appeals before the highest federal and state courts; and who took time off from practice to serve in high elective or appointive office. Typically he practiced in a small partnership, outside the management hierarchies of his principal clients.

The big law firm, and with it the modern career of corporate lawyer, was born of the Big Deals, Big Cases, and increasingly Big State of the industrial era. The agreements to build giant consolidated enterprises—first railroads, and then other sectors such as oil and steel—required highly skilled legal work and many lawyers. So did the defense of such enterprises against lawsuits challenging their very existence, like suits for patent infringements and antitrust violations. Alongside big business arose the administrative agencies of the modern state to regulate it, starting with regulation of railroads and public utilities. All of this created technical, specialized work for lawyers and a demand for law offices with the numbers and expertise to staff a railroad merger or bankruptcy reorganization, defense of a massive antitrust action, or public-utility rate-making hearing as well as the miscellaneous business of large industrial and financial clients. Over the century, law firms experienced their biggest expansions during merger movements producing Big Deals, rises in litigation (especially with other corporations and against the government), and above all, with expansions of the regulatory state.

With the multi-specialist law firm developed the career of corporate lawyer. Paul Cravath's New York firm pioneered the model of a meritocratic career hierarchy, of associates recruited from high-ranking (white Protestant) graduates of elite law schools, paid a salary, who competed with one another for partnership, and as partners formed a lifetime membership with the firm (Galanter and Palay 1991).

The actual work of the corporate bar over the century, of course, has ranged enormously in interest, complexity, and importance. At one end is the wholly mundane, technical work of regulatory compliance or contract administration, making small adjustments for each new transaction to standardized forms like bond indentures or securities registration statements (in complex transactions) and purchase-and-supply contracts (in simple ones.) At the other is the design and negotiation with opposite numbers in industry or government of new structures of contractual or regulatory architecture. At one end in conflict management is routine processing of low-stakes repetitive litigation like suits against railroads for grade-crossing accidents or damage to livestock, or employment-discrimination claims or minor union grievances; at the other are the huge cases that can bankrupt a company or ensure its dominance: a competitor's challenge to its patents, a mass-tort class-action against its principal product, a major antitrust suit, a prolonged and bitter strike. At one end in mediating state-business relations is helping to design and draft the legislative and administrative frameworks that will govern whole industries, such as the basic acts setting the ground rules for allocating broadcast spectra and regulating competition in the communications industry; or drafting the codes of industrial governance under the New Deal's National Industrial Relations Act. At the other is the daily grind of processing clients' applications for administrative orders and exemptions and piloting them through the technical mazes of agency bureaucracies.

The social role of lawyers in and around business enterprises has hardly been confined to "the traditional lawyers' role" of furnishing narrowly defined, distinctively "legal" services such as representing clients in courts, predicting judicial decisions, interpreting statutes and regulations, and drafting and planning to obtain favorable and to avoid unpleasant legal consequences. In the United States, lawyers have also been active as promoters of business enterprise, as middlemen with access to sources of venture capital for entrepreneurs, as advisers to investors on profitable opportunities, and as investors and speculators in their own right. Lawyers have taken active roles in enterprises as directors or managers and have used positions as executors and trustees and as directors of financial intermediaries like banks and insurance companies to steer capital into favored local ventures. Lawyer are likewise active in the construction of public policies—especially those yielding favorable promotional and regulatory environments for their clients—as intermediaries and lobbyists before legislative and administrative bodies or local authorities and even (without much pedantic fussing about conflicts of interest) as actual members of such bodies or authorities.[5]

As Hurst pointed out, private lawyers performed quasi-public tasks in their ordinary practice roles. As counselors, they advised clients on whether to fight regulations or comply with them; to bring or defend cases brought against them or settle them; to treat labor or competitors as adverse parties or potential partners. They were also "private legislators" in the sense that they drafted the form documents for governance of relations with other entities their clients dealt with, such as suppliers, employees, shareholders, and consumers (Hurst 1950, 342–52).

How did it come about that *lawyers* were in a position to perform, and did perform, all these roles? In Britain, continental Europe, and Japan, state bureaucrats negotiate the design and enforcement of regulations directly with corporate managers, rather than through lawyers; private lawyers are rarely conspicuous public intellectuals, compared to economists, journalists, academics, and literary figures; and they rarely become senior ministers of state. Even in Germany, where law-trained officials dominate the bureaucracy, they are lawyers who have chosen public careers, not "advocates." In the United States the central state apparatus developed late, only after (and partly as a response to) the emergence of giant corporations. Suspicion and devaluation of public careers inhibited the development of an elite corps of civil servants with high prestige; unlike its parliamentary cousin, congressional government favored patronage appointees and part-time amateurs in government agencies.

Corporate lawyers did a lot of the design of the legal forms of state-business relations that in Europe was done by central bureaucracies. Much of the work of governance, in what Skowronek (1982) has called the "state of courts and parties," was administered through courts: basic private law was court-made common law, and the highest law was court-declared constitutional law; courts administered the general body of corporate law and had to ratify and enforce contracts between corporate shareholders, managers, and creditors; courts in their equity jurisdiction governed bankrupt corporations, which at one time included nearly every American railroad, and approved or disapproved consolidations; regulation of monopoly was accomplished through the (awkward) forms of criminal law and private lawsuits. All this made work for private lawyers.

Being closely connected to political life, lawyers were thus also natural candidates for public jobs and moved easily in and out of office. The work entrusted to senior career ministers in Europe devolved upon lawyers in the United States. Since the founding of the republic, about two-thirds of the U.S. Senate and half the House of Representatives have been lawyers (Friedman 1985b, 647), and lawyers are the largest occupational group in most state legislatures as well (Miller 1995, 62–63). Constitutional argument, the favored rhetorical medium for the discussion and settlement of large issues of the distribution of political authority and the proper scope of the national and regulatory states, was peculiarly the province of lawyers. And lawyers were invaluable links between business and the state because they had experience in politics and government and contacts in the capitals, and between business and foreign countries because (for much of the century) they were among the few Americans who traveled abroad.

To show how such connections between private practices and public concerns have been worked out in the United States, I will sketch a brief ideal-typical account of the evolution of elite corporate law practice in the United States. My account is largely based on New York City examples, with some side trips into other jurisdictions.

Phase 1: Competition. The first phase (the mid-to-late-nineteenth-century norm, iterated repeatedly in the development of new industrial sectors in the twentieth century) was that of competition among many relatively small ventures (railroads, street railroads, oil companies, timber companies, insurance companies, extractive industries, etc.). In this phase lawyers were active in promotion, helping to assemble investors, to negotiate the participation of each in the venture, and to market the shares as well as to do the required start-up paperwork. A lot of this work was routine: negotiating rights-of-way, collecting debts, dealing with small claims of abutting landowners or creditors. Strategic, as opposed to routine, litigation was used as a method of carrying on competition: filing nuisance suits; challenging the patents, mining claims, or franchises of other companies; resisting such challenges to one's own. Lawyers were busy in the state and federal capitals peddling influence and seeking (and sometimes paying for) favors—subsidies, exemptions, rights-of-way, concessions, monopoly privileges, regulatory breaks, public-works contracts. This tended to be a hustling, aggressive, scrappy, opportunistic, ethically corner-cutting kind of practice.

Phase 2: Consolidation. In this phase (1896–1914 for many large U.S. industries; ten to twenty years earlier for major railroads) some sectors came to be dominated by a few giant firms. Many companies failed; the strategy of the successful ones was to absorb competitors by consolidation (and often to integrate vertically). Lawyers in these shake-outs, especially if they represented winners, became foreign ministers for their clients, negotiating treaties and alliances—pools, cartel agreements, trusts, holding companies, and other forms of consolidated enterprise. In this phase the lawyers moved into a unique strategic position as intermediaries between business and the financial world through their ability to combine personal connections with technical expertise. Lawyers met the demand to craft increasingly complex corporate debt and equity instruments offering different mixes of risk-and-reward and security to different classes of investors (no-par stock, preferred stock, the mortgage on after-acquired property, the debenture indenture, etc.). In doing that work they came to know leading investment houses of the New York and European money markets, and became adept at marketing new issues of stocks and bonds to such investors.

In New York around 1900, such work totally transformed the character of corporate practice. A lawyer like Elihu Root, who for years had mostly occupied himself defending bread-and-butter lawsuits and scrapping with competitors over municipal franchises on behalf of a street railway, would suddenly find himself general counsel of an extensive consolidated empire. In the United States the process of consolidation was often achieved via bankruptcy reorganization. Lawyers, as counsel to creditors' and shareholders' committees of reorganizing enterprises, provided the key links with the financial community and the expertise with legal-financial detail to put these giant deals together. Elite corporate practice moved from solo and two-man partnerships into recognizable predecessors of the modern, multipartner firms with career paths for university-law-school-trained associates, providing a range of specialized services. Interestingly enough, leading lawyers tended to move out of in-house general counsel's offices in this period (though there was also traffic in the other direction) into nominally "independent" firms (nominally because big-firm practice has usually been anchored by one or two main clients—often a bank). Most leading corporate lawyers in this period left litigation entirely. (They were to return, in force, in the 1970s.)

The public activities of this new corporate bar went well beyond seeking special deals for particular clients. As agents of a major structural transformation of the economy, they were now concerned to redesign the basic legal framework to accommodate the new forms of industrial and financial enterprise. This was less a matter of negotiating specific concessions for particular clients (though of course that still continued) than of changing the general law so as to legalize consolidations (e.g., by legislation permitting holding companies, or by narrow interpretations of the antitrust laws), to centralize control in management (e.g., by reducing common law directors' and officers' liabilities, liberalizing standard state-law charter provisions to relax restrictions on corporate powers and capitalization, and authorizing managers to exercise "business judgment" without fear of shareholder suits), and to help suppress militant labor (e.g., by pressing the courts to recognize new forms of corporate "property" in economic relations that would be protected by injunction, or by using the antitrust laws to prosecute labor "conspiracies").

Phase 3. Statesmanship. Once the corporate empire was assembled, and clients attained a satisfactory market share, the lawyers' job became that of stabilization and legitimation: protecting the client's and the industry's position. That might mean having to engage in defensive litigation against competitors bringing patent or antitrust or unfair competition claims (routine litigation such as accident and contract claims would by now have shifted to in-house lawyers or subcontracted smaller firms) or against government antitrust actions. But it was most likely to entail corporate statesmanship, the effort to construct durable institutional structures that would assure a stable operating environment, especially for industries with high fixed costs. So in this phase many firms, often at the urging of or through the medium of their lawyers, pursued a corporatist politics. They pressed for (or acquieseced in) regulatory schemes that would satiate populist clamor against monopoly while also enforcing their price-fixing agreements and raising costs of entry and operation for their small competitors; cooperative relations with antitrust enforcers who would grant prior clearance to merger plans; national labor standards (outlawing child labor, setting minimum wages and maximum hours) that would remove advantages of competing firms in antilabor states; social wages financed out of general tax revenues that would improve labor relations without their having to pay for it; workers' compensation plans that would quiet labor agitation over safety at acceptable cost; cooperative accords with labor unions who could help to maintain discipline and contain militancy in return for job security and high wages.

In this phase in the United States, lawyers played a critical part in both designing and staffing such institutional arrangements, not only in their roles as counsel for particular firms or trade associations or business policy groups, but as members of civic associations such as the National Civic Federation, which brought together business executives and conservative labor leaders, and finally as lawyers on leave from practice as officials in city, state, and federal governments.

As lawyers made their clients respectable, they did the same for themselves. They put some distance between themselves and their clients, emphasizing their detachment, as when firms prohibited members from investing in client companies. They adopted ethics codes proscribing the more vulgar forms of client-chasing. They devoted themselves to legal science, like codification projects or the "Restatements" of the American Law Institute (a consortium of elite judges, corporate lawyers, and law professors) and law reform.

By no means were all corporate lawyers cooperative corporatist-state builders. Many represented business clients who bitterly opposed arrangements such as the New Deal's schemes of securities, public-utilities, and especially labor regulation, or supported them as long as they thought they could control the regulators and switched to vehement opposition when they could not. Some lawyers were themselves by ideological conviction ferociously opposed to any large federal or government role in the regulation of business. In the 1930s these formed the backbone of the Lawyer's Committee of the Liberty League, whose members counseled their industrial clients to civil disobedience of the orders of the New Deal's new labor board, in the certain (and ultimately mistaken) conviction that the Supreme Court would invalidate the National Labor Relations Act. They led the struggle, embodied in the Walter-Logan Act of 1940 vetoed by President Roosevelt, to burden the administrative process with so much trial-type due process as to bring it to a total halt (Wolfskill 1962; Shamir 1995). Yet by the 1950s most of the New Deal's innovations, which had settled cozily into the familiar tripartite deals between industries, their friends in Congress, and regulatory agencies, had come to be viewed by leading firms as an at least tolerable and often very useful revised framework for a capitalist economy.

Phase 4. Administering routine. Once stable conditions of order were achieved, the new regulatory schemes established and their basic ground rules worked out, there was less scope for lawyer-statesmen. Corporate lawyers became caretakers of the going system. New Deal hotheads "with their hair ablaze" founded Washington firms to serve the capitalists they had thought to tame with regulation (see for example Horsky 1952; Kalman 1990). Younger lawyers often started their careers with a brief term in government to learn the system from the inside. Large-firm corporate practice became still more technical and specialized, much less a matter of negotiating new conventions with the state than of administering existing ones. Lawyers continued to cultivate relations with the bureaucracy; but their main stock in trade became their expertise rather than their contacts, and business firms turned over their political-action work to specialists in lobbying and government relations (Heinz et al. 1993). Practice conditions were stabilized as well: law firms were locked into long-term relationships with major clients and handled virtually all those clients' business; young lawyers entered the firm hoping to stay with it for life.

This approximately describes the system that prevailed for many big-city firms in United States from the end of World War II until the 1970s (see Smigel 1969 for a classic study of the postwar law firms).

Phase 5. Destabilization and reconfiguration. Since about 1975 corporate law practice in the United States has entered a distinctly new phase. The main origins of the new phase are in the severe shocks to the settled corporate-legal order delivered by international competition, by the new mobility of capital and the new volatility of the market for corporate control. These have made business firms anxious to cut costs by dismantling regulation and labor agreements they once accepted as the price of stability. As they became more litigious toward governments, competitors, and unions, more prone to takeovers as targets or raiders, and more driven to financial restructuring to play to the capital markets, these companies' legal costs rose geometrically. Firms have tried to keep these costs down by severing long-term ties with outside firms, bringing most legal work in-house and auctioning off fragments of specialized work—especially complex litigation—to many different outside firms. The result is a whole new style of corporate practice—ruthlessly competitive, powered almost exclusively by the drive for profits, so demanding as to leave no time or energy for other commitments, very lucrative for lawyers and firms who succeed but also very anxiety-producing because so many fail, and mostly indifferent to social responsibility and public values.

The old stable institutional order of law firm practice has dissolved. Lawyers no longer expect a lifetime career in a single firm, but move among firms who bid for their services, and from firms to house counsel's offices, investment banks, accounting firms, and business consulting services. Firms have raised associates' salaries to compete with pay in alternative careers now open to law graduates; but with more pay has also come longer hours of work (eighty hours or more a week in many firms), and lower chances of making partner and of secure tenure even after partnership. Compensation is tied to client-getting ability: "You eat what you kill" (Galanter and Palay 1991).

Meanwhile, the American style of corporate law practice has spread to foreign countries, especially Europe; but in the process it has attracted many competitors: English solicitors' firms, multinational accounting firms, and new European multidisciplinary consortia. Three of the five largest international law firms (with 1,125 to 2,300 lawyers each, and twenty-one to sixty-one offices in different jurisdictions) are American; the other two are English. Accounting firms in the United States now employ more than 5,000 lawyers, doing "legal" work such as giving advice on taxes and bankruptcy organizations. American lawyers are also competing fiercely for a share of the increasingly lucrative business of international arbitration, formerly dominated by Europeans, and promising to bring the mixed blessing of American-style litigation practice to the rest of the world (Dezalay and Garth 1996). In competition with European solicitors and accountants, American lawyers are building the new institutions of international political economy.

In the last decades of the nineteenth century, the elite lawyers' self-conception as Tocqueville's "aristocracy," America's de facto governing class, and trustee for the public interest came under increasing strain from the pressures of their private practices, especially the demands and interests of private clients. As the most successful lawyers were drawn into the orbit of powerful corporate clients like railroads and financial institutions, the strain threatened to destroy the legal elite's public role, or to reduce it to that of tactical and political agent of big business.

Most business lawyers simply acquiesced in that new identity, but the most conspicuous leaders did not; they persisted in trying to salvage a cultural and political leadership role from new practice conditions. They took collective action to restore the public capacity of the profession and to rescue the legal system from corruption. The profession's institutional legacies of this period—modern bar associations, law schools, law firms, ethics codes and disciplinary regimes, administrative commissions, and procedures for reducing patronage in the selection of judges and civil servants were all to some extent products of this collective effort. (So were less admirable attempts to purge the profession of ethnic, immigrant, radical, and plaintiff's personal-injury lawyers believed to endanger its public-service image.) Elite lawyers did occupy high offices of state and often conducted them in a way that transcended the narrow and immediate interest of clients. The highest foreign policy posts for most of our history have been occupied by lawyers on leave from practice, usually New York City corporate practice. Lawyers who have moved into judgeships have sometimes confounded former clients—as well as the presidents who appointed them—by their independent-mindedness. Although organized bar groups have sometimes just been mouthpieces for popular prejudices or powerful client groups, they have also played the role Tocqueville assigned to them as guardians of legalism—of rights to representation and due process for criminals and dissenters, of subsidized access to legal services, and of international human rights—as well as the more positive role of expert advisors on law reform, through such institutions as the American Law Institute and the National Commissioners on Uniform State Laws, organizations of practicing lawyers, judges, and law professors (see generally Halliday 1987; Powell 1988).

This elite took on another major project: building an ideological framework of legal order, a set of overall structuring or ordering principles—rationalizations, justifications, inspiring guiding norms—of the legal system. Lawyers elaborated this project as public intellectuals—judges, office-holders, law reformers, civic activists, treatise-writers, bar leaders—from a variety of public pulpits.

There were actually two rival projects, or visions of ideal legal order. The older was the "classical" ideal being perfected as a legal science of private-law principles in the law schools and their articles and treatises, and in decisions of the courts, especially the federal courts (which corporations being sued by out-of-state litigants had the option of choosing to hear their cases), and as a science of public-law principles in the opinions of state and federal judges and the briefs, speeches, and writings of lawyers appearing before them. The private-law principles called for strict enforcement of all contracts, even such one-sided agreements as employment contracts; tended to limit the liability of companies for industrial accidents; and were hostile to most collective tactics of organized labor, such as strikes and boycotts. The public-law principles, developed out of "due process" clauses in state constitutions and the federal Fourteenth Amendment, produced a rich jurisprudence of constitutional limitations on legislators' and administrators' powers to change the ground rules of economic life, which inspired courts to strike down some "progressive" social legislation such as minimum-wage, maximum-hours, and federal anti–child-labor laws, as well as laws favoring union organizing (see Gillman 1993; Cushman 1998).

The challenge to the classical vision came from the "progressive" ideal that began to emerge in the 1890s, was developed by Progressive reformers and intellectuals, secured beachheads in legislatures and on regulatory commissions and even among some influential judges (Holmes, Brandeis, Cardozo, Learned Hand, and Julian Mack, among others), and achieved its institutional triumphs first at the state and local levels, and at the federal level in the New Deal. The Progressives criticized classical law as biased and inadequate to deal with social problems, and they proposed to replace it with social-science–based expertise applied by administrative commissions.

Both visions of ideal legal order aspired to apolitical universality, an objective basis in science, and autonomy from partisan politics and class warfare. Progressive-minded business lawyers hoped that their double program of engaging in reform politics and institution-building while advising clients to comply with the emerging policies of the administrative state in their own best interests would give their profession a way to serve simultaneously the legitimate interests of clients and the public interest (see, e.g., Berle 1962). Relatively older and more conservative lawyers of the 1890–1940 era, men like James Beck, John W. Davis, and William Guthrie, favored the classical vision, as it gave them a basis in constitutional principle for fighting legislation and regulation that disfavored their clients, and the sympathetic and conveniently final forum of the judiciary in which to make their arguments. In practice, however, classical courts were sometimes a slender reed for business libertarians. The courts were indeed reliably and consistently hostile to labor organizations; but—with notorious exceptions—they upheld most Progressive regulations as valid; and the legislation they did strike down, such as child labor and worker's compensation laws, had often been enacted with strong support from business interests. As many leading lawyers denounced the famous *Lochner* decision invalidating maximum-hours laws for bakers as applauded it. Indeed, business interests and their lawyers were among the driving forces behind much of the administrative state-building efforts of the early part of the century. Business lawyers tended to move back and forth between classical and Progressive visions as political contexts and client interests changed. Classical conservatives swallowed their doubts about the most constitutionally dubious of the New Deal's experiments, the National Industrial Recovery Act, because their major clients initially supported it—and celebrated its invalidation by the Supreme Court after their clients had turned against it (Shamir 1995). Progressive and New Deal regulation was also a huge source of both new business and new opportunities for civic action. The New Deal especially expanded opportunities for lawyers to serve as mediators between business-client interests and the administrative state and to move back and forth between public and private careers (Irons 1982).

At the same time, however, the profession was evolving a conception of its private functions that, over the course of this century, largely pushed aside the public functions. Lawyers increasingly specialized not only by type of case but by clientele: in labor disputes, lawyers made careers representing exclusively management or labor; in tort cases, plaintiffs or defendants. The task of representing underrepresented groups and some notion of the general public interest increasingly devolved upon other specialists: government, public interest, legal aid and "cause" lawyers, and law professors. (See "Public Interest Lawyers," below.) Elite lawyers continued to take time off to serve in public office and to be active in the bar's technical law reform projects such as the American Law Institute's "Restatements"; they assumed a leadership role in the bar's efforts after 1970 to promote subsidized legal services and (through their firms' policies) to supply modest levels of pro bono service; and they have been exceptionally active in some causes such as international human rights. When President Kennedy asked the legal profession in 1963 to create an organ that would commit lawyers' time and efforts to civil rights, some 200 prestigious lawyers immediately signed up to form the Lawyer's Committee for Civil Rights under Law. Yet there has arisen no equivalent to the great projects of 1870–1940 to develop and rationalize a general institutional-ideological architecture of American legalism or to be Progressive lawyer-statesmen designing grand compromise solutions to the factional clashes of society. The closest modern versions of such a project are the neo-liberal project of restoring some version of the "classical" legal order of the late nineteenth century in the United States itself; and the attempts by American lawyers, consultants, world financial institutions, and development agencies to construct liberal-legal institutions (the "Rule of Law") overseas, in developing and ex-Communist societies. The everyday reality for most practitioners is total immersion in the service of private clienteles.

Lawyers for Individuals

The other "hemisphere" of private practice—solo and small-firm lawyers serving individuals and small businesses, is vast and miscellaneous. In 1900, this category encompassed the entire profession save for a few big-city big-business firms. It is still numerically the largest segment of the private bar, but it accounts for a rapidly diminishing share, compared to large-firm corporate practice, of total lawyers' effort and earnings. It has also included some very wealthy and famous members, such as tort plaintiffs' lawyers who are richer than all but a few top corporate lawyers and celebrity trial lawyers like Max Steuer, Louis Nizer, F. Lee Bailey, or Edward Bennett Williams, who take on high-profile clients and cases. Its staple business throughout the century has remained much the same: claims for simple debt and collections, personal injury suits, criminal defense, divorce and other family work, realestate closings, wills and trusts, bankruptcies and foreclosures, and miscellaneous problems of small businesses.

No one has ever tried to write the history of law practice in this hemisphere, and the attempt would take up many volumes. This section focuses on two of the many types of "personal plight" practitioners: solo practitioners and the personal injury bar.

At the bottom of the hierarchy are solo and small-firm practitioners making a precarious living on the brink of unemployment. They are the most vulnerable to business cycle downturns; to competition from non-lawyer organizations such as trust departments, title insurance companies, and accounting firms (since their staple work is real estate work, wills, debt collection, auto accidents, and divorces); to reforms reducing the need for lawyers such as no-fault auto accident and no-fault divorce laws; and to do-it-yourself forms, manuals, and software programs. Carlin's pioneering study described the typical individual practitioner as a self-made son of "an immigrant from Eastern Europe with little or no formal education" (Carlin 1962, 3), the graduate of a low-prestige (often night or part-time) law school, and more likely Jewish than Protestant (Heinz and Laumann 1982, 111–12). While the incomes of partners and associate in corporate practice have been rising dramatically since 1970, the incomes of solo practitioners declined by 30 percent between 1970 and 1985 (Sander and Williams 1989, 475), while their numbers increased by 34 percent from 1980 to 1988 (Curran and Carson 1991, 6). One response to these precarious market conditions has been the organization of franchise law firms, which attempt to realize scale efficiencies and product standardization through consolidation and rationalization of legal work for middle-class individuals (Seron 1996; Van Hoy 1997).

The most dramatic development in this hemisphere of practice, and certainly the one with the broadest and most controversial social effects, is the rise and transformation of personal-injury tort practice, of the plaintiffs' personal injury bar and the insurance-defense specialists who oppose them, and of a mass tort class-action specialty within that bar.

Tort practice hardly existed in the United States before the 1880s. Injured persons rarely sued. The wounded soldiers of industry were compensated, if at all, by small payments from mutual-benefit societies or paternalistic employers. The routine expectation of "total justice" (Friedman 1985a), that someone else could be blamed and should have to pay for accidental injuries, was not yet widely embedded in the culture. Plaintiffs who did sue usually lost or recovered tiny damage awards. Corporate defendants, and employers in particular, had many effective defenses such as rules denying compensation to workers who had been injured by fellow employees or who could be alleged to have "assumed the risk" of injury by taking on a dangerous job or to have contributed to the injury by their own negligence. The sudden rise in tort claims was a response to the enormous carnage caused by industrial technology—railroads, factory machinery, mining operations, streetcars, and eventually automobiles—to workers, passengers, and bystanders, and to the rapid growth of a mostly immigrant urban bar of attorneys, working for contingent fees of 30 to 50 percent of the amounts recovered, willing to take on cases for the injured. Before 1900 the same lawyers often represented whoever first sought to hire them, whether plaintiffs or defendants; that changed when the companies most often sued, like railroads, mining companies, and streetcar companies, began to demand complete loyalty from their lawyers, put them on retainer, and forbade them from representing plaintiffs (see generally Bergstrom 1992; Friedman 1987; Thomas 1999; Munger 1994).

Personal injury practice was never for the ethically fastidious. Plaintiffs' lawyers chased ambulances, hung around hospital rooms and funeral parlors, hired "runners" and policemen and doctors to refer business, and bribed witnesses. Elite lawyers used their control of bar associations to discipline the plaintiffs' bar for "solicitation" and tried to limit contingent fees and keep out of the profession graduates of the night schools where (until mid-century) most plaintiffs' lawyers were trained (Carlin 1966; Auerbach 1976). Company lawyers also developed tricks of their own. They sent agents into hospitals to get injured plaintiffs to sign releases of liability in return for low settlements, smuggled inconvenient witnesses out of town, and deployed a vast and versatile arsenal of procedural weapons to delay cases and exhaust adversaries or to move cases into more sympathetic legal fora than state jury trials, such as the appellate courts and the federal courts (Friedman 1987; Russell [n.d.]; Purcell 1992, 34–45).

Where accidents were common, the mutual interest of injurers and injured in quick and predictable settlement resulted—after much conflict and dissent—in the routinizing of claims processes. For industrial injuries to workers, the tort system was displaced, in part through political compromises negotiated between big businesses and unions and embraced by Progressive reformers, by an administrative no-fault nonjudicial system, Worker's Compensation, which spread to almost all states between 1910 and 1920 (Friedman and Ladinsky 1967).[6] Auto accidents, which had in relatively short order become by far the biggest class of injuries—in 1930 more than 30,000 Americans died in auto accidents (Simon 1997)—remained in the tort system, though the great majority of cases were disposed of without suit by insurance company claims adjusters, and the rest were handled by stables of specialist defense lawyers working in-house or on retainer for insurance companies (Ross 1970).

The first mass-tort cases—involving large numbers of victims injured by the same cause—arose from accidents: fires, floods from bursting dams, sinkings of boats. Litigation of such disaster claims had unpromising beginnings. Victims were often poor, hired local counsel to fight experienced company lawyers, and faced daunting jurisdictional requirements, procedural obstacles, and hostile courts. Only one civil suit was brought in the wake of the Triangle Shirtwaist Fire of 1911, a disaster in which unsafe tenement conditions resulted in the deaths of 145 New York sweatshop laborers. Plaintiffs rested their case after only one day and lost it; the remaining civil suits settled for $75 each (Speiser 1980, 136–37). Few lawyers could risk the costs of taking on such suits, given the probability of loss and low settlements.

The tort bar began to organize itself after World War II. An association of workers' compensation lawyers founded in 1946 added tort practitioners in the 1960s and eventually became the Association of Trial Lawyers of America (ATLA). Between 1951 and 1971 its membership grew from 2,000 members to 25,000, and it became a clearinghouse for information, a means for recruiting cadres of lawyers to take on and coordinate mass tort litigation, and a powerful political interest group with a massive war chest for lobbying legislatures and influencing judicial elections (*Trial*, July–August 1971, 26ff.).

As the tort bar organized, it developed specialties. The first was airplane accident law, a desultory practice area before the 1940s. Stuart Speiser pioneered the role of coordinator and general contractor of teams of plaintiffs' attorneys who represented families of air accident victims from different jurisdictions, helping the lawyers to consolidate cases and prepare a common litigation strategy (Speiser 1980, 196–97, 258–60). In the 1960s, 288 lawyers, representing about 75 percent of the 1,500 plaintiffs who sued the Merrill Company for bad side effects caused by its anticholesterol drug MER/29, combined into a group that drastically cut the costs of litigation by centralizing research and document discovery, deposing witnesses, and finding and preparing scientific experts (Rheingold 1968, 116, 120–22).

Meanwhile, changes in substantive law and procedure had transformed the landscape of tort disputes (for an overview, see Schuck 1995). The courts opened the door to "strict products liability" claims against manufacturers of products alleged to have caused plaintiffs' injuries by ruling that plaintiffs did not have to prove the company was negligent, only that the product was "defective." The "asbestos era" of the federal court system began in 1973, when a federal appeals court ruled that asbestos manufacturers were strictly liable (*Borel v. Fibreboard* [1973]). By 1987 around 50,000 asbestos claims were pending in the nation's courts, by 1992 200,000 claims; to this day some 6,000 to 9,000 new claims are filed annually (Hensler and Peterson 1993, 1004). In the 1970s, the federal courts began to allow the aggregation of asbestos claims as class actions (*Jenkins v. Raymark* [1986]). Patterns established in asbestos litigation rapidly spread to other mass torts litigation, such as DES, Bendectin, the Dalkon Shield, Agent Orange, breast implants, and most recently (and profitably), tobacco.

Mass tort practice as it has evolved has gravitated to an ever smaller number of specialized firms headed by celebrity "Kings of Torts" such as the Peter Angelos firm of Baltimore, which in the 1990s represented more than 10,000 asbestos plaintiffs. In 1995 a *Forbes* list of the twenty-five trial lawyers with the highest incomes listed nine who specialized in mass tort products or accident cases (*Forbes* 1995). The mass-tort lawyers' successes in court, and their growing wealth and political influence, have made them very controversial. Manufacturers anxious to limit exposure to products-liability verdicts have led "tort reform" movements to induce legislatures and judges to make product-liability suits harder to bring and to win and to limit damage awards and attorneys' fees. Tort reformers have accused plaintiffs' lawyers of growing fat on the fees of an out-of-control "litigation explosion" of groundless claims, based on "junk science," brought only to induce settlements, and, by making companies fearful of huge punitive damages awards, tending to stifle innovation and cripple the American economy (see, e.g., Huber 1991). Since 1980 conservative politicians have made "tort reform" and the crusade against plaintiffs' lawyers a centerpiece of their campaigns. In riposte, friends and allies of the plaintiffs' bar portrayed them as populist heroes willing to fight the system of callous corporate wrongdoing on behalf of little guys, who needed the occasional big verdict to cover the high risks of litigation and "send corporate America a message."

More disinterested observers told a less dramatic but equally troubling story. Punitive damages were rarely awarded, usually a low multiple of compensatory damages, and if high, invariably reduced on appeal. Evidence that fear of product liability has had bad macroeconomic effects is weak to nonexistent. Clearly some mass-tort claims (like the Bendectin and, more disputably, the Agent Orange and breast-implant cases) were indeed based on dubious science; in others (like tobacco) the bad science was generated by the corporate defendants (see generally Galanter 1996). The biggest problem with mass tort actions turned out to be that some of them badly disserved not corporations, but the victims themselves. Corporate lawyers came to welcome class actions as a means to consolidate and dispose of all the claims against their clients. Plaintiffs' lawyers developed a strong interest in colluding with their opponents to settle cases quickly for low total damage figures, in order to earn extravagant fees for themselves without having to do much work. Trial judges went along with such collusion, and with plans to prevent individual plaintiffs from "opting out" of class actions and bringing suits on their own, because such arrangements made cases manageable and reduced pressures on dockets (Coffee 1995).

The administrative costs, including lawyers' fees, of adversary procedure in tort cases were always—and still are—appallingly high, likely to consume at least half and often more of the total recovery. This fact alone still keeps most small individual claims out of the tort system, because lawyers cannot afford to litigate them. Yet for all its high costs, the personal-injury lawyer working for a contingent fee has remained the only practical means by which an ordinary individual could confront a powerful corporate entity and effectively seek redress for injuries. Such a person, however, increasingly needs protection from abuse by some of his champions as well as his injurer (Weinstein 1995).

Public Interest Lawyers

This category is the most difficult to define, since all lawyers claim to serve the public interest by effectively representing clients, helping them to realize their freedom and defending them against those who would limit it, particularly the state. My focus here is on broader conceptions of public-interest practice than simply supplying legal services to individuals, however deserving. Client-oriented though it may be, the American legal profession is also known for activism in seeking to bring about changes in the legal ground rules of social life, or to extend coverage under those rules to the previously excluded. I describe here three types of social change lawyers: (1) rights litigators; (2) lawyers as activists in community or group mobilization; and (3) lawyers as representatives of diffuse constituencies in policy formation. These categories overlap considerably. Many lawyers have been involved in all three. Because of space limitations, I must leave out of this essay an enormously important class of lawyers who serve the "public interest"—lawyers working for federal, state, and local governments.

Rights Litigation

The best-known public-interest initiatives of the U.S. legal profession, which are now being widely imitated by activist lawyers in both the advanced and developing societies of the rest of the world, are public campaigns to transform what otherwise might be simply political demands into legal rights, declared and enforced through judicial proceedings.

Ironically, rights-activist litigation in the United States was pioneered by elite lawyers and judges to establish judicial interpretations of private and constitutional law that would fortify rights to ownership and control of business property against (what these elites perceived to be) impulsive populist redistributive or regulatory legislation and trade-union actions such as strikes and boycotts. This movement achieved its most spectacular successes between 1870 and 1937, when lawyers for corporations persuaded state and federal judges to strike down many laws regulating labor relations (such as minimum-wage or maximum-hours laws and laws restricting employers' rights to seek injunctions against labor actions) as violations of basic rights to property and contractual liberty (Forbath 1991). In the 1930s, a group of conservative business lawyers, the National Lawyers Committee of the Liberty League, launched a sustained campaign of test-case litigation to invalidate New Deal legislation (Wolfskill 1962). In the Great Depression of the 1930s, however, such judicially created rights to be free of economic regulation were widely perceived to set rigid and illegitimate restrictions on the government's ability to deal with the emergency and manage the economy. The Liberty League's crusade collapsed when the Supreme Court upheld the New Deal's National Labor Relations (Wagner) Act. Since 1937 business lawyers who want to resist regulation have mostly had to do so by trying to influence legislatures and administrative agencies rather than by asking the courts to recognize constitutional rights to economic liberty.[7]

In a national culture of legalized rights—especially rights declared to be "fundamental" and enshrined in constitutions—and devoted in theory to the liberal ideal of equality of rights in law, it was inevitable that campaigns to improve the status and condition of marginalized and subordinated groups should be cast in terms of equal rights, and that their establishment should be sought through the familiar forms of law.

In this field the pioneers were lawyers for the antislavery cause, and, after the Civil War, for the causes of women's and blacks' civil equality. Reform societies organized to attract patrons and subscribers who would pay for belief in the cause. These funds would defray the costs of lawsuits, while lawyers usually volunteered their time. The next step was to attach the cause to promising clients; or, in appellate proceedings, to ask the court for leave to file briefs as *amici curiae*. This model proved so successful that it has been duplicated repeatedly in modern times by advocates of civil liberties and civil rights. The American Civil Liberties Union (ACLU) was founded in the Red Scare of World War I, when several thousand people, most of them connected to militant labor organizations, were prosecuted by the federal government for impeding the war effort or were deported as undesirable aliens. Supported largely by membership subscriptions and volunteered lawyers' time, the

ACLU since the 1930s has built an impressive record of using the federal courts to prevent persecution of political and religious dissenters by providing them with free legal representation (Walker 1990), and in the process has helped to produce the United States's extraordinarily libertarian (by world standards) regime of judicial protection for free speech.

The most amazing and dramatic use of the model has been by the National Association for the Advancement of Colored People (NAACP) through its Legal Defense Fund ("Inc. Fund"). The NAACP brought and won an important test case, *Buchanan v. Warley* (1917), in its early years. The Inc. Fund's epic journey began in 1930 with a small foundation grant to study the conditions of educational inequality in the South. With a tiny staff of low-paid lawyers headed by Charles Hamilton Houston and Thurgood Marshall, the Fund then embarked on a thirty–year campaign of test-case litigation in the federal courts to try to establish, by gradual degrees, the principle that state-mandated separation of the races in public institutions and places violates the constitutional guarantee of "equal protection of the laws," and by so doing to dismantle the system of legally established racial apartheid in the South. That campaign ended with a moral triumph in 1954, with the Supreme Court's declaration in *Brown v. Board of Education* (1954) that state-mandated segregation of the races in public schooling (and by implication in other public settings as well) was unconstitutional—though it took many more years of protest movements, legal challenges, and federal legislative and executive action before much was done to implement the principle (Tushnet 1987).

The reformers who led these early rights-activist crusades were an interesting alliance of establishment and marginal lawyers. Some were patricians, like the corporate lawyer Moorfield Storey, who headed the first NAACP legal committees. Others were highly educated professionals confined to the margins of their profession by prejudice: the Jewish, black, and female lawyers such as Morris Ernst, Osmond Fraenkel, and Crystal Eastman (the mainstays of the ACLU); Charles Hamilton Houston, Thurgood Marshall, Constance Motley, Robert Carter, and Jack Greenberg of the NAACP; and later but in the same tradition, Ruth Bader Ginsburg of the ACLU's Women's Rights project.

In the 1960s and 1970s, more and more groups followed the strategy of the civil rights movement: to seek declarations of rights in the courts, and then add to further litigation a push for legislation or administrative action. These strategies met with astonishing success. The reformers found surprisingly receptive allies in the—as often as not, Republican-appointed—judges of the U.S. Supreme Court under Chief Justice Earl Warren and lower federal courts: middle-class men who could be provoked to outrage by what test-case litigation revealed of the treatment of marginal and outcast groups in American society. Federal judges embarrassed by the racism and backwardness of the old South, for example, were so revolted by the conditions exposed in Southern prisons, which had been run on the feudal model of slave plantations and tolerated ferocious levels of filth, torture, and coerced labor, that they stretched their legal authority to construct far-reaching remedial orders that placed whole institutions for years under professional reform administrators (Feeley and Rubin 1998). Other judges were provoked to sweeping remedial action by local authorities' obstruction of and resistance to court orders, especially orders to compel school integration. Every act of defiance created more judicial sympathy for the rights-activists, who now appeared as champions of the rule of law against the lawlessness of regularly constituted authorities. Client groups asserting rights to be free from arbitrary or contemptuous treatment by government also found judges receptive to this traditional libertarian strain. Rights litigators were often able to recruit allies in elite law firms to help their causes.

The main beneficiaries of this rights revolution were blacks and women (and, a little later, persons with physical handicaps); but illegitimate children, immigrants, and resident aliens also benefited. The main beneficiaries of the new "procedural due process" rights to fair treatment by the government were criminal defendants, prisoners, juveniles charged with crimes, inmates of mental asylums, welfare recipients, government employees and other claimants to government largesse, such as social-security disability funds, and schoolchildren under discipline.

There was nothing radical about rights-activism on its face. Its basic aims were simply to extend accepted legal principles of equality and fair procedural treatment to groups of persons who had been excluded from their coverage. This might seem a centrist or even conservative program, but once taken seriously and given elite judicial and political backing, it profoundly disrupted existing patterns of hierarchy, authority, and inequality.

Suits brought to achieve declarations of new rights were rapidly followed by more suits for judicial remedial orders, and by lobbying for legislation and executive action to enforce them. Claims of rights to equal opportunity and fair treatment rapidly turned into claims for major redistribution of resources—equalization of public school finances among rich and poor districts, for example—and drastic overhauling of institutions like schools, prisons and mental asylums, and welfare administration, to make those rights effective. Such actions energized a major political backlash against the rights revolution. The Republican party engineered a major electoral realignment based in large part on recruiting voters angered by Warren Court and Democratic administration support for black civil rights, especially school integration orders involving busing, affirmative action plans designed to remedy employment discrimination, the feminist campaigns for equal rights for women and for the constitutionalization of the right to abortion, and expanded protections for criminal defendants. A succession of Republican administrations under Presidents Nixon, Reagan, and Bush gradually replaced the generation of reform-minded federal judges with conservatives committed to reversing, or at least not extending, the proliferation and aggressive enforcement of rights. By the 1990s, reform lawyers who thirty years earlier had fought to get their cases into federal courts now fought to stay out of them.

In some ways rights-activism was an elite reform strategy high above the fray of ordinary politics. For some rights-activist lawyers the important goal was more to vindicate a principle or implement a policy than to advance the interests of a concrete group. Lawyers seeking judicial recognition of the rights of religious dissenters or people accused of crimes rarely identified or even had much contact with actual clienteles (see Casper 1972). This was not invariably so. To build their test cases, NAACP Legal Defense Fund lawyers had to do the arduous and dangerous work of recruiting plaintiffs and organizing suits in the rural South. And though rights-activists were often criticized for over-investing in judicial rule-change and paying too little attention to political mobilization and bureaucratic implementation, in fact they rarely relied on litigation alone to achieve their aims. Litigation was always one strategy among many others, including lobbying, supporting candidates for elections, conducting voting drives, mobilizing allies such as labor organizations, dramatizing causes in the media, grass-roots organizing, and staffing and monitoring enforcement bureaucracies. For example, once a grass-roots civil rights movement had started, the Legal Defense Fund lawyers switched a large part of their efforts from test-case litigation to advancing the goals of the movement and keeping its members out of jail. Still, the natural home of rights-activist lawyers was the courts, especially the upper federal courts.

Community and Social Movement Activism

Rights litigators were the most visible social-change lawyers. Another group of lawyers identified closely with disadvantaged clienteles, and saw themselves fighting shoulder to shoulder with underdogs to reform society and improve their situation from the bottom up.

Until the 1960s such lawyers were generally drawn to the cause of labor, though it did not always entirely welcome them. Through the 1930s the American Federation of Labor (the umbrella organization of craft unions and the dominant voice of labor) pursued the goal of "voluntarism," i.e., laissez-faire; it eschewed any legal aims except the negative ones of defending against employers' legal campaigns against them. Unions did need lawyers to fight court injunctions, criminal contempt proceedings for defying injunctions, and antitrust suits; they found them among left-leaning general practice and business lawyers willing to suffer the stigma of association with organized labor. (Some of those lawyers, such as Clarence Darrow, Donald Richberg, David Lillienthal, and Harold Ickes went on to high posts in the New Deal.) More radical lawyers of the period, mostly from socialist immigrant Jewish households, were drawn to the growing industrial union movement: Maurice Sugar, general counsel of the United Automobile Workers from 1939 to 1947, and Lee Pressman, general counsel of the Congress of Industrial Organizations from 1933 to 1948, for instance. Some radicals (like Pressman) also joined the Communist party. Most joined the National Lawyers' Guild, founded in 1937 as a broad coalition organization of liberal and radical labor, civil rights, and civil liberties lawyers aspiring to be more inclusive than the major bar associations (it admitted Jews, women, and blacks) and to function as an organized counterweight to the conservative politics of the ABA.

After World War II, lawyers with commitments to social reform continued to go into labor law, often after a stint on the National Labor Relations Board staff in Washington. But labor law gradually lost much of its appeal for reformers. Union officials, often Catholic blue-collar workers, tended to be hostile to the Jewish intellectuals who did their legal work, however much they needed them. The federal labor regime created by the New Deal stabilized labor relations by embedding them in legal procedures; this created a steady demand for labor lawyers but also routinized the work of representing unions and deprived it of the romance of a cause. The labor movement lost some of its most intensely committed lawyers when the Taft-Hartley Act of 1947 required a purge of Communists. Incorporated, albeit grudgingly, as a regular partner with business in the postwar economic order, most unions grew more conservative in their aims and ideology, more interested in bread-and-butter bargaining gains than in social transformation, and (in many locals) actively hostile to the new claims of blacks and women for jobs in union-controlled workplaces.

An entirely new field of endeavor, "poverty law" was opened up in the mid-1960s. President Lyndon Johnson created a federally funded Legal Services Program in the Office of Economic Opportunity as part of his War on Poverty. In 1965 the combined budgets of all legal aid societies in the United States totaled $5,375,890 and their combined staffs comprised some 400 full-time lawyers. By 1968 OEO Legal Service had an annual budget of $40 million and had added 2,000 lawyers (Johnson 1974, 188); by 1980 (before President Reagan cut it by a third) the budget was $321 million, supporting 6,000 lawyers. OEO Legal Services also funded "backup centers" in fields such as health and employment discrimination to serve as research centers and information clearinghouses for poverty lawyers in the field. In the early 1970s, charitable foundations (led by the Ford Foundation) began making grants to "public interest firms," about half of whom identified the poor as their principal clientele; by 1975 foundation grants contributed 42 percent of public-interest law firm budgets (Handler, Hollingsworth, and Erlanger 1978, 54).

The new poverty lawyers were a very mixed lot. Like labor and civil-rights–civil-liberties lawyers, some came from left-of-center families and prior backgrounds in social activism. In its early years poverty law practice also attracted high-ranking graduates of elite schools, many of them paid for by

OEO "Reggie" (Reginald Heber Smith) Fellowships. But just as often poverty lawyers came from solo practice or other low-paid "legal rights" jobs like legal aid or public defender practice. Though turnover in Legal Services was always high—few stayed more than four to five years—lawyers who left tended to keep up their activist commitments in other jobs (Handler, Hollingsworth, and Erlanger 1978, 145, 151, 170–74). The lawyers often disagreed about what their objectives should be. Traditional legal aid lawyers and their supporters in the organized bar thought the main mission was a service function, taking care of clients' individual needs and not antagonizing local political or commercial power structures. Others favored a model closer to the Progressive settlement house, of "storefront" services located in poor neighborhoods, combining legal with other social-work services, focused on enabling families to move up and out of poverty. Most of the new lawyers had a more ambitious vision of law as a means to broader social reform, which would work major structural changes in the situation of the poor. An important group favored test-case litigation directed at reforming the indifferent and repressive bureaucracies that served the poor. Others saw litigation as one component of a strategy directed at helping communities of poor people mobilize politically to articulate their own needs and demands and to participate in making and applying policies of the new antipoverty agencies in the cities (see generally Katz 1982; Johnson 1974).

Poverty lawyers involved in reforming the welfare system (1965–73) tried combining all of these strategies. They brought test cases to force welfare bureaucracies to apply their own rules faithfully and fairly and to eliminate arbitrary paternalist regulations; then they helped organize a movement (the National Welfare Rights Organization) of welfare recipients to insist on their rights, in hopes that such claims would overwhelm the bureaucracy and move the government toward a system of unconditional grants. They also sought to repeat the successes of the black civil rights movement, to define the poor as a pariah group subject to unconstitutional discrimination, and to constitutionalize a general substantive right to a guaranteed minimum income. After initial successes on all fronts of its strategy, the movement for welfare rights backfired. As welfare rolls burgeoned—partly because of the lawyers' successes in enrolling eligible families—state and federal governments began to cut back on welfare spending and to impose new requirements. The courts had granted procedural rights to fair hearings, but they refused to create substantive rights to welfare. The nascent political organizations collapsed (Davis 1993).

The new poverty lawyers stirred up a hornets' nest. Established legal aid programs, local bar associations, charitable organizations, and local political machines saw them as threats to their own turf and patronage relations and tried to close them down and restrict their operations to routine individual services. Several governors tried to abolish the programs in their states, after legal services sued the states for violating their own laws and policies. President Reagan tried to abolish the federal program and succeeded in crippling it; it limps onward under many restrictions on its systemic reform activities. The bar associations, however, switched sides and since 1975 have become staunch supporters of legal services, in part because the programs create jobs for lawyers, in part because the bar wants the profession to look good, and in part because lawyers instinctively resist attempts to restrict whom they may represent and by what means.

Lawyers as Policy Entrepreneurs

Lawyers in private practice as well as public office have always been actively involved in designing new policies and the legal machinery to implement them. Lawyers of the Progressive period (1890–1940) invented a new institutional form, the job of legal counsel for the "public interest" group claiming to represent an amorphous and diffuse constituency—Citizens for Good Government, or Public Franchise League, or Committee of One Hundred for the Improvement of Education. As representative of such an abstract "client," the public-interest lawyer naturally had a good deal of discretion about how to deploy his influence. The master of this form of public-interest practice was the Boston lawyer Louis Brandeis, a successful corporate lawyer who was also known as the People's Lawyer for his public-interest causes. Like rights-litigators, Progressive policy entrepreneurs used test-case litigation—though their strategy was to get courts out of the business of declaring rights and to sustain Progressive legislation. Brandeis and the lawyer reformer Florence Kelley brought test cases on behalf of the National Consumers League (which supported maximum-hours and minimum-wage legislation) and also testified before legislatures and administrative commissions in favor of legislative reforms (Strum 1984). (After being appointed to the Supreme Court in 1916, Brandeis continued to direct public-interest crusades from behind the scenes through his agent and disciple, Felix Frankfurter.) The reformers' ultimate goal was usually to set up an expert commission. They were experts at creating publicity. After a scandal revealing some social horror—exploited child labor, tainted meat, railroad bribery of legislators or kickbacks to preferred customers, prostitution rings, insurance fraud—reformers in collaboration with the muckraking press would persuade legislatures to establish commissions with the power to investigate, hold hearings, and make recommendations. These were mostly staffed by part-time amateur volunteers, usually lawyers. Sometimes they turned into permanent administrative agencies.

Brandeis's model has been widely imitated in more recent times. In the late 1960s and early 1970s the model was developed into the role of "public-interest" representative in administrative proceedings. The muckraker and consumer lawyer Ralph Nader, who organized cadres of college-and law-student volunteers to investigate programs and their failures, became the best known and one of the most effective. The mission of the public-interest lawyers was to repair glaring defects in political pluralism—to open up the administrative agencies that the Progressives and New Dealers had created to the broad constituencies they were supposed to serve. Until the late 1960s, administrative agency decision procedures—such as hearings on the construction of energy projects like nuclear power plants, or the granting or renewal of radio or TV licenses—were usually dominated by representatives of the industries they regulated. The new "public-interest" lawyers claimed that other, more diffuse constituencies—TV viewers, lovers of wilderness and the environment, consumers, future generations—also had interests in the decision. The lawyers claimed to represent those interests. With the help of the federal courts, public-interest lawyers were increasingly permitted to intervene in agency proceedings and to challenge agency decisions on judicial review. They have since found a regular place at the table in administrative decision-making processes. In politically congenial administrations, they have been brought in to staff important government posts (McCann 1986; Vogel 1996).

"Public-interest" or "cause" lawyers are by necessity lawyers without organized clienteles, because the people on whose behalf they speak are too weak, diffuse, or unorganized to have a means of aggregating interests and expressing desires. Once a movement or interest group assumes some organic or institutional form, it no longer needs "public-interest" lawyers—it can hire its own. The most successful "public-interest" representatives have managed to turn their abstract constituencies into real ones. The environmental movement, for example, began as a few vanguard activists; but it has used its activism to create a mass middle-class movement, aroused, well-financed, and able to mobilize politically around major initiatives or perceived threats to its core interests. Other examples may be found in the movements for women's rights, disability rights, gay rights, and animal rights. Many public-interest constituencies, however, limit their involvement to writing checks to keep the movements alive; real decision-making power remains with their representatives.

Another institution that has become a reservoir of lawyers for the Progressive policy-making project is the university law school. As a result of the relative weakness of both the state and the organized profession at the time modern law schools began to be organized (1870–1930), the schools have enjoyed an extraordinary degree of independent control over admissions, curricula, examinations, and certification of graduates as eligible to take the bar exam. Like other American faculties they have had to respond to overseers (legislatures in the case of public schools, trustees and alumni in private ones) who have raised questions about hiring radicals (and Jews); but they have never had to submit to direct state or bar control. The independence of law faculties has given law teachers a large degree of latitude to express views and undertake public-interest reform projects that are relatively independent of powerful elements among the bar elite and its clients.[8] Beginning around the 1920s, some law schools became vantage points from which professors could criticize the legal establishment and recommend reforms in judicial doctrine and legislation. (Notable early examples were Harvard professor Zechariah Chafee's critiques of the 1917–1920 Red Scare's prosecution and deportation of radicals for sedition, and a law professors' protest against the Sacco-Vanzetti convictions.) When the New Deal recovery program was launched in 1933, many law professors went off to Washington as full-time officials or part-time consultants to the administration and wrote much of the New Deal legislation. Law school professors also helped pioneer a transformation in private-law doctrine—the expansion of enterprise liability to hold manufacturers of defective products civilly liable to injured consumers. Since the 1960s, law schools have often served as home base to law reform organizations and to rights-activist and public-interest lawyers, who also serve as part of the law school's clinical faculty.

Public-interest law is now no longer a monopoly of progressive (left or center-left, social-democratic) lawyers. In fact, most of the new public-interest organizations and law firms founded since 1980 are conservative in their ideology and mission (Houck 1984). In their view, what the public interest requires is a dismantling of inefficient regulation (especially antidiscrimination law and health, safety, and environmental regulation) and a return to free-market principles that will genuinely serve consumers and create wealth. Such firms are predictably well funded by business groups and borrow all the techniques of the liberal groups, from intervening in agency proceedings to seeking judicial review of agency action. On the academic side as well law the reform agenda is no longer the exclusive province of left-liberals: there is a large, thriving academic industry of neo-liberal legal economics, with its headquarters at the University of Chicago and several of its most prominent scholars serving as federal judges. The policy proposals of this neo-liberal school have influenced almost every corner of common law, constitutional law, the judicial interpretation of statutes (especially the antitrust laws), and administrative policy. Neo-liberalism has produced the closest symbiosis between academic theory and legal doctrine and policy since the Progressive theory-policy alliances of the New Deal.

CONCLUSION: THE SITUATION OF LAWYERS AT THE CENTURY'S END

The twentieth century was in many ways a century of law and lawyers—as it was also of their opposites: war, revolution, anarchy, ethnic conflict, and dictatorship. Law, its forms and language and procedures, has spread like the kudzu vine as the mode of governance of both private social and economic relations and public regulation; and with law has spread the demand for lawyers to administer, interpret, apply, and enforce the law and—just as or more important—work around it and avoid its effects. American modes of law and lawyering—constitutionalism, judicial review of legislation, judicially enforced basic rights, legalized forms of governance with codes and rules replacing informal authority and discretion, legal modes of challenge to government action, class-action lawsuits to police corporate conduct, lawyer-heavy modes of contracting and deal-making, protracted adversary proceedings as a mode of dispute settlement—are proliferating in the global political economy. The "rule of law," along with lawyers to design constitutions and legal institutions and to train lawyers to make it work, and to staff watchdog groups to reform and contain its abuses, has become one of the West's main export commodities to the developing and ex-Communist world.

Such a highly legalized world should be good news for the American legal profession, but it is not entirely so. Lawyers are partly being undone by their own successes. They succeeded in building a powerful profession, requiring a long course of education for entry, with not only a monopoly over traditional fields of practice such as litigation and conveyancing, but the ability to pioneer and colonize new fields, such as practice before administrative agencies, the roles of public-interest intervenor, monitor of structural court-ordered remedies and consent decrees, and "private attorney-general" in public-law litigation and mass-tort class-action practice. Such highly lawyerized practices and procedures are complex and expensive (Kagan 1991 and 1994; Hadfield 2000). Deployed on behalf of clients with money, lawyers' law is very lucrative; but this attracts competing practitioners and drives clients to look for less costly alternatives. Corporate clients pressure outside law firms to hold down costs, or they contract work out to lower-cost firms. They look to arbitration and mediation procedures for alternatives to the high cost of litigation. The plaintiffs' bar is likewise endangered by its extraordinary newfound wealth and success. Defendants press for "tort reform" that will reduce litigation against them by wiping out lawyers' incentives to bring it. Other reformers seek to deflect tort litigation into low-cost administrative processes that will not need lawyers. Deployed against people without much money, like small businesses or plaintiffs or citizens who are claiming against or resisting claims by powerful and well-lawyered adversaries, or who need lawyers to structure simple transactions, lawyers' law looks like a medium of oppression and becomes an object of populist rage. Most middle-class people simply cannot afford lawyers, except in major transactions like house-buying, or major life events like divorce or criminal trouble. In the lives of the poor and outcast, without the random luck of access to free legal advice, law is almost entirely imposition, and an object of resentment. On the supply side, lawyering is a costly occupation. To earn the entry degree to the profession at a private law school, the student without other resources has to incur $100,000 or more of debt. For students in top-tier schools with access to large law firm jobs, some of which now pay beginning associates $140,000 a year, the price of the J.D. is a bargain. For students in the lower tier, facing low-paid legal work if they can find legal work at all, it is a disaster. The hopes raised in the 1960s and 1970s that a public, nonprofit, or prepaid group-insurance sector of legal services for low-and middle-income clients, financed on a scale somewhat comparable to health care, have been dashed, as these sectors have declined in relative share of resources.

The legal profession spent much of the nineteenth century trying to build itself up as a distinctive order: an independent body of self-regulating practitioners, trained in an autonomous body of legal science, with a monopoly over its fields of practice, and practice in a distinctive institutional form, the collegially managed law firm partnership. In the twentieth century these distinctive aspects of a lawyer's professional life have been dissolving and may be on the verge of disappearing altogether. Lawyers no longer lay claim to a distinctive body of general professional knowledge, the doctrines of common and constitutional law; a lawyer's knowledge is now simply the particular bundles of skills, contacts, and regulatory stuff needed to carry on a specialized practice. Lawyers' independence at every level of practice is subordinated to monitoring and bureaucratic supervision by clients or employers. Self-regulation, demonstrably ineffectual, has been supplanted by regulation by outsiders—judges, bar monitors, regulatory agencies, malpractice liability. Collegial management has been partially supplanted by hierarchical management, bureaucratic rules, and contracts rewarding "rainmakers." Other professions have encroached on aspects of lawyers' work, sometimes taking it over altogether, as in the cases of tax preparation and (in many states) real-estate conveyancing. Lawyers are already being swallowed up in Europe and America by accounting firms; and the business lawyer of the future will be one specialist among many in professional-service firms, likely to switch specialties at some point in his or her career, and to move as computer craftsmen now do from firm to firm, work team to work team, as opportunities open up. The solo practice proprietorship—once by far the dominant form of law practice—is vanishing; it will soon probably be found chiefly in the country and in small towns, its functions ceded to high-volume franchised offices, on-line networks for delivering routine legal services, or—increasingly—to paralegals, lay practitioners, and do-it-yourself software programs. For the highly mobile and highly skilled, at least those willing to sacrifice to it all their time and private lives, what lies ahead is a new world of professional opportunities and great financial rewards; for everyone else, it more closely resembles a quicksand of risk and insecurity.[9]

Ultimately a profession must be evaluated by how well it serves its basic goals—in medicine's case, the health of a population; in law's, the provision of justice and the rule of law, the facilitation of private desires and the transactions of economic life—while observing the constraints designed to moderate or avoid their bad effects. The American legal profession, unlike that in many other societies, has always attracted idealists determined to serve and reform the law to make it fulfill its promises of justice equally and efficiently administered. At the century's beginning the reform leaders included lawyers at the summit of the bar, among whose clients were some large corporations. Such lawyers were often elitist, arrogant, and exclusionary; most of them had the ethnic, racial, and gender biases of their class; but they also believed that they had a responsibility to try to solve the large social problems of their time. By mid-century the business lawyers had, outside the area of foreign policy, mostly surrendered their positions of social leadership to become the captives and technical servants of business clienteles. They devoted themselves to working creatively around the law, in order to minimize and even to nullify its effects on clients. Some business lawyers celebrated this role in libertarian terms, as heroically resisting the inefficient and oppressive burdens of regulation on corporate wealth creation. The most optimistic lawyers at the century's end embraced a kind of global Babbitry, believing that whatever served the interests of international business must benefit the rest of the world as well. Probably most saw their role as simply doing their specialized jobs, providing competent client service in a legal system whose public side had advocates too, without thinking very much about the overall justice or efficiency of the social outcomes of their work.

The tasks of public statesmanship and reform passed to other lawyers—public-interest lawyers, government lawyers, and law reformers. This was never more than a small minority of the bar, but their contribution was significant well out of proportion to their numbers. Their legacy was ambiguous. They helped build up the administrative state as a counterweight to business, but they found it was easily captured by business interests; they then tried to open it up to democratic access, but through procedures so heavily legalized as to make it even more complex and opaque and to require yet more expensive legal advice to operate. Lawyers helped staff and gave material aid to the great social movements of the century, which began to bring into full citizenship groups that had always been subordinated or thought not fully human—immigrant industrial workers, African Americans, women, and a host of others—and in the process rewrote the Constitution as a charter of liberal equality. They also helped invent the administrative instruments to protect the natural environment from devastation. But their achievements reaped a bitter harvest in political reaction, and they were largely thwarted in their more ambitious goals of equalizing economic opportunity and democratic access. The labor movement they once supported is in retreat; income, wealth distribution, and even by some measures access to political influence are more unequal now than they were at mid-century. As a result of these disappointments, reform-minded lawyers have become more realistic about the limits and perverse effects of social engineering through law, more cautious and incremental in their goals and strategies. With the growth of identity politics, reform interests have splintered so far that it has become difficult to organize collaborative legal strategies. Conservative public-interest lawyers with conflicting reform agendas have entered the forum.

Historically, American lawyers imagined a great role for themselves as state-builders, as protectors of the Constitution and the common-law framework of rights against both populist and plutocratic excess, and as reformers whose task was to keep the law up to date with social change and fulfill the promise of equal justice. At the end of the twentieth century, the legal profession finds itself somewhat adrift, full of projects to bring the benefits of law and lawyers to foreign societies but lacking ample charters of purposes in its own land. In numbers, talent, technical skill, and overall wealth, the profession is probably more impressive than it has ever been. But its sense of what Brandeis in 1905 called "the opportunity in the law," that "[t]here is a call on the legal profession to do a great work for this country," especially in mediating the "continuing and ever-increasing contest between those who have and those who have not" (Brandeis 1914, 326–27), is—perhaps only temporarily—in recession.

NOTES

1 Contrast other advanced societies like Germany, Japan, and France, where the highest-ranking law graduates enter the civil service; and England, where until very recently the ablest lawyers became barristers (trial lawyers) and then high court judges.

2 They also have some effects in the other direction. The ethics of adversariness and loyalty to clients rather than the public values of the system make American law more open than most legal cultures to maverick lawyers with maverick claims disfavored by the dominant set of public values.

3 The matter is much more complicated than this sentence suggests. There are many causes of legal complexity other than the interests of lawyers and their best-paying clients, perhaps most notably our process of lawmaking by extraordinarily disorderly pluralist bargaining, which tends to produce compromises in the form of deliberate ambiguities in statutory language, exemptions and exceptions, procedural burdens to increase the cost of enforcement and loopholes to reduce its incidence, and endless opportunities for disappointed interest groups to take another bite at the apple, such as judicial review. Also: although the interests of high-end lawyers favor complex and expensive procedures, the interests of their clients may not, or may favor them only selectively.

4 Along with statutory and profession-approved delegalization has come delegalization unilaterally mandated by contract—as companies increasingly insert into the standard-form contract clauses relegating all disputes to arbitration, often in panels chosen by the industry. These have become common in contracts with employees, between securities dealers and their customers, and between software sellers and purchasers, and they are intended to repel class-action lawsuits and big damage awards.

5 Occasionally what we might call the "traditional" and "entrepreneurial" roles of lawyers merged, as when a lawyer was appointed to manage a company as its receiver, or more subtly when a lawyer actually created marketable value for a company by certifying to investors that its bond issues were valid.

6 This system was supposed to do away with the need for lawyers as well as courts; but lawyers soon came back in to represent injured workers, if only to argue about whether the injury was suffered on or off the job.

7 Recently, however, reflecting the growing influence of free-market neo-liberal ideology on

legal scholars, practitioners, and some judges, interest in the judicial protection of economic rights has begun to revive and to be reflected in court decisions.

8 I say "relatively" because law students depend for employment on the practicing bar, and public law schools depend for funds on the state legislature; if a law school, especially a local law school or public law school, deviates too far from convention, its students will not find jobs. But these constraints seem to be fairly loose, in that law schools can teach many subjects that most practicing lawyers might find too "theoretical" or otherwise of little practical use.

9 It may be that the highest-skilled, most-in-demand recruits to professional services will eventually come to value some combination of time for family life and civic involvements as highly as they do money and professional advancement, and will have the market power to insist that firms adapt their work environments to satisfy these desires.

REFERENCES

Abel, Richard H. 1989. *American Lawyers*. New York: Oxford University Press.

American Bar Association. 1908. *Canons of Ethics*. Baltimore: American Bar Association.

———. 1983. *Model Rules of Professional Conduct*. Chicago: American Bar Association.

American Bar Association Commission on Multi-Disciplinary Practice. 1999. *Report to the House of Delegates*. Chicago: American Bar Association.

American Bar Association Commission on Professionalism. 1986. *"In the Spirit of Public Service. . . ." A Blueprint for the Rekindling of Lawyer Professionalism*. Chicago: American Bar Association.

Auerbach, Jerold S. 1976. *Unequal Justice: Lawyers and Social Change in Modern America*. New York: Oxford University Press.

Bates v. State Bar of Arizona, 433 U.S. 350 (1977).

Bergstrom, Randoph. 1992. *Courting Danger: Injury and Law in New York City, 1870–1910*. Ithaca, N.Y.: Cornell University Press.

Berle, Adolf A. 1962. "Book Review," 76 *Harvard Law Review* 430–32.

Borel v. Fibreboard et al., 493 F.2d 1076 (5th Cir. 1973).

Brandeis, Louis D. 1914. *Business: A Profession*. Boston: Small, Maynard and Co.

Brint, Steven. 1994. *In an Age of Experts: The Changing Role of Intellectuals in Public and Private Life*. Princeton, N.J.: Princeton University Press.

Brown v. Board of Education, 347 U.S. 483 (1954).

Buchanan v. Warley, 245 U.S. 60 (1917).

Carlin, Jerome. 1962. *Lawyers on Their Own: A Study of Individual Practitioners in Chicago*. New Brunswick, N.J.: Rutgers University Press.

———. 1966. *Lawyers' Ethics: A Survey of the New York City Bar*. New York: Russell Sage Foundation.

Casper, Jonathan D. 1972. *Lawyers before the Warren Court: Civil Liberties and Civil Rights, 1957–66*. Urbana: University of Illinois Press.

Coffee, John C. Jr. 1995. "Class Wars: The Dilemma of the Mass Tort Class Action," 95 *Columbia Law Review* 1343.

Curran, Barbara A., and Clara N. Carson. 1991. *Supplement to the Lawyer Statistical Report: The U.S. Legal Profession in 1998*. Chicago: American Bar Association.

Cushman, Barry. 1998. *Rethinking the New Deal Court*. New York: Oxford University Press.
Davis, Martha. 1993. *Brutal Need: Lawyers and the Welfare Rights Movement, 1960–1973*. New Haven, Conn.: Yale University Press.
Derber, Charles. 1982. *Professionals as Workers: Mental Labor in Advance Capitalism*. Boston: G.K. Hall.
Dezalay, Yves, and Bryant Garth. 1996. *Dealing in Virtue: International Commercial Arbitration and the Construction of a Transnational Legal Order*. Chicago: University of Chicago Press.
Drachman, Virginia G. 1998. *Sisters in Law: Women Lawyers in Modern American History*. Cambridge: Harvard University Press.
Epstein, Cynthia Fuchs. 1993. *Women in Law*. 2d ed. Urbana: University of Illinois Press.
Feeley, Malcolm M., and Edward J. Rubin. 1998. *Judicial Policymaking and the Modern State: How the Courts Reformed America's Prisons*. Cambridge: Cambridge University Press.
Forbath, William. 1991. *Law and the Shaping of the American Labor Movement*. Cambridge: Harvard University Press.
Forbes. 1995. 6 November 1995, 160.
Friedman, Lawrence. 1985a. *Total Justice*. New York: Russell Sage Foundation.
———. 1985b. *A History of American Law*. New York: Simon & Schuster.
———. 1987. "Civil Wrongs: Personal Injury Law in the Late 19th Century," 1987 *American Bar Foundation Research Journal* 351.
Friedman, Lawrence, and Jack Ladinsky. 1967. "Social Change and the Law of Industrial Accidents," 67 *Columbia Law Review* 30.
Friedman, Lawrence, and Robert V. Percival. 1981. *The Roots of Justice: Crime and Punishment in Alameda County, 1870–1910*. Chapel Hill: University of North Carolina Press.
Galanter, Marc. 1974. "Why the 'Haves' Come Out Ahead: Speculations on the Limits of Legal Change," 9 *Law and Society Review* 96–160.
———. 1996. "Real World Torts: An Antidote to Anecdote," 55 *Maryland Law Review* 1093.
Galanter, Marc, and Thomas Palay. 1991. *Tournament of Lawyers: The Transformation of the Big Law Firm*. Chicago: University of Chicago Press.
Gideon v. Wainwright, 373 U.S. 335 (1963).
Gillman, Howard. 1993. *The Constitution Besieged*. Durham, N.C.: Duke University Press.
Goldfarb v. Virginia State Bar, 421 U.S. 773 (1975).
Grossberg, Michael. 1997. "The Politics of Professionalism: The Creation of Legal Aid and the Strains of Political Liberalism in America, 1900–1930." In *Lawyers and the Rise of Western Political Liberalism*, ed. Terence C. Halliday and Lucien Karpik, 305–47. New York: Oxford University Press.
Hadfield, Gillian. 2000. "The Price of Law: How the Market for Lawyers Distorts the Justice System," 98 *Michigan Law Review* 953–1006.
Halliday, Terence. 1987. *Beyond Monopoly: Lawyers, State Crises and Professional Empowerment*. Chicago: University of Chicago Press.

Handler, Joel, Ellen Jane Hollingsworth, and Howard S. Erlanger. 1978. *Lawyers and the Pursuit of Legal Rights*. New York: Academic Press.

Heinz, John P., and Edward O. Laumann. 1982. *Chicago Lawyers: The Social Structure of the Bar*. New York: Russell Sage Foundation and American Bar Foundation.

Heinz, John P., Edward O. Laumann, Robert L. Nelson, and Ethan Michaelson. 1998. "The Changing Character of Lawyers' Work: Chicago in 1975 and 1995," 32 *Law & Society Review* 751–75.

Heinz, John P., Edward O. Laumann, Robert L. Nelson, and Robert H. Salisbury. 1993. *The Hollow Core: Private Interests in National Policymaking*. Cambridge: Harvard University Press.

Hensler, Deborah R. 1991. *Compensation for Accidental Injuries in the United States*. Santa Monica, Calif.: Rand Institute for Civil Justice.

Hensler, Deborah R., and Mark A. Peterson. 1993. "Understanding Mass Personal Injury Litigation: A Socio-Legal Analysis," 59 *Brooklyn Law Review* 960.

Horsky, Charles A. 1952. *The Washington Lawyer*. Boston: Little, Brown.

Houck, Oliver A. 1984. "With Charity for All," 93 *Yale Law Journal* 1415.

Huber, Peter W. 1991. *Galileo's Revenge: Junk Science in the Courtroom*. New York: Basic Books.

Hurst, James Willard. 1950. *The Growth of American Law: The Lawmakers*. Boston: Little, Brown.

Hyman, Harold H. 1998. *Craftsmanship and Character: A History of the Vinson & Elkins Law Firm of Houston, 1917–1977*. Athens: University of Georgia Press.

Irons, Peter H. 1982. *The New Deal Lawyers*. Princeton, N.J.: Princeton University Press.

Jenkins v. Raymark Industries, 782 F.2d 468 (5th Cir. 1986).

Johnson, Earl Jr. 1974. *Justice and Reform: The Formative Years of the OEO Legal Services Program*. New York: Russell Sage Foundation.

Kagan, Robert A. 1991. "Adversarial Legalism and American Government," 10 *Journal of Policy Analysis and Management* 369.

———. 1994. "Do Lawyers Cause Adversarial Legalism? A Preliminary Inquiry," 19 *Law & Social Inquiry* 1.

Kalman, Laura. 1990. *Abe Fortas: A Biography*. New Haven, Conn.: Yale University Press.

Katz, Jack. 1982. *Poor People's Lawyers in Transition*. New Brunswick, N.J.: Rutgers University Press.

Krause, Elliott A. 1996. *Death of the Guilds: Professions, States and the Advance of Capitalism*. New Haven, Conn.: Yale University Press.

Larson, Magali Sarfatti. 1977. *The Rise of Professionalism: A Sociological Analysis*. Berkeley: University of California Press.

Linowitz, Sol. 1994. *The Betrayed Profession: Lawyering at the End of the Twentieth Century*. New York: C. Scribner's Sons.

Maguire, John M. 1928. *The Lance of Justice: A Semi-Centennial History of the Legal Aid Society*. Cambridge: Harvard University Press.

McCann, Michael W. 1986. *Taking Reform Seriously: Perspectives on Public Interest Liberalism*. Ithaca, N.Y.: Cornell University Press.

Miller, Mark C. 1995. *The High Priests of American Politics: The Role of Lawyers in American Political Institutions*. Knoxville: University of Tennessee Press.

Moley, Raymond. 1930. *Our Criminal Courts*. New York: Minton, Balch.

Munger, Frank. 1994. "Miners and Lawyers: Law Practice and Class Conflict in Appalachia, 1872–1920." In *Lawyers in a Postmodern World*, ed. Maureen Cain and Christine Harrington, 185–228. New York: New York University Press.

Nonet, Philippe. 1969. *Administrative Justice: Advocacy and Change in a Government Agency*. New York: Russell Sage.

Osiel, Mark. 1989. "Lawyers as Aristocrats, Monopolists, and Entrepreneurs," 103 *Harvard Law Review* 2009–66.

Posner, Richard A. 1998. "Professionalisms," 40 *Arizona Law Review* 1–15.

Powell, Michael J. 1986. "Professional Divestiture: The Cession of Responsibility for Lawyer Discipline," 1986 *American Bar Foundation Research Journal* 31.

———. 1988. *From Patrician to Professional Elite: The Transformation of the New York City Bar Association*. New York: Russell Sage.

Purcell, Edward A. Jr. 1992. *Litigation and Inequality: Federal Diversity Litigation in Industrial America, 1870–1958*. New York: Oxford University Press.

Ramos, Manuel R. 1994. "Malpractice: The Profession's Dirty Little Secret," 47 *Vanderbilt Law Review* 1657.

Rheingold, Paul R. 1968. "The MER/29 Story—An Instance of Successful Mass Disaster Litigation," 56 *California Law Review* 116.

Rhode, Deborah A. 1981. "Policing the Professional Monopoly: A Constitutional and Empirical Analysis of Unauthorized Practice Prohibitions," 34 *Stanford Law Review* 1.

———. 1994. "Institutionalizing Ethics," 44 *Case Western Reserve Law Review* 665.

Rosenthal, Douglas. 1974. *Lawyer and Client—Who's in Charge?* New York: Russell Sage.

Ross, H. Laurence. 1970. *Settled Out of Court: The Social Process of Insurance Claims Adjustments*. Chicago: Aldine.

Russell, Thomas. [n.d.] "Blood on the Tracks: Turn of the Century Streetcar Injuries, Claims, and Litigation in Alameda County, California." Unpublished manuscript on file with the author.

Sander, R.H., and D. Williams. 1989. "Why Are There So Many Lawyers? Perspectives on a Turbulent Market," 14 *Law & Social Inquiry* 431–79.

Schuck, Peter H. 1995. "Mass Torts: An Institutional Evolutionist Perspective," 80 *Cornell Law Review* 941.

Seron, Carroll. 1996. *The Business of Practicing Law: The Work Lives of Solo and Small-Firm Attorneys*. Philadelphia: Temple University Press.

Shamir, Ronen. 1995. *Managing Legal Uncertainty: Elite Lawyers in the New Deal*. Durham, N.C.: Duke University Press.

Silver, James W. 1964. *Mississippi: The Closed Society*. New York: Harcourt Brace.

Simon, Jonathan. 1997. "Driving Governmentality: Automobile Accidents, Insurance, and the Challenge to Social Order in the Inter-War Years, 1919–1941," 4 *Connecticut Insurance Law Journal* 251.

Skowronek, Stephen. 1982. *Building a New American State: The Expansion of National Administrative Capacities, 1877–1920*. Cambridge: Cambridge University Press.

Smigel, Edwin. 1969. *The Wall Street Lawyer: Professional Organization Man?* Bloomington: Indiana University Press.

Smith, J. Clay Jr. 1993. *Emancipation: The Making of the Black Lawyer, 1844–1944.* Philadelphia: University of Pennsylvania Press.

Speiser, Stuart M. 1980. *Lawsuit.* New York: Horizon Press.

Stevens, Robert B. 1983. *Law School.* New York: Oxford University Press.

Strum, Philippa. 1984. *Louis D. Brandeis: Justice for the People.* Cambridge: Harvard University Press.

Stumpf, Harry. 1975. *Community Politics and Legal Services: The Other Side of the Law.* Beverly Hills, Calif.: Sage Publications.

Thomas, William G. 1999. *Lawyering for the Railroad: Business, Law and Power in the New South.* Baton Rouge: Louisiana State University Press.

Tushnet, Mark V. 1987. *The NAACP's Legal Strategy against Segregated Education, 1925—1950.* Chapel Hill: University of North Carolina Press.

Van Hoy, Jerry. 1997. *Franchise Law Firms and the Transformation of Personal Legal Services.* Westport, Conn.: Quorum Books.

Vogel, David A. 1996. "The Public Interest Movement and the American Reform Tradition." In Vogel, *Kindred Strangers,* 141–65. Princeton, N.J.: Princeton University Press.

Walker, Samuel. 1990. *In Defense of American Liberties: A History of the ACLU.* New York: Oxford University Press.

Weiler, Paul C. 1991. *Medical Malpractice on Trial.* Cambridge: Harvard University Press.

Weinstein, Jack B. 1995. *Individual Justice in Mass Tort Litigations: The Effect of Class Actions, Consolidations, and Other Multiparty Devices.* Evanston, Ill.: Northwestern University Press.

Wilkins, David B. 1992. "Who Should Regulate Lawyers?" 105 *Harvard Law Review* 799.

Wilkins, David B., and Mitu Gulati. 1996. "Why Are There So Few Black Lawyers in Corporate Law Firms? An Institutional Analysis," 84 *California Law Review* 493.

Wolfskill, George. 1962. *The Revolt of the Conservatives: A History of the American Liberty League, 1934–1940.* Boston: Houghton Mifflin.

Professing Law

ELITE LAW SCHOOL PROFESSORS IN THE TWENTIETH CENTURY

Laura Kalman

DEJA VU ALL OVER AGAIN

HISTORIANS LOVE TO show the new is old. It is one of our favorite parlor games. We take what someone (often a sociologist, political scientist, or lawyer) has identified as a recent problem and demonstrate it predates time.

I thought of this when I read Judge Harry Edwards's essay, "The Growing Disjunction between Legal Education and the Legal Profession" (1992).[1] At a time when an ABA Task Force had been charged with studying ways of "narrowing the gap" between law schools and the profession (Report 1992),[2] Judge Edwards argued its mission was impossible. According to him, "law schools and law firms are moving in opposite directions." The former should "be training ethical practitioners and producing scholarship that judges, legislators, and practitioners can use," while the latter "should be ensuring that associates practice law in an ethical manner." He maintains, however, "many law schools—especially the so-called 'elite' ones—have abandoned their proper place, by emphasizing abstract theory at the expense of practical scholarship and pedagogy." They are filled with "'law professors' hired from graduate schools, wholly lacking in legal experience or training, who use the law school as a bully pulpit from which to pour scorn upon the legal profession." Equally unfortunately, numerous law firms "have also abandoned their place, by pursuing profit above all else." In sum, schools move "toward pure theory," firms toward "pure commerce." Each

I thank all who commented on this paper when I presented it at the Amherst Conference on Law 2000, Arizona State University College of Law, and UCLA Law School. I am especially grateful to Richard Abel, Marianne Constable, Daniel Ernst, William L.F. Felstiner, W. Randall Garr, Sarah Barringer Gordon, Pnina Lahav, William LaPiana, Jonathan Rose, Austin Sarat, John Henry Schlegel, Christopher Tomlins, and Evan Young.

has forsaken "the middle ground" of "ethical practice" both should occupy (Edwards 1992, 34).

Here we have the classic fin-de-siècle dirge. As Richard Hofstadter reported in the 1950s about the bar at the end of the nineteenth century: "Lawyers kept saying that the law had lost much of its distinctly professional character and had become a business. Exactly how much truth lay in their laments cannot be ascertained until we know more about the history of the profession; but whether or not their conclusions were founded upon a false sentimentalization of an earlier era, many lawyers were convinced that their profession had declined in its intellectual standards and in its moral and social position" (Hofstadter 1955, 158; and see generally Gordon 1983; Simon 1985). We still do not possess sufficient evidence to evaluate nineteenth-century attorneys' assumptions. What we *do* know is that lawyers have been repeating such wails of woe ever since.[3]

Ditto, lawyers on law professors—and not just in the United States. In England, where law professors have never possessed the influence on law and the profession they have historically exercised in most civil law countries (e.g., Van Caenegem 1987, 53–54, 64–65, 87; Tong 1999, 377), William Twining tells us that in recent years some of the most prestigious London law firms have preferred to hire university graduates who have not concentrated on law study: "The legal profession had discovered belatedly that law graduates could not bowl" (Twining 1994, 164). Thus Robert Gordon need devote only one footnote to this aspect of Judge Edwards's complaint, which he dismisses: "The practitioners' complaint about legal scholars as unworldly, hypertheoretical airheads is an ancient genre" (1993, 2105 n. 75; and see Gee and Jackson 1977, 719–62, 927–64). Recall what happened when Christopher Columbus Langdell and Charles Eliot inaugurated the era of the professional law teacher by introducing the case method and hiring James Barr Ames directly out of law school. Many horrified attorneys switched their allegiance from Harvard to Boston University, which had been founded "in protest against what were thought new-fangled methods," and where practitioner-lecturers predominated as teachers (LaPiana 1994, 16; Williston 1940, 72).[4]

Even Harvard housed many skeptics. For example, John Chipman Gray, that part-time practitioner hired to offset Ames (Stevens 1983, 47 n. 32), warned Eliot in 1883: "The idols of the cave which a school bred lawyer is sure to substitute for the facts may be much better material for intellectual gymnastics than the facts themselves and may call forth more enthusiasm in the pupils, but a school where the majority of the professors shuns and despises the contact with actual facts, has got the seeds of ruin in it and will and ought to go to the devil" (LaPiana 1994, 19).

Ever since then, American judges, lawyers, nonlawyers, law students, and even some academic lawyers have mocked those law professors who would place "idols in the cave." Compare "town-gown" relations between medical school professors and private practitioners: despite practitioners' fears that academic doctors would steal their patients, the two groups maintained cordial and cooperative relations from the turn of the century through the 1960s (Ludmerer 1999, 117–18, 172; but cf. Starr 1982, 353–54). Law professors' relationship with practitioners has been rockier. Sometimes the critics of academic lawyers have made more noise than others. But the drumbeat of complaint has never ceased.

Meanwhile their colleagues elsewhere in the university have made their own parlor game out of ridiculing law professors. The law school "no more" belonged in the modern university, Thorstein Veblen famously declared, "than a school of fencing or dancing" (1918, 211). Social scientists and humanists have long found common ground in sniping that law professors receive twice the pay for half the teaching.[5] (For some reason, law professors' high salaries seem to irritate humanists and social scientists more than the princely amounts paid to professors of medicine, engineering, and business). And what about the real dirty little secret of academic lawyers? As late as 1981, Yale Law School's Bruce Ackerman thought other professors might not know it. "We put ourselves forward as professors of law at Yale University (to pick a name at random)," Ackerman said. "Yet even knowledgeable outsiders do not always recognize that lawyers become professors on the basis of a publication standard that embarrasses their colleagues in the rest of the university" (1981, 1135).

Parlor games are fun, and they serve a purpose. But continuity is never the whole story. That Americans have long wanted to "kill all the lawyers" (Bloomfield 1976, 137–38) should not prevent us from focusing on why the prestige of the legal profession has dipped so dramatically in the quarter century since Watergate (Black and Rothman 1998, 835). That lawyers have long proclaimed law has become a business should not divert us from the possibility that the "crisis" in elite law firms Judge Edwards bemoans may be "the real thing—not in the sense of marking a decisive break from professional ideals," but because structural changes in the last twenty years "are transforming big firms and their world in fundamental ways" (Galanter and Palay 1991, 3). And so, too, that elite law professors have long been dismissed as overpaid "airheads" should not deter us from flagging points in which they experienced unusual stress.

In this chapter, I examine periods of strain in the twentieth century between elite law professors and other university academics in the humanities and social sciences,[6] as well as between elite academic lawyers and the profession. I tend to treat the large-firm practitioners who so frequently represent the "profession" and the bar as synonymous; I do not know how much of what I say is applicable to lawyers who work in small firms, government, or corporations. I also do not know (though I doubt) whether much (if anything) that I say reflects the situation at law schools that are not "top-tier." I concentrate on law professors at the leading institutions for three reasons. First, Judge Edwards does. Second, they are the teachers about whose lives we possess the most published information. Third, since the law-school world is uniquely hierarchical, what happens in the first tier *may* possess unusual significance for legal education as a whole.[7]

Prior to the most recent season of discontent (1980–1993), I count two "genuine" (1906–1922 and the 1930s) and one "faux" (1968–1973) times of special tension for law professor's vis-à-vis other university professors and/or the bar. During the first four intervals, politics contributed to the alienation between academic lawyers and the bar. When the professors stepped left, the practitioners stepped away. Further, during the 1930s, the late 1960s and early 1970s, and the Reagan-Bush years, a sense law professors did not understand their disciplines, or wanted to exploit them, caused friction between law professors and other academics. After examining these periods, I turn to the present situation.

TIMES OF TENSION, 1900–1980

1906–1922

The first interval occurred between 1906 and 1922, when academic education was replacing apprenticeship as the principal mode of entry to the profession, and featured acrimony between law professors and the bar. The period opened with the fight at the American Bar Association (ABA) meeting between lawyers and academics over whether to reprint Roscoe Pound's 1906 address attacking America's judicial system (Pound 1906, 398). Opponents characterized Professor Pound's lecture, "The Causes of Popular Dissatisfaction with the Administration of Justice," as a "drastic attack" (Hull 1997, 64). For invigorated law professors such as John Henry Wigmore, however, Pound's speech was "the spark that kindled the white flame of progress" (Hull 1997, 64).

The next highlight, of course, was Pound's call for a sociological jurisprudence. Here Pound, allying himself with other law professors (Johnson 1978, 101) and with progressive lawyers, such as Brandeis, who sought to make law a public profession and attune the bar to the public interest, set out the agenda for the century's law professors (see generally Fetner 1977). Academic lawyers must teach students law was a tool of progressive social change (in the words of Felix Frankfurter, "show them the law as an instrument and not an end of organized humanity"—Frankfurter 1999 [1915], 677); and they must incorporate into law the insights of the social sciences.

Embracing what a later generation of law and society scholars would consider sociolegal research, Pound urged a shift from an analysis of "law in the books," or legal doctrine per se, to an investigation of "law in action," or the social and empirical effects of rules and doctrines (Pound 1910). He encouraged all those affiliated with the legal profession to recognize that "legal principles are not absolute, but are relative to time and place" and to treat them "as instruments rather than eternal pigeonholes into which all human relations must be made to fit" (Pound 1913, 365). Only then would law become a "science of social engineering." Further, Pound urged the legal profession to reach out to the social sciences in the interest of public service (Stevens 1971, 538). Indeed, he was certain that the "want of teamwork" between law and the social sciences explained "the backwardness of law in meeting social ends" (Pound 1912, 510). Judges and lawyers must cease being "legal monks" and seek guidance from other disciplines in making law an instrument of social policy. Law professors must lead the way: according to Pound, in fact, "[t]he remedy is in our law schools," and "the modern teacher of law should be a student of sociology, economics, and politics" (Hull 1997, 67).

Strong words, these, establishing a divide between the bar and the professors over both politics, or reform, and interdisciplinarity, or the relationship between law and other disciplines. The Association of American Law Schools (AALS) and the American Bar Association had met jointly since 1900. When, in 1914, the ABA shifted the date to October and into the academic year, law professors cried foul (Auerbach 1971, 567; Seavey 1950, 153). They began holding their own meetings separately, widening "an already existing gulf between law teachers and the members of the practicing bar" (Harno 1980, 100). Is it coincidental that in his 1914 AALS address, Wesley N. Hohfeld called for the transformation of some law schools into juristic centers, staffed by "a class of university jurists—legal pathologists and surgeons, we might call them—who shall have a far greater share and influence than at present in prescribing for our [social] ills" (Hohfeld 1914, 88)? Clearly, law professors thought law reform was too important to be left to the lawyers and judges.

The following year, one leading Wall Street lawyer told Columbia Law School Dean Harlan Fiske Stone he had been talking "with lawyers resentful of professors at the school who criticized courts and disparaged judges" (Auerbach 1971, 570). In 1916, Elihu Root used an ABA dinner celebrating his career to decry the presence of "half-baked and conceited theorists" in law schools, who "think they know better what law ought to be . . . than the people of England and America working out their laws through centuries of life" (Auerbach 1971, 572).

Jerold Auerbach maintains that despite "the dialogue of disagreement" between reform-minded professors and the profession, "both sides knew that impractical theorists were training quite practical lawyers" (1971, 568, 571).[8] That may be true. Certainly, the "practical lawyers" received assistance from the new student-edited law reviews, which featured doctrinal work exploring and clarifying (always with an eye to improving) the internal logic of legal rules, principles, and institutions (Swygert and Bruce 1985). Still, I wonder. In his famous 1921 Carnegie Foundation report on legal education, "Training for the *Public* Profession of Law," Alfred Reed maintained that the elite "progressive schools . . . [had] come to be more and more out of touch with the . . . relatively conservative practitioners" (Packer and Ehrlich 1972, 217).

Most Ph.D.s, however, did not share the bar's disdain. They would have been more likely to agree with Josef Redlich. In his 1914 report on legal education for the Carnegie Commission, Redlich hailed the "undoubtedly increasing influence" of university law professors "as constituting one of the most encouraging features of American public life" (quoted in Woodward 1968, 717). And why should social scientists feel otherwise? As Dorothy Ross and John Schlegel have stressed, they too were busy transforming their disciplines during this period (Ross 1991; Schlegel 1985, 313–14, 319–20). Professionalization and a new emphasis on scientific method and objectivity were distancing, while not divorcing, the social sciences from national ideology (Ross 1991, 468).

Insofar as they thought about the professionalization and progressivism of academic lawyers, or Pound's description of sociological jurisprudence as a movement for "pragmatism in law" (Pound 1908, 609–10), social scientists proved enthusiastic. The sociologist Edward Ross claimed credit for starting Pound down the road toward sociological jurisprudence (Hull 1997, 55). At a moment when historians such as Charles Beard and political scientists such as Frank Goodnow and Ernst Freund had moved beyond the cautious constitutional realism of the Gilded Age (Belz 1969, 127; Belz 1971; Comment 1962) and Robert LaFollete was hailing the use of experts in government (Carrington and King 1997, 325), sociological jurisprudence seemed a welcome internal acknowledgment of the relationship between law and politics. Economists called for the cross-fertilization of law and economics at the same time Pound urged the cross-fertilization of social science with law (Duxbury 1995, 310–20). Progressive institutionalists such as John R. Commons drew upon sociological jurisprudence (Furner 1993, 236; see also Hovenkamp 1990). When John Dewey followed Pound to the dais at Columbia in 1922 to urge a progressive, pragmatic, antiformalist, and empirical approach to law, he was undoubtedly simply acting as a cheerleader for developments he thought were already beginning to take root in the law school (Schlegel 1995, 24).

The Realist Period

But they were not. It turned out that sociological jurisprudence made no attempt to change the law schools and to bring what was taught there any closer to the social sciences. To paraphrase Karl Llewellyn, inside the law school classroom, sociological jurisprudence remained "bare" of most of that which was significant in the social sciences (Llewellyn 1930, 435 n. 3). This failure of sociological jurisprudence became clear during the second part of the realist period, the second moment of tension.[9]

The 1920s and the first part of the realist era proved a good time for law professors. Social scientists became still more welcoming in the 1920s. To cite but one example, Daniel Ernst has shown that realists such as Herman Oliphant, Walter Wheeler Cook, Walter Nelles, and Thurman Arnold, and economists such as Commons, his students, and neo-Veblenians, "turned to each other as fellow critics and debunkers of the status quo" in labor law and "found much that was congenial in each other's work" (Ernst 1993, 76).

University presidents, such as Nicholas Murray Butler at Columbia, James Rowland Angell at Yale, and Frank Goodnow at Johns Hopkins, also jumped on the realist bandwagon. With Butler's backing, Columbia Law School imported a University of Chicago economist, Leon Marshall, to supervise its renowned study to reorganize the curriculum along "functional" lines instead of legal categories. The law school was "most generously assisted" by scholars in other Columbia departments as it labored for two years to determine what was wrong with the law schools (Goebel 1955, 300; Currie 1955; Twining 1973, 43–51; Kalman 1986, 68–75; Oliphant 1928a). Written by Herman Oliphant, the final report charged traditional legal education with obscuring the social policy behind legal rules; creating a barrier between law and the social sciences; classifying human relations in legal categories "too broad to give intimacy of view and too old adequately to disclose contemporary problems"; and sharpening the dichotomy between substantive law and procedure (Kalman 1986, 70, quoting Oliphant).

Butler was the first university administrator to lose interest: when he passed over Oliphant to choose Young Smith as dean of the law school in 1928, he signaled a "thumbs down" reaction to the realists' proposal to relinquish training practitioners and become a "community of scholars" dedicated "to the non-professional study of law." Oliphant, Marshall, Hessel Yntema, Underhill Moore, and William O. Douglas left Columbia in a huff. Yale and Johns Hopkins eagerly stepped into the breach (Goebel 1955, 301–4).[10] Their university administrations actually did battle to see who could hire more of Columbia's "mutineers" (Kalman 1986, 112, quoting a member of Yale's Prudential Committee). (Imagine a similar scenario had Harvard's tenured critical legal scholars resigned in protest during the 1980s!)

Already at Johns Hopkins, but still listed on the Yale Law School faculty, Cook talked Oliphant and Hessel Yntema, in whom Yale was interested, into accepting the offer of Goodnow, one of Cook's political science teachers, and joining Cook and Marshall in founding the Johns Hopkins Institute of Law (Schlegel 1995, 150–58). The Institute would devote itself exclusively "to scientific research,—to the digging up of new stuff," Oliphant explained to Justice Harlan Fiske Stone, who had deserted him to endorse Smith in the deanship battle. "If, incidentally, it trains an occasional law teacher or research worker not needed to staff itself, that will be wholly incidental, nothing but a byproduct in its main job to increase the fund of human knowledge in law and all the related social sciences" (Oliphant 1928b).

Underhill Moore and William O. Douglas moved from Columbia to Yale, where Dean Robert Maynard Hutchins had already hired three faculty members without law degrees—the psychologist Donald Slesinger; the political scientist Walter Dodd; and the economist Walton Hamilton. Here as elsewhere, Angell, a functional psychologist, warmly supported Hutchins, even teaming up with him and the dean of the medical school to secure funding for Yale's Institute of Human Relations to undertake empirical research harnessing the social and behavioral sciences to law and medicine. Small wonder that Hutchins spoke of the possibility "that the Law School may slowly become a branch of the department of social science in the graduate school" (Kalman 1986, 109–10).

All this sounded hopeful, but what was probably more important for the history of law teachers in the long run was the hiring of the proto-contemporary "law and" academic lawyer: the realist Robert Lee Hale. He studied economics as an undergraduate at Harvard, graduated from Harvard Law School, practiced law for three years, and then entered Columbia's doctoral program in economics, determined to unite law and economics. That he did, in both teaching and research: Hale would later become the darling of critical legal scholars for his exposition of the emptiness of the ideas of property rights and liberty and his attack on the public/private distinction (Fetner 1977, 520–24; Fried 1998).

Hale's career demonstrated the value of advanced training in disciplines other than the law. In the judgment of Barbara Fried, "Hale was a better economist than either Richard Ely or John Commons, and, unlike either of them, had the benefit of both formal legal training and a strong analytical bent of mind" (Fried 1998, 8). Yet, as Hale recognized, no one educated in "law/or" (as a lawyer or economist) would likely possess his teaching and research trajectory (Fetner 1977, 527). Nor was it clear those were enviable: Richard Posner has reminded us that Hale's work "was ignored for decades" (Posner 1997, 1157). The *American Bar Association Journal*, for example, cancelled his column about legal and economic theory as it came to question whether "creative economic criticism fitted in with the general plan of the *Journal* or with the intellectual interests of a large majority of its readers" (Fetner 1977, 527–28).

Nevertheless, tension between elite academic lawyers and attorneys was slight during the 1920s, cooperation plentiful. Hale responded tolerantly to an attorney who accused him of "Bolshevistic ideas" (Fetner 1977, 527–28). In West Virginia and Connecticut, law professors, attorneys, and judges combined forces to work on the judicial council movement "for more scientific judicial administration" (Arnold 1929a, 208–9; Arnold 1929b). Academic lawyers also joined with lions of the bar and eminent judges to form the American Law Institute (ALI). All groups would work together to restate the common law in order to clarify and simplify it, while promoting "those changes which will tend better to adapt the laws to the needs of life" (Hull 1990, 81–82). At decade's end, the elite lawyers in the ABA joined with law professors at prestigious schools to beat back a proposal by the dean of Suffolk Law School that half the members of each law school faculty be practitioners (Stevens 1983, 176).

Meanwhile, the relationship between reformist law professors and like-minded judges became "almost symbiotic" (Fetner 1977, 514). Judge Learned Hand assured those in the Association of American Law Schools that "at the present you as scholars are somewhat the mode," and through tactful encouragement and reasoned judiciousness, might make judges "your easy captives" (Fetner 1977, 511). Benjamin Cardozo, who missed no opportunity to trumpet his reliance on academic lawyers (Polenberg 1997, 83–90), declared himself delighted that "[j]udges have at last awakened . . . to the treasures buried in law reviews" (Swygert and Bruce 1985, 789). Privately, Chief Justice Taft, no reformer, might rail constantly against legal scholarship, disdaining articles critical of the Court as "the way the academicians . . . get even with us"; dismissing "another Commission of University Professors . . . engaged in reversing the Supreme Court"; derogating Justices Brandeis, Stone, and Holmes's "claques in the law school contingent"; and disparaging opinions with law review citations. Nevertheless, it was during this period, Robert Post has shown, that former Dean Stone, sensing "that the Court's institutional prestige to declare law required the supplementation of expertise, even as the Court was in the very act of deciding a question of law . . . broke the barrier against citing law reviews in Supreme Court opinions" (Post 2001, 1364, 1365, 1378, 1376). By mid-decade, "the impact of law reviews on judicial decision making was well-recognized" (Swygert and Bruce 1985, 788; and see Kaye 1989), and commentators were certain a Supreme Court justice was "hurt" whenever "the *Harvard Law Review* declared his latest decision *wrong*" (Swygert and Bruce 1985, 789).

In contrast, the portion of the 1930s during which legal realism and the Depression overlapped proved a period in which, for one reason or another, nobody except Franklin Roosevelt and his New Dealers had much use for academic lawyers. The accord between the law professors, practitioners, and judges disappeared. During the second part of the realist era, as the ALI trimmed its ambitions for the Restatement, modernist professors turned on the project (White 1997, 33–47). They also turned against the lawyers. For Yale Law School Dean Charles E. Clark, the Depression proved "the corporation lawyer of the past decade must give way to the public counsel of the next" (Kalman 1986, 117). "If our simian ancestors had been lawyers,"

Clark's counterpart at Minnesota complained, "we should still be walking on all fours" (Stein 1980, 102). Progressive professors such as William O. Douglas, Abe Fortas, and Frankfurter sometimes seemed to blame the entire Depression on the country's conservative judges and corporate bar, who attacked them and New Deal legislation (see, e.g., Kalman 1990, 54–61).

If it was "hard to exaggerate the sense of professional jubilation" with which leading corporate attorneys such as John W. Davis greeted the Supreme Court's decision invalidating the New Deal's National Recovery Administration (Shamir 1995, 65), it was equally difficult to overstate such lawyers' contempt for law professors. Davis scorned the "wild men" in the law schools, "whose social, economic and legal principles I distrust" (Auerbach 1976, 166). Even Jerome Frank, former corporate lawyer turned realist and New Dealer, who liked the professors' principles, thought they did an awful job of training students for practice; called for a clinical legal education, which would place the law office at the core of the curriculum; and urged academic lawyers to practice law for five years before they began teaching (see, e.g., Frank 1933a; 1933b; 1947; 1951). (He was not dissuaded by reminders that legal education had historically occurred on the cheap in large classes; that clinical "lawyer-schools" would prove too expensive; or that some of Frank's favorite realists lacked any experience in law practice—Kalman 1986, 172–75.)

Then there was the old guard among the law professors. When one alumnus complained the realists had taken over Harvard in the mid-1930s, Dean Roscoe Pound irately protested that "to attribute the views of the so-called realists to the Harvard Law School, which generally is looked at as standing out against that movement is a grave mistake" (Kalman 1986, 57). At the same time, Arthur Corbin was griping to the young Turks at Yale that, thanks to them, it would be "very easy to turn this school into a second rate school of 'political science,' something that would be violently disapproved by the men who made this school, by substantially all of its graduates, and (as I believe) by most of the professors" (Kalman 1986, 139).

Such complaints about "realistic" legal education from professors who preferred doctrinalism in the classroom, and in the profession, were peculiar. "Harvard-baiting" lay at the root of developments at Yale and Columbia Law Schools, where realism was seized upon in part to promote product differentiation and to challenge Langdell's hegemony (Duxbury 1995, 139, 140). Yet while the legal education in New Haven and on the upper West Side differed somewhat from that parceled out in Cambridge since 1870, the similarities proved more striking (Kalman 1986, 45–97).

On the one hand, the realists changed the titles of their casebooks "from 'Cases on X' to 'Cases and Materials on Y'" (Stevens 1983, 158). On the other, there was widespread agreement that with but a few exceptions, realist casebooks made ineffective use of the social sciences and did not significantly depart from their precursors. Thus when it came to discuss the weight some realist professors placed on the desirability of incorporating "nonlegal" materials in its 1932 report on recent developments in law teaching, the Harvard Law School faculty reveled in playing "gotcha": "Consequently, one would expect recent casebooks prepared by these teachers to contain a considerable amount of such materials. However, while some materials are presented in some recent volumes; they are not very extensive; and there seems to be little difference between the recently published casebooks of the 'functionalists' and those of the 'traditionalists' in this regard" (Kalman 1986, 92).

However little pedagogy was changing in the 1930s, as realism moved outside the law school and into the realm of national government, academic lawyers' influence was indisputably increasing exponentially (Shamir 1995, 133–37). When they spoke, policy makers were listening. It was the rare established corporate lawyer, such as Frank or Tom Corcoran, who found important places in the New Deal, though some of their younger colleagues, such as Alger Hiss, did. The pattern was for the law professors, such as William O. Douglas, to go to Washington themselves, or to send their protégés, as Douglas did "the little Hot Dogs," and Frankfurter did the "Happy Hot Dogs" (White 1986a; Kalman 1990, 27).

Predictably, the elite bar's hostility to the law professors and realism grew with its antipathy to the New Deal. Describing the tension between the professors and practitioners as "acute," Auerbach, who credited the Yale and Columbia realists with launching an "unnerving critique of professional values," explained that when the Roosevelt Administration began "to recruit from law faculties and among recent graduates, rather than from the established bar, elite lawyers knew that their public influence and control had waned. Legal Realism rubbed salt in their wounds" (Auerbach 1976, 165, 166).[11] Leave aside the vexed question of whether legal realism was the jurisprudential analogue of the New Deal.[12] What is important is that conservative lawyers, and surely judges too, *perceived* a connection between realism and the New Deal as they reviewed the activities of the "law-teachers-turned-experts in the direct and indirect service of the state," which only increased their antipathy to realism (Shamir 1995, 136).

Meanwhile, inside the university, administrators who had once seemed so open to legal realism left or lost interest. Angell became increasingly unenthusiastic about Yale Law School as budgetary problems and the government service of its professors overwhelmed him during Clark's second term as dean, beginning in 1933. "My observation leads me to believe that law faculties tend to harbor relatively more men of leftward-looking political tendencies than are found in academic groups generally," he concluded in his last report as president, after expressing his embarrassment over the activities of his professors. "It is at variance, I should say, with the prevailing trend in bar and bench and probably reflects the theoretical, as contrasted with the practical attitudes of mind" (Kalman 1986, 134, and see 120–34).

At Johns Hopkins, Goodnow retired the year of the Crash. The physicist who succeeded him responded to the Depression by issuing pronouncements that the Institute was not "essential to the whole university" and must not be supported at "the expense of the real University" (Schlegel 1995, 191). The Hopkins Institute closed its doors in 1933, two years after Yale Law School had severed its connection with the Institute of Human Relations.

Few mourned those developments deeply, many grieved not at all. It was not simply that everyone understood the Depression dampened prospects for funding empirical research. Skepticism about such work had begun to appear before financial exigency as the realists retreated to the law school from the larger university. Most law professors, including those who had once embraced it, ultimately concluded that empiricism had been "oversold" (Stevens 1983, 139; Kalman 1986, 34–35; Schlegel 1995, 201–5; Twining 1973, 63–66).

Realists had little good to say about the nonquantitative social sciences either. Richard Morris's seminal study of the history of American law during the colonial period (1930), for example, represented an attempt to formulate broad hypotheses subsequent historians might test, not a guide for the twentieth-century judge into the full detail of the American legal system when it was younger. The book so troubled Karl Llewellyn, who preferred the more particularistic, legalistic, and presentist history of his colleague Julius Goebel (Nelson 1982, 459), that he described it as "depressing and grotesque," sniffing that "Dr. Morris does not seem aware that he is not a lawyer" (Llewellyn 1931, 731 n. 3). The nation's most disenchanted former realist, Robert Maynard Hutchins, denounced his own earlier work with a psychologist, saying it had yielded only pleasant social contacts and "data absolutely raw. We did not know what facts to look for, or why we wanted them, or what to do with them after we got them" (Hutchins 1934, 512–13). Young Smith, who had become dean of Columbia protesting that, *pace* the "mutineers," he really did support the union of law with the social sciences, had had enough by 1930. He now contended that the once dissatisfied legal scholar who detoured into the social sciences frequently returned "with a feeling of relief to the more settled and orderly domain of law" (Kalman 1986, 74).

Relief, perhaps, but satisfaction? How, then, to explain all those law review articles in the 1930s challenging "Langdellian" doctrinalism and Harvard "conceptualism" and espousing the importance of "integrating" law with social sciences, or the founding by law professors of their first interdisciplinary journal, *Law and Contemporary Problems*, in 1933? Armchair bloviations, especially since most realists stuck to doctrinal scholarship?

I think not. The realists could both "do" doctrinal work and advocate interdisciplinarity without seeming hypocritical because they were committed to doing what they knew how to do best and at the same time they recognized their best was not good enough. Exactly what they hoped the social sciences would do for law always remained unclear (Duxbury 1995, 130). The social sciences had undergone dramatic changes in the wake of World War I, as social scientists became captivated by the method of natural scientists and came to find the idea of the scholar as advocate and reformer, which animated most realist law professors, unscientific (see, e.g., Schlegel 1995; Ross 1991, 320–30, 390–470; Ross 1994a). But in the context of the period, it was reasonable for law professors to continue to think that the social sciences (defined broadly, to include history) could prove useful to law students and lawyers as they considered policy questions and confronted the interdependence of law and society. It was at least as feasible an assumption as, say, the idea that law would benefit from "restatement." The notion that law and other disciplines were intertwined *had* produced some helpful results, such as Hale's use of institutionalist economics to shatter the public/private distinction, and nothing better had come along to take its place. And so, though the love affair had not gone smoothly, those law professors who fancied themselves in the vanguard still mooned over the social sciences.

But not after social scient*ists*. In fact, the 1930s are significant partly for the development of mutual hostility between law professors and the rest of the university. Other academics returned academic lawyers' skepticism. John Henry Schlegel blames the demise of the Hopkins Institute on the arts and sciences faculty: "That group was envious of the Institute's fancy salaries, scared that its University was falling apart, and angry that a group of newcomers was receiving such special treatment" (Schlegel 1995, 209). Social scientists treated Underhill Moore, the realist most determined to make use of their insights, as an amateur (Schlegel 1995, 142–44).

Almost everywhere else, with a few exceptions, such as Wisconsin and Chicago (Hartog 1994, 379; Duxbury 1995, 330–31), the pattern seemed the same: law professors, who made overtures to "outside" scholars, were spurned.[13] When Columbia's Albert Jacobs tried to consolidate social science findings and the law of family relations in one of the most innovative casebooks of the 1930s, psychologists condemned him (Kalman 1986, 89). Felix Cohen experienced the same fate when he appealed to anthropologists (Tsuk 1996). Labor economists collided with their former allies, the legal realists, over collective bargaining during the New Deal (Ernst 1993, 79–80).

The problem was that law professors and social scientists were strutting their stuff in the 1930s, and professionalization and bravado blocked progress. Perhaps the coincidence of the call for an alliance between law and social science with the emergence of the law professor as governmental troubleshooter/policy-maker contributed to the emergence of what Mark Tushnet calls "the 'lawyer as astrophysicist' assumption: We are people who have a generalized intelligence and can absorb and utilize the products of any other discipline in which we happen to become interested" (Tushnet 1988, 31). In practical terms, "any lawyer can read a physics book over the weekend and send a rocket to the moon on Monday" (Frickey 1988, 68). In the 1930s, Daniel Ernst has observed, the assumption was still in its infancy: law professors and lawyers did not yet think they were astrophysicists, but they had come to believe they could appreciate the implications of astrophysics for public policy better than anyone else (Ernst, personal communication, 1999). As Felix Frankfurter would have put it, the academic lawyer must be "on top," the expert "on tap" (Frankfurter 1930, 161).

Thus academic lawyers decided they need not follow the example of Robert Hale and pursue advanced study in *one* discipline or even work with someone in another discipline. Law professors could simply scavenge whatever they needed from other disciplines. That, of course, left them open to criticism from other academics, who were surely already jealous of their higher salaries at a time of financial crisis and general insecurity; of their influence on the policy makers and reform-minded judges Roosevelt appointed; and of their relatively wide array of alternatives to teaching, which included practice and government service.

Their choice also left law professors susceptible to allegations from more traditional doctrinalists that the social science experts did not approve of interdisciplinary legal scholarship and found it "second-rate." And yet those latter attacks themselves reflected a sense of vulnerability. For though most realists had failed at it, they had indeed "demonstrated, in principle, that interdisciplinary legal study was a virtue beyond a doubt." While toppling neither Harvard nor Langdell, they had managed to place "law and" atop a pedestal of its own (Duxbury 1995, 92–93), one on which it remained after "the Germans reduced their courts to tools of the Nazi Party, [and] even the most skeptical lawyers felt compelled to reassert the idea of legal autonomy" (Gordon 1975, 38; Purcell 1969, 438–43; Purcell 1973, 159–78). And so academic lawyers stayed inside the law schools, isolated from other academics and from the profession.

1968–1973

University of Virginia Law School Professor Thomas Bergin ushered in the next apparent period of tension in 1968. In a celebrated article, Bergin declared the law professor "a man divided against himself." He was a victim of an "intellectual schizophrenia," which had him "devoutly believing he could be an authentic academic" and a trainer of practitioners. When feeling "a raw lusting for academic respectability," the professor found himself "voting for the abolition of required courses, deploring the case method, establishing research centers, loving the social sciences, teaching the far-out seminars, aching to reform the law, and secretly wishing to be named to a modest federal post such as Secretary of State." He then offered one of the many "law and" electives in the law school catalogues that Bergin believed academic lawyers, who generally lacked advanced training in other disciplines, were utterly incompetent to teach. But when his "Hessian trainer side" appeared, and he wanted to train attorneys for private practice, Bergin said, the professor did "not want all the courses to be required—only the grim ones"; combed the advance sheets; and identified himself as a "lawyer" (Bergin 1968, 637, 646–48; and see Twining 1967, 397–98).

To make matters worse, even in his "authentic academic" phase the law teacher must continue training potential lawyers to parse cases. That meant, Bergin said, that teaching distracted him from doing writing worthy of an academic. According to Bergin, "we have so little authentic scholarship in our law schools that we are lucky not to be driven out of the academic herd." In his "Hessian-trainer phase," however, the law professor must still "produce vast tonnages of trivia each year in the name of scholarship," which diverted him from adequately training lawyers. The end result was a legal education that did not serve students, the university, the bar, or society (Bergin 1968, 645–46, 643).

Bergin dated the origins of the schizophrenia back a quarter century to the *Yale Law Journal* piece, "Legal Training and Public Policy: Professional Training in the Public Interest," by Harold Lasswell and Myres McDougal (1943). He interpreted Lasswell and McDougal's proclamation that legal education could serve democracy only by becoming "conscious, efficient and systematic training for policy-making" (Lasswell and McDougal 1943, 206) as "chiefly a call for the reform of law through the academizing of legal training." With the Lasswell-McDougal article, Bergin argued, "legal education's academic man reached maturity" and confronted the Hessian-trainer side of himself, who had long existed (Bergin 1968, 642).

Bergin rightly pointed to a "malaise in legal education today—the feeling that legal education is failing in some critical way to do its job" (1968, 657). Indeed, while the years from 1968 to 1973 witnessed "a crisis of values in legal education" (Stone 1971, 392), I do not consider it a period of tension between groups because virtually everyone involved (though for different reasons, to be sure) echoed Bergin. The president of the American Bar Association for 1969–70 would repeatedly use his "President's Page" to say: "From all sides—the judiciary, the practicing bar, and the law schools themselves, including both teachers and students—we hear expressions of growing dissatisfaction with legal education and an intense interest in exploring and initiating change" (Segal 1969b; 1969a; 1970).

This was, after all, a period that began with the chair of the AALS curriculum committee calling for something drastic quickly not only because "law students over the country are reaching the point of open revolt, but also . . . [because] law faculties themselves, particularly the younger members, share with the student the view that legal education is too rigid, too uniform, too narrow, too repetitious and too long" (Stevens 1971, 544). And, newly appointed Chief Justice Warren Burger added, too inadequate, leaving as legal education did "amateurs to learn their craft in the courtroom" (Balbach 1972, 601; Burger 1973). It was an era that ended with the "Carrington Report" and the Carnegie Commission endorsing something that looked like a two-year J.D. degree (both reprinted in Packer and Ehrlich 1972), which law school deans vigorously and successfully fought (Stevens 1983, 242; Stolz 1973, 40–46), leaving "lawyer competency" "the magic elixir" for the rest of the 1970s (Gee and Jackson 1977, 924).

It was a time in which Ralph Nader took to the pages of *The New Republic* to denounce law schools for equipping lawyers for nothing beyond "furtherance of their acquisitive drives" and for training hired guns who labored "for polluters, not antipolluters, for sellers, not consumers, for corporations, not citizens, for labor leaders, not rank and file, for, not against, rate increases or weak standards before government agencies, for highway builders, not displaced residents, for, not against judicial and administrative delay, for preferential business access to government and against equal citizen access to the same government, for agricultural subsidies to the rich, not food stamps for the poor, for tax and quota privileges, not for equity and free trade" (Nader 1969, 21). Corporate law firms raised salaries and expanded pro bono programs to attract the best and brightest law students (Auerbach 1976, 278–79; Nader 1969, 22–23; Cahn and Camper 1970, 1005; Comment 1970). The *American Bar Association Journal* carried articles about the best law students titled "Will They Enter Private Practice?" (Garret and Pennington 1971; Robson 1970; McGonagle 1970) and reported that none of the thirty-nine law review editors at Harvard Law School "expected to enter private practice" (Green 1970, 659; and see Vanderwicken 1971, 77. The implication was that they were not just deferring practice to take clerkships, either).

Student complaints about legal education, ever chronic (Stolz 1973, 41), swelled to a roar. In her 1969 commencement address at Hastings, the valedictorian questioned whether the "last three years [have] not been to a large extent, a waste of my time" (Savoy 1970, 444–45 n. 1). The following year, Duncan Kennedy characterized the law professor as "a truly extraordinary narcissistic phenomenon" who enjoyed "the element of destructive aggression, of terrorism in teaching law" (Kennedy 1970, 73). In comparison, a member of the class of 1972 sounded positively generous in telling Robert Stevens that for all their self-confidence, law professors "haven't got a very clear idea of why they are teaching or what they are teaching or what value their teaching will have" (Stevens 1973, 639). Shades of Karl Llewellyn![14]

Under these circumstances, it is not surprising that even after they had added all the new electives on poverty, urban development, civil rights, and psychiatry designed to appeal to "a generation whose conquering sign is relevance" (McGee 1969, 42), academic lawyers remained edgy. Though he himself had done his share of "cause-lawyering," Charles Black was scared. According to him, he and his colleagues had been anxious for the past quarter century, but as they confronted the student activists of the late 1960s, "many teachers now seem to feel not so much discontent as panic" (Black 1970, 506).[15] "[L]aw schools are up against the wall," AALS President Albert Conard lamented (1970, 366).

But so was every other discipline. As Conard recognized, "the whole of higher education is on the defensive" (1970, 366). Compared to other professors in the social sciences and humanities (Kalman 1996, 55–56), academic lawyers (Austin 1998, xvi), like their medical school colleagues (Ludmerer 1999, 242), had little to fear.

Liberal law professors—and most self-identified as such (Hetrick and Turner 1973)—capitalized on students' attraction to the Warren Court's "rights revolution" (Kalman 1996, 49–58). Academic lawyers could preach that if all aspects of society—even law firms—were on the verge of revolution, they also remained viable candidates for reform. And they could believe that the scholarship they did produce affected equally the political liberals who had entered the judiciary since the New Deal and lawyers (Kalman 1996, 49). Law professors moved as easily between their own world and the more "practical" one of activists, lawyers, and courts as realist scholars had in and out of the New Deal (R. Gordon 1993, 2107 n. 77; Posner 1993a, 1648).

Further, law professors did not feel intellectually besieged. In their minds, they could take what they wanted from other disciplines without toppling the citadel. Neither they and historians nor they and literature professors yet had anything positive to say to each other: this was a time when historians delighted in charging that judges and lawyers wrote "law-office history,"[16] and English professors were busy dethroning the New Criticism (Graff 1987, 240). But the social sciences beckoned. Conard and the two AALS presidents after him were associated with sociolegal research (Garth and Sterling 1998, 462 n. 95), and the 1969 theme of the AALS program was "Contemporary Social Science Research: The Law and the Law Schools."

As that title suggested, during the late 1960s and the early 1970s academic lawyers often declared they had rekindled their relationship with the social sciences (now being reconceptualized as the behavioral sciences—Rose 1999, 161), with which they had continued flirting after the realist period (see Rehbinder 1972). At the University of Chicago, the relationship had blossomed since realism. The funding Chicago's Law and Behavioral Studies Program obtained from the Ford Foundation had made several large-scale empirical projects possible, including most notably the Kalven and Zeisel study of the American jury (1966). And ever since Henry Simons and Aaron Director had become affiliated with the Chicago law faculty in the 1940s, some law professors had embraced economists. So, too, some economists, such as Ronald Coase and Gary Becker, had turned to law. By the late 1960s, Richard Posner was about to hurl modern Law and Economics "like a bomb on the academic legal world" (Duxbury 1995, 395, and see 330–419). Thanks in part to Russell Sage money, the University of Wisconsin Law School also remained hospitable to law and social science (Schlegel 1995, 253). So did the University of Minnesota Law School (Stein 1980, 276). And in the late 1950s, the Yale Law School faculty included two sociologists, Richard Schwartz and Jerome Skolnick. But social science research had not flourished at most law schools in the postwar period, though it was vaguely venerated.

In the late 1960s and early 1970s, however, many law professors outside Hyde Park and Madison believed they were about to consummate the affair with the social sciences, and this time, with practicing lawyers' blessing (Dunn 1969). The University of Minnesota's Carl Auerbach was sure, or so he said at the 1969 AALS meeting, that "the time will come when no law teacher will be regarded as competent who does not possess some competence in some field of social science" (quoted in Mazor 1972, 318). Auerbach urged those who wanted to become academic lawyers to obtain a Ph.D. (Auerbach 1970, 253), an objective that Bergin, who ridiculed the S.J.D., also embraced (Bergin 1968, 652). A summer-session "quick and dirty" course in quantitative Social Science Methods in Legal Education was introduced to draw law professors into the social science world and give them a credential that would legitimate their participation in it (Garth and Sterling 1998, 426). "The benefits of this program are already being seen in law schools throughout the country," the AALS president boasted in 1971 (Fordham 1971, 105).

Perhaps, as Bryant Garth and Joyce Sterling suggest, "the legal world is most receptive to the arguments of social science in periods of rapid change" (1998, 464). With violence and crime apparently zooming, the lawyers found they could secure foundation and governmental support, and they established "the first concentration of interdisciplinary research at American law schools since the 1930s" (White 1986b, 831). As Garth and Sterling ably demonstrate, law professors managed to gain control of "the center of gravity in the field of law and social science" (1998, 461). Yet Garth and Sterling also show that having absorbed what social science and scientists they needed to keep their domain intact, law professors marginalized both (1998, 461; Friedman 1986, 773–79). For the most part, the "assimilated" social scientists were then shunned by those in their disciplines, who had little use for law (Garth and Sterling 1998, 463–64).

Thus the law school embraced just enough reform to preserve law's autonomy.[17] Even at Yale, which had long prided itself on enshrining the social sciences, Duncan Kennedy reported, it was "shocking to hear professors dismiss all disciplines but the law as intellectually shoddy" (Kennedy 1970, 71). Though academic lawyers professed extraordinary enthusiasm for appointees with "ambidexterity in two disciplines" when they filled out questionnaires (Dworkin 1973, 61), they apparently did not do so in faculty meetings (Mazor 1972, 323; Cavers 1972). In 1971, about 3 percent of those listed in the AALS Directory of Law Teachers possessed the Ph.D. along with the law degree; approximately another 10 percent had an M.A. A report that year found "little indication" that "many law schools" had two or more faculty members with advanced training in other disciplines (Mazor 1972, 323–24).[18]

Thus academic lawyers retained ownership of law, colonized sociolegal studies, and basked in the glory of the Warren Court. Further, law professors were still better paid than social scientists and humanists, and their students easily found jobs (see, e.g., Katzman 1968). The job crisis that began in the late 1960s meant that students of the social scientists and the humanists did not. Though law professors suffered angst, they were well off compared to those in the humanities and social sciences.

Oddly, Bergin's piece became the paradigmatic (to use a word law professors were about to begin using endlessly [Tushnet 1979, 1302 n. 33]) statement of the law professor's condition. Virtually every account of the academic lawyer's life published in the past thirty years points to the schizophrenic nature of his (and increasingly her) place in the university. That was unfortunate because, though wonderful, Bergin's essay was misleading.

By my lights, Bergin misinterpreted the Lasswell-McDougal article, which, as he himself admitted, did concern itself "with the improvement of practical vocational mechanics such as rule-learning and case parsing" (1968, 642). Even if he read it correctly, the Lasswell-McDougal "call (if ever made)," Bergin conceded, was nearly universally ignored (1968, 642). It was therefore difficult to see how the article could have created, or even significantly contributed to, a sense of intellectual schizophrenia.

Then, too, there was Bergin's problematic point that the law school is a "hybrid institution" because its denizens pursued their scholarly missions while training practitioners (Barnhizer 1989, 111), while humanists and social scientists replicated themselves. Though one of law professors' favorite observations, it was still counterfactual. How many academics did Bergin and other academic lawyers think professors elsewhere in the university produced? Of twentieth-century American political historians in the postwar period, for example, perhaps no one turned out more "Americanists" than William E. Leuchtenburg of Columbia. Yet when, after more than forty years of teaching, Leuchtenburg came to dedicate a book "to my students who have written about the New Deal era and who have taught me so much," whom he then listed, there were fewer than a hundred names in what is colloquially known as the "Leuchtenburg Mafia" (Leuchtenburg 1995, dedication page). Of course, Leuchtenburg had instructed the graduate students of his colleagues in seminars too. But even when the latter group is added in, the number still seems slight next to the thousands of undergraduates to whom Leuchtenburg taught recent American history, who had no intention of pursuing careers as scholars.[19] Bergin also neglected to mention that *some* elite law professors' students followed them into the academy.

Nor did he make it clear how scholarship diverted the law professor from training practitioners. For all the "law and" electives cluttering the law school curriculum, doctrinal scholarship, which academics still believed aided and influenced judges and lawyers, remained the norm. As always, university legal education did not adequately prepare students for practice. But did that reflect the law professors' preoccupation with scholarship? Probably not, for academic lawyers' duties in that realm were minimal. Law schools did not yet require for tenure much, if anything, in the way of publications, especially compared to other disciplines. At the top of the heap, Harvard was just beginning to demand the one "tenure" article in the late 1960s (Seligman 1978, 126; Stone 1971, 403). Law professors may have spent more time consulting than they did on scholarship.

No matter: in the early 1970s, Bergin renewed his insistence that the law teacher was "the least satisfied professional in America" (Costello 1975, 391, reporting that Bergin made this remark in a 1973 discussion). Considering the misfortune professors elsewhere in the university were suffering, in my opinion he was whining. The law professor lived in relative luxury.

New problems made that clear. When burgeoning law school enrollments (Rudd 1972; Winograd 1973), the product of causes as diverse as the downturn in the economy, the civil rights and feminist movements, the job crisis for academics (and perhaps, Watergate?),[20] became apparent in 1972 and 1973, ABA presidents and most others dropped all discussion of the "crisis of values in legal education." The fact that, in the words of ABA President Leon Jaworski, law had clearly "become the glamour profession of this decade, as the sciences and space technology were in the 1950s and 1960s" (Jaworski 1972), created concern about what his successor delicately referred to as "useful ways to absorb into the profession the record numbers of new lawyers now coming out of the law schools" (Meserve 1972; and see Jaworski 1972; First 1979, 1062–65).

All in all, 1968–1973 was a moment of malaise. It was not zero hour. But Bergin's article resonated for those of his students, and students from other leading law schools, who taught law at elite institutions in the 1980s.

ZERO HOUR? 1980–1993

In contrast to 1968–1973, the tension between the professors and practitioners that Judge Edwards and others have observed lately seems more real. And like the sense of crisis in legal education, it has apparently only grown. How can we explain it?

One way of telling the story might go like this. In 1973, as law schools began to fill up, the law professors, most of whom still labeled themselves political liberals, lost their last hope that the Burger Court would continue what had gone before. For twenty years, academic lawyers had remained under "the spell of the Warren Court" (Sunstein 1995a), their faith in it religious and mystical (Kalman 1996, 2–8). Their devotion to the power of the Court had helped to make constitutional law "the most prestigious field in the legal academy" (Posner 1993a, 1652) and to make the law faculty of an elite law school "the ideal place for a smart boy with a social conscience to go" (Trillin 1984, 83). Now, their trust in the Court wavering, law professors became alienated from the very institution that had once provided so many of them with a sense their mission was noble, the very institution whose work they had assumed their doctrinal scholarship affected (Kalman 1996, 58–59, 87–93).

At the same time, novel political and disciplinary perspectives and classes of people began to appear on law school faculties. Women and people of color were joining law faculties in significant (though hardly overwhelming) numbers (Fossum 1980a, 5532–48; 1980b, 904; Chused 1988; Delgado 1989; Kay 1991; Borthwick and Schau 1991, 191–212; Merritt and Reskin 1997), creating a sense of displacement among old and young boys alike. New political perspectives—ranging from the Critical Legal Studies critique of rights to Law and Economics demonstrations that legal reform often had the unintended consequence of hurting the very beneficiaries it was supposed to help—posed a different set of challenges for the law professors (Kalman 1996, 60–61, 77–94). Further, as it became clear the job crisis in the humanities and social sciences would not end quickly, some who would have become humanists and social scientists in a better market were instead becoming law professors (Minow 1987). Such individuals, a significant number of whom possessed Ph.D.s, proved genuinely interested in interdisciplinary legal studies, which Law and Economics (unlike the intensely doctrinal Critical Legal Studies) made "thoroughly respectable" (Posner 1997, 1146). Apparently, Robert Hale's moment had finally arrived.

Established law professors could not change their sex or their skin color, and they found it difficult to renounce their politics. Consequently, they had two options. Some embraced interdisciplinarity. But it turned out "law and" just made their lives more difficult. For example, ever since the earliest days of legal realism, law professors had struggled to identify principled grounds for judicial decision making. But in the deconstructionist moment of poststructuralist thought, and even in the less threatening time of the interpretive turn, the opposition of subjectivity and objectivity just seemed to be quintessential expressions of the old metaphysics (Kalman 1996, 62–72; Leff 1987, 989).

Other older law professors, and some new ones too, took a second path. Joining forces with the bar, whose calls for clinical and skills training they had fended off as anti-intellectual in the 1970s (Allen 1977, 450), traditionalists began talking more about the law schools' duty to produce competent lawyers (Report on Lawyer Competency 1979). Yet as they battled with the interdisciplinarians and/or members of the Left they charged would make the law school "a colonial outpost of the graduate school" (Allen 1988, 195; Carrington 1992, 789; Carrington 1999, 181–87) and "weaken . . . the symbiotic relationship . . . between the schools on the one hand, and the courts and the profession on the other" (Allen 1983, 404), victory was not forthcoming.

That was apparent when law professors gathered at Yale in 1980 to hold a symposium on "legal scholarship." Though he himself had contributed so much to Law and Economics, Richard Posner defiantly argued in a dazzling paper there that "doctrinal analysis, which is and should remain the core of legal scholarship," was "currently endangered at leading law schools." "The academic lawyer who makes it his business to be learned in the law and expert in parsing cases and statutes is made by . . . [deans at such institutions] to seem a paltry fellow, a Philistine who has shirked the more ambitious and challenging task of mastering political and moral philosophy, economics, history, and other social sciences and humanities so that he can discourse on large questions of justice," he said. Posner would reaffirm the continuation of the crisis in legal scholarship and education at approximately seven-year intervals thereafter (Posner 1981, 1113, 1119; 1987; 1993a; 1993b).

Many joined him in worrying that doctrinal work was coming to seem unprestigious and anti-intellectual. They could point to the fact that it did not often show up in footnotes. "By the 1980s, traditional doctrinal articles are few and far between among the citation elite" (Shapiro 1996, 759), Fred Shapiro reported in a study that unsurprisingly demonstrated that the most-cited law review articles were "published either by professors at one of the 'top-ten' (by conventional opinion) law schools or in a review published at one of these same law schools" (Balkin and Levinson 1996, 850). There was a widespread perception that at the leading law schools doctrinalism was on the defensive, endangered, and in decline (see, e.g., Cramton 1986, 8–9; Kissam 1986, 296–300; Wellington 1987; Farber 1987; Elson 1989, 350; Austin 1998, 14–15, 73, 194).

And in a development that may have seemed equally unsettling to some, who still may have yearned after the social sciences, the two reigning modes of interdisciplinarity were becoming less important. Once law and society and law and economics had been king. But in the 1980s these two "explanatory or 'scientific' *law ands*" were losing out to the "postmodern, interpretive *law ands*" in the citation sweepstakes (Galanter and Edwards 1997, 384).

Further, though its "irreducible normativity" (Rubin 1988, 1853) had long been the "defining feature of legal scholarship," the characteristic that most distinguished it from work in other disciplines (Rubin 1997, 542), postmodernism challenged the law professor's authoritative voice of Olympian prescriptiveness. While some proved more critical in the 1980s of "advocacy masquerading as scholarship" (Bard 1989; and see Tushnet 1981, 1208; Cramton 1986, 7–9), the full-blown "critique of normativity" still lurked in the background (not that it had much impact when it emerged).[21] But many law professors were foregrounding their abandonment of the omniscient voice. Feminist legal theory and Critical Race Theory, like some critical legal scholarship during the middle 1980s, reflected the integration of scholarship with life experience. As younger scholars became interested in narrative, the vertical pronoun was popping up everywhere (Kalman 1996, 125–27). When Susan Estrich began her 1986 article on rape with a story—"Eleven years ago, a man held an ice pick to my throat and said: 'Push over, shut up, or I'll kill you' "—she spoke in a voice readers were unaccustomed to hearing in the *Yale Law Journal* (Estrich 1986, 1087).

As the 1980s progressed, further political ferment deepened the sense of breakdown among law professors. Critical legal scholars at a number of institutions charged they had been illegitimately denied tenure on the basis of their politics, not their publications. Intellectually and sociologically—in scholarship and on faculties—the veneer separating law from politics was very openly stripped away (Kalman 1996, 121–24).

To elite law students who intended to become attorneys, and to the bar, professors seemed so busy among themselves that they had less interest than ever in the practice of law (which was, by many accounts, becoming less satisfying than ever [Rehnquist 1987; Johnson 1993], undoubtedly leading some to take refuge in teaching). Though law students now lined up to work at large law firms (Garth 1989, 433 n. 3), they did not feel their professors approved. Law professors had condemned large firms in the past: recall Adolf Berle's complaint that "legal factories" had "contributed little of thought, less of philosophy and nothing at all of responsibility or idealism" (Berle 1933, 340). Still, some saw something new at work. Judge Edwards's clerks during the 1980s, for example (graduates of Berkeley, Boston University, Buffalo, Duke, Georgetown, Harvard, Michigan, NYU, Stanford, and Yale Law Schools—Edwards 1992, 42 n. 15), were in general agreement that "law school focused much more on the intellectual . . . to the exclusion and indeed the disdain, of the practical" and that most professors acted as if "the graduates who went into practice were those who couldn't get teaching jobs" (Edwards 1993, 61; Ayer 1993). (To be sure, the judge's clerks may not have been representative; Edwards may have chosen them in part because they expressed such sentiment.) Attorneys reported that "scholarship, not teaching, is the be-all and end-all in academia, the coin of the realm; and scholars, even traditional ones, consider law practice the province of the brain dead" (Gordon 1993, 1960).

Even in the late 1960s, law professors had at least found large law firms worthy of exhortation. But the writers in the 1980s who seemed most interested in the big firms were sociolegal scholars who focused on them, often unflatteringly, as social institutions,[22] and journalists in new publications, such as *American Lawyer* and *National Law Journal*, whose mission, one Latham and Watkins partner lamented, was to "shred . . . the secrecy shroud" (Danner 1989, 449; Galanter and Palay 1991, 68–73). Writing in 1985, a law professor maintained that "[t]he philosophic distance traveled since I was a law student in the late 1950's may best be indicated by the fact that, among editors of the *Harvard Law Review* at that time, it was almost universally considered a publication blunder to have published the Hart-Fuller debate in a now classic issue of that review. I recall editors buttressing their views with letters from practitioners who threatened to terminate their subscriptions if the *Review* continued to waste its pages on jurisprudential nonsense instead of on articles designed to aid practitioner research on hot subjects of large law firm litigation" (D'Amato 1985, 982). Law review articles had been expected to aid practitioners.[23] When they did not, attorneys protested, and editors took their complaints seriously (With the Editors 1958, vii). In the 1980s, as some law professors hailed an "increasing division between legal practice and legal education" (Priest 1989, 1983), practitioners complained in vain. Just consider the rave reviews Kenneth Lasson's biting 1990 attack on the pretentiousness of legal scholarship, "Scholarship Amok: Excesses in the Pursuit of Truth and Tenure," won from practitioners (Lasson 1990, 929; "Scholarship Admired" 1991; Lasson 1994, 203–4).

To make matters worse for law professors on the Left and in the center, they were losing the judges and government as well as the lawyers. The Reagan and Bush administrations were transforming the judiciary through the appointment of conservative judges,[24] a number of whom were academics, and were yoking their activities to a jurisprudence of original intent. Republicans in power also faulted the law schools for the liberal judicial activism the Reaganites sought to reverse. Many law professors therefore lost that sense of themselves as the powers behind the judicial throne. Judges were citing their work less, seemingly because they found it less useful (Kalman 1996, 132–38; Sirico and Margulies 1986, 134–35).[25]

As Posner explained, after President Clinton's election:

> The effect was to siphon conservative lawyers from the academy and thus at one and the same time to tug the academy leftward and the judiciary rightward. This effect has been reinforced by the self-selection of leftward-leaning lawyers into academic law. The financial rewards of a commercial practice for top-flight lawyers are very great, and naturally the law students most drawn to such a practice are those with conventional career goals, which emphasize financial success. Opportunities to practice law in an interesting and remunerative fashion in fields like con-

stitutional, poverty, and environmental law are slight unless you're working for the bad guys, and federal legal service in the era of Reagan and Bush was not a congenial alternative for persons of liberal or left inclination. This will now change. But for many years left-leaning lawyers often felt they had no alternative to teaching and so gravitated there and found themselves in an antagonistic relation to the courts, especially the federal courts. (1995, 87)

But it was not just that the profession and government were washing their hands of academic lawyers. Most other academics still wanted no part of them. Law professors with Ph.D.s joined humanists and social scientists in jumping on academic lawyers for their frenzied trendiness. One Gadamer student, who found himself teaching in a law school, believed that the "wholly gratuitous discussions of Nietzsche, Saussure, Derrida, and Foucault" that had become "de rigeur in law review articles about section 1983, contract doctrine, poverty law, and even Uruguayan prisons" reflected a desperate search "for an external, non-legal source of legitimacy or authority" by legal scholars at just the moment their faith in law was crumbling (Collier 1991, 205). Economists viewed lawyers with suspiciousness (Ulen 1997, 463 n. 78). Stanley Fish was sure academic lawyers misunderstood interpretation (Kalman 1996, 113–19). Philosophers parodied their philosophy (Leiter 1992; Nussbaum 1993). Where once historians had condemned "law office history," they now cursed law professors' "history lite" (Flaherty 1995; Kalman 1996, 171–80).

This gulf between them and the university may have bewildered the trendy law professors most—at least, those who did not possess advanced training in another discipline. At some level, they must have anticipated the complaints of doctrinal colleagues, law students, attorneys, and judges. But they were making a real effort to learn from their university colleagues. For example, law professors who wrote about "the Founding" in the 1980s were no longer relying simply on *The Federalist* and textbooks. In fact, academic lawyers with no graduate training in history, who had once ignored the work of historians as important as Charles Beard and Richard Hofstadter, were suddenly falling on J.G.A. Pocock and Gordon Wood (Kalman 1996, 184).

From their perspective, then, academic lawyers were finally allowing interdisciplinarity to breach the autonomy of law. Like the legal realist Underhill Moore, they "wanted to play in the worst of ways" (Schlegel 1995, 145). But since academic lawyers seemed both disingenuous and defensive about what they were doing—using other disciplines for their own purposes—their J.D.-Ph.D. counterparts and colleagues outside the law school seemed more dubious of them than ever (see, e.g., Kalman 1996, 175). To return to our history example, historians thought the law professors so assiduously studying Pocock and Wood were nevertheless ransacking the past for their own presentist purposes (see, e.g., Kerber 1988, 1664–65). Law professors and others in the university were still talking past each other, still engaged in that "dialogue of the deaf" they had been carrying on since the realist period (Burke 1993, 3).

So some academics in other disciplines said that despite its ornamentation, law professors' scholarship had changed not at all. Those were hard words for academic lawyers to hear. As Charles Collier put it: "The plodding, stodgy analyses of judges and doctrinal scholars make the perfect foil for critical, creative legal scholars; but it is scholars *from other disciplines* who induce the anxiety" (Collier 1991, 271).

And then jobs for law professors became harder to come by (Jarvis 1999 [1988], 1079 n. 28). Having shunned attorneys and been shunned by them, by judges, by J.D.-Ph.D.s, and by nonlawyer scholars, were academic lawyers now being abandoned by the legal academy? Small wonder so many everywhere thought the "present situation in legal scholarship" looked so grim in the early 1990s.

Doubtless one could tell a different story. This one, which I will label the standard account, suggests that the perception of disjunction between law professors and practitioners and between law professors and humanists and social scientists grew especially acute between 1980 and 1993. What are the assumptions underlying this story, and how reasonable are they for understanding it?

The standard story supposes that after 1980, law professors lost a common identity. Forget about the disjunction between the professors and practitioners or professors and judges, and focus on the disjunction among professors my account implies. What did the doctrinalist, postmodernist, Rawlsian, and lawyer-economist on the same faculty between 1980 and 1993 share?

Probably more than the story indicates. They had to cope with the same dean and university administration. They had at least some of the same students. Indeed, one problem with the standard story is that it assumes one's politics or credentials determine one's approach to teaching. More likely, student evaluations do, despite their relatively slight importance to personnel decisions, and historically students have hardly proven shy about expressing their preference for "BLACK-LETTER LAW, NOT POLICY" (Abel 1990, 415–16, 447).

Why should we think that the J.D.-Ph.D.s, or the unadorned Ph.D.s, or even the "scholars whose primary interests are 'anything but law' (ABL)" (Johnson 1993, 1239) that Judge Edwards claimed flooded the law school, would present Torts, or, more generally, legal reasoning (which, even in the 1980s, attorneys still thought law schools were teaching well—Garth and Martin 1993, 478, 503, 509), differently from the J.D.s? James White, for example, suggested that at Michigan, during this period, some law professors who possessed just the Ph.D. proved "so conscious of their nonlawyer status" that they displayed greater interest in, and respect for, doctrine than their colleagues who are lawyers" (White 1993, 2180, 2179). Their outsiders' perspective may even have enabled them to conceive of unusually good ways of teaching "the grammar of law talk" ("Waiting for Langdell II" 1996, 142). So, too, some of the teachers who concentrated on doctrine in the classroom were on the Left (Discussion 1985). Perhaps the culture of the law school was sufficient to endow its professors with a shared teaching identity.

In fact, the standard story assumes it did. Running through it are two assumptions—both problematic, but accurate in some ways, in my view—about the period between 1980 and 1993. First, interdisciplinarity "won" out over doctrinalism. Second, Judge Edwards did not need to wring his hands because interdisciplinarity's victory was hollow.

With respect to the apparent triumph of "law and," the standard story throws around terms, such as "traditional doctrinal articles," that dropped out of sight/cite when eclipsed by "theory" in the 1980s. These phrases are arguably so vague as to be meaningless. Did "theory," for example, refer to all theory or just to theory the bar and judiciary found useful? Either way, the implications that law professors did nothing more than sort out students for placement in the hierarchy and that their theoretical work had no impact on legal practice or education were bizarre. Bryant Garth and Joanne Martin point out, for one example, that during the 1980s, theory was transforming both the practice and the teaching of negotiation (Garth and Martin 1993, 499–500, 505). For another, Posner offers a catalogue of the many ways Law and Economics scholarship affected law, judging, and lawyering: "To begin with, it is generally believed that law and economics has transformed antitrust law" (Posner 1993b, 1925). And though most law professors assumed a divide between doctrinal work and scholarship that was interdisciplinary and/or theoretical, there was no reason the former could not incorporate "an appeal to theory and research" in other disciplines (Dworkin 1973, 56).[26]

Further, even if they were cited less frequently, were "traditional doctrinal articles" diminishing in number during the Reagan-Bush years? Opinions varied widely. Michael Saks, Howard Larsen, and Carol Hodne found a drop had occurred, but not a substantial one: where 63.46 percent of law journal contents had been fully or partially devoted to doctrinal analysis in 1960, 59.05 percent were in 1985 (Saks, Larsen, and Hodne 1996, 366). Posner thought doctrinalism's decline "relative, not absolute, and perhaps not even relative; all that may be occurring is a shift in the production of doctrinal scholarship towards scholars at law schools of the second and third tier" (Posner 1995, 94). If so, where did those scholars publish it? According to Mary Ann Glendon, not in the elite law reviews: "The ratio of 'practical' to 'theoretical' essays," by which she presumably meant doctrinal to nondoctrinal articles, "in leading law journals dropped from 4.5:1 in 1960 to 1:1 in 1985" (Glendon 1994, 204). Yet Ariela Gross's study of the *Harvard* and *Columbia Law Reviews* and the *Yale Law Journal* persuaded Robert Gordon that "doctrine is still the staple commodity, even in the reviews edited at fancy schools that go in for the fancy new stuff" (Gordon 1993, 2100). In fact, the study suggested to Gordon that doctrinal scholarship was on the rise in the 1980s (1993, 2100; Ellickson 1998, 161). Reports of the death of the treatise (Simpson 1981), a historic locus of doctrinal scholarship, had also been greatly exaggerated (Allen 1988, 197 n. 17). And many law professors continued to work on American Law Institute Restatements.

Perhaps all these findings are reconcilable. As Paul Campos said, everyone was "to some extent correct in perceiving" that they were "besieged" ("Waiting for Langdell II" 1996, 26). But we lack sufficient information to reconcile them. While it seems that interdisciplinary scholarship possessed more prestige than doctrinal work at leading law schools, and possibly on leading law reviews, it is not clear that interdisciplinarity crowded out doctrinalism.

Was the victory of "law and" as empty as the story suggests? Many legal "metascholars" argued that law professors tried to colonize other disciplines in a vain search for intellectual authority (see, e.g., Collier 1993, 842, 848; Collier 1992; Balkin 1996). At the end of the 1980s, Pierre Schlag protested that "[t]he interdisciplinary travels of traditional legal thought are like a bad European vacation: the substance is Europe, but the form is McDonald's, Holiday Inn, American Express" (Schlag 1990b, 1656). I believe most humanists and social scientists who read the law reviews would have agreed with him. Thus the standard story is correct in pointing out that for all academic lawyers' attempts to bridge it, the gulf between them and the rest of the university remained very much a reality.

And so, as the standard story suggests, did the gulf between law professors and the most powerful in the profession. One possibility the story neglects, however, is that scholarship is more a function of politics than it implies. Like Posner, Robert Gordon believed *most* academic lawyers remained "pretty liberal" during the Reagan-Bush years, and therefore could not expect a hearing from the executive branch, Congress, or the federal courts. "When one has little hope of influencing anybody in power, one's work is likely to turn critical, theoretical, and historical," he reasoned (Gordon 1993, 2107).

That seems a sensible hypothesis. Indeed in this respect, most law professors of the Reagan-Bush years had it worse than the realists of the 1930s. For all the enemies they were making in the profession and judiciary until 1937, the realists assumed New Dealers were paying them heed. Liberal and centrist law professors during the 1980s and early 1990s could make no such assumption. Perhaps their powerlessness liberated them, just as Gordon suggested. Was it so surprising that, as Gordon pointed out, "[m]uch of the concrete prescriptive work in this period was turned out by conservative law-and-economics scholars who could be confident there was a policy audience for it" (R. Gordon 1993, 2107)?

Though I do not doubt the law professors' confidence, I find myself wondering about its basis. How do we tell there was a policy audience? Citation frequency became a standard indicator of audience influence during the 1980s (Shapiro 1985, 1991; Symposium 1996b), as it was in other disciplines (see Leonard 1990, 189–90 n. 29). In some ways, this was understandable. The Reagan-Bush years witnessed the triumph of the "academic superstar." High-profile law professors with the wrong politics might not find a place in the Reagan-Bush administration, but during "the deal decade," as law professors flitted from school to school on "lookover" or "podium-filler" visits,[27] such scholars were likely to receive a multitude of "mega-offers" from other law schools, which they could then use to start a bidding war for themselves. How easier to determine who was worthy of such offers than by focusing on who was most cited? Technology made it cheap and easy to count citations, paradoxically making citation counts a measure of a scholar's value. Though some surmised the dramatic surge in law review symposia reflected a "search for meaning" (Stefanic 1992), the increase may simply have reflected a search for guaranteed publications (generally alongside some big names, who never tired of writing) that could be cited at a time when legal scholars were realizing they had to become more visible in print to receive more outside offers and/or higher salaries.

Still, why should law professors during the Reagan-Bush years have believed citation counts measured "influence" or "impact"? Citation counts offered a useful way of confirming some trends, such as the declining popularity of law and economics and law and society (Symposium 1997; Symposium 1996a, though that observation is itself problematic, since in absolute terms both fields still possessed considerable influence), and the growing prominence (again, relatively speaking) of other "law ands." But one need not be prone to conspiracy theories to believe that scholars tended to cite their friends; articles that appeared in the leading law journals; and those they wanted to impress (Balkin and Levinson 1996).

And to return to the realists, I believe one of their most positive legacies was uncertainty. They may have been more confident about their impact on the New Deal than their own work suggests they should have been. As Posner observes, in the context of his discussion of Law and Economics and antitrust: "It can, to be sure, be argued that all that law and economics *really* did, so far as its impact on the practice of antitrust law was concerned, was to provide conservative judges with a vocabulary and conceptual apparatus that enabled them to reach the results to which they were drawn on political grounds" (Posner 1993b, 1925). (Posner also emphasizes, rightly, that "to enable is to do much"—Posner 1993b, 1925.) The realists reminded us that idiosyncrasy sometimes does play a role in decision making: an opinion, policy, or brief, whatever the citations, is a rationalization of a result the decision maker or lawyer wants to reach. This is not an insight that should paralyze legal scholars, but it should ward off complacency.

Even assuming academic lawyers' work had impact, was the influence positive? Challenging the view that legal scholars no longer impress judges,

William Fisher argues that law professors in the 1970s and 1980s influenced the Supreme Court's interpretation of the Bill of Rights. But that was the bad news. According to Fisher, "the combination of the diversity of the professors' proposals and the Court's tendency to pick up bits and pieces from each has contributed to the jumbled, intellectually unsatisfying character of current doctrine." He concludes that we should be "dismayed to find in Supreme Court opinions shards of the various seemingly incommensurable normative theories developed by law professors" (Fisher 1991, 268, 319, 364–65).

Yet professors have never been certain that scholarship affects policy or practice, much less that it affects them benignly, and they never will be. What judges, lawyers, and other lawmakers say, or have said, about the influence of the treatises and the Restatements written by the great doctrinalists may not reflect reality. The realists should have questioned the impact of their own work on the New Deal. The fact that law professors were more likely than ever to articulate their "legalaboraphobia" ("fear of . . . a law review article falling in an empty forest"—Hirshman 1990, 1034) in the anxious postmodern period of 1980–1993 did not mean it had not always preyed on them.[28]

The standard story raises almost as many questions as it answers. Many of its assumptions, such as its suggestion that doctrinalism was in decline, call out for further research. Nevertheless, on the basis of what we know now, and with the caveats I have outlined, it strikes me as largely accurate in pointing to a high degree of tension during the Reagan-Bush years between most academic lawyers and the profession on the one hand, and other professors on the other. Law professors may have been even more friendless than they were during the 1930s; the realists, at least, had some friends in high places in the Executive Branch.

THE MORE THINGS CHANGE, THE MORE THINGS CHANGE?

If showing everything new is old is historians' favorite parlor game, law professors have one of their own. It involves demonstrating that the more things change, the more they stay the same. That is a different enterprise. Though historians delight in pointing to that shock of similarity with the past, our chief interest is in finding change over time. For us, the past is usually another country; the only lessons of the past are that there are no "lessons of the past."

That observation leads us an obvious question. Assuming the standard story is mostly unexceptionable, as I have argued, did it apply to the Clinton years? It is too soon to do much but raise questions and hazard a tentative answer of "mostly no."

Interestingly, that is the answer of Judge Edwards. In a 1997 speech to the American Law Institute, he indicated that he is "now less pessimistic, for I believe that there are things that can be done and that are being done to improve legal education." He applauded NYU Law School (whose law review subsequently published the speech) for its creation of "a truly integrated model of legal education, one that fully embraces theoretical and doctrinal scholarship, critical legal studies, clinical education, strong involvements with members of the judiciary and practicing bar, a new 'global' law component focused on international issues, and powerful support of public interest ventures." As he sees it, the NYU experience shows that "practical, theory-oriented, and critical legal scholars, along with their clinician counterparts," can "flourish in an environment of mutual respect, sharing equal status and prominence on the faculty" (Edwards 1997, 572).

I share some of his hopefulness. I suspect the tension between law professors and other academics diminished. At the same time, it seems the strain between academic lawyers and the profession increased, but for some new reasons.

Turn first to the relationship between law professors and the profession. In directing our attention to the relationship between politics, law professors' scholarship, and the profession, which has played a large part in our story, Gordon predicted that during the Clinton administration "many more scholars will be doing 'policy'—articles on health care and tort reform, labor policy, tax policy, international trade, and urban policy" and that doctrinal work would become more important "if ever judges come, to seem, once again, sympathetic listeners." Did the focus of academic lawyers' work change significantly between 1993 and 2000, eroding the sense of disjunction between professors, the profession, and judges? Or did, for example, the Republican Senate's successful opposition to so many of the president's judicial appointments and the nature of the Clinton administration's trials (think impeachment and independent counsel—the law review editors certainly seemed to do so, with their frequent symposia on these topics) mean academic lawyers discerned no reason to return to basics (O'Brien 1999)? Or is Gordon correct about the turn to policy, but for reasons different from those he suggests?

It would be helpful to know what legal scholars are told they must publish to receive tenure and post-tenure advances, since a law and economics explanation would stress that the professor will produce what the market demands. Some testimony indicates that entering academic lawyers are advised to "write up a storm" on aspects of policy issues they can research easily on the Internet,[29] though there is also evidence they are told at least one big doctrinal article is still required for tenure. All this is only anecdotal and just reminds us that we lack any information about the impact of technology on scholarly production, which must certainly enter into our calculations for the 1990s (Stefanic 1992, 672).

If there has been a discernible shift to "policy" work, judges and lawmakers may have welcomed it, but I wonder how useful it is to the elite practitioners who complained to Judge Edwards in the early 1990s, even if it fits their politics. Arguably, they faced the most pressure through the decade. "For me, the central eternal verity is that the successful law firms in 1995 will not be practicing law in the same way that successful law firms practiced in 1980, and certainly not as they did in 1970," a partner at Arnold & Porter had predicted at the end of the 1980s. Law practice was about to "undergo the most radical restructuring in its history" (Fitzpatrick 1989, 461).

Time seems to be proving him right. As long as the promotion-to-partner tournament was played in traditional fashion, the firms were able to cope with a world in which the elite law schools "educated," and they "trained," students (see Garth and Martin 1993, 497). With the breakup of the old economics of the law firm, especially since the downturn of 1990–1992, must larger ones demand more, sooner, from their youngest associates? That might create pressure to shift the duty of training, historically a task large law firms willingly assumed (Gee and Jackson 1977, 937–38), to the schools; certainly the ABA Task Force on "Narrowing the Gap" emphasized law faculties should do more in the way of skills training.[30] Perhaps that was because the clinicians made the Task Force their Trojan horse. Still, the gap between elite law professors and the profession may have widened, rather than narrowed, during the Clinton years.[31]

Almost certainly, the gap between law professors with elite credentials and their students, many of whom are future members of the profession, has grown larger.[32] Academic lawyers have worked their way up to elite institutions through a pattern of "colonial service" at "lesser" law schools since the professionalization of law teaching. But historically, Dean Griswold's point about Harvard Law School at the end of his tenure probably applied to most other law faculties: "Our faculties tend to reproduce themselves; and in the process may by the continual inbreeding that is involved be producing even narrower students than they were themselves" (Kalman 1986, 220).

That has changed somewhat. Talk to almost anyone supervising law students who wanted to teach at century's end, and one heard the same lament: students as good as the ones he or she used to place at University of X Law School now had to start at Slippery Rock. It seemed likely that not just the great middle of the profession, but the lower quartile as well, were being taught by graduates of elite law schools with excellent credentials, the right clerkships, and often doctorates. It would be interesting to compare their perceptions of their professors with those of Judge Edwards's earlier clerks. I wonder if students at less prestigious law schools were even more alienated from their professors than were their counterparts at elite institutions.

What about the gap between elite law professors and the rest of the university? At least in terms of credentials, the "interdisciplinary turn" of the early 1990s was apparently sustained through the decade. Twice as many of those in the 1994–95 AALS Directory listed a Ph.D. as had in 1971: of the 8,231 individuals listed, 562 held Ph.D.s, and an additional 1,089 recorded M.A.s (Kalman 1996, 1003).[33] Far more deans of first-quintile law schools in 1996–97 possessed a Ph.D. than did a decade earlier (Bhandari, Cafardi, and Marlin 1998, 340). Some have even suggested that, given the "buyers' market for legal academics," it is "not unlikely that over the coming decade the Ph.D. will become the norm for those entering the world of law teaching" (Galanter and Edwards 1997, 384).[34]

Of course credentials do not necessarily determine one's approach to scholarship, just as they do not define one as a teacher. Ph.D.s and M.A.s aside, what can we say about the interdisciplinary scholarship of the 1990s and its reception by other departments in the university? Many would join John Schlegel in contending that nothing had changed since the 1980s and that law professors were mostly still "using" other disciplines badly (Schlegel 1995, 257; 1996, 981), while humanists and social scientists remained disdainful. They would maintain that legal scholarship emerged from its encounters with other disciplines largely untouched,[35] and perhaps that clinical education is "the only innovation" that has even begun to take hold in American law schools since Langdell (McKay 1977, 995).

My own opinion is different. Call me an optimist, but I saw law professors making genuine progress toward a disciplined interdisciplinarity in the 1990s—an interdisciplinarity that recognizes their location in the law school may compel them to ask questions other academics do not (Kalman 1996, 224).[36] At least, I saw law professors taking what historians said about nuance and evidence more seriously than they ever had (see, e.g., Symposium 1999). Further, perhaps in part because legal scholars now acknowledged their purposes differ from ours (see, e.g., Sunstein 1995b), I discerned a far more welcoming attitude from other academics toward law-types in the 1990s than during the 1980s. At Yale, which has long produced a large number of the nation's law professors, law students and graduate students worked together during the last decade to put out the *Yale Journal of Law and Humanities*. As Hendrik Hartog put it recently: "Everyone is fascinated by law today (including lots of humanistic scholars who have never entered a law school) and disciplinary boundaries no longer work the way they once did. There are now people throughout the university who want to talk with us, work with us, play with us" (Hartog 1998, 394). Perhaps Hartog is more aware of this now that he has moved from a law school to a history department at a university without a law school. It still sounds right to me.

In my view, then, the situation at century's end was one in which law professors occupy a location similar to that they occupied at its beginning. The gap between law professors and other academics was narrower, that between law professors and the profession wider than during the 1930s or the 1980s. While medical schools moved away from the university in the era of cost containment and managed care as they became more dependent on clinical practice (Ludmerer 1999, 231, 335–37, 370–82), elite law schools embraced the university. In fact, as in the early twentieth century, but for different reasons, law professors seemed more a part of the university than they were part of their own profession.

This conclusion is both tentative and speculative, serving, in the end, only to remind us of how little we can claim with certainty about twentieth-century American law professors. Does that matter? Maybe not: to paraphrase Robert Stevens, those "who would seldom be caught with their footnotes down" cheerfully "substitute assumptions for evidence" when they discus law professors and their scholarship" (Stevens 1973, 552–53). Nevertheless, I believe we should combine forces to acquire more data about law professors. At the very least, the search for evidence could give us all—judges, lawyers, law professors, and other academics—the common cause we have so long lacked.

NOTES

1 Judge Edwards had made this complaint earlier (1988) and would continue to voice it (1993, 1994).

2 For the ABA president's complaint that no other profession operated "with so little connection between those who are practicing and those who are the gatekeepers of the profession," see D'Alemberte (1990, 53).

3 As Lawrence Friedman says, the charge that lawyers served "rich, evil clients rather than the public" is difficult to evaluate. "Most lawyers always served mainly themselves, next their clients, last of all their conception of that diffuse, nebulous thing, the public interest. No doubt the Wall Street lawyer sincerely felt he served God by serving Mammon and Morgan. Lawyers have to make a living" (Friedman 1985, 637–38).

4 The American Bar Association and U.S. Bureau of Education's 1891 survey of American law schools provides one indication of how slowly the case method spread across the country (American Bar Association and U.S. Bureau of Education 1999 [1893], 542).

5 At least at Harvard, law professors have been more highly paid than the liberal arts faculty since the nineteenth century (LaPiana 1994, 20; and see Carter 1987, 99). As Dean Thomas Swann told Yale University President Arthur Twining Hadley in 1920: "If we look at the facts we must recognize that the profession of law competes with law teaching, and consequently that a man of first rate ability trained in the law has a greater opportunity to earn money if he abandons teaching than has the historian or the classical scholar of equal ability" (Kalman 1986, 102; and see Johnson 1978, 131). It may even be that for some or all of the period, law professors were better paid than most practitioners. Reminiscing about his days as a student at the University of Illinois College of Law between 1947 and 1950, William Warren recalled that "[o]ur one concern was that there was so little economic opportunity in law practice that we saw ourselves as facing a lifetime of respectable penury. I was glad that I was going into law teaching where . . . I could expect a steady $3,600 a year, rain or shine" (1988, 221–22). Though I have always heard agreement with the portion of the stereotype placing law professors in the classroom less than other university professors, I have never been certain it was correct.

6 I regret that I have so little information about the relationship between law professors and scientists.

7 "We now live in a copycat world in which the limited goal of academic prestige seems to be the dominant value everywhere; this is so even in nearly all of the law schools operated under religious auspices, which might be thought to have a special mission. If elite schools go a particular route, it seems inevitable that nearly every university law school in the land will move or be moved in the same direction. There is now a national market for law teachers, and most new teachers attended one or another of the top-rated schools. Their ideas about teaching law and about legal education were formed at these schools; and their aspirations for a teaching career are not modeled along the lines of a Mr. Chips who devotes himself with great loyalty and dedication,

to students in a particular locale. Law teachers at nonelite schools who are shaped by the elite models will be moved in directions largely counter to the interests of their schools and students" (Cramton 1986, 13). Cramton's words may hold even truer for scholars at nonelite schools now that the job market in law teaching has become tight.

8 But see Schlegel 1985, 313: "[A]ny careful look at law professors as reformers finds them substantially to the right of even the now much maligned progressives."

9 For the purpose of this essay, legal realism began in 1926, with the Columbia Law School curriculum study, and ended in 1938, as the New Deal was coming to a close and as some of the most prominent realists, such as Charles E. Clark, William O. Douglas, and Jerome Frank, were about to receive federal judgeships. By legal realism, I refer not to a broad, frequently intellectually antiformalist and politically progressive movement, which arguably dates back to Holmes (see Fisher, Horwitz, and Reed 1993, xiii–xv, 3–4, 9, 16), but to the realists' attempt to apply some of sociological jurisprudents' insights and their own to legal education. Specifically, the realists sought to bring the social sciences to legal education and to reorient legal education along the lines of the "functional" approach, a term they used to stress the importance of classifying rules, principles, and concepts by factual, social, and economic as well as legal context. By incorporating other disciplines and by studying "law in action"—or, as they might have said, law in the context of its functions—they hoped to make law more efficient, predictable, and just (Kalman 1986, 43–44, 68, 101). I have elsewhere addressed some of the disagreements about defining realism, giving dates to the realist movement, and identifying the realists (Kalman 1997, 1556–60; 1996 13, 250 nn. 1–2).

10 Marshall's appointment was temporary, and it is unclear whether he resigned in protest, as the others did, was fired, or the term of his appointment expired.

11 As Dan Ernst reminds me, less elite lawyers with strong ties to the Democratic party were also miffed by the New Deal's subordination of patronage politics to the pursuit of the best-credentialed lawyers (see Kalman 1990, 32–33).

12 Cf. White (1972) (legal realism was the jurisprudential analogue of the New Deal) with Duxbury (1995, 155): "[W]hile legal realists such as Arnold, Frank, Oliphant, Clark, William O. Douglas and Felix Cohen may have flocked to Washington to work under Roosevelt, they did not necessarily take their realist ideas with them."

13 According to Twining, "lawyers wooed the social scientists before the latter were ready for them" (Twining 1973, 377). That seems to me to describe the situation in the 1930s more accurately than it does earlier decades.

14 "[N]o faculty, and, I believe, not one per cent of instructors, knows what it or they are really trying to educate for" (Llewellyn 1935, 653).

15 According to Stone: "Professor Black's mood is typical; his is the voice of a generation of law teachers who sense that something has gone wrong, that major change is coming, that they are caught up in it, and that they cannot control it" (Stone 1971, 506).

16 "By 'law-office' history, I mean the selection of data favorable to the position advanced without regard or concern for contradictory data or proper evaluation of the relevance of the data proffered" (Kelly 1965, 122 n. 13).

17 As Robert McKay observed in 1976: "The law schools have remained almost exclusively professional in tone, rejecting repeated attempts for the infusion of the social sciences and the humanities" (quoted in Gee and Jackson 1977, 875).

18 Writing in 1977, Gee and Jackson noted that the "interdisciplinarian" law professor remained subordinate to the "traditional legal scholar," with high grades, law review service, and prestigious clerkship experience (1977, 933–34).

19 But see Kronman 1981, 956–57 arguing that there is a "built-in tension" in law teaching "not present in many other university departments" and that the philosophy professor, for example, "does not experience a similar tension in his teaching, having as students only those who have chosen a life identical to his own or [undergraduates] who have not yet made any choice at all." Kronman argued this tension had become has become "pathological" (1993, 265).

20 According to Thomas Ehrlich (1972, 1176): "[M]any more law students than ever before view law school as their second choice. They would have gone to engineering schools or to Ph.D. programs in some other fields but for the perceived economic reality that those alternatives offer little promise of future employment."

21 Schlag 1990a; Symposium 1991. Most recently, Paul Kahn has attacked law professors' work for its normativity, arguing that Edwards and others are wrong in deriding contemporary legal scholarship for being overly theoretical and useless to practitioners. According to Kahn, "the problem is exactly the opposite. Theory has substantially failed to separate itself from practice. The reforms offered by legal theorists may often be impractical, but the central assumption of both the scholar and the lawyer-critic is that reform is the appropriate end of scholarship." Kahn argues that law is "the last area of heresy in the modern academy. . . . The fact that we continue to have on many campuses both a divinity school and a department of religion suggests the unease of allowing a theoretical discipline of religion to extend to Christianity itself. Yet in law, we have only the professional school, without any corresponding academic department" (Kahn 1999, 7, 4). As Austin Sarat points out, Kahn ignores the Legal Studies/Law and Society programs that exist on many campuses (Sarat 2000, 132). I find the assumption of a fundamental difference between departments of religion and divinity schools (and Kahn is hardly alone in comparing the law school to the divinity school) equally problematic. True, the law school resembles the divinity school in that many of its professors are trained practitioners. But the assumption that professors who teach religion outside divinity schools are somehow "neutral" and "objective" strikes me as odd. In the field of Old Testament, Jon Levenson points out, "the emergence of religion departments and Jewish studies programs and departments has further contributed to the dethronement of Christian theology, indeed *any* theology, as the organizing paradigm for the study of the Hebrew Bible." But as he also says, "[i]t is a rare scholar in the field whose past does not include an intense Christian or Jewish commitment" (Levenson 1993, 32, 30). Surely, at least occasionally, that commitment colors teaching and scholarship, even in a religion department. As Frank Michelman would remind us: "As usual, it all depends" (Michelman 1986, 75; see also Kugel 1990, 157, pointing out that most Bible courses, including those taught outside divinity schools, are "in fact exactly the sort of courses you would want to give to a young Protestant clergyman in order to prepare him or her to preach on a given biblical lesson strictly according to Luther's . . . program").

The more important point here, though, is that in legal scholarship, to date, at least, the critique of normativity has proven unsettling, but ineffective. "[I]n the typical 'job talk' . . . aspirants seeking positions in the legal academy routinely feel it necessary to offer proposals for legal reform that correct some deficiency identified in the main body of the talk. Few candidates dare to eliminate such a normative prescription, much less assert the irrelevance of normativity to successful legal scholarship" (Balkin and Levinson 1998, 986 n. 92).

22 See, e.g., Symposium 1985. Galanter and Palay (1991, 137–38) observe that while a generation ago it was "large-firm lawyers who embodied the professional ideal," they were now under attack for abandoning their duties as officers of the court to devote themselves to client interests; subordinating client interests to make money; and forsaking collegiality and self-government. It was not a pretty picture: "The relationship of the large firm to professionalism now seems quite problematic."

23 See, e.g., the remarks of University of Michigan Dean E. Blythe Stason on the occasion of the fiftieth anniversary of the *Michigan Law Review* in 1951–52: "There are four sections—Leading Articles, Notes and Comments, Recent Divisions, and Recent Legal Literature. These several subdivisions have contained many a legal nugget of practical value to the profession. Many hundreds of members of the bench and bar read the *Review* (perhaps several of the leading law reviews) just to keep abreast of professional developments" (Brown 1959, 352).

24 In the Reagan administration alone, Robert Bork, Pasco Bowman, Frank Easterbrook, Douglas Ginsburg, Richard Posner, Antonin Scalia, and Ralph Winter (Wilkinson 1993, 1663).

25 Sirico and Margulies noted a "substantial" decline in the Supreme Court's citation of legal scholarship between 1971–73 and 1981–83 (1986, 134–35).

26 For example, David Rabban, a law professor without a Ph.D., has revised our understanding of the birth of modern civil liberties in a book I wager any historian would be proud to have written (1997).

27 "At leading law schools it is not uncommon to have 25% of the faculty away for at least one semester of a school year," William Warren observes (1988, 224). "What was once stability is now chaos, and appointments committees spend a large percentage of their efforts just scouring the nation for visitors. When Harvard hires ten visitors the effect is not unlike the domino extravaganzas executed by Japanese students, and is eventually felt by Podunk U. which has to hire a downtown lawyer to handle the corporate tax course."

28 While observing "a persistent undercurrent [of] . . . concern" among legal academics about the influence of their work on "the development of the law," Judge Judith Kaye felt it prudent to remind the law professors "that scholarly law review articles going back more than half a century have been devoted to measuring the impact of scholarly law review articles" (1990, 1034).

29 Though Nussbaum does not talk about legal research that utilizes the Internet, she comments: "I have heard with tiresome regularity that junior person Z at school S is 'writing up a storm' and is 'extremely prolific.' Z should have been told to get some training and practice in writing, and not to publish anything at all until it is really finished. One really good article is worth vastly more than five overblown windy self-promoting articles" (1998, 262).

30 The ABA Task Force also suggested that Dean Robert McKay might have been "speaking prophetically" in 1990, when, after writing of the "sharply increased need for law-trained people in the major law firms," he observed that though it was "too much to say that the whole apparatus from legal education through every form of practice, depends on the large firm's somewhat uneasy structure . . . at least we can say that collapse or serious damage to that imposing structure would have serious implications for every element of the legal profession" (Report 1992, 83).

31 Some middle-tier law schools are using their faculty to capitalize on the need for lawyer services, displaying the kind of commercialism we see in modern medical schools (Ludmerer 1999, 340–43). For example, Chicago-Kent has a fee-generating clinic (Laser 1992). The University of Florida College of Law has embraced its dean's enjoinder in his "commercialist manifesto" to become entrepreneurial. It has established a Legal Technology Institute to sell, on a for-profit basis, legal technology to law firms, government agencies, courts, and other legal entities. It is also engaged in a project that "may become the poster child for unabridged commercial enthusiasm . . . active joint venturing with private law firms" through which firms can buy faculty members' time from the law school. Though its dean worries that "the academy will be fearful of change and threatened by entrepreneurial activity," he is convinced that "[w]ith judgment and good taste, every school can become a commercial and educational giant" (Matasar 1996, 807–8, 811). I wonder how the faculty reacts to such experiments.

32 I thank Bill LaPiana for reminding me of this point. For a devastating look at the contemporary law school hiring process from beginning through job talk through end, see Nussbaum 1998.

33 This figure includes everyone listed, though, including librarians, lecturers, and instructors.

34 At least one school that will surely hold out against this trend is the Massachusetts School of Law. For its scathing critique of legal education, which expands on that of Judge Edwards, see Report 1992.

35 Christopher Tomlins persuasively makes the case for this point (Tomlins 2000).

36 Here I agree with Richard Posner, who maintains we should both judge interdisciplinary scholarship "by its best rather than worst examples" and "consider whether legal scholarship would be enriched or impoverished if (to speak only of living nonyoung lawyers whose principal academic appointment is in a law school) such scholars as Bruce Ackerman, William Baxter, Robert Bork, Guido Calabresi, Ronald Dworkin, Frank Easterbrook, Robert Ellickson, Richard Epstein, William Eskridge, Marc Galanter, Mary Ann Glendon, Robert Gordon, Thomas Grey, Henry Hansmann, Morton Horwitz, Thomas Jackson, Duncan Kennedy, Anthony Kronman, Sanford Levinson, Saul Levmore, Catharine MacKinnon, Henry Manne, Frank Michelman, William Ian Miller, Martha Minow, John Noonan, George Priest, Matthew Spitzer, Cass Sunstein,

Roberto Unger, Robin West, G. Edward White, James Boyd White, and others almost too numerous to mention had either been deflected to other fields altogether or been apprenticed to Corbin, Wigmore, Williston, Prosser, or Scott" (Posner 1995, 98–99). My answer would be that not only legal scholarship but other disciplines as well have been enriched by the best of such scholarship. If I am right about the progress toward a more disciplined interdisciplinarity, Judge Edwards should be pleased. "My objection to so-called 'law-and' scholarship is not to the relevance of the 'ands' but to the idea that the 'ands' (as opposed to the 'law') will become the 'ends' of professional education," he emphasizes (Edwards 1994, 565).

REFERENCES

Abel, Richard. 1990. "Evaluating Evaluations: How Should Law Schools Judge Teaching?" 40 *Journal of Legal Education* 407–65.

Ackerman, Bruce. 1981. "The Marketplace of Ideas," 90 *Yale Law Journal* 1131–48.

Allen, Francis. 1977. "The New Anti-Intellectualism in American Legal Education," 28 *Mercer Law Review* 447.

———. 1983. "Legal Scholarship: Present Status and Future Prospects," 33 *Journal of Legal Education* 403.

———. 1988. "The Dolphin and the Peasant: Ill-Tempered, but Brief, Comments on Legal Scholarship." In *Property Law and Legal Education: Essays in Honor of John E. Cribbet*, ed. Peter Hay and Michael Hoeflich. Urbana: University of Illinois Press.

American Bar Association and U.S. Bureau of Education. 1999 [1893]. "Courses of Study in Law Schools in 1891." In Steve Shepard, *The History of Legal Education in the United States: Commentaries and Primary Sources*, vol. 1. Pasadena and Hackensack: Salem Press.

Arnold, Thurman. 1929a. "Judicial Councils," 35 *West Virginia Law Quarterly* 193–212.

———. 1929b. "Bar and Law School United for Research in West Virginia," 15 *American Bar Association Journal* 67–68.

Auerbach, Carl. 1970. "Perspective: Division of Labor in the Law Schools and Education of Law Teachers," 23 *Journal of Legal Education* 251–54.

Auerbach, Jerold. 1971. "Enmity and Amity: Law Teachers and Practioners, 1900–1922," 5 *Perspectives in American History* 551–601.

———. 1976. *Unequal Justice: Lawyers and Social Change in Modern America*. New York: Oxford University Press.

Austin, Arthur. 1998. *The Empire Strikes Back: Outsiders and the Struggle over Legal Education*. New York: New York University Press.

Ayer, Donald. 1993. "Stewardship," 91 *Michigan Law Review* 2150–62.

Balbach, Stanley. 1972. "Legal Education—The Lawyer's Responsibility," 58 *American Bar Association Journal* 600–603.

Balkin, J. M. 1996. "Interdisciplinarity as Colonization," 53 *Washington & Lee Law Review* 949–70.

Balkin, J. M., and Sanford Levinson. 1996. "How to Win Cites and Influence People," 71 *Chicago-Kent Law Review* 841–69.

———. 1998. "The Canons of Constitutional Law," 111 *Harvard Law Review* 63–1024.

Bard, R. L. 1989. "Advocacy Masquerading as Scholarship; or, Why Legal Scholars Cannot Be Trusted," 55 *Brooklyn Law Review* 853–62.

Barnhizer, David. 1989. "The University Ideal and the American Law School," 42 *Rutgers Law Review* 109–76.

Belz, Herman. 1969. "The Constitution in the Gilded Age: The Beginnings of Constitutional Realism in American Scholarship," 13 *American Journal of Legal History* 110–25.

———. 1971. "The Realist Critique of Constitutionalism in the Era of Reform," 15 *American Journal of Legal History* 288–306.

Bergin, Thomas. 1968. "The Law Teacher: A Man Divided against Himself," 54 *Virginia Law Review* 637–57.

Berle, A.A. 1933. "Modern Legal Profession," 9 *Encyclopedia of Social Sciences* 340–45.

Bhandari, Jagdeep, Nicholas Cafardi, and Matthew Marlin. 1998. "Who Are These People? An Empirical Profile of the Nation's Law School Deans," 48 *Journal of Legal Education* 329–64.

Black, Amy, and Stanley Rothman. 1998. "Shall We Kill All the Lawyers First? Insider and Outsider Views of the Legal Profession," 21 *Harvard Journal of Law and Public Policy* 835–60.

Black, Charles. 1970. "Some Notes on Law Schools in the Present Day," 79 *Yale Law Journal* 505–11.

Bloomfield, Maxfield. 1976. *American Lawyers in a Changing Society, 1776–1876*. Cambridge: Harvard University Press.

Borthwick, Robert, and Jordan Schau. 1991. "Gatekeepers of the Profession: An Empirical Profile of the Nation's Law Professors," 24 *U. Mich. J. L. Reform* 191–238.

Brown, Elizabeth Gaspar. 1959. *Legal Education at Michigan 1859–1959*. Ann Arbor: The University of Michigan Law School.

Burger, Warren. 1973. "The Special Skills of Advocacy: Are Specialized Training and Certification of Advocates Essential to Our System of Justice?" 42 *Fordham Law Review* 227–42.

Burke, Peter. 1993. *History and Social Theory*. Ithaca, N.Y.: Cornell University Press.

Cahn, Edgar, and Jean Camper. 1970. "Power to the People or the Profession?—The Public Interest in Public Interest Law," 79 *Yale Law Journal* 1005–48.

Campos, Paul, Pierre Schlag, and Steven Smith. 1996. *Against the Law*. Durham, N.C.: Duke University Press.

Carrington, Paul. 1992. "Butterfly Effects: The Possibilities of Law Teaching in a Democracy," 41 *Duke Law Journal* 741–803.

———. 1999. *Stewards of Democracy: Law as a Public Profession*. Boulder, Colo.: Westview Press.

Carrington, Paul, and Erika King. 1997. "Law and the Wisconsin Idea," 47 *Journal of Legal Education* 297–340.

Carter, W. Burlette. 1997. "Reconstructing Langdell," 32 *Georgia Law Review* 1–139.

Cavers, David. 1972. "'Non-Traditional' Research by Law Teachers: Returns from the Questionnaire of the Council on Law-Related Studies," 24 *Journal of Legal Education* 534–66.

Chused, Richard. 1988. "The Hiring and Retention of Minorities and Women on American Law School Faculties," 137 *University of Pennsylvania Law Review* 537–69.

Collier, Charles. 1991. "The Use and Abuse of Humanistic Theory in Law: Reexamining the Assumptions of Interdisciplinary Scholarship," 41 *Duke Law Journal* 191–273.

———. 1992. "Intellectual Authority and Institutional Authority," 42 *Journal of Legal Education* 151–85.

———. 1993. "Interdisciplinary Legal Scholarship in Search of a Paradigm," 42 *Duke Law Journal* 840–53.

Comment. 1962. "Ernst Freund—Pioneer of Administrative Law," 29 *University of Chicago Law Review* 755–70.

Comment. 1970. "The New Public Interest Lawyers," 79 *Yale Law Journal* 1069–1152.

Conard, Albert. 1970. "Remarks on Induction to the Presidency of the Association of American Law Schools, December 30, 1970," 23 *Journal of Legal Education* 366–68.

Costello, John. 1975. "Another Visit to the Man Divided: A Justification for the Law Teacher's Schizophrenia," 27 *Journal of Legal Education* 390–417.

Cramton, Roger. 1986. "Demystifying Legal Scholarship," 75 *Georgetown Law Journal* 1–17.

Currie, Brainerd. 1955. "The Materials of Law Study, Part III," 8 *Journal of Legal Education* 1–78.

D'Alemberte, Talbot. 1990. "Law School in the Nineties: Talbot D'Alemberte on Legal Education," 76 *American Bar Association* 52–53.

D'Amato, Anthony. 1985. "Whither Jurisprudence?" 6 *Cardozo Law Review* 971–86.

Danner, Bryant. 1989. "Looking at Large Law Firms—Any Role Left for the Law Schools," 64 *Indiana Law Journal* 447–60.

Delgado, Richard. 1989. "Minority Law Professors' Lives," 24 *Harvard Civil Liberties–Civil Rights Law Review* 349–92.

Discussion on Critical Legal Studies at Harvard Law School, A. 1985. Presented by the Harvard Society for Law & Public Policy and The Federalist Society for Law & Public Policy Studies, May 13.

Dunn, Richard. 1969. "Legal Education and the Attitude of Practicing Attorneys," 22 *Journal of Legal Education* 220–26.

Duxbury, Neil. 1995. *Patterns of American Legal Thought*. Oxford: Clarendon.

Dworkin, Ronald. 1973. "Legal Research," 102 *Daedalus* (spring) 53–64.

Edwards, Harry. 1988. "The Role of Legal Education in Shaping the Profession," 38 *Journal of Legal Education* 285–92.

———. 1992. "The Growing Disjunction between Legal Education and the Legal Profession," 91 *Michigan Law Review* 34–78.

———. 1993. "The Growing Disjunction between Legal Education and the Profession: A Postscript," 91 *Michigan Law Review* 2191–2219.

———. 1994. "Another 'Postscript' to the Growing Disjunction between Legal Education and the Profession," 69 *Washington Law Review* 561–72.

———. 1997. "A New Vision for the Legal Profession," 72 *New York University Law Review* 567–77.

Ehrlich, Thomas. 1972. "Manners, Morals and Legal Education," 68 *American Bar Association Journal* 1175–77.

Ellickson, Robert. 1998. "The Market for 'Law-And' Scholarship," 21 *Harvard Journal of Law and Public Policy* 157–70.

Elson, Jon. 1989. "The Case against Legal Scholarship; or, If the Professor Must Publish, Must the Profession Perish?" 39 *Journal of Legal Education* 343–81.

Ernst, Daniel. 1993. "Common Laborers? Industrial Pluralists, Legal Realists, and the Law of Industrial Disputes, 1915–1943," 11 *Law and History Review* 59–100.

Estrich, Susan. 1986. "Rape," 95 *Yale Law Journal* 1087–1184.

Farber, Daniel. 1987. "Brilliance Revisited," 72 *Minnesota Law Review* 367–82.

Fetner, Gerald. 1977. "The Law Teacher as Legal Reformer: 1900–1945," 28 *Journal of Legal Education* 508–31.

First, Harry. 1979. "Competition in the Legal Industry (II): An Antitrust Analysis," 54 *New York University Law Review* 1049–1130.

Fisher, William. 1991. "The Development of Modern American Legal Theory and the Judicial Interpretation of the Bill of Rights." In *A Culture of Rights: The Bill of Rights in Philosophy, Politics, and Law—1791 and 1991,* ed. Michael Lacey and Knud Haakonsen. Cambridge: Cambridge University Press.

Fisher, William, Morton Horwitz, and Thomas Reed. 1993. *American Legal Realism.* New York: Oxford University Press.

Fitzpatrick, James. 1989. "Legal Future Shock: The Role of Large Law Firms by the End of the Century," 64 *Indiana Law Journal* 461–71.

Flaherty, Martin. 1995. "History 'Lite' in Modern American Constitutionalism," 95 *Columbia Law Review* 523–90.

Fordham, Jefferson. 1971. "Eight Years of Challenge and Development in the Life of the Association of American Law Schools," 24 *Journal of Legal Education* 94–105.

Fossum, Donna. 1980a. "Law Professors: A Profile of the Teaching Branch of the Legal Profession," 1980 *American Bar Foundation Research Journal* 501–54.

———. 1980b. "Women Law Professors," 1980 *American Bar Foundation Research Journal* 903–14.

Frank, Jerome. 1933a. "What Constitutes a Good Legal Education?" 19 *American Bar Association Journal* 723–28.

———. 1933b. "Why Not a Clinical Lawyer School?" 81 *University of Pennsylvania Law Review* 907–23.

———. 1947. "A Plea for Lawyer-Schools," 56 *Yale Law Journal* 1303.

———. 1951. "Both Ends against the Middle," 100 *University of Pennsylvania Law Review* 25–47.

Frankfurter, Felix. 1930. *The Public and Its Government.* New Haven, Conn.: Yale University Press.

———. 1999 [1915]. "The Law and the Law Schools." In Steve Shepard, *The History of Legal Education in the United States: Commentaries and Primary Sources,* vol. 1. Pasadena and Hackensack: Salem Press.

Frickey, Philip. 1988. "Constitutional Scholarship: What Next?" 5 *Constitutional Commentary* 67–68.

Fried, Barbara. 1998. *The Progressive Attack on Laissez Faire: Robert Hale and the First Law and Economics Movement.* Cambridge: Harvard University Press.

Friedman, Lawrence. 1985. *A History of American Law.* New York: Simon and Schuster.

———. 1986. "The Law and Society Movement," 38 *Stanford Law Review* 763–80.

Furner, Mary. 1993. "The Republican Tradition and the New Liberalism." In *The State and Social Investigation in Britain and the United States,* ed. Michael Lacey and Mary Furner. Cambridge: Cambridge University Press.

Galanter, Marc, and Mark Alan Edwards. 1997. "Introduction: The Path of the Law *Ands,*" 1997 *Wisconsin Law Review* 374–87.

Galanter, Marc, and Thomas Palay. 1991. *Tournament of Lawyers: The Transformation of the Large Law Firm.* Chicago: University of Chicago Press.

Garret, Michael, and Jean Pennington. 1971. "Will They Enter Private Practice?" 57 *American Bar Association Journal* 663–66.

Garth, Bryant. 1989. "Legal Education and Large Law Firms: Delivering Legality or Solving Problems," 64 *Indiana Law Journal* 433–445.

Garth, Bryant, and Joanne Martin. 1993. "Law Schools and the Construction of Competence," 43 *Journal of Legal Education* 469–509.

Garth, Bryant, and Joyce Sterling. 1998. "From Legal Realism to Law and Society: Reshaping Law for the Last Stages of the Social Activist State," 32 *Law & Society Review* 409–71.

Gawalt, Gerard. 1984. *The New High Priests: Lawyers in Post Civil War America.* Westport, Conn.: Greenwood Press.

Gee, E. Gordon, and Donald Jackson. 1977. "Bridging the Gap: Legal Education and Lawyer Competency," 1977 *Brigham Young University Law Review* 695–990.

Glendon, Mary Ann. 1994. *A Nation of Lawyers: How the Crisis in the Legal Profession Is Transforming American Society.* New York: Farrar, Straus and Giroux, 1994.

Goebel, Julius. 1955. *A History of the School of Law of Columbia University.* New York: Columbia University Press.

Gordon, J. Cunyon. 1993. "A Response from the Visitor from Another Planet," 91 *Michigan Law Review* 1953–69.

Gordon, Robert. 1975. "Introduction: J. Willard Hurst and the Common Law Tradition in American Legal Historiography," 10 *Law & Society Review* 9–55.

———. 1983. "The Independence of Lawyers," 68 *Boston University Law Review* 1–83.

———. 1984. "The Ideal and the Actual in the Law: Fantasies and Practices of New York City Lawyers, 1870–1910." In G. Gawalt, *The New High Priests: Lawyers in Post Civil War America,* 51–74. Westport, Conn.: Greenwood Press.

———. 1993. "Lawyers, Scholars, and the Middle Ground," 91 *Michigan Law Review* 2075–2112.

Graff, Gerald. 1987. *Professing Literature: An Institutional History.* Chicago: University of Chicago Press.

Green, Mark. 1970. "Law Graduates: The New Breed," 210 *The Nation* (June 1) 658–60.

Harno, Albert. 1980. *Legal Education in the United States.* Westport, Conn.: Greenwood Press.

Hartog, Hendrik. 1994. "Snakes in Ireland: A Conversation with James Willard Hurst," 12 *Law and History Review* 370–90.

———. 1998. "Editorial Advisory Board Note," 10 *Yale Journal of Law & Humanities* 392–94.

Hay, Peter, and Michael Hoeflich, eds. 1988. *Property Law and Legal Education: Essays in Honor of John E. Cribbet.* Urbana: University of Illinois Press.

Hetrick, Carl, and Henry Turner. 1973. "Politics and the American Law Professor," 25 *Journal of Legal Education* 342–59.

Hirshman, Linda. 1990. "The Virtue of Liberality in American Communal Life," 88 *Michigan Law Review* 983–1084.

Hofstadter, Richard. 1955. *The Age of Reform: From Bryan to F.D.R.* New York: Vintage.

Hohfeld, Wesley. 1914. "A Vital School of Jurisprudence," 14 *AALS Handbook* 76–139.

Hovenkamp, Herbert. 1990. "The First Great Law & Economics Movement," 42 *Stanford Law Review* 993–1058.

Hull, N.E.H. 1990. "Restatement and Reform: A New Perspective on the Origins of the American Law Institute," 8 *Law and History Review* 55–96.

———. 1997. *Roscoe Pound and Karl Llewellyn: Searching for an American Jurisprudence.* Chicago: University of Chicago Press.

Hutchins, Robert Maynard. 1934. "The Autobiography of an Ex-Law Student," 1 *University of Chicago Law Review* 511–18.

Jarvis, Robert. 1999 [1988]. "Why Law Professors Should Not Be Hessian-Trainers." In Steve Shepard, *The History of Legal Education in the United States: Commentaries and Primary Sources*, vol. 2. Pasadena and Hackensack: Salem Press.

Jaworski, Leon. 1972. "President's Page," 58 *American Bar Association Journal* 325.

Johnson, Alex. 1993. "Think Like A Lawyer, Work Like a Machine: The Dissonance between Law School and Law Practice," 64 *Southern California Law Review* 1231–60.

Johnson, William. 1978. *Schooled Lawyers: A Study in the Clash of Professional Cultures.* New York: New York University Press.

Kahn, Paul. 1999. *The Cultural Study of Law: Reconstructing Legal Scholarship.* Chicago: University of Chicago Press.

Kalman, Laura. 1986. *Legal Realism at Yale, 1927–1960.* Chapel Hill: University of North Carolina Press.

———. 1990. *Abe Fortas: A Biography.* New Haven, Conn.: Yale University Press.

———. 1996. *The Strange Career of Legal Liberalism.* New Haven, Conn.: Yale University Press.

———. 1997. "Eating Spaghetti with a Spoon," 49 *Stanford Law Review* 1547–82.

Kalven, Harry, and Hans Zeisel. 1966. *The American Jury.* Chicago: University of Chicago Press.

Katzman, Martin. 1968. "There Is a Shortage of Lawyers," 21 *Journal of Legal Education* 169–76.

Kay, Herma Hill. 1991. "The Future of Women Law Professors," 77 *Iowa Law Review* 5–18.

Kaye, Judith. 1989. "One Judge's View of Academic Law Review Writing," 40 *Journal of Legal Education* 313–21.

Kelly, Alfred H. 1965. "Clio and the Court—An Illicit Love Affair," 1965 *Supreme Court Review* 119–58.

Kennedy, Duncan. 1970. "How the Law School Fails: A Polemic," 1 *Yale Review of Law and Social Action* 71.

Kerber, Linda. 1988. "Making Republicanism Useful," 97 *Yale Law Journal* 1663–72.

King, Donald. 1999. *Legal Education for the 21st Century.* Littleton, Colo.: Fred B. Rothman & Co.

Kissam, Philip. 1986. "The Decline of Law School Professionalism," 134 *University of Pennsylvania Law Review* 251–324.

Kronman, Anthony. 1981. "Foreword: Legal Scholarship and Moral Education," 90 *Yale Law Journal* 955–69.

———. 1993. *The Lost Lawyer: Failing Ideals of the Legal Profession.* Cambridge: Belknap Press of Harvard University Press.

Kugel, James. 1990. "The Bible in the University." In *The Hebrew Bible and Its Interpreters,* ed. William Propp, Baruch Halpern, and David Noel Freedman. Winona Lake, Ind.: Eisenbrauns.

Lacey, Michael, and Mary Furner, eds. 1993. *The State and Social Investigation in Britain and the United States.* Cambridge: Cambridge University Press.

Lacey, Michael, and Knud Haakonsen, eds. 1991. *A Culture of Rights: The Bill of Rights in Philosophy, Politics, and Law—1791 and 1991.* Cambridge: Cambridge University Press.

LaPiana, William. 1994. *Logic and Experience: The Origin of Modern Legal Education.* New York: Oxford University Press.

Laser, Gary. 1992. "Educating for Professional Competence in the Twenty-First Century: Educational Reform at Chicago-Kent College of Law," 68 *Chicago-Kent Law Review* 243–90.

Lasson, Kenneth. 1990. "Scholarship Amok: Excesses in the Pursuit of Truth and Tenure," 103 *Harvard Law Review* 926–50.

———. 1994. "On Letters & Law Reviews: A Jaded Rejoinder," 24 *Connecticut Law Review* 201–6.

Lasswell, Harold, and Myres McDougal. 1943. "Legal Education and Public Policy: Professional Teaching in the Public Interest," 52 *Yale Law Journal* 203–95.

Leff, Arthur. 1987. "Law And," 97 *Yale L. J.* 989–1011.

Leiter, Brian. 1992. "Intellectual Voyeurism in Legal Scholarship," 4 *Yale Journal of Law and and Humanities* 79–104.

Leonard, James. 1990. "Seein' the Cites: A Guided Tour of Citation Patterns in Recent American Law Review Articles," 34 *St. Louis University Law Journal* 181–239.

Leuchtenburg, William E. 1995. *The FDR Years: On Roosevelt and His Legacy.* New York: Columbia University Press.

Levenson, Jon. 1993. *The Hebrew Bible, The Old Testament, and Historical Criticism: Jews and Christians in Biblical Studies.* Louisville: Westminster/John Knox Press.

Llewellyn, Karl. 1930. "A Realistic Jurisprudence—The Next Step," 30 *Columbia Law Review* 431–65.

———. 1931. "Book Review," 31 *Columbia Law Review* 729–32.

———. 1935. "On What Is Wrong with So-Called Legal Education," 35 *Columbia Law Review* 651–78.

Ludmerer, Kenneth. 1999. *Time to Heal: American Medical Education from the Turn of the Century to Managed Care.* New York: Oxford University Press.

Matasar, Richard. 1996. "A Commercialist Manifesto: Entrepreneurs, Academics, and Purity of the Heart and Soul," 48 *Florida Law Review* 781–811.

Mazor, Lestor. 1972. "The Materials of Law Study: 1971." In *New Directions in Legal Education,* ed. Herbert Packer and Thomas Ehrlich. New York: McGraw-Hill.

McGee, Henry. 1969. "Universities, Law Schools, Communities: Learning or Service or Learning and Service," 22 *Journal of Legal Education* 37–47.
McGonagle, John. 1970. "New Lawyers and New Law Firms," 56 *American Bar Association Journal* 1139–44.
McKay, Robert. 1977. "Law Schools, Lawyers, and Tightly Closed Circles," 1977 *Brigham Young University Law Review* 991–96.
Merritt, Deborah, and Barbara Reskin. 1997. "Sex, Race and Credentials: The Truth about Affirmative Action in Law Faculty Hiring," 97 *Columbia Law Review* 199–247.
Meserve, Robert. 1972. "President's Page," 58 *American Bar Association Journal* 887, 972.
Michelman, Frank. 1986. "The Supreme Court 1985 Term, Foreword: Traces of Self Government," 100 *Harvard Law Review* 17–77.
Minow, Martha. 1987. "Law Turning Outward," 73 *Telos* 79–100.
Morris, Richard. 1930. *Studies in American Legal History, with Special Reference to the Seventeenth and Eighteenth Centuries*. New York: Columbia University Press.
Nader, Ralph. 1969. "Law Schools and Law Firms," *The New Republic,* 11 October, 20–23.
Nelson, William E. 1982. "Standards of Criticism," 60 *Texas Law Review* 447–93.
Nussbaum, Martha. 1993. "The Use and Abuse of Philosophy in Legal Education," 45 *Stanford Law Review* 1627–45.
———. 1998. "Cooking for a Job," 1 *Green Bag* (2d Ser.) 253–64.
O'Brien, David. 1999. "The Great Judicial Stall," *Los Angeles Times,* 5 September, M1.
Oliphant, Herman. 1928a. *Summary of Studies in Legal Education by the Faculty of Law of Columbia University School of Law*. New York: Columbia Law School.
———. 1928b. Letter to Harlan Fiske Stone, June 16, 1928. Harlan Fiske Stone Papers, Library of Congress.
Packer, Herbert, and Thomas Ehrlich, eds. 1972. *New Directions in Legal Education*. New York: McGraw-Hill.
Polenberg, Richard. 1997. *The World of Benjamin Cardozo*. Cambridge: Harvard University Press.
Posner, Richard. 1981. "The Present Situation in Legal Scholarship," 99 *Yale Law Journal* 1113–28.
———. 1987. "The Decline of Law as an Autonomous Discipline: 1962–1987," *Harvard Law Review* 100:761–80.
———. 1993a. "Legal Scholarship Today," 45 *Stanford Law Review* 1647–58.
———. 1993b. "The Deprofessionalization of Legal Teaching and Scholarship," 91 *Michigan Law Review* 1921–28.
———. 1995. *Overcoming Law*. Cambridge: Harvard University Press.
———. 1997. "Roundtable Discussion: The Future of Law and Economics: Looking Forward," 64 *University of Chicago Law Review* 1129–65.
Post, Robert. 2001. "The Supreme Court Opinion as Institutional Practice: Dissent, Legal Scholarship, and Decisionmaking in the Taft Court," 85 *Minnesota Law Review* 1267–1390.
Pound, Roscoe. 1906. "Speech," 29 *American Bar Association Reports* 395–417.
———. 1908. "Mechanical Jurisprudence," 8 *Columbia Law Review* 605–23.
———. 1910. "Law in Books and Law in Action," 44 *American Law Review* 15–36.

———. 1911. "The Scope and Purpose of Sociological Jurisprudence," 24 *Harvard Law Review* 591–619.

———. 1912. "The Scope and Purpose of Sociological Jurisprudence," 25 *Harvard Law Review* 140–68, 489–516.

———. 1913. "Courts and Legislation," 7 *American Political Science Review* 361–83.

Priest, George. 1983. "Social Science Theory and Legal Education: The Law School as University," 33 *Journal of Legal Education* 437–41.

———. 1989. "The Increasing Division between Legal Practice and Legal Education," 37 *Buffalo Law Review* 681–83.

Propp, William, Baruch Halpern, and David Noel Freedman, eds. 1990. *The Hebrew Bible and Its Interpreters*. Winona Lake, Ind.: Eisenbrauns.

Purcell, Edward. 1969. "American Jurisprudence between the Wars: Legal Realism and the Crisis of Democratic Theory," 75 *American Historical Review* 424–46.

———. 1973. *The Crisis of Democratic Theory: Scientific Naturalism & The Problem of Value*. Lexington: University Press of Kentucky.

Rabban, David. 1997. *Free Speech in Its Forgotten Years*. Cambridge: Cambridge University Press.

Reed, Alfred Z. 1972. "Training for the Public Profession of the Law." In *New Directions in Legal Education,* ed. Herbert Packer and Thomas Ehrlich. New York: McGraw-Hill.

Rehbinder, Manfred. 1972. "The Development and Present State of Fact Research in Law in the United States," 24 *Journal of Legal Education* 567–89.

Rehnquist, William. 1987. "The Legal Profession Today," 62 *Indiana Law Journal* 151–57.

Report. 1992. *The Deeply Unsatisfactory Nature of Legal Education Today: A Self-Study Report on the Problems of Legal Education and on the Steps the Massachusetts School of Law Has Taken to Overcome Them*. Amherst: The Massachusetts School of Law.

Report and Recommendation of the Task Force on Lawyer Competency: The Role of the Law Schools. 1979. Chicago: American Bar Association. (Cramton Report)

Report of the Task Force on Law Schools and the Profession: Narrowing the Gap, Legal Education and Professional Development—An Educational Continuum. 1992. Chicago: American Bar Association. (MacCrate Report)

Robson, John. 1970. "Private Lawyers and Public Interest," 56 *American Bar Association Journal* (April) 332–34.

Rose, Jonathan. 1999. "Law after Society," 24 *Law & Social Inquiry* 143–94.

Ross, Dorothy. 1991. *The Origins of American Social Science*. New York: Cambridge University Press.

———. 1994a. *Modernist Impulses in the Human Sciences 1870–1930*. Baltimore: Johns Hopkins University Press.

———. 1994b. "Modernist Social Science in the Land of the New/Old." In Ross, *Modernist Impulses in the Human Sciences 1870–1930*. Baltimore: Johns Hopkins University Press.

Rubin, Edward. 1988. "The Practice and Discourse of Legal Scholarship," 86 *Michigan Law Review* 1835–1905.

———. 1997. "Law And and the Methodology of Law," 1997 *Wisconsin Law Review* 521–65.

Rudd, Millard. 1972. "The Burgeoning Law School Enrollment," 58 *American Bar Association Journal* (February) 146–48.

Saks, Michael, Howard Larsen, and Carol Hodne. 1996. "Is There a Growing Gap among Law, Law Practice, and Legal Scholarship? A Systematic Comparison of Law Review Articles One Generation Apart," 30 *Suffolk University Law Review* 353–77.

Sarat, Austin. 2000. "Redirecting Legal Scholarship in Law Schools," 12 *Yale Journal of Law and Humanities* 129–50.

Savoy, Paul. 1970. "Towards a New Politics of Legal Education," 79 *Yale L. J.* 444–504.

Schlag, Pierre. 1990a. "Normative and Nowhere to Go," 43 *Stanford Law Review* 167–91.

———. 1990b. " 'Le Hors de Texte, C'est Moi': The Politics of Form and the Domestication of Deconstruction," 11 *Cardozo Law Review* 1631–74.

Schlegel, John. 1979. "American Legal Realism and Empirical Social Science: From the Yale Experience," 28 *Buffalo Law Review* 465.

———. 1985. "Between the Harvard Founders and the American Legal Realists: The Professionalization of the American Law Professor," 35 *Journal of Legal Education* 311–25.

———. 1995. *American Legal Realism and Empirical Social Science*. Chapel Hill: University of North Carolina Press.

———. 1996. "Talkin' Dirty: Twining's *Tower* and Kalman's *Strange Career*," 21 *Law & Social Inquiry* 981–1000.

"Scholarship Admired." 1991. 103 *Harvard Law Review* 2085–86.

Seavey, Warren. 1950. "The Association of American Law Schools—In Retrospect," 3 *Journal of Legal Education* 153–73.

Segal, Bernard. 1969a. "President's Page," 55 *American Bar Association Journal* (September) 847, 857.

———. 1969b. "President's Page," 55 *American Bar Association Journal* (December) 1103.

———. 1970. "President's Page," 56 *American Bar Association Journal* (August) 715, 734.

Seligman, Joel. 1978. *The High Citadel: The Influence of Harvard Law School*. Boston: Houghton Mifflin.

Shamir, Ronen. 1995. *Managing Legal Uncertainty: Elite Lawyers in the New Deal*. Durham, N.C.: Duke University Press.

Shapiro, Fred. 1985. "The Most-Cited Law Review Articles," 73 *Cal. L. Rev.* 1540–54.

———. 1991. "The Most-Cited Articles from the *Yale Law Journal*," 100 *Yale Law Journal* 1449–1514.

———. 1996. "The Most-Cited Law Review Articles Revisited," 71 *Chicago-Kent Law Review* 751–79.

Shepard, Steve. 1999. *The History of Legal Education in the United States: Commentaries and Primary Sources*. 2 vols. Pasadena, Calif. and Hackensack, N.J.: Salem Press.

Simon, William. 1985. "Babbitt v. Brandeis: The Decline of the Professional Ideal," 37 *Stanford Law Review* 565–89.

Simpson, A.W.B. 1981. "The Rise and Fall of the Legal Treatise," 48 *University of Chicago Law Review* 632–79.

Sirico, Louis, and Jeffrey Margulies. 1986. "The Citing of Law Reviews by the Supreme Court: An Empirical Study," 34 *UCLA Law Review* 131–47.

Starr, Paul. 1982. *The Social Transformation of American Medicine*. New York: Basic Books.

Stefanic, Jean. 1992. "The Law Review Symposium Issue: Community of Meaning or Re-Inscription of Hierarchy?" 63 *University of Colorado Law Review* 651–81.

Stein, Robert. 1980. *In Pursuit of Excellence: A History of the University of Minnesota Law School*. St. Paul, Minn.: Mason Publishing Company.

Stevens, Robert. 1971. "Two Cheers for 1870: The American Law School," 5 *Perspectives in American History* 405–548.

———. 1973. "Law School and Law Students," 59 *Virginia Law Review* 551–707.

———. 1983. *Law School: Legal Education in America from the 1850s to the 1980s*. Chapel Hill: University of North Carolina Press.

Stolz, Preble. 1973. "The Two-Year Law School: The Day the Music Died," 25 *Journal of Legal Education* 37–46.

Stone, Alan. 1971. "Legal Education on the Couch," 85 *Harvard Law Review* 392–441.

Sunstein, Cass. 1995a. "Tanner Lectures on Human Values (a portion of which were published under the title 'Incompletely Theorized Agreements')," 145 *Harvard Law Review* 1733–72.

———. 1995b. "The Idea of a Useable Past," 95 *Columbia Law Review* 601–8.

Swygert, Michael, and Jon Bruce. 1985. "The Historical Origins, Founding, and Early Development of Student-Edited Law Reviews," 36 *Hastings Law Journal* 739–91.

Symposium. 1985. "The Law Firm as a Social Institution," 37 *Stanford Law Review* 271–659.

———. 1991. "The Critique of Normativity," 139 *University of Pennsylvania Law Review* 801–1075.

———. 1996a. "Law and Economics and Law and Society," 1996 *Wisconsin Law Review* 375–565.

———. 1996b. "Trends in Legal Citations and Scholarship," 71 *Chicago-Kent Law Review* 743–1013.

———. 1997. "The Future of Law and Economics," 64 *University of Chicago Law Review* 1129–1224.

———. 1999. "Moments of Change: Transformation in American Constitutionalism," 108 *Yale Law Journal* 1917–2349.

Tomlins, Christopher. 2000. "Framing the Field of Law's Disciplinary Encounters: An Outside Narrative," 34 *Law and Society Review* 911-67.

Tong, Gao. 1999. "A Comparison of Chinese and U.S. Legal Education." In D. King, *Legal Education for the 21st Century*. Littleton, Colo.: Fred B. Rothman & Co.

Trillin, Calvin. 1984. "A Reporter at Large: Harvard Law," 60 *The New Yorker* (25 March) 53–84.

Tsuk, Dahlia. 1996. "Between Critique and Reform—Felix Cohen on the Indian Question." Unpublished manuscript.

Tushnet, Mark. 1979. "The Dialectics of Legal History," 57 *Texas Law Review* 1295–1305.

———. 1981. "Legal Scholarship: Its Cause and Cure," 90 *Yale Law Journal* 1205–23.

———. 1988. "Constitutional Scholarship: What Next?" 5 *Constitutional Commentary* 28–32.

Twining, William. 1967. "Pericles and the Plumber," 83 *Law Quarterly Review* 396–426.

———. 1973. *Karl Llewellyn and the Realist Movement*. London: Weidenfeld and Nicholson.

———. 1994. *Blackstone's Tower: The English Law School.* London: Sweet & Sons/Sweet & Maxwell.

Ulen, Thomas. 1997. "Firmly Grounded: Economics in the Future of Law," 1997 *Wisconsin Law Review* 433–63.

Van Caenegem, R. C. 1987. *Judges, Legislators and Professors: Chapters in European Legal History.* Cambridge: Cambridge University Press.

Vanderwicken, Peter. 1971. "The Angry Young Lawyers," 84 *Fortune* (September) 74–77, 125–27.

Veblen, Thorstein. 1918. *The Higher Learning in America*. New York: B.W. Huebsch.

"Waiting for Langdell II." 1996. Roundtable Discussion. In *Against the Law*, ed. Paul Campos, Pierre Schlag, and Steven Smith. Durham, N.C.: Duke University Press.

Warren, William. 1988. "Legal Education in the Time of John Cribbet." In *Property Law and Legal Education: Essays in Honor of John E. Cribbet,* ed. Peter Hay and Michael Hoeflich. Urbana: University of Illinois Press.

Wellington, Harry. 1987. "Challenges to Legal Education: The 'Two Cultures' Phenomenon," 37 *Journal of Legal Education* 327–30.

White, G. Edward. 1972. "From Sociological Jurisprudence to Realism: Jurisprudence and Social Change in Early Twentieth Century America," 58 *Virginia Law Review* 999–1028.

———. 1986a. "Felix Frankfurter, The Old Boy Network and the New Deal: The Placement of Elite Lawyers in Public Service in the 1930s," 39 *Arkansas Law Review* 631–67.

———. 1986b. "From Realism to Critical Legal Studies: A Truncated Intellectual History," 40 *Southwestern Law Journal* 831–43.

———. 1997. "The American Law Institute and the Triumph of Modernist Jurisprudence," 15 *Law and History Review* 1–47.

White, James. 1993. "Letter to Judge Harry Edwards," 91 *Michigan Law Review* 2177–90.

Williston, Samuel. 1940. *Life and Law: An Autobiography*. Boston: Little, Brown.

Wilkinson, J. Harvie. 1993. "Legal Education and the Ideal of Analytic Excellence," 45 *Stanford Law Review* 1659–69.

Winograd, Peter. 1973. "Law School Admissions: A Different View," 58 *American Bar Association Journal* 862–65.

"With the Editors." 1958. 71 *Harvard Law Review* vii-viii.

Woodward, Calvin. 1968. "The Limits of Legal Realism: An Historical Perspective," 54 *Virginia Law Review* 689–739.

The Twentieth-Century Discipline of International Law in the United States

David Kennedy

THINKING ABOUT INTERNATIONAL LAW AS A PROFESSIONAL DISCIPLINE

I WOULD LIKE TO TELL TWO stories about twentieth-century international law in the United States that diverge from the historical conventions of the discipline itself: a story about the transformation of the disciplinary vocabulary through successive waves of generational renewal, and a story about the projects pursued by people in the discipline that animated transformation of the broader vocabulary. These stories foreground the professional discipline in the intellectual and social history of the field, to pave the way for understanding the blind spots and biases that accompany disciplinary knowledge.[1]

The history of twentieth-century international law is more conventionally told as a movement of ideas—usually from nineteenth-century formalism about sovereignty to twentieth-century pragmatism—and as the proliferation of new institutional forms and sites for practice—from the great centralized intergovernmental institutions through the specialized agencies of the United Nations system to the more diverse contemporary array of judicial and nongovernmental bodies collectively often referred to as the "international community" or "civil society." The events referred to in these stories—expanded subject matter, new participants, new ways of thinking about sovereignty, new sites for practice—all happened, and they have been of great significance for the profession. From my point of view, however, the stories customarily woven from them are unsatisfying as history and do much to legitimate the discipline's impoverished vocabulary for thinking about international affairs.

These stories overemphasize the degree of change and the instance of novelty in the field, eliding the degree of continuity in the profession's lexicon. They underestimate the extent to which international law has renewed itself by transforming, without significantly departing from, its disciplinary vernacular. They repeatedly underestimate the degree of ambivalence within the field itself, both at particular moments and across the century. In this, these stories are not good history. But they are also bad histories with consequences—reinforcing, defending, apologizing for the participation of international lawyers in governance while discouraging inquiry into the limits of the international legal imagination. They underestimate the field's own dark side, its participation in the construction and defense of violence, parochialism, human rights violation, environmental spoliation, and international conflict of all types. They confuse expansion of the field itself with the achievement of progressive humanism, and they obscure the unfortunate political, social, and economic consequences of the profession's expertise for its practitioners and for those whose imaginations are limited by the taking of the profession's advice.

To correct for these deficiencies, I offer here two types of stories that foreground movements within the discipline itself, and I then suggest the types of blind spots or biases that might plague the discipline and that might be reinforced by these more conventional stories of its progress. Doing so requires a preliminary sense for what we mean by a "profession," a "discipline," or by a "professional vocabulary," "expertise," or "consciousness."

International law is often defined as a set of rules, doctrines, and institutions, perhaps as "the law that governs relations among states." Although this can be helpful, I am more interested in understanding international law as a lived professional practice, as an intellectual discipline, as the culture developed by international lawyers to speak about what they see as the political and social world around them.

I define international law as a group of people sharing professional tools and expertise, as well as a sensibility, viewpoint, and mission. Their disciplinary consciousness or lexicon is composed of typical problems, a stock of understood solutions, a vocabulary for evaluating new ideas, a sense about their own history, and a way of looking at the world. They launch projects of criticism and reform within and against this professional vocabulary. Of course their shared professional sensibility may differ across time, just as international lawyers in different countries may have rather different professional preoccupations or priorities.

Almost as a byproduct of their professional work, international lawyers have developed relatively stylized modes of criticism and reform that express what we interpret as a relatively continuous disciplinary character or style. Over the life of a discipline, common interpretive formulas or traditions emerge—what we often think of as "schools of thought"—that can remain stable for a long time, just as they can unravel.

A common disciplinary vocabulary like this can extend and reinforce the profession's accumulated knowledge about what works and what doesn't, which may be all to the good. But, of course, a disciplinary vocabulary can also have limitations, characteristic blind spots, and biases. A professional vocabulary can have unacknowledged bad effects when it legitimates, explains away, apologizes for, or simply distracts professional attention from injustice. Like other such professional vocabularies, the routine rhetorical practices of international lawyers can place those who use them in bad faith, uncomfortably stretched between what they in some sense know to be true or possible and what they can find words for at that moment within their professional vocabulary.

MAPPING A PROFESSIONAL VOCABULARY

There are no doubt lots of ways to map the vocabulary or expertise of a discipline like international law. One sort of map would stress the world views of participants in the field: what do they see, what do they worry about, what do they remember, how do they understand their history, where do they look for disciplinary inspiration, what do they want? In my own past work, I have tried to compare international lawyers to professionals in other related fields in precisely this sense. We can make a quick comparison:

Public international lawyers look out at the world and see states. They worry about how law will be possible among sovereigns; they remember wars and understand their history as progress from sovereign autonomy to international community, from formal rules to pragmatic principles and institutions. They look to political science for inspiration, and they want improved global governance.

International economic lawyers look out and see buyers and sellers hoping to trade. They worry about the myriad risks of transacting internationally, particularly those caused by governments; they remember the Great Depression and understand their history as progress toward ever lower tariff barriers and an ever more flexible legal/institutional structure for trade bargaining. They look to economics for disciplinary inspiration and they want an ever more reliable free trade regime.

Comparative law professionals look out at the world and see different legal cultures, made up of national systems at different functional stages of development. They worry about professional parochialism and understand their history as a march toward greater knowledge about the influences, similarities, and differences among cultures and developmental phases. They look to sociology or anthropology for inspiration, they eschew any direct hand in governance, and they want greater understanding.

This sort of map may be helpful in identifying the professional blind spots and biases born of specialization. International lawyers in the United States make a particularly interesting discipline for inquiry of this type because they have been relatively isolated from the broad movement of ideas in American law, from the practice of statecraft and the disciplines of the foreign policy intelligentsia, and from their international law counterparts in other countries. To understand the history of the discipline, of course, we need a map that is far more sensitive to relations among disciplines in a particular place and to the relationships between people working within the field and the broader intellectual, political, and social terrain of their society. I have tried to make maps of this sort—intellectual sociologies, if you like; they tend to get really complex really fast, and I won't attempt one here.

Yet another sort of map, however, is more important to the story of disciplinary transformation I would like to tell here. It focuses on developments *within* the field's vocabulary of disputation. This sort of map requires some historical investigation and enough disciplinary continuity to trace changes in a common vocabulary. In mapping the history of international law's vocabulary, I have persistently been struck by the reappearance of classic debates, tensions, and ambivalences that show no sign of resolution. At the same time, for all the diversity in political projects and ideologies represented in the field, international lawyers have for more than a hundred years shared a few basic commitments I would describe as "cosmopolitan," "liberal," and "humanitarian." It is impossible to evaluate the profession's century of achievement without coming to terms with the virtues and vices of both professional equivocation and the broader liberal cosmopolitan tradition to which this profession has been committed.

The ambivalence: it is customary in talking about the intellectual history of a legal field to treat doctrinal conclusions and institutional outcomes as slowly establishing a corpus of best practices or ruling precedents. There will always be paths not taken, of course, and questions that persist, but the point of the exercise is to document whatever clarity there might be about the rules that are in place and about the ups and downs of doctrinal clarity and institutional competence that have led to this point, on the broad understanding that the field is learning, maturing, coming into its own.

International legal histories of this type have generated a number of common assumptions about the field: that international law is predominantly about states and sovereignty, that its dominant interpretive method is rather formal compared to other fields, that consent lies at the heart of its binding force. That "it" is law rather than politics, and international rather than local. That its rules are public rather than private. That the field has progressed, just as international society has progressed, from a period of sovereign autonomy to one of international community, from a time of rules to a period of principles, from a law of doctrines to one of institutions, from governments roped together by treaties to an open-ended process of global governance, from a formal legal method to something more functional, modern, and pragmatic.

I am always struck by the extent to which this is not at all the whole story. For more than a century, international lawyers have imagined each new moment as the overcoming of sovereignty, formalism, autonomy, and politics and as the coming into being of law, pragmatism, and international community. More than a hundred years ago they were already proclaiming the arrival of institutions, pragmatism, community, and globalization. Yet that which has been thought finally overcome continually returns, not only as an evil foe, but also as a newly attractive reform. We need only think of the resurgence of formal attitudes toward law, in doctrines about territory (*uti possedetis*, for example) or in the increasing legalization of the world trading system, to realize that the triumph of antiformalism has been neither rapid nor complete. Indeed, it would be more accurate to say that the discipline sustains interest in these propositions with the deepest ambivalence.

Almost every basic doctrinal proposition in the field is now conceived in at least two voices—a voice of stability, associated vaguely with the past, and an updated or renewing or reform vision that is more complex, relevant, up to date. Looking back, we see a field with a double consciousness about its own materials. There are rules and exceptions, classic positions and new thinking, formal definitions and pragmatic solutions. The discipline is both tenaciously attached to the classic definition of international law as "law among sovereign states" and full of denunciations of international law's fetish-like attachment to states and to "sovereignty."

As a result, it is far more useful in reconstructing the field's intellectual history to identify the debates that continually preoccupy the field, rather than the stockpile of temporary and partial resolutions that litter the disciplinary landscape, and to focus on the voice of the professional that can bring these contradictory tendencies into harmony, at least temporarily, and can reframe particular choices as contributions to disciplinary progress.

More conventional histories of the field understate this ongoing ambivalence, often by spreading its elements out into a historical narrative. Thus, in the most classic and common example, one finds recognition of the enduring commitment to *both* formal sovereign entitlements *and* antiformal efforts to embed international law in a more multifaceted political structure repeatedly explained as the presence of "traditional" and "modern" elements. The more one gets into the materials, the less compelling this story of an incomplete break from the old to the new international law becomes. There were elements of what we would think of as antiformal ideas about sovereignty in the nineteenth century, and formalism remains a potent source of innovation and idealization for the discipline. It would be better to say there was a transformation in the way international lawyers understood the meaning and importance of their ambivalent commitments—a more extreme antagonism between the elements and a stronger practice of displacement and denial in their narration—that accompanied the fall into modernism at the start of the twentieth century.

As a result, we need to think further about the function—the ideological function, for want of a better term—of these conventional stories in the disciplinary vocabulary. It is as if one function of historical narration were quite straightforwardly to lessen awareness of the ambivalence of the field's ongoing commitments. As a result, some terms in the professional lexicon are certified as progressive and community-oriented, others as regressive holdouts for a more primitive world of sovereign autonomy. So long, for example, as formalism remains associated with the nineteenth century and is thought to have characterized a presocial international world of autonomous sovereigns, while antiformalism about sovereignty seems linked to twentieth-century reforms and the emergence of an "international community" for the discipline to interpret and manage, the profession has a sort of default reform proposal ready at hand—when in doubt, deformalize, denounce sovereignty, demand a law embedded in the political. The endurance of this sort of calcified reform imaginary in the discipline's expertise is hard to overestimate.

At the same time, the field also exaggerates the "reality" of the nineteenth-century system and the artificiality or constructed nature of the twentieth-century innovations. The old law was formal, but the old states were really states, real political actors. The new law is more embedded in social life, but its creatures—institutions, individuals, the apparatus of civil society—are constructs, its community an artifice of law. That this sort of thing might affect the way international lawyers see the world around them is easy to imagine. Picture international lawyers coming to the dispute between Israel and the Palestinian Authority, making every effort to achieve a neutral, detached, objective and even-handed attitude. They nevertheless might see two types of claims—formal demands for absolute sovereignty over this or that and more pragmatic demands for international recognition of overlapping competences—and might hear one type of claim as more primitive than the other. And they might see two types of claimants—the one a real, if rather new, state, the other an artificial creation of the international community itself. If you work for the Palestinian Authority and want to make a claim for absolute sovereignty over something, you can anticipate a problem being heard—you are yourself the creation of the modern pragmatic international community, and what you are demanding is not only retrograde, returning us all to an era of autonomous political units, but in some vague way incompatible with your own status. Israel, by contrast, need not claim sovereignty—it *has* sovereignty.

If we look back at international law in the twentieth century, we find this sort of thing going on quite a bit. The arrangement of terms within the professional vocabulary has an impact on the way international lawyers come to imagine the world for which they hope to provide the law. But international lawyers also share a more overt form of common professional consciousness.

The common vision: the most significant element in the international legal imagination is quite simple. When international lawyers look at the world it is self-evident that we have plenty of politics, but only very little law. The idea that we have plenty of law, a kudzu of procedures and norms beneath which only the most tenuous political culture can survive, is simply not on the table. This idea has all sorts of consequences for the field, setting in place a program to expand law and reduce politics, to tame the political with law, rather than the reverse. This program, in turn, has a number of elements: cosmopolitanism, liberalism, and humanism.

A hundred years ago "cosmopolitanism" was termed *l'esprit d'internationalité*. In the 1920s and 1930s, as again in the 1950s, it was reflected in an increasingly federalist interpretation of international organizations, and today it is visible as enthusiasm about "global governance." The idea here is commitment to the general, the global—and not the particular, the local, the cultural. As cosmopolitans, international lawyers are more concerned with the level at which solutions emerge or governance proceeds than with the details of those solutions or the distributive consequences of that governance. Where they govern, they aspire to do so with clean hands, detached from the messy business of arbitrating among political groups. This is an arms'-length government of adjudication and consensual dispute resolution.

The international legal vocabulary imports the problematic of liberal political theory into international affairs. The international lawyer looks out at the world and sees separate, autonomous communities ("states") struggling to relate to a hypothetical "world community," in which they can both remain free and come to be members themselves. International lawyers construct their field around the philosophical question: how is governance possible among free entities in a community? Since relations among states "are" political, and law "is" a national creation of the sovereign, it is difficult to build an international law. They experience this worry both as a philosophical problem to solve (how can there be law among sovereigns?) and as a practical challenge (what should we do next to strengthen law among states?). Like domestic liberal political theory, international law often explains the compatibility of freedom and constraint in contractual terms. At some times the international legal order has seemed a Benthamite machine for maximizing the happiness of the greatest number; at others it has been seen as a Kantian vehicle for protection of fundamental rights.

Liberalism has plenty of associations, and international lawyers have been drawn to all of them at one time or another: a left-of-center faith in the humanitarian potential of federal and universal government, a right-of-center belief in mercantilism and the pacific consequences of commercial freedom, a centrist commitment to technocratic and rational government. They have typically advocated moderate or intermediate solutions to problems of international governance; they have emphasized possible harmony of interests, rational governing techniques, the need to "balance" among opposed considerations, moderation in social reform, self-determination and participation by social groups in decision making.

International lawyers have seen themselves as an avant garde for peace, for social goals and humanitarian causes. The keys here are pragmatism, humanitarianism, functionalism, and universalism. International law, they feel, stands with peace, prosperity, and a forward-looking and pluralist global community, while "politics" is associated with war, with the collapse of commerce, with a primitive parochialism. They stress international law's social and emancipatory potential, its ability to express and further universal human needs/wants/natures/functions, rather than its potential for defending the aggressor or miscreant. They advocate arbitration to replace war, institutions for dispute resolution, and rationalist machinery for collective security, a benevolent and civilizing global governance system. In this they have been ardent reformers, of their discipline and of the world.

To sustain each of these elements—the priority of law over politics and of the global over the local, and the association of international law with humanism and liberalism—requires ongoing intellectual work. At the very least, any ambivalence within the disciplinary vocabulary on any of these points needs to be managed. If the materials with which the professional works foreground sometimes the legal and sometimes the political, a general story about the progressive movement from one to the other will be useful in maintaining a commitment to the omnipresence of the political and the need for law.

So far so good. But we also need also to explore, to map if you like, the vocabulary with which international lawyers have expressed these ambivalences and articulated this common vision. The vocabulary of their expertise, in which they express, formulate, and defend reforms. It is not surprising that as international lawyers have worked to build a legal system outside the state they have pursued issues that parallel the traditional forms of domestic law: legislation, administration, and adjudication. Their efforts to do this might be arranged on a spectrum that ranges from direct efforts to reproduce domestic legal forms and institutions among states to more indirect efforts either to build looser "functional equivalents" to domestic legal institutions or to reinterpret the conditions of statecraft as a more "primitive" version of national law (see fig. 1).

International lawyers have proposed a large number of different techniques

Figure 1. Building International Law

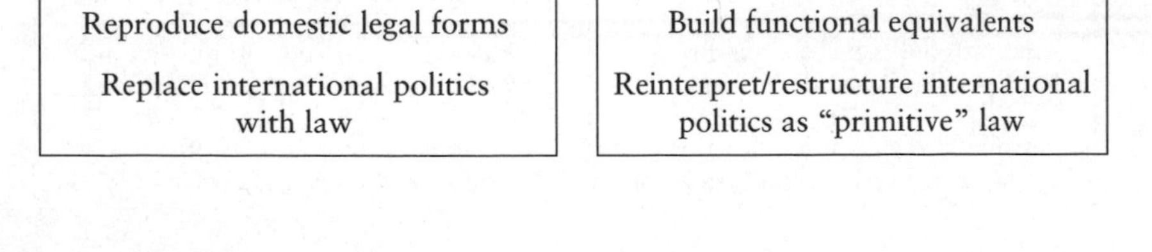

←	→
Reproduce domestic legal forms Replace international politics with law	Build functional equivalents Reinterpret/restructure international politics as "primitive" law

to build international law across this spectrum, covering all three types of legal/political authority: legislative, administrative, and adjudicative. The debates in each of these domains might also be arranged along a spectrum.

Legislation

Here we find work on "sources of law," on the best modes of legislation or codification, on the relative merit of treaty and custom or of rules and principles, and on the relationship between norm generation and enforcement. The spectrum would run from efforts to establish an international legislature with binding powers or to codify an international common law through to softer efforts to expand the domain of stable intersovereign expectations and habits that "function" as norms (see fig. 2).

Figure 2. Building International Legislative Capacity

←	→
Formal codification of law	Stable intersovereign expectations
Treaty	Custom – "soft law"
Rules / Rights	Principles
Norm generation	Norm enforcement
Legislature with binding powers	Plenary with political authority
Unanimity voting – one state one vote	Consensus or weighted voting

Administration

International lawyers (often in more or less strained partnership with the fields of "international institutions" and political science) have worked on the constitutional structure for international bureaucracy; on forms of leadership; on the construction, reform, coordination, and control of an international civil service. The enforcement arm for international law might also be either a

Figure 3. Building An Effective International Administration

←	→
Institutions	Organizations
Legal Personality	The instruments of members
Strong and autonomous civil service	Secondment / Civil servants as clerks
International law enforced through binding adjudication with penalties	Informal enforcement: information sharing to mobilize community shame
Collectively imposed sanctions	Rely on domestic institutions
Focus: Intergovernmental Institutions	Focus: NGOs and civil society

formal equivalent of the domestic state or a more primitive and decentralized functional equivalent based on the mobilization of shame and political pressure within the "international community" (fig. 3).

Adjudication

We find work structuring an international adjudicative process—rules about jurisdiction, enforcement of decisions, and so on. International lawyers speculate about what law might offer to the peaceful settlement of disputes, or about the relative merits of adjudication, arbitration, conciliation, and other dispute settlement formats (fig. 4).

Figure 4. Strengthening the International Judiciary

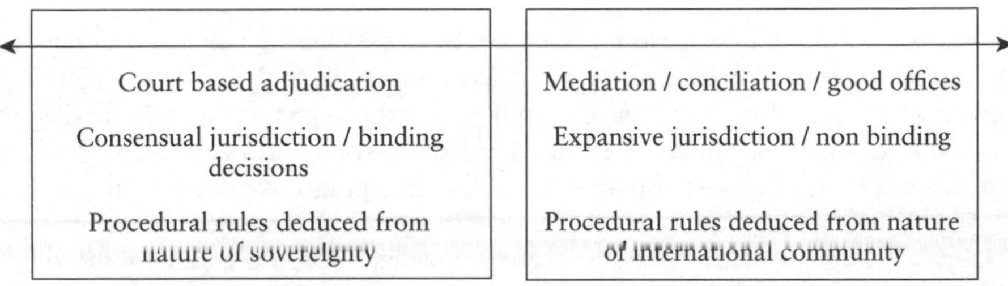

The terms within which these choices are debated are surprisingly consistent across the last century, and the pattern in these debates is also at odds with the idea that the choices are either pragmatic (what will work best in this context) or responsive to immediate historical developments (what will best catch this historical wave). To defend choices in the left-hand columns, international lawyers stress the importance of sovereignty, at least as a current reality, as well as the need to root international law firmly in the consent of sovereigns and the importance of establishing an international law distinct from political calculation. In defending choices in the right-hand columns, international lawyers have stressed the desirability of indirectly sneaking up on sovereignty. In this view, an international law more embedded in its political context will be more likely to dislodge sovereignty and will express more adequately the will of the current and future "international community."

One point stands out about this argumentative practice at this stage. International lawyers tend to defend and criticize relatively modest reforms—very minor movements along the spectrum—in extreme and hyperbolic terms. Think of legislative mechanisms, arrayed from very formal consent-based treaties to the quasi-legislative or persuasive force of "non-binding" agreements. Somewhere along this spectrum we would find people proposing to strengthen the persuasive power of, say, General Assembly recommendations, and people opposed to this idea. This quite modest alteration in the overall scheme of sources, as it is debated, seems to implicate all of the arguments for an embedded law, and all of those for an autonomous law. Proponents of one or the other side characterize the proposals, however "close" they might lie to one another on the spectrum, as implicating all the strengths and weaknesses of the opposite extreme.

The result is, as one might expect, often a great tempest in a teapot, as well as a tendency to disciplinary sectarianism. It would not be too much simply to describe the international lawyer's professional vocabulary as a stockpile of arguments for the hyperbolic defense of modest reforms. But it is nevertheless an exceedingly complex argumentative vocabulary—there are numerous ways of characterizing different reform projects along argumentative trajectories of this sort.

It is quite common, for example, to debate particular reform proposals by arguing about the appropriate boundaries for the discipline. How autonomous should international law be? Is it stronger when it embraces or when it shuns the political? The most basic mode of arguing for or against a given institutional or doctrinal possibility, whether macro ("norm building or administration?") or micro ("should *uti possedetis* trump self-determination in this case?"), is to cast the alternatives as bringing law closer to or further from politics, and then to treat the question as implicating the appropriate boundaries of the field. At this level the arguments for and against a more political international law are intensely familiar and easily presented as a story about progress. Either international law has been too far from politics and must move closer to become effective, or it has become dangerously intermingled with politics and must assert its autonomy to remain potent. Pretty much any choice from the left columns can be defended, relative to its partner on the right-hand side, by stressing the need to keep law pure of politics, just as any choice on the right side can seem a vehicle for merging international law more firmly into the political context. A very similar argumentative structure has developed around a series of boundary issues. For example, how closely should a public law external to states be modeled on national law? Should we be seeking to reproduce the functions of national public law or the forms of national private law or both? Arguments about relations with national law extend from "dualism" with its fully separate international and national legal orders on the left through to "monism," commingling the two legal regimes, on the right.

At one level, international law is not concerned with real people—it is concerned with real problems perhaps, but its agents, subjects, and objects are "states." Still, in pursuing this disciplinary identity, the field has been perennially enmeshed in relations with social movements of various sorts: the peace movement, the women's movement, the environmental movement, the human rights movement, the labor movement, the indigenous people's movement. But how far should this go?

Again, in arguing about the roles of individuals and non-state actors we find a continuum from thinking states the only proper subjects and sovereignty an on/off legal status, through to visions of multiple subjects and the idea of sovereignty as an artificial legal bundle of rights.

International law has seen itself as "public" law, about governing. But there is also a private international legal order, often deeply enmeshed in national law. We find a great deal of work on the "public" nature of international law and on the field's relations with the worlds of economics, the market, mercantilism, trade policy: in the left column, a sharply differentiated public and private law; in the right, a flexible governance partnership with economic law and institutions.

You get the idea. But there is no stopping here—we might continue this list and speak about relations with nationalism, with religion, with values, with the periphery, and so on. In each case we would find a spectrum of analogous arguments; from one universal to a more variable international law, from assimilation of the periphery into a universal humanism through to more normative flexibility and respect for local cultural or religious autonomy.

HOW CAN WE ORGANIZE THESE ARGUMENTS?

In arguing about the relations between international law and neighboring social spheres and in proposing or opposing particular institutional forms, international lawyers return repeatedly to two basic axes of philosophical disputation, each with its own well-developed vocabulary: the relationship law should seek to strike between an international community and sovereign autonomy, and the most effective balance between a more formal and a less formal law (figs. 5 and 6).

There is a relationship between these two primary vocabularies. As a starting point, we could say that international lawyers have predominantly associated sovereign autonomy with formal law and international community with antiformal law. They have tended to see movement from left to right on these spectra as progress—to think that we move from autonomy to community as we move from formal to pragmatic law. There has also always been a (less often voiced) counternarrative, however. Since late in the nineteenth century,

Figure 5. First Primary Spectrum

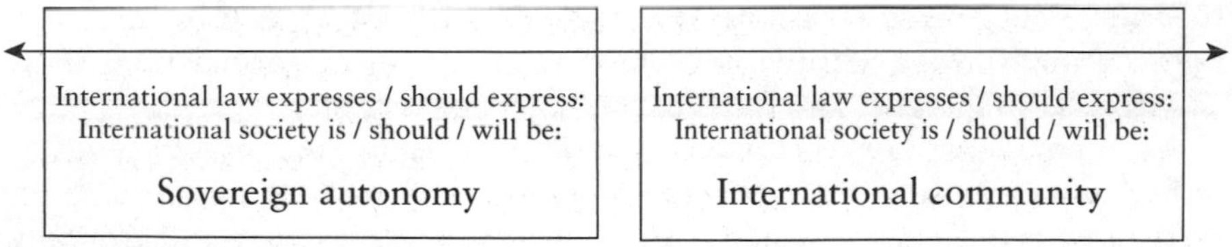

← International law expresses / should express: International society is / should / will be: **Sovereign autonomy**	International law expresses / should express: International society is / should / will be: **International community** →

Figure 6. Second Primary Spectrum

Formal International Law	Antiformal International Law
Sharp distinctions law / politics or national / international	Soft distinctions law / politics or national / international
Autonomous law based in consent	Embedded law based in value
Objective and scientific	Subjective judgment

international lawyers in a variety of places have stressed the centrality of the nation to international law's project and have seen movement to perfect the nation—in Italy, in Germany, but also through extension of the national form and the principle of national equality to extra-European societies in Asia and elsewhere, through self-determination and eventually decolonization—as forward progress from the more integrated, if haphazard and hegemonic, international system of the past.

In developing this story, the terms thought to convey differences along these continua may vary over time. At one point, the difference seemed well captured by the choice between rules, whether codified by treaty or by custom, and "general principles of law" or the new category of "soft law." At a later moment, after inquiry into the "sources of law" no longer seemed so foundational, the entire effort to generate norms—including both rules and principles—seemed to epitomize the left column, while international lawyers drawn to a less formal international law focused more on matters of policy, asking what arrangement fulfilled a desired political or institutional "function" best, rather than what arrangement was normatively persuasive. This sort of transformation has been common in international law across the century. We might represent this sort of change graphically as shown in figure 7.

This sort of transformation is possible because the terms that illustrate the spectrum can be interpreted to lie in various places along it relative to one another. At a more theoretical level, for some time the general difference between formal and informal attitudes about international law seemed captured by the difference between "positivism" and "naturalism." After theories about the nature of international legal obligation came to seem less important than theories about how international law could be most effective, those drawn to both naturalism and positivism seemed relatively more formal than those adopting a "pragmatic" or "functional" approach (fig. 8).

As international lawyers have argued about various reforms, it is unusual to find anyone close to the extreme end of either spectrum. If you thought the situation was and always would remain one of complete sovereign autonomy,

Figure 7. Second Primary Spectrum Revisited

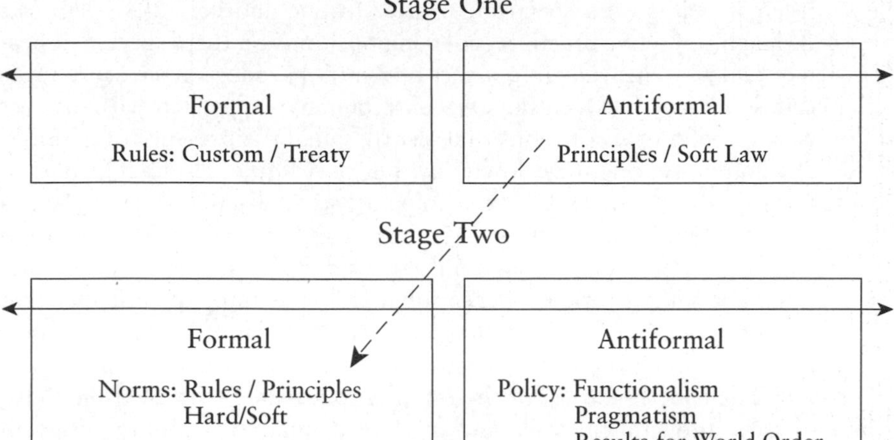

Figure 8. Second Primary Spectrum Revisited II

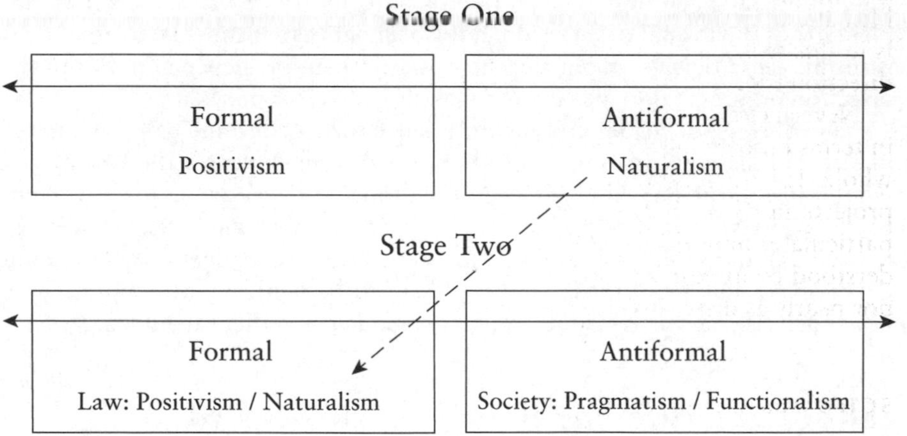

it would be difficult for you to imagine a role for international law. If you thought the international community had fully eliminated the sovereign state, it would be difficult for you to understand how the law that remained could be seen as "international." Being an international lawyer means seeking to bring autonomous sovereigns into community. Most everyone acknowledges the importance of both rules and broader principles; everyone sees a situation for both sovereign autonomy and international community. No international lawyer imagines law in mechanical terms, just as no international lawyer would see it simply as an expression of natural values or religious principles.

If you put these two points together—that no international lawyer is comfortable at the extremes and that particular positions can be reinterpreted to lie at different points on a spectrum relative to one another—the result is a very puzzling interpretive practice. Assessing positions on these spectra in progressive or ethical terms runs into a sort of Zeno's paradox. Since everyone is situated in some way between the extremes, one may approach without ever quite reaching rules or institutions that clearly signal the presence of an international community; one may downplay, but never quite eliminate, rules or institutions that seem to express the imperatives of legal form. Framing a choice between two arrangements—say, custom and treaty—in terms that implicate the larger issues of sovereign autonomy and international community or a formal and an antiformal international law runs into the difficulty that custom and treaty can often be recharacterized to lie elsewhere on the spectrum. Just when one has railed against custom for entrenching the politics of the past and defended treaties for their ability to legislate with the times, custom can seem altogether flexible and modern compared to the requirement that states reach formal consent before anything can be done—a formula guaranteed to produce vague political compromises rather than workable rules. It is a common experience that no sooner is a more functionalist/community-oriented solution reached than it finds itself open to criticism as emblematic of the formal order wedded to sovereignty that must be overcome. It is in this sense that we might say there is a deep ambivalence about both the direction progress takes and the terms with which it is marked.

Nevertheless, doctrinal and institutional reforms continue to be evaluated in terms of these broad arguments about their significance for the system as a whole. It is surprising how rarely international lawyers argue for particular projects in terms of the specific distributional or strategic consequences for particular groups that will result. At the same time, these general terms are understood by almost all those who use them to be neither entirely persuasive nor nearly as dispositive as the arguments made using them would suggest.

SCHOOLS OF THOUGHT IN INTERNATIONAL LAW

Since a wide range of large and small choices are framed to present these boundary issues, it comes as no surprise that international lawyers have repeatedly reflected on them in theoretical terms. To be a "school of thought" in international law means to have a relatively stable position on these broad theoretical questions. No one thinks these will ultimately be defensible positions. On the contrary, people in the field imagine that virtually all the possible positions are already on the table and have been found inadequate. Nevertheless, we are familiar with international lawyers who see autonomous sovereigns behind every bush, and others who see everywhere a community at work. Likewise we know those who think in terms of rules and worry about defending law's autonomy from subjective and political influences, and those who think about principles and policies and worry about ensuring law's links with its context.

Understanding a school of thought in the field means understanding that point on the continuum of different answers—all understood to be bad answers—toward which a given group gravitates. Do they tend to think of law in formal and autonomous terms, do they emphasize that law can only be built among sovereigns by consent, do they worry about diluting law's autonomous contribution to order by freighting it up with other issues and considerations? "Positivists." Do they think of law more fluidly, are they worried about values and context, do they stress the dangers of a law drifting free of the real world? "Naturalists." Do they fall someplace in between, is their instinct to split the difference, do they stress pragmatism over principle? The "eclectic" or "Grotian" tradition (fig. 9).

In traditional textbooks about international law these schools of thought are often introduced by listing ideas or propositions to which people in the schools are thought to adhere. It would be far more accurate to describe what it means to participate in a school of thought by focusing on a person's argumentative default position, his or her instinct in arguing about the field's central questions or basic doctrinal and institutional choices. A "positivist" will start off thinking about any of the choices we have looked at more sympathetic to the left-hand pole, will tend to see anyone less "positivist" than him- or herself as making the errors of the right-hand pole. For a naturalist, the reverse is true. It is not surprising that as argument about these matters goes on, more and more mainstream international lawyers resist identification as either positivists or naturalists, but see themselves instead as "Grotians," instinctively eclectic about all the choices we have looked at. Because all these "eclectics" continue to argue with one another by treating their opponent's position as if it implicated the dangers of an extreme that would give away the project of international law altogether, it is common to think *other* people belong to schools of thought and argue from belief while one's own position reflects a sensible analysis of a specific and nuanced situation.

In each period of renewal and consensus, the field has been arranged in

Figure 9. Some Conventional Schools of Thought about International Law

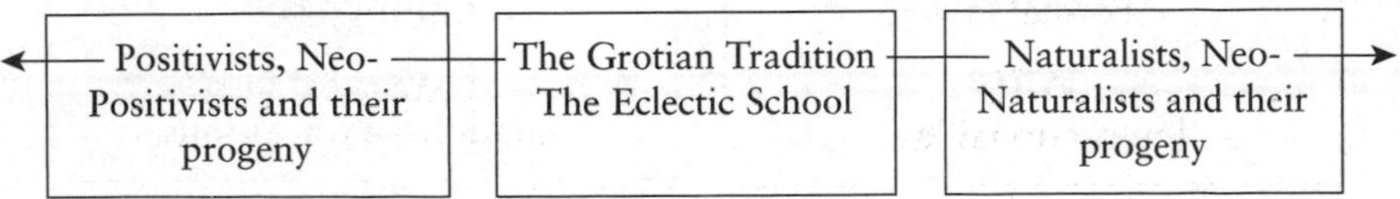

slightly different "schools of thought." During periods of disciplinary crisis the goal of intellectual work is often to rearrange and restabilize the intellectual terrain and the configuration of "schools of thought" is itself up for grabs.

Prior to the Second World War, the United States international law academy thought itself roughly divided into positivist and naturalist schools of thought. These schools were differentiated by their tendency to argue from the formal law and sovereign autonomy poles (positivists) and from informal law and sovereign community poles (naturalists) (fig. 10).

The consensus default during this entire period was toward the left end of both spectrums. It is in this sense that we can call this the age of positivism in international law. There were also dissident voices urging a less formal, more embedded law as both a better expression of political reality and an expression of a higher, more integrated international community. These voices were strongest in the anxious period just after the First World War, when the discipline was most resolute in rejecting the legacy of the Hague System seen to have failed in 1914. They were often associated in the United States with political science rather than law, with progressive Wilsonianism, with support for the League, and with interest in international organizations more generally. They were also strong in the Catholic tradition. Although they faded from the mainstream after the establishment of the Permanent Court and disillusionment with the League, they remained present as a kind of ethical and political counterpoint.

After the Second World War, the terrain changed dramatically. All of prewar international law was in disrepute after 1945—positivists in the United States had largely been isolationist, and the naturalist enthusiasts for the League seemed to have been altogether out of touch with the world of political possibility. Numerous efforts to criticize, reform, and renew the profession were launched in the late 1940s and 1950s. Only in the 1950s did a new consensus begin to emerge; it would last for more than thirty years.

Figure 10. Schools of Thought on American Law, 1925–1939

MAINSTREAM	COUNTERPOINT
Positivists	Naturalists
Sovereign autonomy	International community
Formal law	Informal law
PCIJ International law	League / ILO International relations

In a sense, it is correct to say that after the Second World War everyone was an eclectic, far more flexible in bringing to bear arguments from across the spectrum on any given doctrinal or institutional choice. But there was also a wholesale reorganization of the main intellectual commitments that defined "schools of thought" in the field. Beginning in the 1950s, most international lawyers in the United States rejected both naturalism and positivism in favor of a sensibility influenced by pragmatism, functionalism, American legal realism, and the American legal process school. By 1960, the postwar generation of international lawyers and academics had established two new schools of thought—both of them post-positivist and post-naturalist—between which the subsequent generation of international lawyers in the United States then arranged themselves.

At one end of the new spectrum was the Yale School, dominated first by Harold Laswell and then by Myres McDougal; at the other was the Columbia School, led by Louis Henkin and Oscar Schachter. Just as in the prewar discipline there was a mainstream and a counterpoint; the Columbia School became the mainstream, and the Yale School became the counterpoint.

The Yale School situated itself toward the policy end of the formal/informal law spectrum and toward the sovereign autonomy end of the sovereign autonomy/international community spectrum. The Yale scholars worked self-consciously in the tradition of American legal realism and were most insistent in their critique of formalism—as practiced by both naturalists and positivists. They introduced the word "policy" into the international law vocabulary as an alternative to norms—a category of judgment and political management that stood outside hard and soft law, rules, and principles. As they moved further toward the right side of the formal/antiformal axis, they were also acutely aware of scholars still further from legal form who had abandoned international law altogether for political science. They differentiated themselves from this new political science "realism" by stressing a commitment to *order* among sovereigns, to values and policies, rather than to a Hobbesian individualism among states. By 1960, the Yale School represented a solid alternative that was neither positivist nor naturalist—it combined a strong antiformalism with an insistence on "realism" about sovereign autonomy as the basis for world community. They had broken the link between antiformalism and prewar institutional idealism, as well as the link between sovereign autonomy and prewar formalism about norms.

At the same time, the Columbia School was moving in exactly the opposite direction. These scholars were also critical of prewar positivists—but for their emphasis on isolationism and sovereign autonomy, not for their commitment to norms. They were also post-realist scholars and had a healthy skepticism about the solidity of codification. Their commitment to norms celebrated principles as much as rules, soft law as much as hard, flexible as much as strict interpretation. For those in the Columbia School, the point was to build an international legal order focused on the institutions of the United Nations, to establish a normative fabric that could bridge the gap between East and West, and to establish a flexible institutional locus for decolonization and development in the Third World, outside the cold war divisions. This search for a humanist neutralism required norms—human rights norms, procedural norms, administrative law. Too much policy could easily jeopardize the search for a community acceptable to East, West, and South.

By 1960, the Columbia scholars represented a clear alternative to the Yale School, one that was also neither positivist nor naturalist in the prewar sense. They combined a weak antiformalism with a commitment to neutral norms and humanist institutions as law for the modern international community. They had broken the link between a formal commitment to norms and the insistence on sovereign autonomy that had characterized prewar positivism. But they had also broken the link between a commitment to international community and the idealism of prewar progressives and naturalists. We might illustrate this transformation as shown in figure 11.

This new arrangement lasted more than thirty years, until the end of the cold war in 1989. Since then, the field has been in a new period of anxiety and contestation. Early in this period of anxiety, there were fleeting efforts to revive the Yale School—symbol for a generation of a more flexible alternative to the disciplinary mainstream—just as there had been a variety of neonaturalist revivals in the 1940s. Most leading international lawyers under fifty in the United States, however, are now critical of both the Columbia and the Yale schools.

The field has become a center for political and intellectual contestation. There are military voices, economic voices, populist voices, conservative voices, post-Marxist voices, feminists, queer theorists, scholars whose formation was powerfully inflected by the lit/crit movement, the critical legal studies movement, by neoconservatism, and on and on. National differences are more pronounced—never has the United States international law tradition seemed so idiosyncratic, or been in such sustained methodological and political debate with international lawyers in other traditions.

And yet, although a new disciplinary consensus has not yet emerged, there are strong proposals on the table, both for a new mainstream consensus and for a set of methodological counterpoints. Despite the presence of dissident voices among the field's established players—people like Allott, Berman, Carty, Charlesworth, Chimni, Chinkin, Engle, Frankenberg, Hernandez, Koskenniemi, Langille, Mutua, Onuma, Paul, Tarullo, and Valdes—the beginnings of a new mainstream approach to the field are now visible, proposed largely by people in their forties under the rubrics of "transnational law," "the

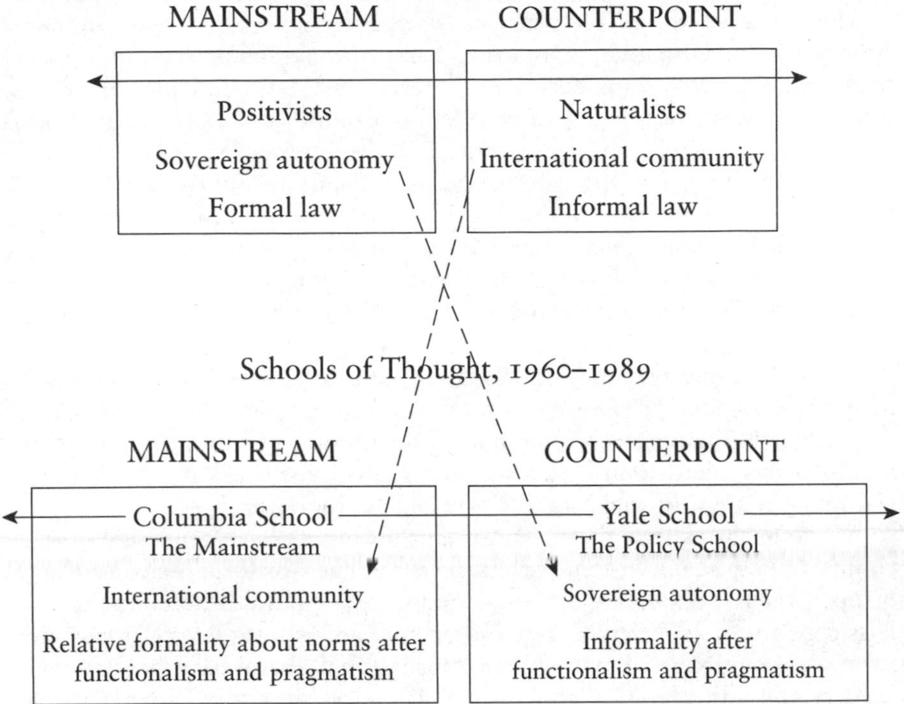

legal process," or "liberalism," terms they borrow from the scholarship of the last great period of anxiety in the 1950s.

These scholars, the leading "new" scholars of my generation—people like Koh, Slaughter, Alvarez, Kingsbury, and Teson—many of them my law school classmates, friends, and colleagues, urge movement toward a new understanding of international community and a new appreciation for an antiformalist international law. In the process, they reaffirm some of the field's most familiar and dogmatic propositions: that sovereignty has eroded, that international law should be understood politically, that the boundary between international and municipal law is porous, that international law may not be as universal as it pretends, that the international regime is better understood as a process or multilevel game than as government by legal norms. They have taken ideas that have been part of disciplinary common sense for a century—pragmatism, antiformalism, interdisciplinarity—and turned them into a fighting faith. This methodological self-confidence announces a political optimism: the end of the cold war will complete the internationalist project, inaugurating a humanitarian "civil society"—an "international community" that will dethrone the state, welcome wider participation, and open international law to the political.

The specific reform proposals on offer differ quite a bit—use domestic courts to enforce international norms, harmonize national regulations rather than seeking international norms, use international law principles to energize a broad coalition of nongovernmental organizations rather than rulemaking by intergovernmental agencies, reimagine the international judiciary as a player in a social game whose currency is legitimation—but the form in which they are presented is broadly similar. They urge greater disaggregation of international law, more reliance on national institutions, more blurring of the lines between law and politics and between national and international law than before. These new mainstream voices criticize the Columbia School for overestimating the role of rules and insist on a revitalized antiformalism. At the same time, however, they criticize the Yale School for straying too close to Morgenthau's political science of autonomous sovereigns. The idea is to break the association between the community orientation of the Columbia school and its overemphasis on rules, while at the same time breaking the Yale association between antiformalism and sovereign autonomy.

As we might expect, these mainstream proposals have generated a set of counterpoints, again written within the discipline's historic lexicon of arguments. Counterpoints have proposed themselves on both the left and the right. Dissident voices of both types coalesce around an insistence on relatively more formal conceptions of law than the transnational-liberal-legal-process mainstream, and rather more skepticism about the possibility of an international community.

Relative to the centrist proponents of "transnational" and "liberal" law, the new counterpoint positions stress the formality of entitlements and the autonomy of actors. On the center-right this comes from "public choice" scholars, often working in the neighboring field of international economic law, who model the emergence of institutional regimes on the basis of game theories rooted in the autonomy of decision makers and sympathetic to the possibility of a formal legal fabric. On the left, we find European scholars nostalgic for the legal culture of formalism and a range of scholars rethinking the field from the perspective of one or another "identity politics." To get purchase against the emerging transnationalist mainstream, these scholars stress the relative stability of their identity positions, for women, as people of color, as Latin Americans, gay and lesbian, indigenous or disabled people, or as Third World nationals, as well as the relative formality of entitlements necessary for their protection. These voices respond both to more extreme assertions of Third-World sovereign autonomy and to assertions of cultural relativism they fear would undermine their aspiration to universal human rights. These human rights enthusiasts have broken the link between relatively formal law and a universalist international community, and in that they have departed from even the Columbia School's mainstream enthusiasm for human rights. But they have also broken the link between a public order system based on the autonomy of actors and the antiformalism of the Yale School.

International lawyers in the United States are on the verge of revising the basic high-low arrangement of positions in their field for the second time since the end of the Second World War. We might chart this proposed reorientation of the field as shown in figure 12.

If we put these realignments together, we can trace changes in the disciplinary lexicon as successive generations rebuild the discipline's mainstream by rearranging central terms, borrowing from and criticizing earlier approaches

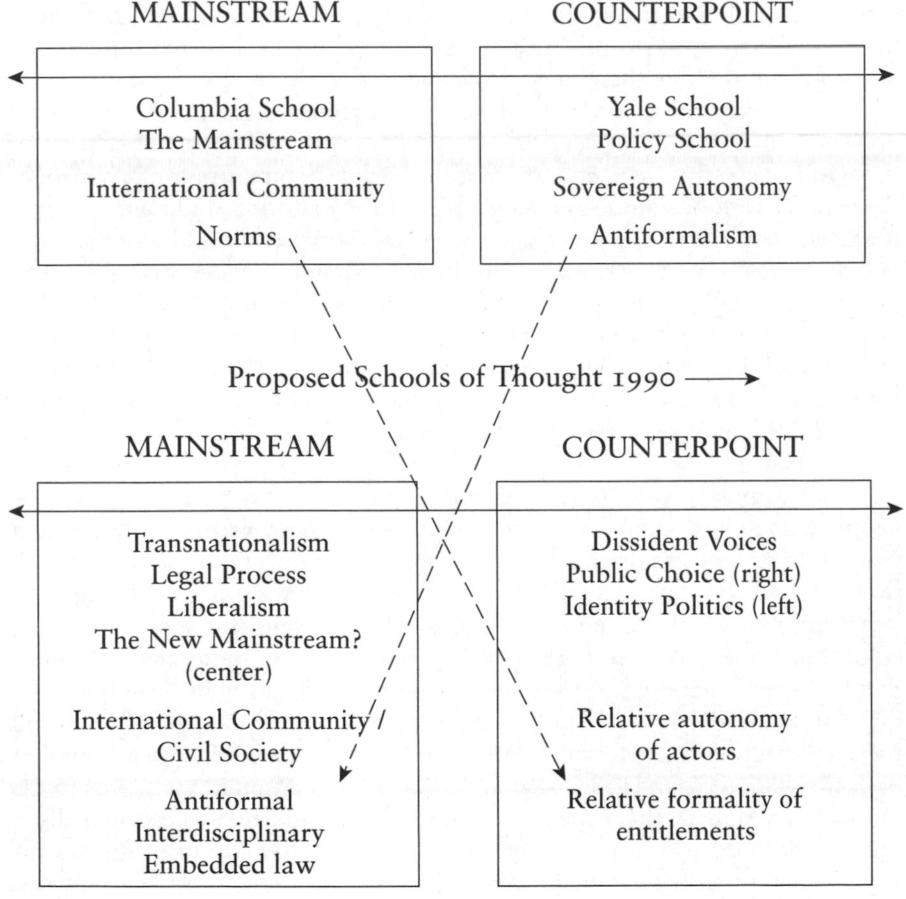

from both the mainstream and the more dissident counterpoint, and focusing attention on different threats external to the field.

BUT HOW DOES THIS VOCABULARY DEVELOP?

An elementary map of the discipline's ambivalences and commitments leaves more questions open than it answers. We should wonder if this vocabulary limits the international law professional in any significant way. An astonishing range of different phenomena have been understood in these terms over the last hundred and more years, and the vocabulary seems repeatedly to renew itself in the face of a postwar anxiety about new political and economic realities. But do the discipline's own reform ideas capture the full range of the politically possible? How compulsory is debate in these terms? Can renewing the field mean something other than a reorganization of this vocabulary? We need further research into the limits this vocabulary poses for the practical and political imagination of people in the profession (although I sketch some tentative suggestions along these lines at the end of this chapter).

It is also difficult to understand how this extremely plastic and repetitive professional vocabulary develops—why does one or another school of thought become the "mainstream," another only a "counterpoint?" Why does the arrangement of schools remain stable for long periods, and then reconfigure itself so dramatically in only a few years? Why, we should wonder, does one or another set of ideas within this broad vocabulary come to dominate at a particular time, and what animates movement among these ideas? The process by which a disciplinary vocabulary is used and transformed remains an extremely human one. Beyond the work of individuals responding to problems with good ideas, we have energy and passion, which can better be understood in the language of power and group struggle.

Of course it comes as no surprise that one set of ideas within a broad disciplinary vocabulary can come to dominate at a particular moment because people with that idea have institutional resources to devote to its implementation. If an American administration pumps money into international institutions to develop interest in the use of international law by national courts, or if a leading law school tenures scholars who promote interest in national courts, or if the American Society of International Law funds study of international law by national court judges, or if important journals have symposia on relations among national judiciaries in various countries—any of these will have an effect on the perceived plausibility of these ideas. We are all familiar with the work of foundations—from the Ford Foundation in the 1960s to the Olin Foundation in the 1990s—inflecting the agenda of professional disciplines. The international law discipline has its own odd lot of institutions scattered about, often with some power to dispense jobs, fancy certificates, visas, medallions and the like. If the United Nations sponsors symposia on Third World Approaches to International Law, or if UNESCO publishes books on the subject, the plausibility of these ideas will be affected. If the author of such a book becomes president of the World Court, some people will read the book, some will reject it, some may try to repeat the gesture, others treat it as spent. The ideas about international law popular at a given moment in some countries are more influential than those popular in others simply because some countries are more powerful. The effects of educational patterns in the metropolis on thinking at the periphery is no less pronounced today than a hundred years ago.

Power in this sense—money, access to institutional resources, relationship to underlying patterns of hegemony and influence—is central to the chance that a given idea will become influential or dominant within the international law profession. We need look no further than the extremely disproportionate effect of ideas developed in the United States since the Second World War. Struggle among individuals and groups over resources—institutional resources, prestige, the resources of perceived plausibility, disciplinary hegemony—and the processes by which these resources are allocated are better explanations for the dominance of some ideas at some times, and for transformations in the disciplinary vocabulary, than either the good-faith pragmatism of innovative individuals or the meritocractic allocation of resources by practitioners and institutions external to the field.

To understand this struggle we need a map of disciplinary groups parallel to our map of the disciplinary lexicon. As a starting point for such a mapping exercise, let me propose three basic sorts of group dynamics within the field of international law: those based on affinity for ideas, those based on professional and personal identity, and those based on struggle for domination.

Common Intellectual Projects and Ideas: The Dynamic of Commitment and Aversion

At the most overt level, many people in the field are animated by their fealty to a set of ideas. They do come to believe in the importance of various intellectual propositions about law or about international society, and they then develop projects to promote these commitments. They try to get other people to share their ideas and to forgo competing ideas. And, of course, people come to believe that other ideas are not as valid or important or useful as their own, and they develop aversions to projects that seem to express commitments with which they disagree. As particular doctrinal or institutional projects come to be associated with one or another of these ideas, those who share the commitment can sometimes be mobilized on its behalf, just as those who do not can often be mobilized against it. Sometimes groups sharing intellectual commitments or aversions develop projects to promote these commitments. It is also common, however, for groups formed on the basis of a shared professional identity or political project to seek allies on the basis of these shared intellectual commitments.

The most important idea around which international lawyers have organized themselves has been the discipline's own broad mission—to construct governance among states, to speak to power from a cosmopolitan point of view, to promote a broadly liberal and rationalist frame for understanding international affairs. Of course, particular groups of international lawyers experience this commitment differently. A group could form around the project of ensuring that little changes in international law, or that everything needs to be rethought for the discipline to survive. Each of the positions mapped in the professional lexicon has also, at one time or another, been the basis for shared commitment and aversion by some international lawyers. Rearranging the field's schools of thought, proposing a new mainstream or counterpoint arrangement of the disciplinary vocabulary—these are all projects of this type. Moreover, the discipline is intellectually and politically porous, so international lawyers in different countries are influenced by the intellectual styles and political preoccupations of the national elites within which they work, and the long march of the tendencies operates in international law as elsewhere.

Identity Groups: The Dynamic of Affiliation and Disaffiliation

If we thought of a professional discipline simply as a group of people sharing a common vision, project, or professional vocabulary, divided by intellectual orientations, commitments, and aversions, we would miss a great deal. The profession is also rife with sociological and political affiliations that are not experienced first as *intellectual* commitments. The field is animated by the seductive power of groups and individuals, as well as by the desires of many professionals to disaffiliate with one or another group of colleagues. Affiliations based on personal and professional identity affect the distribution of ideas in the field as profoundly as do shared intellectual commitments.

We are all familiar with the charismatic power strong teachers or professional leaders can exert on behalf of their methodologies. People can also be attracted or repelled by doctrinal or institutional projects—building courts, working with nongovernmental organizations—because they express particular professional identities: people who build bridges, or like to argue, or always look on the bright side, or like to feel that they are lighting a single candle. Some groups will seem "in" and some will seem "out" at particular moments. Some professional "voices" can seem more fun to speak than others—more sophisticated, more daring, safer, more committed, more powerful, more abject. Maybe the Yale people have all the fun, or the Columbia people are the really serious ones, or the formalists exude the pleasures of negation.

Professionals are often more ready to affiliate with those who share their disciplinary subspecialties and to disaffiliate from those in other departments. Like other fields, international law is also divided by generational affinities: people who remember the Second World War, who worked in European reconstruction, who were affected by Vietnam, who grew up with computers, and so forth. Among the strongest sources of professional identification are the links built through mentor-mentee relations. Like ethnic, class, gender, race, religious, national, or other strong identities within the broader political field, mentor-mentee relationships present, at a micro level, a somewhat independent field of life, of desire, affiliation, and alliance somewhere between the rationalist community and the ambitious individual. In launching projects or proposing intellectual commitments, it is often possible to find allies and enemies by tracing the links among mentees and mentors.

Pursuing Projects: The Will to Dominance and Submission

The discipline is more than groups of people with substantive commitments or professional identifications. The patterns of intellectual commitment and aversion and of professional affiliation and disaffiliation provide a context or terrain in which professionals can pursue projects of dominance and submission with other individuals and groups. New thinking emerges not simply as the result of a disinterested persuasion effort among identity constituencies in the field with different commitments; it is also the result of competition among constituencies within and outside the field for authority, recognition, prestige, and resources. Many such projects are simply the extension into action of an intellectual commitment or professional identity. Others express a will to power that arises outside these common professional characteristics. And the discipline has a will to power of its own, for itself as much as for its vision.

Moreover, although it is less often discussed in these terms, there is also a will to submit that will affect the distribution of ideas and resources in the discipline at any given time. The discipline as a whole may see itself paying fealty to other powers—to politics, say, or to economics. International lawyers may find congenial the role of servant to statecraft, voyeur of power, chronicler of politics, even powerless critic of power, and might be altogether uncomfortable if thrust into the driver's seat. And individual international lawyers may seek out the leadership of others in the profession, regardless of the particular commitments or identifications their projects entail, for the experience of following.

International lawyers often seem to oscillate between a will to rule and abjection in the face of what they interpret as power. Looking back on the field over a century, the disciplinary will to disengage from power is striking. International lawyers coming into the field after 1980, on the other hand, often experienced their elders as having submitted far too happily to a kind of disciplinary detachment from the foreign policy apparatus, and opposition to this willed submission became a force of its own, producing an intense energy to perform as macho and entitled to rule.

International lawyers also participate in a range of political projects outside the field of international law on the basis of their expertise and seek allies in the profession for these efforts. Such projects can be associated with the broad party politics of the society. International lawyers in the United States have been active in supporting both the Democratic and Republican parties, as well as in promoting particular factions within them—Rockefeller Republicans, Stevenson Democrats, and so on. It might make more sense to organize international law in the United States in terms of the political affiliations of its members than in terms of either its internal professional associations or its intellectual commitments. At the moment, American international lawyers on the right tend to be formalists about American sovereign prerogatives and strict interpreters of the commitments of foreign powers, particularly to respect property rights, and the prerogatives of international institutions, but very expansive and policy-oriented when it comes to interpreting restrictions on U.S. power abroad. American international lawyers on the left are more likely to be rule-oriented when it comes to American obligations and far less worried about the formalities of multilateral or international institutional initiatives. Political affiliations of this type contribute to the argumentative instability of the profession's intellectual terrain and to the general sense that everyone is an eclectic or post-intellectual pragmatist. Political efforts of all these types will influence the distribution of ideas and professional affiliations within the discipline.

Commitment, Affiliation, Domination, and the Distribution of Ideas

In mapping the influence of power on the distribution of ideas in a field, it can be helpful to separate these three dimensions—commitment, identification, and domination—for they can operate independently of one another. In the simple case, a person who seeks to make a project out of promoting international law seeks allies among those who share an intellectual commitment to this idea and who share professional identification with others in the field. He or she then seeks to dominate those within and without the field who are less enthusiastic about this project.

But we can easily imagine more complex cases. A person might seek to translate his or her commitment to an intellectual proposition—building courts is better than building administrative agencies—into action as a project by seeking the support of others with whom he or she shares other commitments or identifications. A person or group might seek power by transforming its professional identity—say, those who know about defense policy or appreciate political science—into an intellectual commitment for the field as a whole, and so on.

We are now in a position to supplement the traditional account of the distribution of ideas in the discipline. We began with the constraints of the professional lexicon itself, the language within which professionals pursue projects. Professionals also embellish and transform the discipline's basic arguments in the pursuit of projects, for which they seek allies and resources. We might think of the discipline as a kind of force field animated by some combination of these three elements (fig. 13). There is a common disciplinary mission, viewpoint, and vocabulary. International lawyers share a range of commitments and aversions to particular intellectual propositions within that vocabulary. They affiliate and disaffiliate from a variety of professional identities, some expressing commitments of the field, others provided by the context of their work or by their broader social context. Lawyers pursue projects, efforts to promote intellectual, political, or personal objectives, deploying their expertise in the discipline's vocabulary, seeking alliances with others on the basis of shared commitments, aversions, or affiliations. The status of forces among particular ideas, particular modes of criticism or reform, will often depend on the distribution of forces among groups whose projects, commitments, and affiliations seem implicated.

We should see disciplinary change, then, in at least two different registers—

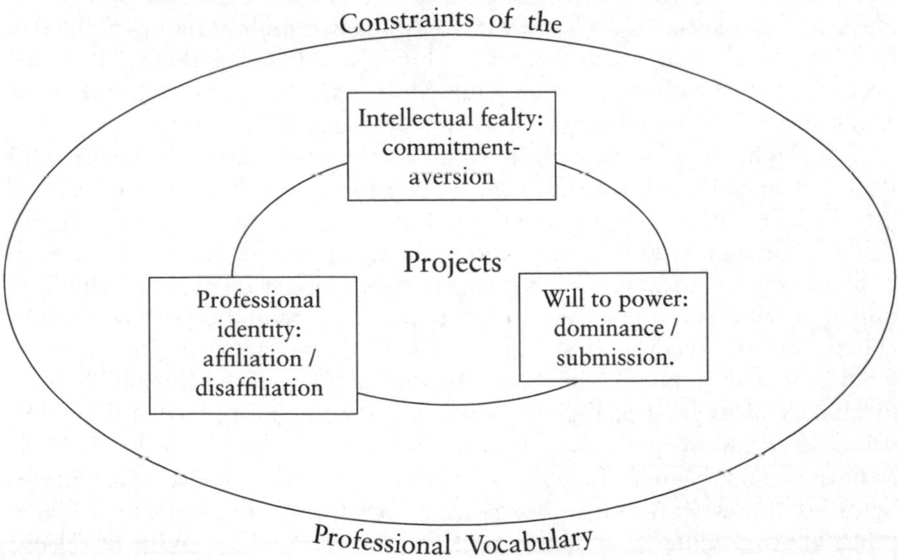

Figure 13

as a transformation in the professional vocabulary, and as a project of people located within the profession. I have looked in some detail here at changes in twentieth-century international law in the first register. Let me now look more briefly at one episode in that transformation as a set of projects pursued by a generation of people.

INTERNATIONAL LAW TODAY: ANXIETY AND THE SEARCH FOR A NEW CONSENSUS

The contemporary bid to establish a new consensus in the field and to end the post–cold war period of anxiety is not only a transformation of the field's professional vocabulary. It is also a product of various projects of affiliation and commitment by individuals and groups within the field. The transnational–legal process–liberalism proposals for a new consensus are all interesting, and many of the specific reform ideas being advanced as exemplars of this new vision may be great ideas. Given the plasticity of the justificatory vocabulary within which they are being proposed, I am confident that many could be implemented without consolidating the broader vision, just as the broad rearrangement of schools of thought being advocated could be achieved without implementing any of the particular reforms. Nevertheless, there are all sorts of alliances between those attached to particular reforms and these general ideas: those opposed to the ideas oppose reforms, reform opponents oppose the ideas, and vice versa. What is needed is a more basic understanding of the patterns of commitment, affiliation, and ambition within which these debates are occurring. Let me illustrate, at least in a loose way, the sorts of influences and engagements that would be part of such an account.

Scholars bidding for mainstream status customarily present dissensus in the field as "methodological." Although this formulation takes the emphasis off the struggle among affiliations and ambitions in the rearrangement of the field's intellectual terrain, it has a certain benign pluralistic feel. Given the arrival into the legal academy of various "methods" for studying law (feminism, policy science, political science, cultural studies, law and economics, public choice, literary theory), it is not surprising that methodological diversity would show up in international law. As long as the goal remains building the machinery of international governance, and the measure remains pragmatic use value, the more methods are brought to bear, the more tools we are likely to have in pursuing our disciplinary project. Of course, it is customary to recognize that these methods sometimes carry with them loose political affiliations, but these differences simply contribute to the field's pluralist or eclectic breadth. In my own experience, however, international lawyers are not blank slates, committed to a broad disciplinary objective and searching around for a useful method to get there. They are people with projects, commitments, and affiliations. They seek and reward allies, punish enemies, and contend with one another as if their differences mattered, both for the field and for themselves.

Proposals for a new consensus in the field uniformly present themselves as broad efforts to help the field achieve its broadest objectives, rather than as the projects of particular individuals or groups. They are so written that all professionals of good sense might share their commitments and affiliate with efforts to realize their implementation. Still, it is easy to distinguish among these scholars those with one or another more specific commitment or affiliation. There are people who want to promote international economic law as a field, who want to affiliate with law teachers in other "tougher" fields, who want to reinterpret international economic law as a somewhat public or constitutional legal order amenable to at least some socially responsible regulatory initiatives. Being seen to be a person who knows about economics or who consorts with law and economics scholars might well advance such a project. Similarly, there are people who want to redeem public international law as a possible partner in managing American foreign policy. To make it a worthy participant in statecraft, they feel they must demonstrate a certain hard-boiled understanding of power, and a rapprochement with the political scientists who have staffed the Democratic party foreign policy establishment might be a good strategy.

The same sort of interpretations might be made of those outside this new mainstream, among those who insist upon the formal entitlements and autonomy of national traditions as expressions of the field's own good sense. There are people who want to redeem the possibility of a Third-World nationalist position, who are drawn to affiliate with people involved in scholarly enterprises drawing on all sorts of postcolonial literary, historical, or cultural theory—not because of a clear idea about how such a "methodology" will advance international law, or even their particular project, but because the milieu seems a productive one for pursuing the project, filled with people with whom they seek affiliation. And there are people who were propelled by deracination to international law, only to begin working out their identity as Latino or Asian or Jewish or gay, and so on. We might recognize scholars opposing transnationalism–legal process–liberalism in the lexicon of "public choice" as vaguely right-of-center people, morally upright, tolerant but scandalized by the messy compromises and seamy deals of political life, who would be horrified by the idea of taking power in either a struggle of identities or a liberal governance regime, within the discipline or in the society. Rather than become a participant in a "regime," such a person might prefer to replace the corrupted world of politics with a more sensible and rational expertise. Where humanitarian values need protection, better a nice clean rule or right.

The most significant projects, affiliations, and commitments moving the international law profession at the moment are generational and political. Both are easy stories to sketch. The generational account picks up as the long engagement between my own generation and our predecessors ends. The displacement of the Yale-Columbia axis by the axis of support for and opposition to transnational–legal process–liberalism is an event in the development of ideas. But people in the field easily recognize it as also a generational phenomenon. The 1960–1989 generation was an extremely cohesive one that entered the field early in the Kennedy administration and only began to lose its grip after the elections of Reagan and Thatcher. Since the end of the cold war they have retreated with remarkable generosity and grace or have reinterpreted themselves as participants in a new generational wave of renewal and engagement for the field. The leaders in the field are now largely my contemporaries, whose formative experiences in the field came after the disappointments of 1968 and Vietnam. At the same time, the field is expanding rapidly, and a much larger and potentially more diverse generation is coming on the scene.

Generational change within a field is rarely smooth. A field can be dominated by people who understand themselves to be part of one generation for thirty or more years, and they can quite suddenly be displaced by another group of people who might differ in age among themselves by as much as twenty years but still see themselves as a single generation. In American international law, this has been extremely pronounced, providing an opportunity to examine how a generation coalesces, announces itself, and displaces its predecessor.

If we are to place this generational story in a social and political context, we might start with the observation that for international law in the United States the 1990s have been like the 1950s. There are certainly contextual similarities: long economic expansion, newly unchallenged global role, a period of national cultural retrenchment, reaffirmation of conventional "family values" against the periodic cycles of modernist sexual and political opening. International lawyers again find themselves defending the machinery of multilateralism against a conventional isolationism translated by hegemony into a unilateral internationalism. We find again a displacement of public law aspirations by the priorities of free-trade economic expansion on the one side, and a creeping tendency to idiosyncratic humanitarian interventions on the other. It is not surprising that we find leading international lawyers today returning also to the ideas and practices of the 1950s—antiformalism, legal process, transnationalism, universal humanism, embrace of international relations, postwar liberal triumphalism, worry about the viability of humanism in a divided and decolonizing world, talk about a liberal world public order, defense of the universal in human rights. For international law, the 1950s were also a time of disciplinary doubt, of postwar anxiety about the viability of collective security, multilateralism, even international law itself, in the new world of "totalitarianism," "ideology," and the cold war. The 1950s saw deep methodological division in the field as scholars trained in the world of cultural modernism, sociological jurisprudence, functionalism, and legal realism struggled to reinvent their field on these new terms in new conditions—people like Hans Morgenthau, Pitman Potter, Josef Kunz, Leo Gross, Hans Kelsen, Myres McDougal, and Philip Jessup.

It was only in the 1960s that a methodological and political consensus settled on the field: the internationalist liberalism of people like Richard Falk, Louis Henkin, Oscar Schachter, Tom Franck, Louis Sohn, and Abe Chayes who consolidated a new mainstream way of thinking against the backdrop of the Yale alternative. In a way, the old public international law simply foundered on the rocks of legal realism and policy science. The new generation hitched their wagons to the foreign policy of the Kennedy era, and to an American-style liberalism with an internationalist and cosmopolitan perspective, at first promised by Kennedy's New Frontier, then by Hammarskjöld's revitalized United Nations. As the liberal consensus on American internationalism dissipated, the field became increasingly marginal, isolated from both the cosmopolitanism of Republican free traders and the increasingly interventionist cold war liberalism of the Democratic party, in Vietnam and elsewhere. Their commitment to the formal rules necessary to criticize American hegemony or to build a regime of coexistence with the Soviet Union isolated them further from American legal scholars in other fields eagerly embracing the world of "policy." There was Ford, there were spurts of energy in the Carter years around human rights and the law of the sea, and then came Thatcher and Reagan and Bush.

Nevertheless, the disciplinary hegemony of the Hammarskjöld liberals in the field of public international law was surprisingly complete and long-lasting. It also had an enormous echo outside the United States, in many ways more than here at home for generations of young lawyers from the Third World, as well as from our industrialized allies and colonies, looking for a safe space between socialism and embrace of the American empire. The international legal scholarship of the 1950s was simply swept away. After 1960 it was routine to assert that all those who had come before had missed the most significant political developments: superpower convergence, decolonization, the emergence of development as a central substantive issue, the existence of cosmopolitan space between the superpowers. The field had been in urgent need of renewal, had suffered from an unhealthy methodological extremism when the practical problems of a newly interdependent world called out for an eclectic *via media*. The discipline's marginal status discouraged dissident voices within the field, even as it established a practice of professional dissidence. A call for "new ideas" in 1959 rather than 1999 would have had many takers—all proposing one or another version of the liberal humanism that would dominate the field for a generation. Their program would have rekindled the modernist and cosmopolitan recipes of the 1920s, enthusiasm about international administration, a chastened collective security, a critique of sovereignty, an embrace of political science, of expertise, a call for renewal.

By the time Clinton was elected, this vision had broken apart—exactly as the isolationist consensus of American international lawyers before the Second World War collapsed after 1941—and for ten years we have been in a period of contestation and disciplinary anxiety. The context in which my disciplinary colleagues urge renewal of the field is one in which international lawyers have fallen far from power. For most in my generation, this is a problem, not an opportunity. The central project common to the new mainstream is an urgent effort to permit international lawyers to return to a position of authority within the American political establishment they have not had in almost a century. The leaders of the field are no longer content to criticize power—they are anxious to exercise it. New ideas are necessary if the field is to give policy makers a workable set of myths and methods, or is to imagine itself into the same social frame as the new governing establishment.

In this sense, the leading "new" scholars of my generation are to the Clinton era of renewed, if chastened, Democratic party foreign policy what the Hammarskjöld generation were to the Kennedy and Johnson administrations. Their shared political project is the defense and development of a benignly hegemonic foreign policy of humanitarian interventions. They share with the Clintonites a way of thinking about markets and human rights, share with Clinton's World Bank appointees a skepticism about neoliberalism, an earnest faith in modest interventionist development policy, and so forth. They seek a more humane (if only marginally more open) immigration, refugee, and asylum policy. Inside American legal culture, they are internationalist about the foreign relations law of the United States, favoring an expanded federal authority in foreign affairs and an increased role for international law in United States courts, even as they favor chaining the State Department to law when it acts abroad. Thus they favor decentralization of judicial adherence to international law—and the use of national, or even local, courts to enforce human rights norms. Anyone and everyone should try Pinochet, for example. But they do not favor decentralization of American executive power in the foreign affairs field—allowing Massachusetts to use its purchasing power to sanction Burma, for example—at least as long as the Democratic party remains in control of the national administration.

There are differences within the group, of course, about this or that intervention, the viability of a criminal court, and so on, but everyone wants U.S. courts to pay more attention to the International Court of Justice, wants the United States to "use" the institutions of multilateral dispute resolution more sincerely and more often. This is not the party of Buchanan or Helms or Perot or Nader—and also not of Rockefeller or Bush Republicanism. It is certainly not the party of Reagan, with his belligerence on cold-war interventions, bilateral or unilateral enthusiasms, his obsession with the Contras, and all that.

For international lawyers to be players in this new political climate, the leaders of my generation concur that the discipline must dump the rule piety and policy skepticism inherited from the Columbia School. A dose of political science would obviously be a good idea, and the transnational–legal process–liberalism school has embraced a strand of the political science academy whose vocabulary converges with their own, worrying about "governance," "regimes," "global management," and so forth. After all, recent Secretaries of State or National Security Advisors have been political scientists or Wall Street attorneys, but none have been international lawyers. These people are skeptical of human-rights dogma—far too unrealistic and formal—but extremely supportive of the human-rights ethic, process, procedures, machinery, just as they are empathetic about culture and poverty and other humanist commitments and enthusiastic about all sorts of efforts to dialog and understand. Unlike some Catholic figures in the field, however, raison d'état rather than social justice is their first commitment. But it is a soft, embedded, humane raison d'état.

The transnational–legal process–liberalism school recognizes that the real players behind globalization are economists or international economic law specialists and understands that an appreciation for economics alongside political science wouldn't hurt. Still, its proponents tend to be people who share the idea, common in the broader liberal intelligentsia, that economics is in some sense bloodless, or has a tin ear for ethics. As members of the governing establishment, they certainly support free trade, but these are not neoliberals of the Washington consensus. They are modest interventionists, interested in tempering free trade with appropriate regulations, sympathetic to the concerns raised by nongovernmental organizations (a new term for labor unions) about the social impact of trade. And so on.

What we have is a generational cohort proposing a new synthesis, animated by a set of overlapping political projects they are pursuing vigorously. They have sought out allies among those sharing one or another of their intellectual commitments—to interdisciplinarity in general, to the importance of economics and political science—among international lawyers, and among those in neighboring fields who have felt that international law had somehow gone astray, needed a cold hard look, a reengagement with policy science. They have cultivated friends among those of their elders who chafed most under the dominance of the Yale-Columbia axis—scholars at New York University, at Harvard, at Michigan, in the west. They have found support among those drawn to their intellectual and professional style, their hip sensibility and apparent political with-it-ness. They have mobilized institutional resources in universities, in law firms, in government. They have worked to mobilize professionals in a number of subdisciplines to generate operational examples of their general ideas—environmental law, refugee affairs, arms control. They have written broad reinterpretations of the field's most basic doctrines and institutions—judicial review, the power of the security council, the role of courts, the function of international institutions. They have sought out and supported mentees and followers, have appealed to the desires of others in the field for energetic leadership. They have presented their suggestions for doctrinal and institutional reforms to one another's practitioner-beings in the hope of confirming adoption. All this is quite normal—had they not done so we might have wondered about the usefulness of their ideas or the depth of their professional commitment and competence.

This emerging professional consensus has been criticized in numerous ways, by people within and without the field, by international lawyers from the United States and elsewhere. Critics have made efforts to mobilize constituencies in opposition, just as the transnational–legal process–liberalism proponents have sought to do on their own behalf. Some of this opposition comes from people proposing other ideas to reorganize the field, some from people opposing one or another of the pet projects of the transnational–legal process–liberalism cohort. This opposition effort has generated two broad types of criticism, neither of which strikes me as terribly convincing, but both of which have been rather effective tools for mobilizing people in the field to opposition.

Some opponents have focused on the broad ideas themselves—the antiformalism, the emphasis on an embedded civil society rather than sovereign autonomy, and so on. The idea here is to demonstrate that something about these ideas is bad for the field as a whole—will drag it too close to politics, blunt its claims to universalism, ignore the continuing importance of states. We might think of this as an effort to develop a "high" church position opposite the new low church of transnational–legal process–liberalism. Where they are antiformal, be formal; where they emphasize community, focus on the continuing value of sovereign autonomy. At the same time, these voices are very concerned not to be mistaken for even more formalist identity and human rights fundamentalists. The result is a vigorous, if rather familiar debate. The difficulty, of course, is that once one places these schools on the broader spectrum from the political science realism/formalism opposed by the new mainstream through the sovereign autonomy/identity fundamentalism opposed by the new dissident voices, the difference between the mainstream and the counterpoint seems less and less one of principle. Indeed, it would not be surprising for the mainstream scholars to find it difficult to understand how what the dissidents are proposing actually differs from what they are proposing—or to hear their dissent as a willful misreading of mainstream intentions.

In arguing about the proper limits of the field—its relations with commerce, the base, politics, and so forth—the new high and low church have developed roughly parallel and opposing accounts of how only their solution can save the field's broad project. The idea here is to find some element in the opponent's broad vision that invalidates the entire project. Doing so often takes the form of associating the ideas of the transnational–legal process–liberals with a set of political consequences and affiliations. Thus, one might argue that antiformalism about international law is inexorably associated with American hegemony or imperium—it was in the 1950s and it is today. In an extreme version, one might say that the Nazis were antiformalist, and so were the colonialists, so it's just bad stuff. The problem with arguments of this type, of course, is that antiformalism has had a quite varied political career in international law—associated with the Left in 1919–1939, with the Right in 1960–1989, and today's transnational–legal process–liberals are quite insistent that it is the perfect set of ideas for a moderate center-left program.

A second strand of criticism takes the emphasis off the ideas altogether and focuses on the association of the transnational–legal process–liberals with a variety of reform efforts, dear to the American political establishment, that these critics oppose. Thus, it is argued that the new American international lawyers are somehow (and the somehow is often rather mysterious) implicated in a broad American plot of domination. Now it is true that these people want to participate in American governance and in America's participation in global governance—but being part of a right-wing conspiracy of global domination could hardly be further from their own intentions. There is no question that the transnational–legal process–liberal group has been assisted powerfully by this association with the American political establishment in their struggle within the American intelligentsia, just as they have often paid a cost for this association abroad. But this association should be understood (and, if you like, opposed) as an alignment, an alliance, an association, rather than as an entailment. For one thing, these people understand themselves to be strident opponents of American adventurism of this sort, themselves critical of American pop-cultural dominance, firmly empathetic to the developing world, supportive of the ethic of human rights everywhere but above all sensitive to the difficulties of cross-cultural understanding and dialog. Theirs will be a regime of differentiated rights and responsibilities—that's the whole point. It might turn out that their ideas had nevertheless been captured by practitioner-beings with completely different agendas, and they had become the unwitting accomplices in a set of political initiatives they did not understand, but this is extremely difficult to demonstrate. The fact that the ideas originate among Americans who want to participate in American government does not, at least to me, suggest that the ideas are tainted, any more than the fact that some idea arose in the colonial encounter taints it always in all contexts. Americans come up with good ideas sometimes, as do colonialists, and ideas turn out to be rather flexible as they migrate about. Nevertheless, a rather successful opposition to transnational–legal process–liberalism has emerged that blends these two strands of criticism. These people are Americans, they propose to strengthen the American foreign policy machinery and participate in it, they are antiformalist about international law and willing to relax commitment to universalism. They are either evil or unwitting accomplices in a project of hegemony.

In my own view, criticism of this sort is at once too sweeping and too wedded to the discipline's own vocabulary. As an intellectual matter, given the instability of the professional lexicon, the effort to uncover political biases in a new school of thought requires going beneath the charges and countercharges that simply deploy arguments across the spectra of the profession's established vocabulary. And the effort to connect ideas in the discipline to political projects requires a more sociologically focused inquiry into the projects of domination, affiliation, and commitment by which ideas are captured by one or another group at a given moment. This will probably require more attention to the particular context and political motivations of the idea's proponents. Efforts to identify the dark side of disciplinary common sense and its capture by groups are important, but they seem unlikely to be accomplished by a silver bullet. Rather, opposition of this type requires an ongoing performance and counterdemonstration, an effort to uncover and make visible the blind spots and political projects firmed up on the more neutral vocabulary of disciplinary renewal and pragmatic persuasion. The audience for this sort of demonstration consists of people in the field who might be mobilized one way or the other. The distribution of ideas in the field will be determined, in large part, by the relative success of various groups and individuals in mobilizing younger people to seek career paths thought to instantiate one or another set of ideas about where the field should head.

My own hope is that as the field rushes to embrace a new consensus, there will remain some who keep doubt alive. It would be better, as I see things, if we could wallow in dissensus and uncertainty a while longer rather than rushing to develop either enthusiasm for the transnational–legal process–liberal project or for its opposition. Both seem unpersuasive except as they have come into power in the field through political activity and alliance, and both seem to share the blind spots and biases of the discipline's professional lexicon. It has been my project while this new consensus has slowly emerged to open a space for a range of critical initiative and alternative voices: to seek alliances, affiliations, power, to permit the development of ideas that did not fit the lexicon of high and low. The point was not to develop an all-points criticism of transnational–legal process–liberalism, nor to propose an alternative, any more than it was to support this emerging mainstream project. The idea is simply to sidestep the preoccupations that generate this sort of transformation in a disciplinary vocabulary that needs to be rethought in a far more daring way.

I have come to this project myself partly by following the energy of younger international lawyers who seem charismatic and whose political and social projects I admire, partly by longstanding aversion to many of the projects of other international lawyers and skepticism about the commitments and projects of the field as a whole. My intuition is a critical one—that in some way the international legal profession has often made the very things it claims to care most about less likely, that the professional discipline is part of the problem, and that the established professional argumentative practice in the field repeatedly places its speaker in a posture of bad faith—overestimating small differences and over-promoting broad arguments about which one is also professionally ambivalent. This intuition, I'm afraid, applies to those of my generational cohorts now proposing a new political and intellectual synthesis for the discipline as well as it does to their most notable opponents.

Unfortunately, this remains, after close to twenty years of collaborative work, a very un-worked-out intuition and a comparatively unsuccessful project. We have started to figure out how the discipline participates in keeping a terribly unjust international order up and running, even as it seeks with great passion to be a voice for humanitarian reform, even as it renews itself constantly to be more effective. But we are just getting started. The difficulty is to figure out how to get beyond rearranging the discipline's own points of reference. This is not just an intellectual difficulty, however. Transforming the discipline, just like reinforcing it, is a project that requires the mobilization of affinities, the building of groups, the staging of controversy, the announcement of opposition, and seductive appeals of recognition, engagement, play. In my experience, thinking against the box the field has built for itself is a performance in a particular context, a project of affiliation and disaffiliation, commitment and aversion, dominance and submission.

A FIRST ALTERNATIVE PICTURE: THE LIMITATIONS OF PROFESSIONAL CONSCIOUSNESS; OR, THE DARK SIDE OF EXPERTISE

One element in that extravernacular effort has been an attempt to map, in a more systematic way, the biases and blind spots that accompany the discipline's vocabulary across a range of efforts to renew or reorient the field. For some years I have been working from the intuition that the discipline's store of professional commitments, practices, and ideas do have very deeply rooted blind spots and biases that are not likely to be overcome by movement among schools of thought in the field of international law, nor by borrowing from the neighboring international disciplines of comparative law, international economic law, or political science. My starting point has been the observation that while international lawyers are largely very nice people, socially quite liberal, committed to making things better, something about the way they conceptualize problems and possible solutions, including their best ideas about how to renew the field and their most critical observations about how things have gone astray, seems nevertheless to strengthen rather than weaken what seems inhumane in our current international arrangements. The blindnesses and biases of the disciplinary vocabulary have been enhanced rather than eliminated by the current generation of enthusiastic renewalists.

One way to describe the limited nature of the professional vocabulary would be to focus on the widespread tendency to disregard what seem background conditions and norms. One might identify across several generations of disciplinary innovation common but mistaken ideas—like the idea that international governance is separate from both the global market and local culture, or is more a matter of public than of private law—that narrow the sense among foreign policy professionals of what is possible and appropriate for foreign policy. Although we know professional disciplines have blind spots—some emphasize public at the expense of private order, governance at the expense of culture, economy at the expense of society, law at the expense of politics—we hope these run-of-the-mill limitations can be corrected by aggressive interdisciplinarity. Unfortunately, blindness to the background can be maintained, even reinforced, in the face of interdisciplinary work. Specialists in all internationalist fields share a sense that governance means the politics of public order, while a background private order builds itself naturally through the work of the economic market. As a result, these specialists underestimate the possibilities for political contestation within the domain of private and economic law and overestimate the impact of globalization on the capacity for governance.

The specific effects of this sort of disciplinary limit will differ over time. Since the cold war, international lawyers in the United States have come to share a diagnosis of the changed conditions for statecraft: international politics has fragmented, involving more diverse actors in myriad new sites; military issues have been tempered, if not replaced, by economic considerations, transforming the meaning of international security; a new politics of ethnicity and nationalism is altering the conditions of both coexistence and cooperation. Despite this interest in context, in expanding the boundaries of the field, in an antiformal or embedded law, they share with their more formal opponents and with their predecessors across a century of disciplinary renewal a conception of what governance *is*, of the distinction between law and politics, and so forth; and these conceptions have consequences for their assessment of today's political possibilities.

For example, international lawyers in the United States today overestimate the military's power to intervene successfully while remaining neutral or disengaged from background local political and culture struggles. They tend to overestimate the technocratic or apolitical nature of economic concerns, including the independence of economic development from background cultural, political, and institutional contexts. A shared sense that cultural background can be disentangled from governance leads specialists to overemphasize the exoticism of ethnic conflict as well as the cosmopolitan character of global governance. The result is a professional tendency to overlook opportunities for an inclusive global politics of identity—for working constructively on the distributional conflicts among groups and individuals that cross borders.

The proliferation of sites for international public policy that contemporary international lawyers embrace has a dark side about which they are more overtly ambivalent. The erosion of the state they see to be transforming the methods and objectives of public policy, eroding the ambitions of public law, expanding private law and private initiative, withering the welfare state under conditions of globalization, inaugurating a democracy deficit, governance by experts, technocracy. Law fragments political choices, spacing them out in bureaucratic phases structured by proliferating standards and rules. Political interests become factors to be balanced in an apparently endless process. In a technocratic private market, the locus for political choice is not so much opened up as rendered invisible. The idea of a "government" promoting a "program" has been replaced by the enlightened management of prosperity, dramatically narrowing the field of participants whose interests are understood to be in contestation internationally—exactly as today's international lawyers celebrate an opening of the policy process to civil society.

Mainstream international lawyers have greeted this trend with a tone of tragic resignation. Something called "globalization," interpreted as a natural fact, has rendered public intervention in the emerging global market more difficult than it was within the welfare state, whether for the environment, labor standards, consumer protection, or redistributive taxation. Although international lawyers often bemoan the weakening of traditional public policy levers in the face of newly mobile capital, their relative resignation contrasts starkly with their enthusiasm for a newly open international political process, as if enthusiasm about new participants were linked to confidence that they can now do little mischief. The link here is a familiar liberal one between democracy and a disempowered state, between strong markets and weak governments. The common theme is a disempowering of public law and the disappearance of background private and commercial affairs from the jurisdictional domain of politics.

My intuition is that we could reject both enthusiasm about the fragmentation of international political life and resignation before the shrinking ambitions of public policy in the face of a growing private sector. But as a policy alternative this is extremely difficult to express or hear in the discipline's conventional lexicon regardless of the school to which one belongs. Rebuilding politics as an alternative to law, or developing a domain of contestation that is *not* law-not-politics, between-not-within states-nonstates, is not part of the discipline's problem set. It is extremely difficult to articulate an opposition to antiformal enthusiasm for a weak global governance system in terms that are not understood to revive the state or disestablish the international market in the name of formal entitlements. But the welfare state often did entrench class, race, or gender privilege within its borders while preventing movement of people, ideas, and capital—all in ways that buttressed inequitable resource distributions across the globe and shrank the global imagination. In some cases a more technocratic politics has been a counterweight to the corrupt tendencies of mass politics and the capture of the welfare state by rent seekers of various sorts. And treating the state apparatus as the *sine qua non* of decolonization has often entrenched gruesome practices in the name of sovereignty. My own suggestion is that resignation about the demobilization of a vigorous public policy indicates that even as welfare states erode, the notion of public policy they exemplified is alive and well: public policy as territorial intervention by "public" authorities against a background of apolitical private initiative. This resignation refuses to treat as political, as public, as open to contestation the institutions and norms that structure that background market.

If we think of the private domain as political, it is not at all obvious that the current situation is one of fragmentation rather than concentration. Global governance may simply have moved from Washington to New York, from the East Side to Wall Street, from Geneva or the Hague to Frankfurt, Hong Kong, and London. Where factors of production are relatively immobile, a locality or private actor may have more capacity to conduct global public policy than either the welfare state or the institutions of international economic law. The question, in other words, is not *whether* politics or *where* politics, but *what* politics. International lawyers, in my view, should care less about whether the state is empowered or eroded, or whether the law is autonomous or embedded, than about the distribution of political power and wealth in global society. Because mainstream international lawyers accept that the political and economic results that flow from a particular system of private initiative are outside the legitimate bounds of contestation, they can be enthusiastic about a disaggregation of the state and the empowerment of diverse actors in an international "civil society" without asking who will win and who will lose by such an arrangement. As a consequence, the turn to political science too often illuminates the structure of the regime without adding to our understanding of its substantive choices.

Technocratic governance, a displacement of public by private, of political alignments by economic rivalries, the unbundling of sovereignty into myriad rights and obligations scattered across a global civil society—all this has transformed international affairs. Today's leading international lawyers stress that this has often meant an opening of international affairs to new actors and concerns, a democratization and proceduralization of international relations, and this may well be positive. But this transformation has also shriveled the range of the politically contestable, confirming as natural the geographic and economic distributions thought to be the inevitable consequences of "the market." Underestimating the political nature of private institutions and initiatives, many mainstream international lawyers have accepted the demobilization of policy making as they have lauded increasing access to its machinery. The result is a professional class unable to develop viable political strategies for the world it has applauded into existence, ratifying the political choices that result from the arrangements of private power to which the state has handed its authority, while still celebrating the expansion of participation in an emasculated public policy process.

If we think about military power, the refusal to engage background norms and conditions is equally striking. Of course, the question of who can project force abroad remains important, undergirding patterns of trade, prosperity, and emiseration. The current generation of renewalists has provided us with a new security vocabulary of budget surpluses or deficits and hard or soft currencies rather than throw weights and silos. We are urged to reimagine missiles as missives, their deployment determined less by Clausewitz than by Hayek or Keynes, their military function shaped more by CNN than by the Pentagon. Like the disestablishment of the state, the economization of security has largely been welcomed by Clinton-era international lawyers. If the liberal peace hypothesis proves correct, the disaggregation of the state into a global market has left the world more secure and free to worry about prosperity. At the same time, economic security seems achievable through technocratic means, sound management and trade deals, and a smorgasbord of alternative dispute resolution mechanisms. Trade wars promise to be friendlier than real wars: they cost less and can be won by lawyers.

In the meantime, today's foreign policy professionals have drummed up all sorts of new uses for military machinery. During the cold war, military interventions and proxy wars were hard-wired to the central problem of global security. Now they float more freely, drifting into limited police actions, humanitarian gestures, and stabilization at the periphery. The military has emerged from the collapse of the welfare state as the only bureaucracy broadly thought capable of acting successfully, so long as the mission does not bleed back into economic or political matters. Seen this way, the military is available for a wide variety of technocratic tasks, but it should be protected from the quagmire of political or social engagement. The military will stabilize borders and prop up states precisely as globalization renders state institutions marginal sites for public policy. International lawyers anxious for a role in the foreign policy apparatus assert that our national interest now coincides with the stability of global governance for a global market. Consequently, the military should become a national contribution to that international order, for which the United States should be thanked and probably reimbursed. At the same time, nothing is very urgent—we could do it or not, it is a moral question, a technical question, maybe we should send the Red Cross instead, or hold a plebiscite, or enforce an embargo. We expect a police action, an air strike, force by permission, with limited objectives and clear avenues of retreat back to the cosmopolis.

The problem is this: our foreign-policy professionals expect a technocratic cosmopolitan governance to have no stakes in local disputes beyond stability, and therefore to deploy force in an unrealistically sanitary way, without political entanglement. But cosmopolitan governance does have stakes in local disputes. Although we should focus on securing prosperity, these new security concerns cannot be engaged without thought to the social and distributional context within which they occur, any more than by military force detached from economic cost and political risk. Economic security need not mean deference to the largest market actors; there are, after all, a number of possible markets, structured by different background values and distributive choices. Defending the stability of a political order necessary for investor confidence requires a set of political choices both among states and among groups or classes within nations, as among the transnational interests of labor or capital or women or men. Moreover, it calls for choices among economic sectors with stakes in different patterns of modernization, among investors with stakes in different patterns of production, trade, and consumption. It is commonly said, for example, that a global market "requires" an emerging market to enforce the "rule of law" to permit "transparency" and "predictability" in market transactions. It sounds very clean, egalitarian, procedural, just like apolitical background rules. But the alternative is neither arbitrary nor chaotic allocations, but a different and often equally predictable allocation of resources, perhaps to local rather than foreign investors, to domestic oligarchs rather than foreign shareholders or vice versa.

Such choices can only be engaged, can only be *seen* beneath the blanket insistence on technical "transparency" once the mainstream tendency to efface background cultural, institutional, or political structures has been overcome. In the recent Banana War between the United States and the European Union, there was a well-established institutional machinery to weigh the technical impact of one or another result on the balance between free trade and protectionism, to assess costs between American producers and European consumers, but no mechanism to examine distributional costs between African, Caribbean, and Central American labor.

The Clinton-era optimism that military deployment can be disentangled from ongoing local political judgment and risk is rooted in the notion shared by contemporary foreign-policy professionals, whether formal or antiformal in their orientation, that cosmopolitan governance projects simply *are* about law rather than politics, about the universal and the rational rather than the local and the passionate. But it turns out that humanitarian intervention and international community policing also require engagement with the distribution of power among groups, along with a political vocabulary for addressing social and economic justice. It is as if the old coexistence mentality that left cold-war internationalists agnostic between liberal and totalitarian regimes had paradoxically reasserted itself as agnosticism between wealth and poverty, between this and that warlord, this dictator and those victims. But long-term economic security cannot be "managed" without attention to distribution, any more than long-term humanitarianism can be enforced without political choices. Humanitarian *aid* is one thing; humanitarian intervention is another. We saw the difficulty in Kosovo—in our odd oscillation between hands-off negotiation and pious criminalization. Both aspire to clean hands—but governance is a messy business, globally as locally.

Today's international lawyers have also placed "culture" center stage in foreign-policy debates, and in many ways rightly so. Cold-war ideological conflict obscured other differences and accentuated traditional modes of interstate politics. The medium for international affairs has become increasingly cultural: Coca-Cola has become more important than the Voice of America or the military establishment; CNN has replaced the embassy cable. Governance is less about norms or sanctions than about communication and persuasion. Like the economization of security and the disaggregation of the state, this cultural turn suggests a model of international affairs more amenable to expertise, a matter of texts and images rather than either guns or butter. Within the cosmopolis, at least, "culture" is about persuasion and communication, governance a matter of deposits and withdrawals from a legitimacy stockpile in an "international community" where everyone speaks the language of missiles and messages, sanctions and sanctimony. Outside the cosmopolis, however, for today's international lawyers of whatever school, culture means a set of local and particularist commitments altogether different from the secular, rational, and pragmatic communicative methods of cosmopolitan governance. Out there, religion and ethnic identity are back, not simply the handmaiden to market rationality and reasoned patriotism, but a range of more primitive, mystical, and irrational creeds.

My international law colleagues tend to take this two ways. Sometimes they reaffirm their cosmopolitan sensibility as a historic liberation from particularism. International economic law defends the liberal spirit of free trade against outbreaks of economic nationalism in the form of subsidies or protectionism. As nationalism "breaks out" or ethnic hatreds "reemerge," internationalists struggle to keep the superego in charge. This cosmopolitanism is tolerant of (if disengaged from) cultural differences, particularly those involving commercial preferences (Germans like beer) or "private" and "consensual" family practices (female genital mutilation). Sometimes the internationalist takes the opposite tack, affirming cultural specificity and insisting on a defense of the West against the rest or speaking for international civilization itself against all that shocks the conscience of mankind.

Either way, there is a problem. As international affairs come to be pursued in cultural terms, both a culturally demobilized "international community" and an artificially unified "West" will find it difficult to govern, for "governance" means participating in the struggle among cultural groups. Cultural identities are at once more than preferences and less than iconoclastic alternatives to modern civilization. They require more than tolerance or exclusion, they must be engaged with more than the promise of participation in an eroding public life through minority rights and self-determination. Thinking about culture this way leaves the local and global groups and institutions that structure distributions of power and wealth outside the field of vision.

International lawyers in the United States today overstate both the contrast between local cultures and the global cosmopolis and the equation of cosmopolitanism with "civilization" and the "West." Internationalists are neither outside culture nor simply "Western." Cultures are not this solid or coherent. In fact, the most interesting issues arise *within* cultures, including *within* the culture of internationalism, often between groups presenting themselves as cosmopolitan or secular and a variety of new gender, race, national, or religious identities. Of course, people do pursue political projects in broad cultural terms, promoting "North" or "South", "Asian" or "Western," the "Islamic" or the "secular," and conflicts are likely to break out along imaginary boundaries of this type. But patterns of communication, migration, and economic development have also produced a Third World in the First and a First World in the Third, have proliferated "Western" sensibilities as well as nationalist resistances of various sorts in a wide variety of places. In short, our international legal establishment is fixated on differences *between*, just when differences *within* have become far more important.

The differences between men and women within both international and national cultures are more significant—also for foreign policy—than the difference between the international and national treatment of women or men, just as differences among men and among women are often more significant than those between them. We need not set these commonplace observations aside when we think internationally. Differences among possible "market" economies or among transnational groups in a global market are more significant than an imaginary line between the market and public life or between North and South. Differences among groups within developing economies are more significant than relations between developed and underdeveloped economies or between global and national markets.

In my view, our mainstream international lawyers across all schools have become too used to thinking that we have a robust international political order with only the thinnest layer of law. The reverse is more accurate—we have a robust process of global law and "governance" without a global politics. Real government is about the political contestation of distribution and justice. Governing an international order means making choices among groups—between finance and production, between capital and labor, between these and those distributors, these and those consumers, between male and female workers. Some of these choices will be national, of course—between Thai and Malaysian producers, for instance—but most will not. Development policy means preferring these investors to those, these public officials to those, not the technocratic extension of a neutral "best practice." To make these choices we need a world that is open to a politics of identity, to struggles over affiliation and distribution among the conflicting and intersecting patterns of group identity in the newly opened international regime.

Putting this together, the suggestion is that our international policy professionals err when they sharply differentiate between national culture and global governance or between global economics and global politics. They err when they isolate politics within a shrinking public sphere, when they assume governance must be built while markets grow naturally, when they treat security as a technical matter, disengaged from social and political context. Our international lawyers, whether formalists or antiformalists, enthusiasts for sovereign autonomy or for a revitalized international community, have systematically underestimated the opportunities for engagement with the background worlds of private law, market institutions, cultural differences. From the fragmentation of international politics, specialists have too readily drawn an optimistic conclusion about global democratization and a pessimistic conclusion about the horizons for public policy. As military issues have been tempered by economic considerations, they have become unduly sanguine about projecting military force abroad without local political engagement, while simultaneously overestimating the amenability of economic security issues to technocratic measures. They increasingly see military force both as an expression of a national interest unwilling to place a single soldier in harm's way and as a technical tool for cosmopolitan governance, able to be extended abroad on the unrealistic condition that the cosmopolis lives up to its promise to govern without political, economic, or cultural entanglement. Whether they are thinking about economic stability among the wealthier powers or development at the periphery, they think of the global economy in strangely depoliticized and technical terms. These misinterpretations often reinforce one another. Only after accepting the attenuation of public-policy capacity in the face of globalization does it make sense to reinterpret security in economic terms turned over to technocrats indifferent to distributive concerns. The result is a decontextualized, deracinated, and depoliticized foreign policy amenable to international legal expertise.

By reinforcing the invisibility of background norms and private arrangements, mainstream international lawyers have taken important areas of political contestation out of the internationalist's vision precisely as the disaggregation of the state makes these norms and institutions the most significant sites for international policy making. They stress the naturalness of current distributions of global wealth and poverty, focusing our attention on participation in public structures precisely when questions of economic justice decided elsewhere become most salient. And they reinforce the stability of cultural identity at precisely the moment diasporic and hybrid experiences make contestation among and within cultural groups the central context for both politics and economics.

In my view, we could rethink the locus of international political contestation and public policy by invigorating debate about what have seemed to be the background rules and structuring institutions of private law, economic life, and local culture. The fragmentation of the state and the geographical expansion of the economy place local and global groups in complex and intersecting new relations. They invite a new global politics of identity. We should judge the global market, like the global political order, by the distribution it effects among today's overlapping cultural, political, and economic groups. The issue is not how to repress or manage national, ethnic, economic, race, gender, or religious claims, containing them within the private or the national domain, but how we can engage them internationally.

It is possible to resist and question this sort of disciplinary blind spot. But doing so often requires departing the discipline's own vocabulary. Stepping outside the professional discipline in this way, moreover, will often mean stepping beyond the easy partnerships of well-established interdisciplinary projects. If international lawyers share a blind spot to global governance that is not cosmopolitan, rational and detached, borrowing from the field of international relations will only help if that field is not also committed to the same idea about what global governance is and is not. Similarly, if international lawyers are blinded by the notion that markets grow naturally while governments must be made, they will get no help from international economic law, a field that shares this central idea. Where international lawyers are limited by their tendency to think of culture as a local phenomenon and of their own work as outside or after the particularities of cultural commitment, they will get no help from comparative law to the extent that discipline shares this vision.

This sort of reconceptualization is a messy and unfinished business that sidesteps the frame of the discipline's own problem set, vocabulary, and arrangement of schools of thought. The intense ambivalence and flexibility of the profession's own vocabulary makes it hard to imagine we will be able to escape professional limitations, assuming we want to, simply by reversing or reorganizing these conventional commitments. Although many people have tried to develop extravernacular projects, in my experience projects that resist this lexicon, that glimpse around its boundaries in various ways, seem to need to be performed, to happen, to be staged. We have a map, if a rudimentary one, of disciplinary renewal. If you seek to improve and update the ambivalent vocabulary with which international lawyers argue hyperbolically for modest reforms, we know where to send you. But new thinking, thinking outside the box, for that so far about all we can say is that sometimes we know it when we hear it.

NOTE

1 I have told the story of twentieth-century international law in the United States more comprehensively in Kennedy 1987, 1997, 1999, and 2000.

REFERENCES

Kennedy, David W. 1987. "The Move to Institutions," 8 *Cardozo Law Review* 841–948.

———. 1997. "International Law and the Nineteenth Century: History of an Illusion," 17 *Quinnipiac Law Review* 99–138.

———. 1999. "The Disciplines of International Law and Policy," 12 *Leiden Journal of International Law* 9–133.

———. 2000. "When Renewal Repeats: Thinking Against the Box," 32 *New York University Journal of International Law and Politics* 335–500.

Index